# The Korean War

PRINCETON STUDIES IN
INTERNATIONAL HISTORY AND POLITICS

*Series Editors*
Jack L. Snyder and Richard H. Ullman

Recent titles:

*From Wealth to Power: The Unusual Origins of America's World Role*
by Fareed Zakaria

*Ideas, Institutions, and the Internal Balance of Power: Agents of Change in Soviet Foreign Policy* by Sarah E. Mendelson

*Disarming Strangers: Nuclear Diplomacy with North Korea* by Leon V. Sigal

*Imagining War: French and British Military Doctrine between the Wars*
by Elizabeth Kier

*Roosevelt and the Munich Crisis: A Study of Political Decision-Making*
by Barbara Rearden Farnham

*Useful Adversaries: Grand Strategy, Domestic Mobilization, and Sino-American Conflict, 1947-1958* by Thomas J. Christensen

*Satellites and Commissars: Strategy and Conflict in the Politics of Soviet-Bloc Trade* by Randall W. Stone

*Does Conquest Pay? The Exploitation of Occupied Industrial Societies*
by Peter Liberman

*Cultural Realism: Strategic Culture and Grand Strategy in Chinese History* by Alastair Iain Johnston

*The Korean War: An International History* by William Stueck

*Cooperation among Democracies: The European Influence on U.S. Foreign Policy* by Thomas Risse-Kappen

*The Sovereign State and Its Competitors: An Analysis of Systems Change*
by Hendrik Spruyt

*America's Mission: The United States and the Worldwide Struggle for Democracy in the Twentieth Century* by Tony Smith

*Who Adjusts? Domestic Sources of Foreign Economic Policy during the Interwar Years* by Beth A. Simmons

*We All Lost the Cold War* by Richard Ned Lebow and Janice Gross Stein

*Mercenaries, Pirates, and Sovereigns: State-Building and Extraterritorial Violence in Early Modern Europe* by Janice E. Thomson

*The Limits of Safety: Organizations, Accidents, and Nuclear Weapons*
by Scott D. Sagan

# The Korean War

## AN INTERNATIONAL HISTORY

• *WILLIAM STUECK* •

PRINCETON UNIVERSITY PRESS

PRINCETON, NEW JERSEY

Copyright © 1995 by Princeton University Press
Published by Princeton University Press, 41 William Street,
Princeton, New Jersey 08540
In the United Kingdom: Princeton University Press, Chichester, West Sussex

All Rights Reserved

Library of Congress Cataloging-in-Publication Data

Stueck, William Whitney, 1945–
The Korean war : an international history / William Stueck
p. cm. — (Princeton studies in international history and politics)
Includes bibliographical references and index.
ISBN 0-03767-1
ISBN 0-691-01624-0 (pbk.)
1. Korean War, 1950–1953. 2. Korean War, 1950–1953—Diplomatic history.
I. Title. II. Series.
DS918.S819 1995 951.904'2—dc20 94-46286 CIP

This book has been composed in Times Roman

Princeton University Press books are printed on acid-free paper and meet the guidelines
for permanence and durability of the Committee on Production Guidelines for Book
Longevity of the Council on Library Resources

Third printing, and first paperback printing, with corrections, 1997

http://pup.princeton.edu

Printed in the United States of America

7 9 10 8 6

• *FOR PAT* •

# CONTENTS

| | |
|---|---|
| LIST OF MAPS | ix |
| ACKNOWLEDGMENTS | xi |
| INTRODUCTION | 3 |
| CHAPTER 1<br>The Origins of the Korean War | 10 |
| CHAPTER 2<br>The Diplomacy of Confrontation and Consolidation | 47 |
| CHAPTER 3<br>Diplomacy Fails: The UN Counteroffensive and<br>Chinese Intervention | 85 |
| CHAPTER 4<br>Limiting the War | 127 |
| CHAPTER 5<br>The Dimensions of Collective Action | 167 |
| CHAPTER 6<br>Armistice Talks: Origins and Initial Stages | 204 |
| CHAPTER 7<br>Progress | 236 |
| CHAPTER 8<br>Deadlock | 268 |
| CHAPTER 9<br>Concluding an Armistice | 308 |
| CHAPTER 10<br>The Korean War as International History | 348 |
| NOTES | 371 |
| BIBLIOGRAPHY<br>Manuscript Sources • Dissertations and Other<br>Unpublished Secondary Works • Government<br>and United Nations Publications • Interviews •<br>Oral Histories • Newspapers and Popular<br>Magazines • Books and Articles | 447 |
| INDEX | 469 |

## LIST OF MAPS

| | |
|---|---:|
| 1. Summer 1950 | 49 |
| 2. UN Offensive, Fall 1950 | 87 |
| 3. November 1950 to January 1951 | 129 |
| 4. Stalemate, July 1, 1951 to July 2, 1953 | 226 |

# ACKNOWLEDGMENTS

IT IS A great pleasure to acknowledge the assistance I have received from individuals and institutions. The Harry S. Truman Library and the National Endowment for the Humanities provided major grants for travel and release time from teaching. The Humanities Center at the University of Georgia funded me through a quarter off from teaching. The American Council for Learned Societies, the American Philosophical Society, and the History Department and Research Foundation at the University of Georgia all provided funding for travel. Given the magnitude of the research involved in this study, there is simply no way I could have done without the support of the above institutions.

The staffs of numerous libraries offered essential assistance in my efforts to exploit their holdings, in some cases greatly expediting the declassification review process of key documents. In particular I would like to thank Kathy Nicastro and Sally Marks of the Diplomatic Branch of the National Archives in Washington, D.C.; Dennis Bilger, Elizabeth Safly, and Edwin Mueller of the Harry S. Truman Library; Marilla B. Guptil of the United Nations Archives; Dacre Cole of the Historical Office of the Department of External Affairs of Canada; Fe Angela Manansalu of the Jose Laurel Memorial Library in Manila; and the entire staff of the Australian National Archives in Dickson, Australia.

Numerous scholars have facilitated my work. In particular, Zhai Qiang, Chen Jian, and Zhang Shuguang assisted me in developing the Chinese side of my story. Zhai translated numerous Chinese documents, and Chen and Zhang gave me access to their unpublished manuscripts on China and the Korean War. All three of these fine historians spent hour after hour sharing their thoughts on Chinese foreign policy, and Chen provided invaluable criticism of my treatment of the subject in an earlier draft. On the Soviet side, Kathryn Weathersby provided translations of many declassified documents and shared her impressive insights on the Soviet Union's foreign policy during the last years of Stalin's rule. British scholars Geoffrey Warner and Rosemary Foot were most generous in referring me to newly available materials and providing criticism of portions of earlier drafts of the manuscript. Lester Langley, William Leary, and Peter Hoffer, all colleagues at the University of Georgia, have provided a combination of criticism and encouragement through many years of toil. Eduard Mark has often given me leads on sources and provided inspiring conversation on the cold war. Melvyn Leffler, John Gaddis, James Matray, and two anonymous readers for the University of North Carolina Press took the time to read a very long manuscript and suggest revisions. John Merrill provided several useful suggestions on chapter 1. Lewis Bateman of the University of North Carolina Press was patient and supportive at every stage of the book's development.

My typist, Bonnie Cary, has patiently and proficiently typed my many drafts, always going the extra mile in accommodating my schedule. Research assistants Leann Grabavoy Almquist and Guo Xixiao have provided timely support in looking up sources. Ms. Guo also helped in converting Chinese names into their modern English-language form and in updating my computer skills. Rita Bernhard did a superb job of copyediting.

Imprint Publications readily granted permission to use portions of an essay I had published previously in their volume *A Revolutionary War*, and the Keck Center for International and Strategic Studies at Claremont-McKenna College did the same for my essay in their *The Korean War: 40-Year Perspectives*.

Finally, I want to thank my wife, Pat, who tolerated first my absence on many lengthy research trips and then my frequent inattention through many years of writing and rewriting. She, more than any other person, made it possible to complete this work through her faith and support.

# The Korean War

• INTRODUCTION •

THE COLD WAR has ended and World War III seems more remote than ever. In looking back over the two generations of intense competition between the United States and the Soviet Union, however, one might easily wonder why another global confrontation did not occur. From the late 1940s to the late 1980s millions of people on both sides lived in constant fear of such an event. These fears were never more intense or widespread over a sustained period than during the Korean War. Though limited in geographical scope to a small Asian country and beginning as a struggle between armies of Koreans, the conflict eventually included combatants representing twenty different governments from six continents. Of the estimated casualties to military personnel, more than half were non-Korean. The war rendered terrible destruction to indigenous peoples and failed to resolve the political division of the country, which remains a source of tension and danger to the present day. Yet it contributed significantly to the evolution of an order that escaped the ultimate horror of a direct clash of superpowers. In its timing, its course, and its outcome, the Korean War served in many ways as a substitute for World War III.

This book addresses the international dimensions of the Korean War, first, through a detailed narrative of its diplomacy and, second, by analyzing its impact on global politics. To the extent that these two purposes can be accomplished through a chronological narrative, they are integrated into the body of the book. When not, the broader effects of the war receive treatment in this introduction and in a concluding chapter.

Several interlocking themes run through the narrative. Most basic is the multilateral nature of the war, both in its origins and its course. The war originated in 1945 with the division of the peninsula into occupation zones by the Soviet Union and the United States, and the perpetuation of that division as a result of the two nation's subsequent failure to agree on terms for unification. The competition that developed between the two powers led to the polarization of Korean politics and the division of the country into two hostile regimes. Meanwhile, the Communists marched to victory in a civil war in neighboring China, and the Soviet-supported North Korean leader, Kim Il-sung, used that conflict as a training ground for an army. With Moscow's help, that army eventually achieved decisive superiority over the government forces sponsored by the United States and the United Nations below the 38th parallel. When, with Soviet approval and aid, Kim's forces invaded the South in an attempt to unite the peninsula under his control, the United States, with UN backing, rushed to stop him. On the UN side, South Korea and the United States provided more than 90 percent of the manpower, but sixteen other governments sent forces of some kind and, unofficially, Japan provided hundreds of laborers in critical Korean industries and in the peninsula's harbors operating dredges, lighters, minesweepers, and even American LSTs (Landing Ship,

Tanks). On the Communist side, the People's Republic of China eventually contributed hundreds of thousands of troops.

Of the foreign participants, the United States and China played by far the largest role in actual fighting, yet several other nations had a major impact on the course of the war. In the Soviet bloc, the Soviet Union itself provided large-scale material assistance to North Korea and China; its pilots flew hundreds of combat missions over the northern reaches of the peninsula; and the presence in Manchuria of army units, plus a substantial portion of its air force, all represented a major deterrent to U.S. action beyond the Yalu River. Soviet posturing in other areas, especially in Europe, achieved a similar end. Soviet diplomats played an active role in the United Nations and elsewhere as advocates of the North Korean and Chinese cause and as intermediaries between their allies and the United States. In the West, at crucial times, U.S. allies, especially Great Britain and Canada, provided counterweights to tendencies in Washington to start along a road of escalation in Korea that could have ended in World War III. In their urging for restraint, the allies received valuable support—at times even leadership—from India and other Asian neutrals.

A second theme centers on the role of the United Nations, which other scholars have written off as little more than an instrument of U.S. policy. To be sure, the international organization often played that role, but just as often it provided the setting for allied and neutral pressure on the United States, an institutional framework within which weaker nations could coordinate their efforts to influence the world's greatest power. Such efforts frequently succeeded, in part because many of those nations had contributed forces to Korea. The UN role in the Korean War merits attention not only as an agency of collective security against "aggression," but as a channel of restraint on a superpower that occasionally flirted with excessively risky endeavors.

A third theme is that participation in the war—its origins or its course or both—was often the result, at least in part, of calculations having little to do with Korea. Soviet leader Joseph Stalin gave Kim the green light in the spring of 1950 primarily to serve his purposes regarding China and Europe. Smaller backers of the UN cause in the fighting contributed largely in hopes of influencing the United States, frequently in places other than Korea.

This point leads to a fourth theme of the book, namely, that the war's impact was global, despite the limited geographical scope of the fighting. This impact originated not in Korea's strategic importance, which was merely regional, but in the challenge posed by the North Korean attack on a land controlled by a government created at the initiative of the United States and the United Nations. Washington assumed that Moscow was intimately involved in Pyongyang's action and that this involvement reflected a new Soviet aggressiveness, as well as a threat to U.S. credibility worldwide. Western European leaders agreed with the U.S. decision to resist "aggression." Like the U.S. leaders, they remembered the failure of the Western democracies during the 1930s to halt the expansionism of Japan, Germany, and Italy before it was too late to avoid a major war. With Soviet and Soviet proxy forces now holding substantial advantages over enemy military units in central and southeastern Europe, the allies of the North Atlantic Treaty Organization (NATO) agreed on the need both to resist the North Korean move and to build up their own armed strength. Over the next three years, the armed forces of NATO countries increased by some three million men; the United States committed six divisions to Europe on a semipermanent basis; and the allies constructed an elaborate infrastructure, organizational as well as material, to support the manpower increases, admitted Turkey and Greece to the fold, and moved far along the path toward accepting West German rearmament. Although Yugoslavia never joined NATO, it received substantial assistance from the United States, Great Britain, and France, it engaged in military staff talks with the United States, Greece, and Turkey, and it signed a defense pact with the two latter nations. More than any other factor, the Western response to the Korean War discouraged Soviet or Soviet proxy forces from moving against Yugoslavia.

The Western response was not limited to Korea and Europe. The United States concluded defense treaties with Japan, the Philippines, Australia, and New Zealand, it greatly expanded military assistance to the French in Indochina, and it took the lead in concluding a lenient peace treaty with Japan in which the Soviets refused to participate and which did not rule out future Japanese rearmament. In the aftermath of the war, the United States also concluded defense pacts with South Korea and Taiwan and initiated formation of the Southeast Asia Treaty Organization. Thus the Korean War played a pivotal role in the rearming of the West and in expanding U.S. military commitments on a global scale. U.S. aid to foreign countries, which before June 1950 had been more economic than military, shifted decisively to the latter category.

The Soviet bloc matched the West with a military buildup of its own. Although statistics on Communist countries are far from definitive, clearly an expansion and modernization of armed forces in the Soviet Union and eastern Europe began in late 1948 and speeded up considerably after the outbreak of war in Korea. By the end of the conflict in 1953, satellite armed forces totaled roughly 1.5 million men. According to a claim made later by Nikita Khrushchev, the Soviet military nearly doubled between 1948 and 1955. Although the claim is probably exaggerated, there is no question that a substantial increase occurred. In addition, army units were motorized and weaponry updated. Soviet air capabilities on and around the periphery of the Eurasian land mass grew enormously.[1]

A fifth theme is that the military buildups in both the West and the Soviet bloc had important economic and political consequences, which, in turn, influenced both the course and final impact of the war. Japan became an essential supplier of material for the UN cause in Korea and this role assisted greatly in Japan's final recovery from World War II and integration into the Western alliance system. In western Europe, higher military spending produced deficits in budgets and dollar accounts that were exacerbated by increased prices in raw materials and reduced economic assistance from the United States. The United States complained of what they considered to be the slow pace of European rearmament, and the Europeans resented U.S. pressure for greater efforts from their already strained economies. Such squabbling, often in public, encouraged leaders on the other side to believe that contradictions in the enemy camp ultimately would tear apart the enemy coalition. For a substantial period, this belief undermined U.S. bargaining power directed toward bringing the Korean War to an end.

Ironically, the popular discontent that emerged within the Soviet bloc in 1953 was, in part, a result of the rearmament drive in eastern Europe, and probably helped to speed Communist concessions for an armistice in Korea. Although Moscow managed to hold together the western portions of its empire, the strains in eastern Europe proved to be of greater magnitude than those between the United States and its European allies. Indeed, those strains joined with the broad Western response to the North Korean attack to provide a strong deterrent on the Kremlin against sanctioning conventional military ventures into territories outside the Soviet sphere of influence. If the world was more heavily armed in 1953 than three years earlier, the likelihood that the two superpowers would stumble into a direct military clash with each other was also substantially reduced. The Korean War raised cold war tensions to new heights, but its impact actually induced Stalin's successors to pursue a measure of détente with the West and with the wayward Communist regime of Josef Broz Tito in Yugoslavia.

The People's Republic of China (PRC) made overtures to the West as well, although they came more slowly and were on a more limited scale. Between Beijing and Washington, the barriers to a constructive relationship proved more difficult to overcome. China and the United States had confronted each other directly in Korea, both on the battlefield and at the negotiating table, and the experience produced lingering bitterness and fears on both sides. The war also provided the occasion for U.S. intervention to prevent the PRC from conquering the last bastion of the Nationalist government on Taiwan. When the PRC became directly involved in Korea, that U.S. policy on Taiwan became locked in place. Without a concession by Washington on this issue, a thaw in Sino-U.S. relations remained all but impossible.

Nonetheless, ongoing animosity between China and the United States did not preclude a drawing apart of Beijing and Moscow. The Korean War contributed enormously to the international prestige of the new China, which fought the world's greatest power to a standstill, and to China's stature in North Korea. The Soviet Union made essential contributions to North Korea's and China's struggle, but Pyongyang and Beijing took on the primary burden of risk and sacrifice. Whereas on the eve of the war the PRC had solicited a strong alliance with the Soviet Union, it emerged from the conflict with renewed self-assurance. Over time, that new stature could only increase the PRC's willingness to steer an independent course in foreign policy. For its part, North Korea was bound to play off its two allies to further its own purposes. Because the Korean War enhanced the long-term prospects for a Sino-Soviet split, led to North Korea's development as a distinct entity, and enabled the anti-Soviet Communist government in Yugoslavia to survive, it undermined the Soviet position as uncontested leader of international communism. Of the great powers, the Soviet Union clearly was the prime loser by virtue of the Korean War.

This and other consequences were partly the result of the war's length of more than three years and its indecisive result. Thus a final theme of this book is that the major actors had numerous opportunities to stunt the broader impact of the war, not to mention its consequences for the peninsula itself. Stalin, for example, might have persuaded the North Koreans to retreat to the prewar boundary during the weeks following the U.S. decision to send combat troops to the peninsula. In all likelihood, such a move would have brought an end to the war during the summer of 1950. That development would have represented a great victory for the United States, but its long-term impact would have been far more limited than what actually occurred. The war also might have ended in the fall of 1950, either with UN troops halting at the 38th parallel after the Inchon landing or with a triumphant march to the Yalu River. Again, these outcomes would have constituted striking victories for the United States. They would have produced differing impacts on international politics as well. U.S. prestige would have emerged less tarnished than it did after the clash with China, and Western and Soviet bloc military preparations probably would have risen more modestly. A successful U.S. effort to unite the peninsula behind a friendly regime would have represented a major blow to the Soviet Union, but one that might have had a less lingering impact than what ultimately came to pass. Finally, the war might have halted in early 1951 with the Chinese stopping their southward advance at the 38th parallel in the summer or fall of the same year, within weeks or months of the commencement of armistice talks, or in the spring of 1952, by which time the prisoner-of-war issue was the only stumbling block to peace. Any of these outcomes would have altered the war's impact on the international scene, as well as on Korea and on domestic developments in China, the United States, and elsewhere.

This brief excursion into the realm of counterfactuals highlights the need to analyze the Korean War in its parts in addition to examining it as a whole. At several times the conflict could have escalated out of control. It also could have ended at roughly the point where it started—as it actually did in July 1953—at the Yalu River or the Sea of Japan, with the peninsula unified under one government, or at the narrow neck just north of Pyongyang and Wonsan. That it started and ended in a particular way, in a particular place, and at a particular time had much to do with military events in Korea, but decisions and developments elsewhere also played a prominent role. Without ignoring indigenous forces, the primary goal of this study is to explain the course of the war from the perspectives of the great powers most prominently involved—the United States, the Soviet Union, and China.

In none of the cases described above is the story a simple one; in all of them, strategic and other peculiarly national concerns, ideology, domestic politics, and personalities played a role. Although ideological confrontation between authoritarian communism and liberal capitalism often appeared to be the most striking reality in the great power contest over Korea, it invariably was filtered through national perspectives, domestic pressures, and individual personalities. Thus ideology usually holds limited explanatory power for specific decisions. A common adherence to Marxism-Leninism drew Stalin and Chinese leader Mao Zedong together against the United States, but the vulnerability of their nations to U.S. power reinforced the bond. At the same time, differing national perspectives often produced divergent priorities. These divergences, in turn, necessitated extended bargaining between the governments, the outcome of which had a notable impact on events in Korea. On the Western side, the process was complicated by the existence of a larger number of actors and more pluralistic political systems. Yet even ideological and national perspectives together fail to capture the complexity of international interaction over Korea. The personality and characters of individual actors played a vital role. Stalin and Mao were willful men who placed strong personal stamps on their governments' policies. The same can be said of North Korea's Kim Il-sung, although his influence with his allies diminished once the war started, and especially after China committed its armies. The best-documented illustration of the impact of personality on the Communist side involves China's decision to enter the war. With PRC leaders—Chinese and Marxist-Leninist to a man—deeply divided over the issue of intervention, Mao took a firm hand in deciding to take on the United States in Korea. In the West, of course, no individual played as dominant a role in government as did Stalin or Mao, but presidents Harry S. Truman and Dwight D. Eisenhower, General Douglas MacArthur, Secretary of State Dean Acheson, and Secretary of Defense George C. Marshall all influenced decisions at particular times in ways that others in their places probably would not have. If the "great man" theory of history represents a distortion, structural approaches placing exclusive weight on ideology or the struggle for power among independent nation states hardly suffice as alternatives.

In a word, although this study provides meaningful generalizations about the nature and impact of the Korean War, it also analyzes the multiplicity of factors that produced specific decisions. More often than not, the precise congregation of forces in any particular case eludes the historian, but I remain convinced that the most consistently useful method in the quest is the careful examination of sources from the period being studied. To a considerable degree, I have based this book on original sources, many of them archival. Yet limited availability and my own limited capacities have produced some boundaries, which I have tried to circumvent when possible through the use of translations and other secondary sources. For the Communist side, I also have drawn extensively on official Western reporting—from Moscow, primarily of the British and the Americans; from Beijing, of the British, and, through the

British and Canadians, the Indians; and from New York, the British, the Americans, the Canadians, and the Australians. In both conception and method, this work combines the qualities of scholarly synthesis and the research monograph.

In seeing this manuscript off to the publisher after many years of labor, I confess to two dominant feelings, neither of which is altogether characteristic of me. First is a feeling of humility over the realization of how little I know about the Korean War, of how much remains to be done by those who will follow me. In particular, I am sensitive to historian Michael Hunt's warning of "the risks of dilettantism" among those who venture into the field of international history; that "cross-over research needs to . . . offer and evaluate evidence with sufficient knowledge and rigor to stand up to the scrutiny of specialists."[2] I can hope only that the specialists in various areas who have examined this study in manuscript form have been sufficiently rigorous in their criticism, and I sufficiently conscientious in responding to it. Second is a feeling of hope that my particular approach to international history will provide information and insights that others have missed, that this study will at least widen the path toward understanding and suggest ways for others to go beyond.

• CHAPTER 1 •

# The Origins of the Korean War

FROM CIVIL WAR TO INTERNATIONAL CONFLICT: 25–30 JUNE 1950

The wet season had begun. Heavy rain fell along much of the 38th parallel, the two-hundred-mile boundary between North and South Korea. In the Ongjin region, an isolated area on Korea's west-central coast, the crackle of small arms fire and the hollow boom of artillery suddenly interrupted the monotonous patter of the raindrops. It was the early hours of Sunday morning, 25 June 1950.

Who started the firing in the predawn hours of this dreary morning remains in doubt. The Ongjin region had long been the setting for border skirmishes between North and South Korean troops, and often the South had initiated the combat. The evidence for this day in June is ambiguous, even contradictory.

What followed the outbreak in Ongjin, however, is less uncertain. By daybreak, North Korean artillery had commenced firing at six other points along the 38th parallel. Soon thousands of North Korean soldiers poured southward. Some troops struck from the sea, landing along South Korea's east coast. By 9:30 in the morning the attackers had seized Kaesong, a key town located on the main railroad line leading to Seoul, South Korea's capital city. Two infantry divisions, with Soviet-built tanks in the vanguard, swarmed the main roads approaching the Uijongbu corridor, another gateway to Seoul. Before noon, YAK fighter planes attacked both the capital and nearby Kimpo airfield. A large-scale invasion was under way.[1]

The attack should have come as no surprise to South Korea or its sponsor, the United States. Top South Korean officials had warned for some time that an invasion was imminent. U.S. observers on the scene, though less alarmist, all recognized the possibility of an assault from the North.

Yet the North Korean onslaught caught the South off guard. Many of South Korea's military leaders were abroad, either in Japan or the United States. Numerous officers assigned to units along the tense boundary were away from their posts on weekend passes, as were many of the U.S. advisers attached to those forces. Of the four divisions and one regiment assigned to border duty, only four regiments and one battalion were positioned along the front. The permanent head of the U.S. advisory group in Korea had recently left the country for reassignment in the United States. His temporary replacement was in Tokyo saying good-bye to family members, who were themselves returning home.

The explanation for this gross lack of preparation rests in the psychology of individuals who, as Harold Joyce Noble, the first secretary of the U.S. embassy in Seoul, later wrote, "had lived so long on the edge of a volcano . . . [that they] had become accustomed to it." "We knew it would explode some day," he recalled, "but as day after day, month after month, and year after year passed and it did not blow up, we could hardly believe that tomorrow would be any different."[2]

"Tomorrow" was different, though, on 25 June 1950, and the failure of South Korean and U.S. officials to prepare for that contingency was to cost them dearly in the days ahead. Had the United States anticipated the offensive, diplomatic moves might have been initiated to discourage it. Even had these failed, the South Koreans and Americans might have taken military precautions that would have reduced the impact of North Korea's early thrusts. As it turned out, the attack greatly confused inexperienced South Korean officers and soldiers, and this confusion proved a tremendous asset to North Korean forces. By midnight on 27 June Seoul's defenses neared collapse, and, in the panic created by a rapid evacuation, South Korean troops blew up a key bridge over the Han River before critical supplies and several military units had escaped across it. The action destroyed any prospect of maintaining a position on the southern bank of the river. More formidable South Korean resistance, especially if reinforced by U.S. air and naval power, would have improved immeasurably the chances for a quick end to hostilities.

The surprise element only partially explains North Korea's rapid advance. The attackers both outgunned and outmanned their opponents. Supplied generously by the Soviet Union, North Korea had 150 medium-sized tanks and a small tactical air force; South Korea had no tanks and virtually no military aircraft. North Korea had a three-to-one numerical advantage in divisional artillery, and its best guns far outranged those of South Korea. Although both sides had a relatively equal number of contestants, tens of thousands of Koreans, hardened by combat in the Chinese civil war, filled North Korea's lead divisions.[3] The war began with Koreans fighting Koreans, but the inequality of the contest had much to do with the relative support given the two sides from beyond Korea's boundaries.

Alarmed, the United States moved quickly to prevent South Korea's extinction. In Tokyo, General Douglas MacArthur, the commander of U.S. forces in the Far East, began shipping arms and ammunition from Japan to South Korea, without even requesting prior approval from Washington. On the evening of 25 June (the morning of 26 June in Korea, which is thirteen hours ahead of America's eastern standard time), President Harry S. Truman ordered U.S. air and naval forces to assist in and protect the evacuation of Americans from South Korea. On the following day, after General MacArthur reported that South Korean forces could not hold Seoul and were in danger of collapse, Truman removed restrictions on U.S. air and naval operations below the 38th parallel. Four days later, after increased air and naval action had failed to halt North Korea's advance, the president committed U.S. ground units to combat on the peninsula.[4]

From almost the beginning, the involvement of the United Nations magnified the international aspects of the conflict. That organization had played a central role in Korea since late 1947, even sponsoring the creation of the Republic of Korea in the South. The United States now sought to perpetuate that role so as to cast its effort to repulse North Korea in a framework of collective security. On 25 June the UN Security Council rejected a neutrally worded measure advanced by Yugoslavia and, instead, adopted a resolution calling for "the immediate cessation of hostilities" on the peninsula, the withdrawal of North Korean forces to the 38th parallel, and "every assistance" from member nations in implementing the resolution. Two days later, with the North Koreans showing no intention of abiding by Security Council action, the council met again—and again the Soviet delegate, despite his veto power, chose not to attend. In his absence, the Security Council considered another U.S. resolution, which called on "members of the United Nations to furnish such assistance to the Republic of Korea as may be necessary to repel the armed attack and to restore international peace and security in the area."[5]

By this time the Security Council had received a report from the UN Commission on Korea (UNCOK), which had been created the previous year by the U.S.-dominated General Assembly. Among other activities, the body was to "observe and report any developments which might lead to, or otherwise involve, military conflict in Korea." UNCOK, whose military observers had returned to Seoul from an inspection tour along the 38th parallel only forty-eight hours before the hostilities began, stated that North Korea was "carrying out a well-planned, concerted and full-scale invasion of South Korea" against forces "deployed on [a] wholly defensive basis in all sectors of the parallel." Limited in numbers, transportation facilities, and familiarity with the terrain and the people, the military observers were in a poor position to render such judgments; moreover, UNCOK was far from nonpartisan in outlook. Nevertheless, the United States now used the UNCOK report to persuade six other Security Council members to support the resolution, the bare minimum needed for passage.[6] Before the end of the month, the British and the Australians had offered their air and naval units stationed in Japan to bolster U.S. and South Korean forces engaged on the peninsula, and Canada, the Netherlands, and New Zealand had offered naval vessels.[7]

More aid was sure to come, as most UN members agreed that the "aggression" could be the first stage in a tragic repetition of events of the 1930s, when Western democracies had stood idly by while dictators swallowed up one small nation after another.[8] K.C.O. Shann, head of the Australian mission at Lake Success, expressed a common thought among UN representatives from non-Communist nations when he wrote home that, "for all sorts of reasons of justice and reciprocity and the long-term effect on the American people toward the rest of the world, it must be hoped that . . . the burden of carrying through . . . is shared amongst the more fortunate of the United Nations."[9] By 3 July forty-one of the fifty-nine UN members had announced their approval of the Security Council action.[10] What had begun as a conflict between Koreans aimed at eradicating the division of their country soon became a struggle of broad international proportions, one that threatened to escalate into a direct confrontation between the West and the Soviet bloc.

Korea and the World Beyond: The Historical Context

That North Korea's attack on June 1950 did not long remain an internal affair is hardly surprising. Frequent invasions and almost perpetual foreign influence mark Korea's long history. China's involvement on the peninsula extends back over two millennia, and the Tang dynasty played a prominent role in Korea's unification thirteen centuries ago. For much of the next twelve hundred years, Korea was a "tributary" state of China, relying on a deferential relationship with that power to preserve its independence. Even so, from the thirteenth through the seventeenth centuries, Korea endured successive invasions from the Mongols, the Japanese, and the Manchus. For two centuries after that, Korea maintained itself as the "hermit kingdom," using its younger brother status in relation to China in the Confucian system of East Asia to maintain its isolation from the rest of the world. In the mid-nineteenth century that system began to break down and with it went Korea's ability to separate itself from outsiders.

"When whales fight, the shrimp in the middle get crushed." So goes an old Korean proverb, and the late nineteenth and early twentieth centuries illustrate its application to the peninsula. This period witnessed a transformation of the balance of power in northeast Asia. The Manchu dynasty of China, staggering from internal decay and Western incursion, could not shield Korea from either a rapidly modernizing Japan or an ever-expansive Russia. After trying for more than a decade to contain China's effort to reinforce its privileged position in Korea, Japan went to war in 1894. Japan's victory effectively eliminated China from the scene.

Now Russia emerged as the protector of Korea's independence. Protection meant exploitation and domination as well, an arrangement the Japanese proved unwilling to accept. In February 1904, after several years of indecisive jockeying over Korea, Japan suddenly attacked and defeated Russian forces at Port Arthur and Inchon. Korea announced its neutrality, but soon found itself occupied by Japanese troops. By this time Japan enjoyed an alliance with Great Britain and the benevolent neutrality of the United States, an emergent power in Asia, which was perfectly willing to concede Korea to Japan in return for the latter's assurances regarding the U.S. position in the Philippines. Following Russia's military defeat at the hands of Japan, the great powers acquiesced in Japan's control of Korea. In 1905 Japan established a protectorate over the hapless nation. Five years later, after the occupying army had largely suppressed indigenous independence movements, Japan annexed the peninsula. The whales had fought, and the victor engulfed the shrimp.[11]

Korea's traditional politics of factionalism hastened its demise. Like China, Korea at the turn of the century was in a state of political disintegration. Its Yi dynasty wallowed in corruption and inefficiency. The monarch offered erratic leadership, and the royal court occupied itself with petty squabbling and a venal quest for the king's favor. The struggle to maintain independence centered, as in China, on efforts to manipulate relations between rival foreign powers. Between 1896 and 1898 the Independence Club, a reform group influenced by American ideas of democracy and constitutionalism, made some gains, but it lacked organizational cohesion and a sufficient commitment to radical change to prevail over well-entrenched elites.[12] Although the monarchy squelched internal pressures for reform, it proved incapable of mobilizing resistance to Japanese incursion. From the establishment of the protectorate in 1905 to Japan's final defeat by the Allies in World War II, Korea never approached success in casting off the foreign yoke.

A flurry of activity did occur in the aftermath of World War I and U.S. President Woodrow Wilson's rhetoric about national self-determination. Korean patriots petitioned the peace conference at Paris and U.S. officials in Washington, while, at home, hundreds of thousands of Koreans demonstrated against Japanese rule. In both Shanghai and Seoul, Nationalist leaders established provisional Korean governments. The Bolshevik revolution in Russia inspired the creation of the Korean Communist movement in Manchuria and eastern Siberia, areas that thousands of Korean exiles had long used as bases for guerrilla activity against the Japanese in their homeland.

Yet these efforts lacked both coordination and substantial international support. The Provisional Government in Shanghai tried to weld together the independence forces, but the exiles were so scattered geographically and so varied in background as to preclude concerted action and harmonious relations among them. During 1921 the fragile coalition of groups represented in the Provisional Government all but disintegrated.

Events of the immediate postwar years manifested two conditions that remained central to the independence movement before 1945 and to Korean politics in general following Korea's liberation from Japan. First was the split between the Left and the Right, between people influenced by Marxism-Leninism, the Soviet Union, and/or the Chinese Communists and those subscribing to Western liberal ideas, Confucianism, or an amalgam of the two. Within Korea, the Communists and non-Communist nationalists achieved a united front in 1927, only to watch it disintegrate four years later. Right- and left-wing components of the exile movement located in Nationalist China combined forces under the Provisional Government early in 1944, but this was the first such alliance in a generation and it turned out to be more apparent than real.

Divisions within the independence movement frequently rested on less exalted grounds than ideology. Factionalism drained strength from Korean patriot organizations, left and right alike. In 1919 the Communist movement split into two factions: the Irkutsk group made up of "Russianized Koreans" who, though of Korean origin, had lived in Russia for some time and attached themselves firmly to the Soviet Communist Party, and the Shanghai group, which generally regarded communism as subservient to the goal of Korea's liberation from Japanese control. By 1945 the Communist exiles were even more divided. The Soviet faction constituted those who had long resided in the Soviet Maritime Province; the Yanan faction, peopled by Koreans who had been active in China between the world wars, had close associations with the Chinese Communists led by Mao Zedong; the Kapsan faction included Koreans who had operated in Manchuria during the 1930s but had moved into Soviet territory during World War II. These groups had limited contact with Communists in Korea, who themselves split into numerous factions.

Unity also eluded right-wing groups. In the mid-1920s feuding within the Provisional Government reached near comical proportions. When President Syngman Rhee halted the flow of money, collected in the United States, to government headquarters in Shanghai, the Provisional Legislative Assembly impeached him, and a five-member board found him guilty as charged. Rhee declared the decision illegal and went on with his fund-raising and lobbying activities in Hawaii and the continental United States, where Koreans also squabbled among themselves. In 1941 some progress occurred toward unity and even toward reconciliation between Rhee and the Provisional Government, but factionalism burst forth two years later when Rhee and his supporters seceded from the United Korean Committee in the United States. The politics of the Koreans in exile mirrored the familial and small-unit relationships that had prevailed in their homeland during the last centuries of the Yi dynasty. This pattern provided a weak foundation for either effective resistance to Japanese rule or an orderly transition to independence once that rule ended.

International conditions between Korea's annexation and World War II also ruled out a serious challenge to Japanese domination of the peninsula. At no time did a great power offer large-scale assistance to independence forces. The Soviet Union and China, the two nations most interested in Korea, lacked the strength to give much help. Both were busy fending off foreign predators and putting their own houses in order. The United States, which had the potential strength to assist Korea, had no inclination to do so. Such action would produce conflict with Japan, which would endanger U.S. trade with and investments in China and Japan and its hold on the Philippines. Without massive international aid, effective Korean resistance to Japanese rule was impossible. Japan held a vast military and economic advantage over the Koreans, and its geographical proximity to the peninsula made the exercise of control a relatively easy task. The poor prospects for success of the Korean independence movement created frustrations within its ranks and reinforced its tendency toward factionalism.[13]

World War II transformed this outlook and produced new, albeit inadequate, efforts among the exiles for a united front. Although the Allies continued to ignore Koreans as instruments in the battle against Japan, the war created an American determination to destroy the Japanese empire and produced conditions in which the Soviet Union could assist in the endeavor.

Moscow's interest in Korea is easily understood. The Soviet Union touches that country's northern frontier, and the peninsula has often been described as a dagger, pointed either at the heart of Japan or at Manchuria and eastern Siberia. In a word, nestled among the three great powers of northeast Asia, Korea is a potential launching pad for offensive operations by one against the others. Like Poland in the West, Korea under Soviet influence could be a source of strength to that power, just as under enemy control it could be a cause of weakness. Although for four decades after 1905 Russia preoccupied itself with defending its western frontiers, once Germany fell in May 1945 the Kremlin naturally turned increased attention eastward toward Korea and Manchuria.

America's interest in Korea is less obvious. During the last half of the nineteenth century, the United States played an active role in opening Korea to the Western powers. In 1871, on the coast of the peninsula near Inchon, a small U.S. expedition fought a pitched battle with Korean soldiers as part of an unsuccessful attempt to commence negotiations with the government on trade and the treatment of shipwrecked sailors.[14] Eleven years later the United States became the first Western nation to sign a "treaty of amity and commerce" with Korea.[15] To Korean leaders subscribing to a Confucian framework of international relations, the United States became an older brother, especially after the elimination of China's presence in the mid-1890s. The Koreans expected the United States to protect them from other great powers. Despite America's "outward thrust" in the generation after its civil war, however, U.S. activities in Korea reflected as much the verve of a few representatives abroad as a sustained interest on the part of Washington. Whereas early in the twentieth century Russia accepted Japanese domination of that country only after defeat in war, the United States accepted it without a quibble, even in the face of pleas from Korea to lend "good offices" under the treaty of 1882.[16] Six thousand miles from U.S. shores, lacking large quantities of crucial resources, and heatedly contested by other nations, Korea received little attention in the United States.

World War II ended this indifference. Although Korea was not central to U.S. postwar plans, it attracted some notice in Washington, and it did so under the assumption that the United States must now play a more active part in international affairs than ever before. U.S. policymakers believed that global instability between 1919 and 1939, and particularly the successful aggressions of Japan, Italy, and Germany during the 1930s, derived largely from the failure of the United States to assume a responsible position in the world community. To avoid a repetition of the present conflict after the defeat of the Axis powers, it was imperative that the United States assume a leading role in world affairs. Korea had not been the troublespot in the interwar period that it had been at the turn of the century, but the projected defeat of Japan in World War II threatened to provoke another great power rivalry over the peninsula. That concern grew early in the war as the Nationalist regime in China pushed for U.S. recognition of the Korean Provisional Government, now based at Chungking, the temporary Chinese capital. To Americans, that pressure represented China's effort to reestablish its position on the peninsula before the Sino-Japanese war, an action that could only create problems with the Soviet Union.[17]

Compounding the potential for trouble was Korea's apparent unpreparedness for independence. With few exceptions, U.S. analysts believed that the factionalism of the exile groups and their shallow roots among Korea's masses made them unlikely instruments for stable self-rule in their homeland.[18] President Franklin D. Roosevelt proposed an international trusteeship for Korea of the sort to be applied to Italian colonies in Africa and Japanese-held French colonies in Indochina. The plan involved multinational participation in Korea—the Soviet Union, China, the United States—as the best means of protecting the interests of all concerned. The great powers would work together to prepare the Korean people for independence.

At international conferences between late 1943 and early 1945, the United States received only partial support for this approach. The British never liked the trusteeship idea, as they feared its application to their own empire.[19] At Cairo in November 1943, Great Britain and China agreed that Korea should "in due course . . . become free and independent." Soon afterward, at Teheran, Roosevelt recorded that Soviet Premier Joseph Stalin accepted the judgment that Korea would require a period of tutelage before gaining independence.[20] Yet other statements by Soviet officials at the time indicate that they were noncommittal on Korea.[21] In early 1945, at Yalta, the U.S. president proposed a trusteeship for the peninsula to include the Soviet Union, the United States, China, and perhaps Great Britain. Stalin gave his oral approval, but showed no enthusiasm.[22]

Long before Yalta, possible Soviet designs had concerned U.S. officials dealing with Korea. In October 1943 a State Department paper concluded that,

> Korea may appear to offer a tempting opportunity [for Stalin] . . . to strengthen enormously the economic resources of the Soviet Far East, to acquire ice-free ports, and to occupy a dominating strategic position in relation both to China and Japan. . . . A Soviet occupation of Korea would create an entirely new strategic situation in the Far East, and its repercussions within China and Japan might be far reaching.[23]

Events of the next twenty months reinforced such fears. Nationalist China, mired in corruption and ineptitude, failed either to fight aggressively against the Japanese on the mainland or to lure their Communist opponents into a unified Chinese government. The growing likelihood that China would remain weak and divided in the postwar period, rather than become the emerging great power and "policeman" as Roosevelt had hoped, caused apprehensions about a power vacuum in northeast Asia that the Soviet Union would fill. This prospect became more alarming after the Yalta conference where Roosevelt, to ensure Soviet assistance in the war against Japan, conceded to

Stalin the Kurile Islands, the southern half of Sakhalin, and special privileges in Manchuria. Only the United States could provide balance in the area. U.S. plans for involvement on the peninsula became increasingly directed toward containing Soviet expansion.

The U.S. concerns were not unfounded. At both Teheran and Yalta, Stalin proved reluctant to be drawn out on the Korean issue, always leaving the initiative to Roosevelt and giving nothing more than vague oral commitments. Roosevelt did not push, as even at Yalta, the end of the Pacific war seemed more than a year away, and other issues were more pressing. Stalin had good reason not to reach detailed agreements on Korea. The Americans gave every indication of wanting to avoid ground operations against Japan on the mainland of northeast Asia. With the Soviets intending to declare war against Japan two or three months after Germany's fall, Stalin probably calculated that his own forces would occupy most or all of Korea, which would put him in a position to bargain for a good deal more than a quarter share in a multipower trusteeship.[24]

In July, at Potsdam, neither side attempted to work out specific arrangements on Korea. Initially, Harry S. Truman, the new U.S. president, held back because of British Prime Minister Winston Churchill's sensitivity about trusteeship, which might be applied to Italian colonies in the Mediterranean and even the British empire.[25] Then, on 23 July, word reached Truman that an atomic bomb would be ready for use against Japan during the first week of August. Hope arose that the weapon would force Japan's surrender before the USSR entered the Pacific war. Washington's relations with Moscow had chilled since the Yalta conference, as the two sides sometimes disagreed on the meaning of the accords reached there. President Truman now contemplated the possibility of shutting the Soviets out of Korea entirely.[26]

Subsequent events belied this hope. During the second week of July, the Japanese had approached Moscow about mediating an end to the war.[27] Aware of the possibility of an early Japanese collapse, and of its potential impact on his nation's share of the spoils in northeast Asia, Stalin pressed his generals to speed up preparations for entry into the war. At Potsdam, he told Truman that his forces would be ready for action in mid-August, but the Soviet declaration of war actually came on the eighth.[28] Soviet troops entered the extreme northeast reaches of Korea before Japan surrendered six days later. British forces concentrated on the southern Pacific and southeast Asia, and the Nationalist Chinese were busy reoccupying Japanese-held territory in their homeland and in northern Indochina. Only the Soviet Union and the United States could occupy Korea, and U.S. ground forces remained several hundred miles from the peninsula. With an airlift and use of speedy naval transports, U.S. units might have landed on the peninsula before their Soviet counterparts moved far southward. But General Douglas MacArthur, commander of U.S. forces in the Far East, wanted to concentrate his armies for the occupation of Japan. Planners in Washington, overestimating the Soviet head start in Korea, did not insist that he alter his plans.[29]

Stalin made no effort to occupy all of Korea. In mid-August, when the

United States proposed the 38th parallel as a dividing line between Soviet and U.S. occupation zones, he readily agreed, even though this arrangement placed under American control two-thirds of the country's population, as well as Seoul, the most important city. Stalin's agreement rested primarily on military conditions in Korea combined with uncertainty regarding U.S. intentions. At the end of the second week of August, the Soviets had only two infantry divisions on the peninsula, and these faced nine Japanese divisions, which showed every indication of intending to fight.[30] Soviet troops occupied only the extreme northeastern tip of Korea, hundreds of miles from Seoul over rugged terrain. If Stalin rejected the 38th parallel, the Americans might airlift troops to Seoul from Okinawa, and what if Japanese troops surrendered to them while continuing to fight the Soviets?[31] Furthermore, occupation south to the 38th parallel would give the Soviets access to coveted warm-water ports and the bulk of the country's industry, including hydroelectric power, as well as a substantial buffer for their own nation's far eastern boundary. Stalin probably viewed the line as a firm one, designating spheres of influence in Korea. On the eve of war with Japan at the turn of the century, Tokyo had proposed the 38th parallel as a possible dividing line between their spheres, but then Russia had been greedy and had paid a high price for its effort to dominate the entire peninsula. Now, with the United States still mobilized for war and holding a monopoly on the atomic bomb, Stalin concluded that the time was not ripe to quibble over a relatively minor issue. He may have believed that a cooperative spirit on Korea would help persuade the United States to concede his nation a significant role in the occupation of Japan, which was of far greater moment.

Soviet-U.S. occupation of Korea, especially without precise agreements on its nature and duration, greatly reduced Korea's prospects for a smooth transition toward independence and unity. As the immediate threat from these common wartime enemies disappeared, the Soviet Union and the United States, now clearly the world's most powerful nations, found it increasingly difficult to reach new agreements or even to execute old ones where these were vague. In Korea, the division of the independence movement into Communist and anti-Communist groups compounded the potential problems in constructing a unified, indigenous government. By early September 1945, when U.S. troops finally arrived on the peninsula, the seeds of future trouble were firmly planted.

## Occupation, Division, and Turmoil

Thousands of Koreans roared approval as U.S. occupation authorities in Seoul lowered the Japanese flag and raised the stars and stripes.[32] U.S. troops had landed in Korea on the previous day, 8 September, a month after Soviet forces had entered the country from the north. Euphoria reigned among Koreans, who had long hungered for independence.

From the beginning, however, the Soviet-U.S. occupation cast dark clouds over Korean hopes. Soviet troops above the 38th parallel behaved so badly that they soon had to travel in threes after dark to protect themselves from outraged natives.[33] U.S. soldiers in the South were a trifle less rapacious, but their commander, Lieutenant General John R. Hodge, proved abysmally insensitive to Korean desires for immediate liberation from their hated Japanese overlords. In the Pacific campaigns against Japan, Hodge had distinguished himself as a capable, hard-driving field commander. Yet his instincts were profoundly conservative, and he had no training or experience in politics, no knowledge of Korea, and little initial guidance from his superiors in Washington or in the Far Eastern Command. His selection as occupation commander derived solely from his XXIV Corps' proximity to Korea when Japan surrendered.[34] They were in Okinawa, six hundred miles away, which was closer than any other major unit not assigned for duty in Japan. His Soviet counterpart in the North, Colonel General Ivan Chistiakov, was a hero of the Soviet Union who had commanded an army at Stalingrad and, for much of the 1930s, had served in the Soviet Far East.[35] Now he quickly replaced Japanese officials with Koreans, many of whom had returned from exile with Soviet forces. In contrast, Hodge proclaimed that Japanese personnel would remain in administrative posts in the U.S. zone until qualified Koreans could be found to replace them. "The greatest need of Koreans today," he declared, "is patience."[36]

"Need" and reality did not coincide. On 10 September throngs of Koreans took to the streets of Seoul to protest Hodge's policy. Two Koreans attempting to seize a police station died at the hands of Japanese military police. Under pressure from Washington, as well as from within South Korea, Hodge ousted the Japanese governor and police chief and replaced them with Americans.[37]

Hodge's other moves overshadowed this gesture. If the hardening of occupation zones into separate political entities was to be averted, two tendencies of Korean politics, ideological polarization and factionalism, had to be contained. The first would magnify Soviet and U.S. fears of the peninsula's domination by the other, eliminating prospects for a compromise settlement in the form of neutralization. Factionalism would subvert possibilities for establishing a coalition of internal forces and would encourage the occupying powers to choose sides in political squabbles in order to maintain order. Because the ideological perspectives of the United States and the Soviet Union differed so radically, they were unlikely to wind up supporting the same groups.

Hodge's actions fostered both phenomena. He refused to recognize or consult the "People's Republic," a self-proclaimed government that attracted much support nationwide. Although dominated by left-wing sympathizers, its leaders tried to establish a broad base by appointing to important positions representatives of the center and the Right, including exiles. Syngman Rhee was designated chairman, albeit without his knowledge or approval. Despite his absence in the United States, he was widely known in Korea and highly respected, in part because of his advanced age—he turned seventy in 1945—

which in Korea's patriarchal society was considered a source of wisdom, and in part because his lineage connected him to the royal family of the Yi dynasty.[38] His membership in the Independence Club many years before, his possession of a Ph.D. from Princeton University, and his tireless lobbying abroad against Japanese domination also contributed to his status. While Soviet occupation authorities made extensive use of the people's committees, which were the local organs of the republic, Hodge, to preserve order in the U.S. zone, maintained the bureaucratic structure of the Japanese. He merely replaced the departed colonial officialdom with Americans and conservative Koreans, many of whom had held minor administrative positions in the previous regime. In discouraging the People's Republic, Hodge broke the first and most promising effort at national cohesion in Korea's recent history.[39]

Hodge encouraged the formation of political parties. The result, as one U.S. officer noted with only moderate exaggeration, was that "every time two Koreans sit down to eat they form a new political party." By early November, 205 groups had registered with the U.S. military government.[40] To encourage order and to undermine the Left, Hodge turned to Korean conservatives, many of whom had collaborated with the Japanese and, on the eve of the U.S. arrival, had formed the Korean Democratic Party to counter the People's Republic. He also pressed for the return to Korea of conservatives Rhee and Kim Ku, the head of the Provisional Government. The former arrived in mid-October, the latter a month later. Although Kim soon proved inept at political maneuver, Rhee excelled both at self-promotion and at blasting the indigenous Communists and the Soviets. The Right remained faction-ridden, but it now had a dynamic leader who rejected the People's Republic and made no pretense of seeking compromise with the Left. Thus prospects for national unification rapidly diminished.[41]

With that said, it remains uncertain that different leadership of the U.S. occupation could have averted a division of the peninsula. In their zone, Soviet authorities initially permitted both non-Communists and domestic Communists, who had no allegiance to the Soviet Union, to participate in government activities. But the Soviets gave no encouragement to the Seoul-based People's Republic and, despite the North's need for rice from the South, greatly restricted economic interaction between the zones. In October, over the objections of most domestic Communists, the Soviet command sponsored the establishment of a northern branch of the party. Two months later, the Soviets simply referred to it as the North Korean Communist Party. Kim Il-sung, an early advocate of creating the organization, became its chairman. A thirty-three-year-old former leader of anti-Japanese guerrillas in Manchuria who spent much of World War II as an officer in a multinational unit in the Soviet army stationed near Khabarovsk, Kim went out of his way to endear himself to Soviet officers early in the occupation.[42] In January 1946 most of the non-Communists, including the prominent Christian leader Cho Man-sik, were purged because of their opposition to trusteeship. Conceivably, these actions were responses to Hodge's moves toward a separate indigenous administration in the South and his favoritism toward anti-Communist groups. More likely, they reflected Stalin's unwillingness, in this "Poland of the East," to risk a unified national government free from Soviet control.[43]

In the spring of 1946 negotiations between the occupation commands tested prospects for peaceful unification. The setting was a joint commission agreed on the previous December at the meeting of foreign ministers in Moscow. The new body was to submit proposals for "the formation of a provisional Korean government" and of a five-year, four-power trusteeship to the prospective trustees—the Soviet Union, the United States, Great Britain, and China. In drawing up recommendations, the commission was to consult with "Korean democratic parties and social organizations." The ultimate authority to judge commission proposals rested with the governments of the occupying powers.[44]

The joint commission quickly divided over the question of consultation with Korean groups. The Soviets wanted to consult only groups supporting the Moscow agreements, that is, trusteeship. Because the Korean Communists had followed the Soviets in supporting trusteeship, and because all moderate and right-wing groups opposed that approach, the Soviet plan would eliminate from consultation all parties free of its influence. The United States rejected this scheme and, with non-Communist leaders organizing a mass campaign against trusteeship, the Americans even hedged on the feasibility of the idea itself. In early May the deadlocked commission adjourned. It did not meet again for more than a year.[45]

Meanwhile, Korean politics became increasingly polarized. Above the 38th parallel the Communist-dominated "Korean National Democratic Front" held firm control. This organization encompassed the three primary factions within the Communist movement: the Soviet group, dominated by Kim Il-sung, which now included both Koreans with extended residences in the USSR before 1945 and the Kapsan faction; the Yanan group, led by Kim Tu-bong; and the domestic faction, whose leader, Pak Hon-yong, operated primarily in the South until 1948. Constant jockeying occurred among these groups, but the Soviet Union remained the ultimate arbiter, much to the benefit of Kim Il-sung. Factionalism never spilled over into North Korean society, although some unrest did exist in both town and country into the spring of 1946. Ultimately, the Soviet army, together with land and labor reform and a massive migration into the U.S. zone—which by 1948 probably exceeded a million people—produced tranquility in the North.[46]

Conditions in the South were far from tranquil. The trusteeship issue provided one source of disruption. Unlike their Soviet counterparts, who mustered Communist support for the Moscow agreement and purged the non-Communist dissenters, U.S. occupation authorities, lacking a firm commitment to authoritarian methods, encountered persistent opposition to trusteeship from their natural allies on the Right. Syngman Rhee had concluded from bitter experience that the United States could not be trusted to act in Korea's interests. As a young man in 1904, he had been sent to the United States by the Korean king, Kojong, to seek the good offices of the U.S. government with Japan under the treaty of 1882. U.S. leaders had concocted flimsy technicalities to justify inaction.[47] Now Rhee and other ultranationalists were hardly unquestioning followers of the U.S. line. Their campaign against trusteeship subsided temporarily after the Joint Commission adjourned in May 1946, but factionalism remained widespread, with Rhee and Kim Ku on the far Right, Kim Kyu-sik in the center, Yo Un-hyong on the moderate Left, and Pak Hon-yong on the radical Left holding the most prominent positions in the scramble for influence. Prodding from the State Department in Washington induced General Hodge to seek a coalition of moderate forces, which, if successful, would undermine Rhee and combat Communist efforts to develop popular backing. Yet Hodge refused to seize control of the police from the Right or to initiate large-scale economic reforms to improve the lot of the peasantry or the urban workers.

The result verged on chaos. Partisan police activity ensured that Rhee's forces would win a sizable majority in any election, as they did in one for an Interim Legislative Assembly in October 1946. But neither the Communists nor the moderate groups accepted the outcome, and when Hodge favored moderates in filling appointive positions in the assembly, he infuriated Rhee without gaining control over the new body. As 1947 dawned, Hodge confronted an increasingly militant Right determined to bring an early end to the U.S. occupation.

The Communists, despite repressive efforts by the police and the U.S. army, continued to exploit depressed economic conditions. In October 1945 Hodge had lowered rents for tenant farmers, who made up a sizable portion of the rural population, but he failed to redistribute land. Without such action, the rural poor stood little chance of advancement. Conditions in the cities were even less encouraging. Between July 1945 and March 1946 prices rose more than five times as rapidly as wages. The system of transporting crops from farm to city was completely inadequate and pricing policies of the occupation encouraged hoarding among the wealthy. Then, during the summer of 1946, floods destroyed 20 percent of the crop. For South Korea's masses, the year since liberation from Japan had been one of unfulfilled expectations. In September urban workers turned to strikes and riots to express their discontent. The unrest spread to the countryside, where landlords became frequent objects of attack. Hundreds of civilians and police died in the turmoil. Such circumstances scarcely provided a framework for productive talks regarding unification, either between the occupation commands or among Korean factions and parties.[48]

## KOREA, THE COLD WAR, AND THE UNITED NATIONS

International politics mirrored the stalemate in Korea. During 1946 Soviet-U.S. relations deteriorated rapidly. Increasingly, U.S. leaders viewed Soviet-imposed Communist governments in Poland, Bulgaria, and Rumania as manifestations of expansive designs in Moscow. February and March saw a hardening of the rhetoric of the two superpowers toward each other. Late March brought a crisis over the presence of Soviet troops in Iran. In May Soviet forces finally withdrew from Iran—and Manchuria as well—but only after considerable U.S. pressure. At the same time, the United States halted reparations shipments from the American to the Soviet, French, and British occupation zones of Germany, which represented a giant step toward a Germany divided into pro-Soviet and pro-Western sectors. In August tensions mounted in the eastern Mediterranean over Soviet demands for a role in the defense of the Dardanelles. Despite Moscow's eventual retreat on this issue, the Mediterranean remained a troublespot because of a Communist-led rebellion in Greece. When in February 1947 Great Britain informed Washington that it soon would withdraw aid to the tottering Greek government, the Truman administration launched major new initiatives to contain Soviet influence. First the United States appropriated $400 million for economic and military assistance to Greece and Turkey. Four months later Secretary of State George C. Marshall proposed massive U.S. economic aid for a depressed Europe, the western portions of which stood threatened by Communist revolution. The cold war was under way.

Despite the sorry state of Soviet-U.S. relations, in mid-1947 Washington made one final effort to break the Korean impasse. In April Marshall approached Soviet foreign minister V. M. Molotov with a proposal to reconvene the Joint Commission. The Soviets agreed, and the body commenced meetings in Seoul the next month. The roadblock over consulting Korean groups soon reappeared. The Soviets continued to insist on the exclusion of parties openly opposing the 1945 Moscow accords, and Rhee, convinced that his prospects were best served by a stalemate in the Joint Commission and the establishment of an independent government in South Korea, campaigned aggressively against trusteeship. Typically, the United States was irate at Rhee but unwilling to suppress his activities. Difficult as he was to get along with, he had impeccable anti-Communist credentials, and he had no peer on the Right as a political operator. With negotiations in the Joint Commission hopelessly deadlocked, U.S. leaders decided in September to dump the Korean problem into the lap of the United Nations General Assembly.

The move reflected U.S. weakness in Korea. Conditions below the 38th parallel had steadily deteriorated. The absence of land reforms combined with the division of the peninsula and the influx of Koreans from the Soviet zone and Japan to produce a depressed economy. The Communists, aided by infiltrators from the North, took full advantage of this situation. Joseph E. Jacobs, the top State Department official on the scene, estimated that "at least thirty percent of the people in South Korea are leftists, following Communist leaders who support the Soviets behind United States lines."[49] During the spring of 1947 the State Department, concerned about Japan's economic recovery and aware of the peninsula's role as food supplier and market for finished goods for that island nation, had developed a plan for major economic assistance to South Korea. But signals from Congress, heavily influenced by fiscal conservatives suspicious of America's expanding role abroad, were so discouraging that the State Department postponed advancing its plan. Military conditions in Korea were no more encouraging than economic ones. North Korea's armed forces were far stronger than those indigenous to the South, and growing U.S. commitments elsewhere, together with recent congressional cuts in the defense budget, forced a reduction in U.S. occupation forces. U.S. military leaders, who previously had regarded Korea's fate as of considerable importance to developments in China and Japan, reluctantly concluded that the United States had "little strategic interest" in maintaining troops in Korea.[50]

Still, the Truman administration believed that it must make some effort to salvage part of Korea. Although the United States should withdraw its troops "as soon as possible," it could not simply "'scuttle' and run."[51] The physical losses resulting from Soviet control of the peninsula were bearable: the United States could neutralize Korea with its air power in Japan and could look elsewhere for new markets and food for that nation. Yet the U.S. stake in Korea was no longer perceived in merely physical terms. Korea was the only country where the Soviets and the Americans confronted each other directly, without the involvement of either an internationally recognized native government or a third foreign power. "It is here," one U.S. diplomat declared in mid-1946, "where a test will be made of whether a democratic competitive system can be adopted to meet the challenge of defeated feudalism, or whether some other system, i.e., Communism, will be stronger."[52] "I fear," a State Department official wrote in September 1947, that U.S. abandonment of Korea "will be interpreted throughout the world as an indication that the United States has decided not to maintain its strong position in the Far East. The result upon Soviet policy toward the United States, both [in] . . . the Far East and . . . in Europe, would . . . be unfortunate."[53] As other nations—friend and foe alike—watched anxiously to see if the United States had the will to sustain a commanding presence outside the Western hemisphere, the surrender of South Korea threatened to jeopardize U.S. credibility worldwide.

The United Nations became the instrument both for a U.S. military withdrawal from Korea and for one last effort to prevent a U.S. debacle there. On the one hand, if the United States presented the case of Korea to the General Assembly under the pretext of expediting the independence of the peninsula, the Soviet Union might find it difficult to oppose UN supervision of democratic procedures to unify the country.[54] The Communists might triumph through such a process, but at least it would be orderly and democratic. Korea would not be abandoned to chaos and civil war. On the other hand, because the United States dominated the General Assembly, Stalin was more likely to oppose UN intervention in Korea, which would pave the way for the creation of an independent state below the 38th parallel. Such an entity would remain vulnerable both to internal disintegration and to outside attack. But limited, well-supervised U.S. economic aid might prevent decay from within. The Soviets might hesitate to unleash North Korean forces against a regime with broad international sanction through the United Nations. The odds were long, but as the Truman administration pressed ahead in its effort to halt communism in western Europe and the Mediterranean, the United Nations option seemed the only honorable means of extricating the United States from a most awkward entanglement. In engaging the international body in Korea, the United States altered the framework of foreign involvement on the peninsula from an essentially bilateral to a multilateral one, a shift of considerable long-term consequence.

The Soviets, having had little success in eastern Europe with free elections and holding a mere third of Korea's population in their zone, opposed a resolution in the General Assembly calling for elections throughout Korea to establish a national assembly. The resolution passed anyway, creating a United Nations Temporary Commission on Korea (UNTCOK) to supervise the process. When the Soviets carried out their threat to deny UNTCOK entry into the North, the United States secured United Nations sanction, through the Interim Committee of the General Assembly, for elections in the South alone directed toward establishment of a "National Government."[55]

This accomplishment required considerable effort by U.S. diplomats. Australia and Canada opposed UN-sponsored elections in the South alone, and India expressed serious doubts about this course. These nations thought that it moved beyond the terms of the General Assembly resolution of the previous fall and would solidify the division of the peninsula, increasing the prospects for future conflict. Moderate South Korea leader Kim Kyu-sik's proposal for a North-South conference on unification provided an attractive stage between the present course of Soviet-U.S. stalemate and clear-cut action to divide Korea. UNTCOK itself anticipated at most that it would be advised to observe elections to establish a consultative assembly in the South. America's handling of the Korean issue within the United Nations produced a cabinet crisis in Canada. Prime Minister W. L. Mackenzie King acquiesced in the U.S. position only when key members of the cabinet threatened to resign and President Truman made a direct appeal. The British went along, too, but without enthusiasm. Only intense lobbying by the United States in the heightened anti-Soviet climate created by the recent Communist coup in Czechoslovakia persuaded most governments to support the U.S. stance. Even so, a third of the delegates abstained in the Interim Committee, a body in which Soviet bloc representatives refused to participate. The episode revealed the United Nations more as an instrument of cold war politics than an agency devoted to facilitating negotiations on divisive issues.[56]

Elections in South Korea took place on 10 May 1948, despite protests by leftists, moderates, and some rightists. A North-South conference did occur in Pyongyang in late April, with Kim Kyu-sik and Kim Ku participating, but the event failed to disrupt the elections. Upon their return to Seoul on 5 May, the two men refused to engage in the campaign, yet they also failed to mount strong resistance to it. Both men, as well as numerous others from the South who went to Pyongyang, were disappointed by the determination of North Korean leaders to control the conference. Thus no broad-based "united front" between northern and southern political groups emerged. Back in Seoul, the two Kims faced considerable official pressure not to aggressively oppose the elections. Ultimately, their failure to participate, together with the highly partisan activities of police and youth groups, enabled Rhee and his allies to win handily.[57] Widespread violence marred the process, and UNTCOK endorsed the election as "a valid expression of the free will of the electorate" only after acrimonious debate and over the objections of Canadian, Australian, and Syrian delegates.[58]

During the ensuing weeks, the newly created "national assembly," with a hundred seats for nonexistent representatives from above the 38th parallel, drafted and approved a constitution for the Republic of Korea (ROK) and elected Rhee its first president. On 15 August, with General MacArthur visiting Seoul for the first time, the republic began its fragile existence.

In its zone, the Soviet Union followed the U.S. lead. On 25 August a "national" election occurred to choose a Supreme People's Assembly. That body met a week later to approve a constitution and formally create a government. In mid-September North Korean Communists in Pyongyang established the Democratic People's Republic of Korea (DPRK), with Kim Il-sung as premier.

With the peninsula housing two indigenous governments, each claiming jurisdiction over the entire country, a major precondition for war was firmly in place. Their ideologies stood at opposite poles, as did their great power sponsors, whose relationship elsewhere continued to deteriorate. Both Korean governments longed for full sovereignty over their divided nation, and with peaceful unification a remote possibility, the path of violence beckoned whichever side could muster the strength to overwhelm its bitter rival.

## THE PRECARIOUS BALANCE

North Korea continued to be more stable than its opponent in the South. Although Kim's leadership in Pyongyang was not beyond challenge, factionalism did nothing to undermine internal order. In contrast, divisions within the Right below the 38th parallel made smooth government operations there impossible. The Korean Democratic Party, which represented the large landholders and held a plurality in the National Assembly in Seoul, resisted Rhee's efforts at domination. The party had backed Rhee for president, but it now attempted to control the government through the legislative branch. It even pushed bills through the lawmaking body that threatened the interests of the state bureaucracy and the police force, which controlled their implementation. Such conflicts revealed the shallowness of Rhee's political base. He could not dodge critical issues, yet the very groups that had helped elect him were often on opposite sides.[59] His stubbornness, reflected in his selection of a cabinet that failed to represent the various groups within the assembly, further undermined his position.

Land reform needed special attention. The U.S. military government had waited until the spring of 1948 to carry out a land redistribution program, hoping that the Koreans would institute such action themselves through their Interim Legislative Assembly. When that body dragged its feet, the Americans finally acted, but only on acreage formerly owned by Japanese. The action was so popular that most candidates in the May 1948 elections advocated its extension to other lands as well. Once in office, however, successful candidates had difficulty agreeing on specific legislation. Meanwhile, in anticipation of the eventual passage of a bill providing for redistribution, many landowners forced tenants to purchase plots on unfavorable terms.[60]

The squabbling in Seoul occurred in the midst of a challenge in the provinces. In the fall of 1948 a revolt on Cheju Island, located off the southern coast of the peninsula, spread to the cities of Yosu and Taegu on the mainland. These incidents were part of a larger pattern of civil disorder that engulfed several coastal and mountainous areas. Rhee responded by imposing martial law over much of South Korea.[61] Aided by North Korea, subversive activities in the South gained their primary impetus from economic conditions and distaste for a government that U.S. ambassador John J. Muccio characterized as "incompetent" and "without strong public support."[62]

Muccio's report reached the U.S. State Department as the Chinese Communists consolidated their hold over Manchuria and North China. To U.S. diplomats, the Communist victory over the Nationalist forces of Jiang Jieshi derived from the corruption and ineptitude of an opponent who refused to implement broad political and economic reforms. U.S. observers saw in Rhee and his government many of the characteristics that had produced Jiang's decline.

Yet the Nationalist government was not a creation of the United States; the Republic of Korea was. To abandon Rhee in his time of trial by withdrawing all American troops from the peninsula would represent a major setback to U.S. prestige. If Korea then followed China along the path of communism the Japanese, responding to prevailing winds, might be difficult to keep in the Western camp. Likewise, America's friends in Europe and the Mediterranean might question U.S. reliability against Soviet penetration.[63] Despite distaste for Rhee, despite the call of the UN General Assembly on 12 December for the withdrawal of foreign troops from Korea "as soon as practicable," and disregarding the Soviet announcement that its forces would depart from North Korea by the end of the year, the United States postponed the removal from the peninsula of seventy-five hundred U.S. soldiers.

In the following June, and in spite of the opposition of Rhee and some officials in the State Department and the UN commission, the last U.S. troops finally did leave.[64] By that time conditions within South Korea appeared less desperate. Farmers had enjoyed a bountiful harvest during the previous fall, a U.S. economic aid program had begun to take hold, and U.S. arms and military advisers had helped strengthen South Korea's army. By some estimates, ROK forces were now "fairly evenly balanced" with those in the North. Through limited economic and military aid and the continuing involvement of UN observers, Washington hoped to deter an attack from the North.[65]

No consensus existed on what should be done if deterrence failed. The Joint Chiefs of Staff regarded as "militarily unsound" any commitment of U.S. troops to the peninsula. Yet exchanges between the State and Army departments, plus planning papers from the latter agency, indicated that some sentiment existed for the deployment of U.S. troops in Korea for political reasons, but only as a last resort as part of a UN force.[66]

Although South Korea had closed the gap in military strength between itself and North Korea, a stable balance remained unlikely. In late 1946 or early 1947 Kim Il-sung had begun dispatching tens of thousands of Koreans to China to assist the Communists in their struggle against Jiang Jieshi. Apparently, the first major Korean unit returned to the homeland in February 1948 and was quickly integrated into North Korea's army. The rapid collapse of Nationalist forces in the Chinese civil war from the fall of 1948 onward meant that many thousands more Korean nationals who had served in Mao's armies might now return home, greatly augmenting North Korea's strength.[67] Furthermore, in March 1949 Pyongyang and Moscow concluded an arms pact in which the latter committed itself to supply an expanded North Korean military machine.[68]

The United States was in no position to help South Korea keep pace with its rival. Domestic politics and prevailing economic thought in Washington put severe limitations on funds available to support foreign policy. During 1948, in typical election-year fashion, Congress had passed a tax cut, overriding President Truman's veto. The chief executive, a believer both in balanced budgets and an expanded welfare state, walked a tightrope in planning expenditures between internal and external needs. In doing so, he held to a defense budget inadequate to protect America's commitments abroad. This fact helps explain the final withdrawal of U.S. troops from Korea in the face of jitters in the State Department. The Mutual Defense Assistance Act of October 1949 did provide funds for arms to South Korea to support a sixty-five-thousand-man army, but the limited materials available for similar programs elsewhere necessitated the establishment of priorities for aid. In such a hierarchy the ROK ranked below friendly powers in western Europe and the Middle East. By mid-June 1950 the South Korean army had adequate supplies to sustain defensive operations for only fifteen days.[69]

U.S. discontent with Rhee also helped to limit the aid provided South Korea. Not only was he the promoter of a police state unsympathetic to economic reform—a land redistribution act did not pass until June 1949, and even then Rhee showed little inclination to implement it—he was determined to unify the peninsula, if necessary by force. In May, partially as an effort to heighten tensions to either prevent the final withdrawal of U.S. troops or to obtain security guarantees from Washington, ROK forces provoked a series of incidents along the 38th parallel. These incidents lasted for the rest of the year, frequently involving large-scale fighting between North and South Korean forces. Washington officials wondered if Rhee's appeals for more arms were not simply a ploy to prepare him for a march north and fulfillment of his destiny as the father of modern Korea.[70]

Suspicions of Rhee aside, unrest within South Korea conditioned U.S. observers to believe that, for the moment, North Korea would limit itself to covert methods in its attempt to destroy the ROK. By the spring of 1950 Rhee's antiguerrilla campaigns had produced reduced subversive activity, but U.S. intelligence believed that this was merely a lull in the ongoing Communist effort to "bore from within."[71] Because officials in the field regarded an early attack from the North as unlikely, those in Washington preoccupied themselves with Communist Chinese preparations for an invasion of Taiwan, Jiang's only remaining bastion, and with possible stepped-up Communist activity in Indochina, where the French struggled to maintain a foothold.[72]

Secretary of State Acheson's treatment of Korea in his National Press Club speech of 12 January 1950 reflected the belief that a North Korean attack was not imminent. "Subversion and penetration" represented the primary threats to South Korea's existence, Acheson claimed, and they could be resisted through limited economic assistance and the promotion of democratic institutions. Beyond Japan, the Ryukyus, and the Philippines, the United States could not guarantee areas in the Western Pacific "against military attack." The people in such areas must rely initially on their own efforts to defend themselves, but then on "the United Nations which so far has not proved a weak read to lean on by . . . [those] who are determined to protect their independence against outside aggression."[73] Acheson would have been wise to omit mention of the U.S. defense perimeter, but his definition merely repeated a public statement by General MacArthur during the previous March and his attention to South Korea hardly suggested a lack of concern.[74] First and foremost, the speech was a response to clamor in the press and the China bloc in Congress for U.S. action to save the Nationalist Chinese regime on Taiwan. Fearing commitment to a losing enterprise that would push the Chinese Communists closer to the Soviet Union, Acheson opposed such action, and President Truman supported him. The Joint Chiefs were more concerned about Taiwan, however, and they persuaded the chief executive to include the words "at this time" to his announcement that the United States had no desire to establish military bases on the island. The military leaders were less worried about Korea, as were pro-Jiang forces in the press and Congress.[75] Under the circumstances, even had the secretary of state been so inclined, he was in no position to speak out more strongly on South Korea.

## The Road to War: The Communist Side

Much about North Korea's evolving plans and the Soviet and Chinese role in them has recently come to light. Kim broached the possibility of an all-out attack on South Korea as early as his March 1949 meetings with Stalin in Moscow. The Soviet leader regarded the idea as premature while U.S. troops remained below the 38th parallel. Although he did not reject the idea in principle, he continued to oppose its early execution for months after the U.S. withdrawal in June, encouraging his client to continue efforts to undermine the ROK through guerrilla activities. Kim persisted in his pressure on Moscow, telling the Soviet ambassador in Pyongyang in January 1950, "I do not sleep at night, thinking about unification."[76] At the end of the month, Stalin began to come around. Two months later Kim arrived again in Moscow, and the Soviet leader finally gave him the go-ahead, contingent on Mao Zedong's approval. Kim received that approval in mid-May on a trip to Beijing. Meanwhile, the Soviet Union provided North Korea with planes, heavy artillery, and tanks, which, along with the influx of as many as sixty thousand Korean soldiers from China, gave Kim's regime clear military superiority over the ROK.[77] In May, the Soviets dispatched a new military team to the DPRK which had greater combat experience than its predecessor. Soviet advisers actually drafted the North Korean plan for attack.[78]

The initiative throughout was squarely on Kim's side. Few Koreans accepted the division of their country, and there was no assurance that unification could occur to the Communists' satisfaction by any means short of an overt North Korean attack. In an attempt to defeat the South through less direct methods, Kim had formed the Democratic Front for the Unification of the Fatherland (DFUF) in June 1949. Between June and September the North sent thirteen hundred well-trained, well-equipped personnel across the 38th parallel, many of whom joined guerrillas already operating in ROK territory. Guerrilla actions quickly spread through mountain regions in the southwest, center, and northeast. But ROK forces launched a counteroffensive at the end of the year, wiping out a large portion of the organized guerrilla units during the first months of 1950. With ROK authorities dragging their feet on land reform, and with former collaborators with the Japanese still prominent in the ROK army and police, prospects for internal subversion were still very much alive. Still, little immediate chance existed of overthrowing the ROK from within, and, if a land reform bill that was passed in June 1949 was finally implemented as planned during the summer of 1950, that chance might diminish even further.[79]

The declining prospects of the guerrillas alone was enough to induce Kim to press for more overt methods of uniting the peninsula, but evidence of growing economic and political interaction between South Korea and Japan made Kim's desire for military action more urgent. Diplomatic activity and trade between South Korea and Japan increased during 1949 and early 1950, and, in February 1950, Rhee even made a two-day trip to Tokyo. Amid talk in the United States about a separate peace treaty with Japan, new initiatives to promote Japan's economic recovery, and possibly that nation's eventual rearming, Pyongyang published and broadcast warnings about the developing linkage between South Korea and its former colonial master. That linkage would not only undermine the DPRK's prospects for taking over the South, but would eventually enhance Rhee's opportunities for marching north.[80] For the moment, however, North Korean military superiority was within reach, and that advantage might be augmented by popular uprisings in the South. Kim had much reason to want early military action against the South.

While North Korea viewed its options in local terms, the Soviet Union was a Eurasian power with its primary foreign interests facing westward. Its interests had been compromised over the previous three years as a result of the belligerent nature of its foreign policy. By the fall of 1949 the implementation of the Marshall Plan, the creation of NATO and an indigenous West German government, and the passage by the U.S. Congress of an arms aid bill for western Europe should have told the Kremlin that the appropriate course was to avoid any action that would further provoke a concerted effort by the United States and its allies.

In addressing the imponderables of Soviet involvement in Korea, it is essential to grasp the context of decision making in Moscow in 1950. Joseph Stalin held the power of decision, both on foreign and domestic matters, but he remained a highly suspicious man, ever wary of the designs of those around him. The purge of Communist Party leaders in Leningrad and Moscow during 1949 and 1950, and his frequent juggling of high-level personnel over the last years of his rule, reflect Stalin's never-ending quest for security within his own house. To him, maintaining his position at the top of the Soviet hierarchy was not simply the way to maximize his personal power; it was his only method of sustaining life itself. Clearly Stalin made foreign policy choices with a keen sense of how they would influence his personal power.[81]

Whatever the range of his authority and depth of his insecurity—perhaps in part *because* of them—Stalin permitted a good deal of internal debate on foreign policy. During 1949 and early 1950 two identifiable lines of argument existed in the Soviet press. One used the party organ, *Pravda*, as its primary mouthpiece, and included such officials as Vyacheslav Molotov and Mikhail Suslov; the other used the government organ, *Izvestiia*, as its main outlet, and drew support from Georgii Malenkov and Lavrentii Beria. The first or "militant" line argued that the capitalist states were inherently hostile toward the Soviet camp and unreliable in carrying out agreements, but that opposition to U.S. policies was on the rise among the peoples and governments of western Europe and that the United States itself suffered from an increasingly debilitating economic crisis. If the Soviet Union continued its pressure on the West, the United States soon would become disillusioned with its own efforts abroad and retreat to the Western Hemisphere. In contrast, the second or "moderate" line downplayed the contradictions within and between the Western powers, as well as the economic problems of the United States. The moderates emphasized American progress in western Europe and the advantages accrued from U.S. economic exploitation of the area. Since Soviet pressure had strengthened the Western alliance, a reduction of international tension was necessary. Conciliatory moves by the Soviet Union would make America's task more difficult in maintaining and consolidating the alliance.[82]

A compromise occurred in December 1949, with the militants accepting the line on peaceful coexistence over an extended period while the moderates conceded the need for continued vigilance at home regarding economic development and military spending, which already had been increased to finance a buildup in eastern Europe. During the first six months of 1950 debate declined in the Soviet press. Apparently, Stalin had decided on a cautious policy in western Europe so as to devote new attention to the more encouraging situation in Asia.[83] This did not mean serious negotiations with the West on Germany or Austria, a letup of political pressure on Tito, with whom Stalin had broken in 1948, or a reduction of propaganda attacks on Western governments.[84] Yet it did involve at least a postponement of any plans to invade Yugoslavia and greater concentration on the Moscow-controlled peace movement in propaganda directed toward western Europe.[85]

But why devote more attention to East Asia? Why not adopt a broad policy of accommodation as the moderates appear to have wanted? Stalin almost certainly viewed the Asian equation from the standpoint of fulfilling three large objectives: first, to maintain his own hold on power at home; second, to reinforce his influence over Communist governments on the Soviet periphery; and, third, to distract American attention and resources from the more important European theater. In the first case, we already have seen Stalin's concern manifested in the internal purges starting in 1949. The maintenance of a high level of international tension through a forward policy in Asia could further discourage any straying from his leadership at home. The same could be said for eastern Europe, where, much to Stalin's dismay, the Tito regime continued to survive. Purges there began in the fall and continued for the remainder of Stalin's reign.[86] Official harassment of British and U.S. diplomats in those countries provides additional evidence of both Stalin's fears and of his determination to seal off the regimes from the outside world.[87] Clearly, his failure to depose Tito and his undoubted knowledge through espionage of U.S. subversive efforts, which probably were far more modest than he thought, gave him concern about the western borderlands.

Concern also existed about developments in the East. The Communists had won in China without consistent Soviet aid or a close relationship with Moscow over the past generation. During the late 1920s the Chinese Communists had abandoned classical Marxist-Leninist doctrine by focusing their activities on the countryside rather than the cities. A decade later Mao Zedong isolated Wang Ming, the leader of the pro-Soviet faction of the party, and eventually forced him into exile in the Soviet Union. In the aftermath of Germany's attack on the Soviet Union in 1941, Mao resisted pressure from Moscow to help secure its eastern flank by taking the offensive against Japan. At the end of the war, the Soviets signed a Treaty of Friendship and Alliance with the Nationalist Chinese government and pressed the Communists to come to terms with that body. Mao negotiated with the Nationalists, but eventually he chose the course of civil war. Stalin aided Mao at several critical points in 1945 and 1946. His greatest fear was always the emergence of a strong united China aligned with the United States, and he never had confidence that his treaty with the Nationalists would prevent that eventuality. Yet he harbored ambivalence toward the Communist victory on the mainland. While pleased with the decline of U.S. influence, he remained concerned that here was a neighbor that might challenge Kremlin leadership over revolutionary forces in Asia and perhaps even elsewhere.[88]

Sino-Soviet relations appeared to be solid as 1949 progressed. At the end of June, on the eve of a visit to Moscow by a high-level Chinese delegation, Mao announced that he would "lean" to the Soviet side in his foreign policy.[89] Stalin then apologized to his Chinese Communist guests for past Soviet failures to support them in their struggle against the Nationalists and agreed to Soviet assistance for Chinese economic reconstruction and the development of an air force.[90] When Mao traveled to Moscow in December, he endured the combination of humiliation and ingratiation that Stalin commonly meted out to his lieutenants at home. Mao's statement that his visit should "create something that . . . not only look[s] nice but taste[s] delicious" initially confused his host, but Stalin eventually grasped that the Chinese leader wanted Soviet military assistance, a formal alliance, and a renegotiation of the Sino-Soviet treaty of 1945.[91]

Stalin continued to distrust Mao's intentions. The Soviet leader had told a top Mao adviser, Liu Shaoqi, during his Moscow visit of the previous summer, that the Chinese Communists should avoid political contacts with the Americans, but he was not persuaded that his advice had been taken to heart. Stalin worried that a Sino-Soviet alliance would ease Mao's fears of the United States and encourage him to believe that he could deal with Washington on a basis of equality. The Chinese then might try to use their relationship with the Americans to undermine the privileged Soviet position in Manchuria and Sinjiang, which Mao clearly wanted to alter. Although Mao received his military alliance, and a loan, Stalin insisted on several secret protocols, which reminded the Chinese of unequal treaties of the past.[92] Stalin's continuing wariness influenced him to pursue a forward policy in Asia and to encourage China to do the same. By drawing the United States deeper into the region, such a course would serve the twofold purpose of perpetuating China's isolation from the West and turning U.S. efforts away from Europe.

What specific actions did Stalin have in mind? Obviously, the North Korean attack was one move, but it was neither the first nor the last one envisioned. By June 1950 Communist parties or governments had taken four actions regarding Asia that fit Stalin's idea of a broad offensive. In mid-January the Soviets walked out of the UN Security Council, allegedly to protest its failure to seat Communist China but probably actually to freeze the Mao regime out of the international organization and as a first step toward complete withdrawal from the UN in favor of establishing a new, Communist-dominated body.[93] Later in the month China, and then the Soviet Union, recognized the Ho Chi Minh government in Vietnam. In mid-February the Communist giants signed a treaty of friendship and alliance. Soon Japan's Communist Party, under pressure from Moscow, departed sharply from its previously "lovable" approach to adopt a more aggressively militant line.[94] Finally, after the Korean venture was well under way, Ho's forces launched a major offensive in Vietnam.[95]

North Korea's attack was clearly the most risky of these moves. U.S. signals on Korea had been ambiguous. During 1949 the United States withdrew its last occupation troops from the peninsula, and it responded coolly to overtures by the Philippines, Nationalist China, and South Korea regarding a "Pacific Pact" along the lines of NATO. In his address on 12 January 1950 Secretary of State Dean Acheson omitted South Korea from the U.S. defense perimeter in the Pacific while suggesting that, if attacked, the ROK could expect help from the United Nations.[96] On several previous occasions U.S. leaders had publicly labeled Korea a testing ground in Asia between communism and democracy, and in June 1949 Truman compared giving economic aid to the ROK to economically assisting western Europe, which was about to receive a military commitment from the United States.[97]

But rhetoric was cheap, military involvement was not. In Asia the United States had studiously avoided the kind of commitment of resources and prestige made in Europe. Between 1947 and 1949 the Truman administration had refused to take direct action in China to prevent a Communist victory in the civil war. Now, at the beginning of 1950, it resisted strong domestic pressure to make a concerted effort to save Taiwan from the Communist onslaught.

Furthermore, U.S. attempts to construct a united front in East Asia had failed. The United States had urged Great Britain, its closest ally, and India, the largest non-Communist state in Asia, to delay recognition of the People's Republic of China.[98] By mid-January 1950, however, both those countries, plus ten others outside the Soviet camp, had recognized the new regime. On Korea, the United States had received support in the UN General Assembly, but that support was more impressive in breadth than in enthusiasm. The Rhee regime did little to endear itself to UN representatives in UNTCOK or its successor, the UN Commission on Korea (UNCOK), established at the end of 1948. Indeed, the South Korean government irritated members of those bodies from India, Australia, Canada, France, and Syria by discouraging their efforts to enhance representative political institutions in the South and to establish contact with North Korean officials. In any event, the lowly rank in their home countries of UNCOK members and their frequent absence from the peninsula suggested a less than exalted place for Korea in the foreign policies of even those nations willing to participate in UN activities there.[99] In the United States, the Truman administration also had difficulty maintaining support for aid to Korea. In mid-January 1950 the House of Representatives actually defeated an economic assistance bill for the ROK.[100] Understandably, Stalin suspected that in a pinch there would be little support for collective intervention to save South Korea.

Stalin made it clear to Kim throughout their deliberations that Kim could not expect direct Soviet intervention on his behalf. According to one Soviet diplomat at the time, Stalin told Kim that, if he ran into trouble with his venture, he would have to look to Beijing not Moscow for aid.[101] Stalin also refused to permit Soviet advisers to accompany North Korean forces in the initial attack.[102] But Stalin did order that North Korea's requests for war materials be met.[103] For his part, Kim assured his Soviet mentors of a quick victory over the South. Not only would the return of Korean soldiers from China, and Soviet arms assistance, give Kim's army a decisive advantage over ROK forces; the North Korean attack would set off an uprising in the South that would undermine resistance to the advancing troops.

Although Stalin gave a tentative green light in April 1950 for a conventional move across the 38th parallel, it surely remained contingent on a variety of factors, both in Korea or elsewhere. Khrushchev's account in his memoirs of Stalin's fear that the United States might "jump in" fits neatly with the widely held image of the Soviet dictator as a cautious actor in the foreign policy sphere, especially when it came to direct military action.[104] Yet if he feared the presence of U.S. soldiers on the peninsula, he probably viewed a variety of other U.S. responses as desirable. At the top of the list was an American military commitment to defend Taiwan, which Stalin surely thought likely in the face of hedges in the hands-off policy regarding the island that appeared in published statements by Truman and Acheson in early January.[105] Additional U.S. moves might include stepped-up aid to the beleaguered anti-Communist forces in Indochina and the Philippines and even a bolstered presence in Japan, which might be countered by a newly militant Communist Party there as well as through the psychological impact of the fall of nearby Korea. What he most certainly did not want was an expanded U.S. effort in Europe, a response he probably thought unlikely because of his estimate of U.S. economic capacities and political strength. He stood willing to accept certain risks, however, owing to his knowledge through espionage of America's lack of readiness for war with the Soviet Union—militarily, politically, and economically—and to his desire to ensure support for his leadership at home and on his eastern and western borders.[106]

As June approached, events confirmed Stalin's inclination. The Rhee regime continued to rest on shaky foundations in its relationship to both the indigenous population and its foreign sponsor, the United States. In April Acheson threatened openly to withdraw U.S. aid unless Rhee held spring elections as scheduled and acted to curb runaway inflation.[107] Early in May Tom Connally, the Democratic chairman of the U.S. Senate Foreign Relations Committee, stated publicly that South Korea probably would be overrun by the Communists "whether we want it to or not." In response to this declaration, Acheson refused to commit the United States to the use of force to prevent such an occurrence.[108] During his visit to Moscow late in the month, UN Secretary-General Trygve Lie failed even to raise the Korean issue with Stalin.[109] On 30 May, in elections for the National Assembly of the ROK, opponents of President Rhee scored major gains, reinforcing the belief in Moscow that when North Korean forces moved across the 38th parallel they would receive widespread indigenous support.[110] Washington's concern about Asia was on the upswing, but its attention centered on Japan and on Southeast Asia, particularly the Philippines and Indochina, where material assistance to the French began in May. Yet this trend was not on a sufficient scale to shift attention from Europe, where spring NATO meetings held an ominous ring. What better method to draw U.S. efforts from the decisive theater of the cold war, to further dampen anti-Communist morale in western Europe, and to solidify China's isolation from the West than a quick, successful, proxy venture in Korea?

Mao was unaware of many of Stalin's calculations, though he knew of the Soviet leader's concerns about the rise of an Asian Tito. Despite the release over the last several years of numerous documents for the prewar period, little has emerged that is definitive on China's role in North Korea's march south in June 1950. Khrushchev's account that Stalin consulted Mao on Kim's plans and that the Chinese leader approved is believable but vague on specifics.[111] Additional evidence indicates that during January 1950 Beijing agreed to return fourteen thousand or more well-equipped Korean troops who had fought in the Chinese civil war.[112] Four months later Kim Il-sung visited Beijing and discussed his desire to attack South Korea.[113] Kim undoubtedly shared with the Chinese his basic intentions, and Mao conveyed his general approval. Kim's relations with the Chinese Communists extended back to the early 1930s when, as a young man, he joined their party. During the next decade, much in his writings and speeches showed a distinct Maoist tint.[114] Although Kim was not immune to the historic big-brother relationship of China to Korea, he was a strong nationalist. There is reason to believe that by 1950 he distrusted the Yanan group within his own party and resented its adulation of Mao. Apparently, Kim did not inform Mao of the early date of his planned move south.[115] As for Mao, nationalism and ideology, plus his indebtedness to Kim for assistance in the Chinese civil war and his desire to impress Stalin, suggest that his response to Kim was largely sympathetic.

Mao's perspective is crucial in comprehending the origins and course of the Korean War. The Chinese leader was a nationalist who, though a Marxist-Leninist for nearly three decades, had during the 1930s and 1940s adapted his ideology to Chinese circumstances and often rejected Soviet advice and demands. He never forgot the instances when Stalin had chosen Soviet interests over the cause of revolution in China, and he always placed a high priority on restoring China to its historic place in the world.[116] Ideology provided a means for achieving that goal and was not a goal in itself.

At the same time Mao's ideology, combined with U.S. support for the Jiang regime during the Chinese civil war, led him to believe that the United States posed a major threat to his nation and his revolution. Despite its failure before 1949 to intervene directly in the civil conflict, Washington now might feel compelled to do so in the face of Jiang's impending defeat. In such a context, Soviet assistance to his regime seemed crucial.[117] The idea that victory was "possible even without international help . . . [was] mistaken," he declared in his "lean to one side" address of 30 June. "In an epoch in which imperialism exists, . . . a genuine people's revolution [cannot] . . . win victory in any country without help from the international revolutionary forces."[118] Although there were limits to the lengths he would go to achieve Soviet assistance, in 1949 and 1950 it clearly ranked at the top of his foreign policy objectives.

Events during the summer and fall of 1949 solidified his commitment to an alliance with the Soviet Union. Liu Shaoqi's trip to Moscow went exceedingly well. Stalin confessed his past errors regarding China, urged the Communists to move quickly to establish a people's republic and to take the lead in promoting revolution in East Asia, and agreed to extend concrete advisory and material aid for their economy and military forces.[119] Meanwhile, the Nationalist Chinese had launched a naval blockade of Shanghai and numerous air raids against the city and surrounding areas. The Truman administration attempted to discourage Jiang from such activities, but it continued to provide him with economic and military assistance, including ships. Mao already knew that the United States was exploring methods of separating Taiwan politically from the mainland. Such activities reinforced Mao's view that the United States had aggressive intentions.[120] Within two months of Liu's return from Moscow in August, Mao commenced planning for his own visit to the Soviet capital.[121] In late October the costly defeat of Mao's forces in their attempt to seize the offshore island of Quemoy from the Nationalists served to emphasize the PRC's need of air and naval assistance from the Soviet Union to ensure final victory in the civil war.[122]

At the turn of the year the Soviets agreed, in principle, to negotiate a military alliance. To avoid appearing overly anxious, Mao directed Chinese Foreign Minister Zhou Enlai to join him in Moscow, but to avoid undue haste. Zhou took more than two weeks to arrive from Beijing.[123] To persuade Stalin of their reliability, the Chinese recognized the Communist-led Democratic Republic of Vietnam and seized U.S. consular compounds in Beijing.[124]

Sino-Soviet negotiations culminated on 14 February in the signing of a military alliance and other agreements. Mao and Zhou left Moscow three days later, while lower-level officials stayed on until April to work out a series of economic arrangements that, among other things, enabled the Soviets to exploit the raw materials of Sinjiang.[125] Most important to Mao was a thirty-year Treaty of Friendship, Alliance, and Mutual Assistance, in which each signatory agreed to provide military and other aid "by all means at its disposal" should Japan "or any state allied with her" attack the other, resulting "in a state of war." Stalin accepted this commitment only after considerable hesitation. He agreed as well to withdraw Soviet military forces from Port Arthur by the end of 1952, relieved perhaps to find that his guests desired a temporary retention of the status quo as a deterrent to U.S. adventurism. He also readily accepted the Chinese request for assistance in defending their coastal cities against continuing Nationalist raids. A Soviet air force division was to be stationed in Shanghai for this purpose.[126] Finally, the Soviet Union agreed to provide loans of $300 million over a five-year span at a 1 percent annual interest rate. To Westerners the amount seemed paltry, yet it was a figure chosen by Mao himself, who worried about becoming overly indebted to foreigners.[127] Although Mao paid a high price for these commitments, including the recognition of Outer Mongolia's independence, he left Moscow having achieved his primary short-term aims.

Mao's concern to guard against U.S. aggression was by no means his only foreign policy objective; nor did its achievement involve simply standing pat within China's mainland boundaries. The nation's offshore islands, most notably Hainan and Taiwan, remained to be taken—indeed, the first was captured in May—and Korea and Indochina, historically areas of Chinese influence, were the scenes of struggle between "progressive" and "imperialist" forces. Mao intended to use half the Soviet loan to purchase naval equipment from Moscow for use in his offensives against Nationalist-held islands.[128]

His adherence to a revolutionary ideology joined with his commitment to his nation's traditional conception of itself as the "Middle Kingdom" to persuade Mao that he also must aid the "anti-imperialist" cause on his borders. Thus, while his top priority following his conclusion of an alliance with the Soviets was to seize control of the offshore islands and rid himself of the last Nationalist strongholds, he did not lose sight of objectives in borderlands to the northeast and south. As agreed in January, Korean soldiers were returned from China to Kim Il-sung during the spring. In addition, as a result of talks with Ho Chi Minh during January and February, PRC leaders ordered the formation of a military advisory group to assist the Communists in Indochina.[129]

In a word, despite the monumental political and economic problems faced at home, Mao's vision, national and ideological alike, prevented him from simply turning inward. He was not as intimately involved in North Korea's plans as Stalin. He even may have harbored reservations about a North Korean move before the planned assault on Taiwan during the spring or summer of 1951. Yet the U.S. refusal to intervene directly on Taiwan to prevent a Communist victory may have encouraged Mao to believe that the Americans would not react decisively in Korea either.[130] Moreover, whether from the perspective of his relationship with Stalin or Kim, or of his revolutionary and nationalist conscience, he was in a weak position to oppose a North Korean offensive. There is even some reason to believe that, during Kim's May 1950 visit to Beijing, Mao offered to position three Chinese armies along the Yalu River as backup for the North Koreans but was assured that the precaution was unnecessary.[131] If the arrangement of the final plans were worked out between Moscow and Pyongyang alone, Beijing was hardly a passive, unwilling, or unwitting outsider.

The last weeks before the attack show the North Koreans engaged in masterful deceit.[132] While new Soviet military advisers made final preparations with a small group of North Korean officials, U.S. and South Korean intelligence picked up various suspicious activities just above the 38th parallel.[133] But Pyongyang made sufficient noise on the political front to distract attention from its plans. Pyongyang radio devoted numerous broadcasts to the guerrilla struggle in the South, characterizing its strength in terms sharply conflicting with reality. Apparently this ploy aimed to mislead the enemy into believing that guerrilla operations remained the chosen method for eliminating the ROK. North Korea also avoided initiating border skirmishes, though in May, when several minor incidents did occur, it blew them way out of proportion, perhaps to pave the way for the later charge that the war began as a result of ROK attacks.

The final political offensive began on 1 June, when the press in Pyongyang proposed that the DFUF renew a unification appeal it had made a year before. The DFUF followed with a call for nationwide elections in two months, culminating in the convening of a national assembly on 15 August. Hearkening back to the proposals of the spring of 1949, the DFUF called for a conference of political leaders from North and South Korea. Neither Rhee and other rightists nor UN officials were to attend, but UNCOK was invited to join others in sending a representative north of the 38th parallel to receive the formal proposal. While Rhee prevented South Korean politicians from participating in that exercise, an UNCOK official managed to cross the border and return with the proposal.[134]

At this point, Pyongyang announced that three DFUF representatives would cross the parallel to make direct contact with South Korean leaders. When they did so, they were immediately arrested and interrogated. Soon they were heard over Seoul radio making propaganda broadcasts for the Rhee regime. As scholar John Merrill has remarked, it remains uncertain whether these were genuine statements or part of "a difficult disinformation scheme." Yet, combined with two other North Korean initiatives, "they completely absorbed the attention of southern officials in the critical days before the war."[135]

Those initiatives included, first, a proposal to exchange two leading southern Communists recently taken into custody by the ROK for Cho Man-sik, the prominent Christian patriot who, since early 1946, had been held under arrest in North Korea; and, second, a merger of the Supreme People's Assembly of the DPRK and the recently elected ROK legislature. Despite an immediate exchange on the first, Rhee placed conditions on the swap that prevented its early implementation.[136] The second proposal got nowhere before the commencement of hostilities.

The June initiatives were designed not as possible alternatives to war but as covers for North Korea's actual intentions. The moves helped maintain the element of surprise for the military offensive, which remained a tightly guarded secret even in the North Korean army, and enhanced DPRK claims of peaceful intentions once the war broke out. Certainly Kim had no intention of conducting serious negotiations toward unification. His talk to a North Korean army unit on 5 June indicates that he expected war in the near future. He told the soldiers that "there is every indication that an all-out war instigated by the U.S. imperialists and the Syngman Rhee puppet clique may break out in our country at any moment.... [If it does,] we must take a decisive counteroffensive at once and deal a deadly blow to the enemy, and drive the U.S. imperialists out of our territory and reunify the country."[137] Provocation, of course, was in the eyes of the beholder, and Kim was determined to maintain the fiction, even within his own army, that South Korea had attacked first. Confident that his military forces were superior to the enemy's, that his attack would spark strong anti-Rhee uprisings in the South, and that the United States would either stand aside or intervene too slowly and on too small a scale to make a difference, Kim saw every reason to seek unification by force.

## The Road to War: The United States

Kim, Stalin, and Mao got more than they bargained for. The North Korean attack came at a time of increasing alarm in Washington over recent international developments and growing pressure on the Truman administration to act decisively in Asia. The Soviet explosion of an atomic device in August 1949 ended the U.S. monopoly over the most potent weapon in human history. Within a few years—1954 was projected to be the year of greatest danger—the Soviets would have a delivery capability and a stockpile of atomic bombs sufficient to render monumental damage to the U.S. homeland. This development would greatly reduce the value of America's atomic arsenal in deterring Soviet conventional military action. It even might encourage a Soviet first strike in the United States to eliminate its industrial superiority, a prospect that led some officials to contemplate preventive war.[138] On the heels of the Soviet atomic test came the Communists' expulsion of the Nationalists from mainland China and the Sino-Soviet treaty of alliance. Soon, U.S. intelligence reported the stationing of Soviet jets in China and the concentration of Chinese forces in provinces along the border of Indochina, where the French struggled indecisively against the Communist-led Vietminh.[139] Communist rebels of Chinese descent stepped up pressure on the British in Malaya, as did the Huks against a corrupt and inept pro-U.S. regime in the Philippines.[140] In the midst of increasing chaos, fears grew over the possible impact on Chinese elements in the Filipino population of a Mao victory in Taiwan, which would eliminate the last bastion of the National government.[141] The Communist threat appeared no less compelling in Burma and Thailand.[142] Pressures mounted within the Truman administration to prevent the Communist conquest of Taiwan, to grant material support to the French in Indochina, which in fact did commence in May, and to bolster military aid to the Philippines and even South Korea.[143] The opposition Republican party in the United States, frustrated by many years of not being in control of the federal government and increasingly influenced by its right wing, pummeled the Democrats over the earlier-than-expected Soviet acquisition of atomic weapons and the "loss" of China. Republican orators, backed by the conservative press, characterized the Truman administration as at best soft on Asian communism, at worst heavily infiltrated by subversives.[144]

The lengthy top-secret document NSC-68, presented to Truman in April 1950, reflected the growing sense of crisis inside the executive branch. While reaffirming the Europe-first strategy, the paper characterized the cold war as an ideological struggle of global proportions. The Soviet Union, its authors asserted, "is animated by a new fanatic faith, antithetical to our own, and seeks to impose its absolute authority over the rest of the world. . . . In the context of the present polarization of power a defeat of free institutions anywhere is a defeat everywhere." However innovative U.S. foreign policy may have been since 1947, the ongoing Communist advance, militarily and politically, now dictated a far greater marshaling of U.S. resources than in the past. With Soviet resources "mobilized close to the maximum possible extent," the United States could not permit a continuation of the huge gap between its potential and its actual capabilities. Closing this gap was essential not only to defend America's immediate boundaries, but to maintain the determination of "our allies or potential allies" to resist "Soviet intimidation" and reject neutrality.[145]

A growing fear for the short term was of global war through miscalculation. As Paul Nitze, the new head of the State Department's Policy Planning Staff and the primary draftsman of NSC-68, wrote in February, recent Kremlin behavior suggested that, more than ever before, the Soviet Union might be willing "to undertake a course of action, including the possible use of force in local areas, which might lead to an accidental outbreak of general military conflict."[146]

The thinking within the national security bureaucracy was not entirely defensive in nature. NSC-68 talked of the "retraction" of Soviet "power and influence from the present perimeter areas around traditional Russian boundaries and the emergence of the satellite countries as entities independent of the U.S.S.R."[147] This was not to be accomplished by war in the traditional sense, but its articulation reflected a growing belief that the United States must take the offensive in the cold war, that the country must not only halt but reverse the recent trend of Soviet success. Stalin's break with Tito in 1948 had created hope that splits also would occur between the Kremlin and other eastern European Communists, and it reinforced hopes that Mao would adopt an independent course in China. By the spring of 1950, however, limited covert operations in eastern Europe had produced few positive results, and a Sino-Soviet split appeared to be years away.[148] During the fall of 1949, U.S. recognition of the new regime in China received active consideration, but PRC treatment of U.S. officials on the mainland was so harsh that, in April 1950, Washington withdrew all that remained.[149] Former Under Secretary of State Robert Lovett, who played a consultant's role to the group that drafted NSC-68, believed that "we should find every weak spot in the enemy's armor, both on the periphery and at the center, and hit him with anything that comes to hand." "Anything . . . short of an all-out effort," he insisted, "is inexcusable."[150]

Although Lovett expressed a common view in the executive branch, the American people and a majority of Congress lacked such a sense of urgency. Their complacency, combined with President Truman's own fiscal conservatism, made the immediate mobilization of resources for the contest impossible.[151] In May the president even talked publicly of reducing defense spending in the coming fiscal year.[152]

The outbreak of war in Korea provided the spark necessary for a move toward implementing NSC-68. Not only did the United States intervene in Korea, it stepped up aid to anti-Communist forces in Indochina and to the beleaguered government of Elpidio Quirino in the Philippines. It also announced that it would defend Taiwan from Communist attack. Such moves made prospects for Sino-U.S. rapprochement more remote than ever, which surely delighted Stalin. The Korean War, however, also provided an impetus for the consolidation and expansion of NATO, for a further movement of Yugoslavia toward the West, for increased covert operations in eastern Europe, for a sustained U.S. military presence in Japan, and, initially at least, for a rejuvenation of spirit in the United Nations, all of which disturbed Moscow.

To the United States, the Korean conflict became a struggle for credibility, to prove that the liberal democracy of people unused to sustained effort abroad could rise to the challenge of international communism. The North Korean offensive across the 38th parallel thrust the peninsula to center stage. Truman, an avid reader of history and a believer that the past held important lessons for the present, declared on 27 June that "the attack upon Korea makes it plain beyond all doubt that Communism has passed beyond the use of subversion to conquer independent nations and will now use armed invasion and war."[153] Korea had become the Manchuria of the 1950s, the place where military aggression first showed its ominous head. Although firm U.S. action in Korea was not of great strategic importance, Acheson wrote a day later, it was "vital . . . as [a] symbol [of the] strength and determination of [the] west." A feeble response would encourage "new aggressive actions elsewhere" and demoralize "countries adjacent to [the] Soviet orbit."[154] To prevent a repetition of the 1930s, when the Western democracies had appeased aggression, thus setting the stage for World War II, the United States must act boldly in several areas.

Still, two key questions remained in weighing the scope of the response within Korea. First, although there was no doubt that the Soviets were behind the North Korean attack, was it an isolated move or part of a larger Soviet military offensive? Second, how much force was needed to repulse North Korea? The State Department's Office of Western European Affairs believed that an attempt must be made to save South Korea, "always assuming that it has a reasonable chance of success within a reasonably short time."[155] Fearful of diverting scarce resources to a strategically remote area, military leaders in Washington initially hesitated to commit U.S. troops to combat. So did General MacArthur in Tokyo. More than two days after the North Korean attack, the latter declared to a visiting official from the United States that anyone who advocated a U.S. challenge to Communist power on the Asian mainland "ought to have his head examined."[156] By 30 June the Far Eastern commander, encouraged by the vigorous response to the crisis from home and anxious to exploit any opportunity to bolster his nation's commitment in the western Pacific, pressed his government for an immediate dispatch of two divisions to Korea. From the start of the crisis, the Joint Chiefs of Staff had taken a back seat to the State Department and the White House; now, with an appeal before them from their prestigious commander-in-the-field, with no sign of Communist preparations for military adventures in other areas, and with hope that America's superior atomic and economic capabilities would deter Soviet actions elsewhere, they conceded to the interventionist tide.[157] The initially stated objective was restoration of the 38th parallel, but the climate within the administration and the domestic pressures for a strong course in Asia augured ill for a policy of restraint.

PROSPECTS

Any effort to roll back communism in Korea, especially with U.S. troops above the 38th parallel, would raise the specter of Soviet or Chinese intervention or both. Neither the Soviet Union nor China wanted to precipitate a direct clash with the United States. Despite the frequently bombastic rhetoric emanating from Moscow, the Soviet Union had a deep sense of insecurity. That nation had lost over 10 percent of its population during World War II, and, although giant strides had been made since the 1920s, it lagged decades behind the United States in industrial output. Although Stalin could maintain huge armies in peacetime, he could hardly muster the military-industrial strength to contest the United States once it had mobilized for war. And in 1950 he lacked the stockpile of atomic weapons and the fleet of long-range bombers necessary to launch a major air offensive against the U.S. homeland. He was anxious to avoid an engagement of Soviet and U.S. military forces at almost any level. In the volatile atmosphere created by the North Korean attack, Stalin decided against a Soviet return to the UN Security Council to block the U.S. effort to engage that body in the ROK cause.[158] Conceivably, he even desired that U.S. intervention in Korea be cast within a UN framework to reduce prospects of a formal declaration of war in Washington, which at some future date might activate the Sino-Soviet treaty requiring direct Soviet military measures.[159] Yet Stalin was far from helpless in influencing events on the peninsula. He could supply the North Koreans with arms and ammunition and provide logistic support and tactical advice behind the lines. Ultimately he could do the same for the armies of Communist China, which, though concentrated on central coastal regions opposite Taiwan, could be moved north in an emergency.

Beijing had reasons of its own to avoid a conflict with the United States. Mao and his cohorts still were consolidating their authority over the Chinese mainland, a task that no government had accomplished for more than a century. They faced problems of economic reconstruction and development that more than matched those of the Soviet Union in 1945. Whereas the Soviet economy lagged far behind that of the United States, it had at least entered the industrial age, an accomplishment that China could not hope to achieve for a generation. Crossing swords with the United States in Korea would present serious liabilities. It could lead to direct U.S. retaliation against the mainland. It would call for a major reallocation of domestic resources and compromise the evolutionary movement toward a socialist society conceived in Mao's "New Democracy." In a speech of 23 June, Chairman Mao declared that "the test of war is basically over." He looked forward to an unhurried process "of country-wide socialist transformation." A day later, the People's Revolutionary Military Council and the Government Administrative Council endorsed a plan to demobilize a portion of the People's Liberation Army over the next six months.[160]

Even so, China was emerging from one of the most momentous revolutions of the twentieth—indeed any—century, and a fundamental aspect of that process was the rebuilding of the pride of a people whose ancient civilization had long been ravaged by foreigners. Most Americans viewed their country's historic relationship to China with a clear conscience, but the Chinese were inclined to regard all Westerners as venal barbarians. To the Communists, the United States topped their list of foreign villains. The leader of the capitalist bloc, the United States continued to recognize and aid the Nationalist government and to prevent the PRC from taking China's seat at the United Nations.[161] The United States also occupied Japan, which, within recent memory, had used Korea as a stepping-stone into China. The desire to reestablish China's traditional role as protector of Korea, and a sense of obligation to Kim for his assistance in the civil war, provided additional reasons for the PRC to take an active interest in the peninsula. If U.S. forces approached China's border, a strong response might appear necessary—for reasons of security, because of national pride and cohesion, and out of fraternal duty.

Moreover, because the Soviet Union was the greatest threat to U.S. security, and western Europe the foremost area of U.S. concern outside the Western Hemisphere, Washington might not unleash the bulk of its military might against China. Short of that eventuality, China's massive armies, operating close to home and with Soviet material support, could hold their own. Mao's doctrines of guerrilla warfare, which emphasized manpower and morale over machinery and advanced weaponry, had served him well against the Japanese and the Nationalists.[162] Thus the nationalistic, ideological, and power realities that provoked the outbreak of war in Korea in June 1950 were bound to make that conflict difficult either to contain or to end.

Perhaps the most encouraging development during the first weeks of the fighting, from the perspective of those wanting to contain the war, was that the United States cast its intervention within a collective framework. To be sure, the United Nations had often served merely as a rubber stamp for U.S. policy. With the Soviets boycotting the Security Council, where they had a veto, that pattern threatened to become more pronounced than ever. Yet America's European allies, while welcoming the initial intervention in Korea, were keenly aware of its dangers. In a positive sense, it could provide a spark to strengthen the West and deter future Soviet adventurism. On the other hand, it could divert U.S. attention and resources from NATO, so much so that the Soviets might move against a highly vulnerable western Europe. If the fighting in Korea could serve as a substitute for World War III, the conflict could also constitute its beginning. In the latter case, no matter what the eventual outcome, Europe would be in shambles. Because Washington solicited a UN role in Korea as a source of international legitimacy, the allies could use the organization as an instrument to contain U.S. action. Should the Soviets refuse to return to the Security Council, the British and French could stalemate that body through their own power of veto. If the General Assembly moved to center stage, the allies could combine with neutrals to encourage U.S. restraint.

In a word, although the outbreak of war in Korea exacerbated global tensions and posed a real danger of uncontrolled escalation, countervailing trends remained on the horizon. Whether those trends would prevail or the world would descend into an unsurpassed orgy of violence depended ultimately on political—both domestic and international—and military calculations in Washington and Moscow; but the maneuvering of diplomats in a young and untested organization, which had failed to prevent the outbreak of fighting in Korea, might exert an important influence on those calculations.

• CHAPTER 2 •

# The Diplomacy of Confrontation and Consolidation

### THE MILITARY CONTEXT

Some thirty-four miles below Seoul, on the main highway and railroad line connecting the capital with the southeastern port of Pusan, lies the tiny agricultural village of Osan. Early on the morning of 5 July 1950 a column of disciplined and well-armed infantry, led by three dozen T-34 tanks of the North Korean 105th Armored Division, pressed southward toward that obscure community. Lacking detailed plans for operations south of Seoul, North Korean forces had been slow to proceed beyond the Han River.[1] In recent days, however, they had captured the city of Suwon from the hopelessly outclassed Republic of Korea army. Yet a new contestant had entered the fray, thus raising South Korean hopes that the tide of battle soon would change.

The first U.S. troops, some four hundred strong, had landed in Korea at Pusan airport on 1 July. Residents there gave them a rousing welcome, cheering and waving American flags and supportive banners at trucks carrying the soldiers from the airport to the railroad station. The next morning the U.S. warriors arrived at Taejon, the temporary capital of the ROK. There they were greeted by Sihn Sung Mo, the acting prime minister, two UN officials, and a South Korean band belting out American tunes. Major General John H. Church, head of U.S. field headquarters at Taejon, had fostered the new climate of confidence, declaring to reporters on the previous afternoon, "We will hurl back the North Koreans, and if the Russkies intervene we will hurl them back too."[2]

On 5 July, as North Korean tanks approached Osan, this confidence was finally given a test. Less than three miles north of the village, on ridges overlooking the main road, the four hundred infantrymen of U.S. "Task Force Smith" lay in wait for the enemy. At 8:16 A.M. U.S. artillery in the rear commenced firing on the tanks. Then the forward troops opened up with bazookas and recoilless rifles. But the tanks did not turn and run: although four of them were either incapacitated or destroyed, twenty-nine others broke through the U.S. line. Three more tanks and two regiments of North Korean infantry followed. By late afternoon the Americans were in disorderly retreat across the rain-swept hills and rice paddies of the Korean countryside.

The skirmish at Osan revealed that the mere appearance of U.S. troops would not reverse the military balance in Korea. American combatants had inadequate firepower to resist Soviet-built tanks, and North Korean soldiers were not intimidated by opponents simply because their skin was white or because, five years earlier, they had overwhelmed the Japanese oppressor. U.S. planes dominated the air, but, operating from distant bases in Japan and in the overcast skies of Korea's rainy season, they proved of limited use on the battlefield. U.S. soldiers, in addition to being poorly equipped, usually lacked prior combat experience and an aggressive spirit. Years of occupation duty in Japan had left them ill-prepared for the task before them. In the first weeks of fighting, United States forces and the remains of the ROK army struggled desperately to maintain a toehold on the peninsula.

By early August the North Koreans had driven all the way to the Naktong River, often little more than thirty miles from Pusan. They pressed down on enemy forces, which clung to the so-called Pusan perimeter, a line encompassing an area some fifty miles wide and a hundred miles deep on the southeastern tip of Korea. North Korean units frequently penetrated U.S. and South Korean positions, even threatening U.S. field headquarters at Taegu. In the last hours of August the North Korean I Corps in the southwest began an offensive that quickly spread across the battlefront. Fighting during the next two weeks resulted in more casualties to U.S. troops, now under the United Nations banner, than during any equivalent period in the war.

Yet over the past month and a half, the United States had executed a buildup of supplies and personnel in Korea. From the end of July on, South Korean and U.S. soldiers at the front outnumbered the North Koreans. The popular uprisings that Kim had anticipated would assist the Communist advance never developed and, despite the DPRK's impressive gains during the first month of combat, its armies also had suffered more than fifty thousand casualties. Without direct Chinese or Soviet intervention, the DPRK had a limited capacity to replace losses. North Korea's lengthy supply lines, combined with U.S. control of the air and sea, hindered the replacement of arms and ammunition. Joining the buildup of U.S. troops in Korea was an influx into Japan of military units from the United States, which would give UN forces an offensive capability.[3]

Meanwhile, Korea held center stage at the United Nations in New York and in the capitals of the superpowers and their leading allies. With the exception of the Nationalists on Taiwan, who saw a broadening conflict as their best hope of recapturing mainland China, everyone wanted to limit the war to Korea. Yet mutual ambitions, fears, and suspicion produced other objectives that directed national policies away from an early end to the fighting. Although the existence of atomic weapons on both sides provided a barrier against unlimited escalation, the high level of tension between the Soviet Union and the United States and the intricacies of their internal politics and alliance relationships discouraged progress toward a diplomatic solution. In both Washington and Moscow, it seemed easier, even safer, to mobilize resources than to pursue accommodation. Some of the Western powers and many Arab and Asian nations saw matters differently, and their voices added a complexity to diplomacy regarding Korea that qualified the prevailing bipolar trend of global politics. Whether those voices would exercise a restraining

**Summer 1950**

- Controlled by U.N.
- ← Communist advances
- Controlled by Communists

Start of North Korean Offensive June 25, 1950

Pusan Perimeter September 14, 1950

influence or, inadvertently, encourage intransigence on the part of the superpowers remained in doubt as the brutal fighting in Korea continued through the summer.

## Early Peace Probes

In wartime military developments usually dictate diplomacy rather than the reverse. Under conditions of extreme ideological conflict, where the contestants deny the other's legitimacy, constructive talks are likely to occur only after protracted stalemate on the battlefield. Only then—and even then perhaps just temporarily—will the belligerents abandon the goal of military victory. During the summer of 1950 the principals in Korea showed little interest in political efforts to end the fighting. North Korea stood too good a chance of military victory. To South Korea, the military balance was so unfavorable as to make diplomacy seem impossible except as an instrument of surrender. U.S. assistance might make surrender unnecessary, eventually even help to produce a conquest of the hated rival in the North.

Truman, Stalin, and Mao all wanted to avoid a military confrontation of the great powers over Korea. On 27 June the U.S. president revealed his desire to localize the conflict in an aide-mémoire to Moscow, the first direct communiqué from the United States to the Soviet government during the crisis. The dispatch avoided any charge of Soviet culpability for the North Korean attack and asked the Kremlin to use its good offices to persuade Pyongyang to withdraw its forces from the South.[4] The Soviet premier refused to do so, clinging to the fiction that South Korea had started the war by launching an offensive north of the 38th parallel and claiming that the conflict was an internal matter, a civil war for Koreans alone to resolve. The Soviet press and radio lambasted the United States for its alleged "aggression" on the peninsula, characterizing Americans as "beasts of Wall Street" and "arrogant U.S. bandits." Chinese Communist propaganda centered on U.S. intervention in the Taiwan strait, labeling the United States a "paper tiger" and asserting that China's millions were "confident that the People's Liberation Army will liberate all the territories of China." Mao also ordered the Thirteenth Army Corps, consisting of four armies, to redeploy from the Central-South Military Region to the Korean border. But neither Stalin nor Mao responded to U.S. intervention in Asia by committing their own forces, which in the early weeks of fighting in Korea would have given Kim a decisive edge. China even halted assertions that it "soon" would liberate Taiwan and it postponed plans for an attack on Jinmen, a small island located off the coast of Fujian Province. Preparations regarding Taiwan shifted to the defensive. Finally, the PRC avoided making specific promises of material aid to North Korea.[5]

Instead of direct negotiations, the superpowers engaged in an oblique exchange of views on Korea. On 6 July Soviet Deputy Foreign Minister Andrei Gromyko approached Sir David Kelly, the British ambassador in Moscow, asking him if his government had any proposals for a settlement. London, which welcomed U.S. resolve in Korea but was anxious to prevent a broader conflict, immediately told Washington about the move.[6] U.S. experts on the Soviet Union, though recognizing the possibility that Gromyko's overture was a ploy designed to "slacken pressure in Korea" by undermining the unity of the "free world," believed that Stalin, having miscalculated the U.S. response to the North Korean attack, might be genuinely interested in ending the conflict. Secretary of State Acheson agreed, and encouraged the British to explore the Soviet position. Nevertheless, he reacted sharply to pressure from Foreign Minister Ernest Bevin to connect restoration of the 38th parallel in Korea to a U.S. withdrawal from the Taiwan strait and U.S. acceptance of

Communist Chinese entry into the United Nations. Acheson instructed Lewis Douglas, the U.S. ambassador in London, "to leave . . . no doubt" in Bevin's mind as to the potential "seriousness" to Anglo-U.S. relations of a split over this issue.[7] The Kremlin proved unwilling to consider an end to the fighting in Korea until Beijing had taken its seat in the Security Council.

India also took a hand in the search for a settlement. That country favored the Security Council resolutions on Korea of late June, which followed logically from India's past support for an independent government below the 38th parallel. New Delhi viewed the North Korean attack as aggression, but Prime Minister Jawaharlal Nehru remained determined to steer an independent course in the cold war. Like the British, he opposed U.S. action to isolate Taiwan, fearing it might broaden the Korean conflict, and he favored PRC admittance to the United Nations. He continued to regard the international organization primarily as an agency of mediation rather than one of collective security. Aristocratic in background and trained at elite schools in England, Nehru held a natural suspicion toward the U.S. political system, with its responsiveness to fickle public opinion. Americans, he wrote to a friend on 3 July, are "apt to be more hysterical as a people than almost any others." Opposition to his position on the Security Council resolutions by respected advisers V. K. Krishna Menon, the Indian high commissioner to the United Kingdom, Sarvepalli Radhakrishnan, the Indian ambassador to the Soviet Union, and elements of his cabinet gave him pause.[8] At the beginning of July Indian diplomats in Moscow and Beijing presented separate plans for a resolution of the Korean conflict. In Moscow Radhakrishnan proposed that, in exchange for PRC entry into the United Nations, the Soviets return to the Security Council and support an immediate cease-fire in Korea, withdrawal of North Korean forces to the 38th parallel, and creation of a "united, independent Korea" through UN mediation. Indian ambassador to Communist China V. M. Panikkar suggested to the Mao government simply that it should be given the Chinese seat in the Security Council as a first step in resolving the Korean issue within that body. Although the Soviet Union rejected Radhakrishnan's overture, China replied favorably to Panikkar's plan. Then, spurred on by reports from Panikkar that the Chinese Communists might be about to attack Taiwan, Nehru made a similar proposal to Stalin and Truman. The Soviet leader accepted it, but Washington demurred.[9]

These early exchanges reflected two major realities of the Korean conflict. First, governments other than those on the peninsula itself held considerable influence over the outcome. The ROK and the DPRK would make their weight felt from time to time, but, as in the past, Korea's ultimate fate was determined abroad, this time in Moscow, Washington, and Beijing by leaders to whom Korea was merely a pawn on a crowded international chessboard. Second, middle-range powers, such as Great Britain and India, had more than a casual interest in the war and hoped to nudge the superpowers and Communist China toward its early termination—or at least away from its extension beyond the peninsula.

If the Communist powers were taken aback by the international response to the North Korean offensive—not only did the United States commit its forces to South Korea's defense but America's European allies and even neutrals like India, Sweden, and Israel supported the action—they were hardly in a rush to end the fighting. With North Korean troops advancing steadily and little immediate risk of a broader conflict, Moscow and Beijing could afford to await developments. In addition to the prospect of a North Korean victory, Stalin may have regarded continued fighting as a means of perpetuating U.S. intervention in the Taiwan strait, thus further alienating Beijing from Washington, and of tying up U.S. forces far away from Europe. Mao himself, though anxious regarding the status of Taiwan, recognized that U.S. action could provide a stimulus to national unity and divert public attention from economic problems within China. As the leader of a revolutionary regime and a believer in the aggressiveness of the United States, he was not about to push for concessions. Rather, he set aside the week of 17–24 July for a "hate America" campaign at home, which concentrated on "unmasking US imperialism," especially on Taiwan. He also stepped up a campaign to suppress "reactionaries and reactionary activities" throughout the country.[10]

The Soviet overture to the British and the Sino-Soviet response to the Indian probe probably reflected a desire to test the diplomatic winds in the West: what were the aims of the opposing camp and was it unified in pursuing them? Although the British response, as communicated to the Soviet Union, revealed no cracks in NATO unity, Moscow realized that London and Washington were not of one mind on terms for ending the Korean conflict. Since January the two governments had diverged on China policy, with the United States continuing to support the Nationalist regime on Taiwan and Great Britain recognizing the Communists on the mainland.[11] With traitors Guy Burgess and Donald Maclean in the British Foreign Office passing documents to Soviet agents on Anglo-U.S. relations, Stalin undoubtedly knew that London had been trying for months to arrange for PRC admittance into the United Nations, just as he likely surmised that America's late June intervention in the Taiwan strait disturbed the Labor government of Clement Attlee.[12] India also had opposed U.S.-China policy for many months, and its effort to link admission of the PRC to the United Nations with a resolution of the Korean crisis demonstrated its continued dissent from aspects of U.S. policy. Mao cultivated the Indians by singling out Ambassador Panikkar for special treatment among the diplomatic corps in Beijing.[13] The Soviets and the Chinese played on British and Indian fears of an expanded war by talking openly of the eventual liberation of Taiwan regardless of the activities of the U.S. Seventh Fleet.[14]

The U.S. response to the Soviet and Indian maneuvers derived from the Truman administration's determination to accept nothing less than restoration of the 38th parallel in Korea. Because U.S. intervention in the Taiwan strait had come in response to the flare-up in Korea, the secretary of state might have regarded a satisfactory resolution of the Korean conflict as reason enough for terminating U.S. involvement in the Chinese civil war. Communist China's admission into the United Nations might have been viewed in the same light, since prior to the North Korean attack the United States had refused either to use its veto to keep the PRC out of the international organization or even to lobby extensively among allies to achieve that result.[15] The United States hoped that resolution of the Taiwan issue and the dispute over Chinese representation in the United Nations would help reduce barriers to a constructive relationship with Communist China. But Acheson now insisted on treating the Korean issue on its merits alone. With U.S. and South Korean troops reeling before the North Korean onslaught, any linkage of Korea to other matters would appear to reward "aggression," thus encouraging Communist military adventures elsewhere. The outbreak of war in Korea also had served to emphasize the importance of Nationalist China's place in the Security Council, as the resolution of 27 June had received the minimum number of votes necessary for passage.[16]

Furthermore, because the Truman administration regarded the North Korean attack as representing a new military dimension to the Soviet menace, Communist control of Taiwan posed more of a threat than before to America's strategic position in the western Pacific.[17] Under international conditions of extreme tension and uncertainty, the availability of the island for Soviet air bases would compromise U.S. control of sea lanes between the Philippines, the Ryukyus, and Japan, as well as threaten U.S. air power stationed on Okinawa. Some State Department officials recognized the political liabilities in the temporary U.S. action to protect Jiang on Taiwan and remained determined to avoid long-term commitment. Yet, on the eve of the outbreak of war in Korea, developments in China and Indochina had produced a reassessment of U.S.-Taiwan policy, which might have led to new U.S. action to save the island even had events on the peninsula not intervened.[18] For the moment, few people in high councils in Washington believed that the United States should risk permitting Taiwan to fall into Communist hands.

Domestic politics reinforced international considerations in producing the U.S. response to peace initiatives regarding Korea. The Republican party had been in a vengeful mood since its defeat in the 1948 election. In the party's drive to seize control of the legislative branch in the upcoming off-year election, Republican leaders were certain to exploit recent U.S. problems in East Asia. Senator Joseph R. McCarthy (Wis.) already had drawn national attention for his attacks on the loyalty of State Department China experts.[19] The president and his political advisers did not want to add fuel to Republican charges by accepting a settlement in Korea that strengthened the Chinese Communists elsewhere.

Electoral politics aside, U.S. diplomats were deeply concerned about partisan controversies over Asian policy. Republicans and "Asia-firsters" in Congress and the press had long agitated for U.S. action to deny the Chinese Communists both control of Taiwan and a seat in the United Nations. Two weeks before the North Korean attack, Assistant Secretary of State Dean Rusk had written to Acheson that the establishment of policies in East Asia "on a broad bipartisan basis" was "of vital importance to the national interest."[20] Internal divisiveness over the U.S. course in the western Pacific could endanger the Truman administration's efforts to maintain its programs to contain communism in western Europe. The threat was not only of congressional emasculation of those programs but of declining confidence across the Atlantic in the reliability of a United States paralyzed by partisan bickering. President Truman's actions in response to the Korean crisis had produced a lull in interparty squabbling and had mobilized public support behind the administration. Flirtation with the British and Indian maneuvers might destroy those salutary developments.

## The United States, the Western Alliance, and the United Nations

To Acheson, the Korean conflict provided an opportunity to consolidate the Western alliance and to develop military strength commensurate with U.S. commitments abroad. The U.S. response to the North Korean attack had eliminated doubts in Europe that the United States would respond forcefully to a Soviet military challenge.[21] By mid-July, however, the continuing North Korean advance and the commitment of tens of thousands of U.S. troops to the Asian theater had turned the initial "elation" in western Europe into what Acheson characterized as "petrified fright." Fears heightened of a similar Communist thrust into West Germany and beyond. With sixty thousand German military police and twenty-seven Soviet divisions in East Germany alone facing twelve poorly equipped and uncoordinated divisions in western Europe, U.S. allies now wondered if NATO "really means anything." While U.S. "intentions" were no longer questioned, U.S. "capabilities" were.[22] From Paris, U.S. ambassador David L. K. Bruce observed that recent events in Korea had reinforced French apprehensions of a Soviet military advance to the English channel. The United States eventually would mount a counteroffensive, but the price of liberating France would be the destruction of the entire country.[23] U.S. representatives reported similar feelings in West Germany.[24] Acheson even showed concern over Japan. After a June visit to Japan, State Department adviser John Foster Dulles had characterized its people as "confused and uncertain."[25] The conservative government of Yoshida Shigeru quickly expressed support for the American stand in Korea, but the opposition Socialist party, which had recently adopted the positions that a peace treaty officially ending World War II in the Pacific should include the Soviet Union, as well as the other belligerents, and that Japan should be neutralized, thus necessitating the withdrawal of U.S. forces, raised questions about support for the United Nations. Acheson believed that this attitude reflected the socialists' fear that "association with the US is dangerous to them."[26]

One remedy for such fears was the rapid buildup of anti-Communist military power. The first step in this process was the augmentation of U.S. armed forces. On 19 July Truman asked Congress for $10 billion for national defense beyond the $14 billion already proposed for fiscal year 1951, removal of the current manpower limit of 2,005,882 on the armed forces, increased military aid to certain friendly nations, and a host of other measures to prepare the economy for "the struggle ahead."[27]

A second step involved a crash program to bolster NATO. This endeavor would raise at least three controversial issues. An expanded U.S. contribution to European defense, especially if this included U.S. ground forces, would provoke debate at home, as Senate ratification of the North Atlantic treaty during the previous year had been based in part on administration assurances that it would *not* station more troops abroad.[28] Fears resulting from the North Korean attack might overcome doubts about altering intentions, but only if the western Europeans demonstrated a willingness to increase contributions to their own defense. Such contributions, in turn, would stir dissension in Europe, where major new military expenditures would require a reduction in the standard of living.

Finally, parity between NATO and Soviet bloc forces in Europe was unlikely to be achieved without West German rearmament. The U.S. Joint Chiefs of Staff had been advocating this measure for months, only to be stymied by the State Department and the White House. In mid-July Acheson and Truman began to alter their views, but they continued to fear political repercussions in western Europe. The French were sure to have deep reservations about West Germany taking up arms. Even the West Germans were likely to have doubts, given the probable impact of rearmament on the prospects for unification. With such potential controversies in mind, U.S. planners commenced a flurry of activity, first among themselves, then in conjunction with their counterparts in western Europe, to seek agreement on how best to counter Communist military strength in what remained the critical area of great power rivalry.[29]

Solidifying the U.S. relationship with Japan constituted another key aspect of the Truman administration's foreign policy. If the United States was to cultivate the friendship of its former enemy, which was central to the U.S. position in the western Pacific, new initiatives appeared essential. The Yoshida government was firmly in place in Tokyo, but economic recovery remained far off, and for the short term, a U.S.-imposed deflationary policy was unhelpful. On the eve of the Korean War, increasing Communist militance had led MacArthur to order repressive countermeasures. Although the country was not in a state of crisis, State Department observers believed that stability necessitated an early end to the U.S. occupation. Fearing the loss of U.S. bases on the otherwise disarmed islands, the Joint Chiefs of Staff delayed movement toward a peace treaty. General MacArthur assuaged this concern somewhat by suggesting that talks for a military alliance proceed simultaneously with those for a peace settlement. Exclusion of the Soviet Union from the treaty-making process would make this procedure feasible. With the outbreak of war in

Korea, Republican John Foster Dulles, who during the previous spring had assumed responsibility for work on the treaty, persuaded Acheson that the project had become more urgent than ever. A peace treaty would set the stage for a formal defensive association between the United States and Japan, and the latter would provide permanence to a U.S. commitment to the Japanese. MacArthur did his part on 8 July when he ordered the creation of a Japanese police reserve and the augmentation of maritime security forces, which constituted a modest beginning to the defeated nation's rearmament.[30]

The secretary of state also sought to emphasize the collective nature of U.S. intervention in Korea. Material support from other nations would relieve the United States of some of the burdens in Korea, would bind friendly nations to the U.S.-initiated venture, and would have a deterrent effect on Moscow. Furthermore, it would undermine Soviet claims that the U.S. effort in Korea had little support among the masses worldwide and would ensure ongoing support within the United States for a collective approach to U.S. foreign policy. Acheson remarked to his Canadian counterpart and long-time friend Lester B. Pearson that, "if the United States had to do all the fighting in Korea, there was a real danger that public opinion [at home] . . . would favour preparing in isolation for the larger conflict ahead and writing its allies off." He and the president were "intensely concerned" that the coming struggle be one of "the free world vs. the Communist world" rather than "the United States vs. the USSR," and the conflict in Korea could represent a turning point in U.S. sentiment on this issue.[31]

The U.S. reaction to the North Korean attack stirred considerable enthusiasm at Lake Success. The previous six months had seen a growing pessimism among UN workers and delegates, who viewed with apprehension the Soviet walkout of the Security Council in January and the inconclusive spring trip to Moscow by Secretary General Trygve Lie. But the U.S. determination to counter the North Korean offensive instilled hope that the organization might indeed be more than "the sum of its members."[32] Talk even circulated of the formation of a UN legion for Korea.[33]

Reality soon intervened. One problem derived from the goal of the U.S. Joint Chiefs for battlefield efficiency. They objected to a proposal by Lie for creation of a committee to stimulate and coordinate aid for the war in Korea and to supervise military operations there. Pentagon officials preferred to leave military plans and their execution solely in the hands of the United States.[34] On 7 July, after much wrangling behind the scenes, the Security Council, with the Soviet delegate still absent, called for creation of a unified command under the United States, which was to receive all contributions to the collective enterprise. President Truman immediately appointed General MacArthur commander of UN forces in Korea.

Two issues emerged between the United States and its allies over the resolution. First was the desire of several governments that no UN forces be used to defend Taiwan. To some officials, the section of the draft resolution welcoming aid from member nations "to assist the Republic of Korea in defending itself against armed attack and thus to restore international peace and security in the area" was too vague in defining the territorial limits of UN action. Second, some observers believed that the resolution's approach of making "forces and other assistance available to a unified command under the United States" took too much authority out of the hands of the United Nations.

In both cases the United States insisted on having its way, though in the first instance the discussion emphasized to the Americans the need to separate the Korean venture from other U.S. action in East Asia; in the second case, the U.S. position expressed a legitimate desire to control the Korean enterprise from Washington rather than Tokyo, where MacArthur's aggressive inclinations might create problems. Still, the centralization of authority in the hands of the United States encouraged others to let it shoulder the primary burden on the peninsula.[35]

Warren R. Austin, the U.S. ambassador to the United Nations, failed to enhance the spirit of cooperation. Formerly a Republican senator, Austin's primary function was to help maintain bipartisan congressional support for the international organization. He was seventy-two years old in 1950 and of declining energy, although his verve in defending moral righteousness and U.S. interests—which to him usually appeared identical—remained considerable. His emotionalism often frayed nerves in other delegations. In resisting changes in the draft resolution creating a UN command, Austin offended several people. He acted so abrasively toward Ambassador Arne Sunde of Norway that one observer believed personal relations "irreconcilably damaged" between the U.S. and Norwegian delegations.[36] In August an Australian diplomat at the United Nations reported home that "the general view here [is] that the time has long since passed when the US Government should have sent Senator Austin back to Vermont to brood amongst his apple trees."[37]

Personalities aside, the desire of the U.S. Joint Chiefs that all military contributions from other nations provide real assistance to operations constituted an ongoing problem in recruiting support for the struggle in Korea. Military planners considered a variety of factors regarding non-U.S. forces—language, diet, religion, equipment, training, and size—in determining who might be approached for contributions. Egypt, for example, had an army of fifty-seven thousand soldiers, but they were Moslems, presenting religious and dietary barriers to integration with U.S. units. Language differences added to the problem of effective interaction, and the Egyptian troops had a "poor" combat efficiency. Afghanistan also had a sizable army but with deficiencies similar to those of Egypt. In these and several other cases of non-U.S. forces, U.S. military leaders deemed direct participation of such forces "undesirable," even if they proved willing.

At times, a nation's commitments elsewhere precluded the contribution of troops to Korea. France's army of half a million soldiers had occupation duties in Austria and Germany, garrison duties in Africa, and combat responsibilities in Indochina, not to mention the task of defending the homeland. Iraq and Iran, particularly the latter, maintained sizable armies, but the Joint Chiefs believed they should be kept at home to guard against "the ever-present danger of Soviet aggression toward the oil fields bordering the Persian Gulf."[38]

At the behest of General MacArthur, the Joint Chiefs determined in late July that minimum acceptable contributions should include "one infantry battalion augmented by appropriate combat and service support, with a total strength of approximately 1,000." These forces "should be fully equipped and should arrive in the field of operations with sixty days level of supplies." "Parent nations should be responsible for full logistic support on a continuing basis," but, where this proved impossible, the forces might be "integrated into the US supply program," with the country that was providing troops agreeing to reimburse the U.S. government.[39]

Believing that the political desirability of broad international participation in the Korean venture should often override military drawbacks, the State Department challenged the Pentagon approach. In early August Acheson went to the National Security Council, where the president agreed that the United States should make every effort to use non-Korean and non-American soldiers, especially from such Asian nations as the Philippines, Thailand, India, and Pakistan.[40] By this time, the Defense Department had reduced to sixteen the number of countries that should be asked to provide combatants. The contributions to be requested varied from two divisions from Great Britain down to a token force of perhaps a hundred men from tiny Luxembourg.[41] The State Department did not limit itself to seeking military assistance for Korea. On 31 July the United States pushed a resolution through the Security Council giving the United Nations Command (UNC) responsibility for determining the relief requirements of Korea's civilian population for administering relief efforts in the field, and calling on other UN organs to help MacArthur fulfill his needs in this area.[42]

Acheson's attempts to strengthen the West did not preclude efforts to end the conflict in Korea, but U.S. preoccupation with consolidating the anti-Communist bloc prevented the United States from launching peace initiatives on its own or pursuing tenaciously the probes of others. To the secretary of state, fruitful talks with the Soviet Union were most likely to occur after the West had established local conditions of political, economic, and military strength.[43] The North Korean attack had occurred because South Korea's progress in the third area had lagged behind advances in the first two. The restoration of peace probably would have to await an improvement in the military position of U.S. forces.

Evidence on the Soviet side offers no reason to dispute this view. Even had the United States offered a trade-off of Taiwan and a seat for Communist China in the United Nations in return for a North Korean retreat to the 38th parallel, there is no certainty that Stalin would have agreed. A U.S. proposal along these lines might have tempted Beijing, but the Soviet premier had no interest in reducing barriers to rapprochement between Communist China and the West or in sowing the seeds of discord between Moscow and Pyongyang, so he might well have balked. In all likelihood, events in Korea were too favorable to the Communist side—and developments elsewhere were not unfavorable enough—to make an early end of the war attractive to the Kremlin.

## Clash in the United Nations

U.S. domination of the Security Council had became sufficiently disconcerting to Stalin to warrant ending the USSR's self-imposed exile from the international body. As a result of the Soviet boycott, the United States had used the Security Council to gain international sanction for its stand in Korea. In June Stalin may have viewed such sanction as advantageous in limiting the war. In any event, a Soviet return at that point might have exacerbated an already explosive situation.[44] A month later conditions had stabilized somewhat, as the United States had clarified its desire to limit the war. With its delegate back in the Security Council, the Soviet Union could veto distasteful resolutions, directly counter U.S. verbal assaults on the Communist world, and perhaps even undermine Western unity on Korea. The "peace" offensive launched during the spring of 1949 had intensified in March 1950 with the commencement of a global effort by Communist parties and various leftist and pacifist committees to collect signatures for the Stockholm Peace Petition, which espoused the banning of atomic warfare. In July the appeal broadened to include the theme "Hands Off Korea." As before, the Security Council could provide a forum for the dissemination of this propaganda.[45]

Yet, as with the Berlin crisis of the previous year, the Kremlin also may have viewed the Security Council as a forum for the peaceful resolution of the Korean issue. Despite the continuing retreat of UN ground forces in Korea, the rapid buildup of U.S. troops and equipment there might prevent a Communist victory. If so, diplomatic initiatives eventually might become necessary either to end a hopeless stalemate on the battlefield or to avert military defeat. On 27 July Soviet representative Jacob Malik informed Trygve Lie that he would return to the council in five days to assume its presidency during August.

The Soviet diplomat quickly clashed with his U.S. counterpart, Warren Austin, and, indeed, with a majority of the entire Security Council. No sooner had he called the 480th session to order than he attempted to shift the agenda from a continuing discussion of Korea to Chinese representation in the United Nations. With millions of Americans watching on their new television sets and hundreds of others roaring approval in person every time the portly Austin or the dignified Briton, Sir Gladwyn Jebb, scored debating points for the West, the supposed peacekeeping body descended into a month-long orgy of procedural battles and inflammatory rhetoric. The Security Council overruled Malik's procedural decisions, but he received support from India on the issue of Chinese representation. He also gave full exposition of Soviet claims that the Korean conflict was a civil war that should be settled solely by internal parties and that U.S. bombing above the 38th parallel involved the brutal destruction of civilian targets.[46]

Malik's maneuvering in the Security Council was part of a larger Soviet effort to draw attention to the U.S. stance on China and to weaken support for the United States in Korea. In mid-August the Permanent Committee of the Peace Movement, a Communist-controlled organization that sought to undermine U.S. efforts to rearm the West, shifted its resources from a mass campaign to collect signatures from people who favored banning the atomic bomb to a worldwide propaganda crusade against UN intervention in Korea.[47] Through the pressure of world opinion, this campaign might soften the U.S. position in Asia, thus paving the way for a settlement in Korea.

Malik's draft resolution of 4 August indicates that the USSR may have desired serious discussions on Korea. Departing from past positions, Malik proposed that Communist China and "representatives of the Korean people" be invited to attend talks on Korea within the Security Council. He did not insist on the formal seating of the Mao regime as a member of the international organ or the expulsion of Nationalist China; he spoke of the Kim and Rhee governments as equals, both of which should participate in the discussions.[48]

This proposal remained a good distance from the U.S. position. Malik clung to the argument that resolution of the Korean conflict should include withdrawal of foreign troops from the peninsula. Because such an event, even if accompanied by a North Korean retreat to the 38th parallel, might encourage a later resumption of the Communist offensive, it clearly was unacceptable to Washington. Malik also insisted that the Rhee and Kim governments be invited simultaneously to attend Security Council meetings. In part, he based his stand on the contention that the council's decision of 25 June to extend an invitation to South Korea alone was illegal because of the absence of two permanent members, the Soviet Union and Communist China. Had the United States accepted this position, it would have conceded the illegality of the resolutions of 25 and 27 June—thus destroying the basis for UN action in Korea—as well as the legitimacy of Beijing's claim to represent China at Lake Success. When on 8 August Malik used his status as president to present, against the rules of procedure, Pyongyang's charge that U.S. bombers were carrying out "barbarous attacks on undefended Korean towns and industrial centers," he gave some credence to the idea that the Communists were more interested in using the United Nations as a forum for their propaganda than for ending the conflict in Korea.[49]

On 21 August, however, with the North Koreans gaining little ground on the battlefield, the Soviet position shifted slightly. In a private meeting of Security Council members Malik implied that South Korea could be invited first to attend discussions on the war so long as no reference was made to the resolution of 25 June and prior agreement was reached to invite North Korea immediately thereafter. Austin and other council representatives demurred, insisting that no invitation be extended to North Korea until the UN "police action" had ended (meaning, presumably, until North Korea had withdrawn to the 38th parallel).[50] When Malik restated his proposal in a formal meeting of the Security Council on 1 September, the other delegates again rejected it.[51]

The host of procedural matters raised during August revealed some of the complications deriving from UN involvement in the Korean affair. The Soviet Union could not accept the legitimacy of the resolutions of 25 and 27 June, and in attacking their status it hardly could avoid raising the issue of Chinese representation. The United States, in turn, bridled at any implication that the resolutions were less than legitimate, and it remained determined to keep the Korean issue separate from that of China's representation in the United Nations. Lastly, because neither North nor South Korea were members of the international organization, since one was recognized by the Communist powers and the other by most nations of the West, and because the principals adhered to sharply divergent accounts of the origins of the present conflict, difficulties were bound to arise over treatment of the two Korean states in UN deliberations. Such problems could not have stymied two superpowers determined to achieve an early termination of the war, but they surely compounded the task of finding some common ground.

Soviet action in the Security Council failed to lead either to progress toward peace or to a weakening of support for U.S. leadership on Korea. Malik's flaunting of the rules of procedure during his presidency actually reinforced unity among non-Communist nations. They saw little reason to believe that the USSR sought to end the conflict on terms other than a victory for North Korea, and they were moving increasingly toward the conclusion that mere restoration of the 38th parallel was inadequate for the maintenance of "peace and security" on the peninsula.

## UNIFICATION OF KOREA CONSIDERED

Unfortunately, these tendencies did nothing to foster prudence within the Truman administration. The United States had announced at the end of June that its intervention in Korea was "solely for the purpose of restoring the Republic of Korea to the status prior to the invasion from the North." Yet the executive branch in Washington soon flirted with an eventual UN military campaign above the 38th parallel, which would set the stage for national unification under a pro-Western government.[52] The State Department split on the issue, with the Policy Planning Staff, still influenced by its former head, Counselor George F. Kennan, opposing a U.S. ground offensive in North Korea and Dean Rusk and John Allison, director of the Division of Northeast Asian Affairs, arguing that the possibility should not be ruled out. The first group believed that such a venture might displease U.S. allies in Europe, bolster Soviet charges of U.S. aggression in Korea, and, worst of all, lead to direct Soviet or Communist Chinese intervention on the peninsula. Allison countered that U.S. failure to punish "aggression" by moving into the North would both eliminate the prospect of fulfilling the Security Council resolution of 27 June, which called for the restoration of "peace and security in the area," and encourage Communist military moves elsewhere.[53]

The last line of thought reflected a widespread fear in the United States that, as the *New York Times* observed on 2 July, "the Soviets can choose to put pressure on almost any point on the periphery [of the Eurasian heartland], sucking in American strength now here, now there, 'bleeding' the United States in a long campaign of attrition."[54] To some analysts, including Secretary of Defense Louis Johnson, Secretary of the Navy Francis B. Matthews, Air Force General Orvil Anderson, and the influential Senator Richard B. Russell (D., Ga.), preventive war against the Soviet Union might represent the only reasonable alternative to such a fate.[55]

Truman and Acheson rejected preventive war, but they sympathized with the common desire to decisively resolve the Korean issue. Since World War II, America's ultimate objective in Korea had always been to make Korea a free and united nation, and its achievement would represent a great victory for the United States over the Soviet Union.[56] To halt UN forces at the 38th parallel would add to the volatile situation within South Korea, where President Rhee already agitated for an all-out military campaign in the North.[57]

The Joint Chiefs believed unification of Korea under a friendly regime would reverse "the dangerous strategic trend in the Far East" over the last year by "disturb[ing] the strategic complex which the USSR is organizing between its own Far Eastern territories and the contiguous areas." Beijing might even reevaluate its "dependent" relationship with Moscow.[58]

General MacArthur's view was still more grandiose. In a meeting in Tokyo on 13 July with generals J. Lawton Collins and Hoyt Vandenberg, the U.S. army and air force chiefs of staff, respectively, the UN commander declared that North Korean forces must be destroyed, not just driven back beyond the 38th parallel. Once this was accomplished, the entire peninsula would be united. He suggested the use of atomic bombs to cut off supply routes into Korea from China and the Soviet Union. "We win here or we lose everywhere," he insisted. "If we win here, we improve the chances of winning everywhere."[59]

The prevailing view within the executive branch in Washington, nonetheless, was that the Soviet Union or China or both would send forces into Korea to prevent UN troops from marching into the northern reaches of the peninsula. From the start of the conflict, U.S. officials had assumed that a direct Soviet-U.S. confrontation in Korea would lead to world war. By August they recognized that the escalating commitment in Korea had left the United States in a poor position to execute its war plan and that, in any case, U.S. forces were sufficiently weak as to raise doubt about the final outcome. At best, Soviet defeat would come after a long and costly struggle in which the U.S. homeland might suffer extensive damage from air attack. The result of a Sino-U.S. clash in Korea was less certain, but it surely would increase the risk of global conflict and tie up major U.S. resources on the peninsula for a substantial period. By mid-August even the hawkish Allison conceded that American unpreparedness for war with the Soviet Union, combined with uncertainties regarding Moscow's and Beijing's intentions, made it too early to commit the United States to a campaign above the 38th parallel.[60]

Yet the option received ongoing consideration. On 10 August, with the UN army still pinned down in the southeastern corner of the peninsula, the Truman administration began laying the political ground work for such a move. On that date Warren Austin asked rhetorically in a speech before the Security Council, "Shall only part of the country [Korea] be assured freedom?" "I think not," he answered. "The United Nations has consistently worked for a unified country, an independent Korea. The United Nations will not want to turn from that objective now." A week later he made a similar pronouncement. Then, at the end of the month, President Truman declared in a radio address that "Koreans have the right to be free, independent, and united." Under UN "guidance," he concluded, the United States would "do [its] part to help them enjoy that right."[61] Increasingly, the State Department viewed the unification of Korea as a method of seizing the offensive in the cold war. As a departmental position paper concluded, a total victory on the peninsula would be "of incalculable importance in Asia and throughout the world." The accomplishment would keenly impress Japan and "stimulate any latent or active differences between Peiping [Beijing] and Moscow." Even "Soviet satellites in Europe" would take notice.[62]

By this time U.S. diplomats had probed European allies on a UN military venture above the 38th parallel and had received a tentative but affirmative response.[63] On 11 September, with General MacArthur on the verge of mounting a counteroffensive in the peninsula, the president approved NSC-81, which called for the advance of UN ground forces into North Korea "provided that at the time of such operations there has been no entry into [that area of] . . . major Soviet or Communist Chinese forces, no announcement of intended entry, nor a threat to counter our operations [there] militarily."[64] The hopes for unification by military means grew out of the assumption that unification by other methods was impossible.

This attitude helped shape the U.S. response to an Indian peace initiative during August. In the middle of the month Sir Benegal Rau, India's delegate to the United Nations, lobbied for creation of a committee of nonpermanent members of the Security Council to study and make proposals regarding Korea's future. Canada instigated the move, seeing it as a possible method of drawing New Delhi closer to the West.[65] The Australian delegation thought the plan "somewhat woolly as . . . are all Indian proposals," but believed it offered the United States and the United Kingdom an opportunity "to rehabilitate themselves in the eyes of Asia, and of India in particular." Since "a clear majority among non-permanent members" were anti-Communist, little chance existed that a report from a committee made up of them would "play into the hands of the Russians."[66] Malik threatened to veto Rau's plan if it included any commitment to the resolutions of 25 and 27 June, while Austin voiced concern that anything short of such a commitment would undermine the validity of those resolutions. The renewed Soviet presence in the Security Council made the General Assembly, where the United States consistently mustered sizable majorities for its schemes and where the great power veto did not apply, a more attractive setting for U.S. maneuvers. And the situation in Korea remained too unclear to warrant final conclusions about that country's future. By 20 September, when the General Assembly was to convene its annual session, circumstances might be different. Discouraged by Austin's response to his plan, and failing to receive encouragement from New Delhi, Rau let his idea die without offering a formal motion.[67]

## THE CHINESE RESPONSE

Austin's comments about a possible UN effort to unite Korea did not pass unnoticed in Communist circles. On 20 August Chinese foreign minister Zhou Enlai sent a message to the United Nations that deviated from past statements emanating from Beijing in its emphasis on Korea rather than Taiwan. Because "Korea is China's neighbor," Zhou declared, "the Chinese people cannot but be concerned about solution of the Korean question."[68] He demanded representation for the PRC while the Korea issue was "being discussed in the Security Council." Two days later, after delegates outside the Soviet bloc rejected Malik's proposal regarding North and South Korean participation in Security Council deliberations, the Soviet representative assaulted U.S. policy in a speech warning that "any continuation of the Korean War will lead inevitably to a widening conflict with consequences, the responsibility for which will be with the United States."[69] Then, on 26 August, an article in the Chinese journal *World Culture* asserted: "The barbarous action of American imperialism and its hangers-on in invading Korea not only menaces peace in Asia and the world in general but seriously threatens the security of China in particular. The Chinese people cannot allow such aggressive acts of American imperialism in Korea."[70] These statements, along with Malik's maneuvers at Lake Success, constituted a "carrot and stick" policy aimed at preventing an eventual UN military campaign in North Korea.

The Chinese reinforced that policy with active preparations for military intervention in Korea. To Mao, U.S. intervention there represented both a challenge and an opportunity for his young government. On the one hand, it might encourage opponents of the Communist revolution remaining on the mainland and Nationalists on Taiwan to become more aggressive. As scholar Chen Jian has remarked, stepped up U.S. activity nearby provided a test of the new regime's "ability to rule China and to safeguard China's prestige and national interests."[71] On the other hand, as an internal directive of the General Information Bureau observed on 29 June, the increased danger from the United States provided a context "favorable for the further awakening of the Chinese people.... We have to hold this opportunity... to start a widespread campaign of propaganda, so that we will be able to educate our people at home and to strike firmly [at] the arrogance of the U.S. imperialist aggressors."[72]

On 4 August, with the "hate American campaign" well underway and several Chinese armies redeployed to Manchuria, Mao told the politburo of the Chinese Communist Party that, "if the U.S. imperialists won the war, they would become more arrogant and would threaten us. . . . We must lend them [the North Koreans] our hands by sending our military volunteers there." The timing would be decided later, but preparations must rapidly proceed.[73] On the next day he informed his generals in the northeast that they must be prepared to fight within a month. Later in August he extended the period of preparation to the end of September, but he also called for twelve armies to be stationed along the Yalu, an increase of eight over his order of early July.[74] Mao feared that the North Koreans had overextended their forces to the south and were vulnerable to a UN counterstrike in their rear.[75]

Although U.S. intelligence picked up the steady movement of Chinese forces northward toward Korea, its reports that Moscow was urging Beijing to intervene on the peninsula and that the Mao regime, facing severe problems of economic reconstruction and development at home, resented the pressure, was apparently erroneous.[76] At this point Stalin probably had mixed feelings about Chinese involvement in Korea. For the short term, this development would further China's dependence on the USSR, yet it would also increase the likelihood of global conflict. For the long term, China's assumption of the major burden in Korea could lead to an erosion of Soviet control over international communism. China might emerge from the venture with considerable prestige and self-confidence, which could only encourage Mao to chart his own course in foreign policy. While Stalin remained willing to see China intervene in Korea under certain circumstances, he probably sought to prevent those conditions from arising.

### The MacArthur Factor and Great Power Diplomacy

General MacArthur's presence in Tokyo magnified Soviet and Chinese fears of a UN counteroffensive in North Korea. As both commander in chief of UN forces in Korea and of U.S. forces in the Far East, MacArthur held considerable leverage over U.S. policy in East Asia. The first post carried with it operational control over U.S., South Korean, and any other forces committed to the UN enterprise in Korea, while the second endowed him with similar authority over U.S. ground, air, and sea forces in the western Pacific. President Truman could veto his orders, but MacArthur's prestige at home with the Joint Chiefs of Staff, important elements of the Republican party, and the public at large made him difficult to control.

The general, now seventy years old, was nearing the end of a long and illustrious career. His record included distinguished service in both world wars and five years as army chief of staff. His first commission in the armed services had come in 1903, giving him seniority over all other active officers, including members of the Joint Chiefs of Staff. Nor were his achievements and ambitions strictly military. After World War II, he became commander of Allied occupation forces in Japan, a post that included not only responsibility for maintaining order in and control over that defeated country but the task of preparing it for an eventual reappearance among the family of nations. He virtually ruled Japan as an independent monarch, and most analysts judged the results favorably. In 1948 he encouraged a campaign among some Republican bigwigs to deliver him the Republican nomination for president of the United States.[77] Although the campaign fizzled, his thirst for high political office endured. "I am ready to serve at any time, in any capacity, anywhere," he proclaimed to a reporter on 25 June 1950.[78] Striking in appearance, magnetic in personality, and, by some accounts, brilliant in intellect, MacArthur also was vain and egotistical. Those serving under him were for the most part sycophants and mediocrities who encouraged his least attractive qualities. Imbued with a strong sense of personal destiny, his lengthy experience in the western Pacific made him a rabid Asia-firster, determined to alter America's traditional slighting of his bailiwick in favor of Europe. The outbreak of war in Korea gave him a long-awaited opportunity to achieve this goal.[79]

MacArthur never had shown sensitivity to the UN role in Korea. In the spring of 1948 he created a minor incident when he refused housing in Japan for members of UNTCOK, who wanted to compose one of their reports in Tokyo.[80] On becoming UN commander, he undermined the collective spirit of the Korean endeavor by providing information in press communiqués that would have been more appropriate in reports to the Security Council.[81] MacArthur was a lone wolf, not well suited to the demands of leadership over a sensitive collective enterprise.

Events involving Taiwan illustrate the difficulty in controlling MacArthur from afar. The willful general had argued for some time that the United States must prevent that island's fall into Communist hands. When, in response to the North Korean attack, President Truman announced that the U.S. Seventh Fleet would temporarily neutralize Taiwan, the Far Eastern commander turned his efforts toward securing a permanent U.S. commitment to defend that territory against attack from the mainland. Here he had the sympathy, if not always the overt support, of Secretary Johnson and the Joint Chiefs. The president and the State Department demurred, at least for the present. To them the Nationalist regime was obnoxious, and U.S. protection of it lacked UN sanction and broad international support.

The Taiwan question presented a particular danger to Anglo-U.S. cooperation. The British remained worried that U.S. action in the Taiwan strait would produce a military confrontation between the United States and Communist China and that such a conflict would make untenable their still lucrative position in Hong Kong and their strategic outpost in Malaya, where Chinese elements of the population engaged in a guerrilla struggle against the established regime. In anticipation of a possible Sino-U.S. crisis, Attlee's Labor government made it clear that Great Britain was not committed to aid the United States in defending Taiwan.[82] Even if Mao did not attack the island, U.S. protection of Jiang exacerbated Communist Chinese hostility to the West and alienated Asian—especially Indian—opinion. As representatives of a nation strapped for resources, British leaders preferred diplomatic finesse, often exercised through the commonwealth, to raw power. Recently independent India loomed as a potential instrument for the maintenance of British influence in Asia, and Britain sought the assistance of its former colonial master in persuading the United States to retreat from Taiwan. On British urging, Truman stated on 19 July, in a well-publicized message to Congress, that current U.S. policy with regard to Taiwan was a temporary expedient "without prejudice to political questions affecting that island."[83] It was hoped that this assurance would keep the issue in the background until the conflict in Korea ended.[84]

On 31 July MacArthur disrupted this effort by traveling to Taipei for talks with Jiang. The Far Eastern commander's statement to the press on returning to Tokyo had strong political overtones. He praised Jiang for his "indomitable determination" to combat communism and declared that the embattled leader's steadfastness "parallels the common interests and purposes of Americans, that all people in the Pacific should be free—not slaves."[85] The generalissimo added his own touch to the occasion, proclaiming that he and MacArthur had laid the groundwork for "Sino-American military cooperation." With his forces "working closely with our old comrade in arms," he asserted, victory was now assured.[86] The U.S. press wondered aloud if Jiang and MacArthur had made secret agreements and if the latter had cleared his activities with Washington.

The incident occurred at a most awkward moment for the State Department, which had just announced the transfer of foreign service officer Karl Lott Rankin from Hong Kong to Taibei to head the U.S. mission there. Although the United States regarded the move as "routine," that Rankin held the position of minister, whereas his predecessor, Robert Strong, was only a first secretary, reflected to many observers a thaw in the Truman administration's cool attitude toward the Jiang regime.[87] This event, together with the MacArthur trip, gave Jacob Malik plenty of ammunition for a propaganda offensive aimed at the United Nations on alleged U.S. "aggression" against China.[88]

Actually the Joint Chiefs had recommended that the Far Eastern commander examine Taiwan's military needs, and the National Security Council had approved. Observers in both the State and Defense departments and in the Central Intelligence Agency feared a Communist assault on the island, and they doubted the capacity of the U.S. Seventh Fleet, the bulk of which was engaged in Korean waters, to repulse such a move.[89] At least partly in response to this concern, President Truman approved the movement of B-29 bombers, some capable of carrying nuclear weapons, across the Pacific to Guam, and Secretary of State Acheson leaked that fact to the press.[90] MacArthur had consulted the Pentagon before flying to Taibei and, although his military superiors encouraged him to send a senior officer rather than go himself, they refused to order him not to make the trip.[91] The State Department did not receive advance notice of MacArthur's plans, which reflected the horrid system of communications between the military and the diplomats while Johnson was secretary of defense. The incident also reflected the difficulty of reconciling MacArthur's position as commander in chief of U.S. forces in the Far East with his capacity as commander of UN forces in Korea. Geographically, the general's responsibilities in the first post were far broader than in the second, yet the U.S. goal of building and maintaining a collective effort in Korea required great finesse in carrying out some of those larger tasks, especially ones related to Taiwan. MacArthur's impatience with the indecisiveness of U.S. policy toward the island, plus his headstrong nature, precluded the graceful juggling of his dual capacity.

A report from foreign-service officers in Taibei increased State Department anxieties regarding the possible aftereffects of MacArthur's excursion. The report warned that the general planned to transfer U.S. fighter squadrons to the island.[92] Because the Joint Chiefs had recently told MacArthur of their proposal to the National Security Council that U.S. planes disperse PRC troop concentrations on the mainland facing Taiwan, the secretary of state feared that "the Proconsul of the East" might actually initiate such action. To guard against this possibility, Truman ordered a message sent to the Far Eastern commander stating that only "the President as Commander-in-Chief" could authorize operations against China.[93] Truman also dispatched Averell Harriman, the new White House adviser on foreign affairs, to Tokyo to explain U.S. policy to MacArthur.

The episode quickly would have become a faint memory in the United States had the petulant field commander not gone public with his discontent over the Truman administration's approach to Taiwan. In response to an invitation to address the yearly meeting of the Veterans of Foreign Wars (VFW), MacArthur dispatched a letter to be read in his absence outlining the strategic importance of the island and rebutting the claim that its defense by the United States would be unpopular in Asia:

> Those who speak thus do not understand the Orient. They do not grant that it is in the pattern of the Oriental psychology to respect and follow aggressive, resolute and dynamic leadership, to quickly turn from a leadership characterized by timidity or vacillation. . . . Nothing in the last five years has so inspired the Far East as the American determination to preserve the bulwarks of our Pacific Ocean's strategic position from future encroachment.[94]

The press received copies of MacArthur's letter to the VFW on 25 August, a day after PRC foreign minister Zhou Enlai sent a telegram to UN Secretary General Lie demanding that the Security Council "condemn . . . and take immediate measures to bring about the complete withdrawal of all United States armed invading forces from Taiwan."[95] There were no such forces, but Mac-

Arthur's letter added credibility to Communist charges and heightened allied fears that the United States was overcommitting itself in Asia at the expense of Europe. Truman ordered the general to withdraw his statement.

The president also took pains to outline publicly the U.S. approach to Taiwan. He reiterated that the Seventh Fleet would be removed from the Taiwan strait once the Korean War had ended and announced that he "would welcome United Nations consideration" of the island's future.[96] Previously the United States had shied away from referring the matter to the international body, but on 29 August, when the Security Council resolved to consider Communist China's accusation of U.S. aggression on Taiwan, the United States voted with the majority.[97]

MacArthur's activities could not help but cause concern in Moscow and Beijing. His moves produced a combination of rage and apprehension among the Chinese Communists, who were anxious to topple Jiang from his last stronghold. The Far Eastern commander's statements regarding the island and the Oriental mentality coincided with a number of critical events: a strafing by U.S. planes of a railroad terminal at Dalizu and an airfield at Andong, both in Manchuria; a speech by Navy Secretary Matthews advocating "a war to compel cooperation for peace" and press reports of other support for the idea in high levels of the Truman administration;[98] and at a time when the Nationalists continued their blockade of the China coast, their attacks on shipping, and their dropping of leaflets on the mainland, all of which conflicted with the U.S. neutralization order of 27 June. President Truman rebuked Matthews, but on 1 September he warned China against intervening in Korea, suggesting that such a move would "spread into general war."[99] Truman's comment sought to prevent Chinese involvement on the peninsula; the air attacks over Manchuria were probably inadvertent; and Washington had no plans for major operations on the mainland against the Beijing regime, nor did it condone Nationalist activities there. Yet, as scholar Allen Whiting has noted, the Mao government, viewing developments through the lens of Communist ideology, may have regarded the events of late August "as part of an overall design to probe the vulnerability of the PRC and to seek its eventual overthrow."[100] The absence of direct diplomatic contacts between Beijing and Washington since the departure of U.S. Consul General O. Edmund Clubb from the Chinese capital in April added to the Truman administration's difficulties in allaying Chinese fears.

Although the Kremlin welcomed MacArthur's assertiveness as a means of holding the Chinese firmly in the Soviet camp and perhaps of embroiling the United States in an Asian quagmire, it probably feared that his belligerence, along with trends in the United States, reflected sinister designs in U.S. policy. Stalin had approved the North Korean attack believing that the United States had written off South Korea. When the Truman administration rushed troops to the peninsula, reversed its policy toward Taiwan, and commenced a campaign to drastically increase U.S. and western European military power, Soviet leaders—inclined toward a conspiratorial view of the capitalist world—

probably suspected a cynical plot to invite a Communist adventure in Korea so as to enable Washington to launch a more aggressive course abroad.[101] Despite Truman's firmness in responding to MacArthur's and Matthews's statements, Stalin may have compared what happened to the two supposedly wayward officials—they were not even demoted—to the punishment that would have been meted out in the Soviet Union for publicly expressing opinions contrary to official policy.[102] If U.S. designs were offensive rather than defensive, a possible voluntary North Korea retreat to the 38th parallel took on an entirely new significance. Such a move would ease the U.S. burden in mounting a campaign above the old boundary, and who could tell just where such a campaign might lead?

Ending the Korean conflict, therefore, was no easy task. Probes of the U.S. position had to avoid conveying to the West any sign of weakness in the Communist world. In taking care to do so, Soviet diplomats made the "stick" more apparent to the opposing camp than the "carrot," thus reducing prospects for serious talks with the United States, which had apprehensions of its own.

### Credits: The United States and Its Allies

It is most unfortunate that a more concerted effort to end the conflict was not made by the superpowers between mid-August and mid-September. By the second week of August the North Korean offensive had lost much of its momentum and each passing day increased the likelihood that UN forces would maintain a toehold on the peninsula indefinitely. With the U.S. buildup on Japan proceeding rapidly, a UN counteroffensive could not be far away. Surely an opportune moment was at hand to end the fighting on the basis of restoration of the 38th parallel. To assuage Communist fears regarding a U.S. military presence in Korea, the United States might have agreed to keep its troops south of the Han River and to withdraw all its soldiers from the peninsula within six months after withdrawal of the North Koreans behind the 38th parallel. U.S. fears of the resumption of hostilities following a U.S. departure might have been eased through the establishment of a demilitarized zone for several miles on each side of the 38th parallel and the stationing in that area of an international police force—or at least an observation team—under the United Nations. Neither the Kim nor the Rhee regimes would have liked such a settlement, but the Soviet Union and the United States had the capacity to force them to accept it.

That no proposals even remotely resembling such a plan emerged reveals the degree of polarization that had occurred in superpower relations. Both were anxious to avoid a direct confrontation with the other, and for the short term they succeeded. Yet their positions prevented an early end to the fighting and, over the longer haul, the continuing hostilities only compounded the risks of a clash between them.

The Truman administration's course did hold some advantages for the

United States. In dampening hopes for an early peace in Korea, it helped mobilize support for augmenting the military strength of the West. By early September, Great Britain and France had taken significant strides to bolster their defense efforts.[103] In the middle of the month, the U.S. Congress passed an $11 billion supplemental appropriations bill to bolster U.S. armed forces and to increase arms assistance to allied nations. The United States also presented to the North Atlantic Council in New York a "one package" proposal to strengthen NATO. The plan envisioned a four-to-six division increase of U.S. troops in Europe, as well as a buildup of British and French strength and the creation of a sizable West German contingent. All units—new and old alike—were to be integrated into a European defense system under a supreme commander and with an international staff. French jitters over German rearmament blocked agreement on a crucial aspect of the U.S. plan, yet acceptance of the principle of integrated forces "under centralized command" represented an important step toward a viable program for the security of western Europe. And France already had withdrawn its opposition to German production of materiel for NATO units and to the organization of a West German police force to match that of the Soviet-sponsored regime in the east. With time, the French might soften their position on German rearmament as well.[104]

The United States also made progress toward strengthening Japan as a bulwark of Western defense. MacArthur's order of early July for the establishment of a seventy-five-thousand-man Japanese Police Reserve Force was initially as much designed to maintain internal order as to ward off any foreign threat, but for the longer term it could become the foundation for a national army. On the economic front, U.S. procurement needs for the struggle in Korea had provided a spark to the Japanese economy. Then, on 7 September, Acheson and Secretary Johnson placed on the president's desk a memorandum outlining governing principles and concrete procedures for negotiating peace and defense agreements with Japan. With months of rancor between the State and Defense departments behind them, U.S. diplomats could now push forward in their effort to solidify the U.S. position in northeast Asia.[105]

Finally, the United States achieved some success in soliciting concrete assistance from nations that supported UN action in Korea. The State Department, to be sure, remained dissatisfied with the Pentagon's performance in this area. Even after President Truman expressed his desire to expedite matters in early August, military officials resisted efforts to encourage offers from Third-World countries. The Defense Department showed only modest interest in using the Organization of American States to generate and coordinate contributions from Latin America, and it opposed any effort to organize, train, and arm the literally thousands of volunteers for service in Korea from non-Communist nations. Although State Department analysts probably underestimated the army's own shortages of manpower, weapons, and ammunition, they recognized the barriers, both material and otherwise, to exploiting the opportunities for collective action in Korea. But their sensitive political antennae made them more anxious than their military counterparts to explore every possibility. The diplomats fumed over reports of fully equipped Turkish troops waiting for orders from abroad to debark for Korea; also angering were reports of resentment in Latin America over the establishment of minimum requirements for contributions, making such contributions impossible. The State Department wanted the United States to assume the cost of supplying and transporting foreign contingents for Korea, but the Pentagon argued that this would set a bad precedent for future UN enterprises. Despite ongoing difficulties, hard interdepartmental bargaining during September produced an agreement that enabled other countries to receive U.S. assistance for contributing to Korea by merely accepting the principle of reimbursement at a later date. By the middle of the month, twenty-nine nations had offered some form of military, economic, or medical assistance.[106]

Several governments committed ground forces despite considerable inconvenience. Great Britain's economy held little slack. Increased insurgent activity in Malaya recently had forced the British to augment their army in Southeast Asia, and the Communist victory in China had made the continued stationing of forces in Hong Kong appear all the more necessary. The dispatch of troops to Korea was a most disagreeable prospect.[107] Yet late in July the British cabinet approved formation of a brigade of troops for service in Korea. When in mid-August the Americans pressed for immediate provision of a ground unit to help maintain the Pusan perimeter, the British rushed two infantry battalions from Hong Kong.[108] Australia had an army of less than fifteen thousand men and defense plans that gave priority to the Middle East and Southeast Asia. The only force it could dispatch quickly to Korea was an understrength infantry battalion on service in occupied Japan. Even this unit would require additional manpower, equipment, and training before being sent into action. Australia offered the battalion anyway.[109] Although it had an army more than twice the size of Australia's, the Quirino government in the Philippines faced a growing Huk insurgency and severe financial problems. Military officials advised against any commitment of troops abroad, as did elements of the opposition Nationalist Party. Yet Foreign Minister Carlos P. Romulo in Manila and Ambassador Mike Elizalde in the United States lobbied successfully to overcome these groups. In mid-September an infantry battalion from the Philippines arrived in Korea.[110] The French and the Greeks offered contingents despite similarly trying circumstances.

Many of the offers were token, and several others were either of such dubious value or of such political sensitivity—or both, as in the case of the Chinese Nationalist offer of thirty-three thousand troops—that they were deferred. Other than Nationalist China, the only Asian states to volunteer troops were Turkey, which did not consider itself Asian at all, and the Philippines and Thailand, neither of which had substantial influence in the region and both of whose troops were poorly trained and equipped for action in Korea. India, whose contribution of troops would have been of great political significance, offered merely a field ambulance unit. Acheson regarded a troop contribution from Pakistan as "outstandingly desirable," yet Prime Minister Liaquat Ali Khan demurred, hinting that only U.S. commitments to his country's defense and to its stand on Kashmir in the UN would produce the desired result.[111]

Several nations offering combat forces hoped for something in return. Turkey, Greece, Australia, and the Philippines all wanted defense commitments from the United States. The attack of Soviet-armed forces in Korea heightened concerns in Turkey and Greece, which faced similarly equipped units on their own borders with Bulgaria (and Albania as well, in the case of Greece). Turkey was particularly insistent in its pressure for admission to NATO. Greece was not far behind. The United States recognized the threat in the Balkans, especially to an internally unstable Greece. Yet sensitive to the fact that the United States and its European allies already had commitments they were not prepared to meet, the State Department tried in vain to discourage appeals for new ones.[112]

Australia, led by Foreign Minister Percy Spender, was the most aggressive of all in pushing for a U.S. defense pact with nations of the southwest Pacific. Fearful of Britain's declining capacity to protect areas far from home and of America's unwillingness to do so outside of Europe, Spender coveted a definite commitment from Washington. So anxious was he to create a favorable image in the United States that he rushed, in late July, without the approval of Prime Minister Robert G. Menzies, who was on the *Queen Mary* in the middle of the Atlantic Ocean, to pledge Australian troops for Korea hours before the British announcement.[113]

The government of Sydney Holland in New Zealand was less intent than Spender on obtaining a defense pact with the United States, but it was genuinely concerned about national security in the face of the Communist advance in Asia. Believing that his country needed to be seen as an actor in its own right rather than merely an adjunct to Great Britain and Australia, Holland speeded up deliberations within his cabinet sufficiently to announce the commitment of an artillery unit to Korea an hour and a half before the Australian move.[114]

The Philippines also desired a treaty of alliance with the United States. The fall of China to communism, coming on the heels of Japanese occupation of the archipelago during World War II, rejuvenated fears among Filipinos that the United States, preoccupied with events in Europe, again would fail to protect their homeland.[115] A more immediate concern was that the Quirino regime needed U.S. assistance to stave off a financial crisis. Dubious regarding the present government's capacity to use aid wisely, the Truman administration had sent a survey mission to investigate conditions. A commitment of troops to Korea might help silence criticism of the Quirino government in the American press and in Congress and also provide leverage to the Philippines in its quest for external support.[116]

Great Britain, France, and other NATO countries already had a defense pact with the United States, but they desired an expanded U.S. military presence in

Europe. A contribution to Korea represented an instrument for maintaining and, it was hoped, augmenting U.S. support for their own region, as well as for influencing UN policies toward the peninsula.[117]

In offering troops for Korea, the Phibun Songhram regime in Thailand had motives similar to its Filipino counterpart. Although it did not expect a formal alliance with the United States and was not in so desperate a condition internally as the Manila regime, the conservative government in Bangkok did have concerns about its standing both at home and on its unsettled borders. Washington already was providing economic and military assistance, but a Thai contribution to Korea was likely to enhance Phibun's place in the scale of U.S. priorities.[118]

South Africa, which offered an air squadron for Korea, had atypical yet strong motives for its action. Since 1948, the United Nations had debated South Africa's racial policies and its claim to the former German colony, South West Africa. As the extremist government of Dr. Daniel Malan moved to implement apartheid, it anticipated increasing difficulty from the international organization. The UN intervention in Korea gave the Malan regime an opportunity, through concrete support for collective action against Communist "aggression," to bolster its standing both at Lake Success and in Washington. The commitment of air support represented "the least possible acceptable gesture" that South Africa believed it could make to achieve this purpose.[119]

Contributions from black Africa might balance South African involvement, at least for propaganda purposes. On 24 July, more than two weeks before the United States had any indication of pending action by Pretoria, Liberia informed the United States of its intention to offer an infantry battalion. Acheson tactfully discouraged a formal offer, however, because of the unit's poor equipment and low level of training.[120] When in early August Ethiopia expressed its desire to contribute a British-trained battalion with English-speaking officers, the State Department was more receptive. But the overture from Ethiopia, whose government in the 1930s had been a victim of the failure of collective security, hardly represented a selfless gesture. The fates of neighboring Eritrea and Somaliland were now in the hands of the United Nations, and Ethiopia was an interested party, especially intent on acquiring the former and thus keen on enhancing its position in the international body. Another method of enhancing its bargaining power was to strengthen its army. Exchanges between Washington and Addis Ababa soon revealed that Ethiopia hoped to receive enough equipment from the United States to arm two or three divisions.[121] Thus a situation emerged here similar to that in relation to many Latin American countries.

The U.S. experience in soliciting assistance in Korea from other countries illustrates the fact that many of the events related to the war had less to do with the peninsula itself than with local conditions hundreds and even thousands of miles away. As one U.S. diplomat observed wryly, the United States must take care that, in seeking aid for the UN effort in Korea, it did not simply spark requests for assistance in equipping national armies.[122]

Whatever the limitations and the eventual price to the United States of its search for concrete support in Korea, initial commitments encouraged U.S. hopes that more would come in the future. Such commitments also helped to counter Communist propaganda designed to pin the label "American imperialism" on the attempt to save the ROK. That accomplishment was of some consequence to Washington, which considered the cold war as much a struggle for the hearts and minds of the world's masses as for the defense of imaginary lines across the European continent or across a remote Asian peninsula.

## The Debit Side

Despite the accomplishments of the Truman administration, the state of U.S. diplomacy, politics, and decision making all left little hope for caution in Korea once the tide of battle shifted. Acheson, the chief architect of U.S. foreign policy, was a man of high character, forceful personality, and intellectual power. His determination to use the conflict as an instrument of future deterrence, however, left him insensitive to the degree to which his diplomatic stance would make the later exercise of restraint a most difficult task.

From the beginning, the secretary of state faced serious constraints on his freedom of maneuver. MacArthur was part of the problem. He disagreed with a Europe-first strategy and, as a result, cared little about preventing the Korean conflict either from expanding into other areas or from involving directly Communist China, the Soviet Union, or both. The commitment to his theater of hundreds of thousands of U.S. troops and a large portion of U.S. air and naval power seemed to him perfectly natural and justified. The idea of halting U.S. ground forces in Korea at the 38th parallel so as to avert Soviet or Chinese intervention never occurred to him.

Washington could always restrain him, but its tangle with him over Taiwan indicated that MacArthur would not hesitate to make his discontents public. Truman emerged from the spat in a strong position domestically. Republicans sought to use the incident to attack the administration's course in Asia, and they received enthusiastic support from the Hearst and McCormick newspaper chains. Yet a national opinion poll revealed that more than three times as many Americans approved of U.S. Taiwan policy as disapproved of it. Most of the published editorials on the MacArthur episode expressed agreement with the president.[123]

The Korean case was different: whereas Americans generally regarded Taiwan as part of China and the conflict over it as part of a civil war, they viewed the ROK as being under attack from an aggressive Communist regime that deserved to be punished. Even more important, whereas Truman had striven to cultivate public support for restraint on the Taiwan issue, he had failed to do so over Korea. From mid-August on his administration actually encouraged public expectations of a UN campaign to unite the peninsula.

The Pentagon often leaned toward MacArthur's views. His seniority, his reputation, his personal dynamism all made him an imposing figure to military leaders at home. They disagreed with his commitment to Asia-first and they were far more aware of America's unpreparedness for global war, yet they had long held reservations about the State Department's cautious policy toward China.[124] They were less sensitive than many diplomats to the rising tide of nationalism in Asia, and they had never believed that U.S. restraint could help lure Beijing away from its close connection to Moscow. With a war on they were anxious to push forward toward military victory.

The evolution of NSC-81 regarding a possible future UN campaign in North Korea reveals that the Joint Chiefs were inclined to give the field commander considerable leeway in his operations. The State Department draft of the paper, dated 31 August, stated that "in no circumstances should . . . [non-Korean forces] be used in the northeastern provinces bordering the Soviet Union or in the area along the Manchurian border."[125] The final draft was a trifle more flexible: "It should be the policy not to include any non-Korean units in any ground forces which may be used [in those regions]."[126] Military planners were responsible for the change, and later events would show that the Joint Chiefs regarded "It should be the policy" as less rigid than "in no circumstances."[127] The farther U.S. ground forces marched into northern Korea, the greater the likelihood of direct Chinese or Soviet intervention.

In addition to the pressures building on Acheson for an effort to unite Korea, other nations failed to provide a restraining influence as they did on Taiwan. Great Britain is a case in point. By early September British foreign minister Ernest Bevin was optimistic that he could temper the more dangerous aspects of U.S. policy toward Asia. Part of this optimism rested in his respect for Acheson, whose British heritage and style often served him better in the staid climate of European capitals than in the free-wheeling atmosphere of Washington. Bevin also derived optimism from apparent British success in bolstering the Truman administration's determination to limit its commitment regarding Taiwan.[128] Bevin hoped that such success would continue and expand to other areas, and he fashioned various tactics to achieve this purpose. The pledge of ground forces to Korea in late July would accumulate some capital in Washington, as would acceptance at home of a greater defense effort. Finally, through maneuvers abroad, especially among commonwealth nations, the British foreign minister sought to build a friendly majority at the United Nations that would counsel restraint in Asia.[129]

Bevin had limited freedom to pursue his goals, as real dangers accompanied his move to influence the United States. In elections during the previous February, the governing Labor Party had suffered substantial losses and now held a slim majority in the House of Commons. Under the forceful leadership of Winston Churchill, the Conservatives smelled blood, and they were bound to jump on any Laborite initiative that smacked of opposition to Britain's ally across the Atlantic.[130] Bevin even suspected U.S. ambassador Lewis Douglas of being in cahoots with Churchill in the campaign to overthrow the government.[131] Yet Bevin's general support for U.S. foreign policy had never been popular with the left wing of his own party, which feared that British defense expenditures would cut into appropriations for domestic programs.[132]

Political trends in the United States posed even greater dangers. Off-year elections were on the horizon, and the Republicans concentrated their offensive against Democratic foreign policy in East Asia. Worse still, as Bevin remarked in a cabinet paper of 30 August:

> American opinion is in a highly emotional state, which is attributable in part to the Korean situation itself and in part to the sense of frustration induced by the feeling that, in fighting North Koreans, Americans are not coming to grips with the real enemy. In such a state of mind the American public is likely to be irrational . . . towards the United Kingdom where our policy diverges from that of the United States.[133]

The Truman administration was unlikely to bend to overt British pressure, and the application of such pressure might spark a reaction in the U.S. public that would compromise the Atlantic alliance. Thus Bevin had to choose his spots carefully, and in doing so he concentrated on U.S.-China policy, which to him posed the most immediate threat of entrapping the West in an Asian quagmire and of compromising England's use of the commonwealth as an instrument for maintaining its global influence.

The British Foreign Office did devote some attention to the future of Korea. As did the U.S. State Department, it saw unification of the peninsula under UN auspices as the ultimate goal, but doubted that the Soviet Union would acquiesce in such a procedure. Although planners in London saw many "explosive possibilities" growing out of a UN military campaign to unify Korea, they thought it too early to establish a policy on the matter. In anticipating the application of pressure on the United States, they focused on the need for establishment of a new UN commission on Korea and for a commitment to nationwide rather than simply North Korean elections as a means of political unification. The fear was that the United States would back Syngman Rhee in his assertion that his government should exercise jurisdiction over all of Korea. The Rhee regime was unpopular in Asia and even in many quarters in the West, and an effort to gain UN support for this approach was certain to stir opposition among non-Communist nations. By mid-August the United Nations Commission on Korea had agreed informally to recommend to the General Assembly a unification plan that would include national elections.[134]

During the summer of 1950, in London and elsewhere in the West, concerns about a final settlement in Korea did not appear to have the urgency of matters directly involving China. As late as mid-August British military leaders estimated that UN forces had only an even chance of maintaining a bridgehead in Korea and, if successful in that enterprise, would take at least three to four months to push North Korean units back to the 38th parallel.[135] Bevin applied little pressure on Washington to commit itself in advance to a course of restraint on the peninsula. Considering his declining health and all the other pressures to which he was subjected, and considering the difficulty of anticipating future developments on the battlefield and their impact on diplomacy, this fact is hardly surprising. It may be regretted, nonetheless, that the British did not join India in attempting to build a non-Communist coalition at the United Nations to encourage U.S. caution in Korea.

In fairness to Acheson, the secretary of state remained wedded to a Europe-first strategy and to averting, if possible, a military confrontation with the Soviets or Chinese. In failing to explore diplomatic solutions to the Korean War, however, and in encouraging hopes of total victory on the peninsula rather than educating public opinion to the dangers of a UN thrust into North Korea, he narrowed his options later on, thus compromising the larger goals of U.S. foreign policy.

### Paths Not Taken: The Soviet Perspective

The motives of Soviet policy are more difficult to identify than those of the United States. Stalin's course failed to undermine Western unity in Korea, to break the momentum toward consolidating NATO and America's relationship with Japan, or to prevent the rapid rearming of the United States. Conceivably, he saw these developments as a means of sustaining his position at home and Soviet dominance over the Communist world. Stalin may have calculated that a high level of tension abroad would assist him in maintaining his firm hold on the Soviet party and state. Continued Soviet hegemony over international communism may have been of special concern.[136] With the United States showing some success in pulling together non-Communist governments, troubles among the Communist states and parties would represent a dangerous setback to the USSR. Forcing the North Koreans into an ignominious retreat before it was militarily necessary hardly would place the Soviet Union in a heroic light before its revolutionary comrades throughout the globe.

Another source of Stalin's failure to take greater initiative to end the Korean conflict may have been the pattern of international events seen within the framework of Marxist-Leninist ideology. On the one hand, this ideology taught that capitalist states were inherently aggressive. A straightforward effort toward peace in Korea based on restoration of the 38th parallel might encourage the United States in its present course of military expansion at home and abroad. This view seemed all the more compelling because, even in late August, the pattern of military events in Korea was by no means clearly established. Chinese generals feared a UN counteroffensive on the west coast of Korea, most likely at Inchon near Seoul. In late August Mao warned Stalin and Kim of this possibility. Yet the Chinese leader suggested military precautions to counter the prospect, not diplomatic concessions. Preoccupied with planning for a military drive against the Pusan perimeter in early September, the Soviets and North Koreans ignored the warning.[137] Even if a successful enemy counteroffensive did occur, more than 200,000 Chinese troops were congregating in Manchuria along the Korean border, and these forces would provide a major barrier to occupation of the entire peninsula by UN contingents. It was understandable that Stalin remained skeptical about making concessions not plainly dictated by battlefield events.[138]

This is particularly true in light of two other aspects of Communist ideology, namely, the belief that inherent conflicts among capitalist states made centrifugal forces at least as potent in their relations as the reverse and the faith that the masses in such nations and in the Third World were seething with discontent and unlikely to follow "reactionary" leaders.[139] Although by the end of August considerable momentum had built up toward rearmament in the West and a consolidation of NATO, this pattern was not nearly so apparent at the time as in retrospect. Rearmament, especially outside the United States, was sure to disrupt habits of domestic consumption, just as rising demand for scarce strategic raw materials, such as tin and rubber, would produce an escalation in prices. Such developments would augment resentments among the laboring classes and stir controversies within and between governments. Certainly the left wing within the Labor Party in the United Kingdom, which before the outbreak of war had been spending 1.5 percent more of its national income on defense than the United States, and the Socialists in France (not to mention the Communists) would bridle over diverting substantial funds from domestic welfare programs to military spending; yet if such diversions were not made—and quickly—resentment would mount in the United States that allies were not assuming their fair share of the defense burden. The question of Germany's rearmament promised to arouse even more controversy in British and French politics—and this controversy would extend to the West German population itself, which was far from united on the idea of contributing directly to the defense of the West.[140]

Communist propaganda also promised to take its toll on Western opinion.[141] One of the strengths of that propaganda rested in its flexibility in appealing to peoples in non-Communist states. To mobilize leftist groups, the Communist press and radio stations emphasized the Soviet desire for peace and warned against "imperialist" efforts to expand military forces. The Stockholm Peace Appeal served as a rallying cry here. In mid-August the Paris office of the "Partisans for Peace" announced that more than 273 million signatures had been collected on the petition to outlaw nuclear warfare, 12 million of which came from France and 2 million from West Germany.[142] To soften resolve among anti-Communist forces in the West, the Soviets also sought to erode confidence in the ability of the United States to protect western Europe from Communist military might. Communist radio broadcasts suggested that UN military setbacks in Korea called into question U.S. military prowess and that escalating U.S. involvement in Asia would compromise the rearmament program for Europe.[143] In France, fears verged on panic, as rumors circulated that a major war was certain if UN forces did not hold in Korea and housewives hurried to augment their stocks of necessities.[144]

The Communist propaganda offensive was, if anything, more formidable in Asia than in Europe. In Asia, the Communists played on the nationalistic sympathies of peoples either still struggling against or only recently liberated from Western colonial rule. The Communists also exploited racial problems in the United States. In late August Radio Moscow characterized "the beastly bombing of peaceful citizens in Korea, racial discrimination, and the oppression of the colored people in the U.S." all as "links in the same chain."[145]

The Soviets reached a far larger audience with their propaganda than did the Americans. Not only was their radio programming more extensive than the Voice of America, both in terms of technical facilities for transmittal over the air waves and broadcasting in Asian languages; their network of parties and other organizations greatly enhanced direct communication with the illiterate masses. Western observers in Asia were unanimous in the belief that the Communists had the upper hand in the propaganda war in Asia.[146]

Propaganda aside, conditions within most non-Communist areas of Asia were ripe for exploitation by revolutionary forces. In Indochina, the United States had begun pouring in economic and military aid to reinforce French efforts, but there remained no evidence that the tide had turned against the Communist-led Vietminh. A major Vietminh offensive was in the works for the fall. In the Philippines, leftist guerrilla forces showed increasing boldness. One U.S. diplomat described official corruption on the islands as "incredibly bad and getting so much more so that one wonders whether there is any integrity left anywhere in the country."[147] The most optimistic U.S. observers conceded that to contain communism in Southeast Asia would require a substantial effort by the United States. To undertake such an effort, Stalin undoubtedly surmised, the United States would be forced to spread its resources very thin, a development that could only weaken U.S. exertions in Europe.

Even in India, whose government Soviet propaganda consistently attacked as reactionary and under the wing of the "Anglo-American imperialists," the Kremlin had little reason to fear a concerted anti-Soviet foreign policy. Nehru had supported the United States in its June intervention in Korea and had taken a firm hand during the previous two years in suppressing the Indian Communist Party. Yet India's support for the PRC's claims to Taiwan and to the Chinese seat in the United Nations and its mediation efforts in Korea surely impressed the Soviets.[148] India's balancing act jibed neatly with Prime Minister Nehru's conception of the national interest, both at home and abroad. In early August the Indian parliament voted unanimously to approve Nehru's support for the UN resolutions on Korea, but the ballot disguised considerable silent opposition. Without the employment of firm discipline within the ruling Congress party, Nehru would have had difficulty prevailing.[149] Domestic politics aside, he recognized that the resolution of India's severe economic problems required that his country avoid foreign conflicts. India's geographic proximity to the larger and stronger Soviet Union and China dictated special caution in dealing with those nations.[150] Furthermore, the Indian prime minister maintained a strong attraction to socialist ideas and a corresponding suspicion toward the capitalist world. The U.S. tendency toward ostentatious displays of wealth deeply offended him.[151]

Nehru was particularly wary of the anti-Soviet camp for its encouragement to "reactionary and military elements in various countries, especially in Asia," and its less than total commitment to racial equality or the independence of colonial areas.[152] U.S. support for French policy in Indochina reflected these elements, as did the case of recently independent Indonesia, where U.S. opposition to the Dutch position had come only after lengthy procrastination and intense pressure from an Indian-led Arab-Asian bloc.[153] His discontent with the U.S. stance in India's dispute with Pakistan over Kashmir, which had been before the UN Security Council since 1948, could not help but affect his attitude in other areas.[154] The Indian leader already had shown impatience with the U.S. refusal to link a settlement in Korea to a U.S. withdrawal from the Taiwan strait and Communist Chinese admission into the United Nations.[155] At a personal level, his visit to the United States during the previous fall had fostered correct but distant relations with U.S. leaders and had not produced the economic assistance for which he had hoped.[156] If he was unlikely to wind up in the Soviet camp, neither was he likely to assist the United States in seeking popular support in Korea or elsewhere in Asia.[157]

Further to the west, conditions gave Stalin little reason to panic. In responding to the Security Council resolutions on Korea of late June, Israel, like India, had departed from its cautious neutral course in the cold war and supported the U.S. position. Establishment of the principle of collective security through the United Nations could prove critical to the ultimate survival of that beleaguered country as could economic assistance from the United States, both from the government and the Jewish community. Yet the Israeli government's support for U.S. policy in Korea provoked strong dissent within both the majority Mapai and minority Mapam parties.[158] Furthermore, Israel had few resources and even fewer friends in the Middle East. Its creation two years earlier had fueled the flames of Arab nationalism, a force that, given Great Britain's past and present position in the region, might increasingly be turned against the West. Although Lebanon, Syria, Jordan, and Iraq issued vague expressions of support for UN action in Korea, Egypt, the most important of the Arab states, did not. A member of the Security Council during 1950, Egypt voted for the resolution of 25 June only because its representative, Mahmoud Fawzi Bey, acted without instructions from Cairo. On orders from home, he abstained on the resolution passed two days later. In explaining his government's position, he revealed a determination to avoid commitment to either of the major blocs and a deep resentment over past UN handling of certain issues. In particular he mentioned the Palestine question, on which the international organization had sponsored partition, thus permitting the creation of Israel, and Britain's occupation of key points in Egypt, on which the Security Council had failed to take a stand.[159] As the summer of 1950 progressed, bilateral negotiations made little progress in resolving the issue of Britain's military bases in Egypt.[160] As the key power of the Arab League, Egypt was unlikely to foster a pro-Western, anti-Soviet bloc in the Middle East.

Neither was Iran. Despite U.S. support for Iran against the Soviet Union in 1946 and the prospect of U.S. economic and military assistance, the government of Prime Minister Ali Razmara was not anxious to throw in its lot with the West. In August Stalin took a step toward reconciliation by releasing several Iranian soldiers captured during border incidents of the previous year. Early the next month the Soviet and Iranian governments announced that they would commence talks to resolve several border disputes. Tensions with Great Britain increased, as Iran refused to ratify an agreement over the sharing of revenues of the Anglo-Persian Oil Company.[161] The Korean conflict fostered the trend toward Soviet-Iranian accommodation. Joseph Waggoner, the second secretary at the U.S. embassy in Tehran, reported in September that,

> as the United Nations forces met with one reverse after another, the realization was re-awakened that Iran is very close to the Soviet Union and might feel the weight of the Soviet army at any time. . . . If the Americans could not quickly subdue the North Korean forces, with bases nearby in Japan, then it was hopeless to expect any American military help in the event of Soviet aggression against their own country. . . . The Soviets quickly seized this psychological change, re-placing the big club with the olive branch.[162]

Stalin may have had more reason to worry about Scandinavia. There traditionally neutral Sweden supported UN action in Korea, and its major political parties united on the need for increased defense spending. Yet Sweden refused to provide troops for the UN effort in Korea, sending merely a field hospital unit. After much speculation in the press that Sweden would join NATO, in mid-August Foreign Minister Osten Unden publicly reaffirmed his nation's commitment to avoiding alliances. If world war came, he declared, Sweden would maintain a policy of "armed neutrality," just as it had done during the two previous such conflicts.[163] Though an irritant to the Soviet Union, Sweden remained an unlikely adversary.

In a word, the global landscape offered the Soviets considerable room for maneuver. The U.S. military buildup was disturbing and events in Korea had not gone as anticipated, yet the Soviet camp remained stronger than its opponents in conventional forces, and political dissension among and within non-Communist nations called into question their prospects for mobilizing resources against the Communist bloc. Even in Korea itself it was too early to tell whether an advantage would emerge for one side over the other in the East-West struggle. For Moscow, a cautious probing of the diplomatic winds at the United Nations seemed worthwhile, but it was imperative that no hint of nervousness escape through Kremlin walls, as such a message to the outside world could compromise Soviet leadership of Asian communism and produce a psychological advantage to the United States in the ongoing cold war.

## Bipolarity and Its Limits

The Korean War is often viewed as an event that extended the bipolarity of international politics to its post-1945 limits. Diplomatic patterns of the summer of 1950 clearly show a trend in this direction. The United States and its NATO allies commenced a major military buildup, Washington moved toward ending the occupation of Japan and creating a military alliance with its former enemy, and several other anti-Communist nations—in the Mediterranean, the Pacific, Southeast Asia, and even Africa—moved to strengthen their relations with the United States. On the Communist side, the Soviet Union and China gave strong vocal support to the North Koreans, and China prepared for a possible direct military intervention on their behalf. U.S. action to protect Taiwan from the Communists reinforced PRC hostility toward and fear of the United States, it helped perpetuate the absence of bilateral communications between the two governments, and it strengthened Beijing's sense of common interest with Moscow. On the part of the leaders of both superpowers, a certain comfort existed in the growing polarization, which provided a degree of focus for domestic and alliance politics that heretofore had seemed unattainable. That comfort, in turn, dulled sensitivity toward the dangers inherent in the perpetuation of fighting in Korea.

There were limits to bipolarization, however, arguably even elements of a countertrend. The Soviet return to the UN Security Council in August symbolized this phenomenon, as it reflected a perception in Moscow that the maintenance of contacts with the non-Communist world in a multilateral setting served its interests.

The most immediate interest, of course, was that the Soviets could prevent resolutions from passing the Security Council, but more generally they could cultivate dissent from the U.S. position. Although they often overestimated prospects in this area and behaved clumsily in attempting to foster them, the Soviets were correct in recognizing among America's NATO partners, as well as India and other neutrals, an uneasiness with U.S. policy in the Korean crisis. The United Nations, as the gathering place of representatives of most governments and the instrument for collective action in Korea, was a convenient forum in which to exploit that unease.

That Stalin had some reason for viewing the matter in this way suggests a complexity to international politics that extends beyond a bipolar framework. On the one hand, that complexity reduced pressure on the Soviet leader to seek a way out of the Korean morass; perhaps it also made the United States disinclined to pursue overtures to the other side for fear of creating false hopes that would impede the drive to mobilize resources in the West. On the other hand, sufficient diversity of thought remained among the Western allies and neutral nations, as well as an institutional basis for collective dissent from the U.S. position, to leave open the prospect that, if the crisis worsened, effective pressure could be brought to bear on the United States to refrain from action that would carry the world over the brink.

• CHAPTER 3 •

# Diplomacy Fails: The UN Counteroffensive and Chinese Intervention

### Inchon

"We drew up a list of every natural and geographic handicap—and Inchon had 'em all," Lieutenant Commander Arlie G. Capps later recalled. "The best I can say is that Inchon is not impossible," Admiral James H. Doyle told General MacArthur only three weeks before the bold UN counteroffensive at that site. "I realize that Inchon is a 5,000 to 1 gamble," MacArthur conceded, "but I am used to taking such odds. We shall land at Inchon and I shall crush them!"[1]

The magnitude of the Inchon gamble was obvious to anyone familiar with the maritime approaches to the city. The main entrepôt for Seoul, Inchon lay twenty-five miles west of the capital on a jagged stretch of coast. The miles of narrow and winding channels leading to the inner harbor had strong currents and a tidal range among the highest on earth. Only once during the month of September—on the fifteenth—was water deep enough to accommodate the twenty-nine-foot draft of American LSTs, and even then for only brief intervals shortly after sunrise and sunset. Easily mined, the channels were flanked by numerous high points ideal for shore batteries. Wolmi Do, a mile-long island with a 350-foot peak rising ominously from its bowels, dominated the sea approaches to Inchon. Seawalls of fourteen to sixteen feet lined the beaches of the mainland at the points most convenient for landing troops. Inchon, in short, was a defender's dream, an invader's nightmare.

Then again, maybe not. The barriers to large-scale amphibious operations at Inchon might give attacking forces the advantage of surprise. Numerous other sites, after all, on both the west and east coasts, lacked the obstacles of Inchon, and, for that very reason, North Korea was more likely to devote greater resources to their defense. Furthermore, Inchon was far enough north to provide UN forces with a deep envelopment of the enemy, the bulk of whose strength was committed against the Pusan perimeter. A successful landing of UN troops at Inchon and their rapid movement eastward to capture Seoul would sever North Korea's communications and trap the Communist army below the 38th parallel, where it could be annihilated. A quick end to the conflict might result at minimal cost in American life and treasure.

Yet officers in MacArthur's staff, in navy and marine contingents of the Far Eastern Command, and in the Pentagon were dubious. They worried not only about the sea approaches to Inchon, but also about the ability of the invaders, once ashore, to sustain the offensive. The city had numerous large buildings from which the enemy could launch deadly rifle and machine gun attacks. Even if UN forces captured Inchon temporarily, they might be overwhelmed after North Korea recovered from its initial surprise and rushed reinforcements to the area. To avert this danger, the U.S. Eighth Army would have to break out of the Pusan perimeter and race northward to join friendly units. The powerful Communist offensive against the Eighth Army at the beginning of September called into question its capacity to accomplish this assignment at an early date.

MacArthur was undaunted by either the doubts of his colleagues or events on the battlefield. On 23 and 24 August the irrepressible commanding general met with his staff, Admiral Forrest Sherman, the chief of naval operations, and General J. Lawton Collins, the army chief of staff, and summoned all his eloquence and prestige to the task of selling the Inchon operation—and for the earliest possible date, 15 September. He succeeded. On 28 August the Joint Chiefs wired their grudging approval of his plans. When ten days later they asked him to reconsider the Inchon offensive in lieu of North Korea's renewed pressure against the Eighth Army, the Far Eastern commander stood firm: "There is no slightest possibility of our forces being ejected from the Pusan beachhead," he declared. Moreover, because MacArthur believed North Korea incapable of a rapid buildup in the Seoul-Inchon area, he was confident that the Inchon operation's success did not depend on the Eighth Army's immediate linkup with the landing force to the north. Military leaders in Washington remained apprehensive, but they gave the go-ahead to the optimistic field commander.[2]

The gamble proceeded on schedule. Just after daybreak on 15 September a battalion of U.S. marines stormed "Green Beach" on the northwestern tip of Wolmi Do. Subdued by a heavy pounding from the sea and air, the enemy offered little resistance. The next wave of marines awaited the late afternoon tide. Then they rushed ashore on the mainland at the northwestern and southwestern ends of the city. By nightfall the attackers had captured more than a third of Inchon.[3]

The follow-up to the initial landings progressed rapidly. On 19 September U.S. marines seized Kimpo airfield on the outskirts of Seoul. A week later UN troops took control of the capital. In the meantime the Eighth Army had broken through North Korean lines in the south, and on 26 September its advanced units joined elements of the U.S. marines near Osan. Communist forces retreated frantically northward. Only about twenty-five thousand of the soldiers reached the 38th parallel, and, as UN troops showed little inclination to halt at that boundary, even those soldiers' safety was not ensured. MacArthur's boldness had paid off. North Korea stood threatened with total extinction.

The Inchon counteroffensive set off a wave of diplomatic activity, within and between the Western and Communist blocs, and between those blocs and Indian-led neutrals. That activity centered in New York, where the UN Gen-

**U.N. Offensive, Fall 1950**

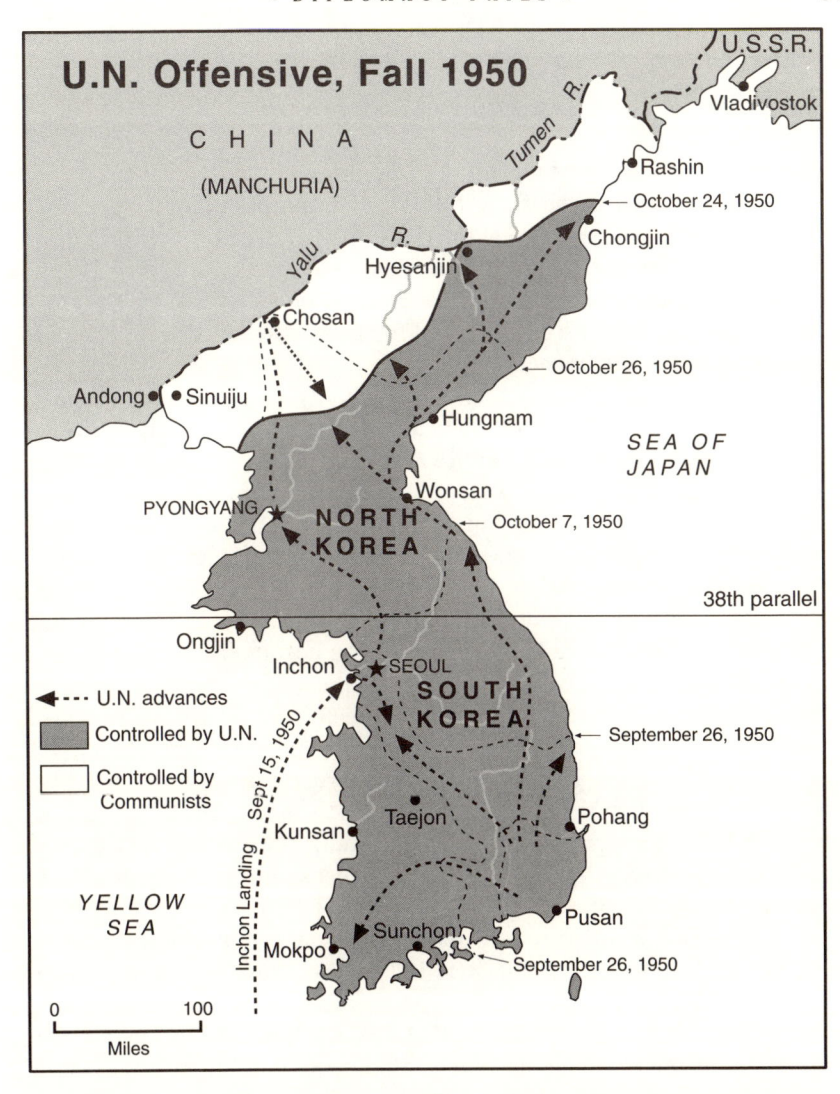

eral Assembly convened on 19 September. An immediate question confronted the United States and its allies: Should UN ground forces cross the 38th parallel and attempt to unify Korea under a friendly government? If the answer was yes, what limits, if any, should apply to UN operations in North Korea, and what diplomatic initiatives should be pursued to pave the way? Facing the Communist powers were the tasks of preventing enemy troops from marching into the North and deciding how to respond if those efforts failed. The challenge for India and other neutrals was to prevent action by either side that would bring in new contestants or expand the fighting beyond the peninsula or both. Whatever the perspective of the individual diplomat or decision maker, all recognized that far more was at stake than the fate of Korea.

## Great Power Diplomacy and the U.S. Decision to Move North

The Inchon landing shaped great power diplomacy as much as it did the military balance in Korea. In the week following the abrupt shift of fortunes on the battlefield, the Soviets signaled at the UN General Assembly that they desired talks on Korea. Soviet Foreign Minister Andrei Vishinsky delivered a keynote address which, though containing the normal quota of insults toward the United States, omitted the past demand for U.S. withdrawal from Korea as a precondition for a settlement there.

Nor did the address directly attack Truman or Acheson. Rather, Vishinsky singled out generals Omar N. Bradley and MacArthur and secretaries Johnson and Matthews "as propagandists for a new war." With the exception of Bradley, all of these officials recently had been reprimanded by the president for being out of step with the administration. Johnson had even been fired. In proceedings to adopt an agenda for the General Assembly, the Soviets did not display their usual vituperation. Jacob Malik referred frequently to his talks of the previous year with U.S. diplomat Philip C. Jessup—which had led to the lifting of the Berlin blockade—to illustrate the accomplishments private negotiations between the great powers might achieve.

Soviet delegates drew attention on the social circuit by acting uncharacteristically friendly and talking openly of the need for a peaceful resolution of the Korean crisis. When at a reception Jessup approached Vishinsky and Malik, the latter told him that they had spent "the best years of our lives" resolving the Berlin issue. Jessup reported to his delegation "that Malik was stating as plainly as they [the Soviets] are apt to do . . . that some negotiations would be welcome."[4]

Battlefield events in Korea were not the only source of this new Soviet tack. Talks among NATO foreign ministers in New York also produced anxiety in the Kremlin. Those discussions centered on methods of strengthening allied military forces in Europe. Measures that held the limelight included creating a unified command; rebuilding defense industries and augmenting national police forces in West Germany; admitting Turkey, Greece, and Spain to NATO; stationing more U.S. troops on the continent; and rearming the West Germans. The most disturbing prospect was the use of German manpower to enlarge NATO military organizations. Although the French and British resisted the U.S. proposal to establish West German divisions within a European army, broad agreement existed on the need for a unified command, additional U.S. soldiers, and increased industrial production and expanded police forces in West Germany. The momentum toward a beefed-up NATO was unmistakable. Recent passage by the U.S. Senate of a supplemental appropriations bill providing more than $15 billion for new defense outlays reinforced this trend.[5]

U.S. plans to bolster the General Assembly was another of Moscow's concerns. On 20 September Acheson delivered his "Uniting for Peace" address to the General Assembly. If the Security Council became paralyzed as a result of a veto by one of its permanent members, he asserted, the General Assembly should be empowered to convene an emergency session on twenty-four hours' notice. That body should establish an observer group to patrol areas threatened by international conflict, and each member nation of the assembly should designate elements of its armed forces to be made available to the United Nations in a crisis.[6] Since the United States dominated the General Assembly, Stalin naturally wished to block the initiative.

U.S. officials feared that the Soviet move for negotiations would stall the momentum toward total victory in Korea, rearmament in the West, and the strengthening of the General Assembly.[7] In New York, Acheson concentrated most intensively on the second of these objectives. He spent seventy-five hours at one stretch in the Waldorf-Astoria Hotel preparing for and participating in talks with European allies, interrupting the marathon only for a brief walk around the block.[8] The discussions centered on NATO. At Pentagon insistence, the United States linked an increased contribution of troops to Europe to its partners' acceptance of German rearmament. The U.S. military was willing to send more soldiers to western Europe to reassure allies and to protect against internal subversion or minor probes from the east, but they believed that defense of the region against a major Soviet attack would require substantial German ground units. After an appeal to the Labor cabinet in London, British Foreign Minister Bevin managed to get support from home for the U.S. plan and for the principles underlying it; other NATO members had similar success, but not France. The idea of Germany—even a divided Germany—again taking up arms was too controversial for the shaky coalition regime of René Pleven to accept, at least before there was substantial progress toward rearmament by the remainder of western Europe and the United States. Acheson spent most of the week and a half following the Inchon landing engaged in intensive discussions about European defense.[9]

Temporarily, the initiative on Korea rested with military planners in Washington and British diplomats in New York. In approving NSC-81 on 11 September, Truman had accepted the idea of a UN military campaign north of the 38th parallel. Before such a campaign could materialize, however, the counteroffensive in Korea had to develop and the response in the United Nations, Moscow, and Beijing had to be gauged.

On 25 September, with UN forces battling for Seoul, the Joint Chiefs sent a draft directive for MacArthur to George C. Marshall, the recently appointed secretary of defense. Based on NSC-81, this document defined the military objective as "destruction of North Korean armed forces." In achieving this goal, UN ground forces could cross the 38th parallel only if at the time they did so there had been "no entry into North Korea by major Soviet or Communist Chinese forces, no announcement of intended entry, nor a threat to counter our operations militarily in North Korea." The draft prohibited UN action "against Manchuria or the USSR" and stated that, "as a matter of policy," only Korean ground forces could operate "in the northeast provinces [of the peninsula] bordering the Soviet Union or in the area along the Manchurian border."[10] General Bradley suggested to Marshall that he clear the directive with the State Department and the president.[11]

State Department officials in Washington questioned the distinction made between military action in Manchuria and the Soviet Union and ground operations in the northern provinces of Korea. When Marshall, who had preceded Acheson as secretary of state and enjoyed great prestige among U.S. diplomats, assured them that this difference sought merely to give the field commander some flexibility if unforeseen circumstances arose in North Korea, they passed on the document, without comment, to Acheson in New York.[12] Preoccupied with NATO affairs, and depending for advice regarding Asia on the hawkish Dean Rusk and John Allison, Acheson approved the directive. He proposed only the addition of a paragraph providing that the "formal extension of sovereignty over North Korea should await action by the United Nations to complete the unification of the country." This provision sought to prevent the Republic of Korea from exerting immediate control over territories above the 38th parallel, where other nations had never recognized its claim of authority. Pushed through the bureaucracy by the army, which feared that any hesitation by UN troops in advancing beyond the 38th parallel would hamper achievement of the new objective of destroying North Korean forces, the directive was wired to MacArthur on the 27th.[13]

Up to this point, prospects seemed good that the Soviet Union and Communist China would avoid direct involvement in Korea. U.S. planners had anticipated such intervention once the military balance shifted in favor of UN forces, but this eventuality did not occur in the days immediately following the Inchon landing. Nor were any clear-cut threats forthcoming of Soviet or Chinese action. From Hong Kong and Taibei, word did filter into the State Department that Beijing would commit troops to Korea if U.S. soldiers advanced north of the 38th parallel.[14] Earlier intelligence reports had indicated that, since July, sizable Chinese ground forces had been moving into Manchuria from distant regions of the country.[15] On 21 September, however, the State Department received through the U.S. embassy in New Delhi the estimate of K. M. Panikkar, the Indian ambassador in Beijing. Based on recent conversations with Zhou Enlai and other Chinese officials—on the Chinese press, on the alleged influence of non-Communist elements in government circles, and on the absence of even "elementary precaution against air raids" in China's coastal cities, Panikkar thought it unlikely that the Mao regime planned to intervene in Korea.[16] James Wilkinson, the U.S. consul general at Hong Kong, followed with reports based on mainland sources that, because the PRC desired entry into the United Nations and was preoccupied with internal reconstruction, it would offer North Korea only limited and indirect support.[17]

This pattern of reporting did not begin to change until the afternoon of 27 September, when Hubert Graves, the counselor at the British embassy in Washington, approached Livingston Merchant, Rusk's top assistant in the

State Department. Graves showed Merchant three telegrams just received from New Delhi, two of which included copies of messages from Panikkar to Nehru. On the basis of conversations with General Nie Rongzhen, the acting chief of staff of the Chinese People's Liberation Army, and Julian Burgin, the Polish ambassador in Beijing, as well as a reinterpretation of a previous conversation with Zhou Enlai, Panikkar now expected China to pursue a policy in North Korea of "indirect intervention." General Nie was especially irate over a recent bombing of Manchuria by U.S. planes; moreover, Zhou's comment on 21 September that, "since the United Nations had no obligations to China, China had no obligations to the United Nations," indicated that Beijing's continuing exclusion from the international body increased the likelihood it would intervene in Korea. The third telegram was a personal appeal from Nehru to Bevin urging that UN ground forces halt at the 38th parallel. Though Graves thought Panikkar a "volatile and an unreliable reporter," his influence on Nehru was disturbing.[18]

This information reached U.S. policymakers too late and was too vague in its implications to hold up the new directive to MacArthur. In all likelihood, Truman, Acheson, and the Joint Chiefs did not learn of the reports until after the directive had been sent to Tokyo.

## Maneuvering at the General Assembly

On 29 September a resolution on the future of Korea finally appeared before the General Assembly, which illustrates how far U.S. leaders had permitted military events and priorities to outpace political considerations. Eight days earlier President Truman had stated publicly that the question of major troop movements beyond the 38th parallel was "a matter for the United Nations to decide."[19] If read broadly, the Security Council resolution of 27 June permitted extensive UN military action in North Korea. Certainly it permitted tactical maneuvers slightly above the 38th parallel to prevent enemy troops from regrouping. At the time the resolution passed, however, its supporters had not anticipated a military effort to unify the peninsula. In Washington the desire to maintain broad unity on Korea outside the Communist bloc dictated approval of a new measure.[20]

Such a measure was not easy to draft, as the United States wanted to avoid committing either itself or the United Nations to any objective that would pin down large numbers of U.S. troops in Korea for an indefinite period or lead to an expanded war. The U.S. delegation at the United Nations sought to avoid openly espousing a position regarding military operations in North Korea until friendly forces reached the 38th parallel. Then a decision could be made on the basis of prevailing conditions, most important, the status of North Korean forces and the anticipated attitudes of Communist China and the Soviet Union.[21]

With UN troops advancing rapidly in the week following the Inchon landing, the British approached the U.S. delegation on the 23d with a proposed resolution for the General Assembly. After consulting with the Americans and making revisions, British delegates presented them with a concrete draft on the following day. Both documents recommended, as the second draft phrased it, that "all necessary steps be taken to ensure conditions of enduring peace throughout the whole of Korea" and that any UN troops entering North Korea should stay only so long as necessary to implement the above.

On the political procedure for achieving unification, the two drafts diverged: whereas the first called for "new elections" for Korea as a whole, the second recommended merely "that elections be held . . . to complete the establishment of a unified, independent, and democratic government of all Korea"; whereas the former provided for two new UN commissions, one to conduct "preliminary discussions with North Korean representatives regarding the political future of Korea" and the other to supervise national elections, the latter designated a single new commission and suggested merely that it take over the tasks of the present commission and "represent the United Nations in bringing about . . . a unified, independent, and democratic" regime over the entire peninsula.[22] The British wanted to start from scratch in creating a government for the entire country, and they preferred to explore the prospects for agreement on unification with North Korea before sending UN troops beyond the 38th parallel. The United States disagreed, wanting instead to conduct new elections in North Korea alone, with the victors taking their seats alongside those already incumbent in the National Assembly in Seoul. The Americans also sought to avoid any negotiations with the Communists that might delay UN military operations in the North. In its studied vagueness, the second draft left the way clear for adoption of the U.S. point of view.

The difference between the two drafts reflected the continuing British tendency to defer to U.S. wishes on Korea so as to ensure Washington's continuing efforts in Europe. The September talks in New York represented a high point in Bevin's efforts to solidify the Anglo-American alliance. On the issue of Chinese representation in the General Assembly he finally broke with the United States by voting for an Indian resolution to admit the Communist regime. (The resolution was rejected by a 33–16–10 count.)[23] Yet this move had been discussed with Washington in advance, the State Department accepted it gracefully, and the vote received little initial comment in the U.S. press.[24] Bevin more than compensated for this break with the United States by persuading the British cabinet to support the principle of German rearmament. The British foreign secretary took the lead in North Atlantic Council meetings in reinforcing Acheson's pressure on the French.[25]

Bevin's talks on Korea with State Department officials in New York reinforced his cooperative mood. He agreed with the American argument that to leave Korea divided at the 38th parallel would represent a victory for the Soviet Union. "Whatever happens to Korea in the end," Bevin wrote to Prime Minister Clement Attlee on the 25th, "we must try to make sure now that just as in the case of the Berlin blockade the Russians are made to realize that they are up against it and to accept that fact."²⁶ Equally important, the Americans assured Bevin and members of the British delegation to the United Nations that they were "anxious to avoid provocation" in North Korea and wished to keep U.S. ground units out of provinces bordering on Manchuria and the Soviet Union.²⁷ The British chiefs of staff in London, especially Field Marshal Sir William Slim, were dubious about any move of non-Korean soldiers beyond the 38th parallel, but Bevin's assurances from New York prevailed with Attlee and his cabinet.²⁸

By 29 September, when a slightly revised resolution was formally submitted to the General Assembly, it had broad backing among non-Communist delegations, including eight cosponsors. Two of these—Pakistan and the Philippines—were Asian.²⁹ India demurred in the face of Panikkar's reports from Beijing, but Acheson and Bevin hoped that Nehru eventually would come around.

The British led the effort to persuade New Delhi. On the 27th Bevin addressed a note directly to Nehru, asserting that the British draft resolution was "far from being provocative" and that there was "no intention to occupy North Korea in strength." He suspected that recent rumblings from China aimed merely to weaken "the front [opposing] North Korean aggression." Sir Archibald Nye, the British high commissioner to India, held private talks with Nehru and Girja S. Bajpai, the secretary general of the Indian Ministry of Foreign Affairs, informing them that the United States wanted to keep its forces away from Chinese and Soviet borders with Korea.³⁰

In New York Bevin explored with Acheson ways of mollifying the Chinese. On the recent accidental bombing of Manchuria, the secretary of state drafted a note for Bevin which he suggested could be sent on to Nehru (who he assumed would communicate it to Beijing). The note expressed U.S. regret over the incident and suggested that representatives of India and Sweden "look into the charges and assess any damage" that they felt appropriate.³¹ Acheson also told Bevin that the General Assembly might hear Communist China on the Korea resolution. Yet he stressed that such a hearing should not delay consideration of the measure, even to give Beijing time to send a representative to New York.³² On 29 September the United States opposed a Security Council resolution, which passed anyway, inviting the PRC to participate in a debate on Taiwan later in the fall.³³

Anglo-U.S. efforts went for naught. India refused to cosponsor the Korean resolution and, in a press conference on the 30th, Nehru announced his opposition to a UN military venture into North Korea "until all other means of settlement have been explored."³⁴ Indications of Chinese intentions grew increasingly disturbing. On the day before Nehru's remarks, the State Department received word, indirectly through the embassy in Moscow, that the Dutch chargé in Beijing believed Chinese officials were considering military intervention in Korea if U.S. troops entered the North.³⁵ On 2 October Wilkinson in Hong Kong sent a partial text of a Zhou Enlai speech of 30 September, which included the assertion that "the Chinese people absolutely will not tolerate foreign aggression nor will they supinely tolerate seeing their neighbors being savagely invaded by foreigners."[36] On the same day as Wilkinson's dispatch, Zhou made this threat more explicit in a midnight conference with Panikkar. He told the Indian ambassador that China would intervene in Korea if U.S. troops crossed the 38th parallel. The State Department got word of this threat early the following day.[37] Washington also received a report, based on air reconnaissance, of a large mechanized convoy moving into North Korea from Manchuria.[38]

Meanwhile, conditions in South Korea and at the United Nations had developed rapidly. On 1 October South Korean units crossed the 38th parallel. Three days before, in response to a report supposedly originating in the U.S. Eighth Army Command that ROK troops would halt at the boundary to regroup, Secretary of Defense Marshall wired MacArthur that he should "feel unhampered tactically and strategically to proceed north of the 38th parallel." This dispatch reflected a new U.S. position, brought on by battlefield developments, to avoid any implication that the movement of UN ground troops into North Korea required prior permission from the General Assembly.[39] At the same time, U.S. diplomats recognized the political advantage to be derived from quick passage of the eight-power resolution on Korea.

Developments at Lake Success threatened to block achievement of this goal. On 2 October Malik and four Soviet allies presented a counterresolution calling for a cease-fire in Korea, withdrawal of foreign troops, free elections throughout the country arranged by a joint North-South commission, and the observance of this process by a UN committee that included representatives of nations bordering on Korea. Sir Benegal Rau, head of the Indian delegation, then proposed the creation of a special subcommittee of the First Committee of the General Assembly to explore a compromise between the two resolutions.[40]

Despite Zhou's warning, despite Rau's stipulation that the prospective subcommittee must submit any proposal by 6 October, and regardless of a favorable Soviet response to the Indian approach, U.S. lobbying helped defeat both the Indian plan by a 32–24 margin, with three abstentions, and the five-power resolution by a more decisive majority. The Arab states, Israel, Mexico, and the Communist bloc were among the nations supporting India. With the effort for compromise defeated, non-Communist nations voted overwhelmingly for the eight-power resolution, both in the First Committee on the 4th and in the General Assembly on the 7th (by 47–5–7 in each case).[41] The United States now had clear authority to lead UN troops into North Korea. This authority came hours after the U.S. First Cavalry Division sent advance patrols into North Korea and only a day before that unit moved in force across the 38th parallel.

The broad support for the eight-power resolution masked considerable unease regarding a UN move into North Korea. Maneuvering at the United Nations and in Western capitals reveals elements of an alliance between America's NATO partners and the Arab-Asian bloc that, under different circumstances later on, would play a pivotal role in the diplomacy of the war. Not only did Rau receive extensive support for his proposal to explore the possibility of a political settlement that would eliminate the need for UN military action in the North; U.S. allies Great Britain, Canada, and the Netherlands expressed doubts about a headlong march beyond South Korea.

By 5 October the foreign and defense ministries in London were in turmoil over General MacArthur's intention to launch an all-out offensive into North Korea. A report of a conversation with General MacArthur from Sir Alvary Gascoigne, the British representative to the U.S. occupation in Japan, heightened long-standing concerns among the chiefs of staff. The UN commander told Gascoigne that the Chinese threat to intervene in Korea was a bluff, and that if they did enter the conflict he "would immediately unleash his air force against towns in Manchuria and North China including Beijing."[42] The military leaders finally put forth a concrete proposal: non-Korean forces should halt in South Korea for one or two weeks to give Western diplomats more time to induce North Korea to surrender and to involve China in negotiations for a settlement. Late on 4 October the chiefs contacted Prime Minister Clement Attlee and Defense Minister Emanuel Shinwell, both of whom were inclined to agree with the idea. Characteristically, Attlee postponed action until talking to Bevin, who had just returned to London from New York.[43]

The foreign secretary believed it would be extremely risky for Great Britain to press the United States to delay the offensive. If Truman deferred to such an appeal and military problems arose later on, the British would take the blame.[44] In his report to the cabinet on his recent meetings in New York, Bevin emphasized that England had had a "steadying influence upon the United States" in recent months but that such influence, to be maintained, "must continue to be unobtrusive."[45] Clearly Bevin counseled Attlee not to press the proposal of the chiefs of staff with the Americans, and the prime minister accepted the recommendation of his top foreign policy adviser.

The chiefs' views did find their way across the Atlantic into the hands of Air Marshall Lord Tedder, chairman of the British Joint Services Mission in Washington, who passed them on to General Bradley. In a formal sense, however, Bevin merely requested assurances from the State Department that the United States still sought to restrict the conflict to Korea and that MacArthur's orders forbade him to mount air attacks in Manchuria or Siberia. Bevin also expressed the hope that there would be a sizable gap between passage of the eight-power resolution by the General Assembly and the crossing of the 38th parallel by non-Korean divisions. U.S. officials were accommodating on the first two points, which involved no concessions, but on the third point said only "that there would be some gap if the Assembly moved promptly to pass the resolution."[46]

In the meantime Canadian diplomats in New York had approached the Americans in an effort to slow down the pace of military events in Korea. Lester Pearson, who was in New York as head of the Canadian delegation to the United Nations, reluctantly opposed the Indian proposal for a special subcommittee to try to reconcile the eight- and five-power resolutions, but he did pursue, in modified form, an idea suggested by Canadian Prime Minister Louis St. Laurent.[47] To the Americans, Pearson proposed follow-up action to the eight-power resolution in which the General Assembly would call on its president, Nasrollah Entezam of Iran, to deliver the resolution to authorities in Pyongyang and, if necessary, conduct discussions with them on its early implementation. It was hoped that the other side would take the use of a civilian channel of communication as a sign of good faith.[48]

The response in Washington was "most unfavourable." Acheson and others in the State Department feared, as Pearson later recorded, that the plan "would interfere with the timetable established by General MacArthur, and give the USSR the opportunity to spin out proceedings here [in New York] with resulting confusion and uncertainty." The Americans had a similar response to a suggestion from the Netherlands, which called for suspension of UN military operations above the 38th parallel until 31 October to give North Korea time to agree to cooperate in implementing the eight-power resolution.[49]

At this juncture Pearson suggested that, following passage of the eight-power resolution, President Entezam simply "issue a formal appeal to North Korean forces to lay down their arms and to cooperate in carrying out the Assembly's recommendation." The Americans appeared to accept this idea, as it involved no further action by the General Assembly, thus reducing prospects for a delay in the offensive into North Korea. Pearson then discussed it with Entezam and Lie, both of whom approved. But on Saturday morning, 7 October, only hours before the vote on the eight-power resolution, Warren Austin approached Entezam and, on the basis of new instructions—apparently from "the highest American quarters"—pressed him "most strongly" not to make any such statement. Already under pressure from the Soviets, who had learned of the plan through a leak to the press, the president retreated, and he informed Pearson too late to enable him to get on the speakers' list and make the proposal himself in the upcoming assembly debate.[50] The disappointed Canadian statesman retired to the Bronx to watch the Yankees pound the Phillies in the World Series.[51]

The episode resulted from the failure of either Acheson—who spent the weekend in Connecticut—or his staff to properly brief Austin. The secretary of state quickly apologized to Pearson, but the incident could not help reinforce allied perceptions of the Americans as "hamhanded" bumblers who were far from having their own house in order.[52]

NATO allies had fully backed the United States in Korea less out of conviction than of fear that anything less might compromise the achievement of critical objectives in Europe. Ironically their anxiety over Korea derived from a recognition that events there could lead to U.S. commitments in Asia which would drastically reduce resources available for Europe, or even to a spreading of the military conflict to that continent long before NATO forces were capable of defending themselves.

## Calculations in Washington, Beijing, and Moscow

Despite America's determination to move forward rapidly in Korea, events of early October stirred much concern in U.S. circles. In Tokyo Admiral Arleigh Burke approached a Japanese counterpart, Admiral Kichisaburo Nomura, who had extensive experience with the Chinese. Burke asked Nomura to evaluate Zhou's warning. The distinguished Japanese seaman and diplomat replied that it was most serious. If non-Korean forces crossed the 38th parallel, the Chinese could intervene. Burke took this estimate to General Charles Willoughby, MacArthur's chief of intelligence, who waved it aside with the observation that Nomura had no special sources of information and was thus merely guessing.[53] Back in Washington, apprehensions appeared in the State Department. Rusk's assistant, Livingston Merchant, thought the Chinese threat should be treated "with extreme seriousness," and Allison's assistant, U. Alexis Johnson, suggested using only South Korean troops above the 38th parallel. O. Edmund Clubb, at the head of the China desk, proposed further consideration of the Indian position.[54]

But Acheson thought military preparations in the field and political events at Lake Success had proceeded too far to warrant delay. He conceded that there was a risk in advancing, but an element of risk had existed in the Korean venture from the beginning. A show of "hesitation and timidity" would increase rather than reduce the danger. The Chinese warning, coming as it did in a private conversation between Zhou and Panikkar, could easily be disavowed and therefore probably represented a bluff. Acheson insisted that circumstances dictated a "firm and courageous" stand.[55]

This response revealed a mixture of condescension and fear toward the Chinese Communists, as well as a deep concern about perceptions of the United States in the Communist world. U.S. analysts had long questioned the capacity of the Communists to unite and rule the mainland. While most observers now conceded that the PRC was likely to be a permanent fixture in China, they also saw it as preoccupied with domestic problems of formidable magnitude and anxious to avoid direct conflict with the United States. The experience with Taiwan during the past summer reinforced this perception, since, despite a good deal of bluster, Beijing had failed to challenge U.S. action to neutralize the island. On the other hand, Acheson and others feared Communist China as a revolutionary force in border areas, especially Southeast Asia, which ultimately could engulf the Third World and undermine the entire structure of international politics. In this sense Communist China was, for the moment, a mere extension of the Soviet Union. To flinch in the face of a threat from Beijing might serve to embolden the Communists at other times and in other places, to lead them to question the will of the United States to maintain a firm course when challenged.

Yet these factors became compelling only as a result of conditions that derived from the Inchon landing. In producing a dramatic reversal of the military balance in Korea, the maneuver left little time for a careful exploration of diplomatic options. By the time the Chinese warning became explicit, non-Korean forces were ready to move across the 38th parallel, and a vote approached on the eight-power resolution in the First Committee of the General Assembly. Under such circumstances, to delay action would have disappointed expectations in the United States in the midst of a congressional election campaign, would have compromised a clear military advantage, and would have constituted an apparent loss of nerve in the face of Communist pressure tactics. The earlier anticipation of Chinese or Soviet intervention in North Korea once the military balance shifted, plus the willingness to halt UN ground forces at the 38th parallel if confronted by such action—or even the threat of such action—fell by the wayside.

The Communist side also proved ill prepared diplomatically to respond to the rapid pace of events after Inchon. China began troop movements northward toward Manchuria in July, and its propaganda regarding Korea became more aggressive in late August. Nevertheless, Mao did not decide to intervene directly on the peninsula until well after 15 September. In the immediate aftermath of Inchon, Kim Il-sung had concentrated on efforts to avert total destruction of his forces in the South and on organizing six new North Korean divisions. He did not make an appeal to Stalin for "direct military aid" until 29 September. Stalin assured him of further arms and weapons shipments and stated that assistance of armed forces would best be in the form of "people's volunteers," about which he should consult China. Kim did not approach Mao for aid until 1 October.[56]

The initial Chinese decision to intervene came on 2 October, and then only after considerable debate in the Politburo Standing Committee of the Chinese Communist Party. Zhou Enlai, Lin Biao, a leading general, and others expressed reservations about intervention. They argued that China remained too weak to fight the greatest industrial power in the world and one, moreover, that possessed the atomic bomb; the PRC, they said, should devote its energies to consolidating its position at home, where the budget deficit and unemployment remained high, where anti-Communist "bandits" continued to control mountainous areas in several provinces, and where numerous offshore islands, including Taiwan, still had not been captured.[57] Mao countered that it would be a disgrace not to assist their neighbor in its time of mortal peril. Furthermore, Mao believed that a direct clash with the United States was inevitable at some point. Indochina, Taiwan, and Korea, other than the Chinese mainland, were likely settings for such a clash. Although Korea presented problems of supply far greater in magnitude than had existed during the Chinese civil war, it was easily the most advantageous of the border areas in which PRC armies could operate. As Zhou later characterized Mao's argument, Korea provided "the most favorable terrain, the closest communications to China, the most convenient material and manpower backup and the most convenient way for us to get indirect Soviet support."[58] In the face of Mao's appeal, the Politburo voted to send Chinese forces to Korea so long as the Soviets agreed to provide air support and military supplies.[59]

Mao wired Stalin on the 2d, the day before Zhou met with Panikkar, announcing China's intention to send troops to Korea.[60] By this time ROK soldiers had crossed the 38th parallel, and MacArthur had sent an ultimatum to Kim demanding unconditional surrender.[61] The lateness of the initial decision, and the divisions within top PRC political and military circles that preceded it, help to explain why, from mid-August through September, Western intelligence reports were so varied regarding Chinese intentions.[62] These factors also explain the timing of Beijing's explicit warning to the United States.

Even the decision of 2 October was not final. Zhou's warning to Panikkar followed the Politburo vote and included a statement that China would not intervene if South Korean troops alone crossed the 38th parallel. Admittedly the statement came at a time when the Chinese fully anticipated a U.S. move beyond the line and while numerous Politburo members held strong reservations about Chinese intervention. In all likelihood Zhou's approach to the Indian diplomat represented an effort to delay the U.S. march northward, thus giving his own forces more time to prepare. Mao also may have hoped through the message to reinforce justification, both at home and abroad, for subsequent Chinese intervention in Korea.[63] He did not issue formal orders to Chinese units in the northeast nor appoint Peng Dehuai to command them until the 8th. Major Chinese forces still did not move across the Yalu River into North Korea. Certainly from 2 October on the scales were heavily weighted toward intervention, but the possibility for a different outcome remained, depending on U.S. behavior, domestic developments, and the Soviet response.

In contrast to Truman on the other side, Mao dominated the deliberations in Beijing.[64] He had enormous prestige as a military leader. Not only did his writings provide a theoretical framework within which weak forces could hope to defeat a materially stronger enemy.[65] His direction of Communist armies against the Nationalists constituted a concrete and successful employment of these theories. Although in the past he had not fought an enemy with atomic weapons, he had defined, as soon as they appeared, their limited significance in war. Obviously reacting to sentiments expressed in his own ranks, Mao lectured cadres in Yanan on 13 August 1945 that atomic bombs could not "decide wars." If they could, he declared, the United States would not have asked for Soviet assistance in the war against Japan. He warned comrades against "a bourgeois world outlook and methodology" and "a bureaucratic style of work divorced from the masses." A year later Mao made his first reference to the atomic bomb as "a paper tiger."[66]

Yet Mao was not oblivious to the weapon's power, nor were his colleagues in the Politburo. In considering possible Chinese intervention in Korea in early August 1950, they discussed at some length the prospect of U.S. use of the bomb. Chinese leaders expressed deep concern, but General Nie reportedly remarked that Soviet possession of the weapon might discourage the

United States from using it. Seven weeks later Nie told Panikkar that, although the United States might kill millions of Chinese and set back the nation's economic development many years, it could not defeat China on land or destroy its essentially rural society.[67] While such statements reflected Mao's thinking, for which he had considerable support, there were doubters.

A key person in Mao's quest for backing at home was Peng Dehuai, the commander and political commissar of the First Field Army and the Northwest Military Region. When Lin Biao declined to command troops in Korea on the grounds of poor health, the Politburo Standing Committee decided on 2 October to ask Peng, who was not present, to take the job. Peng did not arrive in Beijing from Sian in the Northwest until late in the afternoon on the 4th, by which time a meeting of the Politburo Central Committee was in progress. Most at the meeting expressed reservations about intervening in Korea, but Mao held his ground and Peng did not speak. Before the next meeting on the following afternoon, Mao consulted Peng, finding him favorably inclined toward intervention and willing to accept command of Chinese forces in Korea. Mao asked him to express his views at the upcoming meeting, and he agreed. Apparently Peng's subsequent statement decisively shifted the mood of the group.[68]

The scales of judgment on Korea were weighted heavily in favor of intervention, but much with regard to goals and tactics remained to be decided, and here Soviet intentions came into play. In the aftermath of Inchon, Stalin had pressed Mao to dispatch troops to the peninsula, and he had indicated that the Soviet Union would provide air and material support. In his dispatch to Stalin on the 2d, the Chinese leader stated that, until Soviet weapons arrived, his forces would conduct only defensive operations in North Korea. Then a counteroffensive would occur aimed at destroying U.S. forces there. In confronting the possibility of a U.S. attack on China, Mao stated that the real danger would come if the PRC failed early on "to destroy large numbers of American troops in Korea." In such an eventuality, he surmised, the United States would launch major and prolonged attacks on China. Such attacks would disrupt China's economic reconstruction and "cause dissatisfaction among the national bourgeoisie and some other sectors of the people (who are absolutely afraid of war)." At the same time, Mao noted that Chinese troops would be labeled "Volunteers," obviously in the hope that this would reduce prospects for a U.S. declaration of war against the PRC.

Although Mao did not mention the Sino-Soviet treaty of alliance, his discussion of the prospect of a U.S. declaration of war hinted at the obligations created by that agreement; a signatory would be required to assist its partner "by all means at its disposal" if the ally became "involved in a state of war."[69] Mao sought to persuade Stalin that the risks would actually increase should he delay in supplying aid to Chinese troops and that, if the worst came to pass—that is, if the United States declared war on China and launched extended attacks on the mainland—the PRC would expect Soviet intervention on its behalf. On the 8th Mao dispatched Zhou to Moscow in an attempt to reach precise agreement on Soviet assistance.

Zhou finally tracked down Stalin on 10 October at Sochi on the Black Sea. For tactical reasons the Chinese foreign minister began his presentation to the Soviet leader with a statement on why the PRC should not send troops to Korea. China lacked money, armaments, and transportation. If the war became protracted, it would "involve other fraternal countries." Probably sensing a Chinese ploy, Stalin expressed disappointment, explaining why the Soviet Union could not enter the war and why the PRC should. Two weeks earlier, in a message to Mao, he had indicated that both China and the Soviet Union might be drawn into war with the United States and that the two Communist giants should not fear this eventuality. Together, he asserted, they "were stronger than the USA and England, while other capitalist European states with the exception of Germany, which cannot now render any kind of assistance to the USA, do not represent a serious military force." He even implied that war now—rather than "after several years"—might be preferable, as "Japanese militarism" had not yet been "revived."[70] But to Zhou Stalin presented a sharply divergent analysis. His nation was not ready for World War III, although it could deter the United States from expanding a Sino-U.S. conflict in Korea to the mainland. On the other hand, if the United States positioned itself on the border of Manchuria, it would harass China and prevent it from rebuilding the economy of that key region. China also would fear the primary burden of accommodating the exiled DPRK. Stalin concluded by reiterating his promise of large-scale material support for Chinese forces if they went into Korea, but he insisted that Soviet air forces were unprepared in the immediate future to provide cover for PRC troops entering the fray. Zhou refused to commit China to a course in Korea, yet he did agree with Stalin to send a joint telegram to the Central Committee of the Communist Party outlining Soviet commitments. The message stated that it would "take at least two or two-and-a-half months" before Soviet planes could support Chinese troops in Korea.[71]

On receiving the disturbing news from Zhou and Stalin, Mao ordered a halt to all movements by the Thirteenth Army Corps in Manchuria and called Peng, who had already left for Shenyang, back to Beijing for consultations.[72] At another Politburo meeting on the 13th, the PRC reaffirmed the decision to intervene. "If we don't send troops to Korea," Mao reasoned, in a manner remarkably similar to Acheson's regarding a U.S. refusal to send its troops across the 38th parallel, "the reactionary forces in the world will become bolder and that will be disadvantageous to all sides." But Mao also scaled down his initial objectives in Korea. Whereas previously he had talked of quickly wiping out enemy forces, now he planned to "establish a base in the mountainous area north of the Pyongyang-Wonsan line."[73] It was hoped that in the early months of the intervention Chinese troops could concentrate on destroying South Korea forces, which were advancing more rapidly than other UN ground units. Only if non-Korean units entered the extreme northern reaches of the peninsula would Chinese armies launch an early counteroffensive against them.[74] Major Chinese units began crossing the Yalu into Korea on 19 October.

The deliberations in Beijing suggest that, had the United States adopted different tactics in the aftermath of Inchon, Chinese intervention might have been averted altogether. Three issues stand out here: Chinese representation in the United Nations, the status of Taiwan, and the timing of the move of non-Korean forces across the 38th parallel. On all these issues, U.S. actions in the General Assembly showed little flexibility. In the first two cases, U.S. votes hardly could help but stir resentment in Beijing and encourage the Chinese in their belief that, even when the Korean War ended, they would not receive their just desserts. This was especially so given that the stated objective of U.S. intervention in Korea had changed over the past three months from one of restoring the 38th parallel to uniting the peninsula under a friendly government. Press reports from Taiwan of Nationalist plans for operations against the mainland surely encouraged the Communists to view the United States as an aggressive and hypocritical nation.[75] Washington's refusal even to delay a march northward in order to explore a diplomatic settlement in Korea highlighted its aggressiveness. All the maneuvering by Moscow and Beijing to divide the non-Communist world seemed to have been for naught, at least insofar as it was aimed at containing U.S. adventurism.

Under the circumstances Mao rejected the idea that China would be better off staying out of Korea and using a period of peace to rebuild its economy, and he succeeded in fending off doubters within the Politburo. A later *People's Daily* editorial labeled the reasoning of noninterventionists as "erroneous, because it presumes that the enemy will permit us an intervening period and environment for peaceful reconstruction. The U.S. of today is different from the Japan of the past, and there is neither need nor possibility for the United States to stop at Korea for such a long time as Japan did."[76] In a report of 24 October to an organ of the People's Political Consultative Congress, Zhou Enlai pointed out that Korea was an international issue, the loss of which to "U.S. imperialism" would drive "a wedge . . . into the peace camp" and directly threaten China's security. The enemy had lied repeatedly about its intentions in Korea, most recently in a message from British Foreign Minister Bevin, transmitted through Nehru, to the effect that UN troops "would come to a halt when they were 40 miles from the Yalu River." If China permitted them to solidify themselves on its boundary, the PRC would have to station "countless numbers of troops" in the northeast for an indefinite period. This commitment alone would prevent the PRC from devoting much attention to economic reconstruction and development. "On the other hand," Zhou continued, "if we fight back and cause the enemy to get bogged down in a quagmire in Korea, he will no longer be able to attack China, and even his plan to dispatch troops to Western Europe may be upset." This eventuality would increase "internal contradictions" between the United States and its allies, the exact opposite of what would occur if China made concessions.[77]

Mao's decision was a close call, nonetheless, especially once he learned of Soviet reluctance to provide air support. According to one report, the Chinese leader "paced up and down in his room for three days and nights before he came to a decision."[78] Conceivably, a less thoroughly belligerent course on

Washington's part would have made him more receptive to the views of doubters in Beijing. In all likelihood, however, such a course would have involved keeping non-Korean troops below the 38th parallel.

Although China was about to bear the primary burden in Korea, the Soviet Union took the initiative in seeking negotiations with the United States. On 4 October Vasily Kasaniev, a Soviet citizen and employee of the UN Secretariat, extended an invitation for lunch to Hans Engen, a member of Norway's permanent delegation to the United Nations. When they met, Kasaniev brought up the situation in Korea, stating that the eight-power resolution was unacceptable because it permitted U.S. troops to occupy North Korea. For reasons of both security and prestige, Moscow could not tolerate this prospect. It was Engen's understanding, he told Kasaniev, that the United States wanted to remove its soldiers from the peninsula as soon as possible after North Korea's defeat and that Asiatic troops might be called on for occupation duties. Kasaniev responded to this idea with keen interest, and Engen inquired as to what solution the Soviets had in mind. Kasaniev stated that "MacArthur should agree to stop at the 38th parallel. The North Koreans would then lay down their arms and a United Nations Commission would be allowed into North Korea to hold elections, etcetera." Soon after the two men parted, Engen saw Kasaniev and Vishinsky talking together in a corridor.[79]

Engen and Kasaniev met again two days later, again at the latter's initiative. Kasaniev told Engen that Vishinsky was responsive to the notion of an occupation of North Korea by non-U.S. troops. Engen concluded from the conversation that the Soviets wanted negotiations on Korea outside the United Nations. The United States encouraged Engen to continue the contact and to probe Kasaniev on the purpose of their conversations. Engen did so in a meeting on 7 October, and he came away doubting the existence of a "common basis for negotiations." The Soviets, he thought, were seeking to avoid not only a U.S. occupation of North Korea but also the elimination of North Korean authorities. When U.S. troops crossed the 38th parallel, Kasaniev terminated the discussions.[80]

The question here is not so much whether the Soviets were agreeable to talks with the United States—clearly they were—but what purpose those talks were designed to serve. Moscow often sent out feelers through indirect routes, and Kasaniev obviously had access to Vishinsky. But was the Soviet Union willing to accept the elimination of the Communist government in North Korea if U.S. troops stayed out of that area? Could an arrangement have been worked out whereby the North Koreans disarmed and permitted UN authorities above the 38th parallel to supervise elections, and then integrate the territory into the Republic of Korea? The first two meetings indicated that the answer might be yes; however, the final discussion—undoubtedly after Vishinsky had communicated with Moscow, which knew of Beijing's preliminary decision to intervene in Korea—suggested the reverse. Chances are, Stalin's anticipation of Chinese intervention played as important a role as the crossing into North Korea of U.S. troops in the decision to end the exchanges in New York.

The incident emphasizes the constraints on diplomacy created by the torrid rate of military developments following Inchon. Relations between the United States and the Soviet Union were so tense that both sides were extremely sensitive not only to the substance of negotiations but to the form. Neither party would approach the other in a straightforward manner, fearing that it would be interpreted as a sign of weakness. The Americans worried that the Soviets would use talks—or even the prospects for talks—as an instrument for dividing the West and preventing decisive action. Soviet use of the United Nations as the setting for diplomatic maneuvers and the oftentimes public nature of these maneuvers heightened this concern. Thus negotiations invariably took considerable time to develop and even more time to reach a definite conclusion. Because time was short if the U.S. military advantage in Korea was to be exploited, the diplomatic option stood little chance of being fully explored.

Despite Soviet interest in negotiations on Korea, Moscow initially had less difficulty than Beijing in concluding that Chinese intervention in Korea was desirable. Stalin now found himself in a position similar to that of Truman three months earlier. A Soviet-sponsored regime faced extinction, and, if the DPRK went that route, Moscow would suffer a terrible blow to its credibility within its own camp, not to mention in its standing with its enemies. The Soviet Union also would acquire a hostile neighbor that might permit U.S. military bases on its territory. Chinese intervention presumably would not only prevent the destruction of the DPRK, but would occupy the Americans in an area of secondary importance over an extended period, thereby diverting resources that otherwise might be used in Europe. It would further isolate China from the West and exacerbate disagreements over Asia outside the Communist bloc as well. Even if the United States used air power against China and aided the Nationalists in launching an invasion of the mainland from Taiwan, it was highly unlikely that an anti-Communist regime could unite the country. And chaos in China, combined with a continued Soviet presence in Manchuria, was perfectly acceptable to Stalin.

Certain dangers existed, to be sure. Chinese intervention in Korea would increase Beijing's influence on the peninsula and, if successful, greatly bolster China's status in Asia and the Communist world. Over time, such a development could produce a monster on Soviet borders and a challenge to Moscow's claim to leadership within the Communist camp. A more immediate threat was that Beijing pressed Moscow to provide air and material support. Stalin undoubtedly suspected that Mao was trying to draw him into the war. If in response to Chinese intervention in Korea the United States declared war on the PRC, Mao was sure to invoke the Sino-Soviet alliance and expect even greater assistance in an area several thousand miles removed from the critical European theater. Any direct Soviet involvement in fighting with U.S. forces could escalate into total war and, although the USSR might hold initial advantages, its potential strength was far inferior to that of the United States. According to Khrushchev, Stalin was so fearful of a direct Soviet-U.S. clash in

Korea that he preferred North Korea's extinction to the use of his own troops on the peninsula.[81]

Yet for Stalin the weight of the arguments favored Chinese intervention. Concern about China's evolving role yielded to the exigencies of the moment. Fears of uncontrolled escalation were balanced by the fact that, from the beginning of the Korean conflict, President Truman and his counterparts in western Europe had shown a desire to avert a direct confrontation with the Soviets. To reduce the risks in this area, Stalin went back on his promise to grant Mao immediate air cover for his troops. Despite the obvious risk and the desire to reduce it as much as possible, Stalin may have contemplated an early Soviet-U.S. confrontation, so long as the United States was already fully engaged with China, with something less than unmitigated horror. For the moment the West was weak militarily, and its cohesion was fragile. A Sino-U.S. clash in Korea would not only tie down a large number of U.S. forces in Asia; it would place serious, perhaps fatal, strains on the NATO alliance. Surely Stalin's Marxist-Leninist imagination enabled him to envision circumstances in the not-too-distant future in which the balance of political and military forces were enough in his favor to eliminate the need to avoid a direct clash with the United States.[82] In any event, just as Washington feared that a show of weakness or hesitation would embolden the enemy, the Soviet leader probably surmised, as did Mao, that Communist passivity would make the United States more rather than less aggressive.

It is tragic that the United States and China lacked means of direct communication. Since the PRC was about to assume greater risks in Korea than Moscow and since its leaders were divided over intervention, Sino-U.S. negotiations might have produced an understanding. In his warning to Panikkar, Zhou stated explicitly that China would not intervene if South Korean troops alone crossed the 38th parallel. Panikkar, however, was a poor choice as the one to relay the message, both because he was not an American and because he was considered an unreliable reporter in the West. His alarmist reports of the past summer of a possible Chinese assault on Taiwan was a fresh memory.[83]

For several weeks Mao had been looking for ways of communicating privately with the United States. Shortly following Inchon, A. R. Menzies, the head of the Far Eastern Division of the Department of External Affairs in Ottawa, received a story from Roy Peers, an adviser to the Ming Sung Industrial Company, a Chinese shipping enterprise now centered in Hong Kong. Peers stated that Lu Zuofu, the company's manager, had visited Beijing in late August and met with Mao. Mao had told Lu that, although he wanted to avoid war with the United States, he felt a sense of duty to the North Koreans because of their past support against the Japanese and the Nationalists in Manchuria. If U.S. troops crossed the 38th parallel, he would be under considerable pressure to intervene on the peninsula. Mao requested Lu's assistance in informing Washington of these views. Menzies suggested to Peers that "the most convenient channel[s]" for informing Beijing authorities were the Indian ambassador or the British or Dutch chargé d'affaires in China.[84] Regrettably, because the Chinese did not give the last two men access to top officials, they chose to approach the man who was least trustworthy to the Americans.

The absence of direct contacts between Beijing and Washington was an effect rather than a cause of hostile feelings on both sides. Since early in the year, neither party had shown much flexibility toward the other. It is inconceivable that direct exchanges on Korea would have produced a quick resolution of differences on the fate of the peninsula. Yet China's signals to the United States in the immediate aftermath of Inchon might have been sufficiently early and uncompromised by intermediaries of questionable reliability to have bred greater caution in the State Department.[85] That caution, in turn, might have produced stronger determination to keep U.S. troops well clear of China's borders or, less likely, out of North Korea altogether.

### Tension over the Process of Unification

On 9 October, as the U.S. Eighth Army marched across the 38th parallel, General MacArthur broadcast his final call to North Korean authorities "to lay down your arms and cease hostilities" and "to cooperate fully with the United Nations in establishing a unified, independent and democratic government of Korea." Kim Il-sung rejected the call and declared in a radio broadcast that "the Korean People are not standing alone in our struggle and are receiving the absolute support of the Soviet Union and the Chinese People." Almost simultaneously, the foreign minister in Beijing proclaimed that "the American War of invasion in Korea has been a serious menace to the security of Korea from its very start. . . . The Chinese people cannot stand idly by with regard to such a serious situation." Mao already had issued orders for the "Chinese People's Volunteers" (CPV) to enter Korea.[86]

Although the United States was not deterred by Chinese warnings, the Joint Chiefs sent MacArthur an "amplification" of his orders for the campaign in North Korea. Should "major" Chinese units intervene in Korea "without prior announcement," the UN commander was "to continue the action" so long as his forces had "a reasonable chance of success." Any action "against objectives in Chinese territory" still would require prior clearance from Washington. But U.S. intelligence analysts continued to regard as unlikely "full-scale Chinese Communist intervention" unless the Soviet Union opted "for global war." Because the Chinese lacked "requisite air and naval support," they had the capacity to intervene "effectively, but not necessarily decisively."[87]

President Truman's meeting with MacArthur at Wake Island on 15 October added to the atmosphere of optimism in Washington. Held only three weeks before congressional elections, the conference originated in the desire of White House politicos to associate the leader of the Democratic party with the victorious commander in the field.[88] Truman had a strong interest in avoiding a penetrating examination of potentially divisive issues. This put the general in an excellent position to manipulate the president and his entourage. Telling Washington officials what they wanted to hear proved easy for the Far Eastern commander as he was at the peak of his own confidence. "Formal resistance" to the United Nations in Korea, he predicted, would end by Thanksgiving. There was "very little" chance of Chinese or Soviet intervention. China could get only fifty thousand to sixty thousand troops across the Yalu and, without adequate air support, these would be no match for his own forces. The Soviet Union could provide air support but would have difficulty coordinating its planes with Chinese ground operations. Thus not only were the Chinese and the Soviets unlikely to intervene; if they did, UN military strength was perfectly adequate to meet the challenge. MacArthur's audience could not have been more pleased. The presidential party, which included Bradley but not Marshall or Acheson, returned to the United States brimming with confidence in the field commander.[89]

MacArthur left Wake Island in a state of elation.[90] He had hinted during the discussion that he intended to use non-Korean soldiers in the northernmost provinces of the peninsula. When no one questioned him on the matter, he undoubtedly believed he had been given the green light. On 17 October he ordered UN troops to march fifty to a hundred miles into those areas. Seven days later he gave all units the go-ahead to advance to the Yalu. When the Joint Chiefs wired him that this move contradicted his directive of 27 September and requested an explanation, MacArthur asserted "military necessity." He also pointed out that restrictions on the use of non-Korean troops in that directive were labeled only "a matter of policy," and was not a mandatory order. Even that statement had been modified, he declared, by Marshall's dispatch of 29 September stating that he should "feel unhampered tactically and strategically to proceed north of the [38th] parallel." MacArthur concluded his explanation by claiming that the whole issue had been discussed at Wake Island.[91] No one in Washington, from the Pentagon to the Oval Office, stood willing to call to heel the "sorcerer of Inchon."

MacArthur also spoke out at Wake Island on the political dimension of the unification process in Korea. The most immediate question was whether the ROK should exercise civilian authority over territories seized above the 38th parallel. The General Assembly resolution of 12 December 1948 provided a guideline here, and it acknowledged the "effective control and jurisdiction" of the ROK only over "that part of Korea where the Temporary Commission was able to observe and consult," that is, South Korea.[92] Three days before the Wake Island meeting, Acheson expressed concern to Ambassador Muccio over a report that South Korean police were exercising authority in towns located above the old boundary. The secretary of state emphasized that these police should operate only under the authority of the unified command, that the impression should not be conveyed that the ROK was grasping authority over North Korea through its civilian police.[93]

The Interim Committee on Korea moved simultaneously to guard against that prospect. A creation of the eight-power resolution, this body was designed to "consult and advise" the unified command from New York until the more permanent group, the United Nations Commission on the Unification and Rehabilitation of Korea (UNCURK), could gather on the peninsula. On 12 October the Interim Committee passed a resolution proposed by James Plimsoll, the Australian representative, recommending that the unified command "assume provisionally all responsibilities for the government and civil administrations" in North Korea.[94]

Both MacArthur and Muccio disliked this approach, as it would raise the ire of the highly nationalistic Rhee and his supporters. The UN commander followed the ambassador's lead at Wake Island in urging his audience to reject a policy of treating the South Koreans "exactly on the same basis as the North Koreans."[95]

Another issue was whether a national government should grow out of elections held over the entire peninsula or simply above the 38th parallel. In the latter case, the process would be simple: elections would provide representatives for the hundred empty seats in the National Assembly at Seoul, which had been designated for northern areas at the time of the creation of the ROK in 1948. The conduct of national elections would greatly complicate the process, as the constitution of the ROK provided for legislative elections only once every two years, and the last such election had occurred in May 1950. Unless the presently constituted National Assembly took the initiative in providing for national elections—which was unlikely—a UN effort to follow this course would appear to be a repudiation of the republic. It was sure to meet determined resistance from President Rhee. MacArthur and Muccio favored Rhee on this issue, arguing that South Korean cooperation was essential in executing any plan for unification and that the only method of obtaining such cooperation rested in working closely with the ROK.[96]

The State Department had reservations. The Rhee regime was unpopular abroad, where few people believed in its ability to govern the entire peninsula. This was especially the case with India and Australia, which had been represented on UN commissions relating to Korea before the outbreak of hostilities. Although Great Britain had not served on any commissions, its limited experience with the country since World War II had engendered contempt toward Koreans in general, and Rhee's forces in particular. Recent politics within the ROK had reinforced these perceptions. Rhee's bickering with the National Assembly continued, as did the strong-arm tactics of the Youth Corps, whose "goon" squads forcefully impressed civilians into the army while avoiding such service themselves. In early September Rhee and the National Assembly reached an impasse when, against the president's wishes, the legislature passed overwhelmingly a resolution demanding the dismissal of Sihn Sung Mo, the prime minister and defense minister, and Cho Pyung Ok, the home minister. Muccio labored with only limited success to restrain Rhee and his henchmen.[97]

Outside observers also feared that a Rhee government in the North would include former landholders in that area who had fled southward after World War II. These people were likely to attempt a reversal of the land redistribution program, which was bound to produce civil unrest. Foreign diplomats talked about starting from scratch in forming a national government simply in fairness to North Koreans, who had had no say in creating the ROK. The British Foreign Office viewed national elections as a method of disposing of Rhee "without making it necessary to denounce his present government."[98] In Washington, policymakers attempted to balance conflicting pressures. Ultimately they held to the line that, although the unified command rather than the ROK should exercise authority in North Korea until elections were conducted there, those elections alone were adequate for the creation of a national government.

This stand did not survive unchallenged. On 23 October Rhee told a reporter from *U.S. News and World Report* that, despite UN efforts to limit his authority to the South, he was assuming "temporary civil control" over the entire country. The South Korean army and police, he declared, would sample public opinion above the 38th parallel to determine whether his appointees as provincial governors would remain permanently in their positions and whether elections would be conducted in both the North and the South.[99]

A report two days later by the *Times of London* special correspondent in Korea provided confirmation that such a sampling was unlikely to be guided by a scientific spirit. The story asserted that North Korea's rule of Seoul during the past summer had been in the manner of a conquered territory. ROK conduct in liberated territories was no better. Despite the efforts of U.S. officers and UN officials, South Korean police and patriotic organizations continued their vicious persecution of those suspected of collaboration with the late Communist occupation. The reporter described a visit to a village outside Seoul during which he had observed police activity of the most brutal kind. "Interrogation is a neat word" to them, he wrote, "like liquidation: In this case it meant beatings with rifle butts and bamboo sticks, and the insertion of splinters under finger nails."[100]

A storm of protest followed in England.[101] Bevin directed Sir Oliver Franks, the U.K. ambassador in Washington, to convey to Acheson British concern about atrocities and to warn of the possibility that Rhee would provide UNCURK, scheduled to arrive in Korea in mid-November, with a "fait accompli." The U.S. State Department considered Anglo-U.S. differences inconsequential, but the Foreign Office in London suspected Rhee and MacArthur of conspiring in a course that would lead to future trouble.[102]

In the midst of this controversy, Plimsoll in New York quietly searched for agreement on a plan for unification. His scheme provided for early elections in North Korea for an interim legislature there. Representatives from the North and the South would then negotiate a basis for a unified government. National elections would follow for the establishment of that government.[103] The United States was not a member of the Interim Committee, but an American attended its meetings on the pretext that the United States was representing the UN command. U.S. officials at the United Nations lobbied against any deviation from their approach to unification.

The British countered this pressure. Although they had no excuse that would allow them to attend formal meetings, they received reports from Plimsoll and they encouraged Australia and Pakistan, the other commonwealth nation represented on the Interim Committee, to hold firm in opposing U.S. plans. Of the five other representatives, only the Chilean showed sympathy for the Australian and Pakistani position, while the delegates from the Philippines and the Netherlands supported the U.S. line. This left the Thai and Turkish representatives as the swing votes, and they showed no haste in taking sides.[104]

When the commission arrived in Tokyo in mid-November, it immediately requested a meeting with a representative of the UN command. Military officials replied that they could not brief UNCURK on short notice, but MacArthur hosted a luncheon for commission members in which he urged them not to press for new elections below the 38th parallel. Plimsoll learned later that the UN commander had planned, once his forces occupied all of North Korea, to turn over administrative responsibilities there to UNCURK. Lacking the personnel or expertise to carry out such tasks, UNCURK would be forced, in turn, to use ROK personnel for the job, giving Rhee effective authority over the area.[105]

UNCURK finally reached Seoul on 26 November. During the initial discussions there on the political process for unification, the Australian, Pakistani, Chilean, Filipino, and Netherlands representatives clung to their earlier positions. Although the commission took no vote on nationwide elections, the Thai and Turkish delegates now leaned toward opposing them. A slim majority appeared to be emerging in favor of the U.S. position.[106]

The Chinese counteroffensive of late November rendered the debate academic before UNCURK established its position. Yet the disputes of October and November over the unification process in Korea reveal that some of the central issues relating to the peninsula had been left unresolved by the General Assembly resolution of 7 October. Given Rhee's shaky standing in Korea itself and his general obstinacy in the face of both internal and external pressures, it is certain that, even without Chinese intervention, the country would have remained in turmoil and a source of international wrangling for an indefinite period.

Unconventional military activity on the peninsula during October and November reinforces this point. Although by October much of the North Korean army lay in shambles, thousands of soldiers avoided death or capture by retreating to mountainous areas of the South, where they joined anti-ROK guerrillas from the prewar period. The three largest areas of guerrilla activity in South Korea were in the southwest corner of the peninsula, especially in South Cholla Province, long a hotbed of dissent against the Rhee regime; in the central part of Korea just below the 38th parallel; and in the Taebaek range along the east coast south of Samchok. U.S. intelligence estimated that thirty thousand guerrillas operated in rear areas.[107] Thousands more North Korean soldiers fought in small units using guerrilla tactics against the bulk of UN forces, now deployed in the provinces bordering the Soviet Union and Manchuria. The ROK army and police had fought guerrillas in the South for years, frequently with considerable success. With U.S. aid, first from several divisions of troops and later with materials and advice, ROK forces might have succeeded taking over the entire country. Yet the vast mountainous region north of the narrow neck had many advantages for guerrillas, including a close proximity to Manchuria. Even without direct Chinese intervention, MacArthur's prediction that all major opposition to UN forces would end by Thanksgiving and that remaining pockets of resistance would be destroyed by the severe winter said more about the general's extreme self-assurance than about actual conditions in Korea.

### THE UNITED STATES RESPONDS TO CHINESE INTERVENTION

From the last week of October MacArthur had more pressing concerns than Korean guerrillas or the political process for unification. On the 25th ROK units in the northwestern and northeastern sectors alike encountered tough opposition from Chinese soldiers. In the ensuing days UN forces throughout the northern provinces confronted a new enemy. By 6 November MacArthur was so disturbed by the Chinese influx into Korea that he ordered UN bombers to destroy the bridge connecting Sinuiju in Korea with Antung in Manchuria. The Joint Chiefs of Staff contravened this order and directed the postponement of all air operations within five miles of the Chinese border, pointing to an earlier promise by the State Department to consult the British before taking any action that might affect Manchuria. In response, the UN commander cabled Washington with the following plea for support that belied all his optimistic assessments of the past:

> Men and material in large force are pouring across all bridges over the Yalu from Manchuria. This movement not only jeopardizes but threatens the ultimate destruction of the forces under my command.... The only way to stop this reinforcement of the enemy is the destruction of these bridges and the subjection of all installations in the north area supporting the enemy advance to the maximum of our air destruction. Every hour that this is postponed will be paid for dearly in American and other United Nations blood.[108]

Chinese involvement already had set off a flurry of activity in Tokyo and Washington, but on the military side it was far less alarmist than MacArthur's above dispatch. China's last-minute involvement puzzled military analysts. On 28 October General Willoughby in Tokyo wrote that "the auspicious time for intervention has long since passed; it is difficult to believe that such a move, if planned, would have been postponed to a time when remnant North

Korean forces have been reduced to a low point of effectiveness." Three days later General Bradley in the Pentagon observed that China's course seemed to be "halfway between" the marginal or total embroilment expected by military leaders.[109]

On the surface Willoughby's puzzlement may seem surprising. We already have seen that, earlier in the month, he had brushed off Admiral Nomura's surmise that China would intervene because Nomura had no specific evidence to back it up and was basing his belief only on his lengthy experience with China's people and culture. Now concrete evidence existed of such intervention in the form of captured Chinese soldiers, and, moreover, those captured included members of units in several different Chinese armies. The obvious conclusion was that China had intervened on a large scale in Korea. But Willoughby and most others in Far Eastern Command intelligence preferred to believe, or at least to report, that China merely had committed small sections of separate armies.[110] Clearly Willoughby and his subordinates set a higher standard of proof for a conclusion of major Chinese intervention than they did for minor involvement or no involvement at all.

Willoughby may have knowingly falsified intelligence reports, never acknowledging that more than 60,000 Chinese soldiers were in Korea when, in fact, more than 200,000 were there.[111] He was accustomed to telling MacArthur what the general wanted to hear, and he sympathized with his boss's determination to march on to complete victory in Korea.[112] Prussian in bearing, Willoughby was a most unpopular figure among colleagues. Yet he had virtually unlimited access to MacArthur, and this made him an intimidating figure to underlings. Willoughby's intimacy with the UN commander was a reflection of MacArthur's determination to surround himself with people who would not disturb the dreamworld of self-worship in which he so often chose to live.[113]

Chinese behavior should not have puzzled those familiar with Mao's strategy in previous wars. A key point in Maoist thought was the trading of space for time. The ideal moment to attack an enemy of superior firepower came when its forces advanced beyond their major supply bases into rugged terrain lacking easily defensible lines of transportation and communication. Offensives often came in stages, with various fits and starts, rather than all at once. An essay in the 28 October issue of the Chinese weekly *World Culture* revealed some of the implications of Mao's ideas for the current world situation. The author of the essay, Deng Chao, surely sought to relieve domestic anxieties over a conflict with the United States and to convey a warning to that nation; his analysis, however, also fit the framework established by Mao's earlier writings. Deng argued that, with UN troops now far inland, the time was ripe for effective counteraction. Despite the U.S. advantage in metal, its shortage in manpower limited its strength both in Korea and elsewhere. The war against Hitler had proven the inadequacy of air power to defeat an enemy; despite the tremendous tonnage of U.S. bombs dropped on Germany—supposedly the equivalent of 450 A-bombs—what ultimately had destroyed the

Nazi war machine was massive Soviet armies. Even U.S. mobilization at home and similar action by its allies could not match the present manpower capabilities of Communist nations. And the United States no longer had a monopoly on atomic weapons. The concentration of industry in the United States, Great Britain, and France made them especially vulnerable to air attack. The obvious conclusion was that, whether operating locally in Korea or throughout the globe, the Communist powers were adequately prepared for "protracted" war.[114]

State Department observers appeared less bemused by Chinese intervention in Korea than did their military counterparts. O. Edmund Clubb doubted that the scope of Chinese involvement left open the possibility that they would be "promptly bloodied and thrown out by [a] force that they themselves have consistently characterized as 'a paper tiger.'" By 3 November Edward Barrett, the assistant secretary of state for public affairs, was "really alarmist." "Solely on the basis of the very unusual Chinese Communist propaganda campaign of recent days," he concluded that, "at the very least," China planned an intervention in Korea of "a hundred thousand or so" troops. From Hong Kong, Wilkinson, who earlier had thought large-scale Chinese intervention unlikely, expressed second thoughts. On the basis of a "sharp increase" of articles on Korea from the New China News Agency, "a distinctly more bellicose tone toward [the] U.S." in the Chinese press as a whole, and scattered reports of security preparations in northern Chinese cities, he concluded that Beijing most likely intended to wage a guerrilla struggle aimed at preventing UN forces from consolidating their hold on the peninsula.[115]

It took MacArthur's report of 6 November to move top officials in Washington to reconsider U.S. policy in Korea. Although President Truman gave his field commander authority to bomb the south side of the Yalu bridges, he and his advisers had doubts about permitting MacArthur to continue the offensive. Their reservations became more serious when, on 7 November, MacArthur sent another message hinting that the protection of his forces soon might require that his pilots pursue enemy planes operating in Korea back to their home bases in Manchuria.[116] From the start of the conflict in June, U.S. leaders, from the White House to the State Department and the Pentagon, had wanted to limit the U.S. commitment to Korea and to prevent the fighting from expanding into a larger war. Chinese involvement endangered these goals. The problem facing the United States was to assess Beijing's aims and capabilities and then to adopt the course most compatible with U.S. resources and global objectives.

On 8 November the Joint Chiefs informed MacArthur that his present objectives of destroying "North Korean armed forces" might have to be "reexamined." The Far Eastern commander seized this opportunity to plead his case in the strongest possible terms, and in doing so did not hesitate to adjust his estimate of the situation. In a telegram that arrived in Washington before the National Security Council convened on the 9th, MacArthur insisted that any program short of his projected end-the-war offensive, scheduled to commence "on or about November 15," "would condemn us to an indefinite retention of our military forces along difficult defense lines in North Korea and would unquestionably arouse such resentment among South Koreans that their forces would collapse or might even turn against us." "That the Chinese Communists after . . . establishing themselves within North Korea would abide by any delimitations upon further expansion southward," he declared, "would represent wishful thinking at its very worst." On the other hand, "with my air power, now unrestricted so far as Korea is concerned except as to hydroelectric installations, I can deny reinforcements coming across the Yalu in sufficient strength to prevent the destruction of those forces now arrayed against me in North Korea." MacArthur proceeded to compare "the widely reported British desire to appease the Chinese Communists by giving them a strip of Northern Korea" to the appeasement of Hitler at Munich in 1938. "To give up any portion of North Korea to the aggression of the Chinese Communists," he insisted, "would be the greatest defeat of the free world in recent times [and] . . . would bankrupt our leadership and influence in Asia and render untenable our position both politically and militarily." The general pleaded "with all the earnestness that I possess that there be no weakening at this crucial moment and that we press on to complete victory which I believe can be achieved if our determination and indomitable will do not desert us."[117]

MacArthur had several advantages in his quest to maintain a free hand in Korea. First, he was the commander in the field, an official who traditionally received considerable freedom to assess conditions in his theater. For the first time in U.S. history, moreover, the secretary of defense, George C. Marshall, was a military careerist, sure to be sensitive to that tradition. Just as important, in contrast to his superiors at home, who were hesitant and confused, MacArthur had a clear sense of what needed to be done. Washington officials were deeply apprehensive about the impact a confrontation with China would have on Western strength in Europe; however, they lacked definitive information on Chinese intentions and capabilities and shared MacArthur's fear that a show of timidity would embolden the Communists and destroy South Korean morale. The move of non-Korean troops beyond the narrow neck during the second half of October brought the former concern to the forefront, as a halt to or retreat of UN forces could now be attributed only to Chinese intervention rather than to a sensitivity toward approaching China's border.[118] Furthermore, MacArthur was defending an established objective, "the destruction of North Korean armed forces," rather than advocating a new course. Short of a policy's palpable failure, it is always easier to perpetuate a plan than to change one. MacArthur also derived continuing advantage from his brilliant success at Inchon. The Joint Chiefs had questioned his judgment before and had been proved wrong; they were not inclined to challenge him again so soon.

Domestic politics added another dimension to this situation. MacArthur had long been the darling of Republican malcontents over U.S. Asian policy. His smashing victory at Inchon took the edge off partisan attacks during the congressional election campaign, but it also made the thought of restraining him in Korea all the more frightening to Democratic leaders. The passing of the election on 7 November did little to reduce the domestic political pressures on policymaking. Although the Republicans made fewer gains—twenty-eight seats in the House and five in the Senate—than in any off-year election since 1934, the outcome was widely perceived as a defeat for the Democrats. Certainly it encouraged those Republicans who had been most harsh in attacking the U.S. course in Asia. Many analysts, including some Democratic officials, regarded Acheson as the main liability to the administration in the past campaign, putting him in a weak position to take the lead in restraining MacArthur.[119]

Marshall's presence at the head of the Defense Department further weakened Acheson's position. Although on excellent terms with Acheson, Marshall was himself a former secretary of state with high stature in the White House. To many, he was both "the architect of victory" in World War II and the guiding hand behind America's historic departures in foreign policy during 1947 and 1948. In poor health in 1950 and confined to a short workday, he remained, nonetheless, the man to whom people turned for guidance in a crisis. His presence reduced the prospect that Acheson would initiate a proposal to halt the U.S. offensive in Korea.

By the time the National Security Council met on 9 November, Chinese troops in Korea had broken contact with UN forces, thus adding to the difficulty of assessing their strength and intentions. General Walter Bedell Smith, director of the Central Intelligence Agency, presented a new intelligence report estimating that 30,000 to 40,000 Chinese troops were in Korea. Combined with the remaining North Korean units and reinforced by the perhaps 350,000 Chinese soldiers in Manchuria, who probably could be moved to the peninsula in thirty to sixty days, these forces could either halt the UN advance or force a retreat.[120] General Bradley doubted that U.S. air action could prevent substantial reinforcement of Chinese strength in Korea unless U.S. planes operated in Manchuria.

But would China decide to escalate its involvement in Korea? Here policymakers could only speculate about Beijing's objectives. The Joint Chiefs thought three possibilities existed: (1) to safeguard the power complex on the Yalu, which supplied much of Manchuria with electricity, "and possibly to establish a *cordon sanitaire* in North Korea"; (2) to push back UN forces and engage in a war of attrition; or (3) to drive "us off the peninsula." All those present agreed that the State Department should seek direct contacts with the Chinese to probe their intentions and perhaps even to reach a settlement; but MacArthur could continue to operate within Korea as he saw fit.[121]

Acheson's efforts of the next two weeks bore little fruit. He made overtures to China through Sweden, which had relations with Beijing, but to no avail. He hoped that the Chinese delegation, which was on its way to New York to participate in Security Council deliberations on Taiwan, had the authority to discuss Korea. On 8 November the Security Council had invited a representative of the PRC to attend its upcoming discussion on Korea. Although Zhou

Enlai's response was not encouraging, the State Department received a report from New Delhi on 16 November that the Chinese would be arriving in New York in three days and would be empowered to talk about Korea. In fact, the delegation did not arrive until the 24th, the day MacArthur's "end the war offensive" began in Korea (the campaign had been delayed for more than a week because of logistical difficulties). The timing was hardly propitious for the opening of peace talks. In the meantime, the British had had no luck in contacting top Chinese officials through their representative in Beijing.[122]

An alleged Chinese peace plan for Korea did leak from the Polish delegation at the United Nations on 17 November. The plan called for a buffer zone south of the Yalu to be administered by the Kim regime, withdrawal of the U.S. Seventh Fleet from the Taiwan strait and an end to U.S. recognition of the Jiang government, and a formal declaration from Washington withdrawing any further support for that government. Although since early in the month the State Department had been playing with the idea of a buffer zone on both sides of the Yalu, the United States took no initiative in response to the leak.[123]

Indeed, as a result of continuing pressure on the State Department from the Joint Chiefs and Republican supporters of Jiang, plus Rusk's own predilection, the United States had edged toward a less flexible policy on Taiwan. Pressure on the British, who in late September had pushed through the General Assembly a resolution to consider the Taiwan question beginning on 15 November, reflected this trend. In anticipation of this date, the British drafted a resolution calling for a UN commission to study the issue and offer recommendations. It implied that, in making proposals, the body should follow the Cairo declaration of 1943, which advocated the island's return to China. The State Department wanted to keep open the prospect for a recommendation for Taiwan's autonomy. Even when the Korean War ended, the Americans prepared to campaign for the separation of the territory from the mainland or at least its military neutralization. Chinese intervention in Korea served the purpose of hardliners in the United States, as it increased doubts regarding the outcome of the conflict that had sparked U.S. protection of Taiwan. On 15 November, when John Foster Dulles proposed to the First Committee a postponement of discussion on the Taiwan problem, he received nearly unanimous consent.[124]

The Truman administration still made a concerted effort to persuade Beijing that the United States had no aggressive designs. The United States already had cosponsored a resolution in the UN Security Council affirming "the policy of the United Nations to hold the Chinese frontier with Korea inviolate and fully to protect legitimate Chinese and Korean interests in the frontier zone," an obvious reference to electric power facilities on the Yalu. Acheson and Rusk emphasized in well-publicized speeches that the United States had no designs beyond Korea. Truman did the same in a widely covered press conference.[125]

Signals emanating from China, intelligence reports on Korea, and developments in the United Nations and allied capitals heightened concern in the State Department. The Chinese press replied to U.S. efforts at reassurance by reciting the instances since late June in which statements from Washington were later contradicted by U.S. action in Korea. These began with a United Press story of 27 June, which quoted an army spokesman as saying that no U.S. troops would be committed to Korea. Then came reports that U.S. bombing would be restricted to South Korea, that the UN goal was merely to restore the 38th parallel, and, finally, that U.S. troops would halt well short of the Manchurian frontier. "It is quite enough to prove the truth of the adage: 'Never believe a rumor until it is denied,'" the New China News Agency declared on 17 November.[126] Mainland newspapers, journals, and radio broadcasts continued the pattern, established during the last week of October, of mobilizing the Chinese people for protracted war with the United States.[127]

Intelligence reports provided little reassurance. Through the Netherlands, the State Department received an estimate that China already had 160,000 troops in North Korea and 500,000 in Manchuria. The Netherlands embassy in Beijing believed that China wanted to avoid a clash with UN troops, but only if they stayed at least fifty miles from the Manchurian border.[128] The intelligence branch of the State Department provided an alarming scenario. "The most likely Soviet-Chinese course," it believed, included:

> a. Continuation of Chinese-North Korean holding operations in North Korea until . . . preparations have been completed and until prospects of securing U.S. withdrawals from Korea through intimidation and diplomatic maneuvers have been exhausted.
>
> b. In case of the failure of these tactics, increasing unofficial Chinese intervention in Korea to, if necessary, the point of large scale military operations.
>
> c. Increasing Soviet support of the Chinese in equipment, planes, technical advisers, and of necessary "volunteers" to the extent required to prevent a Chinese defeat.[129]

In Tokyo General Willoughby expressed anxiety over growing Chinese strength in the northeast reaches of the peninsula, where the U.S. X Corps was widely dispersed.[130] Under the circumstances MacArthur's splitting of the Eighth Army and the X Corps between western and eastern sectors, respectively, did not inspire confidence in Washington.

U.S. efforts to maintain harmony among allies met with mixed results. The State Department regarded allied unity as critical both in deterring the enemy and in mustering strength in the event of a broadened conflict. Great Britain and France, plus three other smaller nations, did join the United States in cosponsoring a Security Council resolution calling on China to withdraw from Korea. London and Paris, however, were not eager to bring this "six-power resolution" to a vote, as it surely would spark a Soviet veto and even might worsen prospects for an accommodation with Beijing. Sentiment mounted to consider a buffer zone south of the Yalu River. The Indian delegation at Lake Success lobbied for an armistice along the present battle line in Korea, and the Canadians circulated a comparable idea.[131] In Britain, Labor back-benchers pressed Attlee and Bevin to break with the United States. When Acheson approached Bevin, as well as the foreign ministers of France, Canada, the Netherlands, and Australia, regarding the possibility of permitting U.S. planes to pursue enemy aircraft operating in Korea back to their home bases in Manchuria, the replies were uniformly discouraging.[132] Yet General Bradley already had expressed doubt that a military solution could be imposed in Korea without air operations beyond the Yalu.

On 17 November John Paton Davies of the State Department's Policy Planning Staff finally proposed a halt to offensive operations in Korea and a withdrawal of UN forces to the narrow neck of the peninsula just north of Pyongyang and Wonsan.[133] General Charles L. Bolté, the army's assistant chief of staff for plans and operations, believed that support was sufficiently widespread in the State Department that the idea might be put forth in a State-Defense meeting scheduled for 21 November.[134]

Bolté recently had returned from a trip to Japan and Korea. He was the only major official in Washington to have seen MacArthur and visited the battlefront since the Chinese intervention, giving him a strong position to claim his superiors' attention. Under current conditions, he told General Collins, the army chief of staff, UN forces could hold any position in North Korea. Far from shy about venturing into the political realm, Bolté insisted that firmness would deter further "aggression," whereas timidity would produce the opposite result. In words that would have made MacArthur proud, he asserted that "history has proved that negotiating with Communists is as fruitless as it is repulsive." He urged that the Joint Chiefs resist any proposal to alter the field commander's instructions.[135]

Acheson undoubtedly sensed that the military would oppose any initiative to halt MacArthur's impending offensive. In his meeting at the Pentagon on 21 November, the secretary of state did note the anxiety expressed by "friendly" countries in the United Nations about an expanded war, but he went on to say that he had discouraged the British from advancing a concrete proposal for a demilitarized zone and that he had no intention of interfering with MacArthur's directive. Marshall suggested that the United States itself might head off undesirable proposals from its allies by taking the initiative in proposing a demilitarized zone, which would be established only after enemy resistance ceased. On the 24th Washington merely passed on a suggestion to MacArthur that he either halt UN forces on the high ground between ten and twenty-five miles from the Yalu or pull them back from the boundary once the offensive had been completed successfully. South Korean troops would then man the forward positions while other units withdrew to backup locations.[136]

The Far Eastern commander waved this proposal aside, claiming that, militarily, the terrain made the establishment of any line short of the Yalu impossible and that, politically, to accept less than the destruction of "all enemy forces south of Korea's northern boundary would be fraught with most dangerous consequences."[137] This declaration abounded with irony, as MacArthur knew his offensive might fail and assumed that, in such an event, the UN air war would be extended to Manchuria. If it was, he also surmised that the Soviets would take counteraction and that the war would spread.[138] In any event, by the time he received the suggestion from home to halt short of the Yalu, the final offensive had begun. MacArthur had had the last word in Washington. Now the Chinese would have their say on the battlefield. By 28 November Communist forces, more than 200,000 strong, were counterattacking in such force that a suddenly despondent MacArthur reported that his command "now faced . . . conditions beyond its control, . . . an entirely new war."[139]

The United States had played into the hands of the enemy, both militarily and politically. The splitting of UN forces in Korea, and their location in rugged and expansive terrain far from supply bases, greatly diminished their advantage in firepower and mobility. The U.S. failure to pursue a more cautious policy despite strong warning signals gave the Chinese counterattack a modicum of legitimacy outside the Communist world and undermined confidence in U.S. leadership in the West. U.S. Allies had expressed reservations about an aggressive UN campaign in Korea in early October and then again in November, but had succeeded only in discouraging Washington from expanding the conflict into Manchuria. Never again would they—especially the British—prove so deferential to U.S. wishes. In neutral India Nehru became all the more set in his distrust of U.S. designs and judgment regarding Asia. Rather than using India's irritation and fear resulting from China's recent invasion of Tibet to lure New Delhi toward the anti-Communist bloc, the United States reinforced its independence in the cold war and gave impetus to its effort to mobilize an Arab-Asian bloc in the United Nations.[140]

### THE COMMUNIST POWERS FEEL THEIR WAY

What were the prospects between late October and late November for averting a major Sino-U.S. clash? Could a halt to the UN advance in Korea and a more flexible U.S. position on the future of Korea, Taiwan, and Chinese representation in the United Nations have produced a settlement? Answers to these questions must remain speculative and can only be inferred from Mao's telegrams to Stalin and his own subordinates, events on the battlefield, preparations within China, and apparent diplomatic maneuvering, including that of the Soviet Union.

We have seen that Stalin's withdrawal of the offer of air support led Mao to reevaluate his decision to intervene. That decision was reaffirmed and, in response, Stalin again altered his position, committing fighter planes to provide air cover for Chinese troops once they entered Korea.[141] He refused to provide bombers, however, and the Soviet position led Mao to initially adopt a defensive strategy on the peninsula. The Chinese leader did not intend to announce the movement of his troops into the country, but he thought enemy forces might discover their presence before major engagements occurred and that this discovery might bring a halt to the UN advance.[142] Under such circumstances, the Chinese People's Volunteers would spend six months building defensive lines in the northern mountains, during which time they would train and, it was hoped, acquire heavy equipment from the Soviets. They would consider taking offensive action during the next spring, but only after "having achieved an overwhelming air and land superiority over the enemy's troops."[143] If now, in October, enemy forces continued to move northward, advancing beyond Pyongyang and Wonsan into the mountains, Chinese units would engage them, concentrating their effort in the east against the South Koreans, who had rushed ahead of the Americans in the march north and whom Mao and his generals felt confident in defeating.[144]

Had UN forces halted in the area of Pyongyang and Wonsan, a major clash with the Chinese could have been avoided for several months. Conceivably, diplomatic action during those months and, most important, the emergence of a relative balance of military forces in the northern reaches of the peninsula would have discouraged either side from taking the offensive on the battlefield. A stalemate at the narrow neck would have protected the security of China's borders and left some Korean territory under DPRK control, but it would not have achieved Kim's objective of uniting the peninsula under his control; it would not even have left him in a position equal to that before the June attack. Surely he would have pressed for offensive action. No one can say whether Mao, facing divisions at home and a difficult campaign in Korea, which might spark U.S. attacks on China, would have considered his brotherly obligation to Kim or the prestige of his government, at home and abroad, or even his nation's physical security and economic development, as requiring an offensive. Presumably, Stalin would have had input on the matter. Although much about his views remain shrouded in mystery, he clearly wanted to avoid a direct military clash with the United States and undoubtedly grasped the possibility of a U.S. declaration of war against China over Korea, as well as the implications of such an eventuality under the Sino-Soviet treaty of alliance. A year later Mao, unquestionably with his Soviet ally's approval, would accept an armistice line the balance of which was north of the 38th parallel. Yet this was only after China had won some glorious victories on the battlefield and suffered huge losses in manpower.

With UN forces moving rapidly northward during the second half of October, Mao realized that his troops would not have the luxury of digging in in the mountains. By 21 October ROK troops had advanced beyond Pyongyang and Wonsan, and their non-Korean allies were not far behind. This situation provided both a danger and an opportunity for the Chinese, a danger in that they now would have to fight before they were fully equipped with heavy weapons or solid defense lines, an opportunity in that the enemy would be overextended and—in part because of its division between east and west, with a large gap in the middle—extremely vulnerable to counterattacks.

Mao's messages to his field commanders from the 21st to the 23d indicate that he had adopted a more offensive approach. They were now to "seek combat opportunities" and to attempt to "annihilate three or four South Korean divisions."[145] Mao believed that, although the capture of major cities could occur only when Chinese troops received air support, they could win many isolated victories against the enemy, including U.S. units. Such victories would force "the Americans to conduct diplomatic negotiations with us" and prevent them from protecting their own forces in Korea while they were bringing in more divisions from home.[146]

Mao clearly based these dispatches on the assumption that enemy forces, both Korean and otherwise, intended to move rapidly toward the Yalu through territory occupied by Chinese and remnant North Korean armies. Had non-Korean UN troops dug in at the narrow neck while ROK units probed northward, as Washington had understood they would do, Mao might have adjusted his thinking once again. After his "volunteers" had forced a ROK retreat, he might have decided that the time was not ripe to advance on well-established UN lines. Even with the initial UN thrust north of Pyongyang and Wonsan, a retreat of enemy forces to defensive positions might have discouraged Mao from ordering an early offensive. Chinese sources indicate that the CPV broke contact with the enemy in early November to encourage the divided UN forces to extend themselves still further, thus making them more vulnerable to enemy attack.[147] Had MacArthur refused to accommodate his opponents so brilliantly, instead consolidating his forces well south of Chinese positions, a full-blown Sino-U.S. clash might have been averted.

The thesis—later put forth by MacArthur and others—that Mao intervened in Korea only with the assurance, based on information provided by British spies, that the United States would not expand the war, does not jibe with Chinese deliberations or preparations.[148] Mao believed it quite possible that U.S. air attacks on China, even with atomic bombs, would follow its intervention in Korea. According to one account, Stalin was sufficiently fearful of the U.S. reaction to a massive Chinese intervention that he had recommended that the PRC send only about sixty thousand troops to the peninsula.[149] During October and November China took extensive precautions against air attacks in its cities in the northeast.[150]

Nor is the thesis of Chinese assurance against U.S. attack consistent with deliberations within the executive branch in Washington, where the possibility of retaliatory action against China had received ongoing consideration since the end of June. NSC-81/1, signed by President Truman on 11 September, stated that "the United States should not permit itself to become engaged in a general war with Communist China," even if Chinese forces moved south of the 38th parallel. Yet the document envisioned air and naval action against China in such a contingency, and it was ambiguous regarding a response to a clash of UN and Chinese troops in North Korea.[151] Given apparent changes in U.S. policy over the past five months, it is unlikely that either Beijing or Moscow obtained any information through espionage that reassured them about the probable U.S. response to a Chinese offensive in Korea. At most, they could have surmised that the West would be sharply divided if the United States expanded the war—and this they could have learned from reading the *New York Times*.

Thus there is little doubt that the Chinese and the Soviets were deeply worried about the U.S. response to PRC intervention in Korea, and that Mao's military plans were in a state of flux in late October and early November. The question is what, if any, price Beijing and Moscow were willing to pay to prevent an escalating Sino-U.S. clash. One way to address the issue is through an examination of hints in the Communist press and in the diplomatic arena. In its 10–11 November issue, the Hong Kong edition of *Da Gong Bao*, an important Communist newspaper, published a lengthy article outlining three Chinese objectives in its Korean intervention: a withdrawal of foreign troops and nationwide elections on the peninsula, an end of U.S. aid to Jiang, and a halt to alleged rearmament of Japan, as well as a peace treaty with that nation acceptable to China and the Soviet Union.[152] A week later the leak from the Polish delegation at Lake Success omitted any mention of Japan and, on Korea, insisted only on a buffer zone in the north administered by the DPRK. This came six days after Zhou Enlai had rejected a Security Council invitation to participate in discussions on Chinese intervention in Korea, but had proposed that the international body combine its consideration of Korea and Taiwan.[153] A plausible reading of these events is that the Chinese were flexible in their demands and genuinely interested in talks, but were determined to link the issues of Korea and Taiwan and, like the United States, to avoid any show of timidity toward the adversary. The disclosure at Lake Success was readily deniable and obviously forced the Americans to make the next move. Yet it came immediately after the public assurances regarding U.S. intentions by Acheson, Rusk, and Truman and four days following a U.S. request that Sweden use its ambassador in Beijing to feel out the Chinese.[154] In this light, the leak may have represented a countermove to test the diplomatic climate in the West. The PRC delegation to the United Nations, which was to observe discussions on Taiwan (and perhaps Korea), left Beijing on the 14th.[155] Its leisurely trip via Moscow and eastern Europe pushed back its arrival in New York to the 24th, providing a sufficient period for Chinese leaders to gauge the stance of the United States before directly confronting diplomats of the other side.[156]

Because the leak of 17 November came through Polish officials, it is clear that the Soviet Union, which had a closer relationship with Poland than did China, initiated or at least supported the ploy. Determined to avoid direct intervention in Korea, in mid-October, as UN forces moved en masse into North Korea and Chinese rhetoric became more and more threatening toward the West, Stalin merely wished "the Korean people, heroically defending the independence of their country, a successful conclusion to their struggle of many years' duration for the creation of a united, independent, and democratic Korea."[157] Although he modified his earlier stand against providing immediate air support in Korea for Chinese troops, the Soviet MIG-15 fighters that appeared south of the Yalu at the beginning of November restricted themselves to combating UN planes operating near the border.[158] Fearing escalation in Korea, Stalin plainly sought to explore prospects for a peaceful settlement.

Considerations outside Korea helped nudge Stalin in this direction. Despite French foot-dragging, which provoked a heated exchange in meetings of NATO defense ministers at the end of October, and despite widespread doubt in West Germany, German rearmament remained a distinct possibility. Moscow revealed its concern by warning that it would not tolerate the revival of a German army and then by hurriedly calling together Soviet-bloc foreign ministers at Prague to form a united front on the issue. On 3 November the Soviets proposed a meeting of the foreign ministers of Great Britain, France, and the two superpowers to discuss a broad settlement on Germany. By tying down large numbers of U.S. forces in another theater over a lengthy period and further worsening the international climate, an enlarged conflict in Korea might help clear the way in the West for a major German contribution to NATO.[159]

A Japanese peace treaty was another concern in Moscow. On 26 October John Foster Dulles presented to Jacob Malik a memorandum outlining terms for such a pact. These included provision for U.S. military bases in Japan and a reopening of the Taiwan issue, obviously with the prospect of overriding the Cairo declaration. A prolonged conflict in Korea would only solidify the U.S. position on such matters. When Malik got back to Dulles on 20 November with the Soviet reply to the overture, he made "a very definite attempt . . . to create a friendly atmosphere."[160]

The continuing U.S. domination of the United Nations, which had gained momentum since June, also worried Moscow. In early November this domination manifested itself in passage of the "Uniting for Peace" resolution by the General Assembly with only five negative votes. Whether this measure could be translated into an effective instrument against the Communist world remained unclear, but its passage by such a large majority reflected a dangerous trend.[161]

The annual speech celebrating the anniversary of the Bolshevik revolution, delivered on 6 November by Politburo member Nikolai A. Bulganin, reflected a somber mood in Moscow. Whereas Georgi M. Malenkov's address of the previous year had displayed an exuberant tone and had dwelled extensively on developments abroad, Bulganin's centered on the domestic economy and was less high spirited. Both men emphasized the Soviet desire for peace, but Bulganin noted in particular that "Stalin has stated repeatedly that difference of economic systems and ideologies does not exclude cooperation and normal relations between the Soviet Union and the capitalist countries, in particular between the Soviet Union and the United States of America."[162]

If the Soviets were willing to put forth several carrots, as in the above statement or in the Polish leak and the call for talks on Germany, they also were capable of brandishing the stick, as when Bulganin stated—to "stormy, prolonged applause"—that "it is about time for these gentlemen [in the United States] to realize that our people are capable of standing up . . . for the interests of their motherland, if need be with arms in hand."[163] Indeed, Vishinsky's public conduct at the United Nations had returned to its characteristic belligerence. On 2 November he was so polemical in his attack on Dulles that he was rebuked by General Assembly president Nasrollah Entezam.[164]

Soviet diplomacy was moving on several fronts in what appeared to be different directions, a result of Moscow's effort to prepare for various contingencies while, at once, trying to head them off. Events since June had shaken Stalin's confidence in reading U.S. intentions, and thus the circumstances of the fall gave him pause. Could he be sure that a Chinese counteroffensive in Korea would not so enrage the Americans that they would launch a direct attack on the Soviet Union? After all, they made no secret of their view that the real problem in Korea and elsewhere originated in Moscow. Perhaps a new war in Korea would give an upper hand in the United States to the advocates of preventive war. Even if that did not occur, a major buildup of non-Communist military strength—including rearmament in West Germany and Japan—might ensue with resultant long-term dangers to the Soviet Union. The Kremlin therefore may have desired to bargain in several areas, including Korea. At the same time, Stalin remained determined to avoid conveying signs of the jitters to the Americans, who, in any event, might be uninterested in a settlement. Overtures to the West could at least serve to encourage divisions among and within non-Communist nations.

In this area, Soviet feelers merely reinforced the peace movement. On 16 November the Second World Peace Congress convened in Warsaw. The gathering had been postponed forty-eight hours and its location had been changed from Sheffield, England, when the Attlee government denied many of the delegates entry into the country. The Soviet press gave the event wide coverage, claiming representation from eighty nations. The meeting provided the setting for commencement of a new global signature campaign, this time for an appeal far broader than the outlawing of atomic weapons. Among other issues, the appeal called for a five-power peace conference, with the PRC as one of the nations represented; an immediate termination of the war in Korea and a removal of all foreign troops from the peninsula; a withdrawal of U.S. support for the Jiang government; and no remilitarization of Germany and Japan. Couched as an "Address to the United Nations," the appeal recited many of the current foreign policies of the Soviet Union. Beyond the immediate propaganda objective of the congress, the session initiated several organizational changes in the world peace movement. The elaborate structure of a World Peace Council, an executive committee, more than 75 national committees, and 150,000 local groups, constituted to some observers a potential rival to the United Nations.[165]

A final goal of the peace movement was to solidify support for Kremlin policies at home and in the satellites. From 10 November on to the end of the month, the peace campaign enjoyed center stage in the Soviet press and radio.

On the 23d more than half of *Pravda* concentrated on these activities, and five days later a third of the paper had a similar focus. *For a Lasting Peace, For a People's Democracy!*, the widely circulating journal of the Cominform, the Soviet-directed organization of national Communist parties, also devoted much space to the cause.[166] In a tense international climate, the peace crusade would ensure that, if war came, the peoples of the Communist world would view it as having been forced on them and would rally to the sound of trumpets from the Kremlin.

### Responsibilities and Prospects

The maneuvering on both sides during the fateful days of November, and indeed throughout the fall, reveals the depth of division between the West and the Communist world. Each camp faced a dangerous conflict that its top leaders—from Stalin in Moscow and Mao in Beijing to Truman in Washington—wanted to avoid. Each government tried to avert an escalation of the war. That none succeeded is attributable largely to the myriad of forces operating in Washington and Tokyo—the will and influence of a commander in the field whose grasp of Asian realities was badly out of date, the almost pathological concern of U.S. officials to avoid any hint of weakness to the enemy and their desire to win a clear-cut victory in the cold war, their myopic view of a new and dynamic China, and the volatile political climate in the United States, which discouraged prudent choices in foreign policy. It was these factors that produced the reckless UN offensive of late November and forced the Chinese hand. It was the United States, with forces thousands of miles away from its own homeland, that failed to give diplomacy a chance by halting its military advance toward the borders of its primary adversaries. Rather than deterring the Chinese, U.S. aggressiveness provoked them. In fairness to top civilian leaders in Washington, they had no intention of extending U.S. objectives into China. The course they pursued, however, gave Mao reason to suspect otherwise, and it hardly should be surprising that the leader of a highly nationalistic, revolutionary regime chose to lash out in response rather than "sit idly by."

The Korean War remains a conflict for which blame must be widely distributed. Through the summer of 1950 the weight of responsibility belonged with the Communist camp for initiating and perpetuating the military campaign in South Korea. In the autumn, however, the burden shifted squarely to the U.S. side for escalating the battle to the brink of Armageddon. A variety of factors would determine whether the momentum stopped short of the precipice: Who, in the end, would control U.S. policy, Truman or MacArthur? How would the military situation develop in Korea—the worse the fighting went for UN forces, the greater the chance that the United States would push for its extension beyond the peninsula? If the Chinese counteroffensive went well, would Beijing seek to force the enemy out of Korea, as Mao's telegram to Stalin of 20 October suggested he was inclined to do, or would it settle for reestablishing the prewar boundary? Would Stalin remain cautious regarding Soviet participation in the conflict or would a perception of danger or opportunity induce him to expand his nation's role? How aggressively would U.S. allies and the Arab and Asian neutrals press the United States to restrict its military action to Korea and to grant concessions on other issues involving China, and how much would they coordinate their efforts? In a conflict in which battlefield imperatives often held diplomacy hostage, restraint on both sides seemed most likely to emerge under conditions of military balance, a phenomenon which thus far had proved in short supply.

• CHAPTER 4 •

# Limiting the War

### SWINGS OF FORTUNE ON THE BATTLEFIELD

Winter had settled in over the northern reaches of the Korean peninsula. Temperatures rarely climbed above freezing, even along the western coastal plain. In the central mountainous region, where elevations commonly rose more than five thousand feet, the thermometer often dipped well below zero. Snow driven by biting winds added to the arctic quality of what most outsiders considered a primitive wasteland.

It was in this desolate setting that Chinese troops elevated their nation to the status of a major power. To be sure, they lacked the modern advantages of their Western counterparts. They had little heavy artillery or air support. Their small arms, mostly captured from former enemies, came from a myriad of sources—Japan, the Soviet Union, Germany, Canada, Great Britain, the United States. Logistics were primitive, dependent on human and animal transport. Most Chinese combatants crossed the Yalu with a four-day provision of food. Once this was consumed, they had to make do with food from any local sources they could track down. Many soldiers carried only eighty rounds of small arms ammunition and a few hand grenades, supplies that could not be quickly replenished. Clothing was marginal at best: canvas shoes with thin rubber soles and a scarcity of gloves left troops exposed to the brutal winter climate. Communications also left much to be desired. Below the battalion level, contact between Chinese units relied on runners, sound signals by bugle or whistle, and night communication by flare or flashlight. Yet Communist Chinese soldiers were a rugged lot, rigorously led and accustomed to fighting better-equipped foes. Well schooled in the art of guerrilla warfare, they were masters at infiltrating enemy lines and then launching deadly attacks on overextended and temporarily outnumbered opponents. Frequently operating at night, they took full advantage of the darkness to conceal their movements and maintain the element of surprise.[1]

UN forces were ideally dispersed to fall into a Chinese trap. Rather than concentrating his strength for the march to the Yalu, MacArthur had deployed the Eighth Army along the western front and the X Corps in the central highlands. Even after initial battles with a reinforced enemy in late October and early November, the field commander remained supremely confident, determined to fulfill his mission of destroying North Korean resistance as quickly as possible. He made no effort to close the fifty-mile gap separating his forces. Worse still, the Eighth Army and X Corps themselves had diffused their strength over broad fronts in rugged terrain. Especially vulnerable was the

Eighth Army's right flank, which was manned by the highly suspect II Corps of the ROK Army.

Other factors made it impossible to exploit fully the material advantages enjoyed by UN forces. Expertise in air reconnaissance, severely compromised by the demobilization of 1945 and 1946, had yet to achieve peak levels of World War II, and many field commanders operated without detailed maps of the area. Deficient intelligence on terrain and on enemy strength and deployment made tactical planning extremely imprecise. Moreover, in their rush to advance, neither the Eighth Army nor the X Corps built up a substantial reserve of manpower or supplies. To compound the problem, many U.S. soldiers in the west, anticipating victory and anxious to travel light, had discarded steel helmets, bayonets, and entrenching tools.[2]

These men soon regretted their complacency. Within a day after the "home-by-Christmas" offensive commenced on 24 November, the Chinese launched massive counterattacks on the vulnerable right flank of the Eighth Army. In a matter of hours panic swept through the three divisions of the ROK II Corps, sending them southward in disorganized flight, abandoning weapons and supplies by the ton in the mad scramble for safety. U.S. units on the center and left of the UN front remained unaware of the fate of the ROK divisions until late on the 26th. By then, Chinese pressure had driven back the U.S. Second Army Division two miles from forward positions along the Chongchon River. Two days later the entire Eighth Army was in a headlong retreat southward. A week later it quit Pyongyang. Not until mid-December, when it reached the Imjin River just below the 38th parallel, did it pause. To a British observer, U.S. soldiers expressed only one concern: "How soon can we get t'Hell outa this goddam country?" The British found officers and GIs alike characterizing MacArthur in "ribaldries which conveyed, in picturesque but unmistakable terms, their opinion that he was either a dangerous dotard, or an egomaniac determined to be Commander-in-Chief of a world crusade against Communism."[3]

Meanwhile, the X Corps had plunged into a gauntlet of enemy fire along the mountain roads and paths surrounding the frigid Chosin Reservoir. As in the west, the Chinese flanking movement was so complete that UN troops found themselves fighting desperately merely to sustain their southward movement. As the First Marine Division battled to save itself from annihilation, Commanding General O. P. Smith declared to a reporter, "We are not retreating. We are merely attacking in another direction." It took until 11 December for all units, some decimated by casualties, to congregate in the Hamhung-Hungnam area and prepare for evacuation by sea.[4]

The Chinese now faced a choice similar to that of the Americans back in October: whether to cross the 38th parallel and, along with their North Korean allies, attempt to unify the peninsula by military means, or to halt at the old dividing line and settle for a restoration of conditions prior to 25 June. As had been the case with the United States previously, the temptation of total victory proved too great for China to resist. UN forces, having fought out of the initial trap, easily outdistanced the enemy to the 38th parallel; but whether they

## November, 1950 to January, 1951

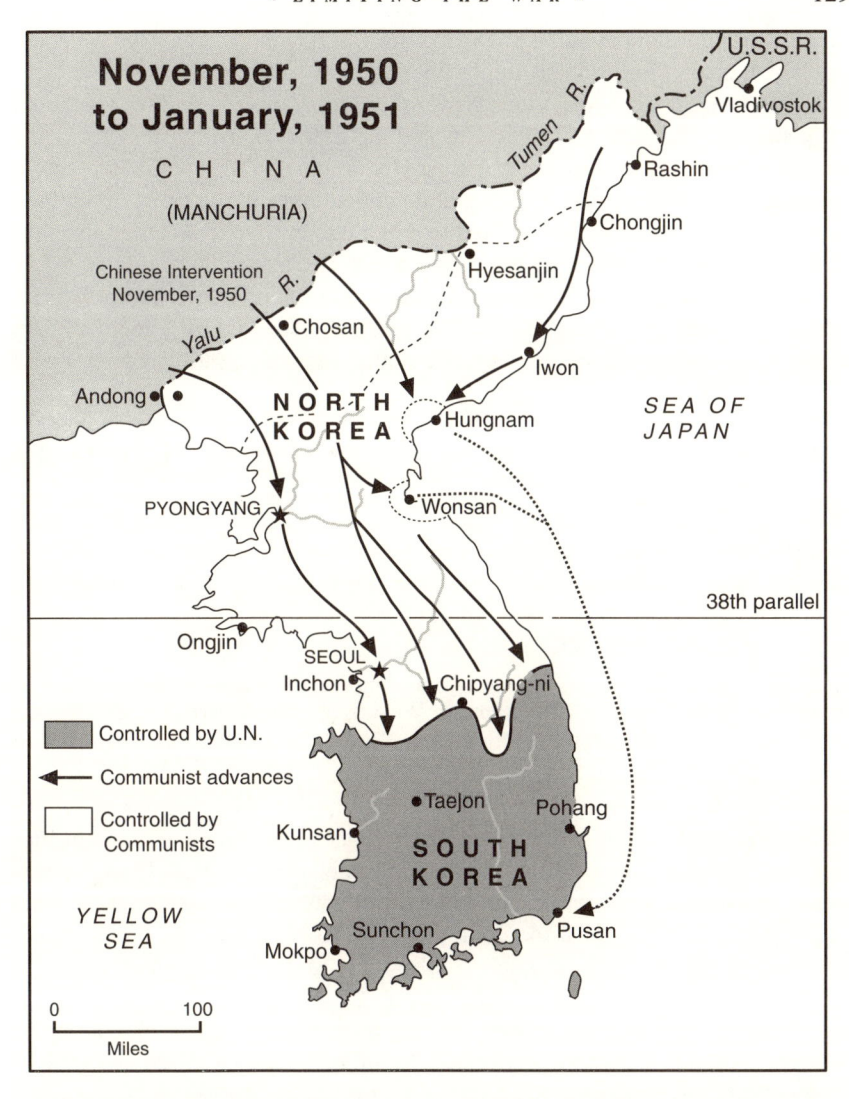

Map features:
- CHINA (MANCHURIA)
- Chinese Intervention November, 1950
- Yalu R., Tumen R.
- Andong, Chosan, Hyesanjin, Rashin, Chongjin, Iwon
- NORTH KOREA
- Hungnam, PYONGYANG, Wonsan
- SEA OF JAPAN
- U.S.S.R., Vladivostok
- 38th parallel
- Ongjin, SEOUL, Inchon, Chipyang-ni
- Controlled by U.N.
- Communist advances
- Controlled by Communists
- Kunsan, Taejon, Pohang
- SOUTH KOREA
- YELLOW SEA
- Mokpo, Sunchon, Pusan
- 0–100 Miles

could hold South Korea against a determined assault remained uncertain. From mid-December Chinese and reconstituted North Korean divisions proceeded southward, while building up a supply network to sustain a new offensive. On New Year's eve they struck, launching massive attacks all along the front. In the west UN troops quickly abandoned Seoul, crossed the Han, and retreated southward all the way to Pyongtaek, seventy miles below the 38th parallel. Further east, in sectors defended by ROK divisions, North Korean units broke open the UN line and penetrated far to the south, where they joined anti-Rhee guerrillas. Reports of these events flowed into Washington from the Far Eastern Command, leading the Joint Chiefs of Staff to fear that friendly forces soon might have to evacuate the peninsula.

Such pessimism proved overblown, fueled, in part, by MacArthur's effort to force his superiors at home to expand the war beyond Korea. By the second week of January Communist supply lines were as fully overextended as those of UN forces during the previous November. In addition to their deficiency in mechanized transport, the Chinese lacked the fighter planes necessary to protect lengthy overland shipments against UN air power. As a result, the supply apparatus from Manchuria had to operate under cover of darkness. Even then, supply stockpiles remained exposed to aerial attack. Arctic weather also took its toll. Robbed of shelter by fiery napalm attacks from UN bombers, inadequately clothed and fed, Communist troops increasingly fell victim to frostbite, trenchfoot, and typhus. Once afflicted, they received little medical care. Those with battlefield wounds fared no better. Morale naturally suffered and, though China drew replacements from a seemingly endless supply of manpower, soaring casualties eventually lowered the quality of soldiers in combat.

As January progressed the UN enemy on the ground became tougher than ever. Sparked by General Matthew B. Ridgway, who took command of the Eighth Army at the end of 1950 following the accidental death of General Walton Walker, and by the heroics of Turkish and British contingents, UN forces gradually regained their aggressive spirit. Making utmost use of superior firepower to counter the Communists' numerical advantage, Ridgway succeeded with limited offensives commencing in late January.[5]

By the beginning of February the Eighth Army was approaching Seoul, and diplomats at the United Nations and in Western capitals were discussing what course to follow if friendly forces reached the 38th parallel. Some observers even argued that the time was ripe for diplomatic initiatives aimed toward a cease-fire. Many analysts remained less sanguine, but there is little doubt that the improvement in UN prospects in Korea reduced the danger of an expanded war. Nor is there any question that the United Nations in New York, by providing a broad multilateral framework within which diplomats could maneuver, had helped to contain the conflict inside Korea's boundaries. Truman's decision of the previous summer to follow his State Department's advice to work through the international body and to use the Korean crisis to reinforce the Western alliance had proven crucial in enabling voices of caution in Washington and elsewhere, especially London, Ottawa, and New Delhi, to lobby effectively against a potentially uncontrollable process of escalation.

## The Challenge to U.S. Leadership

The Chinese counteroffensive produced a major crisis for the Truman administration, both abroad and at home. The Chinese were on the rampage not only militarily in Korea but diplomatically in New York. Wu Xiuquan, head of Beijing's delegation at Lake Success, delivered a blistering attack on the United States in his maiden address to the Security Council on 28 November. U.S. intervention on Taiwan represented "an integral part of the over-all plan of the United States Government to intensify its aggression, control and enslavement of Asian countries," he asserted. "To say that the civil war in Korea would affect the security of the United States is a flagrant, deceitful absurdity."[6] In Tokyo MacArthur rushed to quell criticism of his ill-fated offensive and to press Washington for permission to expand his operations beyond the peninsula. At the beginning of December, in an interview in *U.S. News and World Report*, MacArthur defended his past actions and characterized the prohibition on operations beyond the Yalu as "an enormous handicap, without precedent in military history."[7] Despite pleas from President Truman and Secretary of State Acheson for national unity, several Republican senators pressed for bold new decisions regarding Korea. On the Senate floor, Harry Cain of Washington declared that the field commander should "be given the right to strike wherever military necessity dictates, behind the Yalu River, or anywhere else." Others complained that Acheson was trying to undermine MacArthur. Joseph McCarthy wondered aloud why "the crimson clique in the State Department" directed the war and he asserted that Congress should impeach Truman if the president refused to use Chinese Nationalist forces in Korea.[8]

People in other areas of the non-Communist world expressed concern and often outrage at MacArthur's influence over the U.S. course in Asia. By the time the Chinese counterattacked in Korea, a foreign policy debate had commenced in the House of Commons in London with one-quarter of its members from the Labor Party tabling motions dissenting in some form with Foreign Secretary Ernest Bevin's course abroad. A major source of the dissent rested on distrust of MacArthur's conduct of the Korean War. When China mounted its offensive in Korea, criticism of U.S. leadership spread rapidly in Great Britain, and on the continent as well. In the British Parliament, R. A. Butler, a leading Conservative authority on foreign affairs, reaffirmed his commitment to an alliance with the United States, but insisted that Great Britain "must be heard henceforth [in Washington] with far greater authority."[9] The press in Britain and France disputed MacArthur's push toward the Yalu in the midst of efforts to negotiate a buffer zone in North Korea. Rumors filtered out of government circles in Paris that the United States would be urged to relieve MacArthur as UN commander.[10]

When, in a press conference on 30 November, President Truman stated that use of the atomic bomb in Korea always had been under consideration and implied that the decision on its employment rested with the field commander—which was false—alarm in western Europe and elsewhere reached a new peak. The administration quickly clarified its position, stating that the bomb could be dropped only under the president's orders, but this did little to stem the tide of disapproval outside the United States. Within hours of Truman's statement, British Prime Minister Attlee requested a face-to-face meeting in Washington. French Prime Minister René Pleven and Foreign Minister Robert Schuman rushed across the English channel to coordinate strategy with Attlee and Bevin.[11] Dutch officials also were in close contact with the British Foreign Office and agreed fully that a course of restraint must be pressed on the Americans.[12] The *Nation*'s Howard K. Smith in London characterized Attlee as being "propelled" across the Atlantic "by one of the most amazing political upheavals in Europe since the war[,] . . . a rebellion of free Europe against the kind of leadership America was giving to the West on the Korean issue."[13]

Sentiment in the commonwealth and at the United Nations reinforced the pattern in Europe. The reaction in India to Truman's statement on the atomic bomb was overwhelmingly negative.[14] Sir Girja Bajpai, secretary general of the Ministry of External Affairs, told U.S. Ambassador Loy Henderson that the critical immediate objective in Korea was to avoid the spread of hostilities. Nehru followed with a message to Sir Benegal Rau at the United Nations suggesting a meeting of representatives of the great powers, the linkage of a settlement in Korea to one on Taiwan, and the "absolute necessity" of avoiding use of the atomic bomb.[15] The strongly pro-U.S. foreign minister in Australia, Sir Percy Spender, qualified a statement of support of the United States with the observation that the weapon should be used "only after fullest consultation."[16] When Attlee contacted commonwealth high commissioners in London on 1 December, he encountered unanimous sentiment in favor of an effort to restrain the United States.[17]

Reactions at the United Nations confirmed and expanded on this trend. Even before Truman's ill-considered remark, Britain's Sir Gladwyn Jebb cabled London that "almost everyone [here] blames the recent turn of events to some extent upon MacArthur. The most serious feature is a total lack of confidence in any information emanating from him."[18] Although delegates from Greece, Turkey, Iran, Afghanistan, Saudi Arabia, and Liberia, as well as from Latin American countries, approved Truman's 30 November comments, those from Europe and the commonwealth "appeared greatly shocked" and several from the emergent "Arab-Asian group" expressed concern both that the bomb might be used once more against Asian peoples and that it would precipitate a third world war.[19]

When the Truman-Attlee meetings commenced in Washington on 4 December, the British prime minister carried with him the weight of opinion of a large portion of the non-Communist world. Correspondent Smith in London labeled him "a man of at least temporary power equal to the earth's big two, Truman and Stalin."[20]

### DELIBERATIONS WITHIN THE TRUMAN ADMINISTRATION

By the time Attlee arrived in the U.S. capital, the Truman administration had engaged for nearly a week in high-level meetings on the new crisis in Korea. Decision makers grappled with a host of interrelated questions, from matters narrowly pertinent to military conditions in Korea to broader issues of global strategy: what was the scope of Chinese involvement in Korea? What were the aims of the Chinese and what were their capabilities? Were they willing to negotiate and on what terms? Would their action be followed by Communist moves elsewhere or would it remain isolated like their action in North Korean on 25 June? Could UN forces hold a line across the northern reaches of the peninsula or would they be forced to retreat to the 38th parallel or even farther to the south? Indeed, did they have the capacity to hang on in Korea at all without great risk to their very survival as organized units? What would be the political cost of withdrawal from Korea and how did it compare to the military risks of staying there? Could (or should) Chinese action be countered by introducing new units from outside or by expanding the area of hostilities? How were the Chinese, and particularly the Soviets, likely to react to American or UN air or naval action beyond Korea? How would U.S. allies and other non-Communist countries in the United Nations respond to pressure for such moves? If the war expanded beyond Korea and even Asia, and if it included direct Soviet intervention, how would the United States fare? How, in short, would specific courses related to Korea influence the balance of political and material forces worldwide?

More than ever before, these questions intermingled with domestic politics: How would such courses affect the administration's ability at home to sustain a foreign policy consistent with U.S. interests? Most notably, how would decisions on Korea influence congressional and public support for a U.S. buildup in the critical European theater?

Certain themes quickly emerged within the executive branch in Washington. First came the view that, for the moment, UN forces should attempt to hold on in Korea. On 28 November, in the first National Security Council meeting in the crisis, Acheson declared that an immediate UN withdrawal from Korea would be "disastrous."[21] As the military situation continued to worsen in the days that followed, Secretary of Defense Marshall and the Joint Chiefs backed the State Department in emphasizing that U.S. prestige would suffer a terrible blow if the peninsula were to be abandoned before this became a military necessity.[22] In the face of confusing reports from Tokyo, the administration already had sent U.S. Army Chief of Staff Collins to inspect the front.[23] CIA Director Walter Bedell Smith was the only top official to dispute the decision to stay in Korea; he thought major Soviet moves were likely in more vital areas in the next one to two years and feared, in the meantime, that Moscow would "bleed us to death in Asia while defeating the armament effort in Europe."[24] But Soviet expert George Kennan, who had traveled to Washington from Princeton, New Jersey, to make himself available for consultation, doubted that the Soviets planned military action elsewhere.[25]

A momentary consensus also emerged on the nature and scope of U.S. military operations in Asia. No one wanted a major ground war in China. No new U.S. ground units could be sent to the theater until next spring. Losses in units already in Korea could not be replaced for at least a month.[26] Washington put off a decision on MacArthur's proposal to use Nationalist Chinese troops, fearing the impact of such action on allied unity.[27] The State Department and the Pentagon agreed further that the United States should not use the atomic bomb immediately nor should it take overt action beyond Korea. In adopting these positions, the diplomats emphasized allied opinion, while the military keyed on the difficulty of finding appropriate targets for the atomic bomb and the fear of Soviet or Chinese retaliation, or both, if U.S. planes attacked Manchuria. The Communists had some three hundred military aircraft in Manchuria, about two-thirds of which were bombers. These planes could greatly damage U.S. airfields in Korea and Japan, which would compromise U.S. ability both to strike against enemy troops and supply routes in Korea and to airlift crucial supplies to UN forces on the peninsula.[28] Concerns about overcommitting America's strategic arsenal to Korea and China, as well as the even more fundamental worry about the nation's unpreparedness for war against the Soviet Union, also entered military calculations.[29] Even so, sentiment emerged at the middle levels of the State and Defense bureaucracies for extensive covert operations on mainland China.[30]

The prevailing view against expanding overt military action was clearly subject to change if the Communists unleashed large-scale air attacks on UN units or if those units were forced to evacuate Korea. If the enemy abandoned its restraint in the use of air power from Manchuria, the United States would have to counterattack across the Yalu, possibly with atomic bombs, to protect Japan or to save UN troops in Korea.[31] Pentagon leaders already spoke of retaliation against the Chinese in the aftermath of a forced evacuation of the peninsula. The navy and the air force talked of a naval blockade of China and air attacks against its cities, while the service secretaries proposed a complete naval and economic blockade.[32]

The State Department grew concerned that pessimism in Tokyo was infecting Washington and might hamper the capacity of UN forces to hold in Korea or, worse still, of the United States to pursue a measured response to the challenge from China. The pessimism reached new heights on 3 December when the Joint Chiefs received a wire from General MacArthur that he faced "the entire Chinese nation in an undeclared war and unless some positive and immediate action is taken, . . . steady attrition leading to final destruction [of UN forces] can reasonably be contemplated."[33]

George Kennan provided the lead in countering the trend in an extraordinary display of character matched only by Acheson's response. Before taking leave from the department during the previous summer, Kennan had argued against permitting U.S. troops to cross the 38th parallel. As had become increasingly the case under Acheson's secretaryship, Kennan's counsel was rejected. Now, in December, the United States was paying the price. But Kennan chose the role of sage rather than critic, and Acheson, so often the caustic wit in contending with those who sometimes failed to see the world according to his lights, responded with a grace and wisdom of his own. After a lengthy conversation with the much maligned secretary at his home on the evening of the 3d, Kennan arose early the next morning and penned him a brief note:

> In international, as in private, life what counts most is not really what happens to someone but how he bears what happens to him. . . . almost everything depends from here on out on the manner in which we Americans bear what is unquestionably a major failure and disaster to our national fortunes. If we accept it with

candor, with dignity, with resolve to absorb its lessons and to make it good by redoubled and determined effort—starting all over again, if necessary, along the pattern of Pearl Harbor—we need lose neither our self-confidence nor our allies nor our power for bargaining, eventually, with the Russians. But if we try to conceal from our own people or from our allies the full measure of our misfortune, or permit ourselves to seek relief in any reactions of bluster or petulance or hysteria, we can easily find this crisis resolving itself into an irreparable deterioration of our world position—and of our confidence in ourselves.

When Acheson read the note to his top advisers in the State Department, Assistant Secretary Rusk responded that military leaders were too "dejected," that they needed an infusion of the spirit that the British had displayed in the summer of 1940. At the least, he thought the United States could force the Chinese to pay dearly for their advance in Korea.[34] Rusk and Kennan left for the Pentagon to emphasize to General Marshall the importance of maintaining a position in Korea.[35]

The State Department also adopted a firm but steady position on the diplomatic front, and here the Pentagon stood watch to prevent any wavering. Acheson's initial interpretation of the Chinese offensive in Korea followed MacArthur's line, that it was long planned and not simply a response to the UN march toward the Yalu. The secretary of state wrote to Bevin on 28 November that China's action was "an openly aggressive move designed to destroy UN forces in North Korea." To put diplomatic pressure on China, the six-power resolution calling for its withdrawal from Korea should "receive urgent and favorable action" at Lake Success.[36] When the Soviet Union vetoed that resolution in the Security Council on 30 November, the State Department sought to take the matter before the General Assembly, perhaps even with an amendment labeling Communist China an aggressor. With the British and French opposing the latter option, U.S. diplomats decided momentarily to proceed with the original version of the six-power resolution.[37]

With military conditions deteriorating rapidly in Korea, this course represented little more than "a time-waster." The United States, President Truman and General Marshall believed, should concentrate on exploring possibilities for a cease-fire. Probes at the United Nations soon made it obvious that, in return for a cease-fire at the 38th parallel, Beijing wanted a U.S. withdrawal from Taiwan, admission to the United Nations, and perhaps concessions on the Japanese peace treaty.[38] Although Acheson warned colleagues that on the first two points the United States risked "having the whole world think we are wrong," the Pentagon rejected any thought of surrendering Taiwan to the Communists.[39]

Already under brutal attack in the domestic arena, aware that compromises with Beijing would only further undermine his position at home, and deeply fearful himself of revealing to the Communist world any softening of America's will, Acheson prepared to confront the British over an Asian conflict that threatened to tear apart the Western alliance.

## THE TRUMAN-ATTLEE MEETINGS

Prime Minister Attlee's trip to Washington and back to London via New York and Ottawa symbolized the end of the Bevin era in British foreign policy. Bevin would continue to hold the title of foreign secretary for three more months and would continue to assert himself on occasion, but he was too ill to fly or to carry out the day-to-day functions of policy formation and implementation. With Attlee's momentary emergence at the center of Britain's diplomacy, the Americans encountered a man who lacked strong personal or emotional connection with them. Acheson later described him as an able "but persistently depressing" man whose "thought impressed me as a long, withdrawing, melancholy sigh."[40] He had met Truman at Potsdam in 1945 and the two leaders had gotten on well. Attlee earned the president's trust over the next three years by refusing to break openly with the United States on such issues as atomic energy and Palestine.[41] Yet as a supporter but not the architect of the postwar Anglo-U.S. alliance, he could view the specifics of that relationship with a good deal more detachment than Bevin.

In Washington Attlee tried to maneuver the president into accepting the British point of view. Acheson quickly perceived the Briton's ploy and countered it.[42] As a result, the two sides had to agree to disagree on some issues, but they at least reached understanding of the other's positions; Attlee's probing questions strengthened the cause of restraint in the United States. Acheson sometimes came across to the British as the hard-liner on the U.S. side. Keenly aware of the bureaucratic and domestic political constraints placed on the Truman administration, he sought, first and foremost, to ensure that Attlee left Washington with an appreciation of the dangers posed to the Western alliance by any sharp Anglo-U.S. divergence on Asia.

Disagreement centered on the appropriate stance in possible talks with the Chinese and action in the event UN forces withdrew from Korea. These differences grew out of conflicting perceptions of China's motives in Korea and divergent political pressures in the United States and Great Britain. Attlee argued that China was acting partially out of fear for its security and that it wished to avoid total subservience to the Soviet Union. To encourage a Sino-Soviet split and to avoid getting bogged down in a military engagement in Asia, the United States should accept Beijing's admission to the United Nations and withdraw its protection of Taiwan in return for a settlement in Korea at the 38th parallel.

Acheson disagreed, insisting that Beijing was motivated by Communist ideology and was subservient to Moscow. For the moment the West must act as if the two Communist giants were one. Concessions to the Chinese for a settlement in Korea would encourage them to move elsewhere, undermine confidence in America's reliability in Japan and the Philippines, and confuse or outrage public opinion in the United States, which then would be less likely to support a buildup in Europe. The United States would accept negotiations for a cease-fire along the 38th parallel, he conceded, but would not attempt to initiate talks or make concessions elsewhere to end hostilities. If UN forces had to withdraw from Korea, Communist conquest of the peninsula should not be recognized. A variety of limited actions might be taken against the mainland, including bombing, a naval blockade, aid to anti-Communist guerrilla activity, and support for offensive operations by the Chinese Nationalists.

Attlee countered that such actions would have little impact on China, that the blockade actually might harm the West, and that bombing would provoke retaliation by the Soviet air force and probably escalate into a global war that NATO was not ready to fight. Direct action against China, the prime minister warned, would not be supported by either the United Nations or U.S. allies.[43]

The British made little headway on the issues of Taiwan and Chinese representation in the United Nations, but their arguments against limited war with China impressed Acheson and Marshall, and perhaps Truman as well. Far more than his predecessor, Franklin D. Roosevelt, and his eventual successor, Dwight D. Eisenhower, Truman depended on his top advisers in the area of foreign policy. Their advice on Korea during October and November had been deficient and now, in the midst of a dangerous crisis, some of them were flirting with ideas of immense potential consequence. Attlee's frontal challenge to these ideas exposed Truman to fresh thinking, dramatized to Acheson the political liabilities within the Western alliance and the United Nations of an expansion of the war, and encouraged Marshall to focus on the difficulties of limited military action against China.[44]

The Truman-Attlee talks ended on 8 December. The last meeting began with a report from General Collins, who had just returned from a visit to Korea and Japan. He stated that UN forces were "not in a critical condition" and that the possibility remained for a stand against the Communists somewhere south of Seoul. This estimate relieved some of the tension created by the prospect of an early withdrawal from the peninsula.[45]

The final communiqué of the conference reflected a broad range of Anglo-U.S. agreement, revealed continuing disagreement over Chinese representation in the United Nations, and masked differences in various areas.[46] On Korea, the allies expressed a willingness to end the fighting through negotiations. If the Chinese refused to accept a peaceful solution in Korea, it would be up to the United Nations "to decide how the principles of the Charter [could] . . . best be maintained." The Taiwan question also should be resolved peacefully and with UN involvement, but "in such a way as to safeguard the interests of the people of Formosa and the maintenance of peace and security in the Pacific." As to the atomic bomb, Attlee had wanted a commitment from Truman against its use without prior consultation with and even approval by London. When Acheson and others intervened to point to the storm that such a commitment would produce at home, not to mention the operational problems in an emergency, Attlee settled for a statement that Truman hoped "to keep the Prime Minister at all times informed of developments" that might lead to the weapon's use.[47] Finally, the communiqué expressed Anglo-U.S.

agreement on a rapid buildup of military capabilities, early completion of plans for integrated forces in Europe and appointment of a supreme commander for NATO, and cooperation in the dispensing of raw materials to provide for both "defense and essential civilian needs."[48]

Despite a spirit of cooperation, the pressures of divergent national capabilities and public attitudes and the complications interjected by the sentiments of other parties, especially the French and Germans, ensured that difficulties remained in strengthening the Western alliance. Still, the Attlee entourage could leave Washington feeling it had calmed U.S. officialdom, enhanced British prestige in Europe and the commonwealth, and bolstered the Labor government at home. The Truman administration, in turn, could breathe a sigh of relief that the Anglo-U.S. relationship remained solid and hope that the outcome of the talks would avert a panic in western Europe while conveying signals of firmness and solidarity to the Soviet Union and China.[49]

## Maneuvering at the United Nations

The period from 15 September to the first week in November represented the peak of optimism in the United States regarding the potential of the United Nations as an instrument of collective security. UN forces were on the offensive in Korea and, by the end of October, some nine thousand troops were in action from five nations other than the United States and South Korea. Another twenty-seven thousand men were either on their way to Korea or readying themselves to leave their home countries. Several other nations had offered units to and been accepted by the United Nations Command.[50] In early October the General Assembly passed, by an overwhelming majority, a resolution calling for action to unify the peninsula; a month later that body approved, by a similar vote, the "uniting for peace" resolution.

The Chinese counteroffensive ushered in a new period in the UN's effort to grapple with military conflict.[51] Combating China's seemingly endless supply of manpower represented a far different enterprise than repulsing 100,000 North Korean soldiers. The unease of several nations early in the fall with the impending UN march across the 38th parallel grew into a fear that World War III was just around the corner. Although the United States continued to wield great influence, it increasingly had to adjust its positions to accommodate potential supporters. Divisions within the non-Communist camp became all the more difficult to hide or control, as nations became more determined and better coordinated in their efforts to restrain the United States in Korea. In the process they strained the U.S. relationship with the international body and encouraged the Communist powers to pursue a tough line in Korea, but they also reduced prospects for global conflict.

Much of the initial activity at the United Nations in reaction to the Chinese offensive in Korea focused on the recently arrived delegation from Beijing. Wu Xiuquan proved elusive, rejecting an offer by the Yugoslav delegate Ales

Bebler to serve as mediator, then canceling appointments with Indian representative Sir Benegal Rau on 28 and 30 November.[52] The frustrated Indian diplomat told his U.S. colleague Warren Austin that he doubted the Chinese were "free agents." Britain's Gladwyn Jebb complained that the Chinese delegation was being shielded from contacts with the Western diplomats by Czech and Polish "bodyguards."[53] The Chinese became available only after the Soviet veto of the six-power resolution in the Security Council on 30 November and the impending shift of activity to the General Assembly.

During the first two weeks of December Wu and other members of the Chinese delegation met with Secretary-General Lie and numerous representatives of non-Communist governments. The Chinese clearly had strict instructions from home and regarded a settlement on Taiwan, and probably Beijing's admission to the United Nations, as prerequisites for any agreement on Korea. When on 4 December Zhou Enlai capped recent Chinese press statements with a dispatch demanding Communist Chinese participation in the preparation, drafting, and signing of a Japanese peace treaty, it appeared that a third condition might be added.[54] Lie pressed Wu to accept a cease-fire in Korea before gaining satisfaction on other issues, arguing that otherwise China held little chance for achieving its aims.[55] But in an after-dinner conversation at Lie's home on the 4th, Qiao Guanhua, a Wu assistant and to some observers the real power in the Chinese delegation, insisted that the Korean War could end only if the United States withdrew from the peninsula. He noted the "extreme bitterness" of the Chinese people against the United States for its intervention on Jiang's side in the civil war.[56] Jebb spoke bluntly to Wu and Qiao at a luncheon meeting on the following day. China might be able to push UN forces out of Korea, but it would forfeit any chance of securing Taiwan or gaining entry into the United Nations. It also would face economic and possibly military retaliation by the West.[57]

Coinciding with the effort to engage the Chinese in New York, Rau labored to bring together Arab and Asian nations to pressure the Chinese and the Americans to accept a compromise peace. On 5 December representatives of thirteen countries in New York finally appealed to the Chinese and North Koreans to declare that they would not cross the 38th parallel.[58] These representatives proceeded to devise a plan that they hoped would bring a halt to the dangerous course of events in Asia.

Meanwhile, Nehru was at work in New Delhi. On 30 November Canadian Foreign Minister Lester Pearson approached the Indian prime minister. As "the most influential leader of Asian opinion" and a person who "command[ed] a great fund of good will in western countries," Pearson wrote, Nehru stood "more chance of being heard above the frightening clamour than . . . anyone else in the world today." Pearson suggested that Nehru make a public appeal for a cease-fire and an end to Chinese military intervention in Korea so as to explore "the possibilities of a settlement in which the Government in Beijing could participate."[59] Although Nehru declined to make an overt move, he contacted Attlee on the eve of his departure for the United

States and outlined his views, obviously hoping to influence the upcoming deliberations in Washington.[60] Four-power talks—with the United States, Great Britain, the Soviet Union, and Communist China participating—stood the best chance of producing a settlement, Nehru thought. The first step was to arrange a cease-fire in Korea and establish a demilitarized zone. Then it was essential to admit Communist China to the United Nations and resolve the Taiwan issue in accordance with the Cairo declaration. Nehru also conveyed these appeals to the U.S. government.[61]

On his second day in Washington Attlee wired Nehru encouraging him to propose a cease-fire. The United States would not make the first move, but it would support such an initiative. The British prime minister insisted that U.S. leaders were facing the situation "coolly and calmly" despite severe domestic political pressures.[62] Thus on the 8th Nehru sent Panikkar instructions for an anticipated interview with Zhou Enlai. As before, Nehru saw a cease-fire and a demilitarized zone near the 38th parallel as a crucial step toward broader negotiations, first about the future of Korea, then on the Taiwan issue, and finally regarding China's seat in the United Nations. He wanted his ambassador to caution Zhou against taking a belligerent stand regarding the withdrawal of UN troops from Korea, as this would merely reduce prospects for the achievement of other aims.[63]

Back in New York, the United States sought to push the six-power resolution through the General Assembly. The Americans saw the measure as a means of applying political pressure on the Chinese and of maintaining the prestige and credibility of the United Nations. Yet many others feared that it would further alienate the Chinese and that it represented merely a prelude to U.S. pressure for a resolution condemning China as an aggressor.[64] Despite these reservations, on 7 December, over heated objections from the Communist bloc, the First Committee revised its agenda to place the issue of China's intervention in Korea ahead of the Soviet complaint of U.S. aggression against China.[65]

The Chinese position now appeared to soften, and the efforts of the Arab-Asian group returned temporarily to the forefront. A possible shift in Beijing's stance came on the 7th when Qiao asked M. Gopala Menon of the Indian delegation about the Arab-Asian call for China and North Korea to halt its troops at the 38th parallel. If his government complied, Qiao inquired, what assurance would it have that UN forces would not recross the boundary at a later date?[66] After consulting with U.S. delegates, Rau told Wu, early on the 9th, that he believed the United States was genuinely interested in a cease-fire, a demilitarized zone, and "further negotiations." Wu indicated that Beijing felt the same way, but emphasized that passage of the six-power resolution would "not facilitate matters."[67]

Encouraged, Rau turned to drafting a resolution that would provide for negotiations, satisfy the United States and China, and at least postpone the U.S. push for the six-power resolution. The second of these goals proved the most intractable. In the process of accommodating Washington, he eventually presented two resolutions rather than one, and both were sufficiently watered down to make Chinese acceptance unlikely. The first stated that the president of the General Assembly should "constitute a group of three persons including himself to determine the basis on which a satisfactory cease-fire in Korea can be arranged." The second draft resolution asked that governments unnamed, but clearly including Communist China, "meet . . . and make recommendations for the peaceful settlement of existing issues."[68]

Rau presented these drafts to the First Committee on the 12th. For the first resolution he had twelve cosponsors, which included all those who had participated in the earlier call for the Chinese and the North Koreans to halt at the 38th parallel. The second resolution had identical cosponsors, with the exception of the Philippines, whose government stood at a pivotal stage in talks with Washington on economic and military assistance and thus was susceptible to U.S. arm-twisting. Rau easily persuaded all but the Soviet bloc to give the thirteen-power resolution priority for consideration over a previously submitted Soviet draft calling for the withdrawal of foreign forces from Korea.[69]

This proved a pyrrhic victory. While negotiating with the Americans and his Arab-Asian colleagues, Rau lost touch with the Chinese and the Soviets.[70] His instructions from New Delhi were to avoid proposing any resolutions that did not have the backing of all the major powers.[71] In fact, the Soviet Union strongly opposed the thirteen-power resolution all the way through the First Committee and the General Assembly, which passed the measure on 14 December. Soviet delegate Jacob Malik protested heatedly that the resolution could only be aimed at providing MacArthur's forces with "a breathing spell . . . to regroup and later to attack" Communist troops in Korea.[72] As a result of U.S. objections, the twelve-power resolution, which offered the only inducement to the Chinese to negotiate, was buried in the First Committee.[73] In his haste to mediate, Rau had overestimated his own capacity and that of his colleagues in the Arab-Asian bloc and the commonwealth to influence the principals in Korea.

When the thirteen-power resolution passed, President Entezam of the General Assembly appointed Rau and Pearson to join him on the cease-fire committee. Rau was aware, both from talks in New York and recent reports from Beijing via New Delhi, that prospects for productive talks were nil without a U.S. concession regarding Taiwan; thus he pressed the Truman administration to announce that its stated policy of late August, namely that the Seventh Fleet would protect the island only for the duration of the conflict in Korea, still applied.[74] However, the Americans refused to budge. With the General Assembly in recess after several postponements of discussion on the Taiwan issue, Wu informed Lie on the 15th that the Chinese delegation intended to return home. Despite efforts by Lie and Rau, the Chinese refused to meet with the committee and left the United States on the 19th. The committee contacted Zhou Enlai requesting entry into China, but was rebuffed.[75] On 22 December Zhou released a statement condemning the thirteen-power resolution as illegal, demanding the withdrawal of foreign troops from Korea, and characterizing the cease-fire proposal as a devious U.S. ploy to secure time to regroup its forces for renewed aggression. The Arab and Asian nations had a genuine desire for peace, but they had disregarded the U.S. "intrigue" in seeking "a cease-fire first and negotiations afterward."[76]

Although efforts to bring peace in Korea failed, they were of some use. First, they delayed action on the six-power resolution, the passage of which would have further dimmed prospects for Sino-U.S. talks on Korea and would have encouraged the United States to press for UN condemnation of China and perhaps even sanctions against the PRC. Without an early settlement in Korea, such pressure would develop anyway, but postponing the day of reckoning remained for non-Communist nations the best method of preventing an expanded conflict while averting an open break with Washington. Diplomatic pressure also solidified the Truman administration's inclination to accept a cease-fire along the 38th parallel. On the 15th Acheson authorized the U.S. delegation at the United Nations to communicate to the cease-fire group "a generalized statement of conditions" for an end to the fighting in Korea. The statement provided for establishment of "a demilitarized area across all of Korea approx[imately] 20 miles in width with the southern limit following generally the line of the 38th parallel."[77] The Truman administration had been exploring the possibility of such a settlement since the beginning of the month. Its formal expression to the cease-fire group diminished prospects that the United States would again submit to temptation should the military balance on the peninsula change in its favor.

Finally, pressures from the Arab-Asian group and U.S. allies produced some flexibility in the State Department regarding talks on Asian issues. Acheson avoided a firm position on the scope of any negotiations with the Chinese, but he conceded that such negotiations did not have to concern Korea alone so long as Korea came first and was not connected with other matters. To Canada's Pearson, the new U.S. attitude "offer[ed] some hope of a settlement, or at least of a prolonged debate."[78]

By late December, however, Chinese and North Korean troops stood poised to move en masse across the 38th parallel. When Washington sent feelers to Beijing via Stockholm expressing a willingness to discuss a cease-fire in Korea and, after such was achieved, broader issues on Asia and the western Pacific, the reply was not encouraging.[79] Given the widespread impatience in the United States with a course of restraint, a Communist offensive into South Korea promised to compound difficulties in the quest to limit the war.

## The Perspectives from Beijing, Moscow, and Pyongyang

The three Communist governments involved in Korea had varying perspectives on the Chinese counteroffensive of late November. North Korea sought nothing short of total victory over UN forces, while China and the Soviet Union were more flexible. Just like the Rhee regime in the South during the previous summer, the Kim government had a local view of the conflict, hoping that the intervention of outside forces in its favor would eventually produce national unification under its auspices. Beijing had at least a regional perspective on events in Korea, and Moscow evaluated them in a global context. The two powers agreed on one goal: to prevent the occupation and unification of Korea by hostile forces. From early on in his consideration of intervention in Korea, Mao had gone further, thinking in terms of expelling UN forces from the peninsula; but his indecision regarding tactics during October and early November suggests that pursuit of this objective depended on how battlefield conditions developed.[80] Thus he went through a process regarding the crossing of the 38th parallel in ways similar to that in the United States from July to mid-September. Stalin probably agreed with his Chinese counterpart. Both men hoped they could use the evolving situation in Korea to advance their interests elsewhere, yet the precise nature of those interests sometimes diverged. They agreed that each should play an integral role in shaping any peace treaty with Japan. For China, however, liberating Taiwan was nearly as basic as protecting the Manchurian boundary, and entry into the United Nations was not far behind; the Soviet Union had ambivalent feelings about both these aims. Stalin remained more concerned about the impact of the Korean conflict on the balance of forces along his western periphery, from Scandinavia in the north to the Balkans and Asia minor in the south. Despite the differences here, the course of battle in Korea and the disarray in the West combined to make the maintenance of unity a relatively simple task.

The key decision facing China during the early weeks of its counteroffensive in Korea, which Beijing referred to as its second campaign, was identical to that confronting the United States in the aftermath of Inchon: should its ground forces cross the 38th parallel? As the Americans had done earlier, the Chinese were inclined to answer the question in the affirmative. Pressure from North Korea, the rapid retreat of enemy forces, and events at the United Nations joined to encourage Mao in an aggressive strategy. Kim Il-sung wasted little time before lobbying in Beijing for total military victory on the peninsula. He arrived in the Chinese capital on 3 December and, in a meeting with Mao, Zhou, and Gao Gang, he urged his hosts "not [to] give the enemy a breathing time." Chinese and North Korean forces should seize Pyongyang and Seoul and then press on to push UN forces out of the country. When confronted with expressions of concern about supply problems for Chinese troops, he gave assurances that his subordinates had already been instructed to provide full assistance in this area. He also stated that his reorganized army would be put entirely under the authority of the Chinese People's Volunteers. The next day Mao wired his commanders in the field that the PRC "would negotiate only when the enemy agrees to withdraw from Korea and first to withdraw back to south of the 38th parallel. It is most advantageous that we ... seize Pyongyang [and] Seoul and we will mainly aim at eliminating the enemy [strength] and first of all wipe out the ROK forces. [In doing so] we will be in a stronger position to compel United States imperialists to withdraw from Korea." Mao hoped the war could be won quickly, but he warned that it might be protracted: "We are prepared to fight for at least one year."[81]

Mao's inclination to advance rapidly in Korea strengthened when his forces captured Pyongyang on the 6th and he received a report several days later of an estimate of the situation in Korea by a leading American. On 11 December he wired General Peng that U.S. Army Chief of Staff Collins believed, after a recent trip to Japan and Korea, that "given the current speed and scope of the Chinese and North Korean attack, and given the great losses of the Americans in troops and equipment, as well as low morale," the United States could not "put up a long term defense" on the peninsula.[82] In fact, Collins, if not MacArthur, was more optimistic than the report indicated, but it was consistent with Western press releases coming out of Korea and Japan. Clearly it encouraged Mao to push the Chinese army forward.

Two days later Mao, in his typically hands-on approach to managing the war effort, informed Peng that the United States and its allies were demanding that China halt its forces at the 38th parallel. This represented an attempt "to gain time to regroup their army." If China permitted such a development, it would "be greatly disadvantageous" politically, as it would confer an undesirable legitimacy on the 38th parallel as a political boundary. Thus Peng must advance his troops across the old boundary as rapidly as possible.[83] Despite reports from his generals at the battlefront that Chinese soldiers were exhausted and short of equipment, and ignoring the recommendation of Acting Army Chief of Staff Nie Rongzhen that the CPV halt its moves southward for two months, Mao insisted on continuing the offensive.[84] He recognized, nonetheless, that the fighting was likely to continue for an extended period and that the CPV must be reinforced in manpower and constantly resupplied.[85] Like the United States during the previous summer and fall, China feared the long-term consequences of any failure to exploit a battlefield advantage, but it was the civilian leader at home, unencumbered by an opposition party and confident of his own military judgment, not the commander on the scene, who took the lead in pressing the troops forward.

From the beginning of the counteroffensive in Korea, the Chinese media maintained a confident and belligerent tone.[86] During the second week of December the Chinese press became increasingly explicit regarding aims in Korea. On the 8th a Beijing radio station carried excerpts from a recent speech by Lee Joo Yun, the North Korean ambassador in China, claiming that Chinese and Korean troops would not halt their advance until "the day of driving all invaders from Korea."[87] The New China News Agency reproduced in full Kim Il-sung's recent address celebrating the liberation of Pyongyang. "Final victory" lay ahead, Kim declared, but "we must not allow the enemy any breathing space, the chance to build new lines of defense and the chance to reorganize its troops." "Our heroic People's Army must make swifter attacks," Kim concluded, and "the guerrillas must carry out more activities south of the 38th parallel . . . so that not a single enemy can escape."[88] The New China News Agency followed this report by publishing a message of

General Lin Biao and commanders of the Chinese People's Volunteers calling on their troops "to advance heroically in order to bring about the total annihilation of the imperialist invaders in Korea and in order to help the Korean people to build an independent and united Korea."[89] A *Renmin ribao* (People's daily) editorial on the 17th accused the United States of trying to use negotiations "to get a breathing spell" on the battlefield and rejected the idea of permitting "foreign aggressors" to remain in Korea.[90] Finally, in a statement broadcast by the New China News Agency on 22 December, Foreign Minister Zhou Enlai opined that, when U.S. troops crossed the 38th parallel back in October, "the United States Government . . . obliterated forever this demarcation line of political geography."[91] Beijing clearly had chosen the same course in Korea as had the United States during the previous fall, but PRC leaders did not anticipate as early and as easy a victory as had the Americans before them.

Soviet propaganda followed a pattern similar to that of the Chinese. The U.S. embassy in Moscow characterized the tone of the Soviet press as one of "exuberance and warning."[92] The exuberance derived from the beliefs that the United States was "confused, uncertain, and disheartened," that its allies distrusted U.S. leadership, and that U.S. military power was "threadbare." The Soviet press continued to warn against German rearmament, alleging that the United States was trying to make Germany and perhaps all of western Europe into another Korea.[93] On Korea, *Pravda* hinted that the Soviet Union would become involved in the fighting if the conflict expanded to the Chinese mainland.[94] In the middle of the month, both *Pravda* and *Izvestiia* followed the Chinese lead in publishing Kim Il-sung's fiery speech of the 8th, and *Pravda* and *New Times* stopped accentuating the 38th parallel in their maps of Korea.[95] After President Truman declared a national emergency in the United States on the 15th, a *Pravda* editorial implied that growing tensions abroad would require the establishment of new economic priorities at home.[96]

Rumors at the United Nations had the Soviets trying to restrain the Chinese, but no concrete evidence ever emerged to support that theory. None of the palpable Soviets hints about negotiations that had appeared early the previous fall recurred. The closest gesture to a Soviet move toward peace in Korea was a statement by Jacob Malik at the United Nations on 13 December that the Communist proposal for a withdrawal of all foreign troops from the peninsula included those from China.[97] Given China's dependence on the Soviet Union for heavy equipment should a prolonged war develop—and ultimately on more direct Soviet assistance should it expand on a major scale to the mainland—Beijing was not in a position to disregard pressure for restraint from Moscow, had it existed.

Despite the denial of Soviet and Chinese military doctrine that the atomic bomb was a decisive weapon, and the Chinese emphasis on superior manpower, well led and motivated, to overcome modern arms, neither of the Communist powers could ignore the prospect that the fighting would escalate beyond Korea. Their domestic propaganda alone reveals a sensitivity to the fears of their own populations of a direct conflict with the United States. After Truman's 30 November statement on the atomic bomb, references to possible American use of that weapon diminished in the Chinese and Soviet press.[98] In Manchuria, the construction of air raid shelters, the removal of certain industrial facilities, the augmentation of Soviet air power, and even the influx of Soviet ground forces indicate that Moscow and Beijing actively prepared to counter any U.S. thrust beyond the Yalu.[99] Yet the use of Chinese rather than Soviet troops in Korea, as well as the refusal of the Communists to make full use of their air power against UN ground units on enemy bases in Korea and Japan, indicate a desire to avoid extending the conflict beyond the peninsula.

As December progressed the Soviets and Chinese took comfort in divisions appearing within the United States. Although some sentiment in the United States favored all-out war against China, and Truman himself had declared a national emergency, pushed through Congress new military appropriations, froze Chinese assets in the United States, appointed General Dwight D. Eisenhower the first supreme commander of allied forces in Europe, and announced that additional U.S. troops would be sent to that continent as soon as possible, another segment of opinion leaned toward a "Fortress America" strategy. Such views gained prominent expression in speeches on the 12th by Joseph P. Kennedy, a former ambassador to Great Britain, and on the 20th by former president Herbert Hoover. Kennedy labeled current U.S. foreign policy "suicidal" and called for a withdrawal from Korea and Europe in favor of concentrating on defense of the western hemisphere.[100] Hoover advocated an offshore island strategy in the western Pacific and Europe and, like Kennedy, an emphasis on hemispheric defense.[101] Despite the extensive criticism leveled at such ideas throughout the United States, they also generated considerable support.[102] The internationalist editors of the *New York Times* worried that Hoover's address would "give new impetus to neo-isolationist tendencies in Congress and the country."[103]

The Soviet and Chinese presses harped on the Kennedy and Hoover speeches. On the 17th all major Soviet newspapers carried a large portion of Kennedy's remarks, and a week later *Pravda* reproduced Hoover's talk in full. A *Pravda* editorial chortled that the themes advanced by Kennedy and Hoover demonstrated the failure of Truman's drive to mobilize public opinion behind his aggressive policy.[104] On the 27th in Beijing *Renmin ribao* published an editorial entitled "American Ruling Class Is Confused and Split."[105] Both the Soviet and Chinese media emphasized the impact of Hoover's and Kennedy's assertions on European opinion, which already worried over America's commitment to the continent.[106] These claims aimed partly at reassuring nervous domestic audiences, yet they jibed neatly with the actions and attitudes of the Communist powers in the international arena. The Marxist-Leninist perspective of the government leaders inclined them to stress divisions among capitalist nations, and the traditional authoritarianism of their cultures made it difficult to measure the weight of dissenting opinion in liberal societies.[107]

That said, much cause existed for optimism in the Communist camp. Dissension within and between capitalist nations reached new heights in the midst of the Chinese counteroffensive in Korea, and there was no telling when it would peak. In western Europe, divisions regarding West German rearmament grew by leaps and bounds, with the intricate blend of Soviet scare tactics and hints of prospects for ending Europe's division playing a key role. The Prague meeting of Eastern bloc leaders in late October and the Soviet call for a four-power conference of foreign ministers on Germany early the next month had a noticeable impact on public opinion in western Europe. This development, in turn, encouraged West German Chancellor Konrad Adenauer, who favored rearmament but faced much popular opposition, to push for more concessions regarding his government's authority in relation to the occupying powers. With Great Britain and France already dubious about permitting West Germany to rearm, such pressure could hardly smooth the way to early agreement.[108]

To Stalin, the most disturbing trend probably existed in the Balkans and Asia minor, where Greece and Turkey continued to move toward integration into the Western alliance, and Yugoslavia drew increasingly closer to normalizing its relations with non-Communist neighbors and solidifying its ties with the United States.

Even so, conditions within Yugoslavia and Greece were shaky, and countervailing developments nearby augured well for Soviet interests. Widespread famine threatened Yugoslavia and made it difficult for Yugoslav Prime Minister Tito to feed his army.[109] Political and economic stability in Greece remained tenuous, in part because of long-standing government policies and in part because of financial pressures deriving from a military buildup after the outbreak of war in Korea.[110] The Cominform even engaged in a war of nerves against the two countries, which produced substantial concern in the West.[111] Indeed, since 1949, major military buildups had occurred in the Hungarian, Bulgarian, and Rumanian armed forces, and these processes were directed primarily against Yugoslavia. In January 1951 the Soviets organized war games in Budapest, their stated purpose being to prepare for a coordinated military invasion of Yugoslavia.[112]

It remains unlikely that Stalin ever verged on implementing such plans, especially after June 1950, yet threatening tactics against Yugoslavia and Greece could produce countermeasures that would disrupt their economies. Such tactics could also serve as a warning to the United States of the vulnerability of Europe's "soft underbelly," thus deterring Washington from expanding the conflict in northeast Asia. Middle Eastern nations and Italy needed little reminder of their vulnerability. People there lost much confidence in U.S. military prowess with the rapid retreat of UN troops in Korea.[113] By the time of this retreat, Iran already had concluded a trade agreement with the Soviet Union and cut off Voice of America and British Broadcasting Company transmissions into the country.[114] Only Turkey combined a stable home front with a firm pro-U.S. foreign policy, and the Soviets adapted to this unique circumstance with a measure of détente, permitting Sophia to resolve a dispute over the disposition of Turkish refugees in Bulgaria.[115]

Overall, prospects for chaos or neutralism appeared at least as favorable as for stability or a hostile alliance on the southwestern periphery of the Soviet Union. Total military defeat for the United Nations in Korea could only magnify concern throughout Europe and Asia about the prudence of aligning with the United States in the cold war, and it would prevent the United States from claiming that it had achieved its initial objective of saving the southern half of the peninsula.

The irony of international events of late 1950 is that, temporarily, allied pressure on the United States both discouraged Washington from expanding the war in Korea and encouraged Beijing and Moscow to pursue it below the 38th parallel; the offensive into South Korea, in turn, intensified pressure in the United States to widen the conflict. During the first month of the new year, therefore, the world stood closer to Armageddon than at any moment since 1945. Events on the battlefield in Korea and in the UN General Assembly at Lake Success would do much to determine whether the United States would step back from the brink or plunge headlong into the abyss.

## Anglo-U.S. Tensions

Recent events in Asia and Europe frightened British Minister of War John Strachey. Chinese and North Korean troops had crossed the 38th parallel on their way to what appeared to be total victory over UN forces. In such circumstances, the Americans seemed determined to carry the war into China. In Europe, the United States pressed for the early rearmament of West Germany, before NATO countries closed the gap between their own military strength and that of the Eastern bloc. Soviet propaganda hinted ominously that the Kremlin would not tolerate a West German army. If the United States had its way in the current crisis, Strachey wrote to Foreign Minister Ernest Bevin on the second day of the new year, general war probably would occur within the next two years. Although the United States eventually might prevail, the conflict would "almost certainly [be] fatal [to Great Britain], in the most literal sense of the term." In a third world war, the Soviet Union would occupy Europe to the English channel and, even without nuclear weapons, "would render the whole southern and south-western parts of Britain, including London, uninhabitable or at least 'unworkable.'" The Attlee government had two choices: it could follow the United States into a war with China, thus risking a Soviet military offensive in the West, or it could "move independently in [the] UN organization and elsewhere." To Strachey, the only sane choice was the latter. Whatever its drawbacks, the alternative meant self-destruction.[116]

Strachey's memorandum gained wide circulation at the cabinet and subcabinet levels.[117] Bevin thought its analysis overdrawn, yet to Kenneth Younger, the minister of state at the Foreign Office and an increasingly influential voice given his boss's illness, much of it made sense. Younger was less alarmed than Strachey over Germany, as he believed correctly that U.S. allies had persuaded Washington to retreat from its earlier insistence that West German rearmament proceed simultaneously with a U.S. buildup in Europe. However, with the United States pressing for a UN resolution condemning China as an aggressor and calling for sanctions against her, Korea was another matter. In Bevin's presence, Younger urged Attlee to oppose the U.S. push for a limited war against China. When Bevin "wailed almost tearfully that this . . . [would mean] the end of the U.S./U.K. alliance," Younger wrote in his diary, "the prime minister pulled him up rather sharply." Although Attlee refused to inform Truman that Britain would resist sanctions against China, he instructed Ambassador Franks to warn Acheson that British support for a UN resolution condemning China could not be assumed.[118] Even Bevin favored pressure on the United States. He supported the UN cease-fire group's proposal for an approach to Beijing on Korea and other Far Eastern problems, and he believed that the establishment of a unified position at the upcoming meeting of commonwealth prime ministers in London could influence American public opinion.[119]

The British had reason to worry. The Communist New Year's offensive in Korea occurred in the midst of heightened pressure on the Truman administration from Tokyo and at home for direct action against China. MacArthur had pressed for some time for moves beyond Korea. After failing to convince Washington in mid-December to immediately reinforce the Korean theater, the UN commander intensified his promotion of what his leading biographer labels a "false dilemma."[120] The United States could "blockade the coast of China," "destroy by naval gunfire and air bombardment China's industrial capacity to wage war," and use Jiang Jieshi's forces in Korea "for diversionary action" against the mainland; or, the United States could continue its present course in Korea, resulting in either a forced evacuation of the peninsula or the total destruction of U.S. and allied ground forces fighting there.

MacArthur left little doubt as to the preferred method of resolving the dilemma. With China fully committed in Korea, the United States could do nothing to "further aggravate" Sino-U.S. relations. MacArthur believed that "a Soviet decision to precipitate a general war [probably] would depend solely upon its own estimate of relative strengths and capabilities" rather than on U.S. action outside Korea. Furthermore, a forced evacuation of Korea without direct military action against China "would have the most adverse effect upon the people of Asia," would require "a material reinforcement of the forces now in this theater" in order to hold the offshore island chain, and "would at once release the bulk of the Chinese forces now [in Korea] . . . for action elsewhere." "I understand thoroughly the demand for European security," he claimed, "and [I] fully concur in doing everything possible in that sector but not to the point of accepting defeat anywhere else—an acceptance which I am sure could not fail to insure later defeat in Europe itself."[121]

On 3 January 1951 Admiral Forrest Sherman, the chief of naval operations, proposed measures to the Joint Chiefs that bore similarities to MacArthur's. Sherman wanted to reexamine present limitations on operations related to Korea, keeping in mind only the need to avert hostilities with the Soviet Union until the United States was more fully armed. "As soon as our position in Korea is stabilized, or when we have evacuated Korea," the United States should institute a naval blockade of China. Air and naval attacks on the mainland should occur only if the Chinese Communists attacked U.S. forces beyond Korea. For now, the United States should remove restrictions on Nationalist Chinese operations against the mainland, provide logistic support to anti-Communist guerrillas there, and initiate periodic aerial reconnaissance over Manchuria and along the China coast. If the United Nations refused to support these measures, Washington should act unilaterally.[122] Nine days later, in the midst of another testy exchange with Tokyo, the Joint Chiefs "tentatively agreed" to Sherman's proposals, and Secretary of Defense Marshall placed them on the agenda of the National Security Council meeting scheduled for the 17th. The military leaders also wanted to "press now for UN action branding Communist China an aggressor."[123]

Top administration officials debated these proposals with great earnestness when the National Security Council met with the president on 17 January. Acheson questioned the effectiveness of a naval blockade and Chinese Nationalist action on the mainland and expressed fear of their impact on America's Europe-first strategy. Marshall and Bradley countered by emphasizing the mounting pressure in the United States to retaliate against China. The secretary of defense insisted that the United States give top priority to its own interests, not those of the United Nations or Great Britain. Robert J. Strong, representing the National Security Resources Board, chimed in that a naval blockade would reap havoc on China's internal communications and place "a heavy burden and drain" on the Soviet Union. Confronted with sharp divisions among his leading advisers, Truman postponed a decision, directing the Joint Chiefs to prepare an assessment of the likely military impact of Chinese Nationalist action against the mainland. The State Department was to analyze the political implications of such a course.[124]

London officialdom was well aware of MacArthur's proclivities, of the pessimism of the Joint Chiefs about the prospects of holding fast in Korea, and of the intense pressure in the United States for action against China. Throughout January the British labored furiously to restrain the United States, moving on several interrelated fronts. In bilateral relations, they pressed the Americans for a determined effort to stay in Korea. Ambassador Franks wrote from Washington that "it would be much easier to get the Americans to think and act sensibly . . . when the ability of UN forces to defend a position successfully has been demonstrated."[125] The reverse also was true, and London was receiving disturbing reports from Tokyo. On 31 December Sir Alvary Gascoigne, the British political representative in Japan, expressed concern about UN authorities "continually and actively publicizing their views" of the supposedly "vast and increasing numerical superiority of Communist Chinese formations poised for an attack" into South Korea. Gascoigne doubted the accuracy of such estimates. He believed they had a destructive impact on the morale of UN troops and derived from the need for an alibi in the event of defeat.[126] Dispatches during the early days of the Communist New Year's offensive implied that the UN retreat southward was a good deal more rapid than necessary.[127] On the 8th Prime Minister Attlee wrote to President Truman, reminding him that an understanding had been reached at their December meetings that "we should fight it out in Korea and try to localize the conflict." Attlee requested "an authoritative indication of the intentions of the United States Government in this respect."[128]

British prodding merely reinforced the Truman administration in its policy to hold fast in Korea. Acheson never wavered on this point; neither did Rusk. Not so the Joint Chiefs of Staff, whose concern about defending Japan made them wary of the dangers of withdrawing UN forces from Korea with the Chinese hot in pursuit. If defeat in Korea was inevitable without either expanding the war or reinforcing UN units, a withdrawal from the peninsula before Communist armies pressed down on the old Pusan perimeter seemed prudent to ensure that U.S. divisions arrived intact in Japan.[129] When the Joint Chiefs met with Lord Tedder on the 12th, they gave the impression that they wanted out of Korea.[130]

In reality, the tide of sentiment was about to turn, once and for all, in favor of a determined stand. The president already had before him a draft message to MacArthur outlining the political advantages of staying in Korea.[131] Generals Collins and Vandenberg were about to depart from Washington to examine conditions on the peninsula. The disparity between General Ridgway's reports from the front and MacArthur's from Tokyo (combined perhaps with British admonitions) had produced doubts about the gloomy estimates of the UN commander.[132] In Korea Collins and Vandenberg found the "Eighth Army in good shape and improving daily under Ridgway's leadership." After reviewing the situation with the Tokyo command, the visitors from the Joint Chiefs received MacArthur's assurance that his forces "could hold a beachhead in Korea indefinitely."[133] By the 19th U.S. leaders recognized that no dilemma existed between total withdrawal and expanding the war.

## Delay in Condemning China

The issue of expanding the war remained a divisive one in Anglo-U.S. relations, as the United States continued its campaign in the UN General Assembly for a resolution condemning China as an aggressor. Acheson had told Bevin on the 5th that he regarded the measure as essential. A failure to act would "be the beginning of the end of the UN just as the end of the League of Nations started with their [sic] failure to take any action against Japan and Italy in similar circumstances." Perhaps more important, public opinion at home indicated that "a failure of the UN to recognize this aggression would create a wave of isolationism in this country which would jeopardize all that we are trying to do with and for the Atlantic Pact countries."[134] The British feared that passage of such a resolution would represent the initial step in a U.S. drive for sanctions against China. Acheson's analogy to the 1930s was hardly reassuring, given that the League had passed high-sounding resolutions against Japan and Italy only to see them fail for lack of an effective follow-up. In resisting U.S. pressure, London combined direct appeals to Washington with maneuvering among commonwealth governments and at the General Assembly. In doing so, the Attlee regime tested the durability of the Atlantic alliance and demonstrated vividly the broad international dimensions of the Korean conflict.

Great Britain was not alone in its doubts about a resolution to condemn China. During December 1950 the United States had made its intention clear to press for such a measure should Chinese troops cross the 38th parallel. Canada's Lester Pearson regarded such a resolution as advisable only after exhausting all possibilities for a negotiated settlement. In the last days of 1950, when the U.S. State Department commenced pressure on the Canadians and the British for support in condemning China, London and Ottawa prepared a delaying action.[135]

They had plenty of company. When on 3 January Ambassador Austin met with fellow cosponsors of the six-power resolution, which the Soviets had vetoed in the Security Council, he found little support for early passage of an aggressor resolution. His colleagues believed, however, that members of the Arab-Asian group, with the exception of Indonesia and India, eventually might go along with it; they reasoned that if the United Nations first approached China with the principles for a Korean settlement that the cease-fire group was then formulating, and if, after a reasonable period, Beijing made no reply, then a resolution condemning China might be more acceptable. The next day, with Austin's report on the January 3 meeting before him, Acheson concluded that, so long as the proposed principles with which to approach Beijing proved acceptable, the United States should support "the intermediate step."[136]

U.S. allies and the Arab-Asian group now faced the task of formulating principles that would be favorably received in both Washington and Beijing. The complicated dynamics of personal and government interaction at Lake Success, and between Lake Success and London, where the commonwealth prime ministers convened on 4 January, produced much confusion and revealed poignantly the impossibility of isolating events in Korea from a range of other issues. The most important result of the process was to delay consideration of a resolution condemning China until the time of greatest danger to UN forces on the peninsula had passed.

When the First Committee of the General Assembly reconvened on 3 January, the cease-fire group had not yet agreed on principles for a settlement in Korea. Indian delegate Benegal Rau refused to support an initiative without first gaining clearance from Prime Minister Nehru, who was flying to London.[137] Once there, Nehru discovered it would take time to reach unanimity among his commonwealth colleagues. A variety of factors blocked consensus. Australia and New Zealand feared that splitting with the Americans on Korea would impair their goal of a defense pact with the United States. Canada and Great Britain did not want to compromise their alliance relationships with the United States. Though Pakistan and India were new Asian nations determined to protect their independence in relations with the great powers, religious animosities between their peoples combined with territorial proximity to limit their cooperation with each other. The most promising method for the prime ministers to hide their differences while avoiding a split with the United States was to delay UN consideration of a resolution condemning China. On the 5th they wired New York requesting a week's postponement in their consideration of the principles.[138] Jebb, Australian delegate K.C.O. Shann, and Pearson thought the maneuver "clumsy and high-handed."[139] Yet Washington proved tolerant.

In London Nehru lobbied for measures that the Chinese might accept, while the other prime ministers tried to accommodate him without endangering a break with the United States. The ministers concentrated on the five principles circulated privately by the cease-fire group. These included a cease-fire; a staged withdrawal of foreign forces from Korea; UN administration of the peninsula until the General Assembly established machinery for elections to form a national government; and creation by the General Assembly of "an appropriate body," including representatives of the Soviet, U.S., Communist Chinese, and British governments, to discuss "a settlement for issues affecting the Far East."[140] Nehru thought the Chinese would reject a dominant UN role in administering and unifying Korea and, as central issues in any conference on regional matters, would want explicit reference to Taiwan and Chinese representation in the United Nations, as well as mention of the Cairo declaration of 1943.[141] On the 8th the ministers received word from Indian Ambassador Panikkar in Beijing that his hosts would not consider a settlement in Korea separately from one on Taiwan. With that, Bevin offered a plan that eliminated a cease-fire as a precondition for talks.[142]

Pearson reacted with "surprise and consternation" to the plan, informing Canadian Prime Minister Louis St. Laurent in London that there was not "a chance in the world" the United States would go along. In Washington Acheson quickly confirmed this point, but he agreed to consider a revision of the principles circulated earlier by the cease-fire group so long as India cosponsored them. The prime ministers returned to a modified version of those principles.[143]

By midday on the 11th Nehru had agreed on a statement of principles, and the United States had consented to support these measures in the First Committee. The statement finessed the issue of UN involvement in the peacemaking and unification process in Korea. Although the last principle did not mention the Cairo declaration, it stated that four-power discussions on problems after agreement on a cease-fire should seek settlements "in conformity with existing international obligations" and should cover Taiwan and Chinese representation in the international organization.[144] When the First Committee considered the principles that afternoon, Rau announced that India considered the wording to mean that the Taiwan issue would be resolved on the basis of the Cairo declaration.[145]

All that remained was to guide the principles through the First Committee and present them to Beijing. These apparently simple tasks turned the First Committee into a veritable circus. First some Arab and Asian cosponsors of the draft twelve-power resolution of the previous month expressed resentment that the statement of principles was taking priority over their own handiwork. Then, when Israeli Abba Eban stepped forward with a draft resolution on principles, Arab delegates balked. Once these snags were overcome, the Chinese Nationalist delegate introduced an amendment to replace the People's Republic of China with his own government in the group of four powers in order to negotiate on broad issues in the Far East.[146] The statement of principles did not pass intact through the First Committee until the 13th.[147] The process delayed U.S. pressure for a resolution condemning China for two more days.

U.S. leaders neither expected nor desired a favorable Chinese response to the UN statement of principles. They were in no mood to bargain with Beijing, and they knew the affirmative U.S. vote in the First Committee would cause a storm in Congress, which was in the midst of its so-called Great Debate over President Truman's expressed intention to send more U.S. ground units to Europe.[148] The response on Capitol Hill was not long in coming. Robert Taft, the Senate minority leader, denounced U.S. support for the five principles as "a shocking step."[149] Democratic senator Tom Connally, who, as chairman of the Foreign Relations Committee, was sometimes regarded as a spokesman for the administration in the upper house, expressed reservations about the principles.[150] It was a great relief to the State Department when China rejected the statement on the 17th, again charging that the call for a cease-fire in Korea before broader negotiations were intact would merely provide U.S. troops with "a breathing space" and "help the United States to maintain and extend its aggression."[151]

This response gave Washington the green light to present its resolution to the General Assembly condemning China, which the United States tabled in the First Committee on the 20th. For Great Britain and others, the sticking point in the draft was not the branding of China as an aggressor—which was unlikely in itself to produce an expanded war—but the call in paragraph 8 for "a committee . . . as a matter of urgency to consider additional measures to be employed to meet this aggression and to report thereon to the General Assembly."[152] The Truman administration disclaimed any immediate intention to expand the combat beyond Korea, but it did consider having the United Nations impose a "selective embargo on export[s] to China" that included, as an "irreducible minimum," items "directly serving Chi[nese] warmaking potential."[153] The Truman administration's haste derived from domestic pressures. On the 19th the House of Representatives, in a nearly unanimous vote, passed a resolution calling on the United Nations to declare China an aggressor. The Senate stood poised for similar action early the next week.[154]

Meanwhile, Canada, India, and Great Britain all approached China requesting clarification of its response to the principles approved by the First Committee.[155] On the 22d Rau in New York received Zhou Enlai's reply, which he immediately read to the First Committee. The Chinese elaboration appeared more hopeful than the initial response five days earlier. Zhou now stated that "a cease-fire for a limited period could be agreed upon at the first meeting of the Seven-Nation Conference and put into effect so that negotiations could proceed further." The call for a seven-nation conference adhered to the earlier Chinese proposal to add representatives from India, Egypt, and France to the four powers designated in the First Committee, but the remainder of the statement indicated that the fighting in Korea could be stopped temporarily before a settlement emerged regarding Taiwan. The statement also implied that Chinese troops would be withdrawn from Korea once foreign forces on the UN side departed.[156] A day later Chinese Vice Minister for Foreign Affairs Zhang Hanfu modified this point in a meeting with Panikkar, stating that, as soon as agreement for the withdrawal of foreign troops was reached and was being carried out, China would "assume responsibility for [the] return of Chinese volunteers" (Panikkar's words). Zhang also said that principles for resolving Korea's internal problems could be determined by the seven-power conference rather than by the Koreans themselves, as previously demanded.[157]

These Chinese moves heightened opposition to quick passage of the U.S. draft resolution. On the 22d Rau proposed a forty-eight-hour adjournment of the First Committee to study Zhou's new message. With that, Canada's Pearson wrote in his diary, Austin "broke loose with an ill-tempered and abusive statement." The outburst destroyed any prospect to avert delay, as Rau's motion immediately passed by a 27–23–6 margin. Pearson regarded this outcome as "one of the most severe moral defeats the United States has had," as most of its "reliable allies"—that is, its NATO partners—sided with the plurality.[158] After the recess, Rau presented a revised draft of the twelve-power resolution of the Arab-Asian bloc, which had been moved six weeks earlier but never voted on.[159] In London the British cabinet decided to oppose the U.S. resolution in its present form.[160]

These events hardly spelled doom for the U.S. position. Other "white" members of the commonwealth, plus most NATO countries, already had decided that, in a pinch, they would support the U.S. resolution.[161] The Arab-Asian offering drew relatively narrow support, given its failure even to put forth a cease-fire in Korea as a prerequisite to broader talks on East Asia.[162] The British government, moreover, was deeply divided on the U.S. resolution, with most Foreign Office personnel, including Ambassador Franks in Washington and Jebb in New York, and Chancellor of the Exchequer Hugh Gaitskill inclined to support it. Prime Minister Attlee leaned toward abstention.[163] The cabinet decision certainly was subject to change.

U.S. diplomats took that decision with the utmost seriousness. Clearly it reflected growing disillusionment in British opinion with the direction of U.S. policy at a time when the United States needed a larger effort from the United Kingdom to help sustain European rearmament. Attlee supported such an effort, but the Labor Left promised to raise objections, as did important sectors of the public once they realized that increased military expenditures would require cuts in domestic programs.[164]

The British stand derived in part from sensitivity to Asian, especially Indian, opinion.[165] Although Nehru's self-righteous preaching to the West irritated U.S. policymakers, they recognized his influence in Asia and did not want to anger him unnecessarily. Most important, a British vote against the U.S. resolution, which might encourage France to demur as well, could provoke a dangerous reaction in Congress and the public against an expanded commitment of U.S. forces to western Europe.

A concerted effort by the Truman administration over recent weeks, combined with support from the popular and nonpartisan General Eisenhower, who was on the verge of returning from a European tour, gave momentum to the cause for a U.S. buildup across the Atlantic; but considerable sentiment remained in Congress that the legislative body should limit presidential prerogative on the matter.[166] Fear spread in the executive branch that this sentiment was a mask for isolationism. A show of dissent on Korea from Europe threatened to break open the dam.

On the 26th the Americans showed flexibility at Lake Success. In the midst of proposals by the Israelis and the British to amend paragraph 8, and a Canadian six-step plan toward a peaceful settlement of Far Eastern issues, including Korea, State Department officials presented their own amendment to the disputed paragraph. Under this scheme, the committee considering "additional measures . . . to meet . . . [Chinese] aggression" could postpone its report to the General Assembly if a "Good Offices Committee," created to pursue a peaceful conclusion of the Korean conflict, made "satisfactory progress in its efforts."[167] Just as important, Austin stated in the First Committee on the next day that the resolution would not give MacArthur any new authority and that the committee called for in paragraph 8 could only make recommendations to the General Assembly. The larger body itself would determine whether these recommendations would be made to member nations. Austin also gave assurances that the committee would offer no recommendations for additional measures until a further effort for peace had been tried and failed.[168]

The U.S. resolution now moved rapidly toward adoption by the General Assembly. The British cabinet withdrew its opposition.[169] Threatening comments from Beijing that condemnation of China by the United Nations would eliminate any chance for negotiations had little effect at Lake Success.[170] On the 30th the First Committee rejected the twelve-power resolution while approving the amended U.S. proposal by 44–7–9. Two days later the General Assembly passed the U.S. resolution by a nearly identical count. Outside the Communist world, only India and Burma voted "nay." In the Arab-Asian bloc, Lebanon, Iraq, and Iran voted in the affirmative.[171] For the first time in its brief history, the United Nations had condemned a nation for "aggression."

### The Communist Side: Challenge and Response

China's reaction was not long in coming. On 2 February Zhou Enlai released a statement labeling the U.S. resolution "illegal, slanderous, null and void," and "shameful, aggressive, reactionary and imperialist" to boot. The idea of a Good Offices Committee to seek negotiations for a settlement in Korea represented "a naked deceit."[172] A day later Zhou summoned Ambassador Panikkar and told him that the Americans did not comprehend the seriousness of what they had done, that the conflict might now spread, and that Beijing would have nothing to do with the Good Offices Committee so long as China was branded an aggressor by the United Nations.[173]

What was the impact of UN condemnation of the PRC on the prospects for peace in Korea? New materials from the Chinese side, examined in conjunction with Chinese behavior both before and after passage of the resolution, point toward some definite conclusions. During January Chinese diplomacy on Korea went through two phases. In the first, Beijing showed little interest in negotiations. The Mao regime and the populace in general appeared to be in a euphoric mood over Chinese successes in Korea and showed no inclination to bargain.[174] The New Year's day editorial in *Renmin ribao* proclaimed that, "by conscientious effort, China can become a first-class world military power like the Soviet Union."[175] With the "liberation" of Seoul three days later, the same paper exclaimed: "March on, the Korean people's army and the Chinese People's Volunteers! March on for the independence and freedom of Korea, for the security of China and the East! March on to Taejon, Taegu and Pusan! And, if the Americans refuse to go, push them into the ocean!"[176]

Charles Burton Marshall of the U.S. State Department received a more sober portrait of PRC attitudes through an indirect contact with a Chinese national known only as a person "identified with non-communist elements of the Peiping [*sic*] regime." In one exchange early in the month through a "second party," recently identified as Professor George A. Taylor of the University of Washington, the Chinese party stated that the current government had three factions: "The Moscow-oriented Communists (Stalinists); China-oriented (native) Communists; and non-Communists." "A small inner group" held close ties to Moscow and thought global war inevitable. Mao, though "much in the Russian camp," still might be prevailed on to pursue an independent course. The third group saw two possible courses—to persuade Mao to adopt a more conciliatory attitude toward the United States or, failing that, to join with the second group in a coup d'etat against the first. To pursue either of these courses, the third group needed assurances from Washington that it would not block a settlement of the Taiwan issue or Communist China's admission to the United Nations. The Korean conflict could be resolved through a simultaneous withdrawal of foreign troops and then the establishment of a UN commission, with Communist Chinese representation, to supervise creation of a government for a united country. Marshall responded that China must offer some gesture of good faith before the United States could explore a settlement along these lines.[177]

By the middle of the month Marshall's Chinese contact seemed persuaded that Mao was "irretrievably" in the Moscow camp, that "the only course [for the dissidents] was to precipitate a revolt." The problem was that the PRC was isolated from the non-Communist world. Admission to the United Nations would strengthen the argument of "the non-Stalinist forces" that that world had not barred the door to friendship with China. Again, Marshall pointed to the impossibility of such a U.S. initiative before some alteration of Chinese behavior.[178]

Chinese diplomacy entered a second stage on the 17th, when Beijing replied to the five principles proposed by the United Nations. Rather than simply wiring its reply to New York, the Foreign Ministry also summoned the Indian and Swedish ambassadors and the British chargé, presenting them with copies of the text of Zhou Enlai's message. Zhou received Panikkar personally and talked with him at some length.[179] In content, the response stood a good distance from the five principles, but elaborations on the 22d and 23d narrowed the gap. On the 26th both Mao and Zhou attended a reception at the Indian embassy celebrating the first anniversary of the Republic of India. Mao even gave a brief speech.[180] Obviously the Chinese were cultivating India and, to a lesser degree, Great Britain.

Charles Burton Marshall's continuing indirect contact with a Chinese National reinforced the view that Beijing was interested in negotiations. On the 30th Marshall received a report from Professor Taylor on a recent telephone conversation with the "third party," who had abandoned talk of an attempt to overthrow Mao. Rather, he referred to a letter he had received, dated two weeks earlier, from a person with top-level connections in Beijing. Supposedly those in power in Beijing had altered their belief that war was "inevitable." A Sino-U.S. accommodation now seemed possible. As a sign of good faith, Communist forces in Korea would withdraw northward with the intention of evacuating Seoul uncontested and retreating to the 38th parallel.[181]

The Chinese leadership had reason to modify its attitude around mid-January, as the Communist offensive had bogged down in Korea. According to a later Chinese account, General Peng decided that his forces must halt their advance, that the North Koreans and the Soviet ambassador in Pyongyang protested, but that Mao and then Stalin supported the CPV commander's judgment.[182] At the same time, U.S. support for the five principles provided hope that some PRC aims could be achieved through diplomatic means. If the information Marshall received from the Chinese side on divisions within the

PRC was accurate (the beginning, in February, of tough new action in China to suppress "counter revolutionaries" suggests that it was), Mao may have felt some pressure at home to show flexibility on Korea.[183] In the international arena, such a maneuver would heighten pressure on the United States to make concessions and reduce prospects for passage of the aggressor resolution by the United Nations.

No evidence indicates, however, that Chinese troops in Korea ever gave up ground for other than military reasons or that Chinese or North Korean political leaders ever stood willing to withdraw their forces to the 38th parallel to achieve a cease-fire and broader talks.[184] Quite the contrary. Throughout the second half of January, Mao underestimated the strength of enemy forces. So did his field commanders, at least until UN troops launched a counteroffensive on the 25th.[185] Two days later, with his forces fighting desperately to hold positions south of Seoul, General Peng suggested to Mao that he seek a temporary cease-fire even if it meant agreeing on a retreat of friendly units by 15 to 30 kilometers. Peng believed that his forces needed two months to rebuild ammunition and food supplies before resuming the offensive, but Mao ordered him to counterattack immediately. This fourth campaign, Mao argued, might persuade "the enemy . . . to negotiate with us for settling the Korean problem" on terms favorable to the PRC and the DPRK. In contrast, if negotiations started now, with enemy forces advancing northward, China and North Korea would be at a disadvantage.[186]

Mao's effort during the middle of the month to test the diplomatic winds outside the Communist world was a tactical maneuver grounded in domestic and international developments, rather than a reflection of his abandonment of hopes for total victory in Korea. The Communist Chinese had overcome tactical military setbacks many times before. In Korea they had not yet drawn on their vast manpower reserves, they had not received the heavy equipment from the Soviets that they expected, and they had not fully exploited the potential for guerrilla warfare behind UN lines.[187] With improved weather conditions in the spring, an increased numerical superiority, and better equipment, the Communists again might press their advantage on the battlefield against an impatient, divided, and dispirited United Nations. Mao's estimation of his side's long-term military prospects in Korea made the second half of January an inappropriate moment for a cease-fire or any other agreement on Korea.

Thus passage of the aggressor resolution provided the occasion for, but was not the cause of, China's denunciation of negotiations. Although this affront to China's national pride generated real outrage in Beijing, several months later, after a far heavier Chinese investment in Korea had only produced a further shift in favor of UN forces, the Mao regime began armistice talks despite the recent call by the UN General Assembly for economic sanctions against the PRC. Then China saved face by accepting discussions between commanders in the field rather than between the PRC and DPRK, on the one hand, and a designated negotiating committee of the United Nations, on the other. Such a course was more palatable in July than in February in part because General Ridgway had replaced the belligerent MacArthur in Tokyo, but the altered military balance and Mao's perceptions of that balance constituted the primary motivation for the contrasting responses. As with the United States in November of the previous year, military realities were not sufficiently compelling in January or February to produce an alteration of aims that had been established in a previous period of euphoria. Passage of the aggressor resolution merely hindered the evolution of a negotiating process that had little chance for early success.

The Soviets made no effort to alter Chinese actions. At the United Nations the Soviet delegation supported the Arab-Asian resolution, but in contrast to its behavior in the aftermath of the Inchon landing of the previous September and the less spectacular UN counterattacks of the coming May and June, it did nothing to encourage the Americans to negotiate on Korea.[188] Soviet propaganda regarding the United States reached new heights of vituperation. In an address of 21 January commemorating Lenin's death, Peter Pospelov, director of the Marx-Engels Institute, departed from corresponding speeches of the past four years in concentrating exclusively on the United States. Pospelov's address on the same occasion in 1950 had stressed peaceful coexistence. With Stalin and other Politburo members looking on, he now launched a spirited attack on "American ruling circles" for their past crimes against the Russian people and for the "giddy speed" with which they were now thrusting their own people "into the abyss of a new third world war."[189] *New York Times* correspondent Harrison Salisbury reported that, "Never before from the stage of the Bolshoi Theater at one of the most formal state and party annual occasions . . . had Americans been attacked in tones so acidulous, so vigorous and so sweeping."[190] U.S. observers interpreted this speech and the larger propaganda drive against the United States as an effort, first, to promote a war scare to wreak havoc in the Atlantic alliance and, second, to prepare Soviet citizenry for war.[191]

In the former case, U.S. analysts were certainly correct, in the latter probably so. Stalin's *Pravda* interview of 16 February and its subsequent use by the world peace movement and Communist parties outside the Soviet Union revealed the central thrust of Moscow's campaign to divide the West. In his first major statement on international affairs since January 1949, Stalin began by attacking recent assertions by British Prime Minister Attlee that the Soviet Union had failed to demobilize its troops after World War II. Stalin then lambasted the UN resolution condemning China. "The American aggressors," he asserted, were turning the international body "into an instrument of war." World war was not "inevitable," however, as the peoples of the world still could "take the cause of peace into their own hands and . . . defend it to the end."[192] The statement preceded by less than a week the opening in East Berlin of the first meeting of the World Peace Council, the recently formed agency of the Soviet peace movement, which some Western analysts viewed as a potential competitor of the United Nations. At this meeting—and in the ensuing months—spokesmen for the movement stressed Stalin's call on the masses to "take the cause of peace into their own hands." Although attention was given to Korea and the Japanese peace treaty, Communist propaganda in Europe placed primary emphasis on German rearmament, which not only posed the greatest threat to Soviet security but represented the most broadly divisive issue in the West.[193] Within the Soviet Union and eastern Europe, the prospect of German rearmament could also help to justify added emphasis on defense spending and heavy industry.

Yet other evidence suggests that Stalin actually believed in an increased likelihood of war. Karel Kaplan, once a member of the Communist Party of Czechoslovakia and later a defector to the West, has written of an incident of January 1951, described to him by a participant, Alexej Cepicka, then the minister of defense in Czechoslovakia. Stalin assembled at the Kremlin top-level delegations "from all countries of the Soviet bloc." (It is not clear if China was included.) The Soviet leader told his audience that their side had a temporary military advantage in Europe, that this advantage should be exploited to seize control of the western portions of the continent. Since the opportunity would last for only three to four years, Communist nations must further concentrate efforts toward mobilizing their resources for war.[194]

The story must be treated with caution. Even if the incident occurred as Kaplan says, it does not necessarily follow that Stalin had made a decision to attack western Europe. Perhaps he merely wanted to provide a rationale to tighten Soviet supervision of satellite governments or for a larger defense effort in eastern Europe, both of which soon followed.[195]

Even so, the alleged meeting occurred during a militant period of Soviet propaganda. Stalin's *Pravda* interview included an ominous shift in the Soviet line regarding the peace movement. Whereas in the past the standard position had been that "peace" forces would triumph over those promoting war, Stalin now hedged his bets. Although Stalin did not explicitly rule out peace in Korea or anywhere else, he may have been informing the Soviet public and Communist audiences abroad that global war was a distinct possibility.[196]

This interpretation jibes with a report received by the U.S. State Department in early March through Terry Duce, a vice president of the American Arabian Oil Company. Prepared by an unidentified member of Duce's firm, the report described a conversation of 21 February with two Soviet diplomats shortly after their departure from Moscow. "The most important thing they had to say," the businessman concluded, "is that the Russians are fully reconciled to going to war with the United States this year if events should seem to justify such action.... They are convinced that if an all-out showdown comes, the bulk of world opinion will be with them and against the United States." Events after the summer of 1950 had demonstrated both "America's fundamental weakness militarily" and "its political stupidity." The Soviets would go to war immediately to prevent "a serious American attempt to rearm Germany and the rest of Western Europe." Given the dispersal of Soviet industry and recent improvements in Soviet air defense, American's atomic superiority "would not be decisive." With isolationist sentiment widespread in the United States, total war would stir opposition there, and the Soviet explosion of several atomic bombs on U.S. soil would spark even further dissension. As for the conflict in Korea, the Soviets were delighted with America's continuing expenditure of resources in an indecisive area, with the possibility of an even greater expenditure if measures were taken against mainland China, and with the continuing dissension in the West provoked by the war.[197]

The incident probably represented an exercise in deterrence by the Soviets. Surely Stalin did not want a global conflict. Yet neither was he anxious to reduce tensions with the United States. In all likelihood he would have initiated military action in Europe only if confronted by a concrete move toward West German rearmament in the face of widespread public dissent among U.S. allies. Only then would the combination of immediate opportunity and longer-term danger be sufficient to warrant a calculated move toward war.[198] In the meantime the generally hard line in Soviet foreign policy, including that in Korea, promised to reap substantial dividends, thus dissuading Moscow from any attempt to modify Chinese aims.

For the moment Beijing needed little pressure or encouragement to cling to its own aims. If anything, the PRC's primary concern in relation to the Soviet Union was to ensure its commitment to a broad interpretation of its obligations under the alliance concluded during February of the previous year. Zhou Enlai's *Pravda* article celebrating the first anniversary of the alliance illustrates this concern. In an attack on America's movement toward a separate peace treaty with Japan, Zhou accused the United States of attempting to use the island nation "as a base and its people as cannon fodder, to facilitate the continuation and extension of their criminal actions of invading Korea and Taiwan and intervening in Vietnam and Southeast Asia." "It is precisely this scheme of American imperialism," Zhou declared, "that the Sino-Soviet Treaty of Friendship, Alliance, and Mutual Assistance resolutely opposes."[199] That this expansive interpretation of the treaty appeared in *Pravda* suggests that the Soviets wanted to warn the United States about the implications of a broader war. On the other hand, *Pravda*'s own editorial in celebration of the anniversary was less explicit regarding the international boundaries of the alliance, indicating a Soviet determination to maintain flexibility.[200] For Beijing's part, Zhou's assertiveness was entirely consistent with China's continuing pursuit of total victory in Korea, which was in no way affected by UN passage of the aggressor resolution.

## THE AGGRESSOR RESOLUTION: RESPONSE OUTSIDE THE COMMUNIST CAMP

"All our efforts failed in the end before the big stick of the United States," Indian leader Nehru wrote privately as the aggressor resolution moved inexorably toward passage.[201] Several days later Sir Girja S. Bajpai at the Indian Ministry of Foreign Affairs told Warwick F. Chipman, the Canadian high commissioner in New Delhi, that the U.S. resolution, combined with statements against China by U.S. public officials, engendered "'a feeling in this part of the world that the growing issue is one of Asia against the rest, or the East versus the West.'" Based on this and other recent comments in the Indian press, Chipman reported to Ottawa that, "if the West is not careful, China instead of being regarded as a menace will be looked on as a rallying point for an independent East."[202]

In a reflective paper written in the aftermath of the resolution's passage, Escott Reid, an assistant to Pearson in the Canadian Department of External Affairs, surmised that "the cost of preserving the appearance of unity [within the West] has been great." Allied governments had given public support to U.S. policies that they considered "ill-advised, if not dangerous" and that lacked support in important elements of the private sector. If these patterns continued, Reid concluded, "the foundations of the North Atlantic Community will be weakened."[203]

The *New York Times* reported similar thoughts about "the future of the United Nations." Many delegates at Lake Success believed that, "unless somehow the dilemma posed by Chinese aggression could be resolved and divisions in the non-Communist world repaired," the organization might be relegated to addressing only "matters outside the mainstream of world events."[204]

CBS commentator Eric Sevareid offered a sharply contrasting perspective. Traversing the world scene from the vantage point of Washington, Sevareid began his remarks on the evening of 2 February by describing the atmosphere of the previous November, when "the Chinese suddenly invaded Korea and the great UN army was put to flight." "There was a terrible feeling," Sevareid recalled, "that the whole structure of the Free World was about to collapse. . . . We started down a descending psychological spiral and Stalin must have rubbed his hands with incredulous joy." Yet now, Sevareid declared, "nearly all the private, as well as public talk, here in the capital, is confident talk—on Korea, on Europe, on the United Nations and the Western alliance, and on America's military production. Nowhere, except in Korea, is the physical situation much changed. But the psychological situation has changed tremendously."[205]

Sevareid ignored Asian opinion, but his analysis captured a crucial reality that Nehru, Reid, and many UN delegates missed. The international climate had changed perceptibly since late in the previous year, and that change augured well if not for world peace then certainly for the avoidance of an expanded war. Events from late November through the second week of January had pushed the world closer to global conflict than at any time since 1945. Now a steadiness returned to international politics that had nearly disappeared in the midst of the Chinese advance in Korea.

This steadiness derived partly from the emergence of a degree of military balance in Korea. By the beginning of February, UN ground forces were within ten miles of Seoul, and diplomats abroad were thinking more about what would happen when they reached the 38th parallel than when they evacuated the peninsula. With conditions there no longer desperate, pressures in the United States for an expanded war against China temporarily subsided.

General Eisenhower's tour of Europe and his return to the United States at the end of January, plus French Prime Minister René Pleven's trip to Washington late in the same month, also fostered steadiness. On both sides of the Atlantic, the newly appointed NATO commander's winning personality helped to persuade doubters regarding the necessity of a rapid military buildup in western Europe. With several governments there now committed to sharply increased defense expenditures, the United States could swallow more gracefully a gradual move toward German rearmament.[206] Meanwhile, Pleven's warm public reception in Washington flattered fragile French egos while building mutual understanding on the sensitive German question, the war in Indochina, which had taken a turn for the better, and the dispensing of scarce raw materials.[207]

On Japan events were somewhat less dramatic, but January saw substantial progress toward a peace settlement with a country playing a critical role in the U.S. effort in Korea. On the 10th President Truman approved a memorandum that identified Japan's integration into an anti-Communist alliance system as the primary purpose of such a settlement. Two weeks later John Foster Dulles left for Japan to commence negotiations for a peace treaty and other agreements. On 9 February, after twelve days of hard bargaining, Dulles would initial five preliminary agreements with the Japanese and prepare to fly to the Philippines and Australia to win broad support for his handiwork.[208]

Finally, passage of the aggressor resolution by the General Assembly ensured that the United Nations would continue to play a key role in U.S. decisions on the Korean issue. That body had proved instrumental in tempering the U.S. course during the days of deepest gloom in Korea. In the process of guiding the resolution through the First Committee, the United States had committed itself to working through the international organization regarding sanctions against China and to giving priority to efforts for negotiations with the enemy. In so doing, the Truman administration retained an institutional barrier between itself and congressional and public opinion that could discourage brash and ill-considered action again in the future.[209] With the Chinese still harboring ambitions to push enemy forces out of Korea, this fact could prove of considerable long-term significance.

Still, the UN role in Korea represented, at best, a mixed blessing to U.S. decision makers.[210] For the first time in the history of its involvement on the Korean issue, the United Nations had become something more than an instrument of U.S. policy. The United States continued to be influential in dealing with Korea, but, far more than before, other non-Communist nations now used the organization to influence the United States. Because of allied pressure, Washington had first postponed and then amended its resolution. The Arab-Asian bloc also exerted influence, especially through its impact on the western Europeans, the British in particular, and the Canadians. Whatever their disappointment with the passage of the U.S. resolution and the defeat of their own, they remained determined to use the United Nations in attempting to contain and end the war. To the United States, therefore, the international organization had assumed a very different role in Korea than that originally intended. Since American opinion was often less flexible regarding acceptable terms for a settlement than that in western Europe and the Arab-Asian bloc, the UN role was just as likely to be a burden as an asset in U.S. policymaking.

Even for the detached observer, diplomacy at the United Nations had its negative qualities. The open display of disunity in the General Assembly encouraged the Soviet Union and China to push their advantages to the limit. It also magnified public awareness outside the Communist world of disagreements between the United States and its allies, thus adding to pressures on governments to hold to uncompromising positions. Yet public disunity was an effect not a cause of differences within the West, and between it and the Arab-Asian bloc. Given their ideological perspective, the Communist powers were prone, in any event, to overestimate conflict outside their own bloc. Arguably, the availability of a setting for intensive, multinational interaction helped to fashion compromises that contained differences and averted disarray.

The quadrilateral relationship among the commonwealth powers of Australia, Canada, India, and the United Kingdom illustrates this point. Within this group were America's two closest allies (Canada and the United Kingdom), a soon-to-be ally (Australia), and a neutral harboring strong suspicions toward the West (India). While India eventually split with the other three on the aggressor resolution, the UN and commonwealth formats proved useful in negotiating the five principles and blunting America's rage against China. Throughout the process, Canada's Pearson played the deft hand of mediator. When the commonwealth prime ministers in London moved dangerously far from the U.S. position on principles for a cease-fire in Korea, it was Pearson from New York, through St. Laurent, who persuaded them (Nehru, in particular) to move back on track. Lacking the imperial past of the British or the reflexive condescension toward dark-skinned peoples of the Australians, the Canadians achieved an intimacy with the Indians surpassing that of other Westerners.

Canada did so without compromising its relationship with its allies. Despite the U.S. State Department's occasional irritation over Pearson's maneuvering behind its back, Canadian-U.S. relations never reached a crisis, thus testifying to Pearson's keen sense of how far he could go in pursuing an independent course. Ambassador Franks in Washington paid the Canadian foreign minister a rare compliment on 27 January when he advised the British Foreign Office that "it still remains a good first rough check on what will really inflict serious damage on Anglo-American relations and what will not to see whether Canada is with us or with the United States. If the former, the situation is nearly always under control; if the latter this may not be so."[211]

Australia played a lesser yet still significant role. Although Prime Minister Robert Menzies tended to follow the British lead on Korea, Foreign Minister Percy Spender was the real architect of Australian policy. Viewing the world from "down under," Spender doubted that either British power or interests were adequate for the protection of Australia's security needs. He wanted an independent relationship with the United States. In the crisis over the aggressor resolution, Spender labored diligently—and ultimately successfully—to prevent Menzies from breaking with Washington.[212] Meanwhile, K.C.O. Shann, the Australian delegate at Lake Success, kept close watch on efforts to amend the U.S. resolution. He became particularly concerned when Great Britain and Canada pressed for a provision that the Good Offices Committee would seek talks for a definite period before any consideration of sanctions by the Collective Measures Committee. Shann pointed out to Jebb that placing a time limit on the quest for negotiations actually might accomplish the opposite of what was intended. That is, U.S. allies wanted to postpone sanctions—and even their formal consideration—for as long as possible, an objective that would be better pursued by approaching negotiations with the Chinese as an ongoing possibility rather than something to be declared a failure at a precise moment.[213] To Jebb, the point was well taken and it helped to narrow the gap between London and Washington, especially after Austin in the First Committee committed the United States to the pursuit of negotiations with China.[214]

Thus a retrospective assessment of the ten-week period following the start of the Chinese counteroffensive reveals a positive role for the United Nations and reasons for measured optimism regarding the future that went undetected by many observers at the time. If in early February 1951 the Korean War remained a dangerous and destructive phenomenon on the world scene, the road to Armageddon was a good deal longer than it had been during the previous two months. And a young and much maligned international organization had served an admirable, perhaps crucial function in the gradual retreat from the brink.

• C H A P T E R   5 •

# The Dimensions of Collective Action

### Toward Military Stalemate

On 11 February CPV forces resumed the offensive on Korea's central front, ripping through two ROK divisions and opening a sizable wedge in UN lines. Observers on the UN side watched nervously for signs of the "bug-out fever" that had consumed many Eighth Army units during the previous December. By the 13th CPV troops had encircled the Twenty-third Infantry Regiment, commanded by Colonel Paul L. Freeman, which was dug in on high ground just south of Chipyong-ni.[1]

Located thirty-two miles east of Seoul, Chipyong-ni was a town of several brick-and-frame structures plus a few dozen thatch houses, many of which already lay in ruin. An east-west railroad track and two main roads ran through the community, giving it regional significance as a center for transportation and communications. Snow-covered hills surrounded Chipyong-ni, in some cases rising more than eight hundred feet above the valley. On the night of the 13th fighting hit the town with a vengeance.

Colonel Freeman previously had requested authority to retreat southward, and his immediate superiors had agreed. General Ridgway demurred, insisting that the regiment, even if encircled, could be supplied by airdrop. Well fortified on ideal defensive terrain and having superior firepower, including air support, Freeman's regiment could break the momentum of the counteroffensive while inflicting massive casualties on the opposition's vastly superior numbers. The regiment stayed and fought.

CPV troops struck Freeman's unit from the south. For two days the Chinese launched one mass attack after another. Despite some local victories, they failed to force their opponents into a general retreat. Late in the afternoon on the 15th a U.S. task force, with flank protection from the Twenty-seventh Commonwealth Brigade, moved up to Chipyong-ni to break the siege. An exhausted, seriously injured Colonel Freeman declared triumphantly, "Every time the Chinese banzaied us, we banzaied them right back. We hurt 'em bad." French troops—"crazy fools," he called them admiringly—received special accolades for their stand on the western end of the regiment's position.[2] UN losses numbered in the hundreds, but they were minuscule compared to those the Chinese suffered. CPV commander Deng Hua had underestimated the size of enemy units at Chipyong-ni, and their determination to stand and fight. He also had failed to anticipate the ability of UN units to the south to reinforce the town.[3]

The battle of Chipyong-ni provided a dramatic manifestation of an emergent pattern in Korea. Outnumbered UN ground units with uncontested air support dug in and confronted CPV forces, which attacked in "mass waves" of humanity. The result was huge casualties and limited territorial gains for the Chinese. Within a week the offensive had spent its force, and General Ridgway was preparing an early counterstroke, appropriately code-named "Operation Killer," which began on 21 February. As a British officer had noted two weeks earlier, Ridgway's strategy was "homicidal not geographical."[4]

Yet in maintaining pressure on the enemy in well-coordinated, limited operations, Ridgway also pushed his troops gradually forward. By 1 March UN units had driven their adversaries northward across the Han. Two weeks later the Communists evacuated Seoul. By the third week of April UN divisions were slightly north of the 38th parallel in all sectors except the relatively insignificant Ongjin region in the extreme west.

Still, the Chinese had not abandoned hope of victory. CPV commander Peng Dehuai had never wanted to launch the February offensive, but Mao had insisted, hoping to create advantageous conditions for negotiating a Korean settlement. When the offensive failed, Peng returned to Beijing for consultations. Mao told him, "Win a quick victory if you can; if you can't, win a slow one."[5] He now believed that China must prepare for at least two more years of fighting, and he approved Peng's plea for authority to adopt a mobile defense while preparing for a new thrust southward. Peng would evacuate positions he could not hold before suffering huge casualties, counterattacking where possible before the enemy could dig into new positions. It was hoped that such tactics would minimize his own loses, slow the UN advance, and buy time to move supplies and reinforcements to the front.[6]

During March and early April the Chinese sent three new army groups to Korea, two of which were equipped with Soviet-supplied heavy weapons.[7] On 6 April Peng informed his generals of his desire to move soon. His intelligence indicated a buildup by the enemy in preparation for an offensive of its own. The CPV would do best to attack first, before UN units had been fully reinforced. A week later Mao approved Peng's operational plan. On 22 April, with UN forces advancing in the center of the peninsula near Chorwan and Kumwha, the Chinese launched massive counterattacks, thus beginning the first phase of their spring offensive. Peng hoped to destroy three U.S. and two ROK divisions, plus three British and Turkish brigades. In the central sector Chinese units bludgeoned the ROK Sixth Division into a disorganized retreat, opening a huge gap in the UN line. By the 26th UN forces had plugged this hole, but the main thrust of the Chinese effort had developed in the direction of Seoul further to the west. As late as the 28th the fate of the ROK capital remained in doubt. The Chinese drove the defenders to within four miles of the city.[8]

The advance took a tremendous toll on the CPV, as UN troops gave up ground stubbornly. The Twenty-ninth British Infantry Brigade was especially dogged in engaging three Chinese divisions near the 38th parallel for three days, while friendly forces established new lines further to the south. Its

Gloucestershire regiment fought so heroically against overwhelming odds that General James Van Fleet, the new commander of the Eighth Army, characterized the effort as "the most outstanding example of unit bravery in modern warfare."[9] By 26 April Peng wanted to terminate the offensive. Mao initially demurred, but subsequent Chinese thrusts southward soon persuaded him of the futility of continuing attacks in the west. The first phase of the spring offensive ended before the end of the month. The Communists had suffered an estimated seventy thousand casualties, ten times that of the enemy, and had advanced the battle line an average of merely thirty-five miles.

The Communists still enjoyed an advantage over the UN command in a ratio of nearly three to two, and their stock of supplies remained adequate for the planned second phase, which began on 16 May. Typically, early Chinese thrusts concentrated on ROK units, some of which disintegrated, leaving a giant hole in the UN line and enabling the Communists to capture large quantities of weapons and ammunition. But again UN firepower took its toll. Within four days the main front had stabilized, and UN forces had begun a counteroffensive. Despite a slowdown because of wet weather, by the end of the month the UN advance had cleared South Korea of organized enemy units in all but the extreme northwest. The CPV had suffered even more casualties than before and, for the first time, substantial numbers of Chinese soldiers had surrendered. The new prisoners of war (POWs) reported that soldiers in their units had resorted to eating grass and roots because of the exhaustion of their normal rations. U.S. corps commanders noticed a marked deterioration in the morale of enemy soldiers, an increasing number of whom previously had fought in Nationalist Chinese armies.[10]

General Ridgway, who in mid-April had replaced MacArthur in Tokyo, and Van Fleet had no intention of halting UN forces on the 38th parallel, which had little to commend it as a military boundary. During June they pushed their way slowly northward until the battle line extended nearly forty miles into North Korea on the east coast and from fifteen to twenty-five miles elsewhere east of the Imjin River.

The field commanders doubted the feasibility of major offensives beyond that point. By mid-June CPV forces had regrouped. Despite their heavy losses, they had far greater troop reserves than did the United Nations, and their logistical problems diminished while the opposition's grew as the front moved northward.[11] As the first anniversary of the outbreak of war approached, the military conflict had turned into a bloody stalemate along relatively natural lines of defense and across the center of the peninsula not far from where it had begun.

Meanwhile, representatives of non-Communist governments at the United Nations and elsewhere labored to bring the fighting to an end or at least to prevent its expansion beyond Korea. Such labors included probes of Communist China's position, as well as counters by western European and Arab-Asian diplomats to U.S. pressure for UN sanctions against the PRC. The first effort bore little fruit, and the second met with only partial success. The diplomatic process did take time, however. As during the two months following the Chinese counteroffensive of late November 1950, the delays engendered by the intricacies of multilateral diplomacy reduced prospects that the Truman administration would give in to voices, at home or in Tokyo, seeking to extend the war to China.

With U.S. casualties mounting in Korea, those voices persisted. When President Truman fired General MacArthur in April, they reached a new intensity. Yet because the delaying tactics of U.S. allies had prevented the United Nations from committing itself to additional and potentially destabilizing measures against China, Truman retained relatively safe options for increasing pressure on the enemy in order to satisfy immediate needs on the home front. In the long run such options were no substitute for an end to the fighting in Korea, but the emerging stalemate on the battlefield and the growing strength of the Western alliance provided a context within which the dominant parties on both sides finally might seek to bargain at the negotiating table.

### The UN Committees: Good Offices and Additional Measures

In the aftermath of the General Assembly's adoption of the resolution condemning China, most activity on Korea that took place in New York centered around the Good Offices Committee (GOC) and its effort to arrange for negotiations with Beijing. The GOC operated in close consultation with an ad hoc committee of members of the Collective Measures Committee, a body created under the "Uniting for Peace" resolution of the previous November. The ad hoc group, best known as the Additional Measures Committee (AMC), included an American who, not wanting an indefinite postponement of sanctions against China should it prove unwilling to negotiate on acceptable terms, closely monitored GOC progress.

Problems in constituting the GOC delayed its effort to contact China until the middle of February. Many UN delegates had assumed that the GOC would retain the personnel of the cease-fire group created the previous December. Yet India and Canada refused to serve, believing the committee had little chance of success with the Chinese.[12]

Iran's Entezam, too, had strong doubts about the GOC's prospects, but paragraph 7 of the aggressor resolution designated the president of the General Assembly as the organizer of the committee, so he did not have the luxury of declining service.[13] With the Americans and the British pressing to get the GOC under way, he made no effort to stall. A patient and mild-mannered diplomat who had served in the League of Nations during the 1930s and the United Nations since its founding, he proceeded to recruit two new members. First he sought a representative from a nation that enjoyed diplomatic relations with the PRC. Such a person would enable the GOC to communicate indirectly with Beijing through his own country's diplomatic machinery. As the delegate from the only non-Communist nation other than India enjoying full diplomatic relations with Beijing, and with the added advantage of having abstained on the aggressor resolution, Sven Grafstrom of Sweden was the logical choice. He accepted membership on the 6th.[14] Six days later Luis Padilla Nervo of Mexico agreed to fill the third position. Since his country already held membership in the AMC, he provided a direct line of communication with that body.[15]

The GOC first attempted to approach the PRC on the 14th. Grafstrom sent his Foreign Ministry a message from Entezam as president of the General Assembly (rather than as a member of the GOC) and intended for the Chinese government. Grafstrom asked his superiors to relay the message to either the Chinese ambassador in Stockholm or the Swedish ambassador in Beijing or to both, with the understanding that it would be communicated to China's Foreign Ministry. The message emphasized the need for establishing personal contact between the United Nations and the PRC. The latter was not expected to deal officially with the GOC. Rather, the PRC could designate a representative to meet with Entezam in New York; or such a representative could meet with Entezam someplace outside China and the United States; or Entezam could meet with such a person in China. Swedish officials delivered this message to the Chinese embassy in Stockholm on the 15th and to the Chinese Foreign Ministry in Beijing two days later.[16]

Despite several follow-up efforts, Entezam failed to get a response from the PRC. During the first three weeks of March, Swedish and Indian diplomats in Beijing received word from the Chinese that they intended to make no reply at all.[17] According to Panikkar, however, they remained interested in another method of contact, perhaps a seven-power conference.[18] By the second week of April Entezam had temporarily exhausted all avenues for approaching China.[19] Much sentiment already existed at Lake Success that the GOC must be treated as "a broken reed."[20] U.S. allies looked anxiously for other methods of negotiating with the PRC.

Although the Truman administration honored its commitment of late January to give priority to the GOC, concern remained that the United States soon might press for action by the AMC.[21] As early as 6 February Assistant Secretary of State John Hickerson stated publicly that the United States had "some hope" of gaining UN approval for selective economic sanctions against China.[22] Eight days later the *New York Times* reported that the United States intended to ask the AMC to recommend a limited trade embargo against China that would include petroleum products, military equipment, and machinery for the manufacture of such equipment.[23]

On the same day a conversation between Dean Rusk and Canada's Hume Wrong provided further grounds for concern by a close U.S. ally and adept operator at the United Nations. With Ernest Bevin largely out of the picture in British foreign policy, and the Labor Left more aggressive than ever in the British cabinet, the old intimacy in Anglo-U.S. relations had temporarily subsided, leaving the Canadians as the closest confidants of the beleaguered U.S.

State Department. In response to a Canadian request for an update on U.S. objectives in Korea specifically and in East Asia in general, Rusk told Wrong that the United States sought to keep the war in Korea limited, that it had no intention of carrying military operations to China or even of launching a major ground offensive beyond the 38th parallel. At the same time the United States did not want to ease the PRC's task in consolidating authority on the mainland. The United States hoped that that regime would fall, but intended to avoid overt action to accomplish that goal. Recent intelligence, Rusk went on, indicated that serious divisions existed within the government in Beijing, that although the pro-Moscow faction was now in control and Soviet influence in Manchuria was pervasive, Chinese resentment toward their ally was widespread. The best way to foster this resentment was not to make concessions to China. Quite the opposite: a firm stand, combined with the rendering of costly defeats to Chinese armies on the battlefield, would force Beijing to "realize the cost of living with the USSR," thus encouraging a split.[24]

In defining as a key objective the desire to drive a wedge between China and the Soviet Union, Rusk placed the United States on the side of prevailing sentiment in Ottawa, London, and most other capitals outside the Communist world. Yet his emphasis on tough rather than flexible tactics in achieving this goal contrasted sharply with the views of the bulk of America's allies. The most disturbing point to the Canadians was that the logic of the U.S. position could produce a call for more extensive action against China at any time. If the U.S. analysis proved incorrect, such action could create greater rigidity and aggressiveness in Beijing, thereby sparking a process of escalation of the conflict that could easily get out of control.

Such a chain of events was not difficult to visualize. Since China had limited economic means for retaliating against economic sanctions by the United Nations, it might counter with political or military measures or both, probably involving Hong Kong and Southeast Asia. These could vary in degree from stepped-up efforts to foment unrest in Hong Kong, Malaya, Indochina, and Burma to direct military action against those areas. In the last case, the resisting forces could suffer defeat. The United Kingdom already showed concern about the effect of U.S. trade restrictions on the economic and political stability of Hong Kong.[25] Whatever the outcome of an expanded war in East Asia, the Soviet Union might try to exploit the situation with moves elsewhere. Such actions, in turn, might produce a direct Soviet-U.S. confrontation.[26]

The more severe the economic sanctions, the greater the likelihood of strong Chinese counteraction—or so the British and others believed. U.S. allies hoped to keep the issue out of the international organization entirely, preferring to work quietly through a Paris-based Consultative Group created in 1949 and including the major western European nations, the United States, and Canada.[27] In response to the outbreak of war in Korea, NATO countries had tightened restrictions on exports to China, but the Europeans had not followed America's lead in December 1950 in placing an embargo on all goods to that country.[28] The United States recognized the difficulty of achieving broad adherence among both its allies and the Arab-Asian neutrals, so it pressed for a more selective embargo.[29] The Americans were more sanguine than their friends regarding the impact that a widely supported embargo on petroleum products and supplies related to railroad construction and maintenance would have on China's capacity to sustain military action in Southeast Asia. In contrast to the limited sanctions the League of Nations had imposed on Italy in response to its aggression against Ethiopia, the United States now proposed economic measures only to reinforce UN military action, which was already draining China's resources.[30]

U.S. insistence on holding meetings of the AMC reinforced allied fears. Acheson viewed the AMC as an "instrument for full and sober consideration of countermeasures" against China which, by its "very existence . . . carries with it [an] element of pressure" on the Communists.[31] U.S. prodding led to a meeting of the AMC on 16 February. The ad hoc group was supposed to have fourteen members, the same as the Collective Measures Committee, but Yugoslavia and Burma refused to serve. A balance emerged, with Australia, Belgium, Canada, Egypt, France, and the United Kingdom working to delay any recommendation for new action against China, while Brazil, Mexico, the Philippines, Turkey, and Venezuela followed the U.S. lead.[32]

The first meeting augured well for those predisposed toward caution, as it resulted in the establishment of a bureau of three members—Turkey, Belgium, and Australia—to draw up a program of work and to maintain liaison with the GOC. With the GOC seeking to make contact with the PRC, the bureau relegated itself to compiling a list of possible measures that could be taken against China.

When the GOC showed no progress in its efforts, the United States tried to nudge the AMC forward, but it only succeeded, on 8 March, in persuading that body to appoint a subcommittee of five members, again with a balance in favor of delay, to give detailed study to the bureau's list.[33] Meanwhile, Australia, the United Kingdom, and Canada lobbied quietly to direct the AMC toward seeking new commitments of support from UN members for action within Korea as a method of stalling consideration of more dangerous measures.[34]

During the second half of March the U.S. delegation at Lake Success increased pressure to move the subcommittee along in its consideration of economic sanctions. The Americans objected to the subcommittee concentrating its attention on military matters, fearing that any report in this area would simply fuel new calls in the United States for direct attacks on China; they also believed that the securing of additional contributions for Korea from UN members was handled best at the bilateral level.[35]

Rumblings in Congress nudged the Truman administration toward sanctions. Since the previous summer a sizable movement had existed in the legislative branch to cut off Marshall Plan aid to countries that continued to export "war-useful" materials to the Communist bloc. The president had intervened in September to ensure that the matter stayed under his control. Events since that time had, in the minds of some, only added to the urgency of choking off certain exports to the Communists. On 9 March Senator James P. Kem (R., Mo.) wrote to Truman urging action on the matter. Three days later Kem raised the question on the Senate floor, providing the occasion for some fulsome oratory by several Republican colleagues.[36] No immediate follow-up occurred, but the time was approaching when powerful elements in Congress again would press the issue. U.S. allies had reason to fear that Washington soon might insist that the AMC act on economic sanctions.

## Peace Probes Outside the GOC

In some quarters the prospect of economic sanctions joined with conditions in Korea to provide a sense of urgency to the quest for negotiations with the Communists. By mid-March UN ground forces in Korea approached the 38th parallel along most of the front. Despite British efforts to secure a commitment from the United States to halt major UN ground operations at the old boundary, President Truman had announced on 15 February that crossing the line was a matter for MacArthur to decide.[37] A day later, in a private briefing of representatives of nations with troops in Korea, Rusk provided only marginal reassurance. He conceded that Chinese intervention had made impossible the use of force to achieve the political objective of unifying the peninsula. The United States did not plan major efforts to seize territory above the 38th parallel. When the question of a massive crossing of the line became "a more immediate problem," the United States would consider the issue in depth and consult with countries participating on the UN side. Meanwhile, UN forces would continue to conduct "an aggressive defense," and this tactic would include thrusts into North Korea.[38]

MacArthur added to the unease in allied quarters. On 20 February he stated publicly that he would not "arbitrarily execute" his authority to cross the 38th parallel "if cogent political reasons" were advanced to halt at that point or if there was "any reasonable possibility" of a limitation being put on his ground operations beyond that line.[39] On 7 March he noted to the press that, without a loosening of restrictions "upon our freedom of counteroffensive action" or a buildup of "our organizational strength," a military stalemate was on the horizon in Korea. He hinted that political leaders at home needed to make new decisions aimed at averting this prospect.[40] Eight days later MacArthur told Hugh Baillie of the United Press that the terrain around the 38th parallel did not lend itself to "positional warfare" by the forces now available to him. Forces adequate to that task and with the proper logistical support could advance to and hold the Yalu boundary. In choosing a course, his superiors in the United States "must not ignore the heavy cost in allied blood which a protracted and indecisive campaign would entail."[41] Western Europeans recognized such statements as pressure on Washington to permit another attempt at the forceful unification of Korea.

Worse was still to come. On the 16th Rusk assured representatives of nations contributing forces to the United Nations in Korea that there had been no change in the Truman administration's attitudes since his statement to them a month before, that "unless there should be a spectacular UN breakthrough" in the fighting, "which was highly unlikely," the United States had no intention of launching a large-scale offensive into North Korea.[42] Five days later, the State Department distributed to allies a draft text of a statement on UN policies in Korea. Its terminology was tough, using the word *aggressors* to refer to the Chinese Communists and North Koreans, avoiding any explicit mention of the 38th parallel, and referring approvingly to the General Assembly resolution of 7 October 1950, which tacitly sanctioned the subsequent UN military effort to unify the peninsula. Yet the draft also included a paragraph that implied a willingness to halt the fighting short of military victory and another suggesting that a settlement in Korea could open the way to a resolution of other disputes in East Asia.[43] Unfortunately a draft also went to MacArthur. On the 24th, before Washington had released it to the press, the UN commander issued a statement of his own.

The statement was cocky and insulting. MacArthur gloated over the recent tactical successes of UN forces, asserting that they showed "Red China" to be lacking "the industrial capacity to provide adequately many critical items essential to the conduct of modern war." "Even under the inhibitions which now restrict activity of the United Nations forces," China had been unable to conquer Korea. Beijing "must by now be painfully aware" that should the United Nations abandon its effort to restrict the fighting to Korea, China would face "the risk of imminent military collapse" on the peninsula. The aging general remained magnanimous: "I stand ready . . . to confer . . . with the Commander-in-Chief of the enemy forces in an earnest effort to find any military means whereby the realization of the political objectives of the United Nations in Korea . . . might be accomplished without further bloodshed."[44]

The declaration hinted at the impending use of force to achieve the political objective of unification and it dampened any prospect that issuance of the statement being prepared in Washington would deliver the Communists to the negotiating table. The Truman administration informed allies that MacArthur's comments were "unauthorized and unexpected," but it issued no direct public rebuke and it discouraged a move within the Arab-Asian bloc for an appeal to UN forces not to cross the 38th parallel.[45] Although Secretary of Defense Marshall implied to the press that no attempt would be made to advance to the Yalu, he also stated that no geographical limits existed on movements of UN troops across the 38th parallel provided they did not risk the security of the command.[46] Such statements were designed, in part, to maintain pressure on the enemy; but they also created the jitters in allied capitals, where fears spread that a moment for compromise settlement might pass that would not soon reappear.

The prospect of an enemy counteroffensive in Korea heightened such fears. Throughout March U.S. observers reported a sizable Communist buildup north of the 38th parallel. The immediate justification for UN tactical maneuvers above that line centered on the desirability of making this buildup as difficult as possible.[47] Even if repulsed, major offensive action by China would produce a rise in U.S. casualties and increase pressure within the United States for decisive military action to end the conflict.[48]

Signals from the Communist side offered only limited hope for success in the quest for negotiations. Aside from reports through Sweden for the GOC, information on PRC attitudes usually originated with India's Panikkar. In late February he expressed pessimism regarding the current Chinese attitude. Beijing remained deeply suspicious of U.S. intentions, especially those of MacArthur, and probably would negotiate only if UN forces suffered a reversal in Korea. Stalin's *Pravda* interview during the middle of the month had persuaded Beijing that it could count on Soviet material support if the UN military advance in Korea continued.[49] Panikkar's views did not change substantially in March, though he believed that the Chinese might discuss a seven-power conference through a medium other than the GOC and that their suspicions of the West might be allayed somewhat through an authoritative statement of aims from the United States and the United Kingdom.[50]

By the second week of March UN Secretary-General Lie was sufficiently pessimistic about the prospects for negotiations through an approach to China that he proposed overtures to North Korea or the Soviet Union. Talks with the Kim government offered a means for avoiding the difficult issue of China's demands outside Korea. The problem was how to contact North Korea. Lie suggested that the Soviets might serve as go-betweens and that the Americans might approach them in Paris, where preliminary discussions were in progress on a possible conference of foreign ministers to deal with Germany and other European issues.[51]

Although an effort to contact North Korea soon faded into the background among would-be peacemakers, Soviet representatives at the United Nations quietly encouraged a U.S. approach to Andrei Gromyko, the head of the USSR delegation in Paris.[52] At the beginning of April the State Department instructed Soviet expert Charles Bohlen, a member of the U.S. delegation there, to make an informal overture to a low-level Soviet diplomat.[53] On the 5th Bohlen approached Soviet delegate Vladimir Semenov, but received the impression that his government believed that a new offensive in Korea might make it unnecessary to accept a compromise peace.[54] The U.S. diplomat heard nothing more on the matter until the 21st, the eve of the first Chinese spring offensive in Korea, when Semenov again implied to him that the Soviets anticipated a Communist military victory on the peninsula and that any further conversations on Korea should be pursued with Gromyko. When Chinese armies moved in Korea soon thereafter, the United States decided the time was not right for a follow-up approach.[55]

It is possible that MacArthur's declaration of 24 March, coupled with ambiguous statements in Washington regarding U.S. intentions, discouraged the Soviets or the Chinese or both from pursuing negotiations. Both Communist powers were extremely sensitive to the application of overt pressure. Never did the United States indicate firmly that it would accept an armistice at the 38th parallel. In fact, throughout March, Chinese leaders believed that the United States was planning a major offensive beyond that line.[56] If the Kremlin was trying to persuade Beijing to negotiate, statements emanating from Washington and Tokyo did not make its task any easier. The Chinese press was particularly spirited in its rebuttal to MacArthur's "shameless boast" regarding the balance of forces in Korea.[57]

Yet there is no evidence in Communist propaganda or in Soviet or Chinese maneuvering behind the scenes that Moscow or Beijing was willing to consider a settlement in Korea without certain demands: a withdrawal of foreign troops from the peninsula, U.S. concessions on Taiwan, and Chinese representation in the United Nations.[58] Their expressions of interest in a seven-power conference suggested their continuing pressure for concessions on these issues, as this arena would surround the United States with nations sympathetic to the Communist position on the last two points. Peng Dehuai's memoirs indicate that Mao still anticipated military victory in Korea.[59] A Mao telegram to Stalin of 1 March confirms the point, although it makes clear that the Chinese leader now expected the war to go on for at least two more years. Recent developments on the battlefield clearly indicated that the enemies would not leave Korea "unless a large portion of their troops were annihilated," Mao wrote, and this goal would "take time" to accomplish. He saw the rotation of Chinese armies in Korea in three groups as a means of countering recent enemy attrition tactics.[60] In all likelihood, he did not want negotiations immediately because he thought the CPV military position would improve in the future, thus increasing his prospects for obtaining favorable terms at the bargaining table.

The Soviets may have had less confidence on this matter than the Chinese and encouraged ongoing contacts with the Americans on Korea so as to expedite the path to negotiations should they become desirable in the future. Perhaps Soviet flirtation with talks at Paris indicated a desire to link a settlement in Korea with one regarding Germany. Perhaps tension existed between the Communist giants over the Soviet failure to deliver adequate heavy equipment to the Chinese. Before the Communist spring offensives, however, it is doubtful that Washington's tactics destroyed an opportunity to reach an acceptable settlement or to sow the seeds of dissension between Moscow and Beijing. For the moment Washington's approach actually may have promoted the latter goal.

During late March and early April a statement of aims on Korea served as the focal point for allied discussion over a possible peace initiative. The British and the Canadians expressed reservations about the proposed draft circulated by the United States on 21 March. Pearson recommended a series of revisions, including conforming the statement more closely with the five principles approved by the UN First Committee on 13 January and elimination of the word *aggressors* in referring to China and North Korea.[61] The British took a different tack, informing the United States that they were considering a new peace initiative and requesting that the United States postpone the release of its statement until the cabinet had made a decision on the matter.[62]

On the 30th Herbert Morrison, the new British foreign minister, finally approached the United States with the outline for an initiative.[63] Although the United States did not reject his proposal out of hand, the recommendations never held much appeal to the State Department. The United States anticipated difficulties working out the specifics of a proposed declaration that included not only nations with troops in the UN command but India and Sweden as well. The State Department feared that the final product would be so diluted as to give the Communist side an advantage in any negotiations that followed. Moreover, the third step in the plan, which called on the Soviets and Chinese to suggest proposals for a peaceful settlement in Korea, would enable the Communists to seize the diplomatic initiative by advancing positions that were unacceptable to the United States but attractive to other contributors to the UN effort on the peninsula.[64] In particular, the Truman administration wanted to avoid a return to the five principles of January. While the British draft text of a multipower declaration that was advanced to the State Department on 10 April omitted any reference to issues other than Korea, its call for a six-power conference (dropping only Egypt from the earlier Chinese proposal) left the two allies a good distance from agreement.[65]

To add further complexity to the efforts to negotiate on Korea, the Arab-Asian bloc continued discussing a possible appeal to both sides not to advance their troops beyond the 38th parallel. Since the United States feared that an appeal alone, coming outside established UN channels, would lower the prestige of the international organization and that implementation of such an appeal would place UN military forces at a disadvantage, it lobbied against the move. Resenting the plan to bypass the GOC, Padilla Nervo and Grafstrom joined in the U.S. endeavor.[66]

But before any of the maneuvering aimed at a new gesture for peace in Korea bore fruit, an event occurred in Washington which, along with Communist action in Korea that soon followed, temporarily shifted momentum back toward consideration of additional measures against China. In the wee hours of the morning of 11 April President Truman relieved MacArthur of all his commands.

## The Firing of MacArthur

The UN commander's declaration of 24 March, which blocked a possible peace initiative from Washington, often has been cited as commencing the final train of events leading to his dismissal.[67] Truman wrote in his memoirs that this act represented a direct challenge to the president's position as commander in chief, that he decided then that MacArthur must be relieved. The only remaining questions were how and when.[68] Yet Truman revealed this thought to no one at the time, nor did he commit it to paper until days after the actual dismissal.[69] The only immediate action taken was for the Joint Chiefs to wire MacArthur with a reminder of the president's directive of 6 December 1950 that "officials overseas, including military commanders and diplomatic representatives, should . . . exercise extreme caution in public statements, . . . clear all but routine statements with their departments, and . . . refrain from direct communication in military or foreign policy with newspapers, magazines, or other publicity media in the United States."[70] This was more than had been done in response to MacArthur's other pronouncements during the past several weeks, but, given the blatant nature of the offense, it represented a mild rebuke. The Truman administration had little confidence in the success of a peace initiative before another Communist offensive in Korea, and its exploration in this area was based in part on a desire to mollify its allies.[71] In all likelihood it was subsequent events in Washington, Tokyo, and elsewhere that sealed MacArthur's fate.

Sustained deliberations in the executive branch over the impetuous general's fate did not commence until the afternoon of 5 April, after Republican congressman Joseph W. Martin read, on the floor of the lower house, a letter that MacArthur had sent him dated 20 March. In it, MacArthur responded to a request from the politician for a reaction to a speech of his attacking U.S. policy in Asia and Europe and proposing that Jiang Jieshi receive U.S. backing for an invasion of the mainland. MacArthur expressed agreement with Martin's views and concluded with his common refrain about Asia being the key "battlefield" in the struggle against communism, in which there was "no substitute for victory."[72] Also on the 5th the *London Daily Telegraph* published an interview with MacArthur in which he complained of restrictions on his military operations.[73] Finally, the 5 April issue of *The Freeman*, a conservative U.S. magazine, carried a statement attributed to MacArthur implying that Washington was to blame for the failure to make greater use of ROK manpower in the Korean fighting.[74] As the Pentagon was anxious to increase the ROK contribution to the UN cause and had merely followed MacArthur's advice in refusing to train and arm new South Korean units, this charge was particularly annoying to the Joint Chiefs.[75]

General Bradley quickly got word that Truman was upset with release of the letter to Martin and he called together the Joint Chiefs—except General Collins, who was out of town—to discuss possible action. On the next morning, a Friday, the president called in Bradley, Marshall, Acheson, and White House National Security Adviser Averell Harriman and asked for their advice. Acheson favored MacArthur's dismissal while Bradley and Marshall were opposed. Harriman was ambivalent. Even the secretary of state counseled the president to move cautiously until he had the support of all his leading advisers. Meetings among top officials continued through the afternoon and into the weekend. Late on Sunday the Joint Chiefs finally agreed that, "from a military point of view only," MacArthur should be fired. On the following day, with Bradley, Marshall, Acheson, and Harriman all in essential agreement, Truman told them of his decision to relieve the general and directed that they draft the appropriate orders.[76]

It is a fair guess that the events of 5 April, combined with Senate passage on the previous day of a resolution endorsing the dispatch of four new U.S. divisions to Europe, pushed Truman to the verge of decisive action against MacArthur. With the most immediate threat from Congress to the administration's European strategy out of the way, and with the field commander's public dissent from established policy showing no sign of abatement, the president moved with greater vigor than before.[77]

As a result of Korea and other issues, however, his standing with the public was at or near an all-time low, and he was well aware of the domestic storm a tangle with MacArthur would provoke.[78] In weathering the storm, he surely grasped the importance of support from his top military advisers. Although Marshall and the Joint Chiefs never actually recommended MacArthur's dismissal, they did say it was advisable for military reasons. Had they refused to do so, the president might have tried less drastic methods of restraining the field commander.

Bradley and Marshall hesitated to advocate a decisive move for a variety of reasons. For one thing, although MacArthur's stature had declined since generals Collins's and Vandenberg's January visit to Japan and Korea, Washington shared his impatience with limited war. Despite the improvement in UN military fortunes, plans for an expansion of the war continued in the Pentagon as concern remained regarding an indefinite commitment of substantial U.S. forces to Korea.[79] Even if an armistice became possible, protecting it against future aggression would be difficult on a peninsula divided across the middle. With military conditions fluid in late February and March, the Joint Chiefs resisted State Department efforts to define the U.S. position explicitly regarding the 38th parallel.[80] On 15 March, in a discussion with State Department representatives, General Collins and Admiral Sherman spoke in tentative yet positive terms about a UN advance to Pyongyang or the narrow neck.[81] More than their counterparts at the State Department, the soldiers understood MacArthur's perspective even if they did not fully subscribe to his positions or methods of expressing them. Furthermore, fear existed that the relief of MacArthur would jeopardize the defense program then before Congress and negotiations for a Japanese peace treaty, which were at a critical stage. Perhaps most important of all, Bradley and Marshall feared that MacArthur's dismissal would politicize the Joint Chiefs. These were tired old men who did not relish being principals in the domestic furor MacArthur's dismissal was certain to generate. In the end, and despite Truman's refusal to take a stand until all his subordinates had done so, they did sense his preference, and this probably influenced their final position.[82]

Personal dynamics aside, the key substantive issue to the military men revolved around recent reports of a sizable buildup of air power in Manchuria and the movement into the region of three Soviet army divisions.[83] Up to this point, the Communists had restricted their air war to contesting UN air and naval missions directed at North Korea. A departure from this limited activity to support major CPV efforts to push southward might shift the military balance against the United Nations. Attacks on South Korean ports, on UN supply lines, or on Japan itself also were possibilities. In countering such dangers, the UN command would have to move quickly, and this would require authority for its planes to pursue enemy aircraft back to their bases in Manchuria. On 5 April the Joint Chiefs drafted a new directive to MacArthur granting him this authority and the president approved it, but they did not dispatch it to Tokyo.[84] Two days earlier Rusk had informed representatives with troops fighting on the UN side in Korea that the United States would respond in any way possible to a large-scale Communist air offensive.[85] Soon thereafter, Truman sent an air force squadron to the western Pacific armed with atomic weapons.[86]

U.S. officials in Washington did not trust MacArthur with broadened authority. They feared that he would use a new directive to justify action beyond Korea that was not really necessary, thus needlessly expanding the conflict. Retaining final authority in Washington, in the Joint Chiefs or even the president, would reduce this possibility; yet this approach still might leave decision makers facing a quick judgment based on information provided by MacArthur. And what if direct communication between Washington and Tokyo lapsed temporarily? Changing commanders in Tokyo became a means of protecting UN forces while, at the same time, containing the war except under truly extreme circumstances.[87]

Allied opinion probably influenced Truman and his advisers. Although no foreign government requested the general's relief, by late afternoon on the 6th key State and Defense Department officials knew that granting expanded authority to the UN commander would be difficult to sell to other NATO members, at least while MacArthur retained that post. At that time, Sir Oliver Franks met with Bradley and Admiral Sherman from the Joint Chiefs and Rusk and Paul Nitze from the State Department. He had just received the British government's "preliminary" views on retaliatory bombing. Not only did the British believe that prior consultation at the ministerial level should occur among the allies; so should a warning to the Chinese "for the immediate cessation of their air attacks." Military leaders in London doubted that the danger of a Communist air offensive was as great as the Americans claimed. "We are inclined to think that the major danger is MacArthur's rashness and political irresponsibility, rather than massive air attacks from outside Korea," Morrison informed Franks, "though there is of course a connection between the two inasmuch as the first may provoke the second."[88] Earlier in the day diplomats from four other NATO countries had "cornered" Assistant Secretary of State John Hickerson to express concern about granting MacArthur new authority.[89] Acheson already advocated MacArthur's recall, but events of the 6th were not the first demonstration of how the general's presence in Tokyo complicated allied relationships. On the previous day Franks had approached Rusk with a message from London reflecting what he called the "MacArthuritis" there. The message emphasized the need to avoid even the hint of a desire or intention to extend hostilities beyond Korea, and it complained about an upcoming operation by the U.S. Seventh Fleet off the China coast opposite Taiwan.[90] Minimally, the allied viewpoint reinforced the concerns of U.S. leaders as they gingerly approached a most difficult decision.

## The Domestic Response

Despite the buildup of rumors days before Truman's relief of MacArthur, announcement of the decision produced widespread shock in the United States. Nationalist Chinese Ambassador Wellington Koo recorded in his diary that "it came . . . as a thunderbolt out of a clear sky." Speculation following the events of 5 April had inclined to the view that the president would merely rebuke the general.[91]

Still, Republican critics of administration policy in Asia, already braced to counter that possibility, shifted easily to expressions of outrage and condemnation of the dismissal. Senator McCarthy favored impeachment of the president. Reports spread that Republican leaders in Congress were considering impeachment proceedings against Acheson as well. Movements developed to invite the deposed military hero to address a joint meeting of the House and Senate and to conduct hearings to investigate recent U.S. policy toward Asia.[92] On a radio talk show, Republican Senator Homer Capehart (Ind.) and Democratic counterparts Herbert Lehman (N.Y.) and Hubert Humphrey (Minn.) became so heated in an exchange over the MacArthur affair that moderator Blair Moody had to intervene to avert a brawl.[93] A presidential aide seeking comic relief imagined the festivities that would accompany MacArthur's triumphant return to Washington. They included the "burning of the Constitution," the "lynching of Secretary Acheson," and a "21-atomic bomb salute," all climaxed by "300 nude D.A.R.'s leap[ing] from [the] Washington monument." (The Daughters of the American Revolution had passed a resolution praising MacArthur and expressing confidence in his "defense of American principles.")[94]

The Democrats did not shy away from the battle. The administration soon put out word that it was prepared to counter the deluge.[95] Republican Senator Richard M. Nixon of California, always on the lookout for dirty tricks employed by the enemy, complained that the Democrats were planning one of history's most reprehensible "smear campaigns" against the general.[96] The president made only a limited effort to avoid the fray. In a speech on the 14th he called on Democrats to put patriotism above politics, but then launched a spirited attack on Republican critics of his foreign policy: "they want defense without spending any money; they want us to wage war without an army; they want us to have victory without taking any risks, and they want us to try to run the whole world and run it without friends."[97] Eric Sevareid of CBS remarked wearily, "Washington is a place that can never, for very long, deny itself indulgence in the wild pleasures of party politics."[98]

Partisanship aside, the MacArthur controversy raised fundamental questions regarding U.S. strategy abroad. In a national radio address on the 11th Truman outlined the rationale behind his course in Asia. He opposed more direct action against China because this would entangle the United States "in a vast conflict on the continent of Asia," thus making "our task ... immeasurably more difficult all over the world." The fundamental though unstated premise here was that other parts of the world, especially Europe, held more importance to the United States than did continental East Asia. Truman continued that "our [current] efforts in Korea," coupled with the rapid buildup of military forces by non-Communist nations, would both "blunt the will of the Chinese Communists to continue the struggle" in Korea and discourage them and their allies "from undertaking new acts of aggression elsewhere." The point was twofold: first, the war could be brought to a successful conclusion without expanding the effort; second, to repulse aggression, not to destroy its source, constituted success. In a word, the president advocated a limited war, limited both in the force employed and in the aims sought.[99]

MacArthur's reply came eight days later. Before a packed house in Congress and to a nationwide radio and television audience, the general delivered a stirring address that moved many of his listeners to tears. He reduced his strategy for winning the war—that is, unifying Korea—to four proposals: an intensified economic embargo of China; a naval blockade of the China coast; air reconnaissance over China; and an end to restrictions on Chinese Nationalist operations against the mainland, plus logistical support for such operations. These were far from unlimited means—he did not advocate the use of atomic bombs or, in this case, the bombing of Manchuria, and he denied that he had ever "given a thought" to using U.S. ground forces on mainland China; yet they were means far broader than those presently acceptable to Truman. A failure to employ them, MacArthur insisted, would condemn the United States to "an indecisive campaign, with its terrible and constant attrition upon our forces." For the United States to continue its present course "could only produce new demands" from the enemy. Unworried about an expanded war, MacArthur asserted that China was "already engaging with the maximum power it can commit and the Soviet will not necessarily mesh its actions with our moves." He declared in closing that he had ended fifty-two years of military service and that, like the soldier in an army ballad popular during his days as a student at West Point, he would now "just fade away—an old soldier who tried to do his duty as God gave him the light to see that duty."[100]

With public opinion polls and congressional mail indicating strong sympathy for MacArthur, Republican leaders were not about to let him fade away, and he was not about to resist their beckoning call.[101] The next step in this great drama of American democracy was to commence in early May, when two Senate committees opened joint hearings on U.S. policy in Asia, with MacArthur and top administration officials as the star witnesses. In this context the opposing positions were certain to be subjected to careful scrutiny.

## THE INTERNATIONAL RESPONSE

MacArthur's dismissal received widespread attention abroad, especially in countries with a stake in the Korean War. Both inside the Communist bloc and elsewhere, the response was largely favorable, although several exceptions existed in the latter case and the anticipated impact of Truman's action differed substantially from place to place.

With the exception of Spain, where opinion favored MacArthur, the reaction in western Europe was overwhelmingly pro-Truman.[102] Europeans welcomed MacArthur's dismissal with a giant "sigh of relief." The *New Yorker*'s correspondent in London wrote that "anti-American propaganda in Europe had just taken its heaviest, most punishing wallop."[103] In the British House of Commons, news of the general's firing brought enthusiastic cheers.[104] The West German, French, and Italian responses were less frenzied though equally unanimous in approval.[105] In Greece and Turkey, Truman's move came as a shock, but it received broad support. Despite the admiration for MacArthur's unyielding stand against communism, people in those countries remembered best the Truman Doctrine and the Greek-Turkish aid program of 1947.[106]

Government officials sought to keep a low profile on the MacArthur issue, fearing that public displays of satisfaction would foster antagonism in the United States, where Truman's critics argued that European, especially British, pressure had sparked his action. This view received much support throughout the world, thus adding to concern among European leaders that their countries would become scapegoats in the orgy of popular recrimination that was sweeping the United States.[107]

The Communist press from Moscow westward also emphasized the role of America's NATO partners. Although leading Soviet publications did not editorialize on MacArthur's demise until 18 April, newscasts out of Moscow and eastern European capitals quickly expounded on the event. East Berlin radio chortled that MacArthur's removal constituted "proof of the concrete power of the peoples, of the reality of the existence of the world peace movement." Schuman and Attlee were pro-MacArthur, "but under the pressure of their peoples they had to protest to Truman." The Soviet European Service followed with a threefold explanation of the U.S. decision: "Firstly, they would like to conceal the failure of their disastrous policy in the Far East by throwing the blame on MacArthur. Secondly, they thus hope to embolden their European allies, who have become frightened at the indignation of their peoples. Thirdly, they thus want to drown the voice of the Peace Partisans who demand a peaceful settlement in Korea."[108] The Communist press argued uniformly that no change had occurred in U.S. policy.

The Chinese put less emphasis on European pressure in explaining MacArthur's fall, which it claimed resulted "from the iron blows dealt by the Chinese and Korean peoples." Still, "American aggressors" had failed to learn the lesson. U.S. planes continued to infringe on Chinese territory, the press asserted indignantly, sometimes strafing or even bombing towns and cities. So the United States had not abandoned its attempts to expand the war.[109]

Anti-Communist governments in Asia were less certain that U.S. policy would remain firm in the region. The Japanese considered MacArthur a wise and benevolent ruler who had championed their interests abroad through times of great vulnerability. Now, as one Canadian analyst on the scene remarked, "their country has been reduced from the rank of Five Stars to the rank of Three Stars in the American scheme of things."[110] Not only was General Ridgway of far less stature than his predecessor; he was largely unknown to the Japanese. "The keynote of the Japanese nation," a U.S. correspondent reported, was "anxiety."[111] To Filipinos, MacArthur was a hero who had delivered on his promise during World War II to return and liberate their nation from the Japanese. More recently he had promoted the Nationalist cause on Taiwan, which many Filipino leaders thought crucial to the security of their own islands. Newspapers in Manila immediately rallied to MacArthur's defense, and President Quirino invited him to visit his country.[112] Chinese officials on Taiwan were circumspect in public statements on Truman's decision, but they viewed it as representing a rejection of U.S. support for a Nationalist invasion of the mainland, just as ROK leaders in Korea saw it as undermining their hopes for the unification of their country.[113]

Yet after the initial shock of the dismissal, its impact in these countries subsided. Whatever their doubts about the direction of U.S. policy, they had little place else to go. The commencement of the Communist spring offensive on the 22d relieved ROK officials of anxieties about an early armistice. The Filipino government was on the verge of receiving new economic assistance from the United States, and MacArthur's favorable mention of the Philippines in his address to Congress provided invaluable publicity.[114] The Nationalist regime on Taiwan anticipated a U.S. military mission and expanded material aid. On the 24th the Pentagon announced that Taiwan now ranked equally to western Europe in priority for weapons and ammunition shipments.[115] To assuage Japanese fears, John Foster Dulles rushed to Tokyo with assurances that progress toward an early peace treaty would in no way be interrupted. Ridgway's reassuring statements upon his arrival on the 14th also helped.[116]

Elements in Western nations who had hoped that MacArthur's departure would produce more flexibility in both Washington and on the Communist side were soon disappointed. The United States moved quickly to convey to friend and foe alike that U.S. policy remained unchanged. It rejected a British proposal for Chinese Communist participation in a Japanese peace treaty; it discouraged proposals by Rau for a four-power conference on Korea and other issues; and it turned down a request by Morrison for a declaration of UN aims in Korea.[117] Nor did the Truman administration retreat from its insistence, under certain conditions, on retaliatory bombing of Manchurian bases. Truman had learned a lesson from the furor over his comments the previous November about the possible use of atomic weapons, that subtlety in conveying threats of an expanded war was essential in maintaining allied unity. Under intense domestic pressure, however, and still concerned about the enemy buildup in Manchuria, the president warned in his address to the nation of 11 April that the enemy would "bear the responsibility" for subsequent developments if it escalated its use of air power against UN forces.[118] Finally, the United States increased pressure at the United Nations for an early move by the AMC for economic sanctions against China.[119] For both domestic and international reasons, the State Department moved to demonstrate that U.S. policy remained firm. Acheson actually expected to "cash in" on MacArthur's firing by pressing for British and other support for certain U.S. positions that had previously been opposed.[120]

The Communists did make one move that temporarily raised hopes at the United Nations. On the 15th North Korean Foreign Minister Pak Hon-yong sent identical messages to the presidents of the Security Council and the General Assembly. Most of the communiqué concentrated on lambasting the United States and "Syngman Rhee followers" for alleged atrocities in Korea. Pak concluded by demanding settlement of the Korean conflict through procedures advocated by the World Peace Council at its February conference in East Berlin. The conference had called for a meeting of all powers concerned with the peninsula, including the "Big Five" (that is, permanent members of the Security Council, the PRC being China's representative). North Korea called for the withdrawal of all foreign forces from Korea to permit the indigenous peoples to settle their own affairs. The message made no specific reference to Taiwan, a point that satellite diplomats at Lake Success emphasized in conversations with the Western press.[121]

The message aroused considerable interest, especially in the Arab-Asian group and the GOC. Rau suggested that the Arab-Asian group seek contact with North Korea.[122] The Indian government had already instructed Panikkar to broach to the Chinese the idea of a new peace initiative based on the five principles enunciated by the United Nations in January. After a meeting on the 18th with the Chinese vice minister of foreign affairs, Panikkar submitted a pessimistic report. The PRC official asserted that any chance for peace required a change in U.S. policy. Apparently the Chinese were angry over an alleged attack on the mainland by some two hundred U.S. bombers based on Taiwan.[123] Yet GOC members lacked confidence in Panikkar, and they derived encouragement for an approach to North Korea from a conversation at a reception at Lake Success on the 20th. The primary actor in this informal exchange was Constantin Zinchenko, a Soviet citizen and member of the UN secretariat. Others present included Padilla Nervo, Arne Sunde of Norway,

Lambertus Palar of Indonesia, and Ernest Gross of the United States. On several occasions Zinchenko insisted that the North Korean message should be "followed up."[124] This incident, combined with the facts that the North Korean message had been in Russian and had not been published or even commented on in the Chinese press, appeared encouraging to GOC members. The start of the Communist spring offensive in Korea on the 22d, however, strengthened the U.S. case that the North Korean message "was a scurrilous document."[125]

The North Korean communiqué hardly constituted a palpable shift in the Communist position. Although it made no mention of issues outside Korea, the February resolutions of the World Peace Council to which the message referred did do so.[126] Despite the elimination of such neutrals as India and Egypt, a five-power conference would still leave the United States to negotiate with four nations sympathetic toward Beijing's position regarding Taiwan and Chinese representation at the United Nations.

North Korea's maneuver probably sought to test U.S. firmness in the aftermath of MacArthur's dismissal. The Soviets viewed Truman's action as a result of allied pressure and hoped that more of the same would alter U.S. aims in Korea.[127] North Korea's message to the United Nations and the Soviet follow-up also may have sought to counter the improved U.S. image abroad produced by MacArthur's firing. To respond to the U.S. move simply by launching a long-planned military offensive in Korea might harm the Communist propaganda machine, while an act that appeared to some as a peace probe, coupled with continued claims of ongoing U.S. air attacks on the mainland, might help redress the balance. (China revealed concern about its image abroad on the 18th, when it announced its offer to famine-plagued India of one million tons of rice, this at a time when the Truman administration's proposal to send wheat to that country had been bottled up in Congress for weeks.[128]) Finally, the North Korean move may have aimed to get the jump on UNCURK, which recently had been discussing a possible peace overture to the Kim regime. The Soviets undoubtedly knew of this discussion through Zinchenko, and again they may have regarded it as a potential embarrassment should it culminate in action just before the Chinese offensive.[129] The achievement of any of these purposes, of course, would make any U.S. attempt to expand the war more difficult, either with air action beyond the Yalu or ground operations substantially north of the 38th parallel.

### Increasing Pressure on China

In the United States, the North Korean communiqué attracted only passing interest. In dealing with the war on an international level, the Truman administration preoccupied itself with the issues of retaliatory bombing of Manchuria and UN economic sanctions against China. Controversies between the

United States and its allies lasted well into May, demonstrating the limited impact of MacArthur's dismissal on relationships among the NATO powers. The British took the lead in trying to restrain the Americans.

One might expect that disagreement in the Western camp over retaliatory action against Manchuria would have subsided once MacArthur was fired. General Ridgway was a traditional soldier who accepted his government's desire to limit the war. He was unlikely to overreact to a Communist move or to present exaggerated reports to Washington.[130] Furthermore, the likelihood was slim that Beijing or Moscow would approve an air offensive against UN troops. Although orders for retaliatory attacks on Manchuria had not been issued to the UN commander before 11 April, widespread rumors in the press suggested that they had. Since the U.S. State Department had informed India that such retaliation would occur if the Communists broadened the air war in Korea, it was a good bet that the Chinese understood the risk entailed in that action.[131] (After information on U.S. policy leaked out through the U.S. delegation to the United Nations on the 25th, there could be little doubt that China grasped this point.[132]) Unless the Communist powers actually wanted an expanded war, they were unlikely to use their air power more aggressively.

Yet this was not how matters appeared at the time to America's NATO allies. The tremendous domestic pressures faced by the Truman administration provide the major explanation. In the aftermath of MacArthur's dismissal, such astute observers of the U.S. scene as Sir Oliver Franks and Hume Wrong were quick to warn their home offices that for several weeks it would be extremely difficult for Truman and his advisers to give ground on any issue involving Asia.[133] The British and Canadian ambassadors recognized the good intentions of U.S. leaders, but for many foreign observers it was not difficult to envision beleaguered decision makers in Washington taking ill-considered action that could produce a global conflict. Sizable air and naval maneuvers conducted by the United States off the south and east coasts of China on 11 and 13 April were hardly reassuring.[134]

On 12 April General Bradley informed Franks and Lord Tedder that President Truman had approved attacks on Manchuria in the event of a major Communist air offensive in Korea. In the face of a report of such an offensive, the Joint Chiefs would assess the information and, upon "determining that the conditions contemplated had actually taken place," would authorize immediate retaliation. If political leaders were readily available, they would be consulted in advance of the decision.[135]

British officials protested. To them, the only totally satisfactory procedure was for the United States to consult them for approval after an actual Communist attack had occurred. In addition, the British did not believe that the Communists had the capacity to launch a major air offensive or that they would be prepared to mount a large-scale ground offensive in Korea until June, estimates that called into question the need to make an early decision on retaliation.[136] A series of exchanges on the issue began that included other allied governments as well and ended in mid-May in only partial agreement.

The Chinese spring offensive created a sense of urgency on the U.S. side. On the 26th the Joint Chiefs wired Ridgway inquiring as to the advisability of granting him authority now to bomb Manchuria and the Shantung peninsula in the event of a Communist air offensive against UN troops in Korea. The UN commander replied affirmatively.[137] He also wanted to conduct air reconnaissance of Chinese air bases in Manchuria and Shantung. Washington quickly granted this last request, but the first generated considerable discussion in the executive branch. Ridgway finally received his authority, although on very restricted grounds. The Joint Chiefs' reply to Tokyo on the 28th emphasized that "if at all possible you should seek JCS advice before taking action and in any case you should inform the JCS immediately and withhold publicity until notification of allies has taken place."[138] This meant that Ridgway was to gain prior approval from higher authority unless telecommunications between his command and Washington were temporarily cut off.[139] This loophole conflicted with State Department assurances to nations with troops in Korea that any decision to bomb outside the peninsula would be made in Washington. So U.S. diplomats set about informing those countries of the slight change.[140]

The United States emphasized to allied governments that it would make every effort to consult them in advance of action in Manchuria, and the United Kingdom, as the most insistent nation regarding such consultation, labored to establish machinery to give a quick reply in the event of a crisis. On 10 May British Foreign Minister Herbert Morrison, with the approval of a cabinet now devoid of strong representation from the Labor Left, informed Acheson that his government accepted "in principle" the idea of retaliatory bombing on Manchurian bases.[141] Yet his government could not "divest" itself of responsibility for a decision in a particular case on a matter of such importance. He assured Acheson that once informed of the details of Communist action, the British government could reply "at very short notice" and suggested that any U.S. decision should be "subject to confirmation" by the president just as any British one would require approval by the prime minister.[142] The United States refused to bend further.[143] Fortunately, circumstances never arose in which the consultative process was put to the test.

The issue of economic sanctions against China was in one way more difficult for the allies than that of retaliatory bombing of Manchuria. Because sanctions involved a UN committee with a dozen members and, potentially, a vote in the General Assembly, it could not be dealt with largely in private. If the United States pushed hard for UN sanctions, its allies would either have to submit or to make their opposition public, thus incurring the ire of U.S. opinion. The potential existed for a crisis in the Western alliance comparable to that which occurred in January over the aggressor resolution.

MacArthur's dismissal hastened the day of reckoning. On 14 April Acheson directed the U.S. mission at the United Nations to press for a session of the AMC subcommittee and seek its approval of a recommendation to the full committee to "consider immediately and urgently possible economic measures" against China. Acheson hoped that the AMC could meet on the 18th and approve soon thereafter a recommendation to the General Assembly for economic sanctions. Such "a new manifestation of UN determination" on Korea, the secretary of state wrote, might persuade Beijing to seek a peaceful settlement rather than launch another offensive.[144]

This calculation provided the lesser of two reasons for the U.S. move. The State Department had believed for some time that a course of firmness was the most likely way to bring the Communists to the negotiating table. In the aftermath of MacArthur's firing, Washington needed to convey to the other side in no uncertain terms that no weakening had occurred in the U.S. position. Yet the firing also magnified pressure at home to show firmness, and the rush to convene the AMC to consider economic sanctions was closely tied to the administration's desire to show initiative before MacArthur's address to Congress on the 19th. Acheson's previous concern to avoid the revelation of strong divisions in the allied camp now held lower priority than that of strengthening the administration's domestic position against the anticipated onslaught by MacArthur.[145]

When the subcommittee finally met on the 17th, Britain's Jebb, Australia's Shann, and France's Lacoste all opposed a quick move toward sanctions, which they thought would undermine prospects for negotiations with China. Recognizing the Truman administration's immediate problem at home, and fearing that stubborn resistance would provoke more extreme action, Jebb offered a compromise. The subcommittee would adjourn until the following afternoon, giving its members time to consult their governments. On reconvening, it would propose a study of a selective embargo and a meeting of the full AMC. The U.S. delegation could leak information to the press on the apparent movement toward sanctions that would become public prior to MacArthur's appearance before Congress.[146] The Americans accepted the proposal, the subcommittee meeting on the next day went as planned, and the morning newspapers on 19 April dutifully carried the story; but this merely postponed the day of reckoning.[147]

Allied diplomats delayed a full meeting of the AMC until 3 May. Continuing objections in London and Paris to railroading sanctions through the United Nations, plus uncertainty as to whether even a simple majority in the AMC favored new measures against China, encouraged caution among the Americans.[148] Despite the delay, the AMC convened without any prior agreement on a course of action among its leading members. The British and French still believed the timing poor, as by early May UN forces had blunted the first phase of the Chinese offensive in Korea and hopes returned that a propitious moment for negotiations was near. They also opposed America's "vague formula" for an embargo on petroleum, atomic energy materials, arms, ammunition, and implements of war, and articles of use in making such products, with each country determining what particular items it would cut off and how it would enforce restrictions. The United Kingdom and France both favored a brief and specific list of items to be embargoed. In addition, Britain wanted a UN declaration of aims in Korea to coincide with any new action against China. The initial meeting of the AMC revealed a considerable variety of opinion. Only the Brazilian, Turkish, Filipino, and Venezuelan representatives supported the United States.[149]

Developments within the United States emphasized the danger to the Western alliance of a continued division on sanctions. The MacArthur controversy aggravated long-standing U.S. resentments over the comparatively meager European contributions to the struggle against communism. Senator Capehart reflected these attitudes on 2 May when he called for an ultimatum demanding greater assistance to the Korean effort from UN members other than the United States. If such aid was not forthcoming, Capehart declared, the United States should withdraw its troops from the peninsula.[150] MacArthur's testimony before the Senate Armed Services and Foreign Relations committees, which began the next day, fueled nationalistic sentiments. He referred to the contributions of U.S. allies in Korea as "token," he asserted that a large quantity of strategic materials was flowing into China through Hong Kong, and he stated that, if America's allies refused to acquiesce in his strategy for victory in Korea, the United States should go it alone.[151] The otherwise anti-MacArthur *New York Times* supported the general on the matter of shipments to China via Hong Kong. "This is a point at which the integrity and common sense of the United Nations are involved," the editors wrote. "No one in his senses can urge that the way to deal with aggression is to arm it."[152] On the 9th Senator Kem proposed an amendment to an appropriations bill that would terminate U.S. economic aid to countries selling war materials to Communist nations.[153]

Opposition to the U.S. position in the AMC was now on the brink of collapse. When the committee met on the 7th, Jebb stated that his government might support the U.S. proposal.[154] Three days later Morrison informed Acheson of such support.[155] As on most issues involving Korea, others in the Western bloc quickly followed suit. On the 14th the AMC approved a recommendation to the General Assembly for a selective embargo on China. Only Egypt's abstention prevented unanimity.[156]

Ironically, the Attlee government's concessions to the United States derived in part from events on its own home front. On 2 May Conservatives in the House of Commons began a campaign, first, to find out precisely what strategic goods were being shipped to China through Hong Kong and, second, to ensure that British policy was in line with that of the United States. The Laborites responded clumsily, giving incomplete information and assurances, some of which turned out to be false. Particularly embarrassing were revelations that shipments into China from the British colony, especially of rubber from Malaya and Singapore, had increased during the first quarter of 1951 and had continued into April. Rubber exports were important to the Malayan economy, and their rising price since the outbreak of war in Korea had provided a stimulus that undermined Communist efforts at subversion. An embargo on rubber to China and on other items normally shipped through Hong Kong might encourage the Mao regime to increase pressure on the British possessions. Yet in revealing publicly what the British already were doing to restrict trade with China and that those actions did not go as far as the U.S. proposals, the parliamentary debate on sanctions subverted two past justifications for resisting economic measures through the United Nations. Holding a narrow majority in the House of Commons and, in all likelihood, facing a general election later in the year, the Labor government was not in a strong position to withstand a determined Conservative offensive on the issue.[157]

A crisis in Britain's relations with Iran reinforced pressures on the Attlee government to support UN sanctions against China. In late April the extreme nationalist Mohammed Mossadeq became prime minister in Tehran and quickly nationalized Iran's oil reserves. The act followed protracted efforts by Iran to negotiate an agreement with the Anglo-Persian Oil Company that would give the country a larger share of the profits derived from exploitation of its petroleum resources. In a reversal of roles in East Asia, Washington had long counseled London to bend toward nationalist aims in Iran. With a sizable economic stake in the Iranian oil business—not to mention the political implications regarding other parts of its empire—the United Kingdom now needed support from a dubious U.S. State Department to apply pressure that would salvage a portion of its investment in Persia. Resistance to U.S. policy in Korea might undermine such support.[158]

With the British in line and the AMC virtually unanimous on selective economic sanctions, the United States had little difficulty pushing a resolution through the General Assembly. Soviet bloc representatives declined to participate in the voting, claiming that the resolution was illegal, and seven representatives in the Arab-Asian group plus Sweden abstained. In contrast to the resolution branding China an aggressor, no one opposed the new measure, which passed on 18 May. India's Rau expressed a common view among the non-Communist states that refused to support sanctions, arguing that the embargo was already in effect among key nations and that its formal implementation through the United Nations would create "another psychological hurdle" to peace.[159]

The passage of time would undermine both of these arguments. The embargo by non-Communist countries, to be sure, was never air tight. Despite U.S. pressure, Ceylon never agreed to place an embargo on rubber. Some smuggling into China continued from Macao, Thailand, and Burma. Much of China's initial losses in trade were eventually replaced by members of the Soviet bloc. Still, passage of the resolution encouraged many nations to strengthen their machinery for preventing strategic items from reaching the PRC.[160] This effort produced a significant, albeit temporary and indecisive burden on the operation of China's economy.[161] If this result failed to yield an early peace in Korea, it probably reduced China's capacity for intervention in Southeast Asia and drained other Communist nations of resources that might have been used elsewhere. Any psychological impetus that the resolution might have given China to continue the war did not prevent the PRC from commencing armistice talks less than two months later.

Although the General Assembly vote of 18 May averted a dangerous crisis in the Western alliance, it did not end tensions regarding the proper course in Asia. For some time, the MacArthur controversy had appeared to be pushing the Truman administration into commitments that might dampen prospects for a negotiated settlement in Korea and might even produce an expanded war. At the ongoing Senate hearings, Secretary of Defense Marshall spoke of U.S. determination to prevent Communist China from seizing Taiwan or from gaining entry into the United Nations in terms that left little hope for flexibility.[162] This position was far from welcome to western European governments. So were announcements of the dispatch of a U.S. military mission to Taiwan, an increase in military aid to the Jiang regime, and the establishment of a priority for such aid equal to that for NATO countries.[163]

Then, on the same day the General Assembly recommended economic sanctions against China and a day following a *New York Times* report of a call by Jiang Jieshi to open a second front on the mainland, Assistant Secretary of State Rusk delivered a speech in New York that raised the level of vituperation against Communist China and even implied that the United States would support action to undermine the Mao regime. The PRC was "a Slavic Manchukuo on a larger scale," Rusk declared. "It is not the Government of China. It does not pass the first test. It is not Chinese." He pledged that the United States would "not acquiesce in the degradation which is being forced upon . . . [our friends in China]."[164] Marshall already had announced that the new assistance to the Chinese Nationalists was strictly for the defense of Taiwan, and the State Department followed up Rusk's address with assurances that it reflected no change in U.S. policy.[165] Yet with Truman administration officials applying new pressure for economic sanctions and espousing hard-line policies on Taiwan and Chinese representation in the United Nations, with MacArthur expressing approval of an apparent shift in the administration's course in Asia, and with Jiang talking openly of establishing a second front on the mainland, U.S. allies understandably feared that President Truman was adopting the policies of the very man he recently had fired.[166]

The worries were overblown. For months, the Truman administration had favored UN economic sanctions against China and had envisioned stepped-up military assistance to Jiang.[167] Despite its overt adherence to the five principles on Korea stipulated in January, the United States had never intended to make concessions on Taiwan as part of a negotiated settlement of the war. The Americans had anticipated the initiation of retaliatory bombing against Manchuria under certain conditions for some time. Rusk's rhetoric to the contrary notwithstanding, and despite ongoing study within the executive branch of logistical support for offensive operations by the Nationalists, the U.S. government never planned more than limited covert aid to anti-Communist groups on mainland China.[168] The MacArthur furor induced the United States to press harder on some matters and with greater fanfare, but, in any event, the massive Chinese offensives of 22 April and 16 May would have produced some counteraction by Washington.[169]

As in the past February, the allies underestimated their accomplishment simply in delaying new moves against China, as postponement left several initiatives open that would not automatically expand the war. In April and May the Truman administration could use these relatively safe measures to help assuage the anger and frustration of the American public and Congress and to send certain warning signals to the enemy.

Still, American anger and frustration could not be contained forever. At the Senate hearings, General Bradley indicated that the Truman administration had no intention of restricting U.S. operations if the war continued indefinitely. The present strategy, as outlined by top officials, was to persuade the Communists to accept peace in Korea by making the war excessively costly to them. But if that strategy did not produce the desired result, then another might be adopted. Bradley conceded that the differences between MacArthur and the administration were essentially over timing.[170]

### The Collective Effort in Korea

The key source of impatience was the drain Korea imposed on America's human resources. With no end in sight to the fighting, Pentagon officials grew concerned about replacements for U.S. troops, some of whom had been in combat since the previous summer. At the same time military leaders, still fearing Communist action in another area, remained determined not to slow down the buildup of U.S. forces in the more important European theater.[171] The public and Congress became concerned over mounting casualties in Korea, which by May numbered more than sixty thousand Americans.

Such concerns led the United States to examine critically the contributions made by others to the UN effort in Korea. In early May South Korea and the United States contributed over 80 percent of total UN ground troops. In his Senate testimony MacArthur claimed that the elimination of military contributions from other nations "would have no material effect upon the tactical situation."[172] Given allied criticism of the way the United States was conducting the war, such characterizations invariably fostered public resentment. Republican senators magnified such sentiment by badgering administration witnesses at the widely reported Senate hearings about the comparatively small burden being borne by other non-Communist nations in Korea.[173]

MacArthur's assessment of foreign contributions to the UN side was unfair to several countries. Considering the limited economic resources of such nations as the United Kingdom, Turkey, Greece, the Philippines, and Thailand—plus the military problems they faced at or closer to home—their aid to the Korean enterprise was hardly token. Senate partisans of Jiang Jieshi were fond of mentioning that the total number of non-U.S., non-Korean troops actually sent was less than the offer of thirty-three thousand Nationalist Chinese soldiers, which had been declined.[174] Yet a few thousand well-led, highly motivated, and fully equipped troops from the United Kingdom, Turkey, or

France were worth far more than larger numbers of men on Taiwan, who were poorly trained and armed and of dubious morale. MacArthur's remark that non-U.S. and non-Korean units in the fighting had no impact on the tactical situation was a bitter pill to swallow for the countrymen of the Gloucestershire battalion that suffered over 90 percent casualties in the first phase of the Chinese spring offensive in order to delay the enemy advance in a crucial sector; or for survivors of the French and Turkish units that had paid so dearly for their gallant efforts during earlier Chinese offensives.

That said—and despite the contribution of nonmilitary items to the UN cause by a majority of member governments—the burden for combat rested largely in the hands of the United States and South Korea.[175] The Truman administration itself bore some responsibility for this situation. Because of Pentagon doubts about the worth of contributions from most countries, the United States had been clumsy in soliciting assistance during the first two months of the war, when a psychological moment existed to secure foreign contributions.[176] In the fall, when military conditions turned sharply in favor of UN forces, the United States, thinking the fighting nearly over, reduced its efforts to secure new commitments. In November the State Department nailed down offers of battalions from Ethiopia and Colombia, and these contingents arrived in Korea during the following May and June; but, on the Pentagon's initiative, the United States induced Greece to unload a ship of arms and men destined for Korea before it left home. As a result of this premature move, the Greeks never sent more than a battalion to Korea, despite their initial offer of a brigade.[177] Largely because of divisions within the Department of Defense, renewed efforts to secure commitments did not pick up until February 1951. With a UN withdrawal from Korea now appearing unlikely and the enemy having massive reserves of manpower, U.S. military leaders hoped to attract offers that would significantly reduce the burden of the United States.[178] The conduct of the war had stirred controversy among non-Communist nations, however, and this fact complicated efforts to attract new contributors.

Yet U.S. problems in recruiting combat units from other countries derived primarily from geographical factors, the widespread scarcity of resources for modern military operations, the larger pattern of international politics, which was influenced but not fundamentally reshaped by the Korean conflict, and broad historical forces. Outside the Communist camp, the United States had taken on the major responsibility for Korea after World War II. From 1947 on, other nations gave political support to U.S. initiatives, but their involvement was always secondary, even for those who served on UN commissions in Korea. America's preeminence in wealth and power made it unlikely that the outbreak of war on the peninsula would alter this fact.

Of the three nations in closest proximity to Korea, two, Communist China and the Soviet Union, were on the other side of the hostilities, and the third, Japan, though providing a supply base and some manpower and ships for logistical support, was unable to contribute troops for compelling political reasons. Other countries were located anywhere from several hundred to several thousand miles from Korea, and most of them had more pressing problems that required attention. Israel, with its tiny population and with larger and hostile neighbors on three sides, is the most obvious example. Pakistan, engaged as it was in border disputes with Afghanistan and the larger and more powerful India, is another. Greece and Turkey, which did make significant contributions to Korea, were limited by tense conditions in the Balkans, just as western European nations felt constrained by the inferiority of their own forces to those of the Soviet bloc to the east.[179]

To neutral countries, political considerations dictated against a contribution of troops. Yugoslavia was receiving much needed economic and military assistance from the United States and was in the process of improving its relations with Italy, Greece, and Turkey.[180] Yugoslav diplomats consulted frequently and sympathetically with Americans on a variety of issues, including the Korean War. That conflict, with its obvious implications regarding the Balkans, had drawn the United States and Yugoslavia closer together than ever before. Yet President Tito remained determined to pursue an independent course in the cold war. In the immediate aftermath of North Korea's attack of the previous June, he had explained to U.S. ambassador George Allen that, if Moscow decided to invade his country, it "would make every effort to picture Yugoslavia as [an] instrument of Western aggression aimed against [the] Cominform and would seek to justify [the] attack as [a] necessary defensive measure." Tito felt compelled to "make it abundantly clear to 'progressive opinion' that such allegations had no foundation whatsoever."[181] In any event, border tensions with Hungary, Bulgaria, Rumania, and Albania, plus fears of Soviet-inspired subversion within Yugoslavia, precluded open support for the West on issues far from home. Sweden also sympathized with the UN effort to repulse "aggression" in Korea. Some elements in the country continued to advocate a military contribution and perhaps even entry into NATO. Dominated by the Social Democrats, however, the government persisted in the more cautious course of armed neutrality established during the two world wars.[182]

Most nations of the Arab-Asian group were of similar mind, willing to express support for the initial action in Korea, but determined to avoid commitments that would fundamentally undermine their middle course in the East-West conflict. Eight members of the loosely knit group offered no material aid to the UN enterprise in Korea.[183] India donated a field hospital; but then, as the war lingered on and Nehru and Rau persisted in their efforts at mediation, India sent a similar hospital to the other side as well. U.S. resistance to Arab-Asian attempts at mediation hardened most of the governments in their determination to avoid commitments to the West. In the Arab world, continuing U.S. support for Israel and the ongoing failure of the British to resolve the issues of military bases with Egypt or of oil revenues with Iran fueled anti-Western nationalism.[184]

Pakistan was an exception of sorts to the pattern of sentiment in the Arab-Asian group. Since its creation in 1947, this Moslem nation had sought military and economic aid from the United States. Having little to show for its efforts, the government of Liaquat Ali Khan now expressed interest in contributing a division or two of troops to Korea, but only if the United States supported Pakistan's claims on the Kashmir and Pushtunistan issues. Despite its irritation with India's neutralism and its desire for military bases in Pakistan, which would be useful for the defense of the Middle East and, in the event of global war, for launching air attacks deep into the Soviet Union, the United States refused to cut a deal. Such a ploy would totally alienate India and Afghanistan and encourage war in south Asia, thus increasing the risk of Soviet or Chinese penetration of the area or even infiltration by both.[185]

The U.S. State Department concentrated its efforts in recruiting troops for Korea on Latin America and commonwealth nations other than the United Kingdom. In the second area only Canada and New Zealand responded favorably, the former agreeing to expand its presence in Korea from a battalion to the reinforced infantry brigade it had promised during the previous summer and the latter offering to augment slightly its Sixteenth Field Regiment already in the fray.[186] This result was more positive than the outcome in Latin America. U.S. officials paid special attention to Bolivia, Chile, Uruguay, Mexico, Peru, and Brazil. (Argentina under the Perón regime was an unlikely prospect.) The Bolivian government announced it would send troops to Korea, only to reverse itself before a clamor of public protest. The government in Uruguay, which had once appeared to be on the verge of making an offer, procrastinated as a result of pressure from the opposition Blanco Party and from neighboring Argentina. Chile and Mexico parried U.S. overtures with claims that their public opinion was not ready to support troop commitments abroad, and Peru and Brazil expressed interest in contributing to Korea but only in return for substantial U.S. military and economic assistance. Brazil presented a shopping list that called into question its seriousness in the negotiations for aid to Korea. Despite a concerted effort, including a conference of Latin American foreign ministers in Washington early in the spring, U.S. diplomats failed to secure any new offers from below the Rio Grande.[187]

The meager results of U.S. recruiting efforts in Latin America arose from a host of forces. First and foremost, Latin America was a grievously poor region made up of weak nations that lacked any tradition of direct involvement in conflicts thousands of miles beyond their borders. Only Brazil and Mexico had sent forces abroad during World War II. In the early postwar years, the region had remained on the periphery in the contest to fashion a new international order. Despite its commitments through the Rio pact and the Organization of American States, the United States, secure in the belief that no immediate threat existed in the Western hemisphere, directed little of its largess toward its southern neighbors. This neglect fostered resentment in Latin America and perpetuated feelings of detachment from the world at large. Tired of being taken for granted by their big brother in the north, lacking the economic foundation to maintain modern armies, and facing the condition of reimbursement for any U.S. assistance received to equip their forces for

Korea, the Latin republics hedged when asked to provide cannon fodder for a U.S. crusade in a remote land.

This left South Korea as a potential source of additional manpower. The Pentagon gave ongoing consideration to this possibility not only because of the pressing need for troops but because the Rhee regime constantly agitated for a larger army. In mid-December 1950, as Communist forces moved rapidly southward toward the 38th parallel, the ROK requested arms for the many thousands of its citizens who had some military training but lacked weapons.[188] Three weeks later the Joint Chiefs of Staff asked MacArthur for his opinion on providing rifles and other small arms, which was all that was available in the United States, to enable the ROK to augment its army. In the midst of his campaign to persuade Washington that it must either expand the war or withdraw from Korea, the UN commander replied, "In view of the restricted size of the battlefield in which we may operate in the near future," the weapons could be better used to equip the National Police Reserve of Japan. Available manpower in South Korea should be employed as replacements "for losses in existing ROK units."[189] The Joint Chiefs followed this recommendation.

Despite Rhee's occasional outbursts, the issue lay dormant until early April, when MacArthur suggested in his interview with *The Freeman* magazine that South Korean manpower was not being fully exploited. Rhee responded with a stepped-up campaign in the United States, where his representatives pressed for equipment for ten new divisions. He launched a similar drive in Korea, backed by a National Assembly resolution.[190] U.S. officials faced a dilemma. They were dubious about arming more South Koreans because of the unavailability of competent Korean officers to train them and lead them in battle. Rhee anticipated this objection by proposing that U.S. officers command the new units, but generals Ridgway and Van Fleet demurred, citing the language barrier, the inherent problem of authority when men of one sovereign nation attempted to command those of another, and the large number of U.S. officers required to give such a system a chance to work.[191] Yet U.S. leaders did not want to release information to sustain their position in the face of partisan attacks in the United States, where Asia-firsters viewed the problem as rooted in supply shortages deriving from an overcommitment of resources to Europe.[192] Revelations of incompetence in the ROK armed forces, which extended upward to top echelons of the ministry of defense, would have a demoralizing effect in South Korea and on the UN effort in general. The collapse of the ROK Sixth Division and its abandonment to the enemy of large quantities of arms amidst the Chinese offensive of late April made the Americans all the more determined to ride out the political storm rather than attempt to rectify immediate manpower shortages by establishing more Korean units.[193] Over the long term, however, the Joint Chiefs specifically, and the Truman administration as a whole, hoped that the ROK army could be built up sufficiently "to assume the major part of the burden of UN forces" in Korea.[194]

All things considered—the gross state of military unpreparedness in the West on the eve of the Korean War, the ongoing commitments of several countries in other parts of the world, the limited resources of most nations to support troops in foreign combat, and the immaturity of ROK military institutions—the United States was fortunate to be able to draw nearly half the manpower for UN armies in Korea from non-U.S. sources. That many Americans of the time did not see the matter in this light reflected the lingering impact of their own long history of limited involvement abroad and the resulting uneasiness with the burdens of superpower status that their nation had so recently acquired.

## The Growth of the Western Alliance

Turmoil in the United States and disagreements between Washington and allied governments during the spring of 1951 produced a good deal more smoke than fire. The overall result of intense allied exchanges during May and early June was a narrowing of differences on several key issues. Other than Korea, the outstanding areas of negotiation included West German rearmament, the price and availability of strategic raw materials, the relationship of Greece and Turkey to NATO, and a Japanese peace treaty. On the last three issues, the spring brought steady progress toward accommodation within the anti-Communist bloc; on the first, Soviet efforts to further a split among the Atlantic powers failed, although barriers remained to a resolution.

By sparking a drive for rearmament in the West, the Korean War greatly stimulated demand for strategic raw materials, which created shortages and fueled inflation. This, in turn, threatened western Europe's economic recovery and fostered resentment over America's advantage in competing for scarce resources. Early in 1951 the United States, Great Britain, and France initiated an International Materials Conference to recommend methods of rationalizing the distribution of key commodities. Although the conference had authority only to advise, the U.S. government helped matters along by reducing its purchases of certain items, especially rubber, tin, and wool, the prices of which dropped sharply beginning in March. Other items were slower to respond, and in late April the Labor Left in Great Britain included the raw material situation prominently in its indictment of U.S. leadership. Yet in late April and early May Charles E. Wilson, the director of Defense Mobilization in the United States, toured Europe, and the trip proved reassuring. Most observers anticipated further improvement after 1 July, when a Controlled Materials Plan was scheduled to commence with restrictions designed to curb prices of aluminum, copper, and steel.[195]

Similar hopes existed on the matter of Greece's and Turkey's place in the Western alliance. The admission of the two Mediterranean powers to associate status in NATO during the fall of 1950 had failed to satisfy them, especially Turkey. The heroic performance of its troops in Korea boosted Turkey's national pride and heightened expectations among the Turks that they would be rewarded with full membership in the Western alliance or a security treaty with its strongest member.[196] Yet smaller nations in NATO remained opposed to expanding their commitments to exposed areas hundreds of miles away, and they feared that a U.S. commitment to do so would merely lessen the resources available to defend northern Europe.[197] The U.S. Joint Chiefs also doubted the prudence of further extending their nation's commitments.[198]

In February the wheels of government in Washington began to turn toward accommodating Turkey's and Greece's desires. A conference of U.S. ambassadors to the region, held during the third week of the month, concluded that, if a formal commitment was not soon offered to Turkey, that country would probably "veer towards . . . neutralism." A U.S. commitment need not involve U.S. troops and it would ensure, in the event of war with the Soviet Union, the utilization of Turkey's army, the strongest in the region, plus U.S. access to key air and naval bases on Turkish soil. A new security arrangement with Turkey would require one with Greece as well.[199] At the end of the month, Ambassador Alan Kirk offered similar advice from Moscow.[200]

In April, with reports from the field expressing increasing urgency on the matter, the State Department obtained Pentagon agreement to offer Greece and Turkey full membership in NATO. The initial diplomatic groundwork for such a course would be laid through approaches to Great Britain and France.[201] In mid-May word leaked to the press indicating that London and Paris were receptive.[202]

Many issues remained to be ironed out, including the divisive question of command responsibility in the eastern Mediterranean, where the British still sought preeminence; but a trend clearly had emerged toward extending the Western alliance into the region.[203] Although plans for Yugoslavia were less grandiose than for Greece and Turkey, continuing tensions on its border with Bulgaria generated new assistance from the United States, Great Britain, and France, including funds for the purchase of military equipment.[204] Italy, already a member of NATO, adopted a $400 million rearmament program that ignored restrictions placed on it in its peace treaties with the victors of World War II.[205] In a word, the spring of 1951 brought substantial progress toward a coordinated buildup of anti-Soviet forces in the Mediterranean.

Clear-cut progress also occurred in America's quest for a generous peace treaty with Japan, one that would permit both a continued U.S. military presence in the islands and a Japanese contribution to its own defense. Early in the year the chief U.S. negotiator, John Foster Dulles, had hammered out tentative agreements with the Japanese, who, among other things, were none too anxious to commit to rearmament.[206] By May Dulles had gone a long way toward achieving support for the agreements from Australia and New Zealand by offering them the security pacts they desired. Although no such offer had been made to the Philippines, the United States always could do so in a pinch, and this would go a long way toward securing support from the Quirino regime.[207]

Great Britain proved more difficult. It was already upset about being excluded from a pact involving the United States, Australia, and New Zealand, and it remained dubious about a Japanese peace treaty that excluded Communist China, left the Taiwan issue unresolved, and lacked economic restrictions designed to contain Japanese competition for the trade of Asia. Yet, during May, Anglo-U.S. bargaining narrowed the gap. The British agreed to postpone a determination of Taiwan's fate while the Korean War continued, which also eliminated temporarily an acrimonious issue in the United Nations. London might accept the exclusion of Communist China from a treaty if the Americans also conceded the nonparticipation of Nationalist China. The United States could reduce British apprehensions about Japanese commercial competition by endorsing some limitations on Japan's shipbuilding.[208] In early June Dulles visited London. In the middle of the month he announced that agreement had been reached on all major issues involving the treaty.[209] Reparations remained a stumbling block to several nations in the western Pacific, but there could be little doubt that the United States had taken giant steps toward achieving a central objective of its strategy in East Asia, namely, the integration of Japan into an anti-Communist security system.

The rearmament of Germany was the most divisive issue of all, and the first half of 1951 hardly brought it close to resolution. Serious differences continued among NATO members, with French officials taking the lead in expressing fears of a resurgent Germany.[210] In West Germany the Adenauer government stood fast on preconditions for rearmament, and public opinion remained divided despite a slight shift in favor of the idea.[211] Even so, several encouraging developments had occurred. In March the occupying powers and West Germany reached agreement on a plan for the European Coal and Steel Community. Early the next month the congressional debate ended in the United States on stationing additional U.S. troops in Europe. During May a division of these troops arrived on the continent, and progress continued in plans for sending three more divisions from the United States and two from Great Britain by the end of the year. With the steady advance of rearmament programs on both sides of the Atlantic, the prospect remained of a gradual decline in fears of a German military buildup among the liberal democracies to the west.[212]

The most immediate danger during the spring centered on the Soviet effort to split the allies through its call for a foreign ministers' conference on the future of Germany. Unenthusiastic about multilateral negotiations with the Soviets, the United States insisted that German rearmament could be discussed only as part of the larger issue of European security; but western European opinion prevented the Americans from rejecting Soviet overtures out of hand. In early March a meeting of deputy foreign ministers began in Paris to consider an agenda for a higher-level conference at a later date. Washington feared that the ongoing Soviet peace campaign would create false hopes in the Western democracies for a united, disarmed, and neutral Germany, and that such sentiment would reverse the momentum toward restoring the balance of military power on the continent. Occasional displays of flexibility on the U.S. side, however, combined with the persistent intransigence of the Soviets to produce solidarity in the Western camp. With the passing of French elections on 17 June, in which the Communist Party actually lost ground, the Western deputies moved decisively to adjourn the talks without agreement on an agenda.[213]

Despite the trend toward consolidation in the West, divisions persisted and were unlikely to disappear. The nationalistic mood of the U.S. Congress posed a particular danger. In early June it passed legislation providing for an end to economic and financial assistance to nations exporting strategic materials to the Soviet Union or its satellites. The measure brought a wave of criticism from abroad, especially from western Europe. Fortunately, a loophole enabled the Truman administration to postpone its implementation for ninety days while efforts were made for its repeal.[214] But mere passage of the legislation inevitably fostered resentment toward the United States, which was already in the process of drastically reducing Marshall Plan aid. These cuts, combined with increases in military spending and in the price of raw materials resulting from the Korean War, had produced an increasingly difficult situation in France.[215] Given the democratic political systems under which the Western allies operated, the public airing of disputes was sure to continue, thus complicating their resolution and encouraging efforts at exploitation by the other side.

Still, a significant narrowing of divisions had occurred. While the Truman administration remained on the defensive at home, it accumulated a solid record in the international arena during the winter and spring of 1951. Gradual stabilization of the military front in Korea provided an essential context here, as it enabled Truman to combine firmness with sufficient restraint in order to prevent a deterioration in the Western alliance. This dual course of firmness and restraint, which U.S. policymakers outlined in great depth at the Senate hearings on MacArthur's dismissal, provided a framework for a Korean armistice roughly along prewar boundaries. To their credit, the Joint Chiefs, especially General Bradley, resisted the temptation arising from the rout of the Chinese spring offensives to raise their goal to the destruction of enemy forces.[216] In early June General Van Fleet announced the end of the "pursuit phase" of recent UN ground operations in Korea, and Secretary of State Acheson testified in the Senate hearings that the United States would accept an armistice at or near the 38th parallel if there were "reliable assurances" that the fighting "would not be resumed."[217] These statements temporarily took the edge off pressure from London and at the United Nations for a new declaration of aims on Korea.[218]

What remained was for the Communist powers to show a willingness to talk along lines more accommodating than the ones advanced since the previous November. During that time, Mao had consistently underestimated the strength of enemy forces while overestimating their ambitions. With conditions on the peninsula now moving clearly toward military stabilization, the prospect that he would reevaluate old estimates improved by the day. With trends in Korea and in several other important areas moving in an undesirable direction, Stalin also had reason to take another look at his policy toward the war. If Mao and Stalin altered their views, Kim would have little choice but to go along. Thus as summer approached, the risk of an expanded war shrunk to its lowest point since before Chinese troops began moving across the Yalu.

• CHAPTER 6 •

# Armistice Talks: Origins and Initial Stages

PRELIMINARY SIGNALING

Wednesday, 2 May, struck most New Yorkers as a relatively uneventful day. Skies were clear and temperatures unseasonably warm, yet a mere 6,238 baseball fans showed up at Ebbets Field in Brooklyn to see the Dodgers take on the lowly Pirates, and fewer than five thousand trekked to the Polo Grounds in the Bronx to watch the Giants blast the hapless Cubs. Few residents were surprised to hear that a Senate investigating committee viewed their city as one of the nation's "major centers of organized crime" and former mayor William O'Dwyer as at best a dupe of leading racketeers. Some derived hope from reports of a Chinese retreat in Korea, but news of enemy setbacks had come in the past without resolution of the war. Although the UN Security Council met at Lake Success, it dealt exclusively with the Palestine question. News on Korea from UN headquarters covered U.S. preparations to push in the AMC for a limited embargo against China and efforts to rebut continuing Soviet charges that the war had begun with ROK attacks north of the 38th parallel.[1] Yet shortly after the Security Council adjourned at 5:30 on that lovely spring afternoon, a chance incident occurred that set in motion diplomatic machinery aimed at negotiations on Korea.

Thomas Cory and Frank Corrigan of the U.S. delegation to the United Nations needed a ride into Manhattan. Jacob Malik, the USSR representative, invited the Americans to ride with him and his assistant, Semen K. Tsarapkin. The forty-five minute journey provided the opportunity for an informal discussion that ranged in topic from the comparative virtues of the political and economic systems of the United States and the Soviet Union to the outstanding foreign policy issues between them. Although Malik was "a charming and cordial host," he and Tsarapkin shot the usual barbs about soft, luxury-ridden Americans, who lacked the noble qualities of their own countrymen, and they insisted that the sole source of Soviet-U.S. disputes was U.S. aggressiveness. Malik noted particularly the U.S. construction of military bases on the Soviet periphery. On Korea, Washington did not want peace, as capitalists on Wall Street were profiting from the war. Cory demurred and asked for suggestions as to how the conflict might be ended. Malik replied that Soviet and U.S. diplomats in Paris might take up the issue. He emphasized that this was not a proposal, but that the United States knew well the Soviet Union's favorable attitude toward bilateral talks between the superpowers. Later in the conversation, Malik and Tsarapkin inquired on the whereabouts of such U.S. experts on the Soviet Union as George Kennan, Charles Bohlen, Elbridge Durbrow, and Charles Thayer. When informed that Thayer, who had previously served in Korea, was now in Germany, Malik joked that the transfer of U.S. officials from Korea to Germany might be worth studying. This, and the earlier reference to the talks in Paris, represented neither the first nor the last hints that those two divided nations might be linked together in negotiations. Recognizing possible significance in what had been said, the Americans dispatched a detailed report to Washington.[2]

With the first stage of the Chinese offensive in Korea in shambles, the U.S. State Department took immediate interest in the incident. John Paton Davies of the Policy Planning Staff proposed that Kennan be asked to approach Malik.[3] Although Kennan did not currently hold an official position, he could "speak with authority and in confidence for the Government." Davies thought it unlikely that the Soviets would publicize Kennan-Malik conversations for propaganda purposes as they had done with the multilateral talks in Moscow on the Berlin crisis of 1948.[4] Recalling Philip Jessup's constructive exchange with Malik on the Berlin blockade in 1949, Acheson gained the president's approval to implement Davies's proposal and Kennan consented to make the overture.[5]

Meanwhile, rumors spread of Soviet peace feelers. Diplomats and newsmen in the West noted Soviet press coverage of a cease-fire resolution presented to the U.S. Senate on 17 May. In a move that received little attention in the U.S. media, Edwin C. Johnson, an otherwise obscure Democratic senator from Colorado, called for an end to the fighting in Korea and a withdrawal of foreign troops from the peninsula by the end of the year.[6] *Pravda* published the resolution in full on the 19th and a day later joined other Soviet newspapers in claiming that it showed war weariness in some circles in the United States.[7] In response to a newspaper report, Sven Grafstrom of the Swedish delegation and the GOC confirmed that he had received a message from his government indicating that the Soviets were willing to discuss a cease-fire in Korea based on the situation before the outbreak of hostilities. A story also circulated that Malik had told two U.S. delegates that the war could be ended through direct talks between the Soviet Union and the United States.[8]

These reports advanced hopes at the United Nations that an armistice was near. Not only did the Soviets appear to be probing for talks; U.S. officials were openly distinguishing between the long-term aim of Korean unification and more modest and immediate military goals. U.S. delegates at Lake Success had talked in such terms for weeks. On the 22d General Bradley did the same in testimony at the MacArthur hearings.[9]

The Soviets moved slowly and in secret, denying publicly that they had made any overtures for discussions on Korea and balking at arranging for Malik to meet with Kennan through U.S. diplomats at the United Nations. Kennan finally wrote to Tsarapkin, asking for assistance and suggesting that a disguised message be left with his secretary in Princeton, New Jersey, while he was away on a brief trip to California. A message came on the 29th that Malik would receive the American at his residence on Long Island two days later.[10]

Kennan drove to Long Island on the 31st. His meeting began inauspiciously when Malik dumped a tray of fruit and wine in his lap. Undeterred, Kennan opened a discussion of Korea. Although Malik frequently departed from that issue, he probed the American's views on U.S. terms. Kennan noted that, although the withdrawal of foreign troops from the peninsula "was desirable" eventually, it was not possible immediately. Nor could resolution of China's "wider differences" with the United States be linked to an armistice in Korea. He suggested that the two sides might end the fighting "approximately" where it was "now taking place." Malik referred frequently to Chinese attitudes, leading Kennan to conclude that they "inhibited" the Soviets in discussing Korea. Nonetheless, Malik expressed interest in another meeting, which the two men agreed would occur in six days, giving the Soviet diplomat time to consult Moscow.[11]

Kennan described his reception on 5 June as "if anything even more cordial and with a greater freedom of exchange" than before. Malik stated that his government "wanted a peaceful solution [in Korea] and at the earliest possible moment." He recommended that the United States contact the DPRK and the PRC. Kennan remarked that his government would have difficulty relying on anything those regimes promised. Whereas he regarded the Soviets as holding "a serious and responsible attitude toward what they conceived to be their own interests," the Chinese were an "excited, irresponsible people." Malik retorted that the Americans had been responsible for exciting the Chinese.

Yet Kennan remained hopeful. Unlike in the first meeting, Malik did not raise such matters as the withdrawal of foreign troops from Korea or other long-standing Communist demands. Kennan thought that Moscow already had pressured Beijing and Pyongyang "to show themselves amenable to proposals for a cease-fire." The American surmised that, "with firmness and persistence on our part and at a cost in nerves and temper no greater than that which was involved in the final settlement of the Berlin blockade," the United States might secure an armistice in Korea.[12]

U.S. efforts to contact the Chinese produced less encouraging results than the overture to the Soviet Union. In early May the State Department sent Charles Burton Marshall to Hong Kong. Earlier in the year he had conducted indirect and exploratory exchanges with a Chinese national who allegedly had a line of communication to Beijing.[13] Now it was hoped that Marshall's appearance in Hong Kong would signal the PRC that the United States was interested in talking.[14] On his arrival he put out the word quietly—and proceeded from 9 to 23 May to meet numerous Chinese, at least two of whom, he believed, could pass on the word to mainland officials.[15]

The most significant conversation took place on the 17th in a lounge at the Peninsula Hotel on Kowloon, where Marshall was staying. The name of Marshall's guest on that day remains classified, but he was described in the published portion of the American's notes as the one with "the surest channel to persons near the center of authority in Peking." Marshall began the discussion by outlining possible steps toward formal negotiations on Korea. The other party responded by asking if Marshall could assure him that the United States would not alter its presently moderate course in the midst of efforts to arrange those talks. Marshall said no, pointing out that the U.S. military buildup would reach its peak "in about 18 months" and that any nation's attitude "in the fullness of [its] strength] was likely to be different than at other times." Marshall's caller retorted "that it would be difficult, perhaps out of the question," for his nation to end the war "if the United States and its allies should crow about the matter as if it were a victory; that the Chinese could not swallow pride." Marshall assured him that Korea was of "marginal" significance to the United States and that his government "would not be likely to waste a lot of time crowing about a secondary development." In any event, Washington was not now seeking victory but, "as far as possible," the reestablishment of conditions that existed before the North Korean attack. He added that "lightening for the Chinese the burden of their consciousness of not being able to finish what they started ... was beyond our capability." "The conversation ended," Marshall recorded, "with a grave exchange of good wishes."[16]

The U.S. envoy waited in Hong Kong for another week. When he received no word that the PRC wanted to talk, he returned to the United States. Marshall concluded that the Korean War had not weakened the PRC—indeed, that it had aided the Communist government in "fastening controls on the populace"—that the Soviet "grip" on Beijing had been "greatly strengthened," and that Mao was unlikely to seek an end to the conflict "except as the result of a Moscow decision." His pessimism regarding that possibility led him to suggest an expanded covert effort on the mainland "to bring down the Peiping [Beijing] regime."[17]

Marshall left Hong Kong before the debacle of the second Communist spring offensive in Korea. In early June hints emerged of a shift in Chinese or Soviet attitudes or in both. At the beginning of the month an article entitled "On Peaceful Coexistence" appeared in the journal *People's China*. Author Soong Jingling, the widow of Sun Yat-sen and now a vice chairman of the powerful Central People's Government Council, declared that peaceful coexistence was possible between different political and economic systems if a willingness existed on both sides "to meet the other fellow half way."[18] Soon thereafter came Malik's second meeting with Kennan. Then the State Department learned from its consulate in Hong Kong that Marshall's conferee of 17 May had received a letter from Beijing "expressing guarded interest" in ongoing talks.[19]

Thus by mid-June Beijing and Moscow had shown some interest in the seed planted by the Americans. In the prevailing atmosphere of mistrust and recrimination between the Communist powers and the West, neither the Chinese nor the Soviets were about to risk a sign of weakness by pushing that seed toward premature growth. Given the determination in Beijing not to "swallow pride," the Kremlin was bound eventually to assume the more prominent role in the nurturing process. Washington remained willing to move forward slowly but was ever conscious of anxiety among allies that it would let an opportunity slip away.

### Toward Armistice Talks

Despite Malik's assertion to Kennan on 5 June that the Soviets desired peace in Korea, the Americans heard little more from the Communist side through the middle of the month. Although the U.S. consulate in Hong Kong received a message from the Chinese national to whom Marshall had spoken, Washington did not immediately follow up this lead, as the State Department was about to seek contact with China through its embassy in Moscow.[20] At Lake Success, the GOC launched its own initiative to contact the Communist powers, first directly through Malik and then through the new Swedish ambassador to China, who was about to leave Stockholm for Beijing. But Malik refused to see GOC members, and before the Swedish diplomat could take action in Beijing the Soviets launched an initiative of their own that quickly gained center stage.[21]

UN officials had tried for some time to get Malik to appear on their weekly radio program, "The Price of Peace." During the second week of June he finally agreed to do so. Normally, broadcasts were taped ten days in advance of the program, which in this case was to be aired on Saturday evening, the 23d. Malik, however, did not permit a taping until the night before. Seated at his desk in the Soviet delegation on Park Avenue, with Stalin's portrait dominating the background, Malik recorded the speech in Russian for later release to an international audience. The next morning he repeated the exercise in English. Americans heard this version over the radio that evening.[22]

Most of the address simply repeated charges against the policies of the United States and its allies, which would "inevitably lead to fresh international conflicts" and perhaps world war. The Soviet Union based "its policy on the possibility of the peaceful coexistence of . . . socialism and capitalism," but its efforts for peace in Korea fell short in the face of Western provocations. "As a first step" toward settling the armed conflict there, discussions should start "between the belligerents for a cease-fire and an armistice providing for the mutual withdrawal of forces from the 38th parallel." Malik said nothing regarding the withdrawal of foreign troops, Taiwan, or China's seat in the United Nations.[23]

Malik's words on Korea drew widespread attention in the West. Foreign ministers Pearson in Ottawa and Schuman in Paris responded enthusiastically, as did Trygve Lie, who immediately returned to New York from a vacation in Norway. In London Morrison was more cautious, as were officials in Washington, who, ever fearful of raising false hopes, questioned whether the speech was "more than propaganda." If it was, the State Department remarked blandly, "adequate means for discussing an end to the conflict are available."[24]

Whatever their doubts, U.S. policymakers recognized that the next move was theirs, and they directed U.S. diplomats in New York and Moscow to seek clarification of Malik's remarks. Malik proved elusive, but on the 27th Ambassador Kirk met with Andrei Gromyko, who recently had returned to Moscow from the now defunct Paris talks. Gromyko made it clear that his government envisaged negotiations between the opposing commands in Korea on military questions alone, that broader issues involving the future of Korea could be discussed following the conclusion of an armistice.[25]

Though encouraged by this exchange, Washington still faced the problem of how to commence negotiations. General Ridgway could propose a meeting in Korea to opposing military commanders. Yet this might convey the impression that the United States was asking for an armistice, which at best the enemy would use for propaganda purposes and at worst would take as a sign of weakness. Alternatively, the Truman administration could seek clarification through a public statement defining the attitude of the United States and the United Nations toward a cease-fire. But this might produce, first, a series of public exchanges, which were unlikely to lead to peace, and, second, charges among U.S. allies that, by seeking to score points in the propaganda war, the United States was ruining a genuine Soviet effort to stop the fighting.[26]

Washington chose the first approach, directing Ridgway to broadcast a message on the 29th to the Communist commanders in the field. Carefully drafted to avoid a sign of weakness on the UN side or an unacceptable loss of face on the other end, the message stated:

> I am informed that you may wish a meeting to discuss an armistice providing for the cessation of hostilities and all acts of armed force in Korea, with adequate guarantees for the maintenance of such armistice.
>
> Upon the receipt of word from you that such a meeting is desired I shall be prepared to name my representative. I would also at that time suggest a date at which he could meet with your representative. I propose that such a meeting could take place aboard a Danish hospital ship in Wonsan Harbor.[27]

The Communists replied favorably three days later, proposing an initial meeting between 10 and 15 July and a change in site to Kaesong, the ancient capital of Korea, which was located just below the 38th parallel on unoccupied ground.

The UN command hoped to meet before the 10th, and it saw disadvantages in the proposed site. Although Kaesong was technically in "no man's land," the Communists held the high ground just to the north and could move into the town at any moment. Since Kaesong was south of the 38th parallel and had been the first town captured by the North Koreans in their offensive a year earlier, its choice also would provide the Communists with a propaganda advantage. It was impossible, however, to find a perfect location on the ground in Korea. Most sites between the lines would interfere with the fighting, whereas locations to the north or south would present one side with difficulties regarding access and communications, not to mention prestige. A neutral ship in Wonsan Harbor would approach ideal conditions, but it was understandable why the Communists were reluctant to talk on the vessel of a NATO member.[28] In the interest of moving quickly toward negotiations, therefore, the UN command accepted the Communist counterproposal on a meeting place.[29] To avoid appearing anxious, General Ridgway agreed to commence talks on the 10th and requested a preliminary meeting of liaison officers five days earlier, "or as soon thereafter as possible." The Communists agreed on the 8th and the meeting occurred as planned. Regular negotiations began two days later.[30]

After the complex cat-and-mouse games that had occurred between the two sides over the past year, the final path to the negotiating table seemed strangely direct. In an international system characterized by extreme tension, this was so only because of the emergence of a stable battlefront in Korea and after intricate diplomatic spadework on both sides over the previous two months. If agreement merely to discuss an armistice entailed such preparation, agreement on its precise nature was bound to require considerable time and effort.

## The U.S. and Allied Perspectives

At the end of June Secretary of State Acheson thought that the chance for peace in Korea was "at least fifty-fifty."[31] Recent Communist propaganda had downplayed demands on Taiwan, PRC admission to the United Nations, and the withdrawal of foreign troops from Korea. Gromyko had indicated a desire for talks on military issues between commanders in the field, a framework more conducive to straightforward discussion of an armistice than a multilateral conference that included at least one neutral and an ally who sympathized with parts of the Communist position. The United States was on the verge of negotiations with the Communists under conditions it had long sought.

U.S. leaders were far from euphoric in anticipation. Whatever the outcome of talks, top policymakers assumed that any Communist moves toward conciliation were purely tactical, that the intense struggle between East and West would continue. Indeed, an armistice in Korea might produce stepped-up Communist action in other areas, with Yugoslavia, Iran, Burma, and Indochina the most likely settings.[32] Lieutenant General O. P. Weyland, the commander of U.S. air forces in the Far East, was one high-level doubter regarding the timeliness of an armistice. Weyland thought that the UN command's initiation of a proposal for talks "weakened our bargaining position at the outset." UN forces were "in an excellent military position" and the conflict provided "an invaluable training area" for U.S. forces as well as a climate at home in which the U.S. military machine could continue to expand. On the political side, the ongoing engagement was "discrediting Communist philosophy and aims" and "effecting a schism between the USSR and Red China." On the other hand, the Communists, particularly the Chinese, stood to gain from an end to the fighting. Their commitment of resources to the peninsula had caused them to lose the initiative elsewhere, especially in Indochina. Should the war end in Korea, Beijing could shift its attention to that area, where U.S. intervention would be difficult. If the French were driven out of Indochina, Weyland surmised, "Siam, Malaya, Hong Kong, Burma, India, Pakistan, Iran, and the Middle East will come successfully under Communist expansion."[33] Washington officials held some of the same concerns, although they differed sharply on the prudence of continuing to tie down large numbers of U.S. forces in Korea. In fact, they derived satisfaction from recent indications that, after weeks of polls that showed a majority—or at least a hefty plurality—of Americans favoring MacArthur's strategy in Korea, public opinion had shifted toward approving a truce along the 38th parallel.[34] Yet awareness of potential advantages in prolonging the fighting produced a toughness in approaching the negotiations which, if not always pervasive, would make its weight felt in the months ahead.

For the moment, U.S. leaders were perhaps most concerned that talks would create unreasonable hopes in the West. Military men feared a repeat of the rapid demobilization of U.S. armed forces after World War II. General Ridgway expressed alarm about appearances in the media of such phrases as "'Let's Get the Boys Back Home' and 'the War Weary Troops.'"[35] At a cabinet meeting in Washington, General Marshall declared that the worst danger to the United States was a letdown in the defense buildup.[36] People who for months had struggled to contain popular sentiment in favor of broadening the Korean War suddenly geared up to ensure continued support for the preparedness program.

Policymakers already had put the final touches on instructions to General Ridgway regarding armistice terms. These terms had evolved over many months, beginning in mid-December 1950, when the United States passed on preliminary conditions to the UN cease-fire group.[37] In late May the State Department shared its latest draft with the British and, over the next month, refined it in consultation with London and the Pentagon. On the last day of June the Joint Chiefs communicated the U.S. position to Tokyo.[38]

The message outlined the military purposes of an armistice, the role it was likely to play in the future of Korea, and the topical boundaries of the upcoming talks. An armistice was to end the fighting, provide assurances against its resumption, and protect the future security of UN forces. Since the Communists were unlikely to "agree to an acceptable permanent settlement of the Korean problem," armistice arrangements must "be acceptable to us over an extended period of time." Finally, negotiations were to be "severely restricted to military questions," barring such issues as a permanent settlement in Korea, the fate of Taiwan, or Chinese representation at the United Nations.[39] Military personnel exclusively would conduct the talks. Washington vetoed Ridgway's plan to station William Sebald, the State Department's political adviser to the occupation of Japan, and Ambassador Muccio at the UNC base camp in Korea, fearing it would undermine the distinction about to be made between military and political issues.[40]

To carry out the first two parts of this policy, certain specific arrangements were "essential." "A Military Armistice Commission of mixed membership" must supervise all agreements, and it must have "free and unlimited access to the whole of Korea." Both sides must agree to "cease the introduction into Korea of any reinforcing air, ground or naval units or personnel . . . [and] to refrain from increasing the level of war equipment and material existing in Korea." The armistice must provide for a demilitarized zone roughly twenty miles wide and "based generally upon the position of the opposing forces." This represented an alteration in the U.S. position of the previous December, which had identified the 38th parallel as the southern boundary of the zone. Now Ridgway could begin by demanding that the Communists "withdraw twenty miles or more along the entire front," but he could alter this stance and even agree to some withdrawals on the UN side so long as he did not jeopardize the "strong military position" of his forces. Lastly, POWs should be exchanged on a one-for-one basis "as expeditiously as possible."[41]

The Americans anticipated Communist resistance in at least three areas. Given the sensitivity of Communist governments to the free movement of foreigners within their own territory, they were bound to oppose a supervisory body with "free and unlimited access" to the entire peninsula. The United States realized that it might have to settle for inspection of key points, such as the Yalu bridges, railroad junctions, and major ports. The U.S. position on an armistice line was also likely to cause problems. Malik had called for an armistice based on a mutual withdrawal of forces from the 38th parallel, and Acheson had made public statements both before and after the Soviet diplomat's speech of 23 June indicating that the United States agreed.[42] But the 38th parallel was an indefensible line. Since the Americans lacked faith in Communist intentions, acceptance of the 38th parallel as a basis for a cease-fire would undermine the durability of the peace that followed just as would the absence of broad inspection in the North.

The U.S. position on the POW issue derived from similar concerns. The United Nations held some 150,000 POWs, whereas the Communists had fewer than 10,000. An all-for-all exchange, which was the established procedure in international law, would give the Communists a much greater opportunity to strengthen their forces. Unlimited inspection might protect against this danger, but this might not be feasible. Avoidance of "wholesale repatriation," at least initially, obviously was desirable.[43]

Washington recognized that it would draw fire from neutrals and its NATO allies if its positions appeared extreme or inflexible. Several delegates at the

United Nations were already promoting a post-armistice conference to discuss a broad settlement in Korea, East Asia, and perhaps even Europe. Encouraged by Malik's optimism in private conversations, many people at the United Nations thought an early armistice likely. When Americans urged caution, they encountered criticism for encouraging suspicions of the Soviets.[44] Washington held no illusions that it had free reign in the conduct of negotiations. It cautioned Ridgway that, even though he could adopt positions initially that were more favorable to the United Nations than the minimum conditions, he must avoid a breakdown or stalemate of talks in circumstances that would "cause world opinion to question our good faith."[45]

The ROK government tugged the United States in the opposite direction. Since its inception in 1948 the Rhee regime had frequently embarrassed the United States, and the outbreak of conventional war on the peninsula during 1950 had brought its inadequacies to international attention more than ever before. Reports of mass executions of political prisoners and civilians by the ROK police and army gained widespread attention in December 1950 and again in the following spring.[46] The furor in the second case was particularly damaging. The incident that sparked the controversy grew out of the ongoing guerrilla activity behind UN lines. As was the case before June 1950, the southwest corner of Korea was a center of this struggle. In February a ROK battalion, responding to a guerrilla raid on a police outpost, descended on the tiny hamlet of Shim Um Mium. The soldiers, long suspicious of the sentiments of local residents, shot between five hundred and a thousand people, including numerous women and children. The National Assembly got wind of the massacre and began an investigation. The international press did the same in mid-April. Later in the month Rhee dismissed two cabinet members, Cho Pyung Ok, the Home Minister who had been widely criticized for the mass executions of the previous year, and Kim Joon Yun, the Minister of Justice. Defense Minister Sihn Sung Mo survived this housecleaning, but soon fell over a brewing scandal involving the misuse of funds by the armed forces.[47] Two more ministers suffered similar fates shortly thereafter.

These events did nothing to improve relations between Rhee and the legislative branch. Three of Rhee's new appointees had served in the Japanese regime in Korea, and most fit the familiar pattern of being mere instruments of the president.[48] In early May a meeting of the National Assembly ended in a melee between opponents and supporters of the aging president. The altercation began when one member called another a snake. The former wound up in the hospital, bitten in the face.[49] Bickering between Rhee's partisans and detractors showed no signs of ebbing. In mid-June another legislative investigating committee charged that, during the past six months, more than fifty thousand ROK draftees had died of starvation or disease in training camps. The committee blamed this tragedy on the misappropriation of supplies by the ROK National Defense Corps. The government retorted that the figures were grossly distorted, but it did arrest nine officers for embezzlement, forgery, and neglect of duty. U.S. analysts worried that, unless progress was made toward internal political stability, the recent victories on the battlefield eventually would go for naught.[50]

Through all this turmoil, Rhee continued his campaign to expand the ROK army in preparation for a march to the Yalu. As Australian James Plimsoll noted, Rhee's conception of building an indigenous army went little beyond putting rifles in the hands of his countrymen and sending them into battle.[51] By early April 1951 one British diplomat was so frustrated with Rhee's tantrums that he wrote home suggesting someone "put the old man's head in a bag and keep it there."[52] A month later Rhee publicly denounced the British, allegedly for bringing about MacArthur's dismissal and for persuading the United States to halt UN troops near the 38th parallel. The *London Times* carried the story, which caused considerable stir in a British public already disturbed by reports of atrocities by the ROK army and police.[53] One irate British soldier in Korea wrote the following to Foreign Secretary Morrison:

> Put yourself in my position, . . . a reservist, called back to the armed forces, parted from my family, to take part in a conflict in which my whole train of thoughts said was wrong when the UN forces crossed the [38th] parallel for the first time. The stand the 29th brigade made on the Imjin River in the last week in April, our casualties heavy, and so very fresh in my mind. Am I to go into the next conflict and possibly become a battle-casualty, for a cause one is not in full agreement with? knowing that President Syngman Rhee decries the efforts we have made, tells the world that the British are unwelcome, and the sacrifices made thought so very little of?[54]

Although British diplomats alternated between anger and condescension in their attitudes toward ROK leaders, one Foreign Office official, R. S. Milward, comprehended the source of their intense emotions on unification:

> The division of Korea hamstrung the country economically . . . [and] caused even graver political distortion. [From the start,] the presence of a rival state on Korean soil . . . organized increasingly for the purpose of overthrowing the southern republic, [had dominated the Rhee regime's thinking.] The highly trained North Korean army . . . and the continually renewed guerrilla bands sent from the north into southern territory perpetually disturbed or threatened law, order, prosperity, culture and whatever made independence enjoyable or life worth living. . . . These factors combined with the parochial outlook inherent in human nature to make the Koreans, and especially the Korean government, regard the continued existence of a Communist North Korea as the supreme evil. They quite genuinely do not understand how a sword once drawn against this evil can be sheathed till the evil is destroyed.[55]

Understandable or not, Rhee's campaign to pursue the war to total victory was something the United Nations could not endorse or, beyond certain bounds, tolerate. The United States bore the brunt of the task of reigning him in. Since mid-February, when the recovery of UN forces on the peninsula had produced widespread discussion in the West about a settlement along the 38th parallel, Ambassador Muccio had warned Washington that any effort to implement this approach "would bring a violent explosion from all Koreans" and would create serious problems in "controlling ROK forces."[56] Despite the absence of formal negotiations with the enemy, the Rhee regime pressed throughout the winter and spring for a U.S. commitment to fight on until Korea was unified. The State Department assured ROK diplomats of America's continuing commitment to unification, but distinguished between military and political methods for its achievement.[57] With prospects for unification through diplomacy virtually nil, the U.S. position was hardly reassuring. To Rhee, it made the campaign to arm ten new South Korean divisions all the more compelling.

In response to rumors of impending negotiations for a cease-fire in late May and early June, the South Korean government launched a massive effort to mobilize the public to resist any halt in the fighting short of the Yalu. Rhee promised Muccio on 5 June that he would take care to avoid making provocative statements to the press, but he soon resumed his veiled threats of drastic action should the United Nations attempt to deny his countrymen in their quest for unity. Cabinet members quickly joined in, and the National Assembly managed a rare show of cooperation with the president by unanimously passing a resolution endorsing a continuing fight for an "independent and unified country." Mass demonstrations appeared in Pusan, which, despite the recapture of Seoul in March, remained the seat of government.[58] At the end of June the cabinet announced that a cease-fire must include a Chinese withdrawal from Korea; the disarming of the North Korean Communists and a UN guarantee that no third power would assist them either militarily or financially; and recognition of "the national sovereignty and territorial integrity of the Republic of Korea."[59] The private assurance by the ROK ambassador in Washington, Dr. Yu Chan Yang, that however much these points differed from the U.S. position, still his government would cooperate with the United States, failed to allay concern. Muccio wired home on the first day of talks: "I doubt whether [the] ROK Govt [*sic*] will take overt action of [a] serious nature. On the other hand, Rhee has committed himself so far in opposition [to the] whole idea of [a] ceasefire that he cannot [very] well publicly reverse himself when faced with a *fait accompli*."[60]

The United States hoped that including a ROK representative on the UN negotiating team at Kaesong, permitting Dr. Yang to participate in the regular State Department briefings of ambassadors from nations with troops in Korea, and constant reassurances of U.S. support after a cease-fire would persuade Rhee and his allies not to take extreme measures. Theoretically, given ROK dependence on the United States for its survival, Washington held the upper hand. Yet Rhee was a highly emotional man whose erratic behavior could produce a dangerous crisis at any moment. Only time would tell whether the United States could balance his and his government's demands against its own priorities and those of America's NATO allies.

## The Perspectives of the Communist Powers

Communist nations involved in Korea avoided open dissension among themselves. Less than two days after Malik's address of 23 June, a *Renmin ribao* editorial endorsed his proposal on Korea. On the first of July, after Ridgway expressed interest in negotiations, the same paper declared that, while the "Chinese people" had always wanted a peaceful settlement in Korea, "it was not until recently . . . [that] . . . severe blows to the American army . . . [and] . . . the general demands for peace of the peoples of the world" led the U.S. government to "consider accepting the reasonable peace proposals of Malik."[61] The North Koreans were slower to react and less direct in their endorsement, waiting until 27 June to alter their propaganda in radio broadcasts from the slogan "drive the enemy into the sea" to "drive the enemy to the 38th parallel."[62] Early the next month Kim Il-sung joined Peng Dehuai, the commander of Chinese forces in Korea, in replying affirmatively to Ridgway's overture.[63]

Contemporary observers outside the Soviet bloc and scholars since have assumed that differences, even tension, existed among the three governments and peoples. The DPRK's tardy and oblique response to Malik's address indicates to some that it was unhappy with the move toward negotiations, possibly even that it was not consulted in advance.[64] The North Korean government had a more passionate commitment to the unification of the peninsula than did the other two powers and it may have wanted to fight on, despite the tremendous pounding it was taking from the air. Its dependence on outside aid, however, gave it little influence in defining the Communist position in Korea unless it had the support of at least one of the larger powers. In Malik's first discussion with Kennan, it was the Chinese who came across as the Soviets' concern, not the North Koreans.

In reality, by early June Mao and Peng had scaled back their ambitions in Korea, and Kim Il-sung had agreed after the kind of bargaining that was common in an alliance relationship. As historian Zhang Shuguang has observed, Chinese Communist armies had fought "battles unprecedented in their military history." Mao's military doctrines called for lengthy defensive operations before switching to major counteroffensives. "Tactically," Chinese forces "were to fight a flexible mobile warfare rather than pitched battles." In Korea, however, the CPV had commenced a large-scale offensive merely five weeks after entering the conflict in October 1950. That operation had been forced on them, but the three offensives from January to May 1951 had not. By late May Mao realized that such operations were futile, even dangerous, given UN superiority in firepower and mobility on the ground, air, and sea.[65] Rather than attempting to destroy enemy units of division size all at once, Chinese leaders now concluded that the CPV should engage in more limited operations that would eliminate UN forces slowly over an extended period. Kim, who arrived in Beijing on 3 June, wanted immediate preparations for another offensive, as did some of Peng's commanders. Peng eventually agreed to such preparations but only to drive the enemy below the 38th parallel. Apparently, Kim demanded this objective as a price for going along with armistice talks. The North Korean leader would accept a cease-fire along the prewar boundary if combined with a gradual foreign troop withdrawal from the peninsula. Chinese and North Korea leaders both had advanced knowledge of Malik's address of 23 June, although Kim's approval was not without reluctance.[66] China, after all, having intervened in Korea at a time when enemy forces were approaching the Yalu, could claim more plausibly than North Korea that a settlement along the 38th parallel represented a victory.

North Korea's reluctance, it appears, was a major reason for Kim and Gao Gang making a subsequent trip to Moscow, where they talked at length with Stalin about the military balance in Korea and their host agreed on an attempt to end the war through negotiations.[67] In all likelihood, the Soviet lead in proposing talks was a face-saving device for China and North Korea, which in response to military pressure were about to retreat from past demands. The delay between Malik's last talk with Kennan and his radio address reflected the difficulty in achieving a consensus among the Communist powers but also a desire to avoid any sign of haste, to create a situation in which the United States would appear to be asking the PRC and the DPRK for peace, and to ensure that the UN counteroffensive in Korea had indeed ended.

Although Mao took the lead with Kim in pressing for negotiations, he probably regarded them as necessary only because Moscow had failed to provide sufficient heavy equipment for Korea to make military victory possible. The Soviet Union, to be sure, had played a critical part in discouraging U.S. attacks on China, both through its military presence in Manchuria and its own eastern provinces and through threats that it would intervene openly in Korea should the United States expand the war.[68] By the spring Soviet pilots were flying numerous missions over the peninsula, and they were rushing to train their Chinese compatriots to fly jet fighters. New Chinese soldiers in Korea had some modern Soviet weapons. Yet Communist armies remained far inferior to the enemy in artillery and mechanized support, and the air power in Manchuria was used primarily against UN planes operating well north of the battlefield. In June Xu Xiangqian, the chief of staff of the Chinese army, went to Moscow to plead for more and better equipment. The Soviets, making do with an economy of distinctly limited capacity, placing highest priority on augmenting their strength in Europe, and anxious to keep China in a subordinate position, required payment for much of their aid, a portion of which was financed through mass donation campaigns in China.[69]

Other reasons existed for discontent within the Communist triad, though the closed nature of the societies involved kept them better hidden from outside view than squabbles in the West. Despite the careful preparations of political cadres attached to the CPV regarding troop interaction with the indigenous population, the presence of hundreds of thousands of Chinese soldiers in Korea and their increasing dependence for food on local sources produced tension between them and the Korean people. The relationship between the Chinese high command and the North Korean government was not always smooth. Kim Il-sung was every bit as nationalistic as Rhee, and it surely was galling to him to have in his midst a foreign military apparatus with control over field operations and perhaps a good deal more. According to a later Soviet report, Kim sometimes complained that Pak Il-u, the North Korean army representative to CPV headquarters and a member of the Yanan faction of Korean Communists, behaved as if he were "the personal representative of Mao Zedong." For their part, the Chinese in North Korea were far from shy about intriguing against Kim, whose reputation had suffered tremendously as a result of the debacle of the previous fall. Peng Dehuai himself "was not ashamed to express his low opinion of [Kim's] . . . military capabilities." As for the North Korean leadership, many blamed the Chinese for the failure to drive UN forces off the peninsula in early 1951.[70] Balancing the Chinese presence were thousands of Soviet officers and civilian officials, who were accustomed to unchallenged status in the foreign community of North Korea. Undoubtedly they had mixed feelings toward their Chinese comrades.[71]

In China the mounting cost of the Korean campaign increased dependence on the Soviet Union. Mao's Communists were rightfully proud of their accomplishments in the recent civil war, in which they had achieved victory with timely though minimal aid and encouragement from outside. Now, locked in combat with the most powerful nation in the world and receiving limited assistance from abroad, they adopted drastic measures to develop their heavy industries; these required a good deal of oversight from Soviet technicians. As the base for Communist air operations in Korea, Manchuria also endured an augmented Soviet military presence. Here the Soviets were in a no-win situation: the Chinese wanted, even demanded, assistance, yet their extreme nationalism made them resent foreign involvement in, and at times direction of, operations within their own borders.[72]

An exchange that occurred during the first half of July between Ambassador Panikkar and N. V. Roschin, his Soviet counterpart, illustrates this point. Western diplomats in Beijing had approached Panikkar expressing concern over the ill-treatment suffered at the hands of Chinese officialdom. The Indian agreed to approach Roschin to see if he might intervene on their behalf with the Chinese government. When Panikkar outlined to him the injustices being endured by Western representatives, Roschin replied "astonishingly" (according to Lionel H. Lamb, the British chargé) that his countrymen were having most of the same difficulties. Among other problems, the movements of Soviet nationals were restricted just as much as those of Westerners.[73]

Despite such strains, the Chinese and the Soviets needed each other just as did the United States and its allies. The short-term differences between China and the Soviet Union were probably no more severe than those within the Western alliance. The Soviets, however belatedly, had agreed to provide more modern heavy equipment for Korea than it had before. Such recent material, in addition to the Japanese and U.S. equipment of World War II vintage that the Chinese had used all along, began appearing on the battlefield during the fall. Although the Chinese got a good deal less material than they desired, the Soviets did agree in June to a new trade agreement, which provided for a much increased exchange of goods.[74]

Whatever their other differences, both the PRC and the USSR recognized distinct advantages in seeking negotiations on Korea—or at least dangerous disadvantages in not doing so. By early June it was painfully obvious that, without a major buildup of forces, the Communists lacked the capacity to drive the United Nations off the peninsula. A war of attrition eventually might break the will of the United States to continue the fight in Korea, but it was just as likely to produce such pressure on the Truman administration that it would expand the war. Certainly much of the testimony in the MacArthur hearings suggested this latter possibility.[75] The risks of such a development grew so long as there was little prospect for a negotiated settlement; so did the rapid growth of Western military might. By June U.S. armed forces had nearly doubled since the outbreak of war, and the growth promised to continue. Although much of the initial buildup went to Korea, more and more was now directed toward the Atlantic, the Mediterranean, and western Europe. Air bases in Great Britain and Iceland were well along in their preparation for war, and new or larger bases in western Europe, North Africa, and the Middle East were either under construction or being discussed. Italy had granted or was about to grant to the United States the right to use naval bases and, with Greece and Turkey moving toward full membership in NATO, the U.S. air and naval presence was bound to increase further to the east.[76] All this was in addition to the slower yet steady increase in military spending in western Europe and the possibility of West German and even Japanese rearmament. In equipping modern armed forces, North America and western Europe were outdistancing the Soviet bloc on a scale of two to one.[77] This mobilization of resources might magnify political dissension within and between Western nations, but recently such dissension had not kept pace with the strengthening of the anti-Communist alliance. The buildup in western Europe, the likely expansion of NATO to the eastern Mediterranean, and the progress toward a lenient peace treaty with Japan—the latter of which Chinese propaganda had devoted particular attention to in recent months—threatened to overwhelm the centrifugal forces operating within the capitalist world. The commencement of negotiations might stall and even reverse this trend.

Communist China's more direct involvement in Korea, its exclusion from and censure by the United Nations, and U.S. ties with its archenemy on Taiwan probably made it slower than the Soviet Union to abandon hopes of achieving its larger aims. But numerous signals since mid-April—the firing of MacArthur, a string of public statements by high U.S. officials, several private overtures, and the halt of the UN counteroffensive in Korea in early June—indicated a U.S. willingness to end the war roughly where it had begun. Moreover, conditions within China made the heavy expenditure of manpower and material in Korea a gnawing burden. By June the shortage of raw cotton—in part a result of the drying up of sources in the West—halted work in textile mills for more than two weeks; a massive donation campaign was under way to finance purchase of heavy weapons from the Soviet Union; and a widespread purge of "counterrevolutionaries" was well advanced. Although anti-Communist guerrilla forces had been weakened, the central government still lacked complete physical and ideological control over the country. By early June the Kremlin did not have to apply pressure to lure the Chinese to the negotiating table.[78]

That said, neither of the Communist powers showed any sign of desperation to bring the fighting to an end. The leisurely pace with which the Chinese moved toward negotiations and their start of preparations during the second week of July for a September offensive suggests they perceived time as being on their side.[79] Talks themselves might break the momentum toward Western consolidation and reduce the danger of an expanded war. The Soviet Union certainly had not given up hope in the effectiveness of its peace propaganda, a fact illustrated by its introduction in mid-July of a new English-language journal, *News*, which placed particular emphasis on Anglo-U.S. differences.[80] The use of a public forum—that is, a radio address by Malik—rather than continued private overtures as the instrument for delivering the belligerents to the bargaining table indicated that negotiations were at least partly conceived as a measure in the ongoing propaganda war against Western governments.

Furthermore, although the balance of forces in Korea indicated that none of the belligerents had won or could win a total military victory, the Communists believed that new battlefield tactics might wear down the enemy's will and eventually produce political concessions. The Chinese were accustomed to altering their tactics in the face of unpleasant realities without changing their ultimate goals. Their slow movement away from the course set the previous December—far slower than the U.S. retrenchment on Korea at the end of 1950—reflected in part Mao's self-confidence as a military leader, in part the real importance of his ultimate aims regarding Taiwan and Korea. Even if the more patient approach of destroying the enemy "piecemeal" rather than in "large bodies," as Peng Dehuai characterized it in his memoirs, failed to produce a unified peninsula under Communist control, such an approach still might influence the specific terms of an armistice, which would have both symbolic and concrete significance of considerable magnitude.[81] This being the case, and considering that Beijing had tacitly retreated from earlier demands merely to begin negotiations, the face-conscious Chinese were bound to contest every point with great determination.

Finally, Stalin may have seen certain advantages in a continuation of fighting in Korea. The conflict both tied down significant U.S. resources and occupied the Chinese near Soviet borders, where they could be closely watched. With major sections of Southeast Asia in a state of revolutionary turmoil, an end to the Korean War would free more of China's resources to enhance that process, a development that might further undermine Soviet influence over Asian communism.[82]

It would be an oversimplification to say that the Communist powers uniformly did or did not want an armistice during the summer of 1951. North Korea was lukewarm to the idea, while China and the Soviet Union were favorably inclined but hardly anxious. As the Central Committee of the Chinese Communist Party put it in instructions on 3 July:

> [We] have compelled the enemy to recognize our strength and give up its original aggression plans so that [we] have safeguarded the security of both the Democratic People's Republic of Korea and the People's Republic of China. . . . [With the U.S./UN forces encountering] grave difficulties in the battlefields, they have to ask for an immediate cease-fire. Therefore, it will benefit both sides to achieve a cessation of hostilities right now.[83]

Although the passage reveals a measure of wishful thinking on the part of Chinese leaders regarding the balance of military forces in Korea, it does indicate an expectation of and a desire for an end to the fighting, and these feelings probably were replicated in Moscow. Yet much would depend on the stance of the other side once formal talks began, on events within the United States, and on developing international trends of opinion on Korea and other issues, especially Germany and Japan.[84] In a meeting of CPV commanders on 25 June Peng asserted that the interests of the United States were too spread out across the globe to enable it to maintain its current effort in Korea indefinitely. Already, an economic crisis loomed in the United States, and a peace movement had picked up momentum. In Peng's mind, the Americans were poorly positioned to wage a protracted war on the peninsula.[85] Given the steady deterioration of relations between East and West over the last two years, the complications inherent in resolving issues among several governments, two key ones of which (the PRC and the DPRK) lacked formal relations with a third (the United States), and the vast cultural and ideological barriers separating the two sides, George Kennan perhaps was overly optimistic when he predicted that the shooting could be stopped with no greater difficulty than had the blockade of Berlin.

## Testing Wills

Before talks commenced, Communist troops occupied the Kaesong area, giving them control of the movements by and physical arrangements for the enemy delegation. On 10 July the Communists detained for an hour the convoy of jeeps carrying most UNC personnel to the conference site, claiming, "We must make preparations to insure your safety." In reality, they were completing arrangements in Kaesong to create an impression that the United Nations was suing for peace. As the convoy entered town—each of its vehicles showing a large white flag as previously agreed—three jeeps loaded with Communist officers dressed in full regalia appeared to lead the procession. It then wound through the war-torn streets with, as one U.S. participant later recalled, the officers assuming "the demeanor of conquerors." Communist cameramen snapped dozens of pictures for distribution throughout Asia.[86]

Vice Admiral Turner Joy traveled to Kaesong by helicopter. When he landed he encountered a "reception committee . . . armed to the teeth." He and his top assistants joined their jeep convoy waiting nearby and were led to what was designated UNC headquarters in Kaesong, a two-and-a-half-story building on top of a hill, without furnishings or modern conveniences and with armed North Korean soldiers "dotting the grounds."[87] Presently members of the UNC party got back into their jeeps and proceeded, again in Communist tow, to a building nearby, which once had housed the most expensive restaurant in town. Now it was to serve as the site for negotiations. Inside, Admiral Joy met General Nam Il, the chief North Korean negotiator. Stiffly the two men and their subordinates exchanged introductions and credentials. Once seated, Joy found himself peering northward—in Oriental cultures, the victor faced south—and directly into the eyes of the much shorter Nam. The Communists had provided the leading enemy spokesman with an abnormally low chair, their own with an exceedingly high one. Joy soon retrieved a chair of normal size, but, as he later recalled, "not before Communist photographers had exposed reels of film."[88]

Under Communist arrangements, members of the UNC delegation had no freedom to move about. When during a recess Joy attempted to send a courier to communicate with his base camp at Munsan-ni, twenty-one miles away by road, Communist guards delayed him sufficiently to prevent his completion of the mission.[89]

Ridgway had served in China earlier in his career and was sensitive to the Oriental concern about face. On the eve of the armistice talks, he had emphasized to his negotiating team the importance of leaving their enemy counterparts with easy avenues of withdrawal from stated positions.[90] After receiving a report of the first session, however, he realized he had erred in agreeing to direct negotiations without a delineation of conditions in the conference area. The task now was to seek redress without appearing excessively belligerent, either to the enemy or to an audience of allies and neutrals worldwide. He instructed Joy to press two points: first, that the UNC required "free access to the conference site from the Imjin River area during daylight hours"; second, that twenty newsmen henceforth would be attached to the UNC delegation. If the Communists refuse to concede these points, UNC negotiators would "recess the conference."[91] On the 11th "considerable agreement" emerged on the first point, but the Communists refused to concede the second.[92] When, on the next morning, Communists at their checkpoint in Panmunjom six miles east of Kaesong halted the UNC convoy and denied passage to the twenty newsmen on board, the convoy returned to Munsan-ni.[93] A day later Ridgway proposed over the Armed Forces Radio a five-mile neutral zone around Kaesong in which the two sides would refrain from hostile action. The actual area of the conference and the roads within the zone leading to and from the site would be "completely free of armed personnel." Inside the zone the number of people from each delegation would be restricted at any one time to 150, but its composition would "be at the discretion of its commander."[94]

The Communists took two days to reply, conceding the point on newsmen and the principles of a neutral zone and a conference area, asking only that details on the last point be worked out "through a meeting of both delegations." At such a meeting later in the day the two sides agreed to prohibit armed personnel in the conference area, which was to cover a half-mile radius around the conference house. All military forces were to be eliminated from the larger neutral zone, "except those necessary for military police duty and armed only for this function."[95] The Americans had won the first test of wills, one that might have been averted, or resolved with less publicity, had Ridgway and his superiors in Washington shown more patience in getting to the conference table.

This initial skirmish indicated the Communists' determination to take advantage of every opportunity offered them. Oriental culture aside, they had much reason to grasp whatever symbols of victory they could. They had recently experienced setbacks on the battlefield and faced considerable uncertainty as to enemy intentions. On 2 July Mao wired Peng, Gao, and Kim urging a rapid buildup of ammunition at the battlefront over the next ten days. In part this was in the event the negotiations led to quick agreement, in which case the two sides might not be permitted to reinforce their troops. Yet Mao devoted most of his message to a warning of possible enemy offensives, either along the main front, in the air over North Korea, or at key ports above the 38th parallel on either the east or west coast. The UNC might make such moves in an attempt to force the Communists to accept unfavorable terms.[96] Any sign of weakness at the negotiating table might encourage the enemy to become more aggressive.

Beyond this concern, the Communists had failed twice to unify the peninsula under their control. The United Nations had also failed in this respect, but its initial reason for intervention in the war—to repulse "aggression"—had been achieved, and at far less cost to the West than to North Korea and China, if not to South Korea. The Chinese Communists also had failed to capture Taiwan. Failure on the Communist side was a constant reminder of China's and Korea's limited capacities to dictate their own futures, to liberate themselves from the shackles of Western influence and power. It was critical—for national pride, for the legitimacy at home of the PRC and the DPRK, and to maintain an image of strength abroad—to put the best possible face on the negotiating process, to accumulate all the symbols if not the concrete manifestations of victory, and, at all cost, to avert any implication of defeat. To the Communists, in short, the negotiating process was war by other means.[97]

The recess and its aftermath produced signs of differences between the North Korean and Chinese negotiators. Unlike the UNC contingent, which the Americans dominated despite the presence of one South Korean, the Communists put forth Nam as their leader. This was a facade, as behind the scenes in North Korea the Chinese established a "negotiation direction group" led by Vice Foreign Minister Li Kenong and Qiao Guanhua, head of the International Information Bureau of the Foreign Ministry. The North Koreans agreed that this group, which communicated daily with Beijing, would direct the negotiations.[98] UNC liaison officers sensed this reality in a meeting at Panmunjom on the 13th. After Nam made a statement on UN newsmen at Kaesong, the Chinese representative revealed a note in Chinese characters. When the North Korean "reached for it," Ridgway reported to Washington, "the Chinese said: 'I will handle this' and pushed aside the North Korean's arm. The manner of the Chinese was that of a superior to an inferior who had interrupted at a time when interruption was not desired. The Chinese then read his paper in English." In substance, the message differed little from that of the North Korean, but its tone was more accommodating.[99]

When meetings at Kaesong resumed on the 15th, both North Korean and Chinese delegates were businesslike. When discussion moved to the agenda and Joy developed the distinction between the 38th parallel, to which the Communists demanded specific reference, and a defensible line, the Chinese showed particular interest.[100] On the next day the Communists agreed to drop mention of the 38th parallel on the agenda, although they emphasized that they were not abandoning their insistence on that point as the military armistice line. At the end of the morning and afternoon sessions, the chief Chinese delegate, Lieutenant General Deng Hua, "smiled and nodded" to his opposite on the UN side, a gesture that was notably absent from Nam's demeanor.[101]

Signs of divergence in the Communist camp remained subtle, and its concession of the 16th occurred only after a UNC retreat of the previous day, when Joy proposed an abbreviated agenda. Two items were omitted: arrangement for the International Committee of the Red Cross (ICRC) to visit prisoner-of-war camps, a touchy issue for the Communists since it involved travel in their territory and inspection of their treatment of POWs by members of an alien organization, and an explicit call for acceptance of the "principle of inspection within Korea by military observer teams," which represented a major instrument in the U.S. plan for preventing the resumption of hostilities once an armistice was signed. The Communists continued to quibble about details and to demand inclusion of the item "withdrawal of all armed forces of foreign countries from Korea."[102]

Negotiations quickly centered on the last question. On the 25th, with Joy refusing to budge after a three-day recess initiated by the Communists, Nam proposed a new agenda item, "recommendation to the governments of the countries on both sides." This would involve proposals for a post-armistice conference within a specified time "to negotiate on questions of withdrawal by stages of all foreign armed forces from Korea."[103] On the next day the two sides agreed on a five-part agenda:

1. Adoption of agenda.
2. Fixing a military demarcation line, between both sides so as to establish a demilitarized zone as a basic condition for a cessation of hostilities in Korea.
3. Concrete arrangements for the realization of cease fire and armistice in Korea, including the composition, authority and functions of a supervising organization for carrying out the terms of a cease fire and armistice.
4. Arrangements relating to prisoners of war.
5. Recommendations to the governments of the countries concerned on both sides.[104]

Joy then proposed that negotiations proceed item by item through the agenda, beginning with item 2. Nam agreed, but reserved the right to propose alternative procedures as circumstances dictated during the course of the talks.[105]

After more than two weeks of acrimonious maneuvering, the opposing sides stood ready to discuss the terms of an armistice. Their readiness reflected their recognition that the balance of military power on the peninsula was unlikely to change in their favor without undesirable risks and commitments of resources. Their determination to test enemy resolve at every step reflected the enormous cultural, ideological, and circumstantial gaps that separated them.

### Continued Posturing

Negotiating an armistice line was bound to be difficult. Acheson's statement three days after Malik's June 23 proposal for an armistice based on a mutual withdrawal of forces from the 38th parallel indicated America's willingness to accept that line; however, the remark represented an imprecise generalization rather than a carefully worded statement of policy.[106] Because of military leaders' concern about the line's defensibility, Ridgway's instructions defined the minimum U.S. position as a twenty-mile demilitarized zone based on the battle line "at the time the armistice arrangements are agreed upon."[107] Since the bulk of the current battle line rested above the 38th parallel and provided strong defensive positions against any push southward, it had both material and symbolic disadvantages to the North Koreans and, to a lesser extent, the Chinese. Despite the Communists' agreement to omit mention of the 38th parallel in the agenda, their statements at the early negotiating sessions, as well as public commentaries emanating from Beijing and Pyongyang, held fast to the demand for a settlement along the prewar boundary. In a message to Mao of 24 July, Peng talked of pushing the enemy south of the 38th parallel and then withdrawing to that line for purposes of negotiating peace. Mao's reply two days later stressed the importance of making "active preparations for the September offensive." On 1 August Mao authorized the movement of

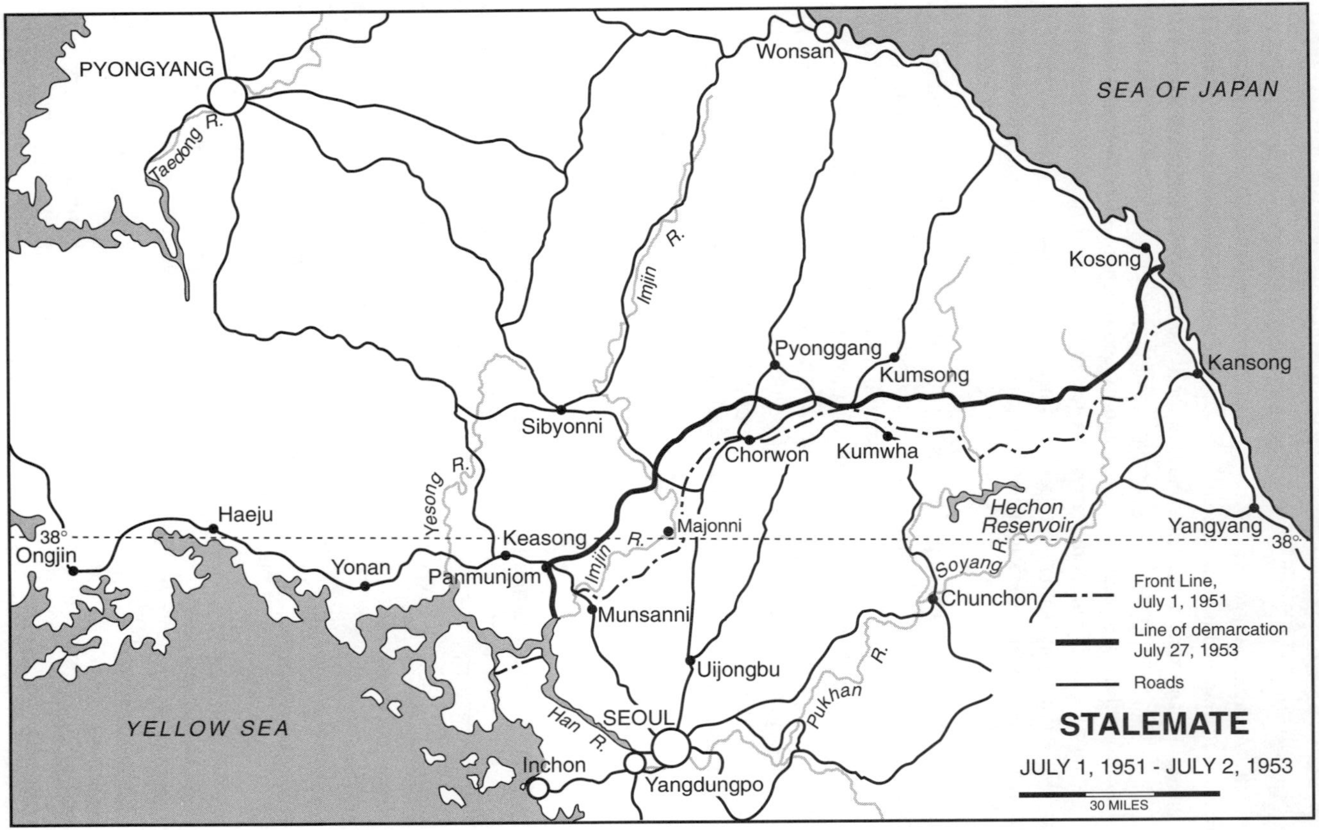
STALEMATE
JULY 1, 1951 - JULY 2, 1953
30 MILES
Front Line, July 1, 1951
Line of demarcation July 27, 1953
Roads
SEA OF JAPAN
YELLOW SEA
PYONGYANG
Taedong R.
Wonsan
Imjin R.
Kosong
Kansong
Pyonggang
Kumsong
Sibyonni
Chorwon
Kumwha
Yesong R.
Hechon Reservoir
Yangyang
Haeju
38°
Keasong
Majonni
Ongjin
Yonan
Panmunjom
Soyang R.
Chunchon
Munsanni
Uijongbu
Pukhan R.
Han R.
SEOUL
Inchon
Yangdungpo

the Twentieth Army Corps into Korea.[108] Clearly the Communists regarded attainment of the 38th parallel as an important objective.

Negotiations on an armistice line began in earnest on 27 July. Instructed to lead with a stance well in excess of the minimum acceptable terms, Joy proposed a boundary substantially north of the battle line. Joy argued that his party dominated both the air above and the sea alongside Korea. Since a cease-fire would include a cessation of military operations in the air and on the sea, as well as on the ground, the Communists would gain more from an end to the fighting than would the UN command—unless, of course, the latter received compensation for terminating its air and sea action against North Korea. That compensation should come on the ground.[109]

Nam labeled Joy's arguments "incredible," "naive and illogical," "one-sided, simple and incorrect." He argued that maintenance by the UNC of the current battle line depended on UN air and naval power, which compensated for the Communist advantage in ground forces. Furthermore, since the battle line shifted north and south of the 38th parallel "all the time," present positions did not reflect "military realities." "On the whole," the lines remained in "the region of the 38[th] parallel," making that point the logical one on which to base an armistice. In concluding, Nam asked: "Seeing that you make such a completely absurd and arrogant statement for what actually have you come here? Have you come here to negotiate for peace or just to look for an excuse for extending the war?"[110]

Joy replied with some vitriol of his own. After referring to his opponent's peroration as "a rude and graceless act," the American lectured Nam on military professionalism:

> Those peoples whose military organizations are respected throughout the world are proud of the reputation for courtesy and for objective mental attitudes. . . . Military men are expected to be sufficiently mature to realize that bluster and bombast phrased in intemperate language do not and cannot affect the facts of any military situation. . . . Rudeness such as you have displayed will lead . . . the United Nations Command Delegation . . . to conclude you have no serious or sincere purpose at this conference.[111]

Joy's scolding temporarily moderated Nam's tone but not his substantive position. The Communists clung to the 38th parallel as an armistice line, while the UNC insisted that that point had no military significance and thus had no place in a purely military agreement. Ridgway assured his representatives at Kaesong that they were merely experiencing "the ancient oriental custom of doggedness in negotiations," that "firmness and patience" were "the only effective counter-measures."[112]

On 4 August an incident occurred indicating extreme carelessness, at the least, on the part of the Communists and, at the most, a desire to terminate the negotiations. As the UNC delegation returned to the conference house at the end of their lunch break, a company of Chinese soldiers, armed with pistols, rifles, grenades, machine guns, and mortars, marched past them.[113] Because the July agreement on the physical surroundings of the talks permitted no armed personnel in the conference area and only lightly armed military police in the larger neutral zone, it was difficult to believe that the action was a mistake. The move probably represented a show of defiance toward what the Communist negotiators considered a ridiculous and insulting UN position on item 2, which they regarded as an infringement of a prior understanding.

The incident infuriated Ridgway. Having entered the talks expecting that they would be conducted on a gentlemanly basis—and being embarrassed as a result—he now momentarily lost his concern about Oriental face.[114] He wanted to "demand" an immediate explanation of "this flagrant violation" of past agreements, "a statement satisfactory to me of the corrective action taken, and acceptable guarantees against a recurrence." Good soldier that he was, the UN commander referred his intended message to the enemy first to his superiors and they toned it down without eliminating its insistence on corrective action.[115] With the talks in temporary recess over the incident and the Communists characterizing it as "accidental" and "trivial," Ridgway wired a description to the Joint Chiefs of the negotiations and of the other side's behavior that, in its intensity and bitterness, reflected poignantly the degree to which the process at Kaesong—and the Korean War as a whole—represented a confrontation of alien cultures and ideologies:

> The discussions are between soldiers. 1/2 of them are Communists who understand only what they want to understand; who consider courtesy as concession and concession as weakness; who are uninhibited in repudiating their own solemn obligations; who view such obligations solely as means for attaining their ends; who attained to power through murderous conspiracy and who remain in power by that and other equally infamous practices.
>
> To sit down with these men and deal with them as with representatives of an enlightened and civilized people is to deride one's own dignity and to invite the disaster their treachery will inevitably bring upon us.
>
> I propose to direct the UNC delegation to govern its utterances accordingly and while remaining, as they have, scrupulously factual and properly temperate in word and deed, to employ such language and methods as these treacherous savages cannot fail to understand, and understanding, respect.

Ridgway proposed to continue the recess until the enemy accepted the creation of a joint inspection team to guarantee agreed-on conditions in the neutral zone.[116]

The Joint Chiefs demurred, permitting the field commander only to insist on a Communist guarantee of neutralization of the Kaesong area.[117] With such a guarantee, and after firm denials by the UNC of Communist charges that its forces had twice breached the neutral zone, the talks resumed on the 10th.[118]

Joy now refused to discuss the 38th parallel as an armistice line. After Nam's lengthy rebuttal, the opposing delegations leered at each other for more than two hours without exchanging a word. Joy broke the silence only to suggest that the talks move on temporarily to item 3 of the agenda. Nam declined.[119] After receiving his delegation's report of the session, Ridgway proposed to Washington an ultimatum to the Communists. If it was not accepted, the UNC would terminate the talks. His superiors objected, emphasizing the importance of leaving the Communists with clear responsibility for any initiative to end negotiations.[120]

During the next six days Nam displayed his usual rhetoric, using the phrase "arrogant and absurd" to characterize the enemy position nineteen times during one seventy-two minute speech; Joy replied in kind, though less repetitively. The Communists showed no sign of strain; indeed, on the 15th the UNC delegation detected a new air of smugness and complacency in their demeanor. Joy suggested the creation of a subcommittee that could discuss an armistice line in a less formal atmosphere. The Communists agreed the next day.[121]

Sparring continued in subcommittee meetings, though at a more rapid pace and with fewer rhetorical flourishes. In the second session the Communists departed from a rigid insistence on the old boundary. Two days later they drew a distinction between the "general area of the battle line," which they adamantly rejected, and the "line of contact." While unsure of the nature of the distinction, Ridgway saw merit in the line of contact as a basis for negotiations. The UN commander now thought that a much narrower demilitarized zone than the twenty miles called for in his current instructions might emerge. Such a zone would be easier to administer while remaining a sufficient barrier to local skirmishes so long as it exceeded the range of small arms. By averting any need for the Communists to withdraw from substantial territory they now occupied, it also would help them save face. The following day they pushed for an agreement on the principle that adjustments in the line of contact could be achieved through advances and withdrawals by both parties in such a manner as to establish a military demarcation line. Ridgway and Joy remained hopeful that progress lurked just around the corner.[122]

This hope came crashing to the ground in the wee hours of the morning of 23 August. Earlier that night, the Communists contacted the UNC base camp at Munsan-ni, claiming that the conference site had just been bombed and strafed. Despite the darkness and rain, the Communists pressed for the UNC to participate in an immediate investigation. On their arrival more than two hours after the alleged incident, the two UNC liaison officers confronted a buzz saw of charges and evidence of a UNC aircraft attack. The physical evidence appeared to be manufactured or inconclusive or both, and the eyewitness accounts were no better, although a plane of other than UNC origin may have flown over or near the conference site around the time of the reported incident. The head Communist liaison officer declared from written notes that future meetings at the delegation, subdelegation, and liaison levels were all off. The Communists subsequently refused to permit an investigation during daylight hours.[123] Their propaganda on alleged UNC violations of the conference area and neutral zone intensified.

For the moment at least, the armistice talks were over.

## WHY?

Ridgway advanced three possible reasons for the Communists breaking off the talks. First, they may have wanted an "excuse" to end negotiations in a manner that would fix blame on the United Nations. They had never desired peace in Korea and had used the conference merely to gain a respite on the battlefield to prepare for a new offensive. Second, the break may have represented "a stalling procedure" in response to such events as the upcoming conference in San Francisco on the Japanese peace treaty and the present Soviet "peace offensive." Such stalling might induce America's European allies to press the United States to soften its position on Korea and elsewhere. Third, the Communists may have sought to "strengthen their propaganda position and regain the initiative in the conduct of negotiations."[124] Joy thought revenge an important consideration because of the other side's loss of face over the incident of 4 August.[125]

In all likelihood, a combination of the second and third reasons most nearly approximated the Communists' motives. The break in armistice talks represented part of a flexible strategy to see the Soviet Union, the PRC, and the DPRK through a period of trial, both in their relations with the outside world and with one another.

The negotiations at Kaesong clearly had not gone as anticipated. As Acheson later conceded, the Communists probably felt tricked by the UNC's rejection of the 38th parallel as an armistice line, which added to their disinclination to abandon it.[126] Yet in an 18 August dispatch to Mao and Peng, chief Chinese delegate Deng Hua showed some sympathy for the battlefront as the basis for an armistice line. Four days later the rest of the negotiating team actually recommended adoption of this position to Beijing.[127] The North Koreans undoubtedly disagreed, and Mao remained unwilling to overrule their position.[128]

Another Communist concern was the embarrassment suffered over UNC counters to their tactics of harassment. The Communists had striven without success to force the UNC to accept responsibility for supposed violations of neutrality arrangements. These efforts centered on UNC air attacks on Communist vehicles showing white flags as they traveled from Pyongyang to Kaesong and on alleged infringements of the neutral zone by armed UNC personnel. In the first case, the UNC suspected the Communists of abusing their privilege of immunity from attacks on trucks supplying their delegation and insisted that immunity applied only when prior notice was given of vehicular movements. In the second case, Communist charges were relatively minor until 19 August, when the leader of a Chinese military police unit patrolling the neutral zone died in an ambush by what the Communists claimed were UNC troops. The UNC countered that none of its personnel bore responsibility for the attack but that South Korean partisans may have been the culprits. This response upset the Communists, who both doubted the UNC conclusion and believed that military authorities should be responsible for the actions of South Korean citizens, even if they are not in uniform.[129]

The Communists could derive little satisfaction from U.S. press reports on the negotiations. In early August, for example, the *New York Times* characterized UNC personnel as believing "that the Communists want an armistice in Korea and, if necessary, will pay a high price to get it."[130] To date, whenever UNC negotiators assumed an unbending position, the Communists had "backed down." *Time* magazine published its story of the Communist retreat at the beginning of talks on conditions in the neutral zone under the bold heading "Red Backdown."[131] A month later *Time* described Nam as "nervously agitated, like a gambler worried by his declining pile of chips."[132] For considerations of bargaining power alone, not to mention face, such an image surely disturbed the Communists.

So did battlefield events after 18 August, when UN forces commenced limited offensives on the central and eastern fronts.[133] Within days of these moves, both sides showed flexibility in the subdelegation meetings. Yet even if the Communists abandoned their stance on the 38th parallel and the Americans dropped their principle of compensation, military conditions would remain a critical factor at the bargaining table, both in determining a precise armistice line and on other issues as well. If the UNC seized more terrain in North Korea, Communist acceptance of "the line of contact" would become more and more disadvantageous. If the UNC maintained uncontested control of the air over most of Korea, it could continue to pound Communist supply lines and bases and even expand its operations against the Yalu dams and dikes that were critical to the irrigation of North Korea's farmlands. A perpetuation of the fighting might become increasingly painful for the Communists, further encouraging a tough U.S. negotiating stance.

Despite the negative aspects of the first ten weeks of talks, the Communists did have reason to believe that eventually the talks could be brought to a successful conclusion. After initiating the shift in negotiations from the delegation to the subdelegation level, the UNC remained adamant on the 38th parallel but showed a desire to consider other lines, even if they departed from the current UNC proposal. Such initiatives may have appeared to the Communists as signs of impatience, as evidence of the U.S. tendency to push issues to a conclusion. The Communists probably surmised that, with time, they could wear down the enemy and achieve better terms. In a speech to a Communist Party organ in early August, Mao argued that the cost in lives to U.S. soldiers, the cost in money, arms, and manpower in what to Washington was a secondary front, and "insurmountable contradictions both in the international and domestic arenas" made Korea an unlikely place for the United States to fight a "protracted war."[134]

From the start of negotiations, military action had played an integral part in the Communist strategy to soften the U.S. position. By late August the UNC believed that the Communists had three armored divisions near the front, the largest stockpile of material amassed during the war, and an increasingly powerful air wing in Manchuria. Communist soldiers captured by the UNC talked frequently of an upcoming "sixth phase offensive."[135] In fact, during the first week of August, the CPV had commenced mobilization for such a campaign. The objective was to push the UNC below the 38th parallel by destroying one U.S. and one ROK division. By 20 August, however, the UNC had begun a limited offensive of its own, and Deng had become wary of prospects for early counteraction. CPV logistics had been hurt badly by enemy bombing and flooding caused by several weeks of rain. Raging waters from North Korean streams had destroyed hundreds of bridges and overwhelmed a large portion of the available storehouses.[136] On 26 August, after pleas from Deng in Korea, Mao informed Peng that there would be no "large-scale counteroffensive in September." He mentioned that Beijing had received a report that the enemy planned to launch an offensive on the west coast of North Korea near Pyongyang and that Peng "should be ready for this."[137] Peng still wanted to take the offensive in early November, but the difficulties the PRC confronted in acquiring from the Soviets adequate heavy weapons of recent vintage placed even this goal in jeopardy.[138] Thus, as the Communists broke the talks at Kaesong, Beijing was becoming less inclined than ever to commit its forces to major military initiatives.

In the days following the break in armistice talks, the Chinese press indicated that the Communists had "suspended," not terminated, the negotiations, and that they might be resumed if the UNC showed contrition for past infractions of the neutral zone. As the days passed, the Communists appeared to reverse an earlier claim that the probe of the alleged bombing of Kaesong was complete, thus hinting at the need to reinvestigate. The UNC remained firm in refusing to offer concessions in order to resume talks, even counterattacking with charges that the Communists had manufactured the incidents.

Communist verbal attacks grew in intensity, and new charges appeared of enemy violations of the neutral zone and even of air attacks on Manchuria.[139] Then, on 29 August, as Stalin wired Mao encouraging him to maintain a firm position, the Soviet Union mounted a new propaganda offensive.[140] All leading newspapers in Moscow published front-page editorials charging that the United States was trying to prolong the war and that its insistence on maintaining troops and bases in Korea was motivated by aggressive intentions against the Soviet Union and China.[141]

The barrage from Moscow was partly in anticipation of the conference on a Japanese peace treaty scheduled to open in San Francisco on 4 September. It was no secret that, once the treaty was signed, the Unites States and Japan expected to establish a military alliance. The Soviets and the Chinese had tried for months to stymie a Western settlement with Japan. The United States now stood on the verge of pulling together a broad coalition of non-Communist states behind a treaty that excluded China, left the Taiwan issue unresolved, dampened prospects for aggrieved nations to collect reparations, and paved the way to both an indefinite U.S. military presence on the archipelago and eventual Japanese rearmament. Yet many outside the Communist world remained dubious or hostile toward the U.S. effort. In Hong Kong and London, commercial circles worried about competition from a resurgent Japan, which already had made great strides forward as a result of the increased demand for finished goods provoked by the Korean War. In the Philippines, Burma, and Indonesia, the reparations issue stirred popular emotions. The United States had reduced fears of Japanese militarism by offering defense pacts to Australia, New Zealand, and the Philippines, but plans for continued U.S. military bases in Japan nourished regional sentiments of "Asia for the Asians." So did the fact that the leading draft of the peace treaty was essentially an Anglo-U.S. product. By mid-August Burma had declined to attend the conference, India leaned in the same direction, and Indonesia had accepted only tentatively and with obvious reluctance.[142]

The combination of danger and opportunity inherent in the final stages of the treaty-making process ensured a major sabotage effort by the Communists. On 11 August the Soviet Union surprised the United States, announcing that it would attend the San Francisco conference. Moscow and Beijing then escalated their propaganda to undermine support for the treaty.[143] The break in the armistice talks represented in part an effort to alarm U.S. allies and jolt such Asian neutrals as India, Burma, and Indonesia, who might then press for a great power conference to resolve outstanding issues in Asia.[144]

To add to the drama, in early September the Communists stepped up military activity in Korea. Communist ground units up to battalion strength probed into "no man's land" at numerous points along the central and western fronts. For the first time, reports filtered into the Western press of sizable numbers of Caucasian (i.e., Russian or European satellite) troops in North Korea. Soviet-built MIGs engaged UNC jets in northwest Korea on a scale far larger than before, a reflection of the success of the Soviet training program for Chinese pilots. YAK fighters strafed sections of UNC lines for the first time in a year. Combined with Communist antiaircraft fire of increased intensity and accuracy, this activity over North Korea looked like the beginning of a drive to contest UNC control of the air.[145]

Korea was not the only place where Communist actions appeared ominous. Yugoslavia complained of a sharp rise in the size and number of border provocations from Albania and Rumania.[146] The East Germans caused the most drastic interruption of traffic into West Berlin since the blockade of 1948–49 when they suddenly made the autobahn into that city a toll road, with an exorbitant tax on all trucks.[147]

The Soviets had no intention of launching an early military offensive into western Europe or the Balkans. Massive efforts were under way to integrate the economies and military machines of the eastern European satellites with the Soviet Union, which included purges of high military and government officials, sizable deportations of intransigent elements of the population, and major dislocations of satellite economies.[148] It remains unlikely that Stalin would have risked all through a premature march westward.

Yet *some* response was necessary to break the momentum toward consolidation of the enemy camp, which extended well beyond conclusion of a Japanese peace treaty. On the eve of the San Francisco conference, the United States signed security pacts with the Philippines, Australia, and New Zealand. In the aftermath of the conference, British and French foreign ministers planned to meet Acheson in Washington to narrow differences over West German rearmament, this to be followed by a full-dress meeting of the NATO council in Ottawa to formally accept Turkey and Greece as full members in the alliance. By this time the U.S. Congress was likely to have passed a defense budget for fiscal 1952 more than four times the size of pre-Korean War military allocations.[149]

All this came after a summer in which the Soviets had directed what one observer called a "half-smile" toward the West. In addition to playing a key role in the commencement of talks on Korea, Moscow permitted publication in *Pravda* of messages from U.S. and British leaders expressing friendship to the Soviet people, it called for an international economic conference to discuss ways of reducing barriers to East-West trade, and it commenced talks in Washington for a settlement of U.S. lend-lease claims extending back to World War II.[150] Unlike its Chinese ally, the Soviet Union harped in its propaganda on the theme of peaceful coexistence.[151]

None of these ploys produced the desired impact on Western policies. By the end of July the Soviet press showed impatience over the commencement of armistice talks failing to produce a slackening of the U.S. defense effort.[152] In late August Soviet demeanor began to turn back toward the implacable hostility more characteristic of Stalin's last years. A war of nerves against the West might create second thoughts among U.S. allies and aid in justifying continued policies of control and exploitation in eastern Europe.

The Soviet turn did nothing to halt the march toward a Japanese peace treaty, which forty-nine countries, including Indonesia and five other Asian and Arab nations, signed on 8 September. Behind the scenes during the San Francisco conference, and in public statements at the end of the conference by Deputy Foreign Minister Gromyko, the head of the USSR delegation, the Soviets indicated that their response to the event would come elsewhere. Most Western analysts took this veiled threat as the preliminary to a Communist offensive in Korea.[153]

That offensive never came. The Communists continued their aggressiveness in the air over North Korea, but they never launched major attacks on UN troops or attempted a large-scale ground offensive. The limited UN offensives of early September, plus the results of local counterattacks by Communist forces, discouraged reconsideration of Mao's 26 August decision to postpone major action. By the end of the second week of September the Communists had suffered more than ten thousand casualties, lost substantial supplies, and given up territory on the central-eastern front.[154] General Peng surely realized that any massive effort to push southward would be suicidal. Adding to the concern were the abysmal conditions in North Korea, where shortages of food and winter clothing were widespread.[155] If unsuccessful, a new offensive would increase Chinese vulnerability, thus worsening the Communist negotiating position. Prudence dictated sufficient offensive action to inflict sizable enemy casualties and, if possible, to recoup recent territorial losses, but without compromising continued defensive efforts to construct a network of trenches and tunnels to protect troops from UN artillery and bombing. No evidence indicates that the Soviets, who were resisting Chinese and North Korean appeals for more munitions and modern military technology, pushed their allies for more aggressive action.

The Communists had overplayed their hand at Kaesong. Their belligerent tactics had solidified UNC determination not to accept the 38th parallel as an armistice line and produced a break in talks at a time when the military advantage rested with the enemy. Just as during the previous January, when the United Nations had advanced its five principles, Mao had miscalculated. In both cases, pressures within his own camp influenced his course, but so, too, did his conviction that superior manpower, both in numbers and in commitment to a cause, would prevail over superior technology. Now, in September, his task was to lure the UNC back to the negotiating table without an unacceptable loss of face.

## • CHAPTER 7 •

# Progress

### THE ROAD BACK

General Ridgway wanted to "categorically refuse" to return to the Kaesong site. The enemy had failed to provide adequate security in the neutral zone, he argued, and the immunity of the larger neutral area from UNC attack provided a military advantage to the other side.[1] With the San Francisco conference in progress, Washington ordered a more cautious approach. The UN commander could propose an alternative location, but in a manner that would not make the United States appear responsible for a final break in negotiations.[2] On 6 September, in a public message to opposing commanders, Ridgway suggested a meeting of liaison officers to discuss a new site.[3] The Communists replied six days later, accusing the enemy of dodging responsibility for violations of the neutral zone and of "creating a pretext for breaking off the negotiation[s]."[4]

On the day before this response, UNC liaison officers sent their Communist counterparts a message that provided a possible basis for resuming talks. In the early morning darkness of 10 September, a U.S. plane had strayed over the neutral zone and machine-gunned buildings near the conference house. The Communists protested and, after an investigation, the UNC concluded that the charge was valid.[5] Admiral Joy expressed regret for the incident and assured the other side that "appropriate disciplinary action" was being taken. The UNC finally had confessed guilt, giving the Communists a face-saving device for a return to the negotiating table. On the 19th they proposed to reopen talks, leaving to the first meeting a discussion of the "unsettled incidents" and the establishment of "appropriate machinery" to ensure the future neutrality of the Kaesong area.[6]

Showing again how his earlier experiences had blurred his sensitivity to enemy face, Ridgway drafted a sharp reply offering only a meeting of liaison officers to discuss "mutually satisfactory" conditions for resumption of talks. Washington vetoed both the harsh tone of his draft and his ongoing request to categorically reject any further negotiations at Kaesong.[7]

Ridgway continued to press for a tough stance, urging that the UNC be permitted to propose a shift of the negotiating site to Songhyon-ni eight miles southeast of Kaesong. If the Communists refused to accept the new site, Ridgway wanted to abrogate the Kaesong neutral zone.[8] General Bradley worried that Washington and the UNC were drifting apart. "When you are so close to those sons-of-bitches," the mild-mannered chairman of the Joint Chiefs of Staff remarked, referring to the Communists, "you [tend to] have different views."⁹ He and others in Washington feared a complete breakdown in talks. Then pressure on the Communists—economic or military or both—would have to be increased, but its effectiveness was uncertain. Doubts existed about continued UNC control of the air over Korea. The enemy was increasing its number of MIGs by a hundred a month, whereas the monthly production of jet fighters in the United States was only thirty-one. Fears also existed about the recent Communist buildup on the ground, especially of armored divisions. Although planners talked of recruiting four more divisions for Korea from other UN members, ongoing overtures to allies left little hope that that goal could be achieved. On the economic side, the British remained dubious regarding either a complete embargo of China or a naval blockade.¹⁰ Certainly a total break in negotiations after the Communists had shown interest in resuming them would place the United States in a weak position to muster support for new action in or beyond Korea.¹¹ Thus Washington allowed Ridgway to proceed only with the proposal to change the site to Songhyon-ni. Bradley decided to make a quick inspection tour of Japan and Korea with the State Department's Charles Bohlen.

The trip produced increased confidence in Washington regarding conditions in Korea. Bohlen reported that "the present military situation is more favorable to the UN than to the enemy" and was likely to stay that way and even grow through the winter. This trend justified "stringing . . . out" the negotiations, "even in endless debate as to site." He and Bradley still feared that "a complete breakdown" would produce strong pressure in the American public for some major military initiative in the war. Since such a move was not justified on military grounds, Bohlen recommended the continued pursuit of an armistice, but with "no great urgency."¹²

In early October Ridgway's tactics began to bear fruit. To back up its proposal for a change of conference site to Songhyon-ni, the UNC commenced a military offensive during the last week of September. Although limited in objective to advances of a few miles, operations were greater in magnitude than any since the previous spring. Despite furious enemy resistance, on 5 and 6 October UN breakthroughs occurred at several points.¹³ On the 3d Mao had ordered his negotiators to reject the demand for a change in the conference site; four days later, however, the Communists proposed an expansion of the neutral area to cover "a rectangular zone" including Kaesong and Munsan and a shift of the location of talks to Panmunjom, with both sides taking responsibility for its protection.¹⁴ Ridgway's suggestion of Songhyon-ni had enabled the Communists to save face in departing from Kaesong by countering with a third possibility. UN military pressure induced them to seize the opportunity without delay.

Ridgway immediately accepted the proposed site, insisting only on a smaller neutral zone and explicit agreements on its nature and security. After a stall over another breach of the neutral zone by UNC planes, which ended with Ridgway's acceptance of responsibility, agreement emerged on the 21st.

As before, the UNC negotiators perceived their Chinese counterparts as in ultimate control of the Communist contingent and more anxious than the North Koreans to resume substantive talks.

On the 25th, more than two months after the Communists suspended the Kaesong talks, the conference reconvened in a tent outside Panmunjom.[15] Ridgway's firmness, moderated by Washington, had paid off. The question remained whether Communist concessions on procedure would be followed by similar moves on substance. The answer would depend not only on calculations of the local military balance but on perceptions of the international political equation and its likely effect on leaders in Washington.

## An Agreement, Kind Of

General Nam and Admiral Joy agreed on the 25th to discuss item 2 at the subdelegation level. After some obligatory sparring between subdelegates over who would first advance a proposal, the UNC presented a map with a four-kilometer demilitarized zone generally following the battle line. The Communists would gain territory in the east but lose even more in the west, including the city of Kaesong. The Communists demurred, but agreed to study the proposal, never mentioning the 38th parallel.[16]

By 8 November differences on item 2 had narrowed considerably. The UNC now offered either a demilitarized zone based on the line of contact or "a predetermined zone" also based on the line of contact but with other conditions: UNC withdrawals from Kosong and Kumsong in the east and central sectors, combined with a Communist retreat in the west to place Kaesong in the demilitarized area. In both cases, the zone would be "subject to revision based on changes in the line of contact prior to [the] signing of [an] armistice." The Communists proposed a demilitarized zone of similar width and based on the present line of contact, but insisted on a veto over subsequent adjustments and refused to consider Kaesong as anything but their own territory.[17]

In Washington the State Department and the Pentagon agreed that the UNC should accept the Communist position on both Kaesong and the armistice line, the only qualification being that an explicit time limit be placed for the resolution of remaining items on the agenda.[18] Ridgway objected, arguing that the UNC should concede on Kaesong only if it stood "inflexibly on the principle that the line of contact as of the effective date of the armistice" must be the line of demarcation.[19]

Political forces at work in the United States, the Western alliance, and the UN General Assembly now in session in Paris militated against firm adherence to Ridgway's principle. At home U.S. leaders feared that America's losses resulting from recent offensives would increase popular pressure for an end to the conflict.[20] By November U.S. casualties in the war approached 100,000. With the Communists accepting the U.S. position on an armistice line, the public was unlikely to show patience toward further delays.[21]

Neither were America's European allies. Great Britain's representatives in Tokyo and Washington enjoyed special access to daily reports on the armistice talks.[22] Despite some reservations about tactics, the British Foreign Office had remained generally supportive of the U.S. position. In September an escalating crisis in the Middle East reinforced this tendency. When the Mossadeq government in Iran refused to abide by a World Court ruling to permit the British to manage Iran's oil fields pending a settlement, London asked the UN Security Council to take up the issue. Great Britain resisted nationalist demands while the United States attempted to mediate. Then, in early October, Egypt served eviction notices on British troops in the Suez Canal zone, and Iraq pressed London for revision of its treaty of alliance.[23] With several showdowns in the region on the horizon, the Attlee regime naturally wanted full U.S. support. Nagging on Korea surely would not engender such a result.[24] Yet important elements of public opinion in Britain wondered if the United States really wanted an armistice on the peninsula. The Labor Left was always ready to believe the worst, but the *Times of London*, not known for anti-Americanism, also expressed concern.[25] During the election campaign of October, which culminated late in the month in a narrow Tory victory and Winston Churchill's return to the prime ministership, both parties emphasized the need for peace. Charges during the campaign that, in power, the Conservatives would be mere puppets of Washington made it especially desirable for Churchill to demonstrate a measure of independence.[26] In early November, in his maiden address to Parliament as the new prime minister, he hinted at a desire for a great power summit, despite the lack of evidence of a similar interest in Washington.[27]

Churchill also labeled the "financial and economic situation" as the most critical issue before the British nation. The follow-up speech of R. A. Butler, now chancellor of the exchequer, reinforced that point, emphasizing the need for the allies "to balance the requirements of defence with the combined resources . . . of the partner countries" of the West and outlining an austerity program at home to contend with economic conditions that had reached crisis proportions.[28] The French government was only days behind the British in introducing austerity measures. One hope for alleviating this crisis was that an end to the war in Korea would lead to reduced prices for raw material imports, loosen the purse strings of the U.S. Congress on foreign economic assistance, and enable the United States to assume more of the military burden in Europe.[29]

Added to the economic distress in western Europe was a nagging fear that the world was edging closer to major war. The Americans seemed more preoccupied than ever with military solutions to global problems. President Truman declared in a speech on 17 September that an agreement with the Soviets was "not worth the paper it is printed on."[30] Early the next month Gordon Dean, chairman of the U.S. Atomic Energy Commission, indicated that the United States had tactical nuclear weapons designed for battlefield situations. Important senators called for their employment in Korea.[31] Speculation arose that the purpose of General Bradley's current visit to Japan and Korea was to consult with field commanders on the matter.[32] Simultaneously, the United States announced that the Soviet Union recently had exploded an atomic bomb, which Stalin confirmed. The Soviet leader made it clear that, in any war between his country and the United States, he intended to use atomic weapons.[33] In late October the popular U.S. magazine, *Collier's*, devoted an issue to an imagined third world war, with Europe providing the key battleground. Rumors abounded of Pentagon involvement in preparation of the story.[34] On the heels of this issue came three well-publicized tests of atomic bombs in the Nevada desert.[35]

With the coming in early November of a meeting of the World Peace Council in Vienna and the convening of the UN General Assembly in Paris, the Truman administration recognized the danger of a new Soviet peace offensive.[36] Not to be outdone, the Americans launched a campaign to reduce armaments. On 7 November Truman outlined a plan in a radio address for reducing the armed forces of all the major powers.[37] Acheson elaborated on the proposal in his maiden speech to the General Assembly on the following day.[38]

The U.S. ploy did little to reduce allied worries.[39] The Europeans knew that Americans considered an armistice in Korea as a first step in reducing tensions with the Soviet Union.[40] When, on 8 November, Vishinsky proposed an end to the fighting in Korea based on a withdrawal of opposing armies to the 38th parallel followed by an early departure of foreign forces from the peninsula, Chinese radio broadcasts referred approvingly to the idea. Fear arose that the Communists were about to revert to a tougher stance in the armistice talks.[41] On 12 November the U.S. State and Defense departments finally decided that a concession was necessary in Korea: the UNC should accept Communist insistence on the current line of contact as the final armistice line, provided that other items on the agenda were settled within a month. The president quickly approved.[42]

Ridgway's reply to his new directive must have reminded Washington of the pleas of his predecessor a year before.[43] The UN commander warned that acceptance of the Communist demand might make major combat operations impossible. Such operations would produce sizable casualties, which, with the armistice line settled, the U.S. public would never tolerate. Even if the UNC rejected Communist pressure for a formal cease-fire upon agreement on item 2, a de facto version would occur, and this would relieve the enemy of the military pressure needed to achieve the settlement of remaining issues. A time limit for resolution of these issues would be ineffective, as its approach would result in irresistible pressure for extension. In the past, Ridgway insisted, UNC resolutions always had produced Communist concessions, and this pattern was likely to continue in the present circumstances. The UN commander pleaded for "more steel and less silk." "With all my conscience," he concluded, "I urge we stand firm."[44] Since the disaster on the Yalu of the previous fall, the admonitions of field commanders had carried less weight in Washington and leaders at the State Department and in the Pentagon refused to reconsider. On the 17th the UNC subdelegation at Panmunjom put forth the new proposal.[45]

Considerable acrimony had characterized recent subdelegation meetings. At one point the chief Chinese negotiator, Major General Xie Fang, called his U.S. counterpart "turtle egg," a particularly contemptuous label in Chinese; later, Xie referred to Admiral Joy as "the senior delegate of your delegation, whose name I forget."[46] Yet once the new UNC proposal appeared on the table the atmosphere changed, and the two sides worked rapidly toward agreement on item 2.

On the 21st the Communist negotiators agreed in principle to the UNC position. Most important, they accepted enemy insistence on the continuation of hostilities until the conclusion of an armistice. With the ironing out of details over the next two days, staff officers took on the task of determining the actual line of contact. The Communists insisted in some cases on their possession of territory held by the UNC. After the Communists conceded in most instances and in others launched quick strikes on the battlefield to back up their assertions, the contestants finally reached agreement. The main delegations met on the 27th to ratify the work of their subordinates.[47] Even then, it took eight more meetings of staff officers to draw the boundaries on large maps of an acceptable demilitarized zone.[48] More than four and a half months after the commencement of talks, the contestants had agreed on an armistice line—provided the remaining issues could be resolved within thirty days.

PERSPECTIVES AND PROSPECTS

On the eve of reaching agreement with the Communists on item 2, Ridgway told Washington that "our future bargaining potential" has been "substantially weakened." "It is particularly debilitating to our prestige and negotiating position," he complained, "to take firm positions, thereby creating widely publicized issues, only to withdraw from our position under pressure." He urged his superiors to communicate to him final positions on the remaining issues and to give him authority to "hold firm . . . even to the point where the enemy breaks off negotiations."[49] In a meeting with the president on his return to Washington in mid-December, Rear Admiral Arleigh Burke, formerly of the UNC delegation, emphasized the need for firmness and patience in dealing with the Communists. In the end, Burke concluded, battlefield events "had much more results at the conference table than anything said at the conference."[50]

Ridgway and his subordinates underestimated their successes, failed to understand that their own overzealousness had been the source of embarrassment, not erratic signals from Washington, which had consistently cautioned against adopting rigid positions, and ignored the fact that the initial arrangements for talks had compromised UNC bargaining power on some matters. On the first point, UNC negotiators had worn down the Communists on numerous issues. The bulk of the line agreed to on 27 November was north of the 38th parallel and also mostly north of the battle line when talks had begun. The UNC had paid dearly in the blood of its soldiers for the advances, but the Communists had suffered much more. The fate of Kaesong represented an exception to the rule that battlefield events had more influence in the negotiations than anything done at the conference table. Initial placement of the city in the neutral zone and UNC tolerance of its remaining there despite subsequent occupation by the enemy gave the latter a distinct advantage in claiming the city as its own. Yet, on balance, maneuvering by the Communists at the commencement of talks combined with their tactics of harassment to stiffen UNC resolve and encourage Ridgway to engage in military action that enhanced his side's position. The overall strengthening of UNC lines of defense during the negotiations more than compensated for the loss of Kaesong.

Did the November concession on the armistice line weaken the UNC position in subsequent negotiations? Firm conclusions are impossible, but clearly the earlier UNC concession on the principle of compensation had not prevented the Communists from departing quickly thereafter from their insistence on the 38th parallel; nor had the subsequent UNC concession on setting an armistice line in advance of an actual cease-fire led the Communists to cling to their call for an end to the shooting before the remaining items on the agenda were resolved.[51] This last UNC concession helped ward off growing dissension in the allied camp over the way the United States was conducting the talks, which was a matter of some importance.

Yet a crucial dimension of Ridgway's argument was that the setting of an armistice line would make sustained military pressure on the enemy impossible. General Van Fleet made this position a self-fulfilling prophecy on 27 November when, without Ridgway's foreknowledge, he ordered his commanders to reduce "operations to the minimum essential to maintain present positions." "Offensive action" was to be taken only "to regain key terrain lost to [future] enemy assault."[52] The order leaked to the press and, despite Washington's denials that a de facto cease-fire was in effect, still the Communists were relieved temporarily of enemy pressure unless they chose to initiate offensive action.[53] Because of the nature of the settlement on item 2, some disappointment was inevitable among UNC soldiers, and for some time Ridgway was under pressure from home to keep down casualties.[54] Even so, Van Fleet's order was neither necessary nor prudent. At best, the resulting decline in casualties helped to relieve pressure from the U.S. public and congressional opinion so that concessions could be made on the unsettled issues.

In all likelihood, Van Fleet's faux pas grew out of the less than happy relationship between the Eighth Army commander and his superior in Tokyo. Ridgway had not been consulted in advance about Van Fleet's appointment during the previous spring. Had he been asked, he would have advised against it. Van Fleet had received his first commission in the army two years before Ridgway, which could not help but make the latter feel uncomfortable in acting as the former's immediate superior. Furthermore, Ridgway did not consider Van Fleet to be particularly capable, nor was he fond of him personally.[55]

Still, U.S. officials recognized that a major advance north of the present battle line was feasible only after a substantial increase in the resources available to the UNC—and this calculation ignored the possibility of augmented Soviet aid to the Communist side. Considering U.S. needs elsewhere and the unlikelihood of sizable new contributions from other UN members, a large-scale buildup of UNC offensive capabilities was not in the cards. With sentiment at the UN General Assembly in Paris against early action outside Korea, a continuation of limited offensives was the only real alternative to the course followed. Although this approach had produced some positive results in the past, they came only after weeks of difficult bargaining. This was so largely because the substance of the issue involved, namely, the location of an armistice line, was of genuine importance to the Communists, just as were at least two of the three items yet to come. Thus the Communists, like the UNC, felt compelled to contest every issue with considerable verve. Had UNC troops moved farther north, making their military advantage all the more apparent, the Communists would have been just as likely to augment their own forces in preparation for counteroffensive action as to grant new concessions at Panmunjom.

In assessing the prospects for an early armistice, therefore, the remaining issues need to be examined. The UNC had agreed to item 5 on the agenda to get the Communists to accept the absence of an item on the withdrawal of foreign troops.[56] The matter involved nothing crucial to either China or the Soviet Union. If both were likely to make passing gestures to North Korean sensibilities, neither was disposed to make the issue a stumbling block to an armistice. The same could be said of the U.S. side, only here the gestures would be directed toward the Rhee regime.[57]

Items 3 and 4 were altogether different. Because the Americans lacked faith in future Communist intentions, they believed that arrangements for the preservation of a cease-fire held considerable importance. In addition to the establishment of a defensible armistice line, restrictions on the buildup of military forces on both sides were paramount. The idea was that maintenance of the present balance of power in Korea would discourage a renewal of hostilities. Crucial to this balance was the U.S. advantage in the air. The inspection of military facilities on both sides would be necessary to enforce restrictions on the size and nature of armed forces, and the United States understood that this might be a sticking point to the Communists.[58] They also recognized the problems that might arise from permitting Communist inspectors to move about freely within South Korea.[59]

In mid-November, as agreement approached on item 2, the State and Defense departments concluded that a statement upon the signing of the armistice might serve as an effective substitute for broad inspection; the statement might read that, in the event of a resumption of hostilities by the other side, the military response would not be restricted to Korea.[60] To achieve full credibility, such a statement would need support from Great Britain and other U.S. allies. The State Department approached the British on 21 November.[61] Because the action the United States anticipated in the event of a breach of the armistice included the imposition of a naval blockade against China and the bombing of China, there was no telling how long interallied exchanges would take. Meanwhile, through their press correspondents at Panmunjom, the Communists indicated that they had no intention of permitting inspection of key facilities behind their lines.[62] Until discussions in the West were concluded on a greater sanctions statement, and unless they led to a U.S. decision that the statement was an acceptable substitute, debates at Panmunjom on item 3 were bound to be long and difficult.

Uncertainty also existed on U.S. policy regarding item 4, the fate of prisoners of war. The Geneva Convention of 1949, which the United States had signed and by which both the UNC and the Communists had announced they would abide, should have made the question easy to resolve. Article 118 read that "prisoners of war shall be released and repatriated without delay after the cessation of hostilities."[63] The United States, fearing establishment of a principle behind which the Soviets could hide in refusing to repatriate all prisoners—as they had with the Germans and Japanese since 1945—even opposed a proposal to permit captives to apply for transfer to another nation willing to accept them.[64]

But in the context of the Korean War many U.S. policymakers regarded an "all-for-all" exchange of prisoners as unfair and repugnant in principle. Despite their announcement to the contrary in July 1950, the Communists had *not* abided by the Geneva Convention, failing to submit lists of prisoners held by their side to the International Committee of the Red Cross (ICRC), permit visits to POW camps by members of that organization, or reveal the location of those camps.[65] They were suspected of having committed numerous atrocities (of which, of course, America's South Korean allies were far from innocent). Moreover, because in July 1951 the UNC held some 150,000 prisoners, many more than were held on the other side, an all-for-all exchange would provide the enemy with a major source of manpower to augment its armies, potentially disrupting the balance of military power on the peninsula.[66] This danger could be reduced by reclassifying some of the Koreans held in UNC camps, roughly 40,000 of whom had been residents of South Korea in June 1950 and had been impressed into the North Korean army either from civilian life or after serving in the ROK armed forces and being captured by the Communists.[67] The UNC could reduce this danger still further by giving Chinese POWs a choice of whether to return to the mainland. Many of these men were former Nationalist soldiers in the Chinese civil war who had been impressed into Communist armies against their will. U.S. observers estimated that more than half of them would choose against repatriation.[68]

UNC adherence to the principle of no forced repatriation also might provide a psychological victory for the West in the cold war. Brigadier General Robert A. McClure, the chief of Psychological Warfare in the U.S. Army, observed in July that the UNC could avoid the heartbreaking experience that occurred after World War II, when Soviet prisoners had been forced to return to their homeland, often against their will and sometimes at the cost of their lives. The United States would derive the advantage in future wars of confronting enemy soldiers who were more likely to surrender because they felt confident of not being repatriated.[69] If the civil aspects of the present fighting in Korea and the recent conflict in China provided an immediate context to apply the principle to the West's advantage, a possible war in Europe matching NATO forces against Soviet bloc armies—including satellite soldiers of dubious loyalty to Moscow—added an obvious future case with perhaps even greater potential for exploitation.[70]

During the summer and fall of 1951 the State and Defense departments in Washington and the UNC in Tokyo devoted considerable attention to the POW issue. By mid-November Ridgway and his superiors at home were confident of the legality and practicability of reclassifying some forty-one thousand Korean prisoners as "civilian internees," although they feared that the Communists would consider release of such persons before an armistice as a "breach of faith" and this would jeopardize the return of prisoners held in North Korea and China.[71] This concern applied with even greater force to insistence on the principle of nonforcible repatriation, which had the added liability of resting on dubious legal foundations. Despite much initial interest in the idea, as item 2 approached resolution the trend in Washington and Tokyo was in favor, except for the category of civilian internees, of eventual acceptance of an all-for-all exchange.[72]

President Truman represented an exception to this trend. He interjected himself only occasionally into the decision-making process on the armistice talks, but at the end of October he expressed reservations about forcing repatriation on prisoners who had cooperated with the UNC or were likely to be "immediately done away with" by the Communists. At the very least, the president thought, the UNC should receive "some major concessions" in return for an all-for-all exchange.[73] Whether Truman's advisers could "educate" him on the complexities of the issue, as one State Department official suggested, remained to be seen.[74]

Also uncertain was the impact of an incident in Korea that occurred only two weeks before agreement was reached on item 2. On 14 November Colonel James Hanley, the chief of the Judge Advocate Section of the Eighth Army, announced that more than 6,000 captured U.S. military personnel had been killed by the Communists since the beginning of the war.[75] In the United States the Hanley statement created widespread horror and outrage over alleged Communist atrocities.[76] Ridgway, who had not authorized Hanley's action, investigated and announced that, despite reports of atrocities involving the death of 6,202 Americans, conclusive evidence had been found in only 365 cases.[77] Yet by connecting Communist atrocities and U.S. fatalities to POWs in such a dramatic fashion, Hanley stirred emotions and through them political forces in the United States that might discourage an accommodating approach on item 4.[78]

Whether inside Korea or elsewhere, the Communists gave little indication that they would put forth extraordinary effort to reach accommodation. The Soviets did reveal anxiety regarding the Western military buildup and, if they needed any reminder of its connection to the continued fighting in Korea, Acheson provided it in his speeches at UN meetings in Paris.[79] With talk spreading in the United States about the use of atomic weapons, with Congress about to pass a $100 million appropriation for exiles from the Communist bloc or others still residing therein either in support of NATO or, more ominously, "for other purposes," and with movement continuing in western Europe and the Mediterranean toward the expansion of the Western alliance, Soviet jitters were understandable.[80] In early November the annual speech on the anniversary of the Bolshevik revolution, delivered this time by Deputy Premier and high Politburo member Lavrentii Beria, suggested genuine concern in the Kremlin regarding international trends. Charles Bohlen, the State Department's leading Soviet expert, viewed Beria's quotation in the speech of Stalin's foreign policy statements of 1927, a year of great Soviet vulnerability, and its extensive treatment of Western rearmament as "defensive and apprehensive" and in striking contrast to earlier "postwar speeches on similar occasions."[81] At the end of the speech Beria used the word *nonaligned* before the standard adjectives *united, democratic,* and *peace-loving* in relation to Germany, perhaps a sign of preparation for Stalin's diplomatic initiative of the following spring aimed at preventing the rearming of a West Germany closely allied to the West.[82]

Anxious or not, Stalin continued to believe he could exploit "contradictions" in the opposing camp. Despite the successful conclusion of a Japanese peace treaty without the participation of the Communist powers and the pending integration of Japan into the U.S. security system, the inclusion in NATO of Greece and Turkey and high-level military talks between the United States and Yugoslavia, and the continuing Western military buildup, enough dissension remained in the West to encourage Stalin to hold firm in most aspects of his foreign policy.[83] Socialists in West Germany had responded favorably to the recent East German campaign for negotiations between the two German governments for the arrangement of national elections.[84] The Labor Left in Great Britain and important elements in France remained dubious about West German rearmament. Negotiations in Bonn and Paris showed only limited progress in resolving problems blocking formation of a European Defense Community that included German divisions.[85] Most important, the economic strains of rearmament in western Europe recently had taken a turn for the worse, which could exacerbate dissension in NATO and halt or even reverse the growth of military budgets.[86]

On Korea itself, U.S. allies remained uneasy about the course the United States was taking, despite the concessions of mid-November. This situation might become even more susceptible to exploitation once items 3 and 4 were on the negotiating table. Certainly it could be used, in combination with timely concessions by the Communists, to reduce prospects for an expanded war. Unlike in the previous fall, Soviet diplomats at the United Nations now showed little friendliness on the social circuit or interest in behind-the-scenes negotiations regarding Korea.[87] Stalin may have feared that an armistice in Korea would only advance the cause of rearmament in western Europe by enabling the United States to allocate more resources to that theater.[88] On 19 November he wired Mao, stating that despite delaying tactics by the Americans at Panmunjom, "the overall international situation" placed them in greater need than the Communist side of "rapidly concluding" an armistice. Thus the Chinese and North Koreans should "pursue a hard line" and avoid any show of haste in the negotiations.[89]

China held a different perspective. In mid-November Lionel Lamb, the British chargé in Beijing, received word of a recent speech by Zhou Enlai. The Chinese foreign minister stated that it had become necessary to negotiate a cease-fire owing to the negative impact of war on the national economy.[90] After many months of activity by the Resist-America-Aid-Korea Committee, including a massive donations campaign directed primarily at the bourgeoisie, and after the arrival of new Soviet aid to Korea, the Communists had all they could do to hold their own in the fighting. With U.S. B-29s flying simulated atomic missions over North Korea during early October and the U.S. public showing considerable sentiment in favor of the use of nuclear weapons, the Chinese undoubtedly grasped the precariousness of their position on the peninsula.[91]

During November the PRC demonstrated its recognition that an ongoing stalemate in Korea would entail increasing sacrifices at home. Early in the month Chen Yun reported to the First National Committee of the People's Political Consultative Conference that investments for economic construction would concentrate on defense measures. He also referred to poor weather conditions in North China that had produced widespread famine and to a national shortage of skilled labor, technicians, and intellectuals, which had compounded the task of supporting military operations in Korea.[92] The committee soon announced the augmentation of the Resist-America-Aid-Korea campaign, an austerity drive tied to new patriotic production measures, and expanded ideological reform.[93] At the end of the year, Mao, showing ongoing concern about morale and discipline at home, would launch the Three Anti–Five Anti campaign against the capitalist classes and bourgeois intellectuals.[94]

Beijing already had canceled plans for a major November offensive, restricting aggressive CPV action to a series of limited tactical thrusts along the battle line. Mao ordered his generals to devote the bulk of their effort to constructing a multilayered system of trenches and tunnels. Peng was to conserve manpower and equipment while holding to current positions and forcing the enemy to expend as many troops and supplies as possible.[95]

Kim Il-sung surely disliked this new defensive-mindedness, but he was in no position to protest. With North Korea suffering from severe food shortages as a result of summer floods, public morale sank to a new low. Kim's dependence on Soviet and Chinese aid reached a high, and his position at home approached that of the Bolsheviks in Russia during the winter of 1918. However painful it was to concede at least temporary defeat for his ambition to dominate the peninsula—and even more to accept an armistice that entailed conceding some territory he had held before the war—such concessions probably appeared essential for his own survival.[96]

If economic conditions in China, the defensive operations of Communist armies in Korea, and the concession on the armistice line at Panmunjom indicated that Beijing desired an end to the war, the adoption of new measures to reinforce the defense effort, the bolstering of Chinese forces on the peninsula, and the determined if flexible negotiating tactics employed in talks with the UNC revealed a continued willingness to accept considerable sacrifice at home to protect the national interest abroad. Mao's opening address to the First National Committee of the People's Political Consultative Conference on 23 October carried a certain defensive tone when discussing the Korean War, which implied that the venture had stirred some dissension among government and party leaders. Still, Mao emphasized the need to face down any "bullying . . . by foreign imperialists." China stood ready to settle the Korean question "by peaceful means" but only if the United States accepted "fair and reasonable" conditions.[97] On 11 November Mao wired Peng that "it would certainly be better if the negotiations . . . succeeded," but went on to state that, if they failed, "we have confidence to continue the war until winning victory."[98] Chinese propaganda acknowledged the Soviet contribution in Korea and overall Sino-Soviet cooperation more than it had during the rest of the year.[99] Increased Soviet support had enabled the Communists to adopt a more aggressive approach in the air war. MIGs appeared over North Korea in greater numbers and demonstrated increasing effectiveness in attacking enemy bombers. In a single week at the end of October the UNC lost five planes in combat, only one less than the number it had lost in the entire war up to that point. Emboldened by recent triumphs, the Communists stationed dozens of their fighters across the Yalu in North Korea and assigned thousands of laborers to construction and repair efforts there.[100] Thus whatever the differences in perspective between Moscow and Beijing, the PRC remained willing and able to stand firm in Korea until the UNC accepted terms that accommodated both China's security needs and its national pride.

While both sides had reason to want peace in Korea, neither was so desperate as to accept it without further hard bargaining at the conference table. As one U.S. correspondent wrote, "only stubborn optimists on both sides were willing to predict any early solution of the whole cease-fire problem."[101]

## Narrowing the Issues

The two sides did make an early effort to resolve remaining differences, especially on item 3. Only a week after discussion on the item began, the Communists accepted the principle of inspection beyond the demilitarized zone. The UNC responded by proposing to move negotiations to the subdelegation level. Nam quickly agreed.[102]

Major differences remained between the two sides. The Communists opposed any rotation of military personnel or replenishment of equipment by either side after the signing of an armistice; the UNC insisted on both so long as neither involved the strengthening of forces. The Communists demanded that the UNC withdraw from islands it occupied off the coast of Korea north of the 38th parallel; the UNC said it would do so only as a trade-off on another issue. On inspection outside the demilitarized zone, the Communists resisted the UNC demand for aerial observation and pushed to replace a joint military armistice commission enjoying unrestricted movements in Korea with a "supervisory organ" peopled by neutral nations and limited to certain "mutually agreed upon" ports of entry. Ridgway wanted neutral inspection teams to be under the authority of a military armistice commission. In internal discussions U.S. policymakers showed flexibility regarding the scope of inspection, but the question of which ports would be open to inspection teams obviously required negotiation. U.S. planners also showed a willingness to give ground on the matter of airfields in North Korea. Although the UNC opposed either the repairing of old ones or the building of new ones after an armistice, Washington surmised that, at most, the Communists would concede the latter point. In any event, the enforcement of restrictions on airfields probably was not feasible over an indefinite period. Here, however, as on the issue of inspection, the final UNC position depended on the outcome of talks between the United States, Great Britain, and other allies on a "greater sanctions statement" warning the Communists against a resumption of hostilities once the armistice was signed.[103]

These talks showed little prospect for early success. In late November Acheson discussed the statement with British Foreign Minister Anthony Eden. Acheson wanted prior agreement on action to be taken if the Communists broke an armistice. U.S. military officials pushed for attacks on Chinese air bases and a naval blockade of the China coast. Eden objected to any prior commitment to specific action. He also thought that all nations with forces in the UNC should be asked to join in the statement.[104]

In mid-December Anglo-U.S. negotiations expanded to include all other contributors to the UNC. By this time the United States had abandoned its quest for agreement on specific action to be taken should a breach of an armistice occur. Yet several contributors to the UNC still had doubts about the U.S. proposal. Canada feared that the statement might encourage the Soviets to try to lure Western military strength to northeast Asia without committing forces there themselves.[105] New Zealand questioned the need for or the desirability of the statement.[106] Australia wanted discussions on the measures to be taken in the event of a major breach of an armistice.[107] With the PRC already engaged in training and supplying Vietminh troops and recent reports indicating a buildup of Chinese forces in Guangxi and Yunnan provinces along the Indochina border, the French wanted to commit signatories to collective action against future "aggression" anywhere.[108]

Great Britain already had further complicated the negotiations by pressing to include India in the statement.[109] By late December the United States was

250 • CHAPTER 7 •

at once optimistic about the prospects for eventual agreement on a statement and uncertain about when such a meeting of minds would occur and what the final product would look like.

Given the uncertainty, Washington refused to concede ground at Panmunjom on the rehabilitation of airfields other than on those unsuitable for jets. When on the 19th the Communists offered a concession on the rotation of troops in exchange for a UNC retreat on airfields, Joy reported to Ridgway that "airfields are clearly the key issue of the armistice."[110] On item 3 alone agreement was yet to be reached on the replenishment of material, the relationship between neutral observers and a military armistice commission, and the extent of inspection; but these all appeared resolvable through further bargaining.

The same might have been said about the POW issue. The Communists had not accepted UNC appeals to begin simultaneous discussions on items 3 and 4 until 11 December. Another week passed before the Communists retreated from their demand for agreement on the principle of an all-for-all exchange of POWs before any swapping of prisoner lists.[111] When the UNC examined the enemy list, it became obvious why the Communists had pressed in advance for the all-for-all principle. The Communists' list showed only 11,559 prisoners in their possession, whereas the UNC classified some 100,000 of its troops as missing in action. During the first months of the war alone, Communist news releases and radio broadcasts had claimed the capture of more than 65,000 enemy troops. In contrast, the Communists reported 188,000 of their soldiers as missing, while the UNC listed 132,000 prisoners and another 37,000 who had recently been reclassified as civilian internees. On the 22d, the first day of discussions on the lists, Rear Admiral Ruthven E. Libby, who had replaced Admiral Burke on the UNC negotiating team, explained that 16,000 more prisoners had turned out to be ROK citizens and also would not be repatriated.[112] Major General Lee Sang Cho protested, arguing that prisoner status should be determined solely on the basis of the uniform worn at the time of capture. Libby counterattacked, knowing that the North Koreans had inducted tens of thousands of captured ROK citizens and soldiers into their army. Although the Americans were not optimistic about the prospects for securing their return, the issue did provide them with a bargaining chip in trying to persuade the Communists to swallow reclassification of more than a third of the prisoners on the UNC side.[113]

If the question of reclassification was likely to be resolved only through prolonged negotiations, the U.S. flirtation with voluntary repatriation threatened to produce a deadlock. The United States still had not adopted a firm position on the matter, but President Truman continued to have strong views.[114] During the second week of December he challenged his advisers in the State and Defense departments on the UNC negotiating position, expressing concern that an armistice in Korea would lead only to a renewed Communist attack at a later date and that this would result in a loss of the peninsula and a resurgence of isolationism in the United States. He feared that during the coming election year it would be difficult to sustain the U.S. rearmament program.[115] An unstated implication of his outlook was that a continuation of the war through 1952 might further U.S. interests.

Truman's top advisers, with the exception of Secretary of State Acheson, who was still in Europe, disagreed. They doubted that the passage of time would lead to an improvement in the U.S. bargaining position in Korea, and they thought that a greater sanctions statement represented an effective deterrent to a renewal of Communist hostilities.[116] This attitude emerged clearly in deliberations on voluntary repatriation. At the end of November Ridgway had wired the Joint Chiefs with a plan to adopt exchange on a one-for-one basis as an initial negotiating position but to retreat eventually to an all-for-all exchange if necessary to secure the return of UNC prisoners.[117] On 3 December the Joint Chiefs recommended the acceptance of this position to Secretary of Defense Lovett.[118] The State Department essentially agreed, although it urged a strong effort "to avoid the forcible return to the Communists of persons whose lives would be endangered thereby."[119]

Given the president's view, however, the State Department and the Pentagon instructed Ridgway to propose a one-for-one exchange until all prisoners and civilians held by the Communists were returned, after which prisoners still in the hands of the UNC would be repatriated on a voluntary basis. The UNC should stick to this position for "as long as possible without precipitating a break" in negotiations.[120] The risk in this approach was, as Ridgway observed, that once the idea of "the right of asylum to POWs" was publicized, it might prove "so appealing to humanitarian sentiment" that the U.S. public would demand its implementation. With the Communists already gearing up their propaganda for an all-for-all exchange, the UNC approached the POW issue with some trepidation.[121]

Admiral Libby did not put voluntary repatriation on the bargaining table until 2 January 1952. By this time the two adversaries had extended, by fifteen days, the deadline for an armistice based on the line of contact of late November 1951. In addition, General Lee had revealed that the reason for the huge disparity between earlier Communist claims of captured ROK soldiers and its current list was his side's policy of "reeducating" and releasing many of them at the front. The UNC jumped on this point with alacrity, claiming that most of these men later turned up in the North Korean army. Libby suggested that in proposing voluntary repatriation he was merely adopting "the principle, advanced and advocated by your side, that a soldier from one side, upon his 'release,' exercise his individual option as to whether he will return to his own side or join the other side." The only differences in practice were that the UNC would await the end of hostilities before giving its prisoners their choice, and the choice would be made under the supervision of a neutral body, the ICRC.[122]

The Communists, who had not anticipated the U.S. position, responded on 4 January with a series of epithets reminiscent of the previous summer.[123] The UNC proposal was "absurd," "useless," and "ridiculous," and they "absolutely" refused to accept it.[124] Radio Beijing labeled it "a brutal and shameless proposition."[125] For weeks the Chinese press had shown impatience with UNC positions at Panmunjom, but now it became more abusive than ever, even warning that they might terminate the talks.[126]

Yet the Communists did not halt the negotiations and, after characterizing the UNC proposal as unworthy of discussion, they soon engaged in precisely that.[127] The Communists harped on Article 118 of the 1949 Geneva Convention, to which in practice they had paid little heed, while the UNC argued a position that appeared to conflict with an agreement to which it had previously adhered.

Whatever the willingness of the Communists to debate the issue, they showed no flexibility as the extended deadline in the agreement on an armistice line passed during the second week of January. Reports in the U.S. press that the United States was on the verge of making concessions on item 4 did not encourage the Communists to bend, but the substance of the issue itself provided plenty of reason for their intransigence.[128] In raising the question of individual freedom of choice, voluntary repatriation struck at the heart of ideological and cultural conflict between East and West. It also confronted the virtual certainty that significant numbers of prisoners held by the UNC would choose not to return to North Korea or mainland China. This result would belie the claims of the Beijing and Pyongyang regimes of having sole legitimacy over their countries. The Chinese were particularly sensitive on this point. When the UNC stated on 15 January that Chinese prisoners should have the choice of returning to Taiwan, the PRC negotiator replied that "if anybody dares to hand over any of the personnel of the CPV captured by the other side to the deadly enemy of the Chinese People [the Nationalists], the Chinese people will never tolerate it and will fight to the end."[129]

The Soviet Union of Joseph Stalin was unlikely to counsel accommodation here. While before World War II the Soviets had concluded numerous agreements on POWs that accepted the principle of voluntary repatriation, at the end of that conflict they insisted on total repatriation of prisoners and displaced persons—and understandably so. In early 1945 more than 5 million Soviet citizens were under foreign authority, some of whom had defected from Soviet armies or fled Soviet territory and were collaborating with the German enemy, a reflection of the Stalin regime's extreme unpopularity in some regions of the USSR. Stalin was determined to retrieve these people. Ultimately—and with U.S. assistance—some 5.2 million people were returned to the Soviet Union, many against their will.[130] Application of the principle of voluntary repatriation in Korea would set a dangerous precedent with implications not only for the future loyalty of Soviet soldiers and citizens, but also for satellite populations in eastern Europe, where U.S. encouragement and aid to dissenting groups was on the rise and ongoing purges indicated continued Soviet concern.[131]

Despite the impasse on POWs at Panmunjom, progress continued on item 3. On the 9th the Communists agreed to the replenishment of war equipment.[132] Two days later the Joint Chiefs informed Ridgway that the UNC should drop its objection to the rehabilitation and construction of airfields if all other issues were resolved. The move reflected Washington's confidence in the effectiveness of the greater sanctions statement and its ultimate acceptability to U.S. allies.[133] By the middle of the month the Pentagon contemplated an eventual return to plenary sessions in order to put forth a "package proposal," with the UNC conceding on airfields and the Communists on POWs.[134] Secretary of State Acheson thought an armistice likely around the end of the month.[135]

The six weeks that had passed since tentative agreement had emerged on item 2 had seen give and take on both sides, though most concessions had come only grudgingly and with the passage of time. An exception was Communist acceptance of the principle of inspection beyond the demilitarized zone, which came in early December. Implementation, of course, would involve inspection in South Korea as well as in the North, and the Communists bargained fiercely on specifics. Yet their early concession on the principle reflected their genuine desire for an armistice.

On the other hand, as the new year arrived, the continuing lull in UN military pressure gave the Communists little reason to hurry. They now had more than 700,000 troops in Korea and supplies far exceeding those of the previous summer. They had taken advantage of the lull in aggressive enemy action to dig in as never before, expanding a system of trenches and tunnels that greatly reduced vulnerability to enemy artillery and air action.[136] Confident of his military position, Mao wired Peng on 28 December that, "so long as we are not afraid of delaying and are not showing anxiety, the enemy cannot play any of its tricks."[137]

### Soviet Probes of Western Cohesion

In early January, while bargaining continued at Panmunjom, the holiday recess of the UN General Assembly ended in Paris. The Soviet Union chose the occasion to probe Western unity on a variety of issues, including Korea. On the 3d Soviet Foreign Minister Andrei Vishinsky took the floor of the First Committee to lambaste the report of the Collective Measures Committee (CMC). Created by the "Uniting for Peace" resolution passed on 3 November 1950, the CMC did not meet until March 1951 or submit a report until the following fall. By this time events in Korea had injected some realism into assessments of the potential of the United Nations as an agent of collective security.[138] Now the report, plus a resolution sponsored by eleven of the fourteen nations represented on the committee and calling for its continuation for another year, became the first item for UN consideration. By articulating the problems inherent in the implementation of broad economic and financial measures, as well as revealing the puny advance commitments nations stood willing to make to a UN military force, the report advertised the limited success of the United States in mobilizing the General Assembly to serve its purpose.[139] Yet the Soviet Union was taking no chances, digging in its heels to resist an extension of the committee's mandate.

In its attack on U.S. policies, Vishinsky's speech of the 3d went far beyond the CMC report. He berated the United States for the $100 million appropriation for exiles from eastern Europe in the Mutual Security Act passed by Congress during the previous fall, and he gloated over tensions within the Western camp on the rearming of West Germany, the Schuman Plan, and high military budgets. After characterizing the U.S. course in Korea as "mere piracy and a mockery of UN principles," he proposed a meeting of the Security Council to consider methods of reducing international tension. Korea was to be the first item on the agenda. Vishinsky closed by repeating recent charges by Beijing that the United States was engaged in maneuvers with remnant Nationalist Chinese forces in Thailand and Burma which indicated that new attacks, sure to be labeled "defensive," were about to be made on the PRC.[140] This last charge, coupled with the buildup of PRC forces in provinces bordering on Southeast Asia, added to fears in Western circles that the Chinese Communists sought a pretext to launch a military offensive into the region.[141]

Vishinsky had reason to believe that Soviet promotion of havoc in the enemy camp would bear fruit. In Western Europe the year began amid fears of inflation and shortages of basic raw materials. Economic conditions fostered increasing impatience with U.S. emphasis on the ongoing military buildup. Over the past year countries there had increased defense budgets on an average of 75 percent, had raised production of munitions by 70 percent, and had improved the combat effectiveness of armed forces by a factor of two or more.[142] Yet, as economic problems worsened in the fall, the U.S. Congress cut by $600 million a request from the Truman administration for foreign economic aid, and some Republican members continued to gripe about allied trade with the Communist bloc.[143] Rumors spread in England that Prime Minister Winston Churchill would receive a cool reception on his upcoming visit to the United States.[144]

The Soviet effort to promote discord in the West included a campaign to promote East-West trade. During the previous fall the Soviets had played an active role in a conference at Singapore on trade with Southeast Asia. The new year found the Soviets sponsoring a major trade exhibit in India and appealing to the Japanese to reopen commercial relations with the Communist bloc, especially China.[145] Many in Japan regarded trade with China as central to recovery. The Korean War had sparked Japan's economy by producing new demand for goods and services connected to the UN military effort; however, with the impending termination of U.S. economic assistance as the occupation drew to a close, with an armistice possible at any time in Korea, and with the question of reparations to be paid to the Philippines, Indonesia, and Burma still unsettled, a need for new markets appeared pressing. Mainland China would provide both buyers for Japan's finished goods and a cheap source of such raw materials as iron ore and coking coal. The British hoped for a revival of Sino-Japanese trade to deflect competition from Southeast Asian markets, while the Republican Right in the United States insisted that, politically, Japan deal exclusively with the Nationalist regime on Taiwan, which implied a downplaying of economic relations with the Communist government. With the peace and security treaties with Japan about to go before the U.S. Senate for ratification and presidential and congressional election campaigns on the horizon, the Truman administration was unlikely to show patience toward Japanese flirtation with Communist China.[146] The dangling by the Communist powers of tempting offers of vast markets and crucial raw materials in the faces of Japanese businessmen had great potential for mischief making. Stalin even opened the new year with a special message to the Japanese people. Other propaganda appeals to Japan and western Europe played up the importance of a "World Economic Conference" being organized in Moscow for April.[147]

Potential for discord within the Western alliance, especially in Anglo-U.S. relations, extended to areas other than economics. The British remained dissatisfied with U.S. rigidity in dealing with the Soviets, believing that it gave them an advantage in the propaganda war. Grumbling also existed over U.S. insistence on one of its own nationals being designated commander of allied naval forces in the Atlantic, over the U.S. buildup of air bases in the British Isles without any agreement for consultations before their use for an atomic attack on the Soviet Union, over lukewarm U.S. support for Britain's policy of resisting nationalist demands in Iran and Egypt, and over Washington's pressure for greater effort to foster military and economic integration on the continent.[148] Further from home, the British objected to U.S. involvement with Chinese Nationalist General Li Mi in Burma and especially to loose talk by U.S. officials on Taiwan about preparations for an invasion of southwest China. London regarded support for General Li as worsening the already faint prospects for a rapprochement with the PRC and even encouraging Beijing to send forces into the region.[149]

Anglo-U.S. differences also existed over Korea. The British Foreign Office remained uneasy about U.S. diplomacy regarding the peninsula, both at Panmunjom and Paris. Unsure of the depth of America's commitment to end the fighting in Korea, dubious about the viability of an armistice, if it did occur, without a rapid follow-up toward political unification, and hopeful that an armistice plus such a move would provide steps toward improving Western relations with China, British planners sought to further their views through the UN General Assembly. The State Department resisted British ideas regarding action through the international organization in anticipation of an armistice and favored creation of a new UN commission, which would include representatives from the United States, three small nations who had contributed to the UN war effort in Korea, and the Soviet Union, if it proved willing to serve, and would report to the General Assembly exclusively on "bringing about a unified, independent and democratic Korea by peaceful means."[150] In contrast, London wanted the General Assembly to pave the way for a peace conference in which both Beijing and Washington would participate and which would begin with Korea but eventually extend to other issues in East Asia.[151] Although Korea did not come up on the General Assembly agenda before the holiday recess, it was bound to do so early in the new year.

Even if the British avoided an open breach with the Americans on Korea, the increasing restiveness of Arab and Asian delegations augured ill for the maintenance of a unified front outside the Communist camp. The first half of the sixth session of the General Assembly had witnessed the most intense criticism to date of the United States by Third-World nations. Most of the attacks came over the failure of the United States to support self-determination when it conflicted with policies of its Western allies. Moslem nations took the lead in pushing complaints against French actions in Morocco and Britain's refusal to withdraw troops from the Suez Canal zone. The Moslems lost in their appeals for consideration of the Moroccan issue by a vote of merely twenty-eight to twenty-three, with seven abstentions.[152]

Clearly the Arab-Asian bloc, which had played such an important role in the previous session of the General Assembly, was back. Although its cohesion was greatest on colonial matters, its members often expressed themselves aggressively on issues of East-West conflict, especially those involving the risk of global war, such as Korea, Germany, and the arms race.[153] In late November Sir Benegal Rau proposed informally the creation of a neutral, three-man "Study Group" chosen on a personal rather than a governmental basis and empowered to contact both sides in the Korean dispute. The group's purpose would be to bring them together after the signing of an armistice in order to negotiate a final settlement. The Indian government refused to put forth the proposal as its own, but both Arab-Asian and commonwealth delegations showed interest, thus reflecting impatience with U.S. reluctance to view an armistice as a stepping-stone to resolution of the broader Korean problem.[154] Whether or not the fighting continued, the Korean issue held considerable potential for dividing the non-Communist world.

In classic Soviet fashion, Vishinsky and Malik proceeded to overplay their hand in Paris. The response to Vishinsky's initial proposal to convene the Security Council and place Korea at the top of the agenda was most encouraging. Despite U.S. lobbying, at least a dozen members outside the Soviet camp either voted against amending the Soviet motion or abstained.[155] The United States did succeed by an overwhelming vote in the First Committee in postponing debate on "the problem of the independence of Korea"; Vishinsky, however, remained unwilling to let the matter rest, interjecting his arguments on Korea into a debate on "measures to combat the threat of a new world war." He asserted that the initial proposals of the Communist side—an immediate cease-fire, a withdrawal of troops from the 38th parallel, and a departure of foreign forces from the peninsula—were eminently reasonable but were rejected by the United States.[156] Now the Americans clung to "unreasonable and unfair proposals" on airfields and POWs. By mentioning the 38th parallel as he had the previous November and by declaring himself on specific aspects of the armistice talks, the Soviet foreign minister probably sought to apply pressure on the United States.[157] This time, however, the ploy convinced many observers who wanted to avoid taking sides that all he was seeking was a replication in a UN forum of the acrimonious debates already in progress at Panmunjom.[158] Vishinsky's vitriolic speech before the First Committee on 17 January added further doubts about Moscow's good faith on either Korea or disarmament.[159] When early in February the sixth session of the General Assembly moved rapidly toward a close, and Malik took over from the homebound Vishinsky the task of upholding Soviet standards for acrimony, the vast majority of Arab-Asian states joined the Western powers in voting to put off debate on Korea.[160]

Soviet prospects outside the United Nations seemed more encouraging. January saw the fall of the Pleven government in France. Although in the middle of the month the National Assembly elected Radical Edgar Faure premier by a four to one majority, Faure's difficulty in persuading the Socialists to join another coalition cabinet left the country incapable of deciding on important issues.[161] One such issue was the status of the Saar, which France had occupied since World War II but which West Germany considered its own. In late January, when France appointed an ambassador to the region, Chancellor Adenauer announced that his government could not cooperate with the European Defense Community until the future status of the Saar was settled satisfactorily. French diplomats expressed dismay as Americans wrung their hands with frustration over the rise of yet another obstacle to a German military contribution to western Europe's defense.[162]

Frustrations also ran from east to west across the Atlantic. As pursuit of the presidential nominations of the major parties heated up in the United States, Europeans watched nervously the progress of Ohio senator Robert Taft in pursuit of the Republican prize. Having Taft, a critic of NATO, in the White House might put a damper on the presence of U.S. ground forces in Europe, not to mention increase the prospects for an expanded war in Asia.[163] When former president Herbert Hoover delivered an address over nationwide radio calling for a withdrawal of most U.S. troops from Europe, the Soviets could barely control their glee, devoting nearly a quarter of an entire issue of *Pravda* to the announcement.[164]

On a less positive note from a Soviet perspective, British Prime Minister Churchill's visit to the United States went rather well. Agreements emerged on raw materials, the exchange of information on atomic energy, America's use of British air bases, and the nationality and authority of a naval commander in the North Atlantic. The aging architect of the special relationship between the United States and Britain during World War II had lost none of his enthusiasm for the connection nor his talent for captivating a U.S. audience. Duly appreciated were his statements before Congress that it was for the best that the United States did not permit the Communists to seize Taiwan and that, if a truce were reached in Korea "only to be broken," the British response in support of the United States would be "prompt, resolute and effective." His promise to support if not fully participate in European integration was met with equal enthusiasm.[165]

Still, a single personality could go only so far in smoothing over national differences. His appeals for U.S. backing on the Middle East received lukewarm receptions. Despite the helpful agreement on raw materials, little chance existed for early U.S. assistance to bail Britain out of its economic difficulties. Churchill's supportive comments regarding U.S. policy in Asia were countered by the ill-timed release in Washington of a letter in which Japanese Prime Minister Yoshida Shigeru assured the United States that, in dealing with China, his government would negotiate treaties exclusively with the Nationalists.[166]

So long as the fighting in Korea continued, widespread fears in England that some irrational act by Washington would escalate into global war would not subside. As negotiations at Panmunjom dragged on, word out of the Pentagon indicated that more and more pressure was building for an attempt to break the stalemate through military action, either within Korea or beyond. In addition to aggravating tensions within the Western alliance, such action would increase casualties, which would heighten dissension in the United States in the midst of an election campaign. Yet to give in to the Communists, especially on the POW issue, would represent a major ideological defeat abroad and would generate criticism of softness at home. Continuation of the present course, on the other hand, would merely perpetuate frustrations that already existed in the United States and had helped to keep President Truman's popularity rating at an all-time low.[167] Thus his administration found itself in the unenviable position, as *New York Times* correspondent Hanson Baldwin observed, of being "damned-if-we-do" and "damned-if-we-don't."[168]

### Washington Makes a Decision on POWs

The dilemmas facing Truman made him angry. In such moods he sometimes uttered sharp remarks to his inquisitors at press conferences or dashed off a belligerent note to a music critic who had panned his daughter's singing. On other occasions he retreated to his private journal, which he kept intermittently during his presidency—and that is what he did on the evening of 27 January. "Dealing with communist governments is like an honest man trying to deal with a numbers racket king or the head of a dope ring," he lamented. "The communist governments . . . have no sense of honor and no moral code." The Chinese had asked for a cease-fire during the previous summer merely to provide an opportunity "to import war materials and resupply their front lines." To the U.S. president, the appropriate course now was "an ultimatum with a ten day expiration limit, informing Moscow that we intend to blockade the China coast from the Korean border to Indo-China, . . . destroy every military base in Manchuria, . . . and if there is further interference we shall eliminate any ports or cities necessary to accomplish our peaceful purposes. . . .

This situation can be avoided [only] by the withdrawal of all Chinese troops from Korea and the stoppage of all supplies and war materials by Russia to Communist China." Having warmed to the task, Truman embellished his prescription with a bit of recent history. "It [was] perfectly plain that the Soviet government does not want peace" around the world. It had "broken every agreement made at Tehran, Yalta, and Potsdam, . . . raped Poland, Roumania, Czeko Slavakia [sic], Hungary, Estonia, and Latvia and Lithuania," and held some three million prisoners from World War II "at slave labor." Such activities "must stop and stop now," Truman concluded. "The free world have [sic] suffered long enough." The Chinese must leave Korea and the Soviets must give "Poland, Estonia, Latvia, Lithuania, Roumania and Hungary their freedom" while halting aid "to the thugs who are attacking the free world." Otherwise there would be "all out war. . . . Moscow, St. Petersburg [Leningrad], Mukden, Vladivostock [sic], Pekin[g] [Beijing], Shanghai, Port Arthur [Lüshun], Dairen [Dalian], Odessa, Stalingrad and every manufacturing plant in China and the Soviet Union will be eliminated."[169]

Truman never took his ideas to his advisers about blowing the Soviets and the Chinese to smithereens. Yet the thoughts he recorded on that January night reveal an important dimension of his state of mind as he approached a crucial decision on the armistice talks in Korea.

Realizing more than ever that the POW issue could become the breaking point in negotiations, U.S. officials pressed forward to establish a final position on it. On 22 January U. Alexis Johnson, the deputy assistant secretary for the Far East, established a working group on the POW question to explore how Communist agreement to voluntary repatriation might be obtained and how, if this proved impossible and negotiations broke down, the administration might cultivate the broadest possible support for the various options that might be chosen.[170] The definition of the group's tasks suggested that the top echelons of the department intended to support the principle of voluntary repatriation.

Debate continued at the working levels. Charles Stelle of the Policy Planning Staff wrote that law was on the side of the Communists and, if approached, U.S. allies would give "a forcefully negative answer" on whether or not voluntary repatriation should be "the sole breaking point of the negotiations." Stelle also doubted that U.S. success on the issue would affect other areas, as "the critical factors influencing defection are always local." Finally, given the limited control by UN forces over the internal working of the POW camps in Korea, it was "impossible . . . to tell who really doesn't want to be returned as opposed to who has been coerced into saying they don't." Many of the prisoners were organized into gangs, led by former Nationalist soldiers who had been forced into Communist armies and then captured in Korea. These leaders conducted "a reign of terror over the other inmates," precluding the possibility of free expression of opinion.[171]

Charles Burton Marshall, also of the Policy Planning Staff, presented a different analysis. He viewed Korean and Chinese POWs separately. To deny

Korean prisoners "protection from the only government which we recognize as legitimate in Korea and to recognize superior a claim to them put forth by a regime which we do not recognize as legitimate . . . would wash out the premises of our whole action in Korea." This issue, Marshall insisted, "gets at the heart of the contention between Communism and the tradition we live by. It bears on the rights of men to make choices and to claim protection." U.S. adherence to the Geneva Convention was "unilateral and self-imposed," not contractual. Given the behavior of the other side, it was in a weak position to claim the document "as obligatory upon us." The Chinese prisoners, however, were a different matter, as the United States was not in Korea "to protect a Chinese regime or to protect Chinese."[172]

Whether out of conviction or knowledge of Truman's inclinations, Marshall's superiors—including Acheson, Nitze, and Bohlen—decided on voluntary repatriation for both Korean and Chinese prisoners.[173] In meetings during the last days of January and the first week of February, the idea of screening prisoners and immediately releasing those who did not want to return home, thus presenting Communist negotiators with a fait accompli, emerged as the favored option.[174]

Military officials disagreed with their State Department colleagues. Fearing an indefinite continuation of hostilities in Korea and dire consequences for UNC prisoners of war, the Joint Chiefs favored acceptance of an all-for-all exchange. But Acheson held firm, reinforced perhaps by a movement in the Senate in favor of a resolution expressing support for voluntary repatriation. Secretary of Defense Lovett eventually agreed not to push the Pentagon point of view with the president.[175]

Reservations continued to exist, even in the State Department. At the German desk, analysts expressed concern that a refusal to repatriate all Communist prisoners in Korea would reduce prospects for Soviet repatriation of the tens of thousands of Germans still held from World War II. In the spring of 1950 the Soviet news agency TASS had announced that all prisoners, except those guilty or suspected of major war crimes, had been repatriated, but the United States and West Germany, not to mention Japan, which had claims of its own, knew differently. If the Americans insisted on voluntary repatriation in Korea, the Soviets might assert that many of its prisoners had been "reeducated and released." The German desk warned that a unilateral release by the UNC of prisoners who chose not to be repatriated would destroy the Geneva Convention and encourage the enemy in a future conflict to do nothing to take care of prisoners, claiming again that they had been "reeducated and released."[176]

Assistant Secretary for Public Affairs Edward W. Barrett also urged caution. The United States knew too little about the numbers of prisoners in Korea who did not want to return, the practicality of various "techniques for segregating them from the others and eventually paroling them," or the "public opinion . . . and even moral factors against leaving our own POWs in enemy hands indefinitely." "Very strong support" now existed at home against forced repatriation, but, if a break in talks occurred over the issue and if casualties continued to mount while UNC prisoners suffered in Communist camps, controversy surely would arise over the administration's commitment "to help some Chinese and North Koreans . . . who were once shooting at us and who surrendered to save their own skins." As to allied opinion, an Office of Intelligence Research survey indicated that voluntary repatriation would *not* be supported if it "became the real choice between a cease-fire and war."[177]

On 8 February, at a meeting with Acheson and Lovett, Truman formally approved the current UNC stand at Panmunjom against forcible repatriation, and instructed his subordinates to continue to examine methods of resolving the issue which would "not require, on the one hand, that we accept the use of force to return prisoners of war strongly objecting to repatriation, or, on the other hand, that the Communists accept the principle of voluntary repatriation."[178] In the weeks that followed, the State Department worked diligently to muster domestic and allied support for this position while exploring the option of releasing prisoners who opposed repatriation without prior knowledge or approval of the Communists.

In part to advance the latter cause, Johnson and General John E. Hull, army vice chief of staff for operations and administration, left for Tokyo and Korea on the 11th. They found Admiral Joy and his negotiating team adamant against the fait accompli approach to the POW issue. Joy believed that Communist acceptance of the principle of no forced repatriation was possible if the United States made the firmness of its position clear, but Admiral Libby was less sanguine.[179]

Johnson and Hull also investigated conditions in UNC prisoner-of-war camps, the bulk of which were located on Koje-do, an island off the south coast of the peninsula some thirty air miles from Pusan. Reports of trouble in the camps had reached the U.S. press and, with a mass screening process looming on the horizon, Washington showed concern.[180]

On Koje-do, the visitors found, as Johnson later put it, "the smell of mutiny in the air."[181] U.S. forces had had little experience in supervising POWs in foreign surroundings, as the United States had entered both world wars after allies had established most of the necessary facilities. The Koje-do compounds had been constructed in early 1951, at a time when secure, friendly territory, well removed from the battlefield, was at a premium. So were top-flight soldiers and officers. Prisoners suffered overcrowding and poor sanitation. Because authorities lacked adequate manpower and expertise, the internal operation of individual compounds rested in the hands of prisoners appointed as "trustees," who effectively had control over the dispensing of goods and services. Prisoners, of course, hailed from two countries experiencing bitter civil conflict. Since up to 1949 many of the Chinese among them had served in Nationalist armies under Jiang Jieshi and many of the Koreans had started out in the ROK army only to be captured and impressed into the North Korean military, loyalties varied, often deriving from immediate circumstances rather than deep conviction. Most trustees were prisoners who expressed strong anti-Communist sentiments, and they maintained authority largely through harsh physical intimidation.[182] The inadequate linguistic skills of the Americans led the UNC to permit "teachers" from Taiwan to operate in Chinese compounds as participants in an indoctrination program, and these people actively promoted the idea of repatriation to the anti-Communist bastion. In the Korean compounds, U.S. supervisors usually depended on ROK guards, who knew the language of the prisoners but lacked the patience necessary to deal effectively with enemy captives intent on making their jobs difficult.

Violence during September 1951 led to the reinforcement and reorganization of security forces, yet by the end of the year supervisory personnel on the island still numbered fewer than ten thousand of the fifteen thousand requested. The screening of thirty-seven thousand Korean prisoners late in the year and their reclassification as civilian internees, coupled with the agreement on an armistice line, heightened tensions. Anti-Communist prisoners recognized both the opportunity and the pressing necessity to organize against repatriation to the Communist side, while the Communists sensed danger to both themselves and the larger cause they espoused.

Unknown to Johnson, Hull, or UNC authorities, once the Communists in North Korea grasped the significance of the POW issue, they began arranging the capture of agents on the battlefield so they would be sent to Koje-do and could help organize activities against prison authorities. A riot on 18 December resulted in fourteen deaths, and the rescreening of civilian internees early in 1952 produced several more incidents. On the day following the Johnson-Hull visit, prisoners in a Communist-controlled compound resisted attempts at screening by ROK teams. In the ensuing melee, seventy-seven inmates died or suffered fatal wounds.[183]

Despite their observations on Koje-do, Johnson and Hull made no effort on their return home to question the prudence of the U.S. position of no forced repatriation.[184] They reported to Truman that the UNC believed that about 5,000 North Koreans and 11,500 Chinese POWs would "violently" resist repatriation to the Communist side. The Chinese prisoners were the biggest problem, both because of their behavior within the camps and their importance to the Communist negotiators at Panmunjom. Ridgway also thought that the Communist position on the battlefield was stronger now than it had been the previous July, although his forces were better prepared to resist an enemy onslaught from the air. The UN commander estimated that, under current conditions, he would need "an additional corps of three divisions" to win a military victory in Korea, and even then only with "greatly increased casualties."[185]

By the end of February U.S. policy on POWs was firmly in place. On the 27th Ridgway wired home arguing strongly against any fait accompli to the Communists on the POW issue and for placing the "safe and speedy return of UNC prisoners" as top priority on item 4. Prospects of getting communist agreement on voluntary repatriation remained poor. The best chance to achieve a settlement while avoiding the forcible return of any prisoners rested in screening all of them, separating from the others those who expressed violent opposition to repatriation to the Communists and removing them from the POW lists, and then offering at Panmunjom an all-for-all exchange on the basis of the revised list.[186] At a top-level meeting in the White House held within hours of receiving Ridgway's message, Truman announced that "the final U.S. position" would be against forcible repatriation. Matthews reported that the State Department had consulted "with our key allies" and that none had expressed opposition to the U.S. position, which was not quite true given an approach by Canadian Ambassador Hume Wrong two weeks earlier.[187] In any case, instructions went out to Ridgway later the same day authorizing him to implement his plan for screening and revising POW lists.[188] The Americans had devised a method of resolving item 4 without formal Communist acceptance of no forced repatriation or sacrifice of the moral high ground through resort to subterfuge.

Throughout the five-week review process on the POW issue, Truman's advisers sensed their leader's disinclination to reexamine his view that prisoners held in UNC camps should not be returned to the enemy against their will. Whatever their own doubts, those advisers were themselves disinclined to "educate" the president—as Johnson had put it the previous fall—on the complexities of the issue.[189] Given later events, it is difficult to condone Lovett's and Acheson's failure on 8 February to outline to the chief executive the reservations circulating in their departments; so too is it hard to accept Hull's and Johnson's failure to impress on him the significance of conditions in the Koje-do camps.

Conditions in the camps derived largely from the inattentiveness of the UNC. Even when trouble began to develop on the island during September 1951 and General Van Fleet visited the scene, the matter did not receive the sustained high-level scrutiny needed to stabilize conditions and bring them into full compliance with the Geneva Convention. Busy men in Washington and Tokyo preoccupied themselves with what seemed to be more pressing issues and the less-than-top-grade officials on Koje-do, unaware of discussions elsewhere about no forced repatriation, made do with a system they felt would soon be dismantled through the signing of an armistice.[190]

By late February 1952, with the POW issue confronting the world, the military situation in Korea stabilized, and trouble in the camps more pronounced than ever, Tokyo and Washington had little excuse for neglect. After the incident of 18 February, Van Fleet, hoping to improve discipline on Koje-do, appointed Brigadier General Francis T. Dodd as commandant. Ridgway sent the Eighth Army commander a stern warning about the potential for embarrassment to the UNC of further outbreaks there, expressing his desire that Van Fleet personally handle the planning of any "mass screening or segregation" of POWs.[191] Yet Dodd had little experience in Asia, knew neither Korean nor Chinese, and received little reinforcement in personnel.[192] Barring a situation of truly crisis proportions, the Joint Chiefs in Washington, Ridgway in Tokyo, and Van Fleet in Korea, who feared a Communist military offensive in mid-April and arranged his activities accordingly, all lacked sufficient commitment to the policy of no forced repatriation to give it high-priority attention.[193] Until May, even the president and the secretary of state failed to appreciate the seriousness of the situation on Koje-do and how it could undermine the propaganda value worldwide of the U.S. stand against forced repatriation. For this ignorance, a portion of the blame must be placed on Johnson, the highest-ranking State Department official to have visited the island.

Finally, a word needs to be said about motivation. Despite the dubious moral foundations of U.S. policy, there is little reason to question Truman's and Acheson's revulsion at the thought of forcing prisoners to return to the Communist fold. This concern, however, fit neatly with a calculation of advantage in the ideological struggle so central to the cold war. As the secretary of state put it in a memorandum to the president of 4 February, "any agreement which would require United States troops to use force to turn over to the Communists prisoners who believe they would face death if returned would be repugnant to our most fundamental moral and humanitarian principles on the importance of the individual, and would seriously jeopardize the psychological warfare position of the United States in its opposition to Communist tyranny."[194]

Domestic political calculations reinforced administrative thinking. As Ridgway anticipated in December 1951, once the principle of repatriation received publicity in the United States, it became difficult to accept a more traditional solution.[195] Before January 1952 occasional expressions of concern appeared in the U.S. press regarding the fate of Communist POWs, but commentators seemed resigned to an all-for-all exchange.[196] During the first two months of 1952, however, almost universal support emerged for the U.S. position on item 4, and a substantial movement appeared in Congress.[197] Still, Truman and his advisers recognized that, if it became clear that their stand was the only barrier to an armistice and perhaps would even expand the fighting in Korea, such support was likely to dwindle.[198] Surely they realized that an ongoing war in Korea could only hurt Democratic prospects in the fall elections, and probably a good deal more than possible Republican attacks on a concession that succeeded in halting U.S. casualties and produced the return of America's long-suffering POWs. The support of international public opinion was recognized as even more problematic.

In the end, the course of the armistice talks during February and the outcome of the recent conference of NATO foreign ministers at Lisbon, from which Acheson returned only hours before the White House meeting on POWs of the 27th, probably inclined officials to believe that, with a few months more hard bargaining, the Communists would concede on item 4.[199] At Panmunjom, the Communists had offered a position on item 5 acceptable to the Unites States, and they had made significant concessions on the permissible size of monthly troop rotations and the number of ports open to inspection teams.[200] In Lisbon NATO allies had reached agreement with the Federal Republic of Germany on its financial contribution to Western defense over the next year and a half, and giant steps had been made toward resolving the thorny problem of restrictions on West German arms production.[201] Germany, of course, was far removed from Korea geographically. To U.S. leaders, who tended to see Moscow's hand behind all that transpired in the Communist world, however, any progress toward integration in western Europe, especially if it involved Germany, was bound to have an impact elsewhere. Since an end to the fighting in Korea was widely considered to represent a fundamental step in reducing East-West tensions, U.S. officials may well have regarded it as a likely Soviet response to ongoing consolidation in western Europe.

Yet given the depth of animosity toward the Communist world that existed in top echelons of the Truman administration, it seems doubtful that even a more pessimistic view of the time required to secure an enemy concession on POWs would have produced a contrary decision. The principle of no forced repatriation touched a sensitive nerve in the White House at a highly charged moment in the cold war. In the president's mind, its continued defense represented an important demonstration of his country's moral superiority in the face of enemy intransigence. As had occurred so often in the past, the prickly chief executive had found an issue worth fighting for.

## Continued Movement

Despite Truman's decision, considerable progress occurred in the armistice talks during March and April. As early as the last week of February, Valerin Zorin, a deputy foreign minister in Moscow, told a diplomat from a neutral nation that an end to the fighting might be near.[202] Yet the Communists had just begun a fierce propaganda campaign charging the UNC with waging bacteriological warfare in North Korea and Manchuria, and the early days of March brought little movement at Panmunjom.[203] At mid-month widespread pessimism existed over prospects for an early armistice among non-Communist observers in Tokyo, Beijing, and the West.[204] Then, amid hints by their press correspondents at Panmunjom that an early resolution of outstanding issues was possible, the Communists began to bargain.[205]

Movement came on both items 3 and 4. On the 15th the Communists hinted strongly that they would drop a demand to inspect classified equipment if the UNC would reduce its insistence on ports of entry for inspection purposes from six to five. Agreement quickly emerged on the scope of inspection of equipment, as well as the number of ports of entry and their specific identity. By the 26th the only issues remaining on item 3 were airfield construction and repair and Soviet membership on the Neutral Nations Supervisory Commission. On 4 April the Communists made a "veiled proposal" for a trade of a UNC concession on the former in return for their own concession on the latter.[206]

The Communists even showed flexibility on the POW issue. As early as 5 March they put forth an ambiguous proposal that Admiral Joy thought might indicate a willingness to accept the UNC definition of "civilian internees." On the 14th the Communists suggested that, once the UNC agreed to the principle of release and repatriation of all POWs, the two sides could move toward agreement on specifics based on data already exchanged. A week later the Communists made their acceptance clear of a UNC list without the personnel reclassified as civilian internees, and on the next day they implied a willingness to make additional adjustments in the final lists. The UNC might eliminate from its list those who had resided in South Korea before the outbreak of war. Further revisions might be made in both lists by substituting civilian internees and perhaps UNC POWs of ROK origin who wished to settle in the DPRK for POWs of ROK origin who wanted to stay in the south. There was no evidence of a Communist willingness to bend on Chinese POWs—quite the contrary—but the constructive tone that had emerged at Panmunjom indicated that, with time, perhaps even in days or weeks rather than months, an accommodation could be reached.[207]

For the rest of the month the two parties sparred over who had made what concessions. The Communists continued to show concern that no Chinese prisoners be sent to Taiwan, and they dwelled on the fact that, although the UNC appeared willing to accept an armistice without specific reference to no forced repatriation, its plan to modify the POW lists before a halt in the fighting amounted to the application of that principle in practice. The UNC, in turn, harped on its claim that the Communists already had put that principle into effect in relation to some fifty thousand South Koreans who now served in the Korean People's Army.[208]

At the beginning of April the Communists accused the UNC of preventing any progress because of its failure to offer "a round figure" of POWs to be repatriated. The UNC replied that such a figure might be in the neighborhood of 116,000, only 16,000 less than the number presented on 18 December 1951 when POW information was first exchanged; but it refused to commit itself to any number before a screening on Koje-do. With that, the Communists proposed a recess to enable both sides to check their final lists.[209] Convinced that agreement was impossible without giving the enemy specific figures and satisfied that the Communists had tacitly approved the conduct of screening, Ridgway gained Washington's approval to carry out the process "at the earliest possible date." Screening began on 8 April.[210]

With the beginning of the screening of POWs, an armistice appeared to be closer than ever before. The cease-fire line would have to be determined precisely, yet because the line of battle had shifted little since December 1951 this matter was unlikely to cause problems. The issues of airfield reconstruction and membership on a neutral inspection body continued to hold up agreement on item 3, yet the UNC had planned for some time to concede on the former issue, and the Communists seemed poised to give ground on the latter—if, that is, agreement could be reached on POWs. Clearly both parties wanted an end to the fighting. The depth of animosity and suspicion between the two sides, however, grounded so deeply in culture, ideology, and historical circumstance, kept the prospects for early accommodation very much in doubt.

• CHAPTER 8 •

# Deadlock

### SCREENING AND ITS AFTERMATH

In screening its prisoners, the UNC tried to produce the highest possible number of repatriates. At UNC request, China and North Korea issued assurances of amnesty to all returning prisoners, which received broad circulation on Koje-do. Officials on the island strove to persuade prisoners that their safety would be protected regardless of their choice, informing them that once they chose they would be segregated from all those who decided differently. The questioners encouraged prisoners to opt for repatriation, emphasizing the inability to guarantee relocation of nonrepatriates to any particular place and the likelihood of their retention for some time after the others went home. Only prisoners claiming that they would violently resist return to the Communists were excluded from the repatriate list.[1]

Despite these efforts, the results of screening differed sharply from the 116,000 figure of repatriates presented tentatively to the Communists early in April. Of the first 105,000 prisoners and civilian internees screened, more than 74,000 stated that they would forcibly resist repatriation. Some 65,000 remained to be questioned, including about 44,000 who either had resisted screening or resided in compounds where leaders objected to the process. Yet even if every one of these people chose repatriation, the total figure of returnees would be only 96,000.[2] U.S. officials understood that the totals would be unacceptable to the Communists and probably would lead them to suspect bad faith on the part of the UNC.[3]

Joy lobbied for rescreening. Ridgway initially objected, but reconsidered after meeting with two Chinese Nationalist interpreters who had been on Koje-do during the screening and claimed that the results regarding Chinese POWs did not reflect their desires. Prisoners in compounds dominated by pro-Nationalist Chinese were so intimidated that, even when separated from their leaders and assured of their safety regardless of their choice, all they could do was repeat "'Taiwan' over and over again." The interpreters estimated that separation of pro-Nationalist leaders from the other POWs "coupled with a period of indoctrination" for the latter would reverse the fifteen to eighty-five proportion of repatriates to nonrepatriates in the Nationalist-controlled compounds.[4] Ridgway sent two officers to Korea to discuss rescreening with General Van Fleet.

Van Fleet persuaded his visitors of the futility of early rescreening. UNC officials lacked the facilities and personnel to carry it out. To build enough new compounds to permit the division of Chinese POWs into smaller units would take two to three weeks. Even then, segregation from the rest of the pro-Nationalist prisoners responsible for the intimidation might prove impossible. Rescreening would produce additional violence, a point driven home by a recent riot in a North Korean compound, which produced seven fatalities.[5] Dodd believed that the numbers produced in the initial effort were within 10 percent of an accurate reflection of POW sentiment.[6]

Ridgway finally advised Washington against immediate rescreening. The Communists were to be informed that approximately seventy thousand prisoners would return to their side, but that, should any of the others later change their mind, they could be returned "at any time until the prisoner exchange is completed." If the Communists refused, the UNC would offer a neutral rescreening of the prospective nonrepatriates. If the Communists remained intransigent, the UNC would offer a "package proposal": a UNC concession on airfields in return for Communist concessions on Soviet representation on the Neutral Nations Supervisory Commission and on POWs.[7]

Washington gave Ridgway authority to implement these proposals but suggested that the UNC rescreen the prisoners before presenting the figures to the Communists.[8] Ridgway rejected this suggestion and even decided against completing the first screening before going to the Communists. He argued that their "increased impatience"—as well as that "of the U.S. and UN public"—dictated against further delay in presenting them with an estimate.[9]

On 19 April the staff officers of the two sides on item 4 reconvened in executive session at Panmunjom. The figures on repatriates presented by the UNC rendered the Communist negotiators temporarily speechless. On recovering from the shock of the strikingly low numbers, the Communists announced that the seventy thousand figure "absolutely by no means can be a basis for further discussion."[10] With the Communists threatening to revert back to the POW lists of 18 December 1951 as the basis for negotiation, the UNC advanced its package proposal on the 28th. The Communists responded with their own package four days later, dropping the demand for Soviet representation on the neutral supervisory organ in return for a concession on airfields, but exempting from repatriation only "captured personnel . . . whose homes are in the area under the control of the detaining side."

The UNC now lost all hope for an early settlement.[11] The exchange of package proposals ushered in the longest period of futility in progress toward an armistice since the talks had begun the previous July. With neither side willing to initiate major new military action, none of the key parties felt much pressure to bend in the negotiations.

## The POW Issue: Style and Substance

Why were the Chinese POWs so important to the Communists? Were there ways of avoiding the impasse that emerged in May? If so, why did the two sides fail to explore such avenues? In addressing these questions, we can do much to illuminate the dynamics of the negotiating process at Panmunjom and the broader nature of the Korean War.

From the beginning of the debate on POWs, Communist negotiators showed particular sensitivity regarding Chinese prisoners. To accept no forced repatriation, the PRC would have to acknowledge the legitimacy of a choice by Chinese citizens between itself and the despised and still dangerous Nationalist government on Taiwan and from the latter again in March 1952. Covert operations against China from Burma and Taiwan had picked up during 1951. Although they represented no immediate threat to overthrow the Communists, they were a constant reminder that Jiang had not abandoned his goal of ruling China.[12] Although most U.S. leaders had given up on that idea, U.S. involvement in the covert activity led the Communists to believe otherwise. The contest for the minds of the Chinese masses was central to the struggle, and the Communists were intent on avoiding any indication that the tide was shifting against them.

Yet similar concerns existed on the Communist side regarding Korean prisoners. Since 1946 civil war had been a part of the Korean scene, it had a strong ideological dimension, and it was a far more even contest than the one in China. Kim Il-sung surely wanted to avoid embarrassment on the POW issue. Why, then, were the Communists willing to give ground on Korean prisoners any more than they were on Chinese? The answer rests in the realities of power within the Communist camp in Korea, the past behavior of the Communists in dealing with POWs, and the course of the negotiations at Panmunjom.

North Korea was the junior partner on the Communist side. The quantities of arms and manpower now required from the outside to maintain North Korea close to its prewar boundaries had grown to grandiose proportions. Chinese soldiers outnumbered North Koreans on the peninsula by nearly three to one. Most of the weapons acquired since the previous summer were of Soviet design or manufacture.[13] The Soviet Union was a great power and China aspired to such status, whereas North Korea could never expect to attain that rank. Concessions regarding inspection beginning in December 1951 and on the withdrawal of foreign troops from Korea after an armistice in February 1952 already had demonstrated a willingness among the Communist giants to sacrifice DPRK interests.

Kim recognized his own limited bargaining power with his allies. So long as the fighting continued, little chance existed of reducing the foreign presence in Korea or of ending the brutal attacks of UNC bombers on the North. Kim spent much of his own time in his underground headquarters, a daily reminder of the ongoing cost of continuing the war. The fact that, even under the system proposed in late March, he anticipated receiving back far more men than would be returned to the ROK may have reduced his concern on the POW issue.

The concession on Korean POWs also fit neatly into the negotiating process as it evolved during the early months of 1952. The UNC had scored propaganda points over the Communist "reeducation" and release at the front of tens of thousands of Korean prisoners who later turned up in the North Korean army. Because U.S. negotiators had characterized this course as akin to voluntary repatriation, acceptance in practice of that principle for Korean POWs appeared as logical compensation for past Communist behavior. Second, a concession on Korean POWs could offset the unyielding Communist position on Chinese POWs, creating a balance on item 4, just as the Communist proposal of early May offered a balanced resolution of item 3. A central problem with the U.S. package plan was that the Communists were to concede on two issues, whereas the UNC was to concede on only one.

The Communists had maneuvered at Panmunjom to create such a situation. On 3 December 1951 they had proposed a neutral supervisory organ as an alternative to the UNC idea of a joint inspection body. When the question of membership on the neutral commission arose during February 1952, the Communists put forth, among others, the Soviet Union. Joy thought the proposal was a ploy to force the UNC to give up inspection altogether.[14] More plausibly, it involved creation of an issue that could later be traded for a UNC concession on airfields. By February the POW question had emerged as a major point in dispute, and the Communists sought to avoid eventually confronting a trade-off of airfields for POWs. Having gone to considerable trouble to maintain a strong bargaining position on the POW issue, the Communists would lose considerable face if they conceded completely on it.

UNC tactics also reduced prospects for agreement on POWs. In a staff officer's meeting on 1 April the UNC built up Communist expectations with the estimate that 116,000 POWs could be returned to Communist China and North Korea.[15] This estimate derived from earlier studies, which represented educated guesses.[16] Two days later, in a meeting of UNC personnel at Munsan-ni, General Dodd placed the figure at only half the total of 170,000 POWs and civilian internees.[17] Providing the Communists with an estimate, it was hoped, would help to secure their tacit approval of the screening process. Yet it was at best careless to present a figure without first checking with authorities on Koje-do.

Certainly it was ill-advised to present the figure of seventy thousand to the Communists based on a screening that was both incomplete in scope and flawed in technique. Again, the course had a rationale. Rescreening would be time-consuming and risky given the conditions on Koje-do. By mid-April the screening process already had taken longer than the UNC had estimated to the Communists, and Ridgway feared that word would leak out regarding the reasons for the continuing recess of talks on item 4, thus increasing the difficulty of cutting a deal.[18]

Ridgway probably had other reasons for his decision. His emotions had gotten the best of him in the past, and something similar may have occurred in April 1952.[19] For some time he had been out of sympathy with aspects of Washington's policies. He longed to take a stand against the Communists, to tell them "this is as far as we will go, no matter what"; he also believed the UNC position on airfields was far more important than that on POWs. In addition to his irritation with his superiors at home, he was angry at the enemy. Communist tactics during the previous summer had quickly broken down his sensitivity to "face," and nothing had happened since to alter his judgment that the Communists were "treacherous savages" lacking any sense of honor.[20] The most maddening activity of the Communists in recent weeks was their charge, which during February became central to their propaganda war, that the UNC was engaging in bacteriological warfare in North Korea and Manchuria by dropping canisters of infected insects from airplanes.[21] Ridgway was about to leave his post in Tokyo to become commander of NATO forces in Europe. The thought of closing out his responsibilities regarding Korea by presenting the Communists with the humiliating seventy thousand figure and following up with the take-it-or-leave-it package proposal may have given him satisfaction.

However ill-advised UNC tactics may have been, it is uncertain that any honest screening process, even if it were preceded by careful preparation to avoid intimidation by sympathizers of the Chinese Nationalists, would have produced figures acceptable to the Communists. By early May the UNC had raised its estimate of those willing to return to the Communist side to between 80,000 and 85,000 simply by counting as repatriates the North Koreans in compounds that resisted screening.[22] A rescreening of Chinese prisoners might have produced a number of Communist repatriates approaching 100,000.[23] A month later, in a meeting with Madame Pandit, Nehru's sister and the head of an Indian cultural delegation touring China, Zhou Enlai hinted that a figure of 100,000 would be satisfactory.[24] Yet never did Zhou or any other PRC official show flexibility on the Chinese prisoners.[25] Rescreening would not have altered the initial choice of a substantial number of these people. Perhaps they could have been hidden among Korean nonrepatriates to avoid any public revelation of their choice. But negotiating such an arrangement required a degree of trust between the principals that was sorely lacking. The UNC even refused to immediately inform the Communists of the upwardly adjusted estimates of repatriates for fear that the enemy would use such estimates to call the entire screening process into question.[26]

Unfortunately, before an account of Zhou's talk with Pandit reached Washington, the negotiations at Panmunjom had resumed public sessions, the UNC had announced to the world the seventy thousand figure on POWs, and U.S. President Truman and British Foreign Minister Eden had issued statements in favor of no forced repatriation.[27] U.S. tactics had made it more difficult for either side to give ground.

## COMMUNIST PERSPECTIVES, KOREA AND ELSEWHERE

The question remains as to whether—and if so how—developments in Korea were related to Communist moves elsewhere. Did the movement toward an armistice during March and April reflect a coordinated strategy between Moscow and Beijing designed, in part, to accomplish other purposes? Or was it an isolated response to local conditions, perhaps even an initiative by the Chinese against Soviet wishes? Was there further room for bargaining on POWs or were the Communists absolutely firm in their insistence on the return of all Chinese prisoners?

It is doubtful that the Communists made concessions at Panmunjom without Stalin's approval. The issue of Soviet membership on the neutral inspection commission directly involved Moscow. Surely both the initial stand and the eventual retreat from it occurred as a result of direct consultations between the two Communist powers. Since the Communist retreat on POWs involved an issue of considerable interest to the DPRK, China is unlikely to have moved without the approval of its senior ally. Conceivably, Communist flexibility on POWs occurred as a result of Soviet initiative.

Stalin may have regarded an armistice in Korea as timely, not as part of a larger thaw with the United States, but as a means of reversing momentum toward the rearming of West Germany and of undermining the limited Western embargo on trade with the Communist world. Wary of possible North Korean objections and of an alliance of Mao and Kim against him, Stalin approached the matter with caution. Yet with Sino-Soviet relations on an even keel now that Moscow was providing major material support for operations in Korea, and with the negotiations at Panmunjom showing perceptible progress early in the year, he may have encouraged the Chinese to seek a compromise on POWs in an effort to further Soviet objectives, especially in Europe.[28]

In early March NATO diplomats anticipated Soviet measures to counter the progress made at the recent meetings in Lisbon toward integrating Germany into the Western alliance.[29] They did not have long to wait. On the 10th, which was the thirteenth anniversary of Stalin's speech to the Eighteenth Party Congress signaling the possibility of a rapprochement with Nazi Germany, Moscow sent identical notes to Washington, London, and Paris. Moderate in tone, the notes departed from past Soviet positions in proposing a united, neutral Germany with "its own national armed forces (land, air, and sea) which are necessary to the defense of the country." Germany could also have its own arms industry and pursue trade and economic development as it saw fit. The proposal on how to elect an all-German government, however, remained vague, as did the one on permanent territorial boundaries.[30]

The Soviet proposal appealed primarily to the Germans. In France, the prospect of a united, armed, and unaligned Germany was frightening. Even in West Germany, the key proposal conflicted with the position of the Adenauer government's leading opponents, the Social Democrats, who were against rearmament. The broadcast of the proposals over Moscow radio and the Soviet failure to include anything new on elections produced suspicion that Stalin's purpose was to cultivate certain groups in West Germany—conservative businessmen, who were also being courted through the Moscow International Economic Conference scheduled for April, former Nazis and military officials in the Third Reich, and neutralists. Since the contractuals and the European Defense Community (EDC) being negotiated between Bonn and the NATO powers included restrictions on West German sovereignty, the Soviet proposals would also appeal to the average German citizen anxious to eliminate barriers to national freedom and unity.[31]

On 25 March London, Washington, and Paris replied jointly to Stalin's initiative, concentrating on obtaining clarification on several points. The hope was that the exchange could be drawn out to extend beyond the signing of the contractuals and the EDC, which was projected for late May.[32]

On 9 April Stalin parried the Western proposal for a UN commission to ensure that conditions necessary for free elections existed throughout Germany, suggesting that the occupying powers themselves take on that task.[33] This note followed two other Soviet initiatives toward the West. First, Stalin declared to U.S. newspaper editors his willingness to resolve all outstanding international issues by "peaceful means" and hinted at the desirability of a meeting of the heads of state of the great powers. Second, the Moscow International Economic Conference opened with the delegates voting to forbid political speeches and assaults on political systems. Michael Nesterov, the president of the Soviet Chamber of Commerce, then proposed a huge expansion of East-West trade.[34] Coming amid a slowdown in the economies of western Europe, produced largely by a decline in exports of finished goods, this proposal held broad appeal outside the Soviet bloc. Western commentators squabbled over whether they were witnessing a "peace offensive" or a "disruptive offensive," but they agreed that a tactical shift had occurred in Soviet policy. An armistice in Korea would add credibility to the campaign as a genuine effort to reduce international tension.[35]

The international events to which the Soviet shift responded were directly pertinent to a debate within the Soviet hierarchy that extended back at least to 1949.[36] The debate centered on the nature of "capitalist encirclement" at a time when, in Europe and East Asia, the capitalist world had been pushed back from Soviet borders. To some officials, most notably Georgi Malenkov and Lavrentii Beria, this development suggested a less aggressive stance on foreign policy, a turning inward to concentrate on improving the lot of the Soviet people. Such a turn would reduce the risk of war between the socialist and capitalist worlds and weaken, perhaps even split apart, the anti-Soviet coalition that had emerged under U.S. leadership.[37]

Although Stalin remained willing to institute tactical shifts in foreign policy to counter undesirable events abroad, those shifts were always so late in developing and so limited in scope and duration as to preclude any genuine thaw in the cold war. In part, this reflected a lack of understanding of the outside world by a man who had traveled little abroad and had all the centuries-old fears and prejudices of Russian governing elites, not to mention the entrapments of Marxist-Leninist ideology. Perhaps even more important, Stalin worried that a sharp decline in international tensions would threaten the foundations of the highly centralized empire he had fashioned—and perhaps even his own rule. During early 1952 a major purge was underway in Georgia. The action appears to have been directed, at least in part, at Beria, a leading

Politburo member and former chief of the Soviet political police, whom Stalin increasingly distrusted.[38]

In his *Economic Problems of Socialism in the USSR*, a series of papers published in early October 1952, Stalin revealed his concern about internal pressures. He directly confronted those "comrades" who argued that wars *between* capitalist countries "have ceased to be inevitable," that the contradictions *between* the socialist and capitalist camps were *more* severe than conflicts *within* the latter camp. Britain and France could not "endlessly tolerate the present situation ... in which American capital is seizing raw materials and markets in the British and French colonies and thereby plotting disaster for the high profits of the British and French capitalists." Nor could "the major vanquished countries, Germany (Western) and Japan," continue "languishing in misery under the jackboot of American imperialism." These smaller capitalist nations would eventually challenge U.S. domination "and force their way to independent development."[39]

Despite these views, the progress early in the year toward West German rearmament, together with the economic strains placed on Communist nations by the Western embargo on strategic items, may have put pressure on Stalin that he felt compelled, at least partially, to accommodate. The Soviet ruler's initiatives were limited in scope. No move occurred to break the prolonged deadlock over an Austrian peace treaty, to loosen impediments to the movements of Western diplomats in the Soviet Union, or to temper the "hate America" campaign in internal propaganda. Indeed, January saw sharply tightened restrictions on Western diplomats, and the late February commencement of charges in the Soviet press that the United States was engaging in bacteriological warfare in Korea and Manchuria represented a hardening of anti-U.S. propaganda.[40] Stalin probably preferred an armistice in Korea and expanded trade with the West, although it is doubtful that he desired a united Germany under anything but Soviet control. For reasons related to his position at home and to the Soviet position on its eastern and western borders, a thaw in the cold war along lines that occurred after his death never entered his mind.

Mao needed little persuading to work toward an armistice on the peninsula. Despite increased Soviet aid during the second half of 1951, the war remained costly to the PRC.[41] Enemy battlefield advances of the fall together with heavy CPV casualties had persuaded Beijing that more manpower must be committed to Korea at a time when collection campaigns at home to support the war tested the limits of public resources.[42] The Three Anti–Five Anti campaign that picked up steam early in the new year represented, in part, efforts to mobilize and to discipline a huge, unwieldy nation faced with the strains of an expensive conflict abroad.[43] The intense propaganda drive against America's alleged use of bacteriological warfare, although partly aimed at a foreign audience, also sought to sustain the ongoing hate-America campaign at home amid an increasingly weary population. The accusations, both in China and Korea, may have aimed to deflect blame from the government to the despised foreigner for the recent prevalence of epidemics of various diseases in northern regions.[44]

China was hardly in desperate straits. With the UNC pursuing less aggressive tactics on the battlefield than during the previous fall, casualties in Korea were down and the Communists were sufficiently well equipped and dug in to discourage the enemy from renewing offensive action. The low level of ground activity enabled the CPV to devote considerable effort to the prevention of epidemics. During March the vast majority of combat troops were inoculated against plagues, typhoid, and smallpox.[45] UNC bombing made the maintenance of adequate supplies at the battlefront difficult but not impossible.[46] Politically, the Chinese had reason for optimism. Despite their refusal to permit neutral inspection to verify their charges, the bacteriological warfare campaign gained a following abroad, especially in the Third World and among neutrals in Europe, and the turmoil on Koje-do hurt U.S. credibility on the POW issue.[47] In the United States Truman had announced his intention not to seek another term in the White House; yet, as the presidential race heated up, this partisan Democrat might feel increasing pressure to end the fighting in Korea. Presidential politics aside, the cost of the war and the rearmament program created increasing difficulties for the U.S. government in controlling wages and prices. In April that effort helped to produce a crisis between labor and management in the steel and oil industries, leading to Truman's seizure of the mills in the first case to prevent them from shutting down and to a strike in the second.[48]

The Communists probably considered that the best opportunity to break the impasse on POWs in their own favor rested in exploiting conditions on Koje-do. Authorities in North Korea maintained contact with hard-core Communist prisoners on the island, and during February, with the POW issue a major point of contention at Panmunjom, agitation in the camps picked up.[49] Despite Ridgway's admonitions to Van Fleet to keep close tabs on conditions, by early May some compounds were so beyond the control of UNC officials and their Communist-led inmates so determined to prevent screening that the process had to be canceled for fear of major violence.[50]

Then, on 7 May, through a combination of careful planning by the intransigent prisoners and General Dodd's carelessness, the Communists captured the commandant and issued a series of demands in return for his release. Through a telephone installed in their compound, Communist POWs used their prisoner as an intermediary between themselves and camp authorities. Encouraged by Dodd and fearful of the consequences of a military operation that might produce high casualties on both sides, Brigadier General Charles F. Colson, the new commandant, agreed to a statement implying that the UNC had failed to provide humane treatment to prisoners, had screened some by force and rearmed others, and had failed to abide by international law.[51]

In the West, news of the Koje-do incident produced a deluge of criticism of the United States.[52] UN delegates were especially critical of U.S. publication of the seventy thousand figure derived from the initial screening. Word that the United States had proposed neutral screening after an armistice mollified them somewhat, but they remained critical of the publicity given to the results of the April screening.[53] Pro-U.S. governments muted their attacks, but many journalists and legislators were less restrained. In England the Churchill government faced a barrage of pointed questions and comments in the newspapers and in the House of Commons regarding the specifics of UNC policy and its implementation on Koje-do.[54]

The Communists were determined to squeeze every drop of advantage out of the situation on Koje-do. At one point they contemplated a major "breakout" from the Communist-held compounds, but the Dodd incident led the UNC to commit additional resources to the island and to dispatch Brigadier General Hayden Boatner, a tough-minded combat commander fluent in Chinese, to bring the compounds under control. The chaos existing there still required weeks to eliminate, and the process resulted in substantial violence. That violence provided more grist for the Communist propaganda mill. By mid-June the last Communist strongholds on the island had collapsed.[55] Yet the Communist campaign to make political capital showed no sign of abating.[56]

Meanwhile, Syngman Rhee had declared martial law over much of South Korea and had jailed numerous members of the National Assembly, providing further embarrassment to the UN cause. Rhee's actions in late May followed several months of difficulties between the South Korean president and the United States. Despite U.S. pleading, he did nothing to improve relations with Japan or to bring inflation under control. He continued to encourage anti-armistice activities below the 38th parallel. By May, with the proceedings deadlocked at Panmunjom, Rhee's determination to stay at the head of his government grabbed the spotlight in U.S.-ROK relations.

The ROK constitution provided for a presidential term of four years, with the legislative branch holding the power of election—or reelection. Doubting his prospects for securing another term through the National Assembly, Rhee sought to amend the constitution to provide for direct popular election of the president. This required action by the National Assembly, which resisted his entreaties. At midnight on 24 May, with time running out for Rhee to devise a method to stay in office, he proclaimed martial law in Pusan, the temporary capital, and in twenty-two counties in the surrounding region.[57]

Rhee's action sparked a wave of protest abroad and a concerted effort by U.S. and UNCURK representatives in South Korea to persuade the aging leader to restore constitutional government. He insisted that a plot existed to overthrow him and subvert the ROK and that foreigners should stay out of South Korea's internal affairs.[58]

The crisis presented a variety of possibilities to the Communists, all of which militated against any offer of early concessions at Panmunjom. Rhee's behavior might undermine the will of nations contributing to the UNC in Korea. He had never had a favorable image abroad, and his flaunting of constitutional processes might provoke new pressures on the United States to end the war or promote alternative leadership in the ROK. If the United States attempted to replace Rhee, chaos might spread in the South, making UNC conduct of the war increasingly difficult. Short of such a drastic eventuality, prolongation of the crisis would sap morale from the ROK army, which had made substantial progress recently and was responsible for holding a large portion of the UNC line.[59] The turmoil in the West over Rhee and conditions on Koje-do eliminated for the moment any danger of expanded UNC military action, either on the ground in Korea or in the air or on the sea beyond the peninsula.[60]

## COMMUNIST PROBES

The crisis over events within South Korea relieved pressure on the Communists to conclude an early armistice, but it also encouraged diplomatic probes in search of concessions. These probes began in May with comments by Zhou to Pandit already mentioned and ended in July with the termination of exchanges between the PRC Foreign Office and the Indian embassy in Beijing, and between Soviet diplomats and Ernest Gross, U.S. deputy representative to the United Nations, in New York.[61]

Zhou's conversation with Pandit on 6 May—and one three days later between Mao and the Indian diplomat—represented a classic Chinese attempt to exploit India's desire to play peacemaker and to influence the United States through its relationship with England. The moment was particularly opportune for China to pursue a channel through New Delhi. Indian-U.S. relations had improved since the previous fall, when Chester Bowles arrived in New Delhi as the U.S. ambassador. Amiable in personality, sensitive to nationalist sentiments in the Third World, and liberal in political persuasion, Bowles quickly befriended Nehru, with notable impact on the relationship between their two nations.[62] Stalin attempted to counter this trend in early April, when he met personally with Indian Ambassador Radhakrishnan as the diplomat was about to return to New Delhi to run for vice president of his country.[63] While Beijing responded evasively to Nehru's suggestion that China accept an impartial investigation of its charges of America's use of bacteriological warfare, Pandit's tour of China provided an opportunity to cultivate Indian sympathies.[64] Mao told Pandit that he was "very keen" for the establishment of full diplomatic relations with London, if only the British would alter some of their policies.[65] Zhou emphasized China's desire to end the Korean War and hinted that the return of 100,000 POWs to the Communists would be acceptable.[66]

A belief that both sides wanted peace spurred Nehru on. In mid-May, he received a letter from Eden indicating that the UNC had offered at Panmunjom a rescreening by neutrals. The Indian leader, whose humanitarianism dictated support for no forced repatriation, grasped the idea of neutral rescreening as a possible method of breaking the impasse and instructed Ambassador Panikkar to pursue the point with Zhou.[67] Panikkar found "some hope" in the initial PRC response to his overture in Beijing.[68] Then, on 14 June, he met for more than two hours with Zhou. Although the Indian ambassador wrote nothing down during the meeting and received nothing in writing from Zhou, he reported to New Delhi that the Chinese foreign minister had made two proposals for a resolution of the POW issue. "Plan A" dodged the principle of no forced repatriation in favor of agreement on a specific number of Communist prisoners to be returned. Panikkar thought that 100,000 would be acceptable so long as it included all the Chinese. If this approach proved unacceptable to the UNC, then "Plan B" could be implemented by releasing all prisoners wishing to return to China and North Korea and transferring the others "without military escort . . . to some neutral place." Both sides would agree to follow the recommendations of "a neutral commission of four" once it had examined these remaining prisoners.[69] The British and the Americans questioned the accuracy of Panikkar's report, but they agreed that Plan B was worth exploring.

Panikkar left Beijing on the 19th to prepare for a new assignment in Egypt. His successor did not arrive immediately to replace him. While London and Washington sought ways to follow up the Panikkar report, Constantin Zinchenko, a Soviet citizen and assistant secretary general at the United Nations, took the initiative in New York.

On the 27th Zinchenko approached the American Ernest Gross about Korea. Although vague on details, Zinchenko expressed hope for an early armistice and advanced ideas that resembled the Plan B reported by Panikkar. Gross informed Washington that his Soviet colleague had spoken more "explicitly" and in a more "unguarded manner" than ever before.[70]

Chinese and Soviet feelers on Korea ended soon afterward. Gross proved unable to meet again with Zinchenko before the latter left New York on 9 July for a vacation in the Soviet Union.[71] On the 14th the British and the Americans received word through India that the Chinese were prepared only to discuss Plan A.[72] At Panmunjom, the Communists failed to put forth any proposal resembling Plan B.[73]

Some people—including members of the Labor Left in England and government and press elites in India—believed that UNC air attacks on Yalu power stations, which commenced on 23 June, explained the demise of Plan B.[74] Previously the UNC had spared these critical facilities for the dispensing of electricity to large portions of North Korea and Manchuria.[75] The Communists, always sensitive to giving ground in negotiations under military pressure, drew back from its exploratory probes on the POW issue. Or so some observers thought.

Another explanation, popular among U.S. and British diplomats, was that Communist feelers never reflected a willingness to return prisoners beyond the round number of at least 100,000, including all the Chinese. In this view, Plan B was largely a figment of Panikkar's imagination. In mid-August a spokesman for the Chinese Foreign Office in Beijing hinted to a representative of the Indian embassy that Panikkar had misinterpreted Zhou's comments in their 14 June meeting.[76]

Panikkar probably embellished Plan B to fit the Indian point of view. Back in New Delhi in early July he stated that the Chinese would never accept a solution on POWs that did not ensure the return of all, or nearly all, the Chinese prisoners.[77] Zhou may have floated the idea of a neutral commission in the hope that the Americans would concoct a method of ensuring through it the numbers the Communists insisted on. Plans A and B may have been part of the same proposal and intended to save *American* face without the Chinese granting any substantive concession.

This leaves Zinchenko's proposal to Gross. The details reported by Gross leave unclear whether it represented a significant departure from the Communist position then on the table at Panmunjom.[78] On leaving New York in mid-July Zinchenko dropped from sight for nearly three years. When he failed to reappear in New York in September as scheduled, UN officials inquired as to his whereabouts and were told that he was ill. He formally resigned his UN post in May 1953, not to resurface until mid-1955 on the staff of *News*, the Soviet English-language journal, amid rumors that he had spent the intervening period in jail. As a person who moved easily among Westerners, he was naturally a target of suspicion in a Soviet Union engulfed in a hate-America campaign.[79] Whether or not his fate was related to his overture to Gross is uncertain, but the possibility remains that Zinchenko exceeded his instructions.[80]

That the stalemate which emerged in July had anything to do with UNC bombing of Yalu power stations is unlikely. To be sure, in mid-July, Mao lectured his negotiators in Korea, who wanted to accept the new UNC figure of eighty-three thousand POWs to be returned, about the need to avoid making concessions under political and military pressure.[81] Yet during both the fall of 1951 and the spring of 1953 Mao continued negotiations and made concessions in the face of such pressure. On those occasions the CPV launched limited face-saving offensives to make the concessions more palatable.[82] It could undoubtedly have done the same in the summer of 1952 had Mao been intent on making concessions to end the war.

The problem rested not in the Communists' unwillingness to bargain while under military pressure, but in the fact that the pressure applied was insufficient to persuade the Communists that concessions were necessary on an issue of considerable importance. That pressure included stepped-up ground operations on the central front in early June and massive bombing operations against portions of Pyongyang and its surroundings on 11 July. The Yalu bombings produced a fifteen-day power blackout in North Korea and a major reduction of electricity available to Manchuria. Attacks on the North Korean capital did considerable damage to Communist supply, production, transportation, and antiaircraft facilities.[83] Yet the bombing failed to reduce significantly the Communists' capacity to hold their positions in Korea. The ground maneuvers were on such a limited scale that territorial gains were minimal and frequently reversed by early counteraction. The Communists completed their tunnel system during the spring, and it proved its worth in the early summer battles.[84]

Nor did the pattern of events outside the Communist world dictate concessions. Not all developments were encouraging to Beijing and Moscow. In South Korea June saw UNC forces on Koje-do gain sufficient control of the POW camps to initiate screening of the previously intransigent prisoners. Early the next month the internal crisis in the ROK moved toward a solution, with Rhee forcing the National Assembly to pass an amendment providing for direct election of a president who theoretically would operate under greater restrictions by the legislative branch.[85] In Europe Stalin's March and April initiatives had failed to prevent the Western powers from signing the contractual and EDC agreements with the Adenauer government in late May.[86] By the end of June all the legislatures of prospective members of the European Coal and Steel Community had ratified its charter, paving the way for its early implementation.[87]

Yet overall the outlook was favorable. The contractual and EDC agreements still had to be ratified by national legislatures, and this was likely to be a time-consuming process. In West Germany and France the prospects for ratification remained uncertain.[88] The rearmament process in western Europe continued to cause political and economic problems, especially in Great Britain and France.[89] In the United States election year politics and tensions growing out of the wage and price controls necessitated by rearmament placed the Truman administration in a precarious situation. In early June steel workers walked off their jobs. Within a month several arms manufacturing plants had closed for lack of steel, and numerous others were on the verge of doing so.[90] All things considered, the United States did not seem to Beijing and Moscow to hold a strong bargaining position in Korea.

For Mao the prospect of a new administration in the United States probably encouraged a waiting game on Korea. This administration, to be sure, might be either softer or tougher in its stance on the war. Yet given Mao's suspicions of the United States and his passionate commitment to elevating China's status, the latter possibility actually may have solidified his inclination to stand firm. There was no guarantee, after all, that a new administration would accept an agreement by its predecessor, especially if the settlement reflected Chinese weakness. Mao may have calculated that he would be better off negotiating an armistice agreement with a new administration than attempting to shrink from a possible confrontation by making an early and politically damaging concession on POWs.[91]

As for the Soviet Union, by the summer of 1952 Stalin's foreign policy was locked in the familiar pattern of consolidating the Soviet buffer in Europe, reinforcing the Sino-Soviet alliance in Asia, and seeking to foster divisions in the West. Purges continued in Czechoslovakia and East Germany as the Soviet bloc moved more decisively than ever to close itself off from the West. On 24 May the third Soviet note on Germany since early March appeared in

Western chancellories, and it carried a sharp tone absent from the first two. On the 26th East Germany imposed new border regulations in the West.[92] Early in July East German Communists voted in a party congress to strengthen the state and augment their armed forces.[93] In part, these moves, combined with renewed harassment of Western traffic into Berlin, represented a war of nerves designed to reinforce doubts about Adenauer's policy of integration with the West. Yet Stalin told Italian Socialist Pietro Nenni that the time was over for bargaining aimed at German unification, that East Germany would now build its own armed forces to match those planned in West Germany.[94]

Stalin remained determined to construct a rocky path for Adenauer and other Western advocates of integration. During the summer, while the hate-America campaign picked up steam in the Soviet Union, Communist activities in western Europe resembled a new popular front, only with the isolation of the United States rather than Nazi Germany as the main objective.[95] Stalin shuffled personnel at the head of Soviet embassies in the West, sending the high-ranking Andrei Gromyko as ambassador to the United Kingdom.[96] At the UN Security Council now meeting in New York, Malik's behavior was relatively mild. The issues he dwelled on as president during June were designed to embarrass the United States in relations with its allies or the Arab-Asian states.[97] In early July, in the UN Economic and Social Council, the Soviet representative spoke at length of the economic benefits to be derived in western Europe through an end to the arms race. Contracts from the Communist bloc for the purchase of capital and consumer goods would provide jobs for hundreds of thousands of Westerners.[98] Back in Europe the Cominform journal published articles criticizing Communist parties for failing to support "peace-loving groups" with whom they might have some policy disagreements on other issues.[99] Speeches at a meeting of the World Peace Congress in East Berlin emphasized U.S. isolation on the issue of rearmament.[100]

Looking eastward Stalin sought to keep Communist China firm in its determination to pursue the Korean War to a successful conclusion. He probably devoted little energy to convincing Mao of the importance of upholding the Communist position on POWs. On that issue, both Communist powers had a significant stake. The question of how much assistance the Soviet Union would provide to the Chinese to help sustain the Korean enterprise while they held the economy together at home and prepared for its long-term development, however, may have required considerable bargaining.

In April a new Chinese military mission had traveled to Moscow to plead for Soviet naval vessels and aircraft, only to be turned away. That result forced the Chinese to continue to limit their military operations in Korea, but it did not compromise their defensive capacity. Peng, now back in Beijing, worked on perfecting a system of rotation of troops and officers between the homeland and Korea. During the summer Mao approved a plan to have all CPV personnel at the front relieved by June 1953, but with an overall increase in Chinese troops in Korea. The war was "a great school," he declared, a far better one than any "military academy."[101]

Mao devoted increasing attention to the home front, where he wanted during 1953 to begin the First Five-Year Plan for economic reconstruction and development. In August 1952 he sent Zhou Enlai and top planners to Moscow to request economic and military aid. Zhou stayed for five weeks; others stayed longer. Zhou got less than he wanted, but the PRC subsequently expanded its use of Stalinist models for development, as well as its public adulation of their author.[102] The agreements included postponement of the Soviet withdrawal from Port Arthur, which reminded Washington that a naval blockade of the China coast might produce a direct confrontation between Soviet and U.S. forces. Stalin also agreed to send five Soviet antiaircraft regiments to Korea, to provide technical assistance for Chinese arms industries, and to supply equipment, paid for by Beijing, for 60 Chinese divisions.[103]

Moscow and Beijing essentially agreed that the war in Korea should continue unless the United States made new concessions. Zhou suggested to Stalin that the fighting might end through agreement to move disputed prisoners to India before their eventual return to the PRC or to continue negotiations on the fate of all or a percentage of prisoners on both sides after a cease-fire. Stalin disliked the first idea and doubted that the Americans would accept the second. Both men showed confidence that China could contain UN forces indefinitely in Korea and that continued fighting prevented the United States from preparing for a new world war, but Zhou worried that North Korean leaders were anxious for an armistice.[104]

### The Struggle for Western Cohesion

If the Communist powers had similar attitudes on Korea, the Western allies struggled increasingly to maintain a united front. Overt dissension arose in late May when Canada protested the dispatch to Koje-do of a company of its troops in the Commonwealth Division in Korea and in late June when widespread criticism followed the UNC bombing of Yalu power stations. In the first case, the spat ended quickly because the turmoil on Koje-do was soon over and the Canadian troops reunited with their commonwealth brethren on the mainland.[105] In part, the flap over the bombing derived from U.S. failure to brief its allies in advance. In London when the controversy broke, Acheson apologized for the "snafu." Soon the United States acceded to the appointment of a British officer to the UN command in Tokyo.[106] The issue of consultation masked a potentially deeper split over how to end the fighting in Korea.

In the United States sentiment shifted in favor of expanded military action. In the press and on Capitol Hill the Yalu bombings received broad support.[107] Between March and July public opinion polls showed an increase in sentiment in favor of bombing air bases in Manchuria from 54 percent to 61 percent and a growth in the desire to terminate armistice talks from 37 percent to 43 percent.[108] Republican election-year attacks on Truman administration foreign policy added weight to those figures. Senator Robert Taft continued his criticism of Democratic timidity in East Asia, and John Foster Dulles, the spokesman for the internationalist wing of the Republican party, resigned from the State Department and launched a stinging attack on the alleged defensiveness of U.S. strategy.[109] When General Eisenhower emerged as the Republican candidate for president in early July, he moved to mend fences with Taft and the party's right wing. The party platform lambasted the Democrats for fighting on in Korea without "hope for victory."[110]

Truman and his top advisers had long resisted domestic pressures to expand the war, but they now faced both the special circumstances of election-year politics and the ever-increasing frustration of inconclusive negotiations with the Communists. During the second week of May Admiral Joy requested authority to suspend negotiations until the enemy accepted the UNC's package proposal.[111] General Clark, who as U.S. high commissioner in Austria after World War II had considerable experience in negotiating with Communists, largely agreed. As he wrote later, the Communists respected only one thing, "FORCE."[112] Always sympathetic to MacArthur's plans to expand the war, he preferred to modify Ridgway's admonition of the previous fall from "more steel and less silk" to "all steel and no silk."[113] But he accepted his role as a subordinate of Washington, and he recognized that events on Koje-do had undermined U.S. credibility on the POW issue. If a unilateral break in negotiations by the UNC produced mounting disunity in the Western camp, the Communists would be less rather than more willing to bargain. Thus the UNC must move cautiously. At the end of May he proposed a step-by-step procedure. The present tactic of spreading out the talks rather than meeting on a day-to-day basis should continue until General Boatner took sufficient control on Koje-do to complete the screening begun in April. Once the UNC had an accurate figure of POWs and civilian internees willing to be repatriated, it would present that information at Panmunjom. If the Communists refused agreement on an armistice during the next week, the UNC would unilaterally recess the talks.[114]

At first Washington refused to entertain a UNC-initiated recess in talks without offering an impartial rescreening before an armistice, a favored approach among leading U.S. allies. By mid-July, however, the Koje-do camps were under control, UNC screening was complete, and final POW figures were in the hands of the Communists. Privately the Chinese had rejected Panikkar's Plan B. Allied pressure for impartial rescreening had subsided because of a Chinese warning to India, Pakistan, Indonesia, Switzerland, and Sweden against sending military observers to Koje-do.[115] While allied sentiment dictated continued efforts to break the impasse at Panmunjom, opinion in Tokyo and the Pentagon moved increasingly toward military solutions.

As always, military planners in the United States had to balance commitments of supplies to Korea against needs elsewhere, and they did so amid concern in the White House and Congress about the growing budget deficit.[116] Still, the mobilization process sparked by the outbreak of war in Korea two years earlier had resulted in a rise in the monthly output of military end items by a factor of five or six. Tanks and planes rolled off production lines at a rapid pace, as did atomic bombs. The United States now had a substantial number of tactical nuclear weapons that could be delivered by fighter aircraft, and the overall stockpile was sufficient to remove scarcity as an objection to their use in or around Korea.[117]

In April the Joint Strategic Survey Committee had proposed that, if no armistice was agreed on soon, the UNC should escalate military action in Korea and against China. This would include the bombing of the Yalu dams and power facilities, a tightened embargo on China or even a naval blockade, and stepped-up covert operations on the mainland. If the Communists expanded air operations in Korea, the UNC should attack air bases in China. The United States should also consider the use of tactical nuclear weapons in Korea and troops from Taiwan.[118]

When Clark succeeded Ridgway in mid-May he immediately explored methods of increasing military pressure on the Communists. Although Clark's orders did not permit bombings on the Yalu, he decided in early June that hydroelectric facilities located elsewhere in North Korea should be hit. Truman then removed prohibitions against attacking the Yalu sites.[119] July and August saw massive attacks on Pyongyang and on targets on or near the Yalu. At the beginning of September, after the Joint Chiefs loosened restrictions on air operations in the extreme northeastern region of Korea close to Soviet territory, UNC planes bombed an oil refinery only eight miles from the border.[120]

Clark also wanted a buildup of UNC ground forces. Washington rejected his proposal for two Nationalist Chinese divisions and delayed until October approval of his request for expansion of the South Korean army. Although the immediate purpose of the latter was to enable native soldiers to bear an increased burden of the fighting, military planners understood that the buildup eventually would add to the offensive potential of UNC forces.[121]

The State Department strove during the summer months to pave the way politically for new action on Korea. To maintain support of a broad coalition of non-Communist nations, the United States had to explore every reasonable angle for an armistice.[122] In late July the State Department wired George Kennan, the new U.S. ambassador in Moscow, outlining a possible overture to Vishinsky or Stalin. The Joint Chiefs communicated the idea to Clark the next day.[123] The diplomat and the military commander agreed that the Soviets would regard it as a sign of weakness, that additional military pressure was the most likely instrument for influencing the Communist stance at Panmunjom. After experiencing for more than two months the extreme isolation of Western embassies in Moscow and the vitriolic press campaign against all things American, Kennan thought a "confident reserve and dignity of bearing" in U.S. diplomacy would be best suited "to strain [the] nerves of people committed to [the] thesis [that] we are slipping."[124] The State Department abandoned the idea of an early diplomatic initiative in Moscow.[125]

During the second half of August the State Department hatched another idea for an initiative on Korea. In part, this plan grew out of Kennan's reaction to the arrival in Moscow on the 17th of a distinguished Chinese delegation. The Chinese had traveled to the Soviet Union, meaning that the former were the "supplicants . . . whose demands and requests led to the meeting." The United States might stimulate new demands by intensifying the military pressure in Korea, but it should balance such action with a "conciliatory gesture . . . to save Chinese face" and provide the Soviets with an alternative to accepting Beijing's demands.[126]

Shortly after Kennan's dispatch, Vincent Hallinan, the Progressive Party candidate for president, proposed a cease-fire in Korea on the basis of the items already agreed on. Negotiations on POWs would continue after the fighting stopped. The proposal appeared in the Communist *Daily Worker* in New York, as well as in the Soviet newspapers *Pravda* and *Izvestiia*.[127]

The Hallinan proposal, with one modification, looked attractive to the State Department. Because a cease-fire would relieve North Korea of air attacks, the Communists would lose any motive to repatriate the twelve thousand prisoners being held by the UNC. With an end to the fighting, pressure in the United States to "bring the boys home" would increase, giving the Communists an advantage in subsequent negotiations on POWs. The United States could eliminate that advantage by insisting on the immediate repatriation of those twelve thousand men in exchange for the eighty-three thousand prisoners held by the UNC who were willing to return to the Communist side. Kennan thought that the idea should be advanced immediately, as did the British Foreign Office.[128] U.S. officials in Tokyo and the Pentagon demurred, setting off an internal debate that lasted until the president made a decision on 24 September.

In Tokyo Clark and Robert Murphy, the U.S. ambassador to Japan, feared that a U.S. initiative in response to Hallinan's proposal would provide the Communists with a major public-relations victory.[129] This concern subsided after 2 September, when Mexico addressed a letter to Trygve Lie proposing a solution similar to that circulating in the State Department, with the added stipulation that nonrepatriates would be admitted temporarily into nations supporting the plan. When "normalcy" returned to the area, these people would be given "assurances" by the government of their country of origin and would be returned to their homeland.[130] The plan would be difficult to execute, but now the United States could take the initiative "without appearing to be doing so in response to the urging of the Progressive Party or the New York *Daily Worker*."[131]

Clark argued that leaving the disposition of nonrepatriates open for "subsequent negotiations" would invite the Communists to include the issue in a post-armistice political conference. With the Communists safe from attack in Korea, they could protract such a conference indefinitely while pressing for a bargain involving a U.S. retreat either on the principle of no forced repatriation or on some other issue.[132]

Unlike Clark, the State Department doubted that the UNC air campaign over North Korea was having a major effect, and it anticipated difficulties on

Korea at the upcoming session of the UN General Assembly.[133] Acheson wanted to use the UN forum to increase pressure on the Communists by inducing the Additional Measures Committee and then the entire assembly to endorse a total trade embargo on China. Securing the support of America's closest allies was the first step in building a consensus for such action. When everyone in this group expressed serious reservations about the U.S. plan, the State Department knew it was in trouble.[134]

On 17 September Acheson met with Lovett, Admiral William Fechteler, the chief of naval operations, and Admiral Libby, who recently had returned from Korea. The Pentagon officials reiterated Clark's arguments and added that, if the POW issue remained unresolved for a substantial period after the shooting stopped, the Communists, having used their invulnerability to enemy attack to build up their military strength in Korea, might resume hostilities.

The secretary of state disagreed. The post-armistice negotiations, he pointed out, would involve numerous issues that were unlikely to be resolved. One more on the table would place no added pressure on U.S. diplomats, especially since the Communists already would have returned UNC prisoners. Perpetuation of the armistice would not depend on eventual conclusion of an agreement on the nonrepatriated POWs. If the Communists wanted to resume the fighting, they could find numerous pretexts on which to base their action, but they would have to do so in the face of a greater sanctions statement threatening enemy counterattacks beyond Korea.

Acheson emphasized the importance of the State Department proposal in strengthening the U.S. position in the UN General Assembly. If advanced by the United States and rejected by the Communists, the proposal would bolster the U.S. case for recessing negotiations and increasing pressure on the Communists. Conversely, the Mexican proposal had attracted considerable attention at the United Nations. If the United States failed to advance a new proposal before the assembly convened, it might face added pressure "to do something more" to obtain an armistice, which could weaken the U.S. negotiating position with the Communists.[135]

A week later, in a meeting of State and Defense officials at the White House, the president stood firm behind the UNC package proposal of 28 April. As he had done during the previous December, he expressed concern that an armistice would compromise the rearmament program.[136] He did not oppose an armistice, but he preferred to seek it through additional military pressure on the Communists. Because the upcoming General Assembly meeting and the November election precluded an early military move, the United States should temporarily restrict itself to presenting to the Communists at Panmunjom several methods of implementing the principle of no forced repatriation and recess the talks indefinitely if none of the suggestions were accepted within about ten days.[137]

On the 28th the UNC delegation at Panmunjom offered five ways of carrying out the principle of no forced repatriation. These methods differed only on the location at which the prisoners would make their choice (the camps themselves or the demilitarized zone), the nature of the personnel on the supervisory teams (ICRC, national Red Cross, neutral nations, joint UNC-Communist personnel, or a combination of these), and the exact procedure once the teams and the prisoners made contact.[138] When on 8 October the Communists rejected all the choices, General William Harrison, now head of the UNC delegation, declared an indefinite recess.[139] In Washington Acheson stated at a press conference that the talks could be resumed any time the Communists accepted one of the UNC proposals on POWs or advanced a new and constructive alternative of their own.[140]

The road to Truman's decision to move toward an indefinite recess without advancing a new substantive proposal on POWs saw a reversal of past positions of the State and Defense departments. Previously the State Department had taken the tougher stance on the issue; now the military insisted on holding firm. Early in the year the UNC had expressed grave reservations about no forced repatriation; now it argued that the principle must be upheld explicitly in an armistice.

Had the State Department's idea been put to the Communists and accepted by them, the likely result would have been unsuccessful post-armistice negotiations on the fate of nonrepatriated POWs, terminated eventually by the United States and followed by the POWs release and shipment to Taiwan. Once the fighting stopped and the two sides had in their custody the POWs choosing repatriation, neither had an interest in giving way. But the United States would want to dispose of the nonrepatriates, both to be relieved of the burden of their care and to demonstrate a commitment to their freedom. Thus the balance of power and interests indicated eventual unilateral action by the United States.[141]

Acheson thought it more likely that the Communists would reject an armistice providing for the repatriation of willing POWs and continuing negotiations on the others.[142] The State Department could live with an armistice without a final settlement on POWs so long as those choosing repatriation were exchanged immediately, but the primary purpose of the proposed U.S. initiative was to solidify the U.S. position at the upcoming UN General Assembly.

Rigidity on the military side is more difficult to explain. The position of top military men early in the year, whether in Washington, Tokyo, or Panmunjom, was that top priority on item 4 should be the safe and early return of POWs held by the other side. So why the opposition to the new State Department proposal?

Individuals probably chose their positions for different reasons. In two key cases, leadership of the UN command in Tokyo and the UNC delegation at Panmunjom, personnel changes had occurred. Even so, it is doubtful that Ridgway would have adopted a position different from the one assumed by Clark. By early 1952 the former was more interested in taking a final, uncompromising stand than in its precise formulation. It is unlikely that he would have changed his mind after Washington identified that position to the Communists in the package proposal. But Clark went one step further than his predecessor. He believed that the Korean War could and should be won through military means.[143] With arms production in high gear in the United States and the possibility of a Republican regime taking over in Washington early the next year, the UN commander had reason to hope for a change in U.S. strategy within the foreseeable future.[144]

So did the Joint Chiefs and the secretary of defense, although it is not clear that any of them preferred to make another attempt to chase Communist armies out of Korea. Still, overall U.S. military strength had expanded greatly in the past year, putting the United States in a better position to intensify pressure in Korea, especially at levels short of an all-out offensive. In contrast, an armistice would compromise the military buildup at home and lead to irresistible pressures to reduce the U.S. presence on the peninsula.[145] Furthermore, the Pentagon probably regarded the nearness of the election as putting the United States at a temporary disadvantage in the armistice talks. Obviously the Communists recognized the pressure on the Truman administration to end the fighting before the votes were cast and wanted to exploit that situation to wring concessions. The Joint Chiefs probably reasoned, given past U.S. retreats, that the State Department and Mexican proposals might not represent the last. If the UNC held firm and the Communists refused to settle, however, a new administration would hold a strong bargaining position. The aftermath of the election would provide an ideal climate for new initiatives, which might induce the Communists to give ground.[146]

A final circumstance was the presence in Washington of Admiral Libby, who in June had left the UNC delegation at Panmunjom. During the previous fall, when the Joint Chiefs had forced concessions on the UNC despite Ridgway's protests, the military men in the field had had no spokesman at the seat of ultimate power. Now they did, and in the person of a man described by one army historian as "a fiery sea dog with a salty tongue . . . [who] combined quickness of mind, common sense, and spirit in an admirable blend."[147] He passionately opposed any new concessions to the Communists.[148]

This leaves President Truman. His position on the POW issue and his strong feelings on dealing with Communists showed no evidence of a shift. On both POWs and U.S. military preparedness the chief executive probably harbored a sense of guilt for having presided over inhumane policies in the first case and dangerous ones in the second in the aftermath of World War II.[149] Truman now stood determined to leave the White House assured that neither the fate of POWs in Korea nor the security of his country had been compromised. Whatever the merits of State Department claims that its proposal protected the POWs from forced return to the Communists, siding with the diplomats seemed risky in the midst of a campaign in which he and his party were being attacked for weakness in Asia. Policy goals and political instincts combined to dictate a firm course in Korea, even if it meant enduring increased pressure at the UN General Assembly.

Truman's decision left the State Department in a quandary over the approaching seventh session. The cool allied response to tightening the economic embargo had already produced a reevaluation of the U.S. course. The original approach had three steps: a resolution expressing support for the UNC position at Panmunjom and calling on the Communists to accept it; then, assuming the Communists demurred, a meeting of the Additional Measures Committee to recommend to the General Assembly a total embargo on China; and finally a second resolution by the entire assembly providing for new sanctions and appealing to members for increased assistance for the UN cause in Korea.[150] Allies objected to the second and third steps.[151] To the State Department, the main alternative involved reducing the process to one step, which closely resembled the first outlined above but added a call to members for larger contributions to the war.[152]

U.S. allies worked hard to avert a split at the General Assembly. They resisted Trygve Lie's pleas for more troops for Korea, as their resources were already stretched thin.[153] Rather, they concentrated on maintaining a united front in opposition to additional measures against China, on exploring the merits of the Mexican proposal, and on delaying debate on Korea in the General Assembly until after the U.S. election on 4 November. The British Foreign Office saw considerable merit in Mexico's plan, but Australia objected as did neutral India.[154] Eden eventually concluded that discussion of the Mexican idea was best avoided at the General Assembly, although whether Mexico would cooperate remained uncertain.[155] London's initiative on the timing of the Korean debate in New York sparked no dissent in the commonwealth and received a favorable response in Washington.[156] Finally, allied efforts persuaded the State Department to postpone a decision regarding concrete action in Korea beyond the initial step of pressing for an innocuous resolution expressing support for the UNC negotiating position.[157]

If interallied diplomacy managed to contain the immediate sources of dissension on Korea, it failed to eliminate other areas of State Department concern regarding the upcoming assembly. The Soviet Union showed no evidence that it would take an accommodating approach. A 25 September conversation with Malik on Korea left Gross with little hope for an early break in the impasse.[158] Sino-Soviet cooperation seemed as close as ever. Although agreements announced on 16 September at the end of Zhou Enlai's visit to Moscow did not mention substantial Soviet economic assistance to the PRC, the hosts accorded the Chinese foreign minister an elaborate send-off at the Moscow airdrome, and he indicated full satisfaction with the course of the negotiations.[159] Not the least hint of division emerged from either the Nineteenth Party Congress in Moscow, which began on 5 October, or the Asian-Pacific Peace Conference, which convened in Beijing three days earlier. Stalin's *Economic Problems of Socialism in the USSR*, published on the eve of the Soviet party congress, emphasized contradictions in the capitalist world in assessing international conditions and celebrated the economic strength of the Communist bloc. Malenkov's lead address to the congress followed closely in Stalin's footsteps.[160] Conceivably, Stalin timed the event to overshadow the Beijing conference, which accommodated delegations from thirty-seven countries and clearly reflected China's emerging leadership role in the Asian-Pacific region.[161] But petty jealousies were unlikely to compromise Sino-Soviet cooperation on Korea.

Perhaps as big an indication as any of what was in store from the Communist side in New York came on the battlefield in Korea. On 6 October CPV forces began one of their largest attacks since the commencement of armistice talks more than a year before. Several Chinese battalions struck at key hills in the western sector above Chorwon. CPV forces suffered huge casualties and failed to achieve their primary objective, but when the enemy counterattacked slightly to the east, they were quick to resist. Fighting in October produced the highest UNC casualties in a year.[162]

As evidence mounted that no break was on the horizon in the Communist stance on Korea, Washington grew particularly concerned about a Soviet move to cultivate the Arab-Asian bloc at the General Assembly, which during the sixth session had abstained or voted against the United States on several important issues, producing some uncomfortably close votes.[163] Now a host of issues involving Third-World relations with the Western colonial powers would provide a severe test to U.S. diplomacy. Acheson and Philip Jessup mapped out a strategy that combined a "moderate" course on colonial issues and a series of private bilateral talks with top Third-World diplomats.[164] Just before the assembly convened on 14 October the secretary of state reversed the U.S. position on the appearance on the General Assembly agenda of the Tunisian and Moroccan issues. Despite strong French objections, he decided to cast the U.S. vote in favor of their inclusion.[165] This was merely the first step in an intricate balancing act that was sure to last for weeks.

The possibility also existed that elements among the conflicting parties on colonial issues would align against the United States on Korea. Such a coalition had failed to jell during the sixth session of the General Assembly only because, from late November 1951 until its end the next February, the armistice talks had shown steady progress. The recess at Panmunjom was likely to provide an irresistible temptation to India to interject itself as a mediator. Given New Delhi's influence among the Arab-Asian powers and within the commonwealth, such a development would complicate the execution of U.S. policy, especially if it was joined by cagey Soviet maneuvering.

The outcome in New York would have no immediate impact on the military balance in Korea, which, more than any other factor, dictated the negotiating positions of the two sides at Panmunjom. Yet the military balance in Korea was linked to political, economic, and military conditions in the rest of the world. The General Assembly had no army divisions, but its proceedings would reveal a good deal about the international political climate. Those revelations would send important signals to Beijing, Moscow, and Washington regarding future possibilities in Korea. For the Communists, there were two key questions: What was the balance between the prospects and risks assumed

292                                          • CHAPTER 8 •

in resisting UNC demands for an armistice? Was time likely to make the United States more or less flexible in its terms, more or less willing to sustain or even expand its military pressure in and around Korea? Unlike in the fall of 1950, a concession to the Americans on Korea would not put enemy forces on their borders. However obnoxious UNC demands on the POW issue, the need to resist them was not so compelling as the need to bloc the UNC march to the Yalu two years before. In such circumstances, events in New York could be crucial in Communist calculations, just as they had been in late 1950 and early 1951. Then divisions in the West had joined with military developments in Korea to foster an ambitious course. Now divisions within the enemy coalition in New York would encourage a firm position on POWs. For the United States, which had a more realistic option of intensifying military or economic pressure or both in and around Korea, the central questions were these: How firm is allied and neutral support for the current UNC stance on POWs? If such support proved solid, did it extend to backing for new pressure on China to achieve Communist concessions at Panmunjom? In helping to answer pivotal questions on both sides, the first meeting of the General Assembly at its sparkling new permanent headquarters in midtown Manhattan could approach in importance the momentous fifth session held two years before.

### Growing Pressure on the United States

Many observers at the General Assembly that convened in mid-October believed time was running out for the resolution of some of the key issues to be addressed. Of special concern was the frigid state of superpower relations symbolized by Moscow's demand for the recall of U.S. Ambassador Kennan, allegedly for remarks he had made in Berlin equating the present climate for Western diplomats in the Soviet Union to that of Hitler's Germany.[166] On Korea talks had recessed indefinitely. In the United States polls indicated broad sentiment in favor of ending the stalemate through a new military offensive.[167]

In this context, the remarks of outgoing Assembly President Luis Padilla Nervo stood out amid the fulsome rhetoric of the politicians and diplomats addressing the opening session. The head of the Mexican delegation thought it "urgent," especially for "the small and medium-sized Powers," to attempt to bring about a reconciliation between the United States and the Soviet Union. He declared that the United Nations had "succeeded [in Korea] in preventing the aggressors from achieving their purpose" and thus "should concentrate on preventing further destruction of life and property." The assembly held "an inescapable obligation to make one more attempt" to bring the Korean War to an end.[168]

Padilla Nervo's words reflected a spirit of independence on the part of a man hailing from a region with twenty votes in the assembly. Although in the past most of these had gone to support U.S. positions, some delegates had shown interest in Arab-Asian mediation efforts on Korea as far back as the fifth session, and the seventh came during a low point in U.S. relations with its southern neighbors.[169]

The Korean War had contributed to this deterioration by increasing the stinginess of the U.S. Congress regarding foreign economic aid and by reinforcing the higher priority for U.S. assistance to countries closer to the center of cold war conflict. In its mutual security program for fiscal year 1953, Congress appropriated merely $72 million for Latin America compared to $4.4 billion for western Europe, $811 million for Asia and the Pacific, and $680 million for the Near East and Africa.[170] Initially the war had sparked demands from the industrialized West for strategic raw materials, elevating prices to the advantage of several Latin nations. Yet the upward trend did not remain steady. When profits did rise, the beneficiaries were often U.S. corporations, which owned much of the mineral-rich properties. Resentment over this situation had led to the nationalization of tin mines in Bolivia. Heated controversy developed in Chile, Brazil, Uruguay, and Mexico over conditions attached to military-aid agreements, which included a promise by recipient governments to facilitate U.S. access to resources of strategic importance. Padilla Nervo's call for an exploration of new approaches to the POW issue could not be written off as an isolated view among Latin American or other delegations. Combined with the Arab-Asians and some of Washington's NATO allies, the Latin Americans might form a majority in the assembly in favor of a compromise solution on Korea.

Acheson responded to this danger with a surprisingly moderate fifty-minute talk on the 16th.[171] He called on the body to support the U.S. position at Panmunjom, but concentrated on colonial and economic issues and refrained from intemperate remarks about the Soviet Union. When the Soviets lobbied to place Korea at the top of the agenda, he did not resist.[172]

Acheson's moderation did nothing to soften the rhetoric of the Soviet bloc. On the 17th the Polish delegate mounted a lengthy attack on the United States, presenting a comprehensive draft resolution that included a four-point program on Korea: an immediate cease-fire, the repatriation of POWs "in accordance with international standards," the withdrawal of foreign troops two or three months after an armistice, and the unification of the peninsula by the "Koreans themselves" under the supervision of nations "immediately interested" and ones "which have not taken part in the war."[173] Vishinsky followed the next day with a spirited critique of the U.S. position on POWs.[174]

The disparity between Acheson's and Vishinsky's positions encouraged delegates from outside the Soviet bloc to step into the breach. Acheson reported to Truman on the 25th that "the outstanding political fact of the assembly thus far has been the domination of the proceedings by the Arab-Asian group, . . . [which] has been exceptionally skillful in allying themselves with both [the] Latin American[s] and [the] Soviets."[175] Although he succeeded in rounding up twenty cosponsors for his resolution supporting the U.S. position at Panmunjom, which he presented to the First Committee on 24 October, he remained uncertain of a "firm majority" on Korea.[176] He had counted on support from America's European and commonwealth allies, and his success in obtaining cosponsors for the U.S. resolution appeared to bear out his calculations. Yet support for the U.S. resolution was infirm, even among several cosponsors. The draft tabled by Acheson explicitly called on China and North Korea to accept the principle of no forced repatriation, which reflected a hardening of the U.S. position since the previous spring, when the Americans had sought to achieve the desired result in practice without an excessive loss of face for the enemy.[177] Washington's commonwealth allies went along publicly with the new U.S. stance, but behind the scenes the British and the Canadians maneuvered for either modification of the twenty-one-power resolution or its replacement by another.[178] During the last week of October they began to focus on efforts by V. K. Krishna Menon of the Indian delegation.

By all accounts Menon was a difficult person.[179] He had served the past five years as India's high commissioner to the United Kingdom. High-strung and ascetic, he was ill-suited to fulfill the ceremonial dimensions of a chief of mission. Insensitive to the feelings of others, yet keenly alert to their slights toward himself—real or imagined—unwilling to delegate responsibility, yet unable to keep up with the details of operating India House, Menon produced a chaotic, scandal-ridden mission.

Prime Minister Nehru, seeking at once to serve his nation's interests while avoiding humiliation of a valued friend, sought to persuade Menon to take sick leave and then to accept a cabinet post or the ambassadorship in Moscow. When these options fell through, Nehru suggested that Menon join the Indian delegation to the UN General Assembly. The latter refused to serve as deputy to Madame Pandit, who already had been assigned to lead the delegation, so Nehru offered him the Korean issue as a special project.[180]

Depressed by Nehru's withdrawal of unbending support and suffering from injuries administered by a speeding London taxicab, Menon arrived in New York "bruised both in body and in spirit." He had to be carried off the airplane.[181] Once on the ground, he depended on a cane in each hand to move about. The immensity of the UN stage and the centrality of the Korean issue rejuvenated him, however, and he soon was working in private for a compromise solution.

As a representative of India, Menon had the advantage over other would-be mediators of membership in both the commonwealth and the Arab-Asian group. In part because he was more at home with British than with Third-World diplomats, in part because he recognized that the way to influence the United States was through its allies, his early efforts centered on the commonwealth.[182] In a meeting of delegates from member nations on the 24th he expressed regret over the First Committee's recent vote to invite a South Korean to participate in the debate and the tabling of the twenty-one-power resolution, which India was unlikely to support. These developments would force most delegates to take sides, complicating mediation efforts. The Communists would regard with suspicion any plan advanced by the United States, so in persuading them that the United Nations had a genuine interest in an armistice, an initiative must emerge from another source. Such an initiative might become possible once the Soviets, the Americans, and some others had "blow[n] off steam" and discovered that such activity "led them nowhere."[183] He did not rule out Indian leadership in such an endeavor, which might entail advancing a "middle-of-the-road" resolution.

It is uncertain when the Communists became aware of his activities. The Soviets maintained a tough stance but with enough hint of flexibility to titillate some delegates outside their camp. Vishinsky's First Committee speech of the 29th concentrated on rebutting Acheson's arguments five days earlier and on highlighting the Communist proposals of 8 October, which stated that "the captured personnel of the Chinese People's Volunteers . . . must all be repatriated home" but also provided that the "tasks of visits, classification, and repatriation can be accomplished under the observance of inspection teams of neutral nations."[184] Some observers wondered if the Communists would accept something less than the return of all the Chinese in enemy hands should a truly neutral method of screening be devised.[185] An erosion of support for the twenty-one-power resolution already was in progress. Reports circulated that several Latin Americans would vote no and that the affirmative votes would number only thirty-eight, nearly a two-thirds majority but substantially less than past support for U.S. conduct in Korea.[186]

Vishinsky was not about to fully reveal his hand. The resolution he tabled merely repeated the earlier Polish proposal for the unification of Korea by Koreans themselves under the supervision of an international commission.[187] Soviet diplomats encouraged Arab-Asian nations to offer an alternative resolution while refusing to endorse anything specific beyond their own handiwork.[188]

The Communists also kept the pot boiling through Chinese contacts with India in Beijing. During the week before Vishinsky's speech, Zhou Enlai called a midnight meeting with Nedgan Raghavan, the new Indian ambassador. Zhou insisted that, although all Chinese prisoners must be returned, they could be transported to some agreed-on point to "be given full assurances of considerate treatment." This at least was the gist of Zhou's comments based on Nehru's reading of his ambassador's report.[189] On the last day of October Zhou had another conversation with Raghavan. The PRC foreign minister appeared to concede that some "secret agents" of Jiang Jieshi among the Chinese POWs could go to Taiwan rather than to the mainland. This was the first instance in which a top Beijing official had suggested a lesser stipulation than that all Chinese POWs be returned.[190]

In New York a variety of ideas circulated in the Arab-Asian group. Indonesia's Lambertus Palar tried to "marry" the twenty-one-power and Soviet draft resolutions, while the Iraqis circulated a draft sounding much like Mexico's plan.[191] At a meeting on 4 November members of the group agreed, according to A. M. Rosenthal of the *New York Times*, that the goal "was to devise a formula . . . that would acknowledge merit in the Communist stand that by international law all prisoners should be sent home, but . . . provides a device under which exceptions would be made for resisting prisoners in this case." Some Third-World delegates talked of synthesizing the plans of the Latin Americans and the Arab-Asian group in a resolution to be sponsored by nations from both regions, an idea reflected by the Iraqi proposal.[192]

In public the United States encouraged the circulation of ideas, while in private it worked to prevent unacceptable ones from reaching the floor of the First Committee. When Vishinsky tabled his resolution, the U.S. delegation lobbied to prevent new proposals from being presented so British Minister of State Selwyn Lloyd and others could press him for an elaboration on Soviet terms. Yet Vishinsky showed no inclination to cooperate, and the Mexicans and Peruvians refused to hold back resolutions of their own.[193] For the moment Acheson and his subordinates did not have to worry about a resolution on Korea being pressed to a vote, as everyone agreed that such action must await the outcome of the U.S. elections on 4 November. Still, with many Third-World nations showing independence and the British, the Canadians, and the French encouraging Menon, the United States was far from in control on the Korean issue. The Americans faced a struggle to secure an endorsement of their policies at Panmunjom and to persuade individual nations to contribute more troops to Korea, never mind to attain majority support for new sanctions against China.

Tension existed within the Western camp on other issues as well, most notably in Franco-U.S. and Franco-German relations. In mid-October Frenchman Edward Herriot, leader of the Radical Party in the National Assembly, announced his opposition to ratification of the EDC. Prime Minister Antoine Pinay issued a statement of support for the May agreements, but rumors circulated that he was in cahoots with Herriot and that Foreign Minister Robert Schuman, a bulwark of the Western alliance, soon would be pushed out of the cabinet. Pinay already was in a spat with the Americans over their pressure to uphold prior commitments on defense spending despite their failure to provide anticipated levels of financial assistance. To hold his cabinet intact, Pinay also had stood firm against any discussion of the Tunisian issue at the UN General Assembly. When the United States voted in favor of placing that matter on the agenda, a wave of anti-U.S. sentiment spread through the French press. The *New York Times* described the atmosphere as "exactly what Joseph Stalin is counting upon, along with economic collapse, when he predicts wars between the 'capitalistic' countries."[194]

Franco-German relations were no better. Tensions continued to build on the Saar question. With the German people determined to see the region back under their control and elections scheduled during the coming year in West Germany, the French found little flexibility in Chancellor Adenauer's negotiating position. Talks broke off in late October, and France announced plans for elections in the Saar under conditions that would ensure victory for pro-French elements.[195]

Differences between France and the United States and West Germany could not help but affect Western rearmament plans. Performance lagged behind the goals set at Lisbon in February, and there was little chance that key western European countries would expand their military spending for fiscal year 1954.[196] Without a major contribution from West Germany, little hope existed of matching Soviet bloc forces to the east.

Trade issues created more dissension in the West. In 1951 imports to the United States from western Europe declined. Americans emphasized Europe's need to improve production and marketing techniques, while Europeans dwelled on the roadblocks to penetration presented by the complicated regulations and procedures confronting foreign producers on the western shores of the Atlantic. President Truman had to intervene in Congress to restrain protectionist sentiments. Trade talks in Geneva in late October 1952 found the United States confronting accusations from allies that its restrictions on food imports violated international agreements. The U.S. delegation could only promise to seek congressional action to repeal the offending measures.[197]

The Soviet Union had long attempted to exploit such divisions, which were aggravated by U.S. pressure to tighten restrictions on trade with the Communist bloc. Although the international trade conference held at Moscow in April had produced few results, the Soviets had reason to hope that commercial questions would continue to sap Western unity.[198] The election of Eisenhower as president of the United States on 4 November reinforced this hope. Republican majorities in both houses of Congress swept in on his coattails, putting the party of protectionism in control of two branches of the federal government for the first time since the early 1930s.

Eisenhower's victory received mixed reviews abroad. Western Europeans feared the president-elect's relationship to the Republican Right and to John Foster Dulles. Most disturbing to them was the general's talk, in a speech he gave in August, of the "liberation" of eastern Europe from the Communist yoke.[199] Concerns varied from the belief that President Eisenhower would follow Robert Taft's lead in pulling back on U.S. commitments abroad, particularly in Europe, to the idea that he would adopt a more aggressive policy toward the Communists, if not in Europe then in Asia at the expense of Europe.[200] Preelection polls indicated that Eisenhower did well on the Korean issue among prospective voters at the same time that they edged toward approval of an offensive strategy to end the war.[201] The candidate's vagueness on Korea did nothing to assuage fears in Europe. On learning of Eisenhower's electoral victory, Churchill told a confidant, "I think this makes war much more probable."[202] As C. L. Sulzberger of the *New York Times* remarked, what western Europeans wanted was "the General Eisenhower it knew," the steady, prudent leader of the wartime coalition and the NATO command.[203] Their uncertainty that this is what they would get guaranteed increased pressures on the U.S. delegation at the United Nations to compromise on the Korean issue.[204] With nothing of consequence occurring on the battlefield in Korea, the Communists could afford to hold to their wait-and-see course.

## BARGAINING AND CONFRONTATION: THE INDIAN RESOLUTION

In the aftermath of the U.S. election, British and French foreign ministers Anthony Eden and Robert Schuman arrived in New York, signaling the readiness of their nation's delegations to move forward on Korea. In Eden's presence, the aspiring mediators coalesced around Menon's ideas. On a matter involving the application of pressure on the United States but on which they themselves lacked a direct interest, Third-World delegates looked for guidance to a major power and intimate of the Americans. The British, in turn, gravitated toward their commonwealth associate. India also had the advantages of a direct line to the PRC and a plan sufficiently vague to have avoided repudiation by the Communists.

Yet the Americans insisted that any armistice agreement contain a high level of specificity on the fate of POWs. Menon's challenge was to remain vague enough to avert Communist rejection while providing adequate precision to avoid U.S. opposition. Since the Americans engaged actively in the development of an Indian proposal while the Soviets preferred to lurk in the background, Menon found himself responding to pressure from the former to put his proposal into concrete form.

On the 7th and 8th Menon outlined his position orally to the Americans. He would create a repatriation commission of four "neutral" nations—Sweden, Switzerland, Poland, and Czechoslovakia—to take custody of POWs after they were transported to a demilitarized zone by the detaining power. Presumably, this arrangement would eliminate Communist suspicions that the UNC was forcibly detaining prisoners. The commission would classify the POWs "as to nationality and domicile," after which they could "return to [their] homelands." The commission was not to use force against prisoners, except as "necessary for the maintenance of discipline in accordance with the Geneva Convention." Decisions of the body were to be by majority vote, and it would appoint an "umpire" to resolve cases on which the regular members were deadlocked. Acheson expressed concern about the imprecision of the proposal, especially on the principle of no forced repatriation and the method of selecting an umpire, and pressed for a written text.[205]

Despite a lengthy attack by Vishinsky in the First Committee on the Mexican and Peruvian proposals, Menon pressed on, encouraged by reports from New Delhi regarding China's views.[206] He continued to receive support from British and Canadian delegates, who believed that the West should not lose an opportunity to align itself with India even if little chance existed for peace in Korea. Pearson and Lloyd worked closely with Menon to refine a draft, but on the 12th they produced a document that was far from acceptable to the United

States. Although it endorsed the principle of no forced repatriation, it also proposed that, after the armistice had been in effect for three months, the military commanders on both sides would recommend to their governments the convening of a political conference to take up any unresolved matters related to POWs.[207] This procedure was likely to result in the indefinite retention of prisoners who did not wish to be repatriated. Despite warnings from Acheson, Eden and Pearson refused to change course.[208] Menon's willingness to accept the principle of no forced repatriation in his draft had broadened support for the Indian initiative among the twenty-one cosponsors of the U.S. resolution. Acheson hoped to swing momentum back toward the twenty-one-power resolution by calling on top Pentagon officials to present their case to wavering commonwealth delegates. If all else failed, he could claim that, as the representative of an outgoing administration, he could not commit the United States to the Indian position.[209]

The Pentagon's judgment was in sufficient disrepute among the British and Canadians to render inconsequential the appearance before them on the 16th of Secretary of Defense Lovett and General Bradley. Their argument that the failure to fully resolve the POW issue *before* an armistice would leave the Communists a pretext for resuming hostilities later on, when their military position had improved, was no more persuasive than it had been to Acheson the previous September.[210]

Nor did Eden accept the argument that the outgoing Truman administration could not commit its successor on the POW issue. The British foreign minister contacted President-elect Eisenhower by telephone and succeeded in reducing his concern about adoption of the Indian resolution.[211] Sympathy expressed by Republican newspapers in New York also persuaded Eden that continued allied pressure on the United States would force a retreat.[212]

State Department officials were not amused. At a press conference late on the 17th Gross sharply criticized the Indian resolution, which had just been circulated in the First Committee.[213] On the morning of the 19th Acheson confronted Eden in an hour-long private meeting. Pearson conferred with Eden shortly after the confrontation, recording in his diary that "these are two people who shouldn't be left alone in the same room to argue."[214] That evening the Americans provoked an extraordinary incident. According to Evelyn Shuckburgh, Eden's private secretary, Acheson and John Hickerson arrived at Eden's suite in the Waldorf-Astoria "a little tight" and asked for strong martinis. Acheson then went after Selwyn Lloyd, who was present, characterizing him as a Welsh lawyer who "had misled and twisted the Americans for weeks." Unless the British fell into line on the Indian resolution, Acheson threatened, "there would be no NATO, no Anglo-American friendship." After referring to his old friend Pearson as "an empty glass of water," he boasted that he would "tear the Indian resolution apart" in his speech next week before the First Committee, thus "debagging that Swami" (meaning Menon). He also noted that, if armistice talks failed in Korea, the United States planned a major military offensive. Showing the strain of a man in his last weeks in office whose foreign policies had provided a major source of the opposition's attack in the recent election campaign, Acheson advised Eden: "Don't you ever appoint a Welsh lawyer as your Minister of State again! All lawyers are failures in foreign policy. Look at myself and John Simon."[215]

Eden was not deterred. On the next day, in a speech before the First Committee, he lauded the Indian effort to find a solution in Korea. He conceded that articles 14 and 17 needed clarification, the first to ensure that the umpire would be a full member of the repatriation commission, the second to ensure that prisoners who opposed repatriation would not be detained indefinitely; but he urged delegates not to insist on perfection. Menon already had acknowledged in his address of the previous day that prisoners could not be held in captivity forever, Eden argued, and his resolution clearly represented progress toward settlement of the one issue blocking an armistice.[216]

Eden's statement revealed the narrowness of Anglo-U.S. differences. The British wanted to give priority to the Indian proposal over the twenty-one-power resolution; the Americans did not, but were willing to go along if articles 14 and 17 in the former were amended to their satisfaction. The British recognized the desirability of amendments, but gave higher priority to passage of the Indian resolution. Despite Acheson's irritation with the allies, it was difficult to imagine him failing to mend the breach with such long-time acquaintances on the Western diplomatic circuit as Eden and Pearson.

Menon was another story. He did not know Acheson well before the seventh General Assembly, and their coming together in New York produced anything but a meeting of minds. As Pearson recorded in his diary, "There are no points of mental or spiritual contact between the practical, incisive, clear-headed Dean, and the vague, metaphysical, missionary Menon."[217] Yet during the second and third weeks of November, the Indian surprised British and Canadian diplomats by demonstrating flexibility in revising early drafts of his resolution. Pearson and Lloyd mediated between Menon and Acheson, often keeping the two men out of direct contact with each other.

The situation did not begin to clarify for several days. On the 21st Acheson departed for a state visit to Ottawa. The American asserted in his memoirs that his private talks with Prime Minister Louis St. Laurent in Ottawa produced a tactical advantage in the diplomatic contest in New York. When he returned to New York on Sunday the 23d, Acheson recalled, he found Pearson "much more cooperative."[218] Pearson contests that view in his own memoirs, claiming that St. Laurent reaffirmed by telephone his support for Pearson's stand.[219] In fact, Pearson *was* in a more cooperative mood upon Acheson's return, but primarily because the two had had a needed respite from each other and because the Canadian found his friend, however touchy, easier to contend with than Ernest Gross, his replacement as head of the U.S. delegation. In addition to his belligerence at twenty-one-power meetings, Gross attempted to pressure the allies by feeding reports to the press exaggerating differences with them.[220]

On the day Acheson returned to New York, Menon offered amendments on both the disputed articles, with the one on Article 14 clearly meeting the U.S. insistence on making the umpire a full member of the repatriation committee.[221] Article 17 remained unsatisfactory, as it failed to provide for the eventual release of prisoners who chose not to return to their homeland. It was not until the 25th that Acheson finally conceded priority to the Indian measure, and then only on the condition that others would press Menon to make additional changes in Article 17.[222]

By this time Vishinsky had clarified the Soviet position in a speech before the First Committee.[223] Initially Soviet-bloc delegates had reserved judgment on the Indian resolution, and the Soviet press had expressed pleasure over the friction it was causing in the Western camp.[224] On the 24th, however, the Soviet foreign minister harshly attacked the measure and its Indian sponsor.[225]

The speech actually complicated Acheson's task. Some allies argued that, since the Menon resolution was unacceptable to the Communists, it no longer had to be fully satisfactory in its content, that it should be passed without further amendment in order to cultivate the Indians.[226] Acheson demurred, but reduced U.S. demands for revision of the Indian's amended Article 17.[227] He agreed to accept its first sentence, which stated that the issue of prisoners not returned to their homeland within ninety days of the signing of an armistice would be referred, "with recommendations for their disposition, including a target date for the termination of their detention," to a political conference of the parties to the conflict.[228] But the second and last sentences would have to be changed. Menon's latest draft read, "If, at the end of a further sixty days, there are any Prisoners of War whose return to their homelands has not been effected or provided for by the political conference, the responsibility for their care and maintenance until the end of their detention shall be transferred to the United Nations."[229] Acheson wanted the time frame reduced from sixty to thirty days, the word *disposition* to replace the word *maintenance*, and the word *agency* to be added at the end.[230] This represented a significant concession for Acheson, as it lacked any explicit acknowledgment that the nonrepatriates were to be freed.

Some furious bargaining remained. Menon accepted inclusion of the word *disposition* and agreed not to oppose an amendment in the First Committee to reduce the sixty days to thirty. Acheson accepted the addition of a clause at the end of the second sentence stating that disposition of remaining prisoners by the United Nations would be "strictly in accordance with international law." By the evening of the 26th an agreement was in place.[231]

The only question remaining was whether, in the face of Communist opposition, the Indians would withdraw the resolution entirely. Left to his own devices, Menon might have chosen withdrawal, his bitterness directed toward the United States for forcing amendments that made his resolution unacceptable to the Communists. Nehru decided otherwise, explaining to his chief ministers that withdrawal would lead to adoption of "a bad and aggressive" measure—meaning the twenty-one-power resolution—while passage of the Indian resolution would "leave the door open for a settlement or at least a consideration of the problem on a new basis."[232]

The Indian resolution passed the First Committee by an overwhelming majority on 1 December. On the next day that body rejected the Soviet resolution and deferred the twenty-one-power, Mexican, and Peruvian measures until a later date. The General Assembly then passed the Indian resolution on the 3d.[233] The Western alliance had held together and the Arab-Asians had supported a resolution by one of their own in the face of opposition by the Communist bloc.

U.S. allies, in conjunction with the Arab-Asian neutrals and some of the Latin Americans, had influenced U.S. policy but not fundamentally. Although the Indian measure had supplanted the twenty-one-power resolution drafted by the United States, the former did endorse the principle of no forced repatriation. If the wording in Article 17 remained vague on the final disposition of nonrepatriates, supporters of the resolution, including Menon himself, acknowledged the need to work out some of the details in negotiations at Panmunjom.[234] The resolution also went beyond UNC proposals advanced at Panmunjom in explicitly releasing prisoners to the custody of a neutral commission before their final disposition, but this was a point that the Communists probably could have won through direct bargaining.

More important, America's colleagues in the non-Communist world again had stalled U.S. desires for additional measures against China. The time spent and difficulty encountered in working out a compromise measure on the POW issue left the Truman administration disinclined to lobby for a sterner resolution in the last days before the General Assembly recessed for Christmas. As in the past, allied and Arab-Asian pressures on the United States cut two ways: they discouraged the Truman administration from any move to expand the war while encouraging the Communists to continue their test of Western endurance.

The question remains of the resolution's impact on relations between the West and the Arab-Asian states, especially India. British and Canadian pleading with the Americans to accommodate Menon derived partly from the assumption that such accommodation would nudge India and other neutrals toward the Western camp in the cold war. The accommodation only after acrimonious bargaining clouds judgments on the accuracy of this assumption. If anything, the process magnified Menon's deeply ingrained suspicions of the United States. In the aftermath of his resolution's passage, he squandered the considerable good will he had accumulated with the American public by openly criticizing the U.S. role in Korea.[235]

That point aside, one experience of limited cooperation could not sweep away the burden of past events and other outstanding issues between the West and the Arab-Asian neutrals. Although the Arab-Asian nations ultimately supported the Indian resolution in the face of Communist opposition, eleven of them abstained on the Soviet resolution.[236] In a speech at Bombay shortly after passage of the Indian resolution, Nehru reaffirmed India's neutrality in the cold war and in another world war should it occur.[237]

Nehru's communiqué to his chief minister, cited earlier, reveals some of the key factors in ongoing neutralism. The Indian leader reiterated his long-standing view that a major source of the current problems in Korea and elsewhere in Asia was America's refusal "to recognize the new China." Nehru acknowledged that recent events suggested "that China is more closely associated with the Soviet Union than might have been thought" and "that there are limits beyond which the U.K. and some other European nations are not prepared to go even under pressure from the U.S.A."; but neither point did overwhelming credit or damage to one side. Indeed, the bulk of Nehru's analysis of foreign issues centered on European colonial policies. After reviewing British and French difficulties from Africa to Southeast Asia, Nehru concluded, "It is very extraordinary how some of the old colonial powers cannot adjust themselves to the new conditions."[238] Within days, nationalist riots broke out in Tunisia and Morocco while, in New York, the French boycotted UN consideration of the status of those territories.[239] Faced with the options of supporting an ally or the Arab-Asian group, which tabled resolutions calling for negotiations directed toward the full independence of both territories, the United States and the United Kingdom clearly chose the former.[240]

At best, Western support for the Indian resolution conveyed to members of the Arab-Asian group a sense of Western flexibility and responsibility on an issue that, short of expanding into global war, was of marginal significance to them. At worst, the display of Western disunity along the way encouraged them in the belief that they could advance their cause by exploiting divisions within that camp.

## The Communist Powers and the Indian Resolution

Soviet and Chinese tactics also merit attention. Vishinsky's rejection of the Indian resolution came at a tense moment among non-Communist delegations. The substance and tone of his attack could relieve some of that tension. Why, then, did the Kremlin choose the 24th for Vishinsky's blistering speech? Why did the Soviets not enter more actively into the bargaining process in New York to counter U.S. pressure on the Indians?

Some believed at the time that China forced the Soviet hand by showing interest in the Indian resolution, that Moscow moved to reject the measure to force Beijing into line.[241] The sequence of events produced suspicions in the West that all was not running smoothly in the Sino-Soviet alliance. Not only did the first word of opposition to the Indian resolution in the Communist camp come from Vishinsky, and in a form that verged on being insulting to the Indians, but the first word of Chinese rejection also came from the Soviet foreign minister. On the 26th Vishinsky announced in the First Committee that the Chinese had informed the Indians of their position two days before.[242]

It was not for two more days that China took a stand publicly in a statement by Zhou Enlai and in an editorial in the party newspaper.[243]

Yet even without a difference of opinion between Moscow and Beijing there were reasons for the Soviets to take the lead. The Chinese had had direct contact with the Indians and had encouraged them to put forth a plan. Understandably, China would want the Soviets to initiate public rejection of the Indian proposal while it privately informed New Delhi of its position. In addition, by the time Vishinsky spoke out, Menon had revised his draft to include a commitment to no forced repatriation and to move toward the Americans on other specifics. With the PRC frozen out of the United Nations, only the Soviets could make a dramatic attempt to halt the process of Americanizing the Indian resolution.

Why the "clumsy" attack on the Indian measure? The Soviets were often clumsy in their tactics at the United Nations, so this instance is hardly unique. Yet another explanation permits greater sensitivity to the conditions existing on 24 November. India had long tried to avoid positions in opposition to either camp in the cold war. New Delhi had made exceptions, to be sure, as in its response to the outbreak of war in Korea in June 1950. Nehru had stated openly that the policy of nonalignment did not preclude India's choosing sides in individual cases.[244] Still, such a stand was not to be taken lightly. Much of India's maneuvering in October and November was designed to avoid making a proposal that either side would reject. Surely the Soviets understood this. They may have calculated that a sharp rebuke to the Indians would induce them to withdraw their resolution or at least resist any additional concessions to the Americans. In fact, the immediate impact of Vishinsky's address *was* to increase pressure on Acheson to accept the Indian resolution without further amendments and to cause the Indians to consider withdrawing their proposal. Menon himself and much of the Indian press blamed the Americans equally with the Soviets for the failure of the proposals to bring peace.[245]

One reading of the minutes of the Zhou-Stalin meetings of the previous summer is that the Chinese were more flexible than the Soviets in involving the Indians in a solution of the POW problem; a more nuanced interpretation is that Zhou used a discussion of the POWs to test Stalin's willingness to aid China in Korea in the face of DPRK wavering.[246] Clearly Mao saw certain uses in an ongoing war: continuing to fight the United States to a standstill increased China's prestige, promoted unity at home, and provided valuable experience for the army. The best guess is that Mao continued to search for solutions on POWs, but remained unwilling to give significant ground. This stance probably was conditioned on Soviet aid for the implementation of China's First Five-Year Plan, which began late in the year using a Stalinist model. In mid-November the pro-Soviet Gao Gang became chairman of a new State Planning Commission in Beijing. The Chinese press glorified Stalin's economic thought and produced an unprecedented volume of propaganda in support of Sino-Soviet friendship.[247]

The only evidence of Chinese flexibility on its POWs held in South Korea came in Zhou's meeting with Raghavan of 31 October in which the PRC foreign minister stated that Jiang's agents among them would not have to be repatriated. Zhou never offered a precise plan, however, nor did he drop his objection to the principle of no forced repatriation. His statement appears to have been a come-on to the Indians to continue their activities in New York. The Communists did not attack Menon's resolution on its initial circulation in the First Committee because they thought the Americans would do the dirty work for them. But by the 24th Menon had moved further toward the U.S. position, and Acheson's return from Ottawa had restored order to the Western deliberations. Thus Vishinsky scrambled to replace Poland's delegate as the first speaker in the afternoon session of the First Committee.[248]

In a word, the Communists sought to encourage activities that would exacerbate divisions in the West, but they opposed concessions on the POW issue. The Soviets and the Chinese had little reason to give ground in a war they were not losing on the battlefield and one that was having a bearable and in some respects salutary impact at home. Events in Korea from late September to early November confirmed the existence of a military stalemate, as the results of tactical offensives by both sides showed the Communists to be in a stronger position than during the previous fall. General Deng Hua, now in command of CPV troops in Korea, had employed an active defense which not only had inflicted thousands of casualties on the enemy but produced minor territorial gains. Mao showed confidence in Deng's tactics, believing that they could eventually force the Americans to make concessions.[249] An increase in Chinese troops in Korea would bring the total by early 1953 to 1.35 million, the highest in the entire war. The stockpiling of ammunition and grain to supply them was well under way.[250]

The election of Eisenhower did lead Mao and his military advisers to conclude that U.S. policy would become more aggressive. During the previous summer, Mao had ordered the Ministry of Foreign Affairs to study the Republican candidate's statements on Korea. Analysts quickly concluded that, if elected, Eisenhower would launch new military action.[251] His postelection activities—a trip to Korea in early December, talk of resolving the stalemate there with "deeds" rather than "words," and his very public agreement to meet with General MacArthur to hear the deposed commander's plan to end the war—reinforced this expectation in the PRC.[252] Stepped-up amphibious training maneuvers off the North Korean and China coasts and Nationalist Chinese raids from offshore islands on PRC-held territories opposite Taiwan had already stirred concern in Beijing.[253] Then, Major General William C. Chase, chief of the U.S. military advisory and assistance group on Taiwan, traveled to Korea for consultations during Eisenhower's stay. At a press conference on his return to Taibei, Chase declared ominously that Eisenhower and U.S. military officials had reviewed strategic conditions throughout the western Pacific.[254]

In December Chinese preparations increased to counter an amphibious assault on the west coast of North Korea, anticipated for the spring of 1953. Maneuvers on the east coast and diversionary attacks on the China coast, it was believed, might accompany that assault. The Chinese viewed enemy use of atomic weapons as unlikely, both because of world opinion and the Soviet Union's retaliatory capability. If Chinese and North Korean forces could repulse an amphibious offensive and inflict heavy casualties, Mao believed, the military situation on the peninsula "would become more stabilized and more favorable to us."[255] Having survived the often dire conditions from late May to November 1951, the Chinese leader was not about to give ground in the more favorable conditions of late 1952.

### EISENHOWER AND THE THREAT OF ESCALATION

The General Assembly recessed for the holidays on 22 December, not to reconvene for more than two months. In the interim, Eisenhower took office in Washington and quickly increased pressure on the Communists. Two weeks after his inauguration, President Eisenhower announced that the Seventh Fleet would no longer protect mainland China from attack by forces on Taiwan.[256] Jiang reaffirmed his determination to recapture the mainland, and General Chase bragged of how the Nationalist army had doubled its fighting efficiency during 1952.[257] In Washington Senator William Knowland, chairman of the Republican Policy Committee, pressed for a naval blockade of China.[258]

European allies had a serious case of the jitters, but the Eisenhower administration continued to hint that new military action was on the horizon. In early March the president called top advisers and congressional leaders to the White House to hear General Van Fleet, the retiring commander of the Eighth Army in Korea, expound on his well-publicized belief that the way to end the war was through military escalation.[259] Eisenhower already had approved an expansion of the ROK army from fourteen to sixteen divisions, and it was no secret that this figure might soon be increased to twenty.[260] In testimony before an open hearing of a congressional committee, Secretary of Defense Charles Wilson hinted that expanded military operations in Korea were near.[261]

The Chinese Communists showed no anxiety. Mao and Zhou made tough statements in rebuttal to Eisenhower's February declaration on Taiwan. Mao asserted that China would fight on in Korea for "any amount of years" to achieve its purposes. Emphasizing contradictions within the capitalist camp, Zhou saw many positive aspects of international events and identified intensification of the anti-America campaign as the top domestic priority for 1953.[262] Even though Mao believed that Nationalist attacks along the China coast were part of Eisenhower's military plans, he told his negotiators in Korea that the PRC "shall let the war drag on until the United States is willing to make compromises."[263] He agreed with the view of his negotiators that China should await a U.S. initiative to reopen talks rather than making the first move.[264]

On 22 February UN commander Mark Clark addressed a letter to Kim Il-sung and Peng Dehuai that could be interpreted as such a move. During the previous December the executive committee of the League of Red Cross Societies in Geneva had passed, on Indian initiative, a resolution calling on both sides in Korea to repatriate sick and wounded POWs as a gesture of good will. Neither side responded immediately to the proposal. In mid-February 1953, however, the U.S. State Department, anticipating that the proposal soon would be raised at the UN General Assembly, pressed Clark to advance it to the Communists. This he did, two days before the body reassembled on the 24th.[265]

Then, on 5 March, before the Communists had responded to the UNC initiative, Stalin died at his suburban home in Kuntsevo after a brief illness. According to his recent Russian biographer, this happened only days before the Soviet leader had decided to advise his Chinese and Korean allies to seek the best deal they could but to try to bring the war to an end.[266] Whether his successors in the Kremlin, and Mao and Kim, would follow Stalin's apparent wishes in the face of U.S. pressure and the uncertainties accompanying his death remained to be seen. At stake was both a halt to the slaughter in Korea and, quite possibly, the prevention of its escalation in intensity and geography.

• CHAPTER 9 •

# Concluding an Armistice

PROLOGUE: THE SUPERPOWER CONTEST FOR WORLD OPINION

Stalin's death did not produce universal optimism outside the Communist world. In western Europe, many saw the dictator as a source of restraint on Soviet foreign policy. The first months after Stalin's death, C. L. Sulzberger reported from Paris, were likely to be ones of great danger. "Should internal ruckuses develop as a result of political or personality schisms not yet visible behind the Iron Curtain," observers feared, "they might very well precipitate a global disaster."[1] In India Nehru was less alarmist, but he did tell Chester Bowles, the outgoing U.S. ambassador, that Soviet foreign policy was likely to be as tough or tougher over the next few months than it had been under Stalin. China might move in the opposite direction, however, especially if it doubted its ally's ability to make a smooth transition to a new leader.[2] Countering Vishinsky's immediate departure as foreign minister was his designation as the Soviet Union's permanent representative to the United Nations and the appointment of Vyacheslav Molotov to the higher post. Methodical, humorless, and deeply suspicious, Molotov resumed the office he had held for a decade before the spring of 1949. In that position he had negotiated the infamous Nazi-Soviet pact, and later executed Soviet foreign policy during the wartime alliance with the West and during its subsequent breakdown. A true Marxist-Leninist, he had been referred to by the architect of the Bolshevik revolution as the "iron behind." Western diplomats preferred "old iron ass," to capture his doggedness in negotiations.[3] His speech at Stalin's funeral on 9 March was comparatively mild in addressing foreign policy issues, as it lacked the usual denunciations of the United States and Western "ruling circles." The speeches given on the same occasion by Malenkov and Beria, the other two members of the new ruling troika, followed the same pattern. Premier Malenkov even emphasized "the possibility of the prolonged coexistence and peaceful competition of two different systems, capitalist and socialist."[4] Yet these hopeful signs did not manifest themselves immediately in the form of action. The following week saw the Communists shoot down two military planes flying near the border between East and West in Europe and fire on a U.S. weather patrol aircraft off the Kamchatka Peninsula in the northern Pacific.[5]

Beginning on 15 March the Kremlin moved dramatically away from the style of Soviet foreign policy of Stalin's last years. First, in a speech to the Supreme Soviet, Malenkov declared that "there is not one disputed . . . question that cannot be decided by peaceful means on the basis of mutual understanding of interested countries." He singled out the United States as among the countries to which this statement applied. Six days later a Moscow radio broadcast departed from the standard line on Germany's defeat in World War II, characterizing it as a result of cooperation among the three allies—the Soviet Union, the United States, and Great Britain. More concretely, the Soviets proposed talks with the British to prevent future air incidents in central Europe and promised to help obtain the release of British civilians held in North Korea.[6] Soon the Soviets invited the United States to join the talks in Germany, and the French and the Americans received similar promises regarding their civilian prisoners in North Korea.[7]

On the 28th the Communists in Korea agreed to the UNC proposal of the previous month to exchange sick and wounded prisoners before the fighting ended.[8] Zhou Enlai followed this move with a cablegram to Lester Pearson, still president of the General Assembly, proposing that negotiations begin immediately at Panmunjom for the exchange of these prisoners and that these talks then proceed to a complete resolution of the POW issue. To indicate that resumed negotiations would not produce the same old impasse, he added a new proposal: "that both sides to the negotiations ... undertake to repatriate immediately after the cessation of hostilities all those prisoners of war in their custody who insist upon repatriation and to hand over the remaining prisoners of war to a neutral state so as to insure a just solution to the question of their repatriation."[9] Mao still anticipated an enemy spring military offensive, but he also regarded the UNC initiative on sick and wounded POWs as a possible feeler by Eisenhower regarding the resumption of negotiations at Panmunjom, which could help the Chinese save face. If nothing else, a favorable response from Beijing would score points with world opinion. It even might induce the United States to abandon plans for new military action in favor of resolving the POW issue.[10]

The Soviets quickly endorsed the proposal and then broke one deadlock in New York by agreeing to Swede Dag Hammarskjold as the new UN secretary-general to replace the retiring Trygve Lie. On the disarmament issue now before the General Assembly, they refrained from polemics and offered three minor amendments to a Western resolution.[11]

Shifts within the Soviet Union reinforced the moves abroad. The hate-America campaign all but disappeared as did the campaign of anti-Semitism and the constant appeals for vigilance against subversives. Hundreds of nonpolitical prisoners received amnesty, and revisions commenced on the penal code. The physicians accused in January of plotting to kill Soviet leaders saw the charges dropped. A group of U.S. newspaper editors, the first to be permitted to visit Moscow since World War II, won a warm reception, and the Soviet foreign ministry informed the U.S. and British embassies of the rescinding of orders that would have forced them to vacate their present quarters.[12] The Soviet press gave great attention to a statement by President Eisenhower about taking recent Communist overtures "at face value."[13]

Zhou's cable to Pearson was enough to send would-be mediators at the United Nations into a frenzy. Menon met with Henry Cabot Lodge, the new head of the U.S. delegation, on 2 April. Disclaiming any thought of transferring negotiations on Korea from Panmunjom to New York, the Indian argued that the General Assembly should still take note of Zhou's message. The Soviets were unlikely to make trouble, as their policy clearly had shifted toward an effort to "make peace." The General Assembly was in recess for the Easter holidays until the 7th, but Lodge had no doubt that, once meetings resumed, the pressure would build for a new discussion of Korea. With the memory still fresh of events of the previous fall, Lodge understood that the best way to prevent this trend from getting out of hand was to move toward a resumption of negotiations at Panmunjom.[14]

On the latter front, Eisenhower and Dulles wanted to move cautiously. Although they had no objection to early negotiations between liaison officers for the repatriation of sick and wounded prisoners, they hesitated to move further until resolution of that issue. As the president remarked privately, "We should use this business of the sick and wounded as a sort of test of good faith on the part of the Soviets."[15] Meanwhile, the United States could seek clarification of Zhou's proposal, which was obscure on the final disposition of prisoners who resisted repatriation. For his part, Dulles remained dubious about an armistice in Korea along the present battle line and flirted with the idea of a military offensive to the narrow neck. If successful, this would provide the UNC with a line to defend that was one-third shorter than the present one and would leave the ROK in control of the vast bulk of the peninsula's resources.[16] Dulles also feared the impact of an armistice in Korea on conditions in Indochina, where the Vietminh was poised for a march into Laos. This prospect rekindled fears that an end to the fighting in Korea would induce the Chinese to increase support for Ho Chi Min to the south. Dulles remarked to White House aide Emmett John Hughes, "I don't think we can get much out of a Korean settlement until we have shown—before all Asia—our clear superiority by giving the Chinese one hell of a licking."[17]

Yet an awareness that no easy or sure military solution existed to the Korean problem helped to nudge Eisenhower toward the negotiating table. On 21 March he directed Secretary of Defense Charles E. Wilson to study the cost of a UN advance to the narrow neck. The president understood that such an advance might require air attacks against Manchuria and the use of nuclear weapons in and beyond Korea. Before the end of the month the Joint Chiefs had expressed doubts about the effectiveness of tactical nuclear weapons against the "well dug in" enemy forces in Korea, had made clear that any UN effort to push north on the ground would produce huge U.S. casualties, and had shown concern that, in the face of a UN offensive, the Soviets might use atomic bombs against the highly vulnerable ports of Inchon and Pusan. In early April a national intelligence estimate and a report by the National Security Council Planning Board emphasized that Chinese forces in Korea and Manchuria, both on the ground and in the air, were sufficiently strong as to make Communist concessions at the negotiating table unlikely.[18]

Still, Communist moves on the diplomatic front provided some grounds for hope. Liaison officers commenced meetings on sick and wounded prisoners on 7 April. Four days later the liaison officers signed an agreement to begin an exchange on the 20th.[19] On the 9th the Communists in Korea proposed the resumption of armistice talks to resolve the POW issue, although on substance they refused to go beyond Zhou's message.[20] Eisenhower realized that, with the Communists appearing anxious to bargain, neither the American people nor U.S. allies—not to mention the Arab-Asian neutrals—would accept an overturning of the armistice terms already agreed on or even a lengthy delay in the resumption of full-fledged negotiations.[21] On the 14th, therefore, Washington leaked to the press that it favored reopening talks at Panmunjom and Switzerland as the neutral guardian of POWs.[22]

By this time the General Assembly had returned to Korea through its debate on a Polish item labeled "Measures to avert the threat of a new world war and measures to strengthen peace and friendship among nations." To counter a Polish draft resolution calling for an immediate cease-fire in Korea and an Indonesian effort to merely amend rather than scrap it entirely, the United States agreed to support a Brazilian draft.[23] This proposal expressed satisfaction over the recent agreement on sick and wounded prisoners and the hope that it would lead to an early armistice. It also provided for a recess of the General Assembly on completion of the current agenda, with the understanding that it would reconvene upon the signing of an armistice or when a majority believed events in Korea required it.

Then something remarkable happened. On 16 April the Poles withdrew their draft and, after prolonging its session through the lunch hour for fear that once delegates left the room the climate of amity might change, the First Committee voted unanimously for the Brazilian measure.[24] Two days later, and after its delegates had read in the morning papers of an agreement to commence armistice negotiations in a week, the General Assembly followed suit.[25]

The Soviet peace offensive did not stand uncontested. In mid-March President Eisenhower, troubled by his inability to seize the initiative in the cold war, had ordered speech writers to commence work on a major address.[26] He delivered the speech, after several rewrites, on 16 April to the American Society of Newspaper Editors. Combining genuine conviction with propaganda, Eisenhower lamented the climate of fear that had been generated by the breakdown of the World War II alliance and the resulting arms race. The worst prospect on the horizon was atomic war, the horrors of which he found no need to describe. On the best prospect, however, he spoke eloquently:

> a life of perpetual fear and tension; a burden of arms draining the wealth and the labor of all peoples; a wasting of strength that defies . . . any system to achieve true abundance and happiness for the peoples of this earth. Every gun that is made, every warship launched, every rocket fired signifies, in the final sense, a theft from those who hunger and are not fed, those who are cold and are not clothed.

With that depressing vision in mind, the president declared that the new leadership in the Kremlin had "a precious opportunity to awaken . . . to the points of peril reached and to help turn the tide of history." "Recent statements and gestures of Soviet leaders," he indicated, could only be "attested by deeds," the first of which "must be the conclusion of an honorable peace in Korea." There were many more: in Korea, "the prompt initiation of political discussions leading to . . . free elections in a united [country]"; in Southeast Asia, "an end to the direct and indirect attacks upon the security of Indochina and Malaya"; in western Europe, peace treaties with Austria and Germany and, in the latter case, "free and secret elections" for the creation of a united country; in eastern Europe, "full independence" from the Soviet yoke; on armaments, a reduction, and in the case of atomic weapons a prohibition, enforced through "a practical system of inspection under the United Nations." Eisenhower concluded with a declaration of his nation's readiness to devote "a substantial percentage of the savings achieved by disarmament to a fund for world aid and reconstruction."[27]

The speech was an immediate success. Both parties in the U.S. Congress lent their applause.[28] Anticipating its appeal abroad, the State Department delivered copies to seventy foreign governments. The Voice of America carried it in more than a dozen languages and on all its frequencies. NATO ministers assembling for a meeting in Paris expressed enthusiasm for Eisenhower's vision. Churchill in London called it "magnificent." While the U.S. president's words generated mixed reactions in Taiwan and South Korea, in India they fell on receptive ears. The government withheld comment, but unofficially many Indians expressed approval of the suggestion that savings on defense expenditures could be directed toward economic development, especially in Third-World countries. In Moscow the daily newspapers carried a TASS report of the address which, though critical, lacked the harsh tone of Soviet ripostes during the Stalin era.[29]

The initial Soviet reaction hardly ended the matter. On 25 April *Pravda* and *Izvestiia* devoted their front pages to an editorial reply. Inside, the Soviet organs reprinted the speech in its entirety, the first such publication of a major pronouncement by a leading Western official since British Foreign Minister Herbert Morrison's questions to the Soviet government in August 1951.[30] Soviet draftsmen proved every bit a match for U.S. speech writers. Beginning, as had Eisenhower, with a recollection of the wartime alliance against "Hitlerite fascism," the piece included France among the allies and omitted Japan from the enemy camp. The essay asserted that Eisenhower's "words on peace" and the seeming ability of all outstanding issues to be resolved conflicted with other parts of the speech. The U.S. president had "threatened unequivocally an 'atomic war'"—a dubious interpretation, to say the least—had "bypassed the Potsdam agreements as a basis for settling the German question, not to mention the vital interests of adjacent countries, [had] ignored the place of the People's Republic of China on Taiwan and in the United Nations, and [had] linked to his proposals a whole series of preliminary conditions," a notable contrast to the position of Soviet leaders. The editorial also pointed to Dulles's more belligerent follow-up speech on the 18th.[31] It ended with an assurance that the Soviets were willing "to assume a proportionate share in settling controversial international issues," but expressed doubt that the United States was willing to do the same.[32]

The armistice talks at Panmunjom, which resumed on the 26th, would provide a test of that assertion. As such, they would contribute mightily to the impact in the West of the latest Soviet peace offensive. They also would help to determine which of Eisenhower's visions of the future would become the reality.

### Initial Sparring at Panmunjom

Zhou Enlai's 30 March statement to the United Nations had suggested that the POW issue could be resolved by turning over all prisoners who did not "insist upon repatriation . . . to a neutral state," and the Communists opened the proceedings with a proposal elaborating on the idea. UNC negotiators disliked three stipulations of the plan: that prisoners not immediately repatriated would be sent to a neutral country; that representatives of the nation of origin of those prisoners then would have six months to persuade them to accept repatriation; and that disposition of any prisoners remaining after the six-month period would be determined by the political conference provided for in the armistice agreement.[33] The proposal lacked any guarantee against indefinite retention, a provision for which, during the previous fall, the Americans had risked a major breach in the Western alliance. General William K. Harrison, the head of the UNC negotiating team, immediately rejected the Communist proposal, labeling it "neither reasonable nor constructive." He attacked the idea of removing prisoners from Korea, as well as the lengthy period for persuasion, arguing that sixty days would be ample. He also noted that the Communists had failed to propose a neutral country to handle the prisoners not immediately repatriated, and he suggested Switzerland.

General Nam Il countered that removing these prisoners from Korea was necessary to eliminate apprehensions about repatriation, which had been drilled into them by the detaining side. It might take time for all POWs to be released, he conceded, but once North Korean and Chinese prisoners were removed from UNC detention and from the scene of their captivity, and given assurances by official representatives of their side, they all would eventually choose repatriation. Unmoved, General Harrison warned the Communists at the beginning of the third session that "we do not intend to become involved in protracted and useless arguments."[34]

On 29 April General Nam became more flexible. He began by stating that the time for explanations to prisoners "may be subject to discussion" and, although he rejected Switzerland as the nation to supervise the process, he expressed his readiness to nominate an Asian neutral.[35] Three days later he mentioned India, Pakistan, Burma, and Indonesia as "suitable" nations.[36]

UNC negotiators remained doubtful that the Communists were serious about an armistice. In addition to the continued gap between the two sides on the substance of the POW issue, the UNC believed that the Communists had withheld at least 375 qualified men from the recent exchange of sick and wounded prisoners.[37] With General Nam refusing to name a neutral state before the UNC accepted the principle of moving POWs out of Korea, U.S. officials grew edgy. On the 3d the Joint Chiefs informed General Clark that Pakistan was acceptable as the neutral state and that the time for explanations could be as long as four months. "If within the next few days" the Communists failed to "indicate a more favorable negotiating attitude," however, Washington would consider "recommendations for bringing matters to a head."[38] In the plenary session on the 4th General Harrison put forth Pakistan as the neutral nation and warned the Communists at both the beginning and end of the session that the time for negotiations was "fast running out."[39] Twice during the first week of May he gave the press gloomy reports on the negotiations.[40] At home Orland K. Armstrong, the newly appointed director of the State Department's Office of Public Affairs, predicted publicly that the United Nations Command soon would release North Korean and Chinese prisoners who wanted to fight the Communists.[41]

The Communists held back at Panmunjom partly for tactical reasons. After observing the pressure applied to the United States during the previous fall by its allies and neutrals, the Communists could not resist an initial test of U.S. resolve. Yet delay also may have occurred because the Communists had not found an Asian neutral that would accept the thankless task of supervising POWs from Korea. On 1 May the U.S. State Department learned that the Soviets had approached Indonesia.[42]

Indonesia's government rested on shaky foundations and it proved unwilling to assume responsibility for supervising POWs from Korea, so the Soviets turned to India.[43] This move showed both the adeptness of new Soviet leaders in diplomatic maneuver and their desire to prevent a break at Panmunjom. Although the Americans were bound to be unenthusiastic about India, rejecting that nation would risk insulting New Delhi.[44]

On 7 May General Nam presented a new eight-point proposal at Panmunjom in which India played a key role. Abandoning the position that one neutral nation serve as host to nonrepatriated POWs while they received explanations from representatives of their country of origin, the Communists accepted the call in the Indian resolution of the previous fall for a five-nation repatriation commission—with Poland, Czechoslovakia, Switzerland, Sweden, and India as members and contributors of supervisory troops.[45] The commission would supervise POWs *within* Korea and would permit explanations to nonrepatriated prisoners for four months, which was a reduction by a third from the previous Communist proposal but still one month longer than the time permitted in the Indian resolution. Following explanations, the disposition of any prisoners not choosing repatriation would rest in the hands of a political conference.

For the Americans the uncertainty regarding final disposition of POWs remained a problem, while the Communist concession on transporting prisoners outside Korea represented progress, as did the reduction of time allotted for explanations. The United States would have preferred Switzerland, Sweden, or Pakistan as a single custodian, or one of the first two joined with India. U.S. officials did not trust India's impartiality if acting alone.[46] The new proposal had the disadvantage of including two Communist nations on the repatriation commission, yet at least they were balanced by Washington's top choices. The Communists probably had the same reservations as the United States about India, and thus wanted two of their own on hand as lobbyists. The five-nation commission also provided the more immediate tactical advantage of following the Indian resolution. The Communists surely hoped that the movement toward that measure would produce overwhelming pressure on the Americans to give ground on the final disposition of prisoners.

## The UNC Response

The new proposal generated strong allied pressure on Washington and edged the Eisenhower administration toward its first major crisis. The British already had grown impatient with U.S. rigidity at the Panmunjom talks.[47] With Eden incapacitated as a result of two recent operations, Churchill was in firm control of British foreign policy, and was in one of his less charitable moods regarding the "special relationship."[48] On a trip to the United States in January, he had found the new leaders in Washington less to his liking than the old. Dulles's "'great slab of a face' he disliked and distrusted," he told private secretary Jock Colville; Eisenhower was "'a real man of limited stature.'"[49] He also distrusted the general orientation of the Republican party.[50] The Korean issue aside, the United States remained unwilling to give the United Kingdom unqualified support in its negotiations with Egypt over Suez, and Eisenhower had the audacity to ask Churchill if he would object to the U.S. president meeting with Stalin alone.[51] When Stalin died and the Soviets commenced their "peace campaign," the prime minister began contemplating a tripartite summit, or even a meeting between himself and Molotov. Despite Eisenhower's cool reaction to the idea, Churchill proposed in the House of Commons on 11 May "a conference on the highest level ... between the leading Powers without long delay" and without the burden of "a ponderous or rigid agenda."[52] Fearing the impact that a summit or the partial settlement of outstanding issues would have on Western defense programs, the Americans were not pleased. Churchill also suggested that the most recent Communist proposal on Korea could form the basis of an agreement.[53] He had already told the Canadians that the United States should abandon its obsession at Panmunjom with details of "method and procedure" and had cautioned Washington against taking any military action that might hamper negotiations.[54] If anything, Canada's Pearson was even more encouraged than the British by the latest Communist offer.[55]

While pressure from London, Ottawa, and the United Nations in New York, where the Communist proposal was well received, tugged the Eisenhower administration in one direction, pressure from the ROK government and the Republican Right at home pulled the opposite way.[56] The UNC response to the 7 May proposal threatened an open breach between Eisenhower and these two ostensible allies. In both cases the potential conflict had deep and complex roots.

Friction between the United States and Syngman Rhee, of course, went back many years, and Eisenhower's relations with the South Korean leader had gotten off to a shaky start when, in December 1952, the president-elect visited the peninsula to fulfill a campaign promise. Dulles advised him to discuss "political matters . . . as little as possible with Rhee."[57] Eisenhower maintained such distance from the ROK president that he nearly created an incident.[58]

When Eisenhower took office, the most pressing issues between the ROK and the United States involved the settlement of accounts regarding advances of Korean currency to U.S. soldiers, through which Rhee hoped to raise sufficient dollars to contain his government's perpetual economic crisis, and the movement of the ROK government from Pusan back to Seoul, which the UNC tried to postpone for security reasons.[59]

These were minor issues compared to disagreement over Korea's continued division, which was sure to arise once armistice talks resumed. The Americans were aware of the problem, but made little effort to resolve it, in part because it seemed irresolvable, in part because, without an armistice on the horizon, it posed no immediate threat to the UNC cause in Korea. With the movement in early April toward resumption of negotiations at Panmunjom, however, Rhee again made ominous noises. In a meeting with Dulles on the 8th Dr. Yang You Chang, the ROK ambassador in Washington, outlined five points that Rhee considered essential for the security of South Korea: "(1) reunification of the peninsula; (2) the withdrawal of Chinese Communist forces; (3) the disarming of North Korean forces; (4) the prevention of any third party from providing arms to the Communists in Korea; and (5) a declaration of the sovereignty of the Republic of Korea and its participation in international discussions regarding the future of Korea." Dulles replied that, although the United States remained committed to unification, it was not obligated to use force in achieving it. When Dulles asked for clarification of some of the five points, Yang raised the question of a mutual security pact between their countries, which he said "would greatly relieve the fears and anxieties of his people." Dulles countered by expressing concern that, since the ROK claimed title to all of Korea, such a pact might require the United States to drive the enemy off the peninsula. An arrangement might be feasible in which the United States agreed only to defend territory below the armistice line, although it would be best to postpone such a measure until all sides had had an opportunity to work out a peaceful settlement for Korea in a political conference. Dulles only agreed to approach President Eisenhower about making a statement assuring the Korean people that his country would not abandon them.[60] Yang had revealed his government's maximum program—the five points—and hinted at a minimum one—a mutual security pact—while Dulles had shown flexibility but had committed himself to nothing. He soon would discover that Rhee played the diplomatic game with a tenacity and a bluster that tested even his own substantial reserves.

Rhee followed up the Yang-Dulles meeting with a letter to Eisenhower, declaring that, if the "so-called free nations . . . [arranged] a peace agreement allowing the Chinese to remain in Korea," his government would ask all armed forces fighting in the UNC that did not want to join in a drive to the Yalu to leave the country. By implication, this included U.S. units.[61] On 24 April he had Yang present an aide-mémoire to the State Department threatening to remove ROK forces from the United Nations Command if it made "any agreement which . . . would either permit or allow Chinese Communists to remain south of the Yalu River, the northern-most boundary of the Republic of Korea."[62]

Rhee also launched a campaign to mobilize support at home. On 2 April the National Assembly unanimously passed a resolution opposing an armistice without unification.[63] That body's Second Vice Chairman, Yoon Chi Yung, expressed official sentiments when he declared that "America is playing into the damn foolish monkey business designed by Great Britain and India's Nehru!" On the 5th, with Eighth Army Commander Maxwell Taylor on the podium, Rhee lectured a gathering of ROK troops on the necessity of fighting on until the nation was reunited.[64] The ROK Foreign Ministry and Office of Public Information spewed propaganda for unification, which South Korean newspapers reproduced and reinforced with editorials. Mass rallies began in Seoul, Pusan, and Inchon.[65]

Western observers were not taken in by this display. They believed that most people in the educated classes and in the rural population wanted peace. South Korea's young men hardly rushed to enlist in the army. As T. K. Critchley, the Australian representative on UNCURK, remarked, Rhee's "arguments would certainly be stronger if the desire of Korean youths to dodge the draft were not so obvious."[66] ROK figures indicated that one in four men required to register for the draft as of the first of the year had failed to do so.[67]

Still, Ellis Briggs, who had replaced John Muccio as U.S. ambassador to the ROK during the previous summer, reminded Washington of the South Korean president's "general unpredictability."[68] Ambassador Briggs and General Clark recognized an element of bluff in Rhee's "'victory or death' act," but understood that he was a proud and passionate man who could not be taken for granted. In late April Clark gave in to Rhee's demand for a representative to the UNC team at Panmunjom who would report to him. Briggs advised the U.S. State Department that an offer of a mutual security pact might be essential to keep Rhee in line.[69] With the ROK army now manning two-thirds of the UNC front against North Korean and Chinese troops, Rhee's admonitions had to be considered.

The Republican Right in the United States reinforced Rhee's pressure on the Eisenhower administration. Republican members of Congress included internationalists, whose attitudes differed little from mainstream Democrats; nationalists, who were at best ambivalent toward U.S. commitments in Europe and to the United Nations, but were often impatient with U.S. restraint in Asia; and those in between, who accepted U.S. involvement in Europe, yet bridled at the shortchanging of Asia. Although individuals sometimes defied easy categorization, the two top Republicans in the Senate, majority leader Robert Taft and majority whip William Knowland, fit into the last two, respectively. Eisenhower and Dulles, both of whom had served in high if nonpartisan positions under Truman, clearly were most comfortable with the first, a fact long recognized by right-wing Republicans.[70] Because the Republicans held a mere one-vote majority in the Senate and a nine-vote majority in the House, the administration needed support from all three groups, and, given the unlikelihood of Republican unanimity on most issues, support was needed from Democrats as well. Theoretically, Eisenhower might have forged a majority based on internationalists in both parties, but this would have required a revamping of Republican leadership in the Senate—a risky enterprise. Even if the president succeeded in that venture, it would have split his own party wide open, diminishing its prospects in the 1954 and 1956 elections and threatening intraparty cooperation on domestic issues, where the president had much in common with the Republican Right. So Eisenhower and Dulles moved on foreign policy issues with a wary eye toward Capitol Hill. The secretary of state met with congressional committees or subcommittees more than a hundred times between 1953 and 1955 and consulted informally with members of the legislative branch on many other occasions.[71]

Lawmakers were in an assertive mood on foreign policy issues after more than a decade of strong presidential leadership. The most striking manifestation of this mood was the "Bricker amendment," named after John W. Bricker, a Republican senator from Ohio.[72] Cosponsored by forty-five Republicans and nineteen Democrats in a resolution introduced in the Senate on 7 January, this proposed constitutional amendment sought to reduce the president's power to conclude agreements with other nations. By early May it appeared certain that the measure would soon be reported to the Senate floor, with the final outcome very much in doubt. The administration also faced a challenge to its budget, the foreign aid and defense portion of which went to Congress on 5 May. To some, including Taft, it did not cut enough from previous Democratic budgets, while to others it reduced defense allotments to dangerous levels.[73] With Styles Bridges, chairman of the Senate Appropriations Committee, reinforcing Taft, passage of anything approximating the administration's plan was far from certain. Eisenhower confronted a difficult struggle in persuading Congress to extend the Reciprocal Trade Agreements Act as well.[74] As if all this were not enough, on 4 May Senator Joseph McCarthy (Wis.) stormed out of a Senate hearing, charging that the State Department was soft on pressing for a halt of traffic into Communist China and the Soviet Union on allied-, usually British-owned vessels.[75]

McCarthy was an extremist, but his tirade symbolized widespread concern in his party about the future of U.S. Asian policy. Many Republicans had long criticized the Democrats for their defensive approach to Asia, and, now that their party had captured the White House, they expected a change. Eisenhower's "unleashing" of Jiang Jieshi in February had raised hopes, yet the follow-up proved less than inspiring, as did the U.S. move to resume negotiations at Panmunjom, which implied a willingness to end the shooting under the present conditions of stalemate.[76] Worse still, on 9 April several newspapers published a story, allegedly based on a high official source (later identified as Dulles), that the administration was considering a UN trusteeship for Taiwan that would entail conceding the mainland to the Communists. The report set off a storm in Washington, and the White House quickly repudiated it.[77] Rumors circulated, however, that once an armistice was signed in Korea, the British and the Indians would engineer PRC admission to the United Nations and the Chinese Communists would increase their intervention in Southeast Asia, where in mid-April the Vietminh invaded Laos.

Thus the Communist proposals at Panmunjom of 7 May came at a time of impatience among many Republicans on Capitol Hill. When Dulles approached Republican members of the Senate Foreign Relations Committee on a tentative response to the Communists, one which would accept an armistice along the current battle line, he found Knowland, Bourke Hickenlooper, and H. Alexander Smith all dubious. Hickenlooper promised he would not "howl" in public; Smith was a team player, who probably could be persuaded; but Knowland remained questionable.[78] If he broke with the administration, much of the Republican Right in the Senate might follow.

Although the administration saw little choice but to go ahead with the armistice line already agreed on, its responsiveness to Rhee and to Republican critics at home was evident in other aspects of the counterproposal presented to the Communists on 13 May.[79] Rhee adamantly opposed parts of a preliminary draft that called for each of the five nations on the repatriation commission to provide custodial forces to supervise prisoners and that placed both Chinese and Korean nonrepatriates under the commission's authority. He refused to allow Communist troops on ROK soil or to turn over Korean nonrepatriates to a neutral state. He also argued that India was not neutral and should not be permitted to send troops to South Korea, even to the off-shore islands. General Clark believed it essential to go along with Rhee, as did generals Harrison and Taylor, Ambassador Briggs, and Robert Murphy, who recently had become political adviser to the UNC in Tokyo. Sir Esler Dening, Britain's ambassador to Japan, felt the same.[80] Faced with the unanimous advice of its representatives in the field and the threat of a Republican revolt at home, the Eisenhower administration gave ground. All Korean nonrepatriates would be "released to civilian status" once an armistice became effective. India alone on the repatriation commission would send troops.

The Eisenhower administration also departed from two provisions in India's UN resolution of the previous fall. First, the UNC now would propose that, after sixty days under the authority of the commission, prisoners who had not chosen repatriation would be "released to civilian status." Second, the commission would function on the basis of unanimity on substantive issues. This meant that, if after sixty days the commission was divided on the desires of an individual prisoner, that prisoner automatically would be released to civilian status in the territory of the detaining side.[81]

While this proposal averted a breach between Rhee and the United States, and between Republicans in the executive and legislative branches in Washington, it produced considerable heat on the Communist side. After studying the proposal overnight, Communist negotiators went to Panmunjom on the 14th armed with a battery of adjectives reminiscent of the early months of armistice talks. "Absolutely unacceptable," "utterly absurd," "indefensible," they cried.[82] Through Beijing radio, New Delhi, and their press correspondents at Panmunjom, the Communists already had circulated hints that the 7 May proposals represented their last concessions.[83] Now they suggested that even those might be withdrawn.[84] Such pressure swung the scales of influence on the Eisenhower administration back toward the NATO allies, but not without the kind of messy public spectacle that had misled Moscow and Beijing so often before.

## The West in Crisis—13–25 May

President Eisenhower observed at a National Security Council meeting on the 13th that the United States was having "considerable difficulties" with its European allies and that relations with the United Kingdom "had become worse in the last few weeks than at any time since the end of the [second world] war"[85] Korea stood at the forefront of issues with the potential for destroying the Western alliance. Few Americans grasped the psychology of Europeans better than Eisenhower did. He understood that many of them feared world war more than anything else, as "it would amount to the obliteration of European civilization." He knew also, as did Europeans, that an escalation of the conflict in Korea, especially if it entailed action beyond the peninsula, represented the one event on the horizon most likely to spread into a global conflagration.[86]

On the day before Eisenhower's remarks, the British opposition leader and former prime minister, Clement Attlee, had addressed the House of Commons. Churchill's speech on the 11th had created irritation in Washington, but Attlee's remarks turned a ripple into a wave. Attlee recited some unpleasant "facts" about the United States. The U.S. system and traditions, he claimed, better suited an "isolationist state" than the world's leading nation. The separation of powers, the lack of unity even within the executive branch, the practice of granting considerable freedom to representatives abroad, the strength of pressure groups at home—all differed sharply from British ways; all made difficult the construction and execution of a coherent foreign policy. At present, Attlee thought, it was hard to tell "who is the more powerful, the President or Senator McCarthy." On Korea, it seemed that General Harrison recently had gone his own way and engaged in unnecessary "haggling" over a reasonable Communist proposal. It was time, Attlee believed, that advisers from other countries contributing forces to the UNC be attached to its negotiating team at Panmunjom. Attlee emphasized Great Britain's need for trade with Communist China and proposed that government's admission to the United Nations following an armistice in Korea.[87]

The Republican Right in the United States was beside itself with indignation. Senator Knowland declared that "our chief ally has joined with certain other UN members in urging a Far Eastern Munich." Rather than submit, the United States "must be prepared to go it alone." Senator McCarthy chimed in that the most disturbing thing about the performance of "Comrade Attlee" was that Prime Minister Churchill and his Conservative Party did not immediately repudiate it. "Let us serve notice on the world today," McCarthy bellowed to spirited applause in Senate galleries, "that we shall never supinely kneel and beg for allies." Senator Everett Dirksen (R., Ill.) suggested that Congress retaliate by cutting foreign aid.[88]

Cooler heads soon came to the fore. Republican senators Smith, John Sherman Cooper, and Alexander Wiley, chairman of the Foreign Relations Committee, all counseled caution.[89] CBS news anchorman Edward R. Murrow provided perspective with the observation that "relations between nations do not depend on speech-making and name-calling. Such relations are determined by cultural, economic, and geographical facts. The British need us to survive and we need them."[90] It was now the task of Eisenhower, as leader of the Western coalition, to put its most important pieces on track. As usual, Korea was central to this process.

To date on Korea, Eisenhower had done a good deal of listening and thinking out loud within the top echelons of his national security apparatus. His tactical maneuvers indicated a preference to end the fighting quickly and without major U.S. losses, but also without making concessions to the enemy. Preliminary staff studies dodged specific cost estimates, but their thrust was that a UNC advance to the narrow neck or the Yalu would require a significant buildup of forces on the peninsula and the use of atomic weapons against China.[91] In part because of public opinion at home, which seemed shaky on enduring new sacrifices in order to achieve total victory, in part because of allied sentiments, and in part because of a personal disposition toward moderation, the president remained dubious about a new military venture.[92] He showed interest in using tactical nuclear weapons against Communist positions at the battlefront, but military officials doubted that such action alone would alter the present balance in Korea.[93] The key questions became these: What were the minimum acceptable conditions for an armistice in Korea? And how long should the United States permit the Panmunjom talks to go on before determining that negotiations could not succeed in attaining these conditions? The May crisis in the Western alliance forced Eisenhower to move toward definitive answers to both questions.

Despite allied lobbying for a return to the Indian resolution, the United States refused to make quick concessions and continued to combine diplomatic activity with military pressure. On the 13th UNC planes commenced attacks on irrigation dams in North Korea, which were crucial to the food supply of Communist troops. By the 16th two dams had been breached, flooding thousands of acres of North Korea's spring rice plantings and temporarily disrupting rail traffic north of Pyongyang.[94] Meanwhile, tired of the propaganda forum the Communists were being provided at Panmunjom and convinced that they had no intention of accepting UNC proposals, General Harrison proposed a four-day recess. With this respite, later extended to the 25th, the Eisenhower administration strove to develop a final negotiating position that would generate support in allied capitals without producing an open breach with powerful Republicans at home or the Rhee regime in South Korea. As acting secretary of state, Walter Bedell Smith remarked in the midst of the process, "We are . . . in a position of trying to reconcile the irreconcilable."[95]

Increasingly, top U.S. officials leaned to the allied side. They knew that, if negotiations broke down over the 13 May proposals, the United States would receive no allied support for new military action. The Joint Chiefs reported on the 19th that, to be successful, such action would require using atomic weapons in Manchuria. In retaliation, the president feared, the Soviets would launch air attacks on a defenseless Japan. General Collins also thought they might hit Pusan and Inchon. In short, global war might result from an all-out U.S. offensive in Korea.[96] The United States stood better prepared than before to fight such a conflict, but its power would be seriously reduced by the defection of European allies and by depletion of its atomic stockpile and bomber fleet in the attack on China.[97] Even without a collapse of NATO, the Soviets could launch major atomic attacks on the United States. According to a National Security Council study, an all-out Soviet offensive could inflict some nine million civilian casualties in the United States and reduce by half the Strategic Air Command's sortie rate.[98] The risks involved in pursuing victory in Korea clearly outweighed the potential gains. As Robert Murphy told General Clark in Tokyo, "If there is a choice between an armistice and difficulties with [the] ROK we must face the latter as the lesser of two evils."[99] Eisenhower agreed, not only with regard to Rhee but also with regard to right-wing Republicans at home.

Washington decided to offer four concessions to the Communists.[100] First, Korean nonrepatriates were not to be released immediately following an armistice, but treated in the same manner as their Chinese brethren. Second, the custodial commission would hold nonrepatriate POWs in custody for ninety rather than sixty days, during which time the two sides would have access to those prisoners. Third, decisions in the commission on individual prisoners would be by majority vote. Finally, prisoners not repatriated by the end of the ninety-day period would be referred to a political conference. Any prisoners remaining after an additional thirty days would be released or have their fate passed on to the UN General Assembly. The third concession provoked the most discussion in Washington, as there was concern that it would result in many of the nonrepatriates eventually being returned to Communist territory. Given the continuing unrest in UNC prisoner-of-war camps and Communist charges of coercion of alleged nonrepatriates, such a result would damage U.S. prestige.[101] Allied pressure to bring the UNC position into line with the Indian resolution prevailed, however, and Washington decided that protection against forced repatriation would have to depend on detailed "terms of reference" for operation of the custodial commission. By restricting the number of Chinese and North Korean officials with access to the prisoners and by regulating the conditions under which interaction occurred, it was hoped that the final number of nonrepatriates to the Communist side would remain close to that produced by the UNC screening of the previous spring.[102]

As their deliberations reached the point of decision, the State Department and the White House kept in close touch with congressional leaders. A major concern on Capitol Hill was that an armistice in Korea would produce overwhelming sentiment at the United Nations for the seating of Communist China. At a news conference on the 14th Eisenhower declared that, "at this moment," he did not believe that the PRC should be admitted to the United Nations after an armistice, but it remained uncertain if U.S. sentiments would carry the day.[103] Five days later Knowland submitted a concurrent resolution to the Senate stating that it was the sense of Congress that, if Communist China were admitted to the United Nations, the United States should withdraw from that organization.[104] In the end, key Republicans decided that their leader deserved some leeway on Korea. In a meeting on the 22d senators Knowland and Smith and Republican Congressman Walter Judd told Bedell Smith that majority rule might suffice in the custodial commission if the allies went along with a tough position on terms of reference.[105] Although relations remained tense between the White House and the Republican leadership in Congress, the administration seemed to have averted an open breach on Korea.[106]

The signs were less hopeful in relations with the ROK. Not only was the United States asking Rhee to make concessions on an armistice; despite the urgings of General Clark and Ambassador Briggs, Washington continued to refuse any guarantee of a mutual defense pact. Although Eisenhower assured Rhee of his commitment to South Korea's security, he argued that recent "ill-considered" statements by ROK officials made it difficult to persuade Congress and the U.S. public of the prudence of such a pact. The one concession offered was to assist the ROK in developing an army of twenty divisions.[107] Rhee was not informed of the new UNC proposals until the morning of the 25th, the very day they were to be presented at Panmunjom. He reacted with shock and adamant opposition, a stance encouraged by his foreign minister,

Pyun Yung Tai.[108] Rhee immediately ordered his delegate to the UNC to boycott the meetings at Panmunjom.[109] General Clark feared that he might release Korean prisoners held below the 38th parallel, a move the UNC was ill-prepared to prevent.[110]

The fear was justified but premature. How much Rhee knew of U.S. plans beyond the proposals of 25 May remains uncertain, but his actions over the next two weeks suggest that he believed it too soon to play his final cards. He may have surmised that the new proposals were as far as the Americans were willing to go and that an even chance existed that the Communists would reject them. Recent hints in the Chinese press indicated that the 7 May proposals represented the final Communist concessions.[111] He probably thought that he still might get what he wanted without taking drastic action.

The Americans, in fact, had decided that their proposals represented their last concessions. If after a week the Communists rejected the proposals and offered no acceptable alternatives, the talks would be "terminated" and the "agreements affecting the Kaesong-Panmunjom-Munsan [neutral] area" voided. The Eisenhower administration did not rule out the possibility of resuming negotiations "at some future time . . . on [the] basis of [the] current draft armistice agreement and currently outstanding UNC proposals," but the momentum in top policymaking circles was clearly toward bringing matters to a head. If negotiations were terminated, the UNC would release "all nonrepatriate POWs" and expand naval and air action against North Korea, including bombings of untouched irrigation dams and attacks on Kaesong, which had become, according to UNC intelligence, "a major advance military base."[112] Eisenhower remained doubtful about a major ground offensive in Korea and atomic attacks on Manchuria, as his top military advisers differed on the appropriate methods of broadening the war. Unlike Truman, Eisenhower never approved the dispatch of atomic weapons to the western Pacific, nor did he discuss publicly the possible use of such weapons in or beyond Korea. Whether on the ground or in the air, a major escalation of UNC operations certainly could not be implemented before the spring of 1954. Yet had negotiations broken down, the president stood ready to approve contingency planning for expanded measures.[113]

Eisenhower appears to have been willing to break the talks in the face of opposition from NATO allies. Following the controversy provoked by Attlee's speech, to be sure, London and Washington both moved to repair the damage. Churchill took a firm hand in the House of Commons to discourage debate on issues that might divide the two governments.[114] General Clark offered to supply Ambassador Dening with a verbatim record of all subsequent meetings at Panmunjom, and, on the 21st, Eisenhower proposed a meeting of U.S., British, and French leaders for the middle of June, a move that received widespread applause in the United Kingdom.[115] Washington consulted "old" commonwealth governments on its new negotiating stance in Korea and even conceded, under pressure, a majority rather than a 4–1 vote as prevailing in the custodial commission. Despite the willingness of the allies to give public support to the new UNC proposals, however, the British and Canadians refused to agree that they should constitute the last concessions to the Communists. Eisenhower warned Churchill of the "most adverse effects upon American public and Congressional opinion" of an allied failure "fully to support a position so clearly reasonable and fair."[116] Washington's instructions to the UNC were to avoid any "public ultimatum," but to make it clear to the Communists that the new proposals represented its "final position."[117] Ambassador Charles Bohlen in Moscow was to arrange to see Molotov and convey the same message.[118] While the rhetoric between London and Washington had cooled down, the seeds of conflict within the Western alliance remained.

### The Communist Perspective—25 May to 17 June

The initial Communist response to the UNC proposal on the 25th was not encouraging. General Harrison emphasized "the gravity of the situation" and suggested a recess until 1 June to give the Communists ample opportunity to consult their governments. General Nam replied that his side could respond by 29 May but would wait the extra time if the UNC desired.[119] Eventually the Communists requested three more days for "administrative reasons," so the talks did not resume until 4 June.[120]

In the interim, the Communist press said little about the UNC proposal. The one exception came on 31 May, when the *People's Daily* in Beijing published an editorial on foreign policy complaining about the Rhee government's recent divulging of the UNC proposal and hinting that the Communists would insist on a return to their own proposal of 7 May.[121]

The Communists were more active on the military front. On 28 May, after three days of heavy shelling, four Communist battalions attacked Turkish units dug in on hills northeast of Panmunjom. After two days of intense combat UNC troops withdrew southward. Then, on 1 and 4 June, the Communists launched major attacks on key hills held by the ROK army in the central and eastern sectors.[122]

These attacks represented the partial implementation of preparations that had begun in April. CPV military commanders doubted the willingness of the Americans to come to terms unless the fighting became more costly to them. Mao still feared enemy amphibious attacks along the North Korean coast, but CPV defensive preparations there during recent months had increased his confidence that such thrusts could be repulsed. Thus major initiatives along the battlefront seemed less risky than they had during the previous year. On 3 April the Central Military Commission in Beijing gave the go-ahead to commence planning. In a reversal of attitudes from the early stages of the war, Chinese field commanders wanted to begin the offensive in early May, whereas Mao insisted that it be postponed until later in the month to give time for careful preparations and to see if the armistice talks bore fruit. On 23 April he wired Peng Dehuai that, "if a cease-fire agreement is reached soon or the truce negotiations requires us to take no more offensive actions, we shall reconsider [the military] action and make a final decision in May."[123] A CPV command instruction of 5 May defined one objective in addition to applying pressure on the enemy in negotiations, namely, to push the armistice line further south to provide "a more favorable strategic position even after the war is over." When the UNC presented its tough counterproposals at Panmunjom on 13 May, CPV commanders wanted to execute their plans immediately, but Beijing insisted that offensive operations be kept on a small scale. Apparently Mao believed that an early offensive on the battlefield might undermine the efforts of U.S. allies to soften Washington's negotiating stance in Korea.[124]

It soon became apparent that Communist attacks of late May were not preliminaries to a massive offensive. On the 4th at Panmunjom, the Communists accepted the essentials of the UNC proposal of 25 May. The wording on the final disposition of nonrepatriate POWs remained ambiguous on whether they could stay in Korea, but it made clear that they would be released after 120 days.[125] UNC negotiators were surprised and delighted that the Communists preferred this solution over referral to the UN General Assembly. Undoubtedly the Communists calculated that they could not win on the issue in the international body. Its airing there would simply publicize the fact that they had given in to nonforcible repatriation and that some prisoners would desert their homeland rather than return to Communist rule. With the Communist concession on the central issue, all that remained were details on the terms of reference, which were resolved over the next four days, and the final drawing of a military demarcation line and demilitarized zone, which the Communists insisted on because of the slight improvement in their position since early 1952. Continuing action on the battlefield indicated that the Communists would seek every small advantage on the second issue—but the operative word here was *small*. After 4 June offensive thrusts by the Communists concentrated on ROK units and were as much a result of doubts of Rhee's willingness to accept an end to the fighting as of a desire to push the final armistice line further south.[126] Without question the Communists wanted an armistice. By the 17th agreement had emerged on the military demarcation line and appeared imminent on the demilitarized zone.[127]

Why did the Communists finally accede to UNC demands on the POW issue? Was the concession a result of pressure by one of the Communist governments on the others or of a consensus among all three? Did U.S. military and diplomatic pressure play a role? In particular, was an alleged U.S. threat of an expanded war and the use of atomic weapons a key factor?

The best guess is that the Communist concession of early June represented part of a larger shift in tactics following Stalin's death, that that shift originated in Moscow but was readily agreed to in Beijing and Pyongyang.[128] Stalin probably intended to approach the Chinese and North Koreans about ending the war before he died, but it is doubtful that the overture occurred before 5 March or that Stalin conceived it in the context of a broad change in tactics. As during the remainder of the war, the DPRK had limited input, eventually influencing its allies only on the question of the fate of Korean prisoners in UNC hands. While the PRC required more careful handling by the Soviet Union, the basic thrust of an initiative on Korea was agreed on between the third and fourth weeks of March during the time the Chinese delegation, headed by Zhou Enlai, was in Moscow to attend Stalin's funeral. A Soviet policy paper of the 19th outlined a new position on POWs in which those resisting repatriation would be transported for screening to a neutral country.[129] In a lengthy meeting on the 21st Zhou worked out an agreement with Soviet leaders on the new initiative. The Chinese and North Koreans would attempt to end the war "on the basis of reasonable compromises with the enemy side."[130] On the 23d Mao wired his negotiators at Panmunjom that, although recent enemy behavior was mostly "provocative and threatening," the UNC proposal of the previous month on the exchange of sick and wounded prisoners might represent an effort "at probing our intention" as a preliminary to making a concession. Thus China should accept the proposal.[131]

The new Soviet leaders had several motives for their initiative. First, a succession struggle was in progress at home, which began with Malenkov at the top of a collective leadership, a hierarchy threatened by Beria until his arrest in June and later, more effectively, by Khrushchev. Political uncertainly provided a strong inducement for Beijing to go along.

The new line had been foreshadowed before the Korean War when both Malenkov and Beria had associated themselves with ideas on Soviet foreign policy that differed from Stalin's inclination during his final years, and certainly from his final testament of the fall of 1952.[132] That testament espoused a continuation of an unwavering attitude toward the West under the assumption that it had and would continue to engender conflict—even war—among the capitalist powers.[133] Although the alternative approach of dividing the West through a less confrontational foreign policy had been downplayed in the Soviet press after early 1950, its quick rise to prominence after Stalin's death suggests that the new leadership had never felt entirely comfortable with the old dictator's course.

These reservations surely mounted as the economic demands placed on the Soviet empire by the Korean War and the accompanying military buildup in the West became all the more burdensome. Overt unrest in eastern Europe was still several months away, but Stalin's successors already perceived a need to moderate the emphasis there on capital construction and heavy industry that the tense international climate seemed to require. Agricultural production had declined significantly during the previous year, and thousands of farmers and businessmen, especially in East Germany, had fled to the West. Food shortages in East Germany were so severe that, in early April 1953, the government instituted rationing.[134] Soviet leaders also may have felt increasing pressure to augment aid to China for the implementation of its First Five-Year Plan, which began during 1953.

The lengthy stay in Moscow of Chinese industrial planners during the months before Stalin's death, the prolonged negotiations for the Sino-Soviet trade agreement signed on 26 March, and the appointment earlier in the month of Vassillii V. Kuznetsov as the new Soviet ambassador to the PRC indicate that complications existed in Sino-Soviet economic relations.[135] In contrast to his predecessor, Alexander S. Panyushkin, Kuznetsov was a high-ranking party official, a full member of the twenty-five-man Presidium. Three days before being appointed ambassador to China, he became a deputy foreign minister.[136] He also had an engineering background. During the spring and summer he would play a pivotal role in negotiating economic and technical assistance agreements for 141 industrial projects in China. Mission accomplished, he returned to Moscow before the end of the year.[137] The Soviet message to the Chinese in March may have been that they could not expect major assistance for their five-year plan unless the Korean War ended.[138]

Compounding the political and economic problems building within the Communist world were indications that the new administration in Washington was not willing to tolerate a continuing stalemate in Korea. These indications did not necessarily dictate concrete concessions, at least not immediately, but they did require diplomatic initiatives to widen cracks in Western unity. Such cracks might put the Americans in a more compromising mood, not only in Korea but elsewhere, especially in Germany. Thus early changes in Soviet foreign policy were more cosmetic than substantive. Even in Korea, the initial concession—that is, to accept screening of POWs—was unlikely to produce many nonrepatriates unless it was combined with well-defined procedures, culminating in the release of prisoners within a reasonable period.

Conceivably the Communists agreed among themselves in March that this last concession might become necessary. What produced its acceptance at Panmunjom, however, was growing unrest in portions of the Soviet empire, plus the emergence over time of a pattern of U.S. intentions and the evolution of negotiations and battlefield events in a manner that enabled the Chinese to give ground without losing face. In the first area Beria's reforms in nationalities policy stirred fears of turmoil in several republics, and the economic course of Walter Ulbricht in East Germany engendered similar concerns about political stability in a key state in the Soviet sphere. In mid-May, despite growing signs of popular unrest and counsels of caution from the Kremlin, Ulbricht increased work norms for industrial laborers in East Germany by 10 percent. On 27 May Soviet leaders met to discuss conditions there. A day later Moscow announced that it had turned East Germany over to civilian control, replacing the commander of Soviet forces with a civilian commissioner. At the beginning of June Ulbricht traveled to Moscow for a series of what turned out to be stormy meetings. Eventually Soviet leaders forced him to adopt reforms that slowed the pace of "forced construction of socialism."[139]

While these events unfolded in the Soviet Union and in Eastern Europe, the United States made it clear that no relaxation of international tension could occur without an armistice in Korea. The Eisenhower administration established this point through public statements by authoritative figures, including the president himself, and through private communications, most notably by Henry Cabot Lodge at the United Nations and Charles Bohlen, who arrived in Moscow as the new U.S. ambassador during the third week of April.[140]

Then, in late May, in the aftermath of the 25 May session at Panmunjom, General Clark addressed a note to generals Kim and Peng conveying his impatience and urging them "to take advantage of the present opportunity." Ambassador Bohlen informed Soviet Foreign Minister Molotov that the new UNC proposals represented "the extreme limit of possible concessions" by his side.[141] General Harrison had assisted in the preparation for this moment through his crisp, authoritative manner in the armistice talks since their resumption a month before.

Preparation also occurred in the realm of military threat. First President Eisenhower declared an end to the U.S. policy of neutralizing the Taiwan strait; next came announcements of the buildup of the ROK army; then came the bombing of irrigation dams in North Korea. Finally, on 21 May, Secretary of State Dulles told Indian Prime Minister Nehru that the collapse of armistice talks probably would lead the United States to "make a stronger rather than a lesser military exertion and this might well extend the area of conflict." Dulles assumed that the message would be passed on to the Chinese.[142] At about the same time, the United States sent warnings to Beijing through the Nationalist government on Taiwan and through UNC officials at Panmunjom that, if an armistice was not concluded in the near future, Eisenhower intended "to remove the restrictions of area and weapons."[143] Whether these threats actually got through to Beijing and Moscow remains uncertain. Nehru denied that he passed on Dulles's statement, although he did urge the Chinese to accept the UNC proposal of 25 May.[144] Nothing has surfaced in China or the Soviet Union to confirm that its leaders received any threatening messages of this kind. Given the weight of other pressures being brought to bear in late May, the explicit threat of an expanded war probably was unnecessary to persuade Beijing and Moscow that the time had come for a final concession on Korea.[145]

Communist intelligence probably indicated that a major UNC offensive before the fall was unlikely, either on the ground in Korea or in the air over Manchuria. If the armistice talks broke down, however, other actions might immediately ensue that would increase the cost to the Communists of continuing the war. The UNC could expand its bombing of North Korean dams and initiate attacks on the heretofore neutral ground around Kaesong, which the Communists had used as a supply base for their forces at the front. The Communists had survived massive UNC bombing of North Korea in the past, to be sure, and they probably could continue to do so. Already they were repairing damaged facilities and lowering the water levels in reservoirs so as to limit flooding if more dams were breached in the future.[146] But the first operation required considerable manpower, and the second reduced the amount of water available for irrigation. Attacks on new targets would add to the burden of an already demoralized population, as well as require new shipments of food and war materials from China and the Soviet Union. The sparseness of the spring harvest in several areas of the former magnified the problem for policymakers in Beijing and Moscow.[147]

Furthermore, if the UNC broke off negotiations at Panmunjom and began a process of gradual military escalation, the Communists would face a choice between continuing an expensive war that they were unlikely to win or making concessions under possibly humiliating conditions. They even might find themselves confronting an enemy with expanded aims. The Communists finally concluded that holding fast on the POW issue was not worth the risk of a continuing and possibly expanded war.

That it took ten days for the Communists to reply to the UNC proposals of 25 May suggests that the eventual concession was by no means a foregone conclusion. In addition to the apparent direction of U.S. policy before the 25th, the Clark and Bohlen messages, the expression of support among U.S. allies for the new proposals, the obvious pressure on Eisenhower to unite the peninsula from within his own party at home and from South Korea, and, less likely, the threats through New Delhi, Taipei, and Panmunjom—all contributed to the Communist decision to give ground.

Even so, not all the pressure on Korea came from the United States, and this fact enabled the Chinese to swallow a major concession. First, at allied urging, the Americans had retreated from their tough terms of 13 May. Ironically, those terms had the useful, if unintended effect of giving the UNC more to concede twelve days later. Then the Chinese timed their concession to come while their forces were on the offensive in Korea, which helped draw attention to the subsequent renegotiation of the armistice line to the Communists' advantage.

But on 18 June, with an armistice apparently only days away, Syngman Rhee thrust himself into the spotlight, calling into question the viability of the agreements so arduously negotiated at Panmunjom—or of any armistice at all.

### The Syngman Rhee Factor

"All hell broke loose, by Rhee's order." So General Clark characterized the release by ROK guards of more than 25,000 of the 35,400 anti-Communist POWs held in camps on the Korean mainland below the 38th parallel. The event occurred in the wee hours of the morning of 18 June. Briefed in advance on what to do once the prison gates opened, the bulk of the prisoners melted into the countryside or nearby cities. Over the next several nights, some 2,000 more prisoners gained their freedom. Fewer than a thousand of the total of more than 27,000 were ever recaptured. Lest anyone doubt the origins of the event, Rhee himself announced, "I have ordered on my own responsibility the release of the anti-Communist Korean prisoners." Over the radio, high ROK officials urged their countrymen to assist the fugitives.[148]

The incident came after two and a half months of growing tension in U.S.-

ROK relations. That tension peaked from 25 May, when, first, the UNC presented new proposals to the enemy and then, ten days later, the Communists largely agreed to them.

The UNC proposals of 25 May were difficult for the South Korean to accept for both substantive and symbolic reasons. They failed to release anti-Communist POWs immediately upon the signing of an armistice, and they permitted Indian troops, which Rhee did not consider neutral, and Communist officials into ROK territory to supervise and question those prisoners, as well as their Chinese counterparts. Largely because the Americans feared Rhee's reaction, they did not inform him of the new offer to the Communists until virtually the moment it was being presented at Panmunjom. To Rhee and Foreign Minister Pyun, this act was a humiliating reminder of America's refusal to treat South Korea as an equal partner in the war. Clark recalled that, after outlining the terms to Rhee, the ROK president became more disturbed than he had ever seen him. "I am deeply disappointed," Rhee told the UN commander. "Your government changes its position often. You pay no attention to the view of the ROK Government."[149] That evening, the combative Pyun told Ambassador Briggs that the proposals represented a "'new Asiatic Munich, except that Korea is not Czechoslovakia' and . . . will never accept them." He implied that "some unilateral action with reference [to] non-repatriate [Korean] prisoners [was] under consideration."[150] Three days later Pyun told another U.S. official that America "had vented all its 'Machiavellianism' on Korea, beginning with [its] 'sell-out' to Japan in 1905–1910." The United States would soon discover that Rhee "represents [the] will of [the] Korean people," Pyun declared menacingly.[151]

With NATO allies standing firm in support of UNC armistice proposals, the United States finally began to give Rhee the attention he deserved. At the end of May Washington decided that Rhee could be offered a mutual security pact.[152] In a letter delivered to the ROK president on 7 June, Eisenhower made the offer to promptly negotiate the pact "after the conclusion and acceptance of an armistice." He also promised economic assistance to rebuild South Korea.[153] Four days later Secretary of State Dulles wrote to Rhee emphasizing the seriousness with which the United States took the goal of peacefully unifying Korea and suggesting that Rhee visit Washington to discuss tactics with top U.S. officials, including President Eisenhower. Rhee was genuinely moved by this overture, but he declined the invitation and proposed that Dulles travel to Korea for talks. Although Dulles regarded such a trip as unwise before Rhee had agreed to accept an armistice, he did decide to send a lesser official, Walter S. Robertson, the assistant secretary of state for the Far East.[154]

Rhee was not about to be mollified by largely symbolic gestures. A lifetime of experience had persuaded him of U.S. unreliability in pursuing Korean goals of unity and independence. At the moment those goals were more inextricably connected than ever, not only because he perceived the Kim Il-sung regime as an extension of the great powers to the north and west, but because the United States was determined to rebuild and rearm Japan. A united Korea would be far better able to resist future incursion by its despised former master to the east. Indeed, a united Korea might even enable the United States to place less reliance on a powerful Japan as a bulwark against Asian communism.[155] Furthermore, within South Korea, Rhee long had taken adamant public stands against an armistice without unification and without a withdrawal of Chinese troops from the peninsula. More recently he had spoken out strongly against permitting Communist and Indian officials and troops below the 38th parallel as members of the neutral nations repatriation commission and of putting anti-Communist Korean prisoners in their hands. Backing down on all these issues would constitute a loss of face that could jeopardize his political survival.[156]

In the aftermath of the Communist concession on the POW issue at Panmunjom, Rhee moved to enhance his ability to act independently of the UNC. He appointed a trusted ally, Lieutenant General Won Yong Duk, as commander of the Provost Marshal General's office, which placed all ROK military police under the Ministry of National Defense rather than the army, whose chief of staff, General Paik Sun-yup, was strongly pro-American. Rhee also called home all ROK army officers serving in the United States.[157]

Rhee acted wisely in taking precautions. His April threats to oppose an armistice had led General Clark to update "Everready," the contingency plan developed during the previous June to take Rhee into protective custody and establish a UNC military government in South Korea.[158] Although in late May Washington rejected the plan for a UNC takeover, it authorized Clark, "in [the] event of internal ROK political or military disaffection against [the] present ROK Government," to "take whatever other steps you deem appropriate to safeguard the integrity and security of your forces."[159] The UN commander took this to mean that, if "the present ROK government cannot be forced to accept the armistice terms," he could establish a more "amenable regime."[160] Yet Rhee's actions of early June rendered the easy execution of a coup against him impossible, making it an extremely unattractive option.[161]

Clark always had been reluctant to risk any move that would produce open conflict between U.S. forces and South Korean troops and military police. Once started, such a conflict would be difficult to contain and certainly would interfere with his primary task of holding the front against the Communists. This concern had led him to oppose implementation of "Everready" during the spring of 1952, and now it made him reluctant even to take precautions against Rhee's possible attempt to release anti-Communist Korean POWs. As he wrote to the Joint Chiefs on 25 May:

> Each of the nine separate locations on the mainland holding Korean non-repatriates has a U.S. Commander with a small staff of U.S. administrative and technical personnel. ROKA [Republic of Korea Army] security battalions provide the overwhelming majority of actual guard forces. While there would be a better chance of maintaining control of the situation if these ROKA units were replaced with

U.S. troops ... any [such] action ... now would only irritate an already sensitive situation. It would be particularly unfortunate if U.S. troops were employed in forceful action against Koreans whose only motive is to resist return to Communist control.[162]

When Korean nonrepatriates began their escape on 18 June, they met with little initial resistance.

Despite the awareness of U.S. officials that Rhee might act to free the Korean nonrepatriates, his actual move came as a shock. Clark wrote to Rhee that the action represented "a unilateral abrogation" of his "personal commitment" to assign "command authority over all land, sea, and air forces" of the ROK to the UN command and of his several reassurances in recent weeks that he "would not take unilateral action ... until full discussion with me."[163] President Eisenhower issued a similar reprimand and warned that, "unless you are prepared immediately and unequivocally to accept the authority of the UN Command to conduct the present hostilities and bring them to a close, it will be necessary to effect another arrangement."[164]

Technically the charge of perfidy was unfounded. Following the appointment of General Won as Provost Marshal, Rhee had put Won in control of ROK security forces at the prison camps. Won came under the authority of the Ministry of Defense rather than the ROK army, which was attached to the UN command. In any event, as Rhee wrote Clark, "if I had revealed to you in advance my idea of setting them [the prisoners] free, it would have only embarrassed you ... [and] spoiled the plan."[165]

For the United States, whether Rhee had broken earlier commitments was academic compared to other problems his action created. The most obvious question was how the Communists would respond. Would they break the talks or demand the impossible, that the escapees from the POW camps be recaptured and turned over to the neutral commission? Rhee complicated the matter by claiming in his press release that "most of the United Nations authorities with whom I have spoken about our desire to release the prisoners are with us in sympathy and principle."[166] The claim was accurate, and it extended all the way to the top, a point that undoubtedly haunted Clark.[167] Its public exposition by Rhee could only increase Communist suspicions that the United States had participated in a conspiracy with the ROK to subvert the agreement negotiated at Panmunjom.

The Communist reaction was not the only concern for the United States. Rhee's letter to Clark revealed that the ROK president was by no means content with his act of defiance. "When the armistice is signed, you and General Taylor will be ... ordered to carry out the terms of [the] armistice," he wrote. "According to the terms, the armies on both sides shall drop back two kilometers.... The ROKA may not be allowed to draw back along with their friendly forces.... Personally I hate it like a poison to tell you I shall have to withdraw the ROKA from your command, but things standing where they are now, there seems to be no alternative."[168] These words represented at once an explicit warning and an invitation to the "full and frank discussion" he had promised earlier.

After an initial fit of temper, President Eisenhower concluded that such talks were essential. Under the present conditions and after all the effort expended by the United States over the past three years, it could not simply withdraw and concede South Korea to the Communists. In a meeting with Dulles on the 18th, ROK Prime Minister Paek Tu Chin and Ambassador You pleaded that Robertson's impending visit to South Korea not be canceled or deferred.[169] After some hesitation, the Eisenhower administration went along. Robertson left Washington on the 22d with instructions to discuss in depth a mutual defense treaty, economic assistance along the lines recommended recently by Dr. Henry Tasca following his special mission to South Korea, and tactics for a post-armistice political conference.[170] On the last point, Robertson was to assure Rhee that the United States would not "become so entangled with the United Nations . . . that we cannot stand shoulder to shoulder with the ROK." But while Robertson was to reaffirm America's determination to work for a united Korea, he was to reject the idea of a withdrawal of foreign forces on the signing of an armistice. The continued pressure of U.S. forces during a political conference, he was to argue, would provide leverage in the quest for unification.[171] This point grew out of a proposal under consideration in the State Department, which provided for unification of the peninsula under the ROK, with the elimination of all foreign troops and bases serving as bait for the Soviets and the Chinese.[172] In a deeper sense the U.S. position against the withdrawal of foreign forces derived from concern that leaving ROK and DPRK forces alone, staring at each other across the narrow demilitarized zone in the middle of the peninsula, would constitute an invitation for further trouble.

By the time Robertson arrived in Korea on the 25th Rhee had presented to Clark "rough outlines" of his negotiating position. The ROK would not sign an armistice, but under certain conditions it would keep its forces under the UNC. The second and third conditions presented minimal difficulties, as they called for a mutual defense pact along the lines of those already concluded by the United States "with other nations of the Pacific Area" and extensive U.S. military and economic aid to the ROK. The key point in the fourth condition, that "no foreign armed force shall enter the Republic of Korea with a view to guarding prisoners of war, nor shall any Communist indoctrinators," would require renegotiating a portion of item 4 with the Communists. This might not prove an insurmountable task if Rhee agreed to the movement of prisoners to the demilitarized zone before their transfer to the custody of the neutral commission. Rhee also showed restraint in assuring Clark that he would not press for the immediate release of the more than eight thousand anti-Communist Koreans remaining in POW camps.[173] This was crucial both because of the danger of clashes between South Korean guards and U.S. soldiers who had been rushed to those camps and because the success of the effort to halt the breakout while significant numbers of prisoners remained in custody was important in persuading the allies and the Communists of America's good faith. Nonetheless, the first of Rhee's conditions presented a major stumbling block, as Rhee demanded that the post-armistice political conference "sit no longer than 90 days." If it broke up without providing for a withdrawal of Chinese forces from the peninsula and "the reunification of Korea," the armistice would "become null and void" and the United States would give "Air and Naval support" for the ROK "advance north."[174] It was Robertson's unenviable task to persuade Rhee to bend on his first and fourth conditions.

Robertson landed in Korea on the third anniversary of the outbreak of war, just after Rhee had delivered a passionate speech against the present armistice agreement to several hundred thousand of his subjects. In a voice choked with emotion, the president demanded the withdrawal of Chinese troops from the peninsula, plus a security guarantee from the United States. Otherwise South Koreans must "unite in spirit and march indomitably, whether others understood us or not."[175] Although Rhee had striven in his public campaign to impress the Americans with Korean sentiments rather than to stir anti-Americanism, his calls for national unity and independence could not help but generate tension between his countrymen and U.S. and UN personnel. From Pusan, the *New York Times* reported a "noticeable change in attitude," as Korean dockworkers threatened to strike, ROK military policemen became "sharper in their manner," and Korean mess boys walked out of their jobs in a U.S. officers' club.[176] From Seoul, the same source observed that Koreans "who have been pushed around generally and looked down upon by the UN troops are beginning to show that they resent it more."[177] For an American entering into this setting, the task was to resist being intimidated without resorting to bluster.

Walter S. Robertson was a former investment banker from Richmond, Virginia. Like many successful businessmen in the United States, he had turned to government service during World War II, first heading the Lend-Lease mission to Australia and later becoming an economic adviser in China. In 1946 he worked there with George C. Marshall on his unsuccessful effort to mediate the civil conflict. Robertson was a stern opponent of Asian communism and a critic of Truman administration policy in the region. Active in "Democrats for Eisenhower" during the fall of 1952, his appointment to head the Far East Division in the State Department constituted both a reward for service to the Eisenhower campaign and a reflection of the Republican administration's determination to at least appear to chart a new course in the western Pacific.[178] No expert on the situation in Korea, his militant anticommunism made him instinctively sympathetic to Rhee, and his roots in the U.S. South gave him a disinclination to confrontation. Since General Clark and Ambassador Briggs were feeling the strain of dealing with President Rhee under tense conditions over several weeks, the situation demanded a fresh face from Washington. Not only did Robertson's arrival enhance Rhee's prestige at home, making it easier for him to give ground; it also enabled Clark to apply subtle pressure from the background while the new man listened to Rhee's tirades and nudged him toward accommodation. At one point the Korean leader burst out to his U.S. visitor, "You are like a hand extended to a drowning man. Please help us find a way out."[179] That was a hopeful sign, but the search was not to prove an easy one.

Washington gave Clark and Robertson considerable tactical leeway. The UN commander could resume armistice talks, which the Communists had recessed on the 20th, and negotiate changes in the draft agreement as he saw fit so long as he adhered "to [the] principle on non-forced repatriation" and undertook "no obligation to the Commies . . . to use force against [the] ROKs to insure their compliance with armistice terms." Clark should not withdraw or agree to withdraw UN forces from Korea, but he could lead Rhee to believe that such a withdrawal or agreement was imminent unless Rhee accepted an armistice.[180]

The Rhee-Robertson talks made little initial progress. On 29 June, after Rhee pushed for an aide-mémoire totally unacceptable to the United States, Robertson informed him that it could not serve as a basis for discussions. Clark applied additional pressure by informing the Korean that the UNC planned to proceed with armistice negotiations.[181] To date the Americans had made only two concessions. First, they agreed to approach the Communists about moving anti-Communist Korean POWs to the demilitarized zone for release to the neutral commission. Anti-Communist Chinese prisoners, however, would be screened by the commission on Cheju Island, where they were presently being held. Second, negotiations for a mutual security pact would commence immediately. For his part Rhee had dropped his demand for the immediate withdrawal of Chinese troops, but he wanted all POWs transported to the demilitarized zone and the pact to be concluded before an armistice. More important, he pushed for an open-ended U.S. commitment "to make democratic Korea strong enough to defend its own strategic peninsula . . . against Communist aggression without depending upon United States manpower." He continued to insist that if a post-armistice political conference did not produce procedures for unifying the peninsula, the United States would join the ROK in a military campaign to achieve the objective.[182]

While Robertson, as he later recalled, developed "almost an involuntary admiration for this old man's absolute, complete, fanatical dedication to saving the independence of his country," Clark grew increasingly irritated with Rhee's "dilatory" tactics.[183] To U.S. publisher Roy W. Howard he wrote that "Rhee is as unscrupulous a dictator as ever lived. . . . Through duplicity and underhanded methods, [he] blocked the armistice which was about to be consummated. . . . During the time that he has blocked an armistice, we have had approximately 25,000 battle casualties."[184] In early July, as Robertson cautioned Washington against issuing statements critical of Rhee and solicited a joint message promoting the U.S. position from such Rhee supporters as General Van Fleet and Senator Knowland, Clark commenced some pressure tactics of his own.[185] On the 1st he held a conference in Tokyo of U.S. military leaders in the UNC, plus General Collins, who had accompanied Robertson from Washington. He followed this action with the movement to Korea of some new U.S. units stationed in Japan, which could help cover a U.S. withdrawal in a hostile environment, with the consolidation of the remaining anti-Communist Korean POWs, and with the slowdown of supplies and equipment to Korea, including the actual suspension of shipments designed to activate the last four divisions in the ROK army's twenty-division program. Eventually he initiated talks between U.S. and ROK officers to discuss the transfer of authority in the event of a U.S. withdrawal.[186] On the 9th, by which time the Communists had agreed to resume plenary meetings at Panmunjom and Robertson had informed Rhee of his intention to leave Korea soon, the ROK leader complained of U.S. psychological warfare tactics aimed at alienating South Koreans "from the government" and causing defections "among his officers and troops."[187]

The Americans never reached complete agreement with Rhee, but Robertson finally received a letter from him that Dulles regarded as a "satisfactory basis for entering into [an] armistice." Problems that remained could be discussed further once the fighting stopped.[188] The letter emerged only after the Americans agreed to press the Communists to accept movement of all the nonrepatriate POWs to the demilitarized zone, where personnel of the neutral commission would determine their final disposition, and after they gave assurances regarding final negotiations for and ratification of a mutual defense pact following an armistice. Rhee in turn stated that, "although we cannot sign [a] truce, we shall not obstruct it, so long as no measures or actions taken under [the] armistice are detrimental of our national survival."[189] Rather than insisting that, if the political conference failed to produce reunification, U.S. forces join with the ROK army in achieving the objective by force, Rhee wrote that "we should like to have specific assurances of moral and material support for an effort with our own armed forces to repel aggressors from Korea."[190] Those assurances never came, and for some time hence Rhee would keep the United States on edge. Yet with the resumption of meetings at Panmunjom on the 10th and Robertson's departure on the 11th, the worst of the storm seemed to have passed.

Outside the peninsula, Rhee's release of Korean prisoners was widely condemned as an irresponsible act by a fanatical nationalist.[191] The move postponed an armistice by several weeks, increasing casualties by tens of thousands and adding millions of dollars in the destruction of property. Rhee's action could have prevented an armistice altogether and produced not only a continuing but an expanded war of inestimable cost. Certainly Rhee was willing to provoke such a conflict if he thought it could achieve his dream of a united country under his control.

What was irresponsible was not necessarily irrational. Rhee was a gambler, but, despite his emotional outbursts about national suicide, he was a shrewd politician who understood, as General Clark put it, "the psychological whammy" he had on the United States. "He knew," the UN commander recalled, "that no matter what happened we could not, after three years of war, after all the blood and treasure we lost, let Korea go to the Reds by default because of a quarrel 'in the family.'"[192] He also knew that Clark and Ambassador Briggs agreed with him about the release of anti-Communist Korean prisoners and that the former had declined to reinforce the camps holding them following Foreign Minister Pyun's hint on 25 May of impending actions there.[193] After the crisis within South Korea during the previous summer, he surely calculated that Clark would hesitate to oust him from power. To be on the safe side, the ROK president shifted personnel so as to reinforce his hold on the government and the police.

Following the release of Korean POWs, Rhee took care to prevent the crisis from escalating out of control. When events in and around the camps led to incidents between Americans and South Koreans, he called a halt to break-out attempts.[194] In negotiations with U.S. officials, Rhee left the most provocative comments to the abrasive Pyun, always positioning himself to mend fences.[195] When the Americans upped the pressure on Rhee and showed evidence of having reached the limits of their bargaining position, the ROK president gave sufficient ground to avoid risk of a total break. Had he been privy to U.S. deliberations, he probably would have held out longer, but with the limited information he had, Rhee concluded rationally that prolonging the crisis might lead to either a successful coup or a U.S. withdrawal.

The threat of withdrawal and the potential internal consequences of that threat were all the more compelling in light of the ROK army's recent performance. In a Communist offensive of mid-June concentrated on ROK forces east of Kumhwa, Chinese units drove the enemy back an average of nearly two miles along an eight-mile front. More limited attacks late in the month took less of a toll, but the Communist buildup on the central and eastern fronts made it apparent that mid-July was likely to see an offensive even larger than the one staged a month earlier.[196] Rhee could not have been optimistic about the result, either on the battlefield or on the spirit of his subordinates in the government and army.

By 9 July, however, Rhee had derived substantial advantages from his actions. In a concrete sense, he got the United States to insist at Panmunjom that no Communist or Indian officials or troops attached to the Neutral Nations Supervisory Commission operate in South Korea. Although he received assurances of U.S. willingness to negotiate a mutual defense pact before the breakout of 18 June, the Americans greatly expedited matters following the event. Although he ultimately received far less than he wanted, Rhee forced the Americans to bargain openly with him, thereby achieving great prestige at home. Perhaps most important of all, he ensured that his ally would never again take him for granted. In a letter to Eisenhower of 27 July, he thanked and congratulated his U.S. counterpart "for the statesmanlike vision with which you have brought the relationships of your powerful nation and of our weaker one onto a basis of honest mutuality and two-way cooperation."[197] The months that followed would demonstrate the substance of this characterization. Whether on the matter of military and economic aid or on strategy for achieving unification short of the use of force, the United States proved more attentive than ever before in working with its ally.

### The Communist Response

Rhee's accommodation of sorts with the Americans did not ensure an armistice. The question remained as to what the Communists intended. Would they use Rhee's release of twenty-seven thousand POWs as an excuse for continuing the war indefinitely or would they, after mandatory expressions of outrage and delays to exploit the incident's propaganda value, still come to terms?

In the immediate aftermath of the POW breakout on 18 June, the Communists showed little inclination to reveal their intentions. Generals Kim and Peng addressed a letter to Clark on the 19th, characterizing the prisoners as having been coerced into leaving the camps by "the South Korean Government and Army directly controlled by your side." The Communist leaders posed three questions: "Is the United Nations Command able to control the South Korean Government and Army? If not, does the armistice in Korea include the Syngman Rhee clique? If it is not included, what assurance is there for the implementation of the armistice agreement on the part of South Korea?" They concluded with an ominous assertion: "If it [the ROK] is included, then your side must be responsible for recovering immediately all the 25,952 prisoners of war . . . who were released and retained under coercion and to be press-ganged into the South Korean Army, and your side must give assurance that similar incidents absolutely will not recur in the future."[198] Although the UNC quickly reinforced the camps with U.S. soldiers, who recaptured a few hundred of the escapees and, in the effort to prevent further breakouts, killed 61 prisoners and wounded 116, it considered the recapture of the bulk of the escapees an impossible task.[199]

The Communist response to Rhee's action could have been more extreme. Although Communist laborers at Panmunjom halted construction of a building to house the armistice-signing ceremony and the Communist press charged the Americans with connivance in the POW escape, no threat emerged to break off negotiations. An editorial of the 23d in the Beijing *People's Daily* merely stated that the incident "has delayed the signing of the Korean armistice agreement."[200] Propaganda broadcasts out of the Chinese capital no longer emphasized U.S. complicity. Rather, their attacks were directed almost solely at Rhee and his government.[201] More encouraging still was a report delivered to Washington on the 29th through the Swedish embassy. Soviet Ambassador Kuznetsov in Beijing had told the Swedish ambassador there that the demand for the recapture of the escaped POWs "should not be taken literally." In Moscow Vishinsky gave the impression to the Swedish ambassador to the Soviet Union that the Kremlin still desired an armistice.[202]

Events soon confirmed the Soviet message. On the 29th General Clark answered the letter of the Communist field commanders, denying foreknowledge of the POW breakout and stating that recovery of the 27,000 escapees would not be possible, just as it "would be [impossible] for your side to recover the 50,000 South Korean prisoners 'released' by your side during the course of the hostilities." Nor could he guarantee that the ROK would accept or adhere to an armistice, but he promised that the UNC would strive to achieve such cooperation. Clark called for the resumption of the armistice talks, which had been recessed nine days earlier.[203] The Communists took until 7 July to answer, in part to approximate Clark's delay in responding to their earlier letter, in part to gauge the trend of negotiations between Rhee and the Americans, and in part to prepare for one last military offensive. On hearing of the breakout of Korean prisoners, General Peng had wired Mao proposing a postponement of the armistice and another offensive thrust against the ROK army. Mao agreed, informing Peng that "wiping out 10,000 South Korean troops is very necessary."[204] Argumentative and occasionally bordering on being insulting, the Communist communiqué of 7 July nonetheless accepted the proposal to resume the talks.[205] Plenary sessions reconvened at Panmunjom on 10 July.

General Nam quickly took the offensive in the renewed negotiations, pressing for explicit UNC assurances on ROK adherence to an armistice and for the recovery of the escaped prisoners. General Harrison was unyielding on the latter point, and on the former he would go no further than to assure the Communists that the UNC would not support the ROK if it broke an armistice. He also revealed that the ROK had agreed to work with the UNC in pursuit of common objectives. The Communists remained dissatisfied with UNC responses. By the 15th Harrison had had enough, charging the Communists with stalling through "a farcical repetition of questions which have already been answered clearly and positively." Meanwhile, he pointed out, "Your side has launched the largest [military] attack since the truce talks began two years ago. . . . Either you need more time to consider our assurances, or you are willfully preventing achievement of the armistice. In either case these meetings are serving no useful purpose."[206]

The second possibility hit closer to the mark. On the night of the 13th, for reasons of both prestige and future deterrence, elements of six CPV divisions attacked ROK positions on the central front. Communist forces pushed the enemy backward up to six miles before U.S. reinforcements helped to stop the drive and regain lost ground.[207] Communist negotiators were not about to come to terms at Panmunjom until the momentum of the military offensive had been halted.

By the 19th such clearly was the case, and the Communists initiated final steps toward an armistice. After outlining his understanding of UNC commitments and reserving the right to refer the question of the escaped Korean prisoners to the political conference, Nam proposed that staff officers work out the remaining details. The UNC agreed after insisting that a date be set for the signing of the armistice. The Communists settled on the 24th, conditional on completion of all preparations.[208] Predictably, those preparations took longer than anticipated, as the two sides continued to bicker over details.[209] On the 27th, however, the signing occurred, and what has been labeled the twentieth century's "nastiest little war" finally drew to a close.[210]

Why did the Communists come to terms? Why, with the Americans refusing to recapture the escaped prisoners or to give definitive assurances of South Korean compliance to an armistice, did the Communists agree to stop the shooting? Continued UNC pressure on the North from the air and sea surely played a role in reminding the Communists of the continuing costs of war, as did the expenditure of manpower and material during the June and July offensives. On the other hand, the gains in real estate secured during those offensives helped to maintain face in the midst of embarrassing concessions at Panmunjom. Those gains against ROK forces, combined with what appeared to be a genuine U.S. effort to restrain the South Korean leadership, made the success of an armistice a distinct possibility.[211] The Communists probably calculated, as did Clark, that further delay would play into Rhee's hands.

That the Communists refused to take the chance of that happening had at least as much to do with events outside Korea. June was a tense month inside the Soviet empire. It began with demonstrations and riots in Czechoslovakia, sparked by a currency reform that virtually wiped out the savings of a substantial portion of the population. Czech authorities suppressed the disorders, but the economic conditions that had provoked them remained.[212] Then, on 16 June, after months of unrest among workers, demonstrations broke out in East Berlin, quickly spreading to 250 towns throughout East Germany. Authorities restored order, this time through a combination of repression and the promise of reforms. Communist officials in Berlin and Moscow blamed Western subversion for the outbreaks, yet Kremlin leaders understood that, throughout eastern Europe, the only way to head off continuing unrest was to institute broad reforms.[213] These would require a reallocation of resources to the civilian sector, as well as extensive Soviet assistance.[214]

Instability within the Kremlin matched that of eastern Europe. Since Stalin's death in Moscow, jockeying for position at the top of the Soviet hierarchy had centered on Beria's quest for supreme power. On 27 June Western observers noticed that a number of tanks and truckloads of soldiers suddenly appeared in Moscow and that Beria failed to attend the ballet at the Bolshoi Theater with other members of the party Presidium. Two weeks later *Pravda* announced his arrest and dismissal from all posts.[215]

The uncertainty created by events in Moscow and eastern Europe and the obvious need to devote resources to civilian economies provided a compelling reason to conclude the fighting in Korea. This was as much the case in Beijing as in Moscow. As the Swedish embassy in China reported during the second week of July, PRC leaders were more anxious than ever for an armistice. Beria's arrest and the trouble in East Germany had shocked them, reinforcing the belief that the country needed a respite from foreign adventures to concentrate on internal economic development.[216]

## REACTIONS AND PROSPECTS

James Reston of the *New York Times* wrote that "seldom in the long story of human conflict has an armistice rested on such bad faith." Reston had traveled to Panmunjom to witness the signing, and he thought representatives of the two sides looked as if they "were signing a declaration of war instead of a truce."[217] As the correspondent for the *Times of London* reported, "There was no pretense at an exchange of courtesies, or even of civility."[218] The delegations entered from opposite sides the large bamboo and wooden structure built especially for the ceremony. There were no bows or handshakes; generals Nam and Harrison barely glanced at each other. The South Koreans did not even show up. The armistice went into effect only twelve hours after the signing, so the contestants continued to pound each other, the Communists with their ground artillery at the front, the UNC with their air and naval power penetrating well into North Korea.[219]

"Vigilance" was the operative word on both sides. In a message aired over Radio Beijing and reinforced in a *People's Daily* editorial, generals Kim and Nam declared that their armies had won "a glorious victory" for the forces of peace and democracy, but they also warned them to "tighten their vigilance" against a possible renewal of aggression from the South.[220] General Clark struck a more somber note, suggesting that the occasion was "a time for prayer, that we may succeed in our difficult endeavor to turn the armistice to the advantage of mankind." "If we extract hope from this occasion," he warned, "it must be diluted with recognition that our salvation requires unrelaxing vigilance and effort."[221] In the United States President Eisenhower delivered a five-minute address to a nationwide radio and television audience. "We have won an armistice on a single battleground, not peace in the world," he emphasized. "We may not now relax our guard nor cease our quest."[222]

For the short term the danger for a renewal of hostilities came from the South. Although on the morning of the armistice Rhee told generals Clark and Taylor and Ambassador Briggs that he was preparing a message for the Korean people informing them that he would "cooperate with the armistice," the statement itself, which appeared on the 28th, was far less than the Americans wanted.[223] If the upcoming political conference failed to unify the peninsula, Rhee declared, "we and the whole world will come to fully realize the futility of peaceful means in solving our problems and then we will be able to pursue our own method of achieving unification with the complete sympathy of world opinion."[224] A day later, in an hour-long interview with Reston, Rhee asserted that it was "inconceivable" that the United States would fail to renew the fighting if the Communists refused to accept unification. The armistice was only "temporary," he insisted, as Korean issues could not be resolved through peaceful means. He warned the Americans not to press him to make concessions to the Communists as they had with Jiang Jieshi in the aftermath of World War II.[225]

Hours before, in Washington, John Foster Dulles had announced that he would soon fly to Korea to conclude negotiations for a mutual defense pact and to discuss a variety of other post-armistice issues. He gave no indication that the United States would support Rhee in any renewal of hostilities, but he did suggest that no concessions would be made to achieve a unified Korea regarding China's seat at the United Nations or the embargo on strategic goods to the PRC. In both cases he referred to a declaration to that effect made earlier in the month at the end of a meeting in Washington of British, French, and U.S. foreign ministers.[226] He also revealed that the United States had agreed to walk out of the political conference after ninety days "should the Communists make it unproductive and use it as a cover for subversive activities."[227]

Rhee's and Dulles's comments sparked a good deal of controversy. Robert Alden of the *New York Times* observed from Seoul that "Dr. Rhee's attitude has been almost patronizing—as if he were giving a little child a bit of candy." Some diplomats there believed that the ROK president had "been encouraged to continue his fight by the steady play of attention that he is receiving from Washington as well as continuing visits to his residence by high U.S. . . . officials."[228]

Receiving far less attention was the fact that the UNC withdrawal from the battlefront to form the southern end of the demilitarized zone had proceeded on schedule, reaching completion seventy-two hours after the signing of the armistice. ROK forces participated in this process just as it had in all the others.

People in the United Kingdom were more interested in Dulles's comments, which to them virtually precluded resolution of the Korean issue. Kingsley Martin, the editor of the London-based *New Statesman and Nation*, warned "that it is dangerous to allow a cease-fire line to harden into a frontier," pointing to the examples of Kashmir and Palestine. He reminded readers "that India and Pakistan cannot indefinitely endure the tension of indecision in Kashmir, while relations between Israel and its neighbors remain dangerously bitter on a frontier that was never intended to do more than recognize a temporary *fait accompli*." Korea would "long remain a danger spot," Martin predicted, "unless from the beginning the United Nations can at least lay down the basis of a program for eventual political collaboration between North and South"; "any hope" for this outcome depended on the admission into the United Nations of the PRC and the lifting of the trade embargo against it.[229] Such views received support in the British press and in both houses of Parliament.[230]

Lester Pearson, still president of the UN General Assembly, had already called for the reconvening of that body on 17 August to discuss the political conference on Korea. While the British government resisted pressure from the Labor opposition to break openly with the United States over China, Lord Salisbury, the acting foreign secretary (with Eden still out of commission), did declare publicly on 29 July that India should participate in the political conference.[231] Rhee was sure to resist that position, and the United States, preoccupied with restraining him on more important issues and not too keen on adding participants beyond the peninsula, was likely to back him up.[232] So within days of the conclusion of an armistice in Korea, the Western allies seemed headed for another difficult round of diplomacy in New York. The *Times of London* editorialized that "Moscow and Beijing must be rubbing their hands more gleefully than for many a long day, reminding each other that peace hath its victories no less renowned than war."[233]

More likely, the Communists breathed a sigh of relief. They had their own internal problems, and the tactics adopted following Stalin's death were in part designed to provide a respite to deal with those problems. The armistice in Korea represented a success of those tactics, and Moscow and Beijing showed no sign of altering course. A *Pravda* editorial of the 28th declared that the armistice proved "that there are no unresolved international issues which cannot be settled by negotiations, by agreement among the interested parties." It expressed a vital concern for the unification of Korea, which should be achieved, to repeat an old refrain, by "the Korean people . . . themselves, without foreign interference."[234] A *People's Daily* editorial out of Beijing lauded "the spirit of negotiation" that had borne fruit in Korea and predicted that "it will not be impossible either to seek a peaceful settlement of other international disputes and long-standing problems."[235]

Such invitations to bargain were certain to strike a responsive chord on issues other than Korea. In Japan, for example, the lower house of the legislature voted unanimously to demand wider trade with the PRC, and Foreign Minister Katsuo Okayaki conceded that, while nothing should be done to undermine the government on Taiwan, trade with the mainland should be considered from a "new angle."[236] Since the armistice would produce a reduction of orders for military supplies from the ROK, Japan had little choice but to seek new markets for its finished products. The armistice in Korea and the interest of the Communist powers in negotiations were also likely to increase the opposition in Japan to large-scale rearmament and perhaps even to the stationing of U.S. forces on the main islands.[237]

In western Europe the armistice in Korea, along with the continuing Soviet peace campaign and the troubles in eastern Europe, threatened to halt the military buildup altogether. As one prominent U.S. analyst observed, the "grand coalition" nurtured so assiduously by the United States since the late 1940s remained incomplete: the European army was "deader than a dodo"— an overstatement—and Chancellor Adenauer, who had followed the U.S. lead in pushing for West German rearmament before negotiations for reunification, confronted an uncertain fate in upcoming elections.[238] On the southern and eastern flank, the conservative government in Italy had just fallen; the Trieste issue continued to separate Italy and Yugoslavia, restricting the latter's coordination of defense plans with NATO; and the Soviets had begun efforts to rebuild bridges to Belgrade, Athens, and Istanbul.[239] U.S. Ambassador Bohlen wrote from Moscow early in July that Soviet moves offered "considerably more dangers than the standard propaganda gestures which we have seen since the end of the [second world] war."[240]

Yet many outside the Communist bloc saw the results of Korea as unlikely to disappear now that the fighting had stopped. In Washington Dulles argued that the United States and, by implication, the entire "Free World," were "infinitely safer" than before. First, the war had established the principle of "collective security [as] . . . something that works." The North Koreans had attacked in June 1950 only because they thought the United States would not fight. The United States had proven them wrong, and in the process North Korea had lost some 1,500 square miles of territory and had seen its cities turned into "hollow husks," its army virtually annihilated, and its population depleted and impoverished. Second, the armistice agreement had established the principle of political asylum, "which has never before been applied to prisoners of war." As a result of U.S. insistence on this principle, Communist armies would be "far less dependable than ever before" and their governments would be "far less likely to use . . . [them] for aggression."[241]

Although most commentators outside the United States ignored Dulles's second point, they commonly dwelled on the first, albeit without the graphic descriptions of North Korea's plight. Amid opposition pressure in the House of Commons to reveal recent understandings between London and Washington, British Minister of State Selwyn Lloyd took time out to extol the UN achievement in Korea: "For the first time since the formation of the United Nations," he noted, "member states have taken up arms in collective resistance to aggression, and the joint action has been successful."[242] In France newspapers of the Right and Center lauded the UN effort in Korea. *Franc-Tireur* described it as "reaffirming a principle, that of preventing armed aggression. What the League of Nations could not do for Ethiopia, the United Nations did for Korea." "What would have happened if Truman had given a free hand to the Communists in Korea?" *L'Aurore* asked rhetorically. "It seems clear enough to us. After Korea it would have been Indochina. After Indochina it would have been the whole of Southeast Asia. And what would have then prevented the Communists, faced with disarmed nations, from attacking Europe?"[243] Turkish Premier Adnan Menderes, speaking as representative for one of the most determined contributors to the UNC among the small powers, declared that troops fighting under the international banner in Korea had "defended . . . their respective homelands."[244] Israeli commentators, whose government had departed from its policy of neutrality to support the UN stand in Korea, celebrated the international body's achievement there in preventing aggression and protecting small nations.[245] Yugoslavia had not sent troops to Korea, but it had privately supported the UN cause there while playing a vital role in resisting Soviet bloc expansion in the Balkans. In a lengthy editorial in *Borba*, the Communist Party newspaper, the Tito government endorsed the theme so prevalent in the West. The Soviet Union had used the Korean War "to 'feel the pulse' of the peace-loving world, to see to what extent it could develop its hegemonistic activity without being countered." The editors criticized Washington's identification of efforts in Korea with "a struggle for the restoration of the regimes of Syngman Rhee, Jiang Jieshi and others" but they commended the West for learning "from its experience prior to World War II . . . that it would be fatal to permit a repetition of Munich."

*Borba* concluded with a note of caution and, in doing so, expressed a view common in the Arab and Asian worlds:

> [The Korean War was] not an isolated episode. . . . It developed . . . because of the abnormal situation in Asia where people and nations very often feel inferior toward the "white," highly developed countries. . . . The solution of the Korean problem should be . . . [part of] the process of normalizing affairs throughout Asia and the Far East, in which the problem of the PRC takes one of the most important positions. . . . It must be made possible for the peoples of Asia to appear on a basis of full equality with the other nations of the world.[246]

Important elements of the U.S. administration, including Eisenhower and Dulles, appreciated the force of this view, but they already had used up much political capital at home to bring Rhee into line with an armistice. That effort had helped to mobilize pro-Jiang forces in Congress and in the Republican party in resistance to a "sell-out" of Nationalist China. Furthermore, the problem in Asia, from Washington's perspective, was not simply one of bringing peoples there into a position of full equality with the West. It also included the problem of Asians themselves treating one another as equals. Western colonialism was a dying phenomenon, but China, a traditional expansionist power indigenous to the region, threatened to take its place. The United States had fought World War II in the Pacific to prevent Japan from dominating the area. Now it was just as determined to deny the new China a position of domination in alliance with the Soviet Union and under the banner of Communist ideology.

The line between granting equality and fostering expansion was not always distinct. If the United States withdrew its protection of Taiwan and the PRC captured that island, eliminating the key remaining barrier to a united China, and, if the United States withdrew its opposition to that regime's admission to the United Nations, no guarantee remained that the newly strengthened Mao government would halt its support for revolutionary forces in Southeast Asia. From the perspective of forty years, with nationalist forces having proven their dominance over international communism, it is easy to say "so what?" To U.S. policymakers at the time, the specter of dynamic expansionist regimes beholden to Beijing spreading from Indochina westward with no end in sight was impossible to contemplate with serenity.

Nor was it clear in 1953—or with the perspective of hindsight for that matter—that concessions to the PRC on Taiwan and membership in the United

Nations would have won its or the Soviet Union's cooperation on the unification of Korea. The U.S. State Department continued to play with the idea of a neutralized peninsula under the ROK. The carrot to the PRC and the USSR was the prospect for withdrawal of U.S. forces from the country, the stick the threat of an aggressive Rhee, determined to unite the peninsula by whatever means necessary and backed by massive U.S. military and economic assistance.[247] Yet Rhee's attitude toward neutralization aside—his reaction when Senator Knowland floated the idea in a televised "Meet the Press" interview in early July was not encouraging—its implementation would involve an expansion in reverse for the Communists, the elimination for the first time of a Communist regime.[248] Since 1947 the Soviets often had supported the withdrawal of foreign forces, but it always had been in circumstances in which, if implemented, the Communists were likely to prevail. After investing much blood and treasure in saving the DPRK from extinction, and with eastern European peoples showing discontent under the Communist yoke, Moscow and Beijing were hardly likely to accept Korean unification on terms that might promote America's rhetoric of liberation. Thus prospects were not good that the armistice in Korea had ushered in a larger process of accommodation, either on the peninsula or in Asia as a whole.

Still, circumstances in Korea had notable contrasts to those in Kashmir and Palestine, Kingsley Martin's admonitions to the contrary notwithstanding. Not only did the destructiveness of conflicts to date in those two areas pale in comparison to that just ended in Korea; each of the superpowers, in conjunction with key allies, were firmly committed in Korea to the defense against attack of one of the contending parties. That situation, though far from a prescription for resolving outstanding issues, represented a hopeful beginning in the management of conflict.[249] And the example of Korea's tragedy and the global crisis it had provoked might give pause to decision makers in Washington and Moscow alike about sponsoring changes elsewhere in the status quo through the blatant use of force across established boundaries.

• CHAPTER 10 •

# The Korean War as International History

### KOREA AS A SUBSTITUTE FOR WORLD WAR III

October 1950 was a pivotal month in the Korean War. Despite Chinese warnings, UN ground forces crossed the 38th parallel and pushed their way toward the Manchurian border. China responded by sending hundreds of thousands of troops to the peninsula. Unaware of Beijing's decision, President Truman and General MacArthur met at mid-month on Wake Island in the Pacific Ocean. Brimming with self-confidence, the UN commander assured his commander in chief and a team of advisers that the war was all but won, that U.S. troops could begin to be reassigned from the theater by the end of the year.

Secretary of the Army Frank Pace was a member of the Truman team at Wake Island. On his return to Washington, he went to Secretary of Defense Marshall's Pentagon office to report General MacArthur's assessment. To Pace's astonishment, the older man expressed concern. "To precipitate an end to the war," he opined, "would not permit us to have a full understanding of the problems we face ahead of us."

"But General Marshall," Pace queried, "do you mean by that the American people would not have fully had the opportunity to grasp the implications of the cold war?"

"I certainly do," Marshall replied. "You didn't live through the end of World War II the way I did, and watch people rush back to their civilian jobs and leave the tanks to rot in the Pacific and the military strength that was built up to fade away."

"I know, General Marshall," Pace admitted, "but a great deal of water has passed under the bridge since then. . . . Would you say I was naive if I said that the American people had learned their lesson?"

"No, Pace, I wouldn't say you were naive," Marshall answered, "I'd say you were incredibly naive."[1]

Little did Marshall know that, by the end of the year, U.S. units in Korea would be fighting for their survival in the face of a Chinese onslaught. With the possible exception of a few days in October almost a dozen years later, the cold war was as close to becoming hot on a global scale as at any time in its forty-year history.

Yet the Korean War did not escalate beyond the country's boundaries. The Soviets, while using many of their own planes and pilots to assist their Chinese and North Korean allies, restricted their operations to the extreme northern reaches of the peninsula. Although U.S. flyers sometimes breached the Yalu River boundary and even strafed airfields in Manchuria, such attacks were limited in scale and clearly contrary to Washington policy.[2] The leaders of the two countries with the greatest capacity to expand the war—Stalin and his successors on the Soviet side, Truman and Eisenhower on the American—consistently preferred to limit the conflict. When pressures on Truman to expand the war became acute in the months following China's intervention in late 1950, U.S. allies joined with Third-World neutrals in the UN General Assembly to discourage U.S. adventurism.

All the while, U.S. and allied armed forces expanded by leaps and bounds. Whereas in the fall of 1950 the Truman administration contemplated cutting in half the Pentagon projection of needs for the remainder of the fiscal year for fear Congress would refuse to provide funding, the acute crisis created by Chinese intervention in Korea reinforced the momentum created by the outbreak of war for a rapid increase in defense outlays. By the middle of 1951 NSC-68 was well on the way toward implementation, and actual U.S. military power had nearly doubled since the outbreak of war twelve months earlier. The buildup continued until the end of the war, and it was reinforced by efforts in western Europe. Although defense spending declined somewhat in the aftermath of an armistice, never again would the United States get caught being as unprepared as it was in June 1950. Clearly "the American people had learned their lesson."

Europe, of course, was the cockpit of the early cold war, the strategic prize that, in the hands of either of the superpowers, would tip the balance in the competition. When the war in Korea began, NATO countries had only fourteen undermanned, poorly equipped, largely uncoordinated army divisions, only two of which were American.[3] Those U.S. divisions were not in Europe as a result of commitments made upon the signing of the North Atlantic treaty in 1949, but because of America's continuing occupation of a portion of Germany.[4] The annual expenditure on defense of the eleven member nations was less than 5.5 percent of their gross national products.[5] Although many regarded a contribution of troops by West Germany as essential to western Europe's defense, the political ramifications of such a contribution were so explosive that no one had officially broached it.[6] Three years later fifteen well-armed divisions were stationed in West Germany alone, six of which were American, and the total military manpower of NATO countries approached seven million.[7] Greece and Turkey had joined the organization, and Yugoslavia had aligned with them. Tito rejected any formal commitment to NATO, but he received considerable military aid from the United States.[8] Despite the continued existence of barriers to West German rearmament, the issue was well advanced toward resolution, with twelve additional front-line divisions the likely result.[9] NATO members now spent more than 12 percent of their gross national products on defense, a significant portion of which was being used to construct the infrastructure needed to serve the increase in manpower and equipment.[10] This included, among other items, air bases, port facilities, oil and gas pipelines, and signal communications units. Finally, the allies had created an institutional framework to provide for integrated planning on an ongoing basis. Most important in this regard was the Supreme Headquarters Allied Powers Europe located outside Paris and headed by a U.S. general.[11] In the context of a crisis thousands of miles away, the United States had transformed a paper commitment to the defense of western Europe, demonstrating an intention to keep major forces on the continent permanently and taking the lead in coordinating their operations with NATO partners.

Despite the buildup, U.S. military leaders continued to regard the military balance in Europe as unfavorable. In his annual report in May 1953 General Ridgway, Eisenhower's successor as NATO commander, concluded that "the disparity between our available forces and those which the Soviet rulers could bring against us [is] so great as to warrant no other conclusion than that a full-scale Soviet attack within the near future would find Allied Command Europe critically weak to accomplish its present mission."[12] Part of the problem was an uncompleted infrastructure, which only recently had received the necessary financing. This deficiency would be largely resolved in the next year. West German rearmament, which Ridgway considered "indispensable," would take three more years before it became significant operationally, by which time NATO's stockpiling of tactical nuclear weapons helped compensate for any conventional weaknesses in relation to Communist forces to the east.[13] Even then there would be a fair share of pessimists who never regarded NATO's strength as adequate to meet the Soviet threat.

The end of the cold war in Western victory has resolved such doubts. No Soviet attack into western Europe ever occurred. In subsequent crises, the region always held firm in the face of Soviet pressure. The integration of West Germany into the Western alliance through the European Coal and Steel Community and NATO facilitated peace, prosperity, and stability on the continent and provided a magnet that, in the long term, helped produce the crumbling of the Soviet bloc.

But was the buildup necessary? Was it needed to contain Soviet expansion or did it merely exacerbate East-West tensions and divert masses of resources on both sides from more constructive ventures? In sparking the buildup, not to mention the tremendous destruction rendered to human life and property, should the Korean War be viewed exclusively as a tragedy, both to the people who fought it and the world that endured its results?

No definitive answers are possible to such questions. Certainly the Korean conflict had its share of tragedy. But there is also reason to believe that it played a stabilizing role in international politics, that without the North Korean attack and the Western response to it a tragedy of far greater magnitude might have occurred.

In developing this hypothesis, Soviet intentions and capabilities following World War II need to be explored. Neither can be determined with certainty; both were subject to change, the former overnight, the latter over time. Yet if we combine what is known about Soviet behavior with what is now suspected of Soviet capabilities, we at least can construct plausible scenarios.

The first point to be made about Soviet behavior is that it was opportunistic, that this opportunism frequently involved the use or the threat of use of military force, and that the Soviets always stood prepared to retreat in the face of superior counterforce or the threat thereof. In Iran and Manchuria during late 1945 and early 1946, the Soviets used occupation forces in attempts to enhance their long-term position. They pulled out in the face of U.S. pressure, however, despite a local advantage, albeit in Iran only after receiving oil concessions from the national government. With Turkey, the Soviets sought a share in movements between the Black and Mediterranean seas plus territorial concessions through aggressive rhetoric and an ominous military presence on that country's borders. Again, the Americans countered with some posturing of their own, and the Soviets never acted out their implied threat.[14] In Berlin the Soviets tried to drive the Westerners out through a blockade, again under favorable local conditions. The Soviets backed down, however, in the face of a Western airlift. In Korea the Soviets gave a client regime the green light and the wherewithal to attack a U.S.-sponsored government. When the attack failed because of U.S. intervention and the United States stood poised to seize the entire peninsula, the Soviets called on the Chinese to prevent the debacle. In all these cases Stalin showed a willingness to use his or an ally's armed forces to expand or to maintain Soviet influence, but he also displayed a desire to avert military confrontation with the United States.

It is not difficult to understand why he wanted to avoid such a confrontation. Until 1949 the United States held a monopoly on atomic weapons, and after that it retained clear superiority in the number of weapons it could inflict on the enemy. The U.S. economy could outproduce its Soviet counterpart on a scale of between three and four to one. With the top leadership in Washington desiring to avoid war with the Soviets, such a conflict was unlikely to have occurred by design.

On the other hand, it could have evolved through miscalculation, all the more so once the Soviets developed a substantial capacity to deliver nuclear weapons to the U.S. homeland. American planners worried about this possibility in early 1950, both as an immediate danger and as an increasing possibility as time passed if the United States failed to augment its military capability.[15] The scenario was a simple one. Holding a local military advantage, Soviet and satellite forces moved into an area outside their sphere, calculating that the United States lacked the ability to respond immediately and directly. So long as enemy forces on the scene were quickly overwhelmed, the Americans would concede the area rather than endure a prolonged struggle, perhaps even a major one. But events did not develop as Moscow anticipated.

One possibility was that the United States would immediately implement its war plan, the centerpiece of which was an atomic offensive against the Soviet Union. If this occurred in 1950, the Soviets would lack a major capacity to retaliate against the U.S. homeland, but as time passed the Soviets would eliminate this weakness and thus might become less inclined to believe that the United States would launch a first strike on them. This development, in turn, would make a Soviet probe into western Europe all the more likely.

Even if the Soviets moved sooner rather than later, the U.S. atomic capability probably was insufficient to quickly knock the enemy out of the war. Soviet forces would occupy most of western Europe and make it difficult for the United States to use Great Britain as a base for its strategic air offensive. At best the conflict would be long and costly.[16]

A second possibility was that all-out war would emerge gradually following a Soviet bloc military thrust that the West initially attempted to counter through piecemeal action. With Soviet bloc forces having a local advantage, the West escalated its response, and Moscow, already committed militarily, refused to back down. By the time Moscow was willing to retreat, Washington, intent on punishing the aggressor, stood unwilling to accept a mere restoration of conditions that existed before the Soviet military initiative. Backed into a corner, Stalin (or a successor) decided to keep fighting. Washington, frustrated by the indecisiveness of the military campaign and pushed forward by irate public opinion, eventually chose to use all its resources against the enemy.

The Balkans was the most likely place for the second of these scenarios to have played out. We know from Bela Kiraly, later an exile but then a member of the Ministry of Defense in Budapest, that a major military buildup occurred in Hungary, Rumania, and Bulgaria from the fall of 1948. Soviet advisers were intimately involved in the enterprise, which was explicitly directed toward an offensive against Yugoslavia. The preparations culminated in January 1951 in elaborate war games in the Hungarian capital. The plans included the participation of Soviet divisions in "the second-echelon strike force," with Hungarian, Rumanian, Albanian, and Bulgarian units constituting the initial thrust. Kiraly observes that "Yugoslavia was supposed to succumb to this anaconda grasp in a matter of days—most probably as gross a miscalculation by Stalin as his former ally Hitler had made."[17] The U.S. intervention in Korea to stymie Kim Il-sung's plans for a quick victory undoubtedly discouraged Stalin from launching an attack on Yugoslavia, although the plans for doing so proceeded for at least seven months after June 1950. Without a North Korean attack and a determined Western response, however, the Soviet leader might well have initiated military action to overthrow the wayward Tito.

The United States would not have responded to such an attack with an implementation of its war plan. Rather, it probably would have supplied the Yugoslavs with weapons, food, and clothing to help them fight a guerrilla war in their rugged mountainous terrain. It is unlikely that such a conflict would have been short. A protracted war in Yugoslavia, which lacks Korea's measure of insularity, its distance from the key theater of the cold war, or its ethnic homogeneity eventually could have spread to other areas of the Balkans and even beyond. In a word, war in the Balkans would have been even more difficult than the one in Korea, both to contain and to end.

By July 1953 the Soviet Union was far less likely than before to initiate or encourage the use of force across established boundaries into areas outside its sphere of influence. Not only had the United States succeeded in preventing the North Koreans from uniting their country; it had rearmed itself and its allies in western Europe, a development that Stalin had neither anticipated nor desired. In response, he had felt compelled to increase the commitment of his own bloc to heavy industry and the modernization of armed forces, so much so that political unrest sprang to the surface in eastern Europe. As a result, Stalin's successors preoccupied themselves with political and economic reform at home and among the satellites, a measure of détente with the United States, and the encouragement of revolution in the Third World. Developments in the last area could produce dangerous tensions, as in 1962 when Soviet leader Nikita Khrushchev decided to place offensive missiles in Cuba. Yet the absence of actual combat between U.S. and Soviet bloc forces enabled the two sides to resolve that crisis relatively quickly.

It was not until 1979 in Afghanistan that the Soviets embarked on a military venture comparable to the one in Korea, only this time it was with their own, not proxy, forces. Again, the outcome was anything but to the Kremlin's liking. In 1979, as in 1950, Soviet action accentuated the military dimension of the cold war. In the earlier case the result was initially to push the world to the brink of war, but eventually to make war a good deal less likely. In the later case the immediate result was to heighten superpower tensions, as the United States provided crucial aid to the Afghan rebels and sharply increased military spending. In the long run, however, the event contributed mightily to the weakening of the Soviet empire sufficiently to end the cold war altogether. Stalin's immediate successors learned the lesson that to arouse the United States from a slumber through blatant military action could prove a costly mistake. It would take more than a generation and a new group of leaders before the Soviet Union would run a repeat performance.

## Korea as Tragedy

If the Korean War should be viewed in part as a substitute for something as bad or even worse, it also must be approached as tragedy, as an event that might have been avoided altogether or ended at a number of points along the way. Although the division of the peninsula after World War II made the conflict possible, it hardly made the war inevitable. A tense situation in the divided country could have existed indefinitely without major war had the United States made its intention clear to defend the ROK in the event of overt attack. As it was, Stalin gave the green light to Kim in the spring of 1950 because he miscalculated the U.S. response.

The war is laden with miscalculation on all sides. A persistent Kim persuaded Stalin that the DPRK would defeat the ROK in a matter of days, partly because of its military superiority, partly because, with the capture of Seoul, the people below the 38th parallel would rise in revolt against the Rhee regime, making a prolonged military campaign unnecessary. No such eruption occurred, and when the resistance continued beyond Seoul, the North Koreans were caught without plans, which slowed their advance during the critical days at the end of June and early July.[18] Late in the summer the North Koreans were so intent on pushing the enemy off the peninsula that they ignored Soviet and Chinese warnings of a counterattack along the west coast.[19] When the attack came the North Koreans were unprepared, and it nearly destroyed their army.

The rapid change in fortunes led to miscalculation on the other side as to the Chinese reaction in the event of a U.S. march into the North. The Americans had never wanted to fight in Korea, they had failed to anticipate North Korea's attack of June, and, now, flush with military success at Inchon, they sought to clean up the Korean mess forever. In their determination to do so, they ignored Chinese warnings and were soon paying the price. So were Koreans, who had to endure an ongoing war of larger dimensions than ever before.

Mao could have ended the war where it had started at the end of the year, but he chose not to, overestimating his military advantage and his ability to use Korea as an instrument for achieving larger aims. In refusing to negotiate on the basis of the five principles put forth by the United Nations in January 1951, Mao missed his best opportunity to achieve his goals beyond the peninsula. It was not until the CPV suffered severe battlefield setbacks during the spring of 1951 that he adjusted his aims to meet military realities. Even then, Chinese tactics in armistice talks served to harden the enemy negotiating position, which, in turn, prolonged the fighting under conditions at least initially disadvantageous to the Communists.

The Americans also miscalculated. At the beginning of talks they failed to anticipate the implications of negotiating an armistice line first, before other issues were resolved. Then, they gave in too easily to public pressure to scale down the fighting at a time when those other issues were still on the table. Finally, the UNC neglected the importance of conditions in the POW camps in the face of its stance on the repatriation of prisoners. That neglect enabled the Communists to create incidents that undermined the legitimacy of the UNC position on prisoners and, along with the military stalemate, made the Communists less likely to come to terms. In the end, however, the Communists miscalculated U.S. firmness on the issue of Chinese POWs, which turned out to be greater than their own.

A certain amount of miscalculation is inherent in international life, given the incomplete data on which most decisions are made. Still, it is essential to ask why specific miscalculations happen at specific times—in our case, why the miscalculations occurred that led to the outbreak of war in Korea in June 1950 and to its continuation until July 1953. Certainly ideology played a key role in shaping the perceptions of the two sides toward each other. Yet individuals espousing similar ideologies often disagreed with each other on critical matters of policy. The ideologies of both sides were sufficiently flexible to permit different conclusions by different people in specific instances. In any event, ideologies are not genetic: individuals subscribe to them for particular purposes at particular times, and they are adaptable to changing circumstances.

There is no better illustration of this point than the case of Mao and Richard Nixon, who stood at opposite ideological poles during the cold war era and, during the early 1950s, held irreconcilable positions on international issues. Yet, a generation later, they proved instrumental in bringing about a rapprochement of their respective countries. Their ideologies remained intact, but the circumstances of their nations, both domestic and international, had changed and thus so did their relationship. In 1950 China was just emerging from a civil war in which the United States had backed the losing side and was in the process of expanding its role abroad. Ideology combined with U.S. behavior and the need to reassert China's historic position dictated to Mao an alliance with the Soviet Union and a forward policy on his borders. Twenty years later China had long since reestablished itself as a great power, the United States was in retreat in Asia, and the Soviet Union constituted an ominous presence in the north. As for Nixon, in 1950 he was a young politician working his way up in a conservative opposition party that had found a promising issue in China's fall to communism. By the 1970s Nixon had reached the pinnacle of politics in his country. Stuck with an unpopular war in Asia and growing problems with America's role as global policeman, President Nixon saw both a need and an opportunity to improve relations with China, now a bitter enemy of the Soviet Union. In explaining the miscalculations that produced the tragedies of Korea, therefore, we must remain sensitive to the unique conditions of the time in which they occurred.

Ideology and historical circumstances played a key role in miscalculations on the Communist side during early 1950. Kim and Stalin overestimated the prospects for internal disruption in South Korea in part because Marxist-Leninist ideology led them to see widespread popular discontent as normal in the capitalist world, especially in colonial or quasi-colonial areas. The recent Communist success in China reinforced this inclination, as Communist leaders had not anticipated the speed with which it had come about. Now they overestimated the strength of the Communist tide in border areas. Stalin underestimated the U.S. response to the North Korean attack, in part because of Washington's failure to intervene directly in China, in part because his ideology encouraged him to doubt that a unified Western reaction was possible, given the inherent contradictions within the capitalist camp and the obvious divisions between Washington and allied governments over Asian policy. Stalin's perception of the United States as being rich and powerful in material things but divided and soft in spirit reinforced his inclination here. Yet ideology merely accentuated perceptions of the United States and its relations with allies, which were not far removed from those of many non-Communist observers in the West.

Further accentuating those perceptions was the belief on the part of Kim and Stalin that an attack on South Korea would serve very positive purposes, for the former that of unifying the country under his control, for the latter that of solidifying his control on the Soviet periphery in the aftermath of Tito's defection in Yugoslavia and Mao's rise in China. In other words, their calculations were in some measure shaped by their appetites. In fairness to them both, U.S. actions and official statements regarding Korea lent themselves to misinterpretation.

Domestic politics, together with strategic factors, go far to explain America's failure to adequately protect its commitment to South Korea. The American people and their representatives in Congress had not yet fully accepted the budgetary implications of their country's recent plunge into the international arena. Congress kept a tight rein on taxes and spending, and President Truman, himself a fiscal conservative, strove to balance domestic and foreign priorities. This pattern joined with America's Europe-first strategy to leave South Korea in a kind of limbo. U.S. leaders, insofar as they thought about the matter, knew that Korea was a tinderbox. Yet many false alarms had sounded in the past and, short of anticipating the precise circumstances under which Korea would explode, they could hardly agree in advance on what was to be done. The State Department, concerned primarily about U.S. credibility abroad if the American creation below the 38th parallel fell before a Communist onslaught, was reasonably attentive, but there were several places on the Soviet periphery where Communist offensives appeared at least as likely to occur. The Pentagon, stuck with inadequate resources and the defense of greater strategic prizes elsewhere, ignored the peninsula as much as possible. Outside the executive branch, there was no powerful lobbyist for Korea's cause. The easiest course was to rationalize the problem away. Korea could be controlled with air power from Japan;[20] North Korea had the capacity to attack but was likely to stick for the moment to covert efforts to bring down the ROK; ROK expressions of alarm were reminiscent of those of Nationalist China and represented efforts to lure the United States into a quagmire. Only when North Korea actually launched its attack could the peninsula get concentrated, sustained attention in Washington. Even then, the outcome would have been far different had there been evidence of impending Communist offensives elsewhere.

The North Korean failure to prepare for a UN counteroffensive late in the summer of 1950, despite the Chinese warning, is explained largely in terms of the psychology of war and the paucity of North Korean reserves. Even when the Americans intervened unexpectedly, the attackers retained a strong chance to drive the enemy off the peninsula, at least temporarily. Time was of the essence, however, and the North Koreans, passionately committed to victory, undoubtedly calculated that their best chance not only of winning but of avoiding defeat was through quick, decisive, offensive action. They simply lacked the manpower and resources both to continue the offensive against the Pusan perimeter and to protect their rear against an enemy counterattack. One cannot help but wonder if the Soviets would have forced on North Korea a more defensive approach, including negotiations, in the aftermath of its unsuccessful offensive of early September had the Inchon landing not occurred in the middle of the month. That is, had MacArthur not insisted on launching the counteroffensive at the earliest possible moment, there is a good chance that the military and diplomatic outcome during the fall would have been very different.

The early date of the counteroffensive and its rapid success left the Chinese unprepared to take immediate action and uncertain as to what course should eventually be adopted. This situation virtually paralyzed PRC efforts at deterrence for the crucial ten days after Inchon. When early Chinese or Soviet moves into Korea, or even clear threats of such moves, did not occur, U.S. planners thought the way was clear to march across the 38th parallel. When the explicit Chinese threats finally came, the momentum on the UN side to continue the offensive northward was too powerful to stop.

Domestic politics, personalities, and lingering U.S. condescension toward the Chinese also played a role in Washington's miscalculation. A halt at the 38th parallel in the midst of a congressional election campaign and without substantial advance preparation of the public risked major political repercussions at home at a time when the Truman administration was already on the defensive for its allegedly timid policy in Asia. Exacerbating the problem was the presence of a victorious general in Tokyo who was sure to make public his objection to any interference with his plans for a continuing offensive. Had the threat of counteraction come from Moscow rather than Beijing, the respect for Soviet military might and the implications of a Soviet-U.S. clash in Korea would have given Washington pause. The idea of China, an economically backward nation just emerging from generations of internal turmoil, confronting the United States in Korea seemed less plausible and thus less necessary to take seriously. Plausibility was further compromised because the explicit threat was transmitted through Panikkar, a diplomat of questionable reliability.

Finally, the fact that the conflict in Korea was part of a larger struggle in which U.S. leaders believed they desperately needed a victory reduced prospects for a more prudent American policy. From the beginning of the war, U.S. leaders had been deeply concerned about the credibility of their foreign policy, not just at home but abroad as well. A clear-cut victory in Korea, one that went beyond containing the Soviet threat, would provide an important psychological boost to U.S. prospects in the cold war. Such concerns dictated U.S. policy until late in November, when the massive Chinese presence in Korea became too obvious for even MacArthur to ignore.

Now it was the Communist side's turn to miscalculate. For Kim the move to push for another try at military unification was reflexive. Unification was the objective for starting the war in the first place. He was not about to let the moment pass without lobbying with his Chinese and Soviet benefactors for a new effort at total victory. For Mao and Stalin, the unification of Korea was not nearly so compelling an objective, and a try at it with Chinese troops could provoke the Americans to take drastic action. But, in any event, Mao doubted the U.S. willingness to settle on the 38th parallel, and his goals of PRC control of Taiwan and admission to the United Nations seemed most likely to be achieved through the establishment of as powerful a position as possible on the peninsula. Perhaps most important of all, Mao was a captive of his own theories of warfare, which emphasized the importance of manpower and morale over technology. At the end of the year his confidence in his own judgment was sufficient to make him overrule his commander in the field, who wanted to halt for lengthy preparations before renewing the offensive into South Korea.

A tragic irony of Korea is that had the Joint Chiefs and civilian leaders in Washington had greater confidence in their judgment in November, they might have restrained their commander in the field in a manner that would have stabilized the military situation in North Korea and promoted a negotiated settlement; in contrast, had Mao had less confidence in his own judgment a month later, he might have followed the advice of his own field commander, again providing an opportunity for military stabilization and negotiations.

As it turned out, it would take six more months and several costly defeats on the battlefield before Mao recognized the impossibility of achieving broader political objectives by military means. Both here and in his side's adoption of excessively aggressive negotiating tactics in the armistice talks, Mao's burning commitment to reestablish China to its rightful place as a great power clouded his judgment.

For Stalin, the miscalculation is less clear-cut. He probably overestimated China's military advantage in Korea in late 1950, but his desire to continue the offensive may have reflected at least as much his calculation that a continuation of the war would serve his purposes in fostering disarray in the West and reinforcing Chinese dependence on the Soviet Union. His ideology led him to exaggerate Western disarray, to underestimate, as before, the degree to which the belligerence of the Communist world would serve to bolster rather than weaken the enemy alliance. Yet he did not miscalculate in his belief that U.S. allies would discourage Washington from expanding the war. The ongoing crisis in Korea did ensure that Beijing would not move independently of Moscow in the international arena. Given Stalin's perennial sense of insecurity in his own house and on Soviet borders, he surely derived comfort from a situation that fostered unity in his own camp.

During the summer of 1951, with the war stalemated at a point near where it had begun, both sides abandoned hope of total victory. They also remained deeply hostile to each other and intent on avoiding any show of weakness, a concern that helped produce a level of belligerence on the Communist side that reinforced U.S. determination to hold to initial positions, and even to adopt ones that increased the difficulty of reaching an agreement. In addition to the fear of revealing any sign of weakness, the continuing underestimation of the U.S. leaders' ability to hold firm in the face of domestic and allied pressures to bring the war to an end helps to explain Communist behavior. It was not until a new administration in Washington seemed willing to abandon military restraint that the Communists finally made a crucial concession on the POW issue in order to conclude an armistice.

Of all the many sources of conflict in the war, none was so charged with ideological content as that over the POWs. Yet even here it was a single personality, that of Harry S. Truman, which converted the issue from one that was resolvable through a few months of hard bargaining into one that produced an indefinite stalemate. Truman's adamance grew out of his experience with the POW issue after World War II, his genuine anger and frustration over Communist behavior, both in Korea and elsewhere, and his determination to leave office with his country fully prepared to defend its interests abroad under conditions that were sure to remain volatile. Still, his commitment evolved over several months, during which time he and his leading advisers permitted the pressure of domestic and alliance politics to whittle away at a limited though significant military advantage—a mistake that his adversaries in Beijing and Moscow would never have made. Through inattention, Washington allowed conditions to develop in the POW camps that could be exploited by the Communists, further reducing pressure on them to settle the issue on UNC terms. With elections approaching in the United States, Mao calculated that time was on his side. He was wrong, perhaps in part because Truman himself was not running for reelection and was concerned primarily about his place in history.

This discussion of miscalculation serves to emphasize the critical role of personalities at various stages of the war. A less determined leader than Kim in North Korea might have backed off from pushing for an attack on South Korea in the face of Stalin's reservations. Stalin might have held to his reservations had it not been for his concerns about the strong and independent personalities at the head of the Communist governments in Yugoslavia and China, and the anticipated impact of a successful North Korean venture on his relationship with them. Less self-assured leaders than MacArthur in Tokyo and Mao in Beijing might have made very different decisions between September and December 1950, thus improving prospects for a quick end to the fighting. Unlike Stalin, Malenkov or Beria in power in the Soviet Union probably would have encouraged Mao to end the war at an earlier date. In Washington Truman often appears indecisive in comparison with leaders on the other side, but on the POW issue his voice proved critical, and it drowned out counsels of caution in both the military and the State Department. Even then, the POW issue could have been resolved during the summer of 1952 had Mao accepted the advice of his negotiators at Panmunjom.

Before leaving the tragedy of the Korean War, one must ask if its prolonged nature was essential in producing the increased level of stability between the superpowers that existed in 1953. Was Frank Pace "incredibly naive" in October 1950 in thinking that the American people had learned their lesson or was George Marshall drawing a false analogy in comparing likely developments after a projected victory in Korea to those in the West following World War II?

With all due respect to Marshall's celebrated sense of history, the chance of going back to June 1950 scales of military spending in the West was unlikely.[21] For one thing, such spending had already increased substantially, and not all of the increase was for operations in Korea. Even without massive Chinese intervention in Korea, the pacification of the entire peninsula would have taken several months, perhaps considerably longer. Such a victory for the United States would have had one crucial difference from that in 1945: it would not have eliminated the primary enemy. The demonstration of a Soviet willingness to use military force to expand its influence would not have been forgotten in western Europe or the United States, unless, of course, Stalin combined an end of the war with a broader effort at rapprochement with the non-Communist world. Evidence does not suggest that the Soviet leader was capable of implementing a thaw in the cold war during his last years. Stalin had backed off from belligerent policies in the past, most recently in Berlin in 1949, but the retreats never encompassed a larger effort to reduce tension with the West compared to what occurred in the aftermath of his death. Short of such an initiative, an increased U.S. military presence in Europe, higher Western defense budgets, and moves toward integration in NATO and West German rearmament were likely to have continued. The reduced scope of operations in Korea would have eased the process in some respects, as the pressure on prices of raw materials and reductions of U.S. economic aid to Europe might have been moderated. Although the military buildup would have been more slowly paced and more limited in scope, the response in and beyond Korea probably would have been sufficient to discourage future Soviet adventurism.

It is a good bet, then, that Korea's contribution to international stability could have been achieved with a much shorter, less destructive course. By any measure, tragedy must remain a major part of the war's legacy.

## Winners and Losers

It would be inadequate to end by arguing simply that the Korean War generated a modicum of international stability in the wake of dangerous conflict, represented a victory of sorts for the United States, a defeat for the Soviet Union, and that its most tragic dimensions resulted from its prolongation through miscalculation on both sides. Those conclusions alone would assure the conflict a central place in the history of the cold war, but they would ignore numerous other dimensions of Korea's impact. It is to these aspects of the war that we now turn through a further exploration of the event's winners and losers.

Perhaps the safest assertion possible in a complex and controversial subject is that the Koreans themselves were the losers, at least for the short term. While for the rest of the world the war was a limited one, both geographically and in weapons employed, for Koreans it was, as scholar Chae-Jin Lee remarks, "a 'total war' in . . . its savage destructiveness and wide-ranging consequences."[22] Historian Bruce Cumings observes:

> In 1953, the Korean peninsula was a smoldering ruin. From Pusan in the South to Sinuiju in the north, Koreans buried their dead, mourned their loses, and sought to draw together the shattered remains of their lives. In the capital at Seoul, hollow buildings stood like skeletons alongside streets paved with weird mixtures of concrete and shrapnel. At American military encampments on the outskirts of the capital, masses of beggars waited to pick through the garbage that foreign soldiers tossed out. In the north, modern edifices scarcely stood anymore; P'yongyang and other cities were heaps of bricks and ashes, factories stood empty, massive dams no longer held their water. People emerged from a mole-like existence in caves and tunnels to find a nightmare in the bright of day.[23]

Korea's losses in the number of people killed, wounded, and missing approached three million, a tenth of the entire population. Another ten million Koreans saw their families divided; five million became refugees. In property, North Korea put its losses at $1.7 billion, South Korea at $2 billion, the equivalent of its gross national product for 1949. North Korea lost some 8,700 industrial plants, South Korea twice that number. Each area saw 600,000 homes destroyed.[24] Adding to the tragedy was the fact that the country remained divided, with little prospect for change in the foreseeable future. During the spring of 1954, to be sure, the main parties held a conference at Geneva on unification, but positions on both sides were sufficiently unyielding to preclude progress.[25]

The most positive light that can be put on the war from the Koreans' perspective is that, once over, it was unlikely to resume. The peninsula was now an armed camp, the world in miniature, but never again would the United States let down its guard there as it had in the year before June 1950. In 1951 it had held firm in negotiations with the other side for several months to ensure that the armistice line would be a defensible one. When the shooting stopped two years later, Washington moved quickly not only to negotiate a security pact with Seoul and to mobilize contributors to the UN war effort to join in the greater sanctions statement; it also maintained sizable forces in Korea and continued to train and arm the much expanded ROK military forces.[26] At the same time, the United States made clear to its ally that any move northward would result in the withdrawal of support. For their part, the Soviets and the Chinese did nothing to encourage Kim Il-sung to repeat his adventure of the summer of 1950. As political scientist B. C. Koh has observed, the war led the North Korean leader to downgrade "the use of military force . . . from a practical to a theoretical option."[27] Although neither side proved scrupulous in abiding by the limitations in the armistice agreements regarding the expansion of armed capabilities, the balance of forces and clarity of purpose of the great powers on both sides served to keep the peace.

If U.S. containment emerged victorious in Korea, America's failure to liberate the North reflected the reemergence of China as a great power in East Asia. In one sense, the Sino-U.S. clash in the war was a stalemate: neither side drove the other from the peninsula. The fighting ended near where it had begun in June 1950. Indeed, China accepted a line the balance of which was north of the 38th parallel, and it ultimately gave way to the United States on the issue of POWs. Despite PRC efforts to influence the post-armistice repatriation process, less than 150 of the Chinese and North Korean prisoners who earlier had said they would resist return to their country of origin changed their minds.[28] Yet the end result represented a marked improvement for the Communists over the battlefield situation of October 1950, when Chinese troops entered the fray.[29] Although Chinese forces had suffered huge casualties and their premodern supply system and weaponry had proven inadequate to sustain the offensives of the winter and spring of 1951, China had forced the strongest nation on earth to compromise in Korea and to accept representatives of the PRC as equals at the bargaining table. "The time has gone forever," General Peng Dehuai declared in a speech of 12 September 1953, "when the Western powers were able to conquer a country in the East merely by mounting several cannons along the coast."[30] No one in the West ever again would dismiss China's power as General MacArthur had in the fall of 1950. During the mid-1960s Washington scrupulously avoided moving ground forces into North Vietnam for fear that such action would provoke direct Chinese intervention.[31]

China's heightened stature manifested itself in numerous other ways. In November 1953 Kim Il-sung led a large delegation to Beijing, where he negotiated agreements for long-term military, economic, and cultural cooperation between the DPRK and the PRC. He thanked his hosts for their "magnificent contributions to the Korean War, which will remain [as] immortal as Korea's mountains and rivers."[32] For their part, the Chinese labeled all the manpower and material provided to North Korea during the war as "gifts" and promised $200 million in aid for reconstruction during the next three years, only $50 million less than that committed by the Soviets.[33] Clearly the war had propelled China to a position of influence in North Korea on a par with that of the Soviet Union.

China's growing influence extended well beyond northeast Asia, a fact illustrated by Zhou Enlai's role in the Geneva and Bandung conferences of 1954 and 1955, respectively. In the first case, the Chinese foreign minister mediated between the French and the Vietminh, ultimately joining with the Soviets to persuade the latter to accept a settlement short of total victory.[34] That statesmanlike position helped pave the way for Zhou to emerge as the dominant personality at the Bandung meeting of African and Asian states, most of which were neutral in the cold war. Zhou's show of tolerance toward the non-Communist states present reinforced the inclination among most of them to regard China's intervention in Korea as a manifestation of the struggle against imperialism rather than of the PRC's alliance with the Soviet Union, which was not invited to Bandung.[35]

Whatever the perceptions of Third-World neutrals, the Korean War significantly elevated China's stature with the Soviet Union. Before China's entry into the fighting, Stalin had regarded the new regime as potentially akin to that in Yugoslavia. After Mao decided to intervene in Korea, the Soviet dictator's attitude had become more respectful and supportive.[36] Stalin's successors, lacking his prestige, became even more solicitous of China's needs. They refused, to be sure, to cancel the PRC's debt for Soviet assistance in Korea, which amounted to $2 billion, a fact never forgotten nor forgiven in Beijing. However, in September 1953, the Soviets promised to assist China in 141 construction projects. Thirteen months later they agreed to extend China a credit of $130 million to begin 15 more industrial ventures and to exchange technical information and provide advisers to advance them, as well as to begin construction of the Chinese portion of a transcontinental railroad. Moscow also agreed to withdraw Soviet military forces from Port Arthur by the end of May 1955 and to liquidate Sino-Soviet joint stock companies, which had been established in 1950 for thirty years but now were regarded by Chinese leaders as providing more profits for their allies than for themselves. Finally, the Soviets turned over as a gift some machine tools and agricultural machines on display in Beijing and promised to assist the Chinese in establishing a 20,000 acre state farm in the province of Heilungkiang in northern Manchuria.[37] Soviet assistance was hardly on the scale of U.S. aid to western Europe between 1948 and 1952, but it was sufficient to provide the foundation for the PRC's First Five-Year Plan.

Yet increased Soviet beneficence also meant increased Soviet influence. Before the Korean War Mao had emphasized a "New Democracy-united front approach" to the recovery and development of China's economy, which included a gradual and peaceful road to socialism, cooperation with the urban bourgeoisie and intelligentsia, preservation of the rich peasant class in the countryside, a continuation of trade with the West, and a measure of balance in attention to heavy and light industry. Despite the ongoing preparations to seize Taiwan, Mao placed demobilization of his armed forces ahead of their modernization. War in Korea changed all this. The controversial nature of Mao's decision to intervene, combined with the magnified danger from abroad, led him to take drastic measures to mobilize the country. The urban bourgeoisie and the wealthy peasants became objects of harsh recrimination. Economic policy turned from recovery and balanced development through a united front with capitalists to rapid nationalization along Stalinist lines. Chinese intellectuals were pushed to the background, as Soviet advisers and party cadres dominated economic planning. Soviet models of economic development were thrust to the forefront as never before. The Americans insisted on sharply reduced trade between China and the West, thus moving Beijing far along the path toward integrating its economy with the Soviet bloc.[38]

The short-term trend did not endure, however. Indeed, China's dependence on the Soviet Union bred strain and resentment that within a decade would tear the alliance apart. In looking back, we can detect signs of strain in 1954 and 1955, in the purge of Chinese leader Gao Gang and in the details of the PRC's five-year plan. Gao was the Manchurian leader who, during the summer of 1949, had traveled to Moscow to negotiate a trade agreement with the Soviet Union for his region. From the fall of 1950 to 1952 he had played a key role in organizing Manchuria for the war effort, only to be brought to Beijing in the latter year as vice premier and chief of the State Planning Commission. In April 1955 Gao was expelled from the party, allegedly for attempting to convert Manchuria into an independent kingdom and for other "antiparty conspiratorial activities." Three months later Ki Fu-chun, Gao's successor at the State Planning Commission, revealed that the five-year plan devoted to heavy industry a portion of China's available capital greater even than the Soviets had committed during their early years in power.[39] In all likelihood, the purge of Gao and the extreme emphasis on heavy industry represented, in part, an effort by Mao to reduce his country's dependence on the Soviets.

Mao's initial choice of an alliance with the Soviets had grown out of his fear of U.S. intentions, and, in an immediate sense, the Korean War exacerbated that fear, thus increasing Chinese dependence. In the war's aftermath, PRC leaders continued to fear U.S. intentions, and they continued to use the Soviet connection for the purpose of deterrence and the advancement of internal economic development, which was critical to the modernization of their armed forces. But, whatever its deficiencies, China's performance in Korea was also a great source of pride and self-confidence. The tardy and often grudging Soviet support for the effort there reaffirmed a lesson Mao had learned during the earlier struggles against the Nationalists and the Japanese, namely, that the Soviet Union was an "Elder Brother" of limited reliability. Stalin's passing from the scene and his replacement by men of more modest stature undoubtedly added to Mao's sense of self-esteem and his willingness, before long, to chart his own path, both at home and abroad.[40]

Mao could not return to conditions of the prewar world, nonetheless, and nowhere was this more apparent than in regard to Taiwan and the offshore islands. On the eve of war, the United States showed no interest in the latter and refused to commit itself to defend the former. When the war began, the United States quickly jumped in to protect Taiwan from Communist attack. When the PRC intervened in Korea, virtually all prospects disappeared that this new U.S. policy would change for the foreseeable future. In the aftermath of war, the PRC probed Nationalist positions on the offshore islands of Jinmen and Matsu only to spark threats from Washington of nuclear retaliation and a formal U.S. commitment to the Nationalists to defend Taiwan. The Soviets proved of little help through this crisis.[41] If the final unification of China was far from inevitable in June 1950, the country's indefinite division had become reality by July 1953. China's adoption of the role of mediator in Indochina in the summer of 1954 and its subsequent retreat on the offshore islands reflected the conclusion in Beijing that it could not afford another military clash with the United States—at least not if given a choice. In 1955 Chinese leaders tried the diplomatic approach by initiating "ambassadorial talks" with the United States at Geneva, but the Americans proved unbending on Taiwan.[42] Even if we ignore the PRC's inability to eject UN forces from Korea, the new China's struggle on the peninsula had a bittersweet quality.

The same can be said of the U.S. victory. On the one hand, that victory extended well beyond Korea itself, as the demonstration of a willingness and an ability to combat "aggression" combined with the military buildup at home and in western Europe to deter such action elsewhere. For the long term, the strains placed on the Sino-Soviet alliance could not help but benefit the United States. In its competition with the Soviet Union, the United States certainly emerged the overall winner. On the other hand, Korea created or deepened certain patterns in U.S. policy toward the Third World that would come back to haunt the United States in the future. Broadly speaking, the problem may be identified as the U.S. response to Third-World nationalism. Washington never developed an effective approach to this phenomenon, in part because of its Europe-first strategy, which placed top priority on nurturing an alliance with the colonial powers, in part because leading Third-World nationalists often espoused communism. By pushing to the forefront in U.S. planning the military aspects of containment and the threat posed by China, the Korean War further diminished prospects for a flexible approach to the Third World that could exploit rather than confront the nationalist tide.

In the Middle East, Egypt represented the most striking example. Following the outbreak of war in Korea, President Truman and top U.S. officials expressed considerable concern over possible Soviet moves in the region. British power was on the decline there, and no other nation had stepped in to balance the ominous Soviet presence to the north. Turkey was willing, but its limited strength and precarious location on Soviet borders put it in some respects in a less advantageous position for military bases than Egypt, which also had one of the world's key waterways, the Suez Canal. Although the United Kingdom already held military bases there, the Egyptian government was anxious to end its privileged status under a treaty of 1936. London dragged its feet and Washington sought to mediate. The Korean War magnified the U.S. inclination to extend a system of collective defense to the area; but, despite impatience with continuing British insensitivity to nationalist sentiment in Egypt, the Americans always wound up backing their ally. Acheson regarded British support on Korea, China, and West German rearmament as critical and was not about to risk it to curry favor with a country that would not even endorse the UN stand against North Korean and Chinese aggression. During the summer and fall of 1951 the United States first fell in behind the United Kingdom in pushing a resolution through the UN Security Council censuring Egypt for resisting transit through the Suez Canal. Washington then joined London in proposing a tripartite Middle Eastern Command that left Cairo in a distinctly subordinate position. Predictably, Egypt rejected the plan.[43] Nationalism took a more extreme turn after a military coup of July 1952, and Egypt's foreign policy increasingly leaned toward the Soviet Union. Given the early U.S. support for the creation of Israel and Israel's growing orientation toward the West after the beginning of war in Korea, relations between Washington and Cairo were bound to be strained.[44] Nonetheless, the growing emphasis on military instruments of containment and on solidifying the Western alliance took an added toll on the relationship.

U.S. relations with China, of course, were affected even more dramatically. Unlike with Egypt, with China it was the United States not Great Britain that had a past legacy to overcome. Eventually, the British position in Hong Kong would have to be resolved, but on the eve of the Korean War the continued U.S. connection with the Nationalist government on Taiwan was the primary concern of the new regime on the mainland. For their part, U.S. policymakers were increasingly alarmed over the Communist threat to Indochina and the recently consummated Sino-Soviet alliance. Although Acheson remained concerned about overcommitment in Asia, about France's insensitivity to nationalist sentiments in Indochina, and about diverting attention in China from Soviet penetration of its northern provinces, a variety of pressures, including domestic politics, edged him ever closer to a more assertive policy. Indeed, U.S. aid to the French in Indochina commenced in May 1950.

The outbreak of war in Korea late the next month produced a snowball effect: within five months it had led to a direct Sino-U.S. confrontation on the peninsula, U.S. intervention to prevent a PRC assault on Taiwan, and deeper U.S. involvement on the French side in Indochina. In all three areas the United States seemed culpable in the eyes of most Third-World nationalists. In the first two, even America's closest allies regarded the U.S. course as ill-advised. Yet in part because of outrage with and fear of China, in part because of domestic opinion, the Truman administration clung to an unbending policy toward the PRC, compromising with allies and Third-World neutrals only on the scope of the war in Korea. During the remainder of the war, a struggle occurred at the United Nations between the United States and most other members over how much pressure to apply on China.

The signing of an armistice in July 1953 did little to soften the U.S. position. Eisenhower had won the election the previous fall partly because of his predecessor's difficulties in Asia. A widespread view in the United States, especially in the Republican party, was that China policy needed tightening, not softening. Eisenhower's "unleashing" of Jiang Jieshi during his first month in office represented as much an effort to mollify important constituencies in his party and the public as to increase pressure on the PRC. In accepting less than total victory in Korea, he used up a good deal of political capital with powerful Republicans in Congress. When the war ended, Eisenhower continued the policy of attempting to isolate Beijing from the non-Communist world. At the United Nations the United States persisted in its view that the PRC be denied admission to the international body and that the economic embargo, which was tougher on China than on the Soviet Union, be maintained. In the former area, the United States succeeded in a strict sense, but only in the face of growing impatience on the part of European allies and Third-World nations. On trade, allies such as Great Britain and Japan, confronted with the choice between pressures from Washington and their own economic needs, increasingly chose in favor of the latter. Many Third-World nations did the same.[45] The apparent U.S. move to the brink of war with the PRC in 1954–1955 and again in 1958 to protect the Nationalist position on the offshore islands also did nothing to inspire confidence abroad in Washington's judgment. Eisenhower and Dulles never lost sight of the desirability of a Sino-Soviet split, but their inclination was to promote it by forcing Beijing, in the short term, to become more rather than less dependent on Moscow. In time, the theory went, this dependence would provoke resentment and rebellion by the junior partner.[46]

The theory had merit, but Washington's rigidity in applying pressure on the PRC exacted a price in America's standing in much of the Third World, where respect and admiration for the new China were widespread, and in the U.S. ability to exploit the Sino-Soviet split during its early years. In the mid-1960s it was the continuing image of China as an aggressive enemy rather than a potential counter to the Soviet Union, the belief that the success for containment in Korea was replicable in Southeast Asia, and the Johnson administration's fear that the loss of another Asian nation to communism would produce dire consequences at home that led to the tragic U.S. escalation in Vietnam.[47] Thus, although Korea taught the United States that it must maintain a high degree of military preparedness, the conflict also set America along the road to overcommitment in Asia, which eventually produced an intervention that ended traumatically in the nation's first defeat in war.

Still, the implications of the Korean War for U.S. standing in the Third World is far from one-sided. The saving of South Korea and Taiwan from communism made the United States few friends in the region. Support for the corrupt, authoritarian regimes of Rhee and Jiang often proved an embarrassment. Eventually, however, the economies of South Korea and Taiwan took off and became models for growth in the developing world. In an area where the Soviet Union and especially the PRC frequently generated greater sympathy than the United States, the economic successes of South Korea and Taiwan were of more than passing significance in the contest between capitalism and socialism.

So was the success of Japan, and the Korean War provided an important jump start to that nation's economy. As historian Roger Dingman has observed, on the eve of war, "Japanese and American Occupation officials had struggled for four years, with indifferent success, to re-ignite the engines of prosperity."[48] During 1949 the Americans had imposed a severe austerity program, which produced a large budget surplus but also fueled unemployment and business failures. Then came the Korean War, during which Japan's gross national product grew at an annual rate of more than 10 percent. Japan's index of industrial production jumped 50 percent. The value of exports rose from

1950 to 1952 by 53 percent, the total value of foreign trade by 84 percent. The source of the boom is clear. Over a four-year period beginning in June 1950, the United States spent almost three billion dollars in Japan on military-related goods and services.

Although the North Korean attack and eventual Chinese intervention increased Japanese concerns about security, the war led to an augmented U.S. military presence in the country and in the region in general. The United States also pressed Japan to rearm. Within two weeks of the outbreak of war, General MacArthur called on Japan to create a 75,000-man national police reserve and to expand by 8,000 men its maritime safety force. Japanese leaders did not realize for some time that the occupation commander intended these moves as the foundation for an army and navy, and they later resisted pressures from Washington to build up their armed forces on a large scale.[49] The successful U.S. defense of South Korea and the American military presence in the area made this stance possible, thus enabling Japan to pursue its economic development relatively unburdened by the commitment of resources to its armed forces.

The war hardly eliminated Japan's problems. The sharply increased international demand for raw materials led to inflated prices on many of the items Japan needed most to produce the finished goods it wanted to sell abroad. At war's end, therefore, Japan continued to have a serious balance of payments deficit.[50] The Sino-U.S. confrontation in Korea made the United States more adamant than ever regarding allied trade with mainland China, thus temporarily restricting Japan's access to a potentially lucrative market and essential supplier of raw materials. Yet Japan received a measure of compensation through easy access to the U.S. domestic market and assistance in penetrating the markets of Southeast Asia. Finally, in 1957, Washington loosened its policy toward allied trade with the PRC.[51] It may be too much to claim that the Korean War was the critical event in Japan's move toward global economic power a generation later, but unquestionably the conflict provided a badly needed stimulus to a nation still largely unrecovered from defeat in World War II.

Given the attention devoted in the body of this book to the role of the United Nations in the diplomacy of the Korean War, it is appropriate to conclude with an assessment of the conflict's impact on that organization. The most obvious point is that the war did not turn the international body into an effective agency of collective security. North Korea's attack of June 1950 came three years after members of the United Nations Military Staff Committee had failed to agree on the nature of an international armed force.[52] The early UN response to the invasion of South Korea produced some hope in non-Communist nations that the international body might become a critical instrument of collective action. Yet by 1953 the largely ineffective efforts of the Collective Measures Committee and the Soviet return to the Security Council called into question the ability of the United Nations to repeat its achievement in Korea. Indeed, the conflict was the lone case in the entire cold war in which the United Nations acted in an official capacity to defend a state under military attack. Even in Korea, less than a third of the total membership contributed military forces, many of the contributions were token in nature, and all of them were motivated by specific calculations of national advantage rather than broad commitments to collective security. The United States dominated the Korean enterprise, but it was unable to build on the venture to provide the United Nations with the wherewithal to protect other states in the future. The trials and tribulations of U.S. diplomacy in the UN General Assembly from late 1950 to the end of the war discouraged such an effort, which, in the face of Soviet opposition and allied reservation, never had much prospect for success anyway.

Nor did the United Nations emerge from Korea with an enhanced reputation for resolving international disputes. The war failed to end Korea's division, and it was instrumental in barring from membership in the United Nations the government in control of the world's most populous nation. With the PRC and the DPRK, not to mention the ROK, standing outside the organization, it hardly could expect to play a key role in future negotiations regarding the peninsula. Even the UN's part at crucial moments in containing the conflict in Korea by restraining the United States was not widely appreciated at the time. The war, in short, did not leave the Unites Nations with a measurably enhanced reputation.[53]

Yet, arguably, its response in Korea saved the United Nations from virtual extinction as a broadly inclusive international organization. On the eve of that conflict, the Soviet Union absented itself from the Security Council allegedly in protest of the Council's failure to grant the new regime in Beijing its rightful occupation of China's seat. Had the North Koreans not launched their attack in late June 1950, that particular issue would have been resolved in a matter of months in the PRC's favor, thus eliminating the Soviet excuse for its boycott. On the other hand, had the United States failed to take the lead in the United Nations in repulsing the North Korean attack, it still would have hardened its previously flexible policy on China's seat. With the PRC frozen out of the United Nations indefinitely, which in all likelihood was precisely what the Soviets wanted, and the organization showing no sign of taking effective action on pivotal issues, Moscow would have had little reason not to withdraw completely and establish an international body of its own. If Soviet bloc countries withdrew from the United Nations, some neutrals probably would have done the same simply to avoid being associated with an organization that lacked representation from one of the two sides in the cold war. Had the United Nations become merely an organization of like-minded states in a sharply divided world, its prospects for remaining a significant force in international politics, or even for survival, certainly would have declined. The UN response to the North Korean attack eliminated this possibility, however, by demonstrating to the Soviets the liabilities entailed in their absence from the organization's key bodies. Paradoxically, the Korean War ensured the Soviet Union's ongoing membership in the United Nations at the same time that it froze out the PRC for an entire generation. But, for the long term development of the United Nations, the former result proved a good deal more significant than the latter.

Thus Korea was a conflict fraught with paradox. It pushed China and the Soviet Union closer together in an immediate sense only to generate forces that afterward would split them apart more rapidly than otherwise would have been the case. It accentuated bipolarity by increasing tensions between the superpowers and making their allies more dependent on them, but also added to the determination of many Third-World neutrals to avoid committing to either side. Although its early stages saw the United States using the United Nations effectively as an instrument of national policy, China's intervention led to others using the organization successfully in the quest to restrain the Americans. That young organization played a critical role in the conflict, but was not really strengthened as a result. China emerged from the war an overall winner, but so too did its arch enemy the United States. Perhaps the greatest paradox of all was that the conflict wrought terrible devastation to Korea, militarized the cold war as never before, and often threatened to escalate out of control, yet at its end the great powers were less likely to become directly embroiled on the battlefield than before it began. Whatever the problems it left unresolved, the war was a defining event in "the long peace" between the Soviet Union and the United States that marked the era following the holocausts of the two world wars.

• NOTES •

ABBREVIATIONS USED IN NOTES

AA     Australian Archives (Mitchell Branch), ACT, Australia
CAB     Cabinet
*CDSP*     *Current Digest of the Soviet Press*
CM     Cabinet Papers
CPR     Carlos P. Romulo Papers, University of the Philippines Library, Quezon City, Metro Manila, The Philippines
*CR*     U.S. Congress, *Congressional Record*
DA     Dean Acheson Papers, Harry S. Truman Library, Independence, Mo.
DDE     Dwight D. Eisenhower Papers, Dwight D. Eisenhower Library, Abilene, Kans.
DDEL     Dwight D. Eisenhower Library, Abilene, Kans.
DEA     Department of External Affairs, Ottawa/Hull, Canada
DEFE     Defense Committee
*DSB*     U.S. Department of State, *Department of State Bulletin*
*DSOD*     U.S. Department of State, Office of Public Opinion Studies, *Daily Summaries of Opinion Development*, Record Group 59, National Archives, Washington, D.C.
EQ     Elpidio Quirino Papers, Ayala Museum and Library, Makati, Metro Manila, The Philippines
*FBIS*     *Foreign Broadcast Information Service*
FEC     Far Eastern Command
FO     Foreign Office
*FR*     U.S. Department of State, *Foreign Relations of the United States*, Washington, D.C.: U.S. Government Printing Office, 1955–1985
GE     George Elsey Papers, Harry S. Truman Library, Independence, Mo.
HAS     H. Alexander Smith Papers, Seeley Mudd Library, Princeton University, Princeton, N.J.
HD     Hugh Dalton Papers, London School of Economics, London, England
*HJCS*     James F. Schnabel and Robert J. Watson, *The History of the Joint Chiefs of Staff*, 4 vols., Wilmington, Del.: Michael Glazier, 1979
HKAN     Headquarters, U.S. Far Eastern Command, Military History Section, "History of the Korean Conflict: Korean Armistice Negotiations (July 1951–May 1952)," unpublished manuscript available in the Modern Military Branch, National Archives, Washington, D.C.
HST     Harry S. Truman Papers, Harry S. Truman Library, Independence, Mo.
HSTL     Harry S. Truman Library, Independence, Mo.
*IS*     U.S. Far Eastern Command, *Intelligence Summaries*, Record Group 260, Washington National Records Center, Suitland, Md.
JFD     John Foster Dulles Papers, Seeley Mudd Library, Princeton University, Princeton, N.J.
KAN     Korean Armistice Negotiations, 1951–1958, Office, Deputy Chief of Staff for Military Operations, Record Group 319, National Archives, Washington, D.C.

| | |
|---|---|
| KP | Korean Project of the Division of Historical Policy Research, U.S. Department of State, Record Group 59, National Archives, Washington, D.C. |
| KYD | Kenneth Younger Diary, The Open University, Milton Keynes, England |
| LC | Library of Congress, Manuscript Division, James Madison Building, Washington, D.C. |
| MSAO | U.S. Department of State, Office of Public Opinion Studies, "Monthly Survey of American Opinion," Record Group 59, National Archives, Washington, D.C. |
| *MSFE* | U.S. Congress, Senate, Armed Services and Foreign Relations Committees, *Military Situation in the Far East*, 82d Cong., 1st session, 1951 |
| *MZM* | Jianguo Yilai Mao Zedong Wengao, *Mao Zedong's Manuscripts Since the Founding of the PRC*, vols. 1–3, Beijing: Central Document Publishing House, 1987 |
| NA | National Archives, Washington, D.C. |
| NSC | National Security Council |
| *NYT* | *The New York Times* |
| *OR* | *Official Records* |
| PAC | Public Archives of Canada, Ottawa, Canada |
| *PPPUS* | U.S. Presidents, *Public Papers of the Presidents of the United States*, Washington, D.C.: U.S. Government Printing Office, 1965–. |
| PRO | Public Records Office, Kew, England |
| PS | "Princeton Seminars," Dean G. Acheson Papers, Harry S. Truman Library, Independence, Mo. |
| PSF | President's Secretary's Files, Harry S. Truman Papers, Truman Library, Independence, Mo. |
| RG | Record Group (National Archives and Washington National Records Center) |
| *SCMP* | U.S. Consulate General, Hong Kong, *Survey of the China Mainland Press* |
| SRRKW | Selected Records Relating to the Korean War, Harry S. Truman Papers, Truman Library, Independence, Mo. |
| TS | Top Secret (now declassified) |
| UNA | United Nations Archives, New York, N.Y. |
| UNC | United Nations Command |
| UNGA | United Nations General Assembly |
| UNSC | United Nations Security Council |
| *USAKW* | U.S. Department of the Army, *United States Army in the Korean War*, 3 vols., Washington, D.C.: U.S. Government Printing Office, 1961–1972 |
| WA | Warren Austin Papers, Bailey-Howe Library, University of Vermont, Burlington, Vt. |
| WIKF | War in Korea File, Department of External Affairs, Ottawa, Canada |
| WNRC | Washington National Records Center, Suitland, Md. |

INTRODUCTION

1. For a dispassionate assessment of Soviet and satellite strength from the late 1940s to the mid-1950s, see Thomas W. Wolfe, *Soviet Power and Europe 1945–1970*, 9–11, 38–49. Wolfe suggests that Khrushchev's figures for 1948 are somewhat low and those for 1955 high, but he does not question the substantial Soviet buildup during the period.

2. Hunt, "The Long Crisis," 138.

CHAPTER 1
THE ORIGINS OF THE KOREAN WAR

1. A few writers have tended to accept North Korea's claim that South Korea commenced hostilities by moving across the 38th parallel with its own forces, although it is rare outside North Korea itself that anyone is heard subscribing to the view that South Korean attacks represented a major offensive. For a detailed discussion of the matter, including a listing of pertinent primary and secondary sources, see Cumings, *Origins of the Korean War*, 2:568–621, 878–88; see also Frank Baldwin's notes in Noble, *Embassy at War*, 313–16. Although Cumings raises important questions about who started the fighting on 25 June, the weight of the evidence points to the North Koreans.

2. Noble, *Embassy at War*, 229.

3. The most detailed comparison of North and South Korean armed forces remains *USAKW*, 1:7–18. Between February 1948 and the spring of 1950, 80,000 to 100,000 soldiers of Korean extraction joined North Korean units after having fought in Communist armies in Manchuria. See Cumings, *Origins of the Korean War*, 2:363.

With the possible exception of Ambassador John J. Muccio, few Americans fully comprehended the disparity between North and South Korean armed forces. For a standard estimate of the balance of forces on the peninsula on the eve of war, see General Headquarters, Supreme Command for the Allied Powers and Far Eastern Command, "General Orientation for the Secretary of Defense and the Chairman of the Joint Chiefs of Staff," 18 June 1950, Box 15, SRRKW.

4. For documentation on the U.S. intervention in Korea, see *FR, 1950*, 7:125–270, and Box 71 of the George Elsey Papers, HSTL. The most detailed secondary account of the intervention is Paige, *Korean Decision*.

5. The two resolutions are reprinted in *FR, 1950*, 7:155–56 and 211.

6. For Security Council debates, including quotes from UNCOK reports, see UNSC, *OR*, 473d meeting, 25 June 1950, and 474th meeting, 27 June 1950. For an outline of UNCOK activities during the first week of hostilities, see W. R. Hodgson (Head of Australian mission in Japan), "United Nations Commission on Korea—Activities Since Outbreaks of Hostilities," 7 July 1950, A1838/T184, 3123/4/5, AA. For a critique of UNCOK operations in Korea in June 1950, see Cumings, *Origins of the Korean War*, 2:547–48.

7. H. Freeman Matthews (deputy under secretary of state) to Dean Acheson (secretary of state), 29 June 1950, Box 4305, 795B.5, RG59, NA.

8. French Foreign Minister Robert Schuman had a reaction common among western European officials when told of the U.S. decision to provide military assistance to South Korea. In an obvious reference to the 1930s, he wept, "Thank God, this will not be a repetition of the past." See Bohlen, *Witness to History*, 291–92.

9. Shann to the Department of External Affairs, 30 June 1950, A1838/T184 (SV), 3123/5/1, AA.

10. Interoffice Memo, Australian Department of External Affairs, 3 July 1950, ibid., 3123/5/2, AA. For U.S. State Department summaries of world reaction, see Acheson's circular intels of 28 and 30 June and 1 July 1950 in Box 2, Classified General Records (Belgrade, Yugoslavia), RG84, WNRC.

11. On Korea's international relations during this period, see Kim and Kim, *Korea and the Politics of Imperialism*; see also Lensen, *Balance of Intrigue*, 2 vols. For background leading up to the period, see Kim, *Last Phase of the East Asian World Order*.

12. Kim, *Korea and the Politics of Imperialism*, 103–18; Lee, *Politics of Korean Nationalism*, 3–85.

13. This account of the Korean independence movement between the world wars is based on Lee, *Politics of Korean Nationalism*, 101–279, which offers the best treatment of the non-Communists; Suh, *Korean Communist Movement*, 3–293; and Lee and Scalapino, *Communism in Korea*, 1:3–232. For an imaginative interpretation of Korean factionalism, see Henderson, *Korea*. In volume 1 of *Origins of the Korean War*, Cumings argues that factionalism in the Communist movement has been overemphasized. He does not deny its existence, however.

14. Chay, *Diplomacy of Asymmetry*, 27–33.

15. Ibid., chap. 2; Lee, *Diplomatic Relations*, chap. 2; Kim, *Last Phase of the East Asian World Order*, chap. 8; Chien, *Opening of Korea*, chap. 6.

16. Recent works on early Korean-U.S. relations include Chay, *Diplomacy of Asymmetry*; Chay, "First Three Decades of American-Korean Relations," and Nahm, "U.S. Policy and Japanese Annexation of Korea," in Kwak, *U.S.-Korean Relations*, 15–53; and Wiltz, "Did the United States Betray Korea," 243–70. Wiltz argues persuasively that the United States did "betray" Korea in refusing to provide its "good offices," although Korean leaders may have expected more than merely a U.S. diplomatic overture to Japan regarding its encroachments on the peninsula.

17. Matray, *Reluctant Crusade*, 8–20.

18. Morris, "Korean Trusteeship," 13–38.

19. Eden, *Memoirs: The Reckoning*, 438; Hull, *Memoirs*, 2:1237.

20. *FR, The Conferences at Cairo and Teheran, 1943*, 449, 869.

21. Ibid., 566; Van Ree, *Socialism in One Zone*, 34–35.

22. *FR, The Conferences at Malta and Yalta, 1945*, 770.

23. "Possible Soviet Attitudes Toward Far Eastern Questions," 2 October 1943, Box 119, Records of Harley A. Notter, 1939–1945, RG59, NA.

24. Van Ree, *Socialism in One Zone*, 34–44.

25. *FR, Conference at Berlin (Potsdam), 1945*, 2:264–66.

26. Matray, *Reluctant Crusade*, 39–46.

27. *FR, Conference at Berlin (Potsdam), 1945*, 1:874, 878; 2:1248; Van Ree, *Socialism in One Zone*, 44–45.

28. *FR, Conference at Berlin (Potsdam), 1945*, 2:1585; Van Ree, *Socialism in One Zone*, 44–45.

29. Sandusky, *America's Parallel*, chap. 8.

30. The initial Soviet invading force suffered nearly five thousand casualties. See Weathersby, "Soviet Policy toward Korea," 185.

31. Sandusky, *America's Parallel*, chap. 8.

32. *NYT*, 10 September 1945, 2.

33. Lauterback, *Danger from the East*, 217.

34. As Commander of the Tenth Army, General Joseph Stilwell might have been in line to head U.S. occupation forces, but in mid-August Hodge's XXIV Corps was removed from this force, apparently because Nationalist Chinese leader Jiang Jieshi objected to Stilwell having control over any U.S. units that might occupy the peninsula or the Chinese coast. See Tuchman, *Stilwell*, 520–21.

35. Van Ree, *Socialism in One Zone*, 54.

36. *NYT*, 12 September 1945, 9.

37. *NYT*, 14 September 1945, 1.

38. Koh, "In Quest of National Unity and Power," 8, 255.

39. Henderson, *Korea*, 126; Cumings, *Origins of the Korean War*, 1:72–79, 153–56.

40. Lauterback, *Danger from the East*, 203.

41. Cumings, *Origins of the Korean War*, 1:72–79, 141–44, 182–93; U.S. Army Forces in Korea, "History of the United States Army Forces in Korea," vol. 2, chaps. 1–2, 4. This unpublished three-volume study was written by members of the historical office in Hodge's command. The largest published primary source on the U.S. occupation is U.S. Department of the Army, Supreme Commander Allied Powers, Japan, *Summation of Non-Military Activities in Japan and Korea*. After the first five volumes, the reports on Korea are published separately as *Summation of U.S. Army Military Government Activities in Korea*, vols. 6–22, and then *South Korean Interim Government Activities*, vols. 23–35. The most extensive unpublished source is RG332, WNRC.

42. See the first installment of Yu Song-Chol's memoirs in *FBIS*, 15 November 1990. Yu, a former general in the North Korean army who was eventually exiled to the Soviet Union, served in the Soviet unit with Kim from 1943 to 1945. Kim was thirty-three years old when he returned to Korea in September 1945.

43. Van Ree, *Socialism in One Zone*, chaps. 4–9; "History of United States Army Forces in Korea," 1:chaps. 1–3. For Kim's early advocacy of a separate organization in the North, see his report of 10 October 1945 in Kim, *Works*, 1:272–92.

44. For the text of the Moscow accords in Korea, see U.S. Department of State, *Moscow Meeting of Foreign Ministers*, 14–16.

45. For U.S. records of the meetings, see RG43, "US-USSR Joint Commission on Korea," NA.

46. Factional struggles within the Korean Communist movement during 1945 and 1946 are covered in Lee and Scalapino, *Communism in Korea*, 1:314–65. On unrest in the North, see Van Ree, *Socialism in One Zone*, 151–54.

47. Wiltz, "Did the United States Betray Korea in 1905?" 251; Chay, *Diplomacy of Asymmetry*, 151.

48. The most up-to-date account of conditions in the South is in Cumings, *Origins of the Korean War*, 1: chaps. 6–10.

49. Jacobs to Marshall, 19 September 1947, *FR, 1947*, 7:802–7.

50. Ibid., 738. U.S. policy toward Korea during 1947 is covered in depth in my *Road to Confrontation*, chap. 3, in Matray, *Reluctant Crusade*, chaps. 5–6, and in McGlothlen, *Controlling the Waves*, 44–55.

51. Butterworth to Lovett, 1 October 1947, *FR, 1947*, 6:820–21.

52. Pauley to Truman, 6 June 1946, *FR, 1946*, 8:713.

53. Sayre to Marshall, 22 September 1947, Box 36, RG84, NA. For other expressions of concern about U.S. prestige, see *FR, 1947*, 6:742–43, 784–85.

54. See, for example, Lt. Col. T. N. Dupuy to General Schuyler, 9 September 1947, 091 Korea (TS), RG319, NA.

55. Matray, *Reluctant Crusade*, 135–46.

56. On UNTCOK, see Gordenker, *United Nations and the Peaceful Unification of Korea*, chap. 3. On India, see Dayal, *India's Role in the Korean Question*, chap. 2. On Australia, see O'Neill, *Australia in the Korean War*, 1:7–10, for a secondary account, and A1838/T184 (SV), 3123/4/5/1 and 3123/4/6, AA, for detailed documentation. The Canadian side is covered in the diaries of Mackenzie King and Lester B. Pearson, then a leading official of the Department of External Affairs and soon to be its head. These diaries are located in the private papers of the two men in the PAC. More readily available sources are Pearson's *Mike*, 2:135–45, and Pickersgill and Foster, *Mackenzie King Record*, 4: chap. 4. For the British side, see FO371/69938, 69939, and 69954 in

the PRO. For an account that places the Korean issue in the context of UN activities at the time, see Luard, *History of the United Nations*, 1:229–39.

57. For a balanced analysis of the Pyongyang conference and the election, see Merrill, *Korea*, 70–82.

58. Hodge to Marshall, 26 June 1948, *FR, 1948*, 6:1229–30. The most detailed account of UNTCOK's role is Gordenker, *United Nations and the Peaceful Unification of Korea*, chap. 4.

59. Kim, *Divided Korea*, 115–32.

60. McCune, *Korea Today*, 129–39.

61. On the Cheju-do and Yosu rebellions, see Merrill, *Korea*, 84–92, 98–129.

62. Muccio to Marshall, 12 November 1948, *FR, 1948*, 6:1326. See also CIA, "Review of the World Situation," 16 December 1948, Box 205, PSF.

63. For two revealing State Department documents on Korea, see Butterworth to Marshall, 4 March 1948, *FR, 1948*, 6:1136–39, and Bishop to Butterworth, 17 December 1948, ibid., 1337–40.

64. Deputy Under Secretary Dean Rusk and Assistant Secretary W. Walton Butterworth warned against a total withdrawal of U.S. troops, but when Ambassador Muccio refused to support them, Secretary of State Dean Acheson submitted to pressure from the Joint Chiefs of Staff. See U. Alexis Johnson Oral History, HSTL; author interview with Rusk, 24 July 1972; Acheson to Muccio, 9 May 1949, and Muccio to Acheson, 11 May 1949, *FR, 1949*, 7:1014, 1018–19. On opposition to U.S. withdrawal within the UN commission, see E. Ranshofen-Wertheimer to the Secretary-General and Assistant Secretary-General, Department of Security Council Affairs, 28 May 1949, DAG-1/2.1.2–2, UNA. On Filipino opposition, see Under Secretary for Foreign Affairs Felino Neri to President Quirino, 18 July 1949, Box: Department of Foreign Affairs, Office of the Secretary, EQ; Romulo, *Third World Soldier at the UN*, 103–4.

65. For various estimates of the balance of forces, see Muccio to Acheson, 11 June 1949, *FR, 1949*, 7:1042; *IS*, 12 and 15 May and 4 and 7 June 1949; Roberts to Department of the Army, 23 April, 13 May, 11 and 18 June 1949, Box C-946, RG59, NA; on U.S. economic and military assistance and appeals for support in the United Nations, see Stueck, *Road to Confrontation*, 158–59.

66. *FR, 1949*, 7:1046–57; Maddocks to Bradley, 23 June 1949, 091 Korea (TS), RG319, NA; Stueck, *Road to Confrontation*, 154–59.

67. Cumings, *Origins of the Korean War*, 2:358–63.

68. Merrill, *Korea*, 143–44.

69. U.S. Department of the Army, *Military Advisers in Korea*, 104.

70. The best accounts of the border fighting are Merrill, *Korea*, 135–43, and Cumings, *Origins of the Korean War*, 2:388–98.

71. U.S. Central Intelligence Agency, "Current Capabilities of the North Korean Regime," 19 June 1950, RG260, WNRC.

72. Stueck, *Road to Confrontation*, 146–51, 169; Schaller, *American Occupation of Japan*, chaps. 13–14.

73. *DSB*, 22 (23 January 1950): 111–16.

74. For MacArthur's statement, see Goulden, *Korea*, 31. For an imaginative yet unpersuasive argument that Acheson intended to give the North Koreans the green light to attack, see Cumings, *Origins of the Korean War*, 2:408–38.

75. For an analysis of domestic political pressures in relation to Taiwan, see my *Road to Confrontation*, 137–43.

76. Terenti Shtykov (Soviet ambassador to North Korea) to Vishinsky, 19 January 1950, in Weathersby, "To Attack, or Not to Attack?" 8.

77. *USAKW*, 1:12; Cumings, *Origins of the Korean War*, 2:445–48, 451; Merrill, *Korea*, 177–78.

78. Khrushchev's *Khrushchev Remembers* (367–70) was the first Soviet source to reveal Soviet involvement in preparation of the attack or even that North Korea had initiated it. The recent release of Soviet documents has confirmed most of Khrushchev's claims and added some important details. For a translation and discussion of "On the Korean War, 1950–53, and the Armistice Negotiations," a report to Soviet leaders dated 9 August 1966, see Weathersby, "New Findings." For a discussion of other evidence from the Soviet side, see Goncharov, Lewis, and Xue, *Uncertain Partners*, chap. 5; Weathersby, "The Soviet Role," "Soviet Aims in Korea," and "To Attack, or Not to Attack?"; Merrill, *Korea*, chap. 1 and 177–79; and Bonwetsch and Kuhfus,"Die Sowjetunion, China und der Koreakrieg," 34–35. I wish to thank my colleague John Haag for translating portions of the Bonwetsch and Kuhfus article.

79. The best accounts of the guerrilla and counterguerrilla campaigns during 1949 and early 1950 are in Merrill, *Korea*, 143–67, and Cumings, *Origins of the Korean War*, 2:268–90, 398–407.

80. For increasing contacts between the ROK and Japan and Pyongyang's expressions of concern about them, see Cumings, *Origins of the Korean War*, 458–65; Merrill, *Korea*, 172–73. The North Koreans entitled their attack plan, presented in Moscow at the end of February, the "Korean people's army preemptive strike plan" (*The Korean Herald*, 30 August 1992, 1; see also *FBIS*, 27 December 1990).

81. On the purges of 1949 and 1950, see Hahn, *Postwar Soviet Politics*, 122–29, 136–39, and Ulam, *Stalin*, 705–14. In characterizing Stalin's inner thoughts during his final declining years, Ulam identifies "two conflicting emotions": the first was "a genuine weariness and a desire to lay down his awesome duties before he would be 'found out' to be incapable of discharging them"; the second was the realization "that a man in his position cannot really retire, that one cannot be a part-time despot" (ibid., 725). For firsthand accounts of Stalin's suspicions of those around him during his last years, see Alliluyeva, *Twenty Letters to a Friend*, 196–200, and Khrushchev, *Khrushchev Remembers*, 246, 275, 279. As Taubman has pointed out (*Stalin's American Policy*, 197), "Seeing enemies all around him was nothing new for Stalin." For secondary accounts that emphasize domestic pressures in the formulation of Soviet foreign policy, see McCagg, *Stalin Embattled*, chap. 14, and Ra'anan, *International Policy Formation in the USSR*.

82. This account of factionalism is based on Letteney, "Foreign Policy Factionalism under Stalin." I wish to thank Jack Snyder of Columbia University for pointing out this work to me. In interpreting the domestic bases of Stalin's foreign policy, I have also drawn on Snyder's "The Gorbachov Revolution," 94–105. On Stalin's personality in his last years, Ulam's *Stalin*, chaps. 13 and 14, was useful.

83. Letteney, "Foreign Policy Factionalism under Stalin," 217. On the Soviet buildup in eastern Europe, see Holloway, *Stalin and the Bomb*, 232, 240–41.

84. See, for example, "Monthly Review of Soviet Tactics, January 1950," 6 February 1950, FO371/868731, PRO.

85. For Soviet preparations to attack Yugoslavia, see Bela K. Kiraly, "The Aborted Soviet Military Plans Against Tito's Yugoslavia," in Vucinich, ed., *At the Brink of War and Peace*, 273–88.

86. Brzezinski, *Soviet Bloc*, 91–97. See also Tismaneanu, *Reinventing Politics*, 39–54.

87. On the harassment of diplomats, see Sir David Kelly (British ambassador to the Soviet Union), "Soviet Union: Quarterly Report, January–March 1950," 30 May 1950, FO371/87609, PRO. For evidence that Stalin had some reason for fearing British and U.S. activities in eastern Europe, see Yurechko, "Containment to Counteroffensive," 67–93.

88. The best sources for background on Sino-Soviet relations are Garver, *Chinese-Soviet Relations*; Westad, *Cold War*; and Goncharov, Lewis, and Xue, *Uncertain Partners*.

89. Mao, *People's Democratic Dictatorship*.

90. Wu, *Eight Years*, 4–5; Chen, "Sino-Soviet Alliance," 13–15.22.

91. For memoirs of the event, see Shi, "I Accompanied Chairman Mao," Federenko, "Stalin-Mao Summit," and Kovalev, "Stalin-Mao Dialogue," pt. 2. The most detailed secondary account is Goncharov, Lewis, and Xue, *Uncertain Partners*. See also Kramer's "The USSR Foreign Ministry's Appraisal," 171–73.

92. Goncharov, Lewis, and Xue, *Uncertain Partners*, chap. 4.

93. Letteney, "Foreign Policy Factionalism under Stalin," 221 n, 260–62. In *Strained Alliance* (chap. 4) Simmons argues vigorously that the Soviets walked out of the Security Council to keep the PRC from entering the United Nations. See also Goncharov, Lewis, and Xue, *Uncertain Partners*, 84–129.

94. Swearingen and Langer, *Red Flag in Japan*, chaps. 18–20.

95. For evidence of Ho's presence in Moscow in early 1950, see Wu, *Eight Years*, 23.

96. On the Pacific pact, see Meyer, *Diplomatic History of the Philippine Republic*, chap. 7, and Mabon, "Elusive Agreements"; also boxes 1.3 and 1.4, Romulo Papers, and box entitled "Department of Foreign Affairs, Specific Subjects," EQ. For Acheson's speech of 12 January 1950, see *DSB*, 22 (23 January 1950): 111–16.

97. *DSB*, 20 (19 June 1949): 783.

98. Martin, *Divided Counsel*, chaps. 15, 17, 20.

99. See Gordenker, *United Nations and the Peaceful Unification of Korea*, and Dayal, *India's Role in the Korean Question*, 64–71; see also the numerous reports of the principal secretaries of UNCOK to the secretary-general in DAG-1/2.1–2-2–6, UN Archives.

100. Matray, *Reluctant Crusade*, 219–21.

101. Goncharov, Lewis, and Xue, *Uncertain Partners*, 145.

102. Weathersby, "Soviet Role," 7–8.

103. Weathersby, "New Findings," 16; Goncharov, Lewis, and Xue, *Uncertain Partners*, 136–48.

104. Khrushchev, *Khrushchev Remembers*, 368.

105. *NYT*, 6 January 1950, 1; *DSB*, 22 (16 January 1950): 80.

106. On U.S. military strength in early 1950, see Trachtenberg, "'Wasting Asset,'" 5–48.

107. *DSB*, 22 (17 April 1950): 602.

108. *FR, 1950*, 7:64–67.

109. UNCOK requested Lie to raise the matter, but the secretary-general declined. See A. B. Jamieson (acting chairman, UNCOK) to Lie, 28 April 1950, DAG 1/2.1.2–4, UN Archives. Lie's explanation, in retrospect fraught with irony, was that "I concentrated attention on a number of more acute problems and above all on the most immediate problem now facing the United Nations, that of the continued participation of the

Soviet Union and the countries of Eastern Europe in the work of various organs of the United Nations. . . . The question of Korea was not mentioned . . . and I felt that it would not be appropriate, in the context of these conversations, to give undue emphasis to this problem."

110. For a dispassionate analysis of the election, see Bertil A. Renborg (principal secretary, UNCOK), to Lie, 15 June 1950, ibid.

111. Evidence from China corroborates Khrushchev's story of PRC Premier and Foreign Minister Zhou Enlai's visit to the Soviet Union in early October 1950, thus adding credibility to his claim that earlier Mao had approved his idea of North Korea's attack. See Chen, "Sino-Soviet Alliance," 21, 30–31.

112. Ibid., 22–23; Nie, *Huiyilu* (Memoirs), 748.

113. Weathersby, "New Findings," 16.

114. Cumings, *Origins of the Korean War*, 2:350–55.

115. Yu, "My Testimony," *FBIS*, 27 December 1990; Goncharov, Lewis, and Xue, *Uncertain Partners*, 145–46, 330 n. 77.

116. See especially Schram, *Mao Tse-tung*, chap. 3; Mancall, *China at the Center*, chap. 9.

117. Zhang, *Deterrence*, chap. 2.

118. Mao, *Selected Works*, 4:416.

119. Zhang, *Deterrence*, 14–21.

120. Stueck, *Road to Confrontation*, 126; Chang, *Friends and Enemies*, 31–32.

121. Chen, "Sino-Soviet Alliance," 16.

122. He, "Last Campaign to Unify China," 5–6.

123. Ibid., 16–19; Mao to the Central Committee of the Chinese Communist Party, 2 January 1950, in *MZM*, 211–12; Goncharov, Lewis, and Xue, *Uncertain Partners*, 84–97.

124. On PRC recognition of the DRV, see Chen, "China and the First Indochina War," 2. On Chinese seizure of U.S. consular compounds in Beijing, see Stueck, *Road to Confrontation*, 133, 135. My interpretation of that event has changed as a result of the documentation that has recently become available on the Chinese side. See Goncharov, Lewis, and Xue, *Uncertain Partners*, 98–99.

125. For a detailed discussion of the agreements, see Goncharov, Lewis, and Xue, *Uncertain Partners*, 111–29.

126. Zhang, *Deterrence*, 32.

127. Ibid.

128. He, "Last Campaign to Unify China," 8–9.

129. Chen, "China and the First Indochina War," 2–6.

130. See Chen, "China's Road to the Korean War," 146.

131. Ibid., 162.

132. Unless otherwise cited, this section is based on Merrill, *Korea*, 172–77.

133. For the recollections of participants in Soviet and North Korean planning, see Lim, *Founding*, 171–74; Yu, "My Testimony," *FBIS*, 27 December 1990.

134. Renborg to Lie and Zinchenko, 16 June 1950, Box 4, DAG-1, 2.1.2, UN Archives.

135. Merrill, *Korea*, 176.

136. Renborg to Lie and Zinchenko, 23 June 1950, Box 4, DAG-1, 2.1.2, UN Archives.

137. Kim, *Works*, 5:421–23. This rhetoric, and that in another talk of 22 June, contrasted sharply with Kim's words to military forces of the previous summer, when

South Korean military actions along the border were on a far larger scale than in May and June 1950. See ibid., 187, 190–91, 424–25, 429.

138. See Trachtenberg, "'Wasting Asset,'" 11–12, and Jervis, "Impact of the Korean War on the Cold War," 564–78.

139. Rusk to Acheson, 26 April 1950, *FR, 1950*, 6:335; *IS*, 6 May 1950; CIA, "Reports of Current Soviet Military Activity in China," 21 April 1950, Box 255, PSF.

140. On the Malayan revolt, see Short, *Communist Insurrection in Malaya*, chap. 8; on conditions in the Philippines, see Kerksvlict, *Huk Rebellion*, chap. 6, and Smith, *Philippine Freedom*, chaps. 6 and 7.

141. For U.S. concerns regarding the Philippines, see Acheson to Truman, 20 April 1950, and Rusk to Webb, 17 May 1950, *FR, 1950*, 6:1440–44, 1450. For evidence of growing concern regarding the psychological dimension of Taiwan's fate, see Rusk to Acheson, 30 May 1950, ibid., 349–51. For a Filipino perspective on Taiwan, see Silvino Lu. Barro to Carlos P. Romulo, 16 October 1950, Box 1.5, CPR.

142. See *FR, 1950*, 6:29.

143. Stueck, *Road to Confrontation*, 146–52, 165–70; for a broad survey of the evolution of U.S. policy toward Southeast Asia, see Hess, *United States' Emergence*, chap. 11.

144. For more on domestic politics and U.S. policy toward Asia, see Kaufman, *Korean War*, 34–37, and Stueck, *Road to Confrontation*, 143–51.

145. *FR, 1950*, 1:235–92; Gaddis, *Strategies of Containment*, chaps. 3–5.

146. *FR, 1950*, 1:145–46; see also Jervis, "Impact of the Korean War on the Cold War," 577.

147. *FR, 1950*, 1:289; see also 252. For a more detailed discussion of this point, see Trachtenberg, "'Wasting Asset,'" 13–16.

148. On U.S. perceptions of prospects in eastern Europe after the Stalin-Tito split, see Heuser, *Western "Containment" Policies*, 13–15, 54–55, 65–67, 76–80.

149. See Stueck, *Road to Confrontation*, 131–37.

150. *FR, 1950*, 1:198.

151. For Secretary of State Acheson's concern about the U.S. public's false sense of security, see ibid., 207.

152. *PPPUS: Harry S. Truman, 1950*, 286.

153. U.S. Department of State, *United States Policy in the Korean Crisis*, 18.

154. Acheson to Kirk, 28 June 1950, RG84, WNRC. See also George F. Kennan, "Possible Further Communist Initiatives in the Light of the Korean Situation," Kennan Papers.

155. Theodore Achilles (director, Office of Western European Affairs), to H. Freeman Matthews (deputy under secretary of state), 26 June 1950, Box 1, KP.

156. Memorandum of Conversation by John Foster Dulles, 1 July 1950, Box 47, JFD.

157. For administration calculations that the Soviet Union probably was not planning a general war in the immediate future or even military probes in other areas, see U.S. National Security Council, "The Position and Actions of the U.S. with respect to Possible Further Soviet Moves in the Light of the Korean Situation," 1 July 1950, 092 Korea, RG330, NA. On hesitation in Washington to commit U.S. troops, see Matray, *Reluctant Crusade*, chap. 10. On the assumption that U.S. nuclear superiority had deterrent value, see Dingman, "Atomic Diplomacy," 51–52.

158. Gromyko, *Memories*, 101–2.

159. Goncharov, Lewis, and Xue, *Uncertain Partners*, 161–62.

160. Weiss, "Storm Around the Cradle," 12–60, 224; Mao, *Selected Works*, 5:38–39. See also the May Day speech of Vice Chairman Liu Shaoqi in Liu Shaoqi, *Collected Works*, 194–95, and Hao and Zhai, "China's Decision to Enter the Korean War," 99.

161. I pointed out earlier that the Soviet walkout from the Security Council in mid-January actually was designed to keep the PRC out of that organ rather than to gain its admission. But the Soviets did consult Mao in advance of making the move, and the Chinese leader approved, albeit without knowing the real Soviet motive (see Mao to the Central Committee, 7 January 1950, in *MZM*, 219). The United States already had announced that it considered the issue of China's seat at the United Nations to be a procedural one, meaning that the great power veto did not apply. Yet Washington also made it clear that it would vote against the PRC taking China's seat. Naturally Beijing regarded the U.S. position as the key in preventing the PRC from taking its rightful place.

162. Mao's idea on warfare presented in his famous trilogy "Strategic Problems of China's Revolutionary War" (1936), "Strategic Problems in the Anti-Japanese Guerrilla War" (1938), and "On Protracted War" (1938) are published in English translations in *Selected Works*, vols. 1–2. A convenient summary may be found in Katzenbach and Hanrahan, "Revolutionary Strategy," 131–46.

## Chapter 2
### The Diplomacy of Confrontation and Consolidation

1. Yu, "My Testimony," *FBIS*, 27 December 1990.

2. *The New York Herald-Tribune*, 1 July 1950, 1.

3. The standard U.S. account of the summer campaigns in Korea is *USAKW*, 1:49–487. On U.S. air operations, see Futrell, *United States Air Force in Korea*, 3–139. For revealing reports on the scale and impact of U.S. bombing and on North Korean casualties, see Joint Daily Sitrep Nos. 44 and 49, 8 and 15 August 1950, Box 262, PSF. Rees's *Korea* is a dated but still useful account of both military and diplomatic events.

4. U.S. Department of State, *United States Policy in the Korean Crisis*, 63.

5. For reports on the Communist press, see CIA, Foreign Broadcast Information Division, "Foreign Radio Comments Related to the Situation in Korea, 4 and 6 July 1950," Box 251, PSF. On Mao's order to send army forces northward, see Hao and Zhai, "China's Decision to Enter the Korean War," 101. On the postponement of plans to attack Jinmen and the shift to a defensive posture regarding Taiwan, see Chen, "China's Road to the Korean War," 185–87.

6. Kelly to Foreign Office, 6 July 1950, F0371/84082, PRO.

7. *FR, 1950*, 6:352.

8. Gopal, *Nehru*, 2:101–3. Sir Eric John Harrison, the Australian High Commissioner to the United Kingdom, reported home the following on 30 June: "U.K. information is that Nehru had a difficult time with his Cabinet before the statement of Indian support [for the second Security Council resolution] was made. He was under some pressure to add to the Indian statement some criticism of the inclusion of Formosa and the Philippines in the Truman declaration." See Harrison to the Department of External Affairs, 30 June 1950, A1838/T184 (SV), 3123/5/1, AA. For an insightful probing of Nehru's views from the U.S. side, see "Nehru's Attitude Toward the United States," an undated paper prepared in the State Department during the fall of 1950 (Box 17, KP).

9. On the British and Indian peace moves, see Acheson, *Present*, 416–20; *FR, 1950*,

7:283–428 passim; Panikkar, *In Two Chinas*, 103; FO371/84081–84084, 84087–91, PRO; on Panikkar's messages from Beijing, see *FR, 1950*, 6:368, 371–72, 374–75.

10. Whiting, *China Crosses the Yalu*, 62; Chen, "China's Strategies," 4.

11. On British policy toward China, see Boardman, *Britain and the People's Republic of China*, 49–52, and Porter, *Britain and the Rise of Communist China*, which are based on published sources; and Martin, *Divided Counsel*, chaps. 17, 20, and 23, and Ovendale, *English-Speaking Alliance*, chap. 7.

12. On Burgess, see Boyle, *Fourth Man*, 1979. On Soviet overtures to the British during May and June, see FO800/511, PRO.

13. J. C. Hutchison (British chargé in Beijing) to Foreign Office, 25 July 1950, FO371/83293, PRO.

14. On Chinese and Soviet scare tactics regarding Taiwan, see Warwick Chipman (Canadian High Commissioner to India) to Pearson, 10 July 1950, vol. 3, WIKF.

15. See the minutes of the second tripartite ministerial meeting of 11 May 1950 at the London conferences in FO800/449, PRO, and Kenneth Younger to Clement Attlee, 29 June 1950, FO800/511, PRO; see also *FR, 1950*, 2:186–87, 207–10, 217–19, 235–43.

16. *FR, 1950*, 2:245–47.

17. Acheson to Paul Nitze, 12 July 1950, DA.

18. Lowe, *Origins of the Korean War*, 153; Chang, *Friends and Enemies*, 73–74.

19. Caridi, *Korean War and American Politics*, 58–64.

20. Rusk to Acheson, 9 June 1950, Records of the Office of Chinese Affairs, Box 15, RG59, NA.

21. See, for example, *NYT*, 2 July 1950, 4:1.

22. Acheson, *Present*, 436; see also Adenauer, *Memoirs*, 271–74; Devillers, "Conflit Vu D'Europe," 1202; and Alexander Werth, *France*, 470–73.

23. Bruce to Acheson, 14 July 1950, Box 4299, RG59, NA.

24. See, for example, U.S. High Commissioner's Office (Frankfort), "West Germany Political Weekly," 28 July 1950, Box 34, Declassified Records, 350, RG84, WNRC.

25. "Summary Report," n.d. (clearly late June or early July 1950), Box 1, Records of the Director of the Office of Northeast Asian Affairs, 1945–53, RG59, NA.

26. "Notes taken by BE on Secretary's report of [Cabinet] meeting," 14 July 1950, DA; Reinhard Drifte, "Japan's Involvement in the Korean War," in Cotton and Neary, *Korean War in History*, 122.

27. John Edward Wiltz, "The Korean War and American Society," in Heller, ed., *Korean War*, 116–18.

28. Williams, *Senate and U.S. Troops in Europe*, 12–27.

29. Lawrence S. Kaplan, "The Korean War and U.S. Foreign Relations: The Case of NATO," in Heller, *Korean War*, 45–57; Acheson, *Present*, 435–45; Egan, "Struggle for the Soul of Faust," 113–66.

30. Acheson, *Present*, 426–35; Schaller, *American Occupation of Japan*, chaps. 15 and 16; Nimmo, *Occupation of Japan*, 4–5, 89–90; Finn, *Winners in Peace*, 263–64.

31. Pearson, "Discussions with Mr. Acheson and Officials in Washington Saturday and Sunday, July 29th and 30th, 1950," vol. 15, Pearson Papers, PAC. Parts of this document are printed in Pearson, *Mike*, 2:149–54.

32. Holmes to A.D.P. Heeney, 1 July 1950, vol. 2, WIKF.

33. A. W. Cordier to Colonel A. G. Katzin, 18 July 1950, DAG-1/2.1.2/4, UNA.

34. Lie, *In the Cause of Peace*, 333–34; *HJCS*, vol. 3, pt. 1, 131–38.

35. For the text of the resolution, see *FR, 1950*, 4:329; on discussions between the United States and its allies, see vol. 2, WIKF.

36. Holmes to Pearson, 8 July 1950, vol. 3, WIKF. For background on Austin, see Mazuzan, *Austin*.

37. K.C.O. Shann (Minister of Australian mission to the UN) to the Department of External Affairs, 18 August 1950, A1838, 852/20/4/2/11, AA.

38. JSPC 853/39, 10 August 1950, 091 Korea (TS), RG319, NA.

39. *FR, 1950*, 7:482 n.

40. See Boxes 43–45 and 4306 in the decimal files of RG59, NA.

41. See JSPC 853/39, 10 August 1950, and Memorandum for General Schuyler from Colonel John M. Willemms, 13 July 1950, 091 Korea (TS), RG 319, MMB, NA.

42. UNSC, *OR*, 479th meeting, 31 July 1950, 2.

43. See, for example, *DSB*, 23 (23 February 1950): 272–74.

44. See above, p. 44.

45. On the peace campaign in the weeks following the outbreak of war in Korea, see *NYT*, 7 July 1950, 3; 22 July 1950, 4; 5 August 1950, 43; 6 August 1950, 4:5; see also CIA, Foreign Broadcast Information Division, "Foreign Radio Comments Related to the Situation in Korea," 2, 10, 17, and 28 July 1950, Box 251, PSF. For background and evolution of the campaign, see Stebbins et al., *United States in World Affairs, 1950*, 153–60.

46. UNSC, *OR*, vols. 5–6, 1950.

47. Shulman, *Stalin's Foreign Policy*, 154–55.

48. UNSC, *OR*, 483d meeting, 4 August 1950, 14.

49. UNSC, *OR*, 484th meeting, 8 August 1950.

50. Austin to Acheson, 21 August 1950, *FR, 1950*, 7:629–30.

51. UNSC, *OR*, 494th meeing, 1 September 1950, 2–9.

52. *DSB*, 23 (10 July 1950): 46.

53. Allison to Rusk, 15 July 1950, and Allison to Nitze, 24 July 1950, *FR, 1950*, 7:393–95, 460–61.

54. *NYT*, 2 July 1950, 4:3.

55. *Time*, 56 (4 September 1950): 12; *NYT*, 1 September 1950, 22; "Scrapbooks," vol. 16, Russell Papers.

56. See Matray, "Truman's Plan," 314–33, and Matray, *Reluctant Crusade*.

57. Rhee to Truman, 19 July 1950, *FR, 1950*, 7:428–30.

58. "Draft Memorandum Prepared in the Department of Defense," 31 July 1950, *FR, 1950*, 7:503–4, 506–7.

59. Collins, *War in Peacetime*, 82–83.

60. See Trachtenberg, *History and Strategy*, chap. 2. On the U.S. war plan and strategic military capability, see *HJCS*, 4:161–77. On Allison's shift, see *FR, 1950*, 7:571–72.

61. *DSB*, 23 (28 August and 11 September 1950): 330–31, 407. On 1 August Acheson sent Austin a draft statement that bore many similarities to the one actually made ten days later. See Acheson to Austin, 1 August 1950, Box 4306, 795B.5, RG59, NA.

62. *FR, 1950*, 7:655–56.

63. "Draft Position Paper for Meeting of Foreign Ministers in September," "United States Delegation Minutes: SRM Pre 4," 30 August, 1950, and "Draft Paper Prepared for the Preliminary Tripartite Conversation of the September Foreign Ministers Meeting," 31 August 1950, *FR, 1950*, 7:656, 776–79, 679–83.

64. "Report by the National Security Council to the President," 9 September 1950, ibid., 716.

65. On the Canadian role, see United Kingdom High Commissioner, Canada, to Commonwealth Relations Office, 5 August 1950, FO371/84083, PRO.

66. See Shann to the Department of External Affairs, 18 August 1950, A1838, 852/20/4/2/11, AA.

67. "Memorandum of Conversation, by James N. Hyde," 11 August 1950, ibid., 555–56; UNSC, OR, 487th meeting, 14 August 1950, 9; NYT, 15 August 1950, 1; 16 August 1950, 1, 5; 19 August 1950, 3; 20 August 1950, 1, 20; 21 August 1950, 1, 5; 22 August 1950, 1; 24 August 1950, 5; "Reminiscences of Ernest R. Gross," 755–805.

68. Quoted in Whiting, *China Crosses the Yalu*, 79.

69. UNSC, OR, 489th meeting, 22 August 1950, 13.

70. Quoted in Whiting, *China Crosses the Yalu*, 84–85.

71. Chen, "China's Road to the Korean War," 181.

72. Quoted in ibid., 183.

73. Bo, *Ruogan Zhongda Jueche yu Shijian de Huigu* (Reflections of certain important decisions and events), 1:43, as quoted in Chen, "Sino-Soviet Alliance," 25.

74. *MZM*, 1:454–55, 469, 485. For translations of several documents of July and August regarding preparations in Manchuria, see Li, Wang, and Chen, "Mao's Dispatch of Chinese Troops," 63–65.

75. Hao and Zhai, "China's Decision to Enter the Korean War," 101.

76. *IS*, 26 August 1950.

77. Schonberger, "The General and the Presidency," 201–19; Schaller, *MacArthur*, 152–54.

78. William R. Matthews, "Diary," 32, Matthews Papers.

79. The definitive biography of MacArthur is James, *Years of MacArthur*; see also Schaller, *MacArthur*.

80. For correspondence on the matter, see DAG-1/2.1.2–2, UNA.

81. See A. W. Cordier to Colonel A. G. Katzin, 18 July 1950, DAG-1/2.1.2–4, UNA.

82. *NYT*, 11 July 1950, 7; 18 July 1950, 6; 21 July 1950, 5. For more details on the British position, see my "Limits of Influence," 68–76.

83. *NYT*, 20 July 1950, 14.

84. On British pressure on the United States regarding Taiwan, and Indian pressure on the British, see FO371/84088, 84089, 84091, 84095, PRO.

85. *NYT*, 1 August 1950, 4.

86. *NYT*, 2 August 1950, 6.

87. *NYT*, 29 July 1950, 5.

88. *NYT*, 3 August 1950, 13.

89. Memoranda of Conversations by Robert P. Joyce, 22 July 1950, and Dean Rusk, 24 July 1950, Box 15, Records of the Office of Chinese Affairs, RG59, NA.

90. Dingman, "Atomic Diplomacy," 62–64.

91. Joint Chiefs to MacArthur, 29 July 1950, 381 Formosa, RG 218, NA; *USAKW*, 3:368–69.

92. Robert Strong to Acheson, 3 August 1950, *FR, 1950*, 6:410–12.

93. Joint Chiefs to MacArthur, 4 August 1950, 381 Formosa, RG 218, NA.

94. *MSFE*, 3475.

95. *NYT*, 25 August 1950, 4.

96. *MSFE*, 3475.

97. *NYT*, 30 August 1950, 5. Deliberations within the Truman administration on Taiwan indicate that U.S. policy was in flux at the time, with the Pentagon arguing strongly against any course that would leave the island in Communist hands and the State Department showing flexibility. That flexibility diminished in September and October. See Stueck, *Road to Confrontation*, 221–22, 246–47.

98. For a key press report, see *NYT*, 1 September 1950, 4:2. Regarding Nationalist activities that conflicted with the neutralization order, see Clubb memo of conversation with Hubert Graves (British embassy), 6 September 1950, Box 21, Records of the Office of Chinese Affairs, RG59, NA.

99. Truman, *Memoirs*, 2:359.

100. Whiting, *China Crosses the Yalu*, 97.

101. This analysis of Soviet policy is based primarily on George, "American Policy-Making," 209–32; and Shulman, *Stalin's Foreign Policy*, chap. 6. Other useful accounts are Ulam, *Expansion and Coexistence*, 496–531; Whiting, *China Crosses the Yalu*, chaps. 4–6; and Simmons, *Strained Alliance*, chap. 6. See also George Kennan's reflections in his paper to the State Department of 8 September 1952 in Box 25, Classified General Records (Belgrade, Yugoslavia), RG84, WNRC.

102. General Orvil Anderson *was* relieved of his post in the Air Force for publicly advocating preventive war, but he was a relatively low-level official.

103. See *NYT*, 20 August 1950, 28; 31 August 1950, 1; 3 September 1950, 23; 6 September 1950, 6.

104. Acheson, *Present*, 437–40; for documents relating to the evolution of NATO, see *FR, 1950*, 3:168–337 passim.

105. Acheson, *Present*, 434–35; Nimmo, *Occupation of Japan*, 4–5, 11, 49, 16–17, 79, 139.

106. United Nations, *Yearbook of the United Nations*, 1950, 226–29. State-Defense conflicts are covered in boxes 4306 and 4307, 795B.5, RG59, NA. The most detailed secondary account is Bohlin, "United States–Latin American Relations," 167–76.

107. Kenneth Younger (Minister of State at the Foreign Office) to Bevin, 11 July 1950, FO371/84091, PRO.

108. *FR, 1950*, 7:578–79.

109. O'Neill, *Australia in the Korean War*, 1:31, 35–44, 86.

110. For a summary of Filipino deliberations, based on published sources, see Meyer, *Diplomatic History*, 129–31. For dissent among the Nacionalistas, see Ramon Diokno to Eulogio Rodriguez, 1 August 1950, Laurel Papers. For Elizaldi's appeal to President Quirino, see Elizalde to Quirino, 2 August 1950, Box: Special Correspondence Elpidio Quirino–J. Elizalde May 1950–1953, EQ.

111. For U.S. dealings with Pakistan on this issue, see Avra Warren (U.S. ambassador to Pakistan) to Acheson, 14, 15, and 16 July and 6 August 1950, and Acheson to Warren, 11 August 1950, Box 4305, 795B.5, RG59, NA. For a secondary account, see Venkataramini, *American Role in Pakistan*, 130–31, 437 n. 4. Turkey was so determined to avoid being considered an Asian nation that it protested to the U.S. State Department over being referred to as such by U.S. officials and in the press (see "Protest of Turkish Ambassador at Public References to Turkey as 'Asiatic Power,'" 5 September 1950, 795.00, Box 4062, RG59, NA).

112. On Turkey and Greece, see *FR, 1950*, 5:410–16, 12:85–89.

113. See ibid., 6:206–23; Spender, *Politics and a Man*, 280–85; Spender, *Exercises in Diplomacy*, 35–48; Watt, *Australian Diplomat*, 173–76; O'Neill, *Australia in the Korean War*, 1:65, 75, 87–88, 109–13.

114. McGibbon, *New Zealand and the Korean War*, 97–98.
115. For a poignant statement of Filipino concerns, see Romulo to Quirino, 1 February 1950, Box 1.4, CPR.
116. The famous mission headed by businessman Daniel Bell arrived in the Philippines on 10 July and stayed for six weeks. For a general account of the mission and concerns in Manila regarding U.S. criticism, see Meyer, *Diplomatic History*, 89–96. For U.S. perceptions, see *FR, 1950*, 6:1423–96. For Ambassador Elizalde's hopes regarding an offer of troops on U.S. opinion, see Elizalde to Quirino, 2 and 8 August 1950, Box: Special Correspondence Elpidio Quirino–J. Elizalde May 1950–1953, EQ.
117. For an astute analysis on this point from the British side, see Franks to Foreign Office, 23 July 1950, FO371/84091, PRO.
118. Darling, *Thailand and the United States*.
119. Bernard C. Carnelby (U.S. chargé d'affaires in South Africa) to the Department of State, 9 August 1950, Box 4305, 795B.5, RG59, NA; see also Noer, *Cold War and Black Liberation*, 18–28.
120. William G. Richardson (U.S. consul in Monrovia) to Department of State, 25 July 1950, and Acheson to U.S. embassy in Liberia, 28 July 1950, Box 4305, 795B.5, RG59, NA.
121. On Ethiopia, see Austin to Acheson, 7 August 1950, and "Memorandum of Conversation: Ethiopian Offer of Assistance to UN Force in Korea and Request for Reimbursable Military Assistance," 11 September 1950, Box 4306, ibid.; UN, *Yearbook, 1950*, 22–23, 363–68, 797–99.
122. "Questions and Answers, First Conference [between generals MacArthur, Vandenberg, and Collins]," 13 July 1950, 091 Korea (TS), RG218, NA; Collins, *War in Peacetime*, 81–83.
123. MSAO, August 1950 and October 1950, RG 59, NA.
124. See Stueck, *Road to Confrontation*, 44–46, 137–43, 149–51.
125. "Draft Memorandum Prepared by the Department of State," 31 August 1950, *FR, 1950*, 7:673.
126. "Report by the National Security Council to the President," 9 September 1950, ibid., 714–15.
127. The Pentagon showed distaste for the idea of halting U.S. forces at the narrow neck as early as 31 July. See "Draft Memorandum Prepared in the Department of Defense," 31 July 1950, ibid., 503.
128. See Diary Entry for 2 September 1950, vol. 38, HD. The entry describes a conversation between Hugh Dalton and Bevin. See also the minutes of a British cabinet meeting of 4 September 1950 in CAB 128/18, PRO. Canada helped here. See Pearson, "Discussion with Mr. Acheson and officials in Washington, Saturday and Sunday, July 29th and 30th, 1950," and Pearson to Acheson, 15 August 1950, vol. 15, Pearson Papers, PAC; see also Stueck, "Limits of Influence," 72–78.
129. Bevin, "Review of the International Situation in Asia in the Light of the Korean Conflict," 30 August 1950, C.P. (50) 200, PRO.
130. For examples of Conservative pressure on the Labor government, see Dalton to the British Foreign Office, 14 August 1950, pt. 2, HD.; *NYT*, 27 July 1950, 1; Boardman, *Britain and the People's Republic of China*, 47.
131. See Diary Entry for 2 September 1950, vol. 38, HD. For context, see Browder and Smith, *Independent*, 335–37.
132. See, for example, Younger diary, 5 August 1950.
133. "Draft Memorandum Prepared by the Department of State," 31 August 1950,

*FR, 1950*, 7:673; see also Franks's perceptive analysis in Franks to British Foreign Office, 23 July 1950, FO371/84091, PRO.

134. See Incoming Cablegram 12211, 11 August 1950, to the Department of External Affairs, AA; text of telegram received from the principal Secretary of the United Nations Commission on Korea, 5 August 1950, DAG1/2.1.2.-4, UNA. For British views, see Bevin, "Korea," and attached "Annex," 31 August 1950, C.P. (50) 193, PRO; see also documents in FO 371/84096, PRO.

135. See the minutes of Chiefs of Staff Committee meetings of 11 and 15 August 1950 in File 34, DEFE 4, PRO.

136. For background on Stalin's concerns on the home front and in the international Communist camp, see notes 81, 82, and 86 for chapter 1.

137. Chinese concerns are covered in Zhang, "Military Romanticism," 65–68.

138. The service secretaries in Washington, despite their awareness of plans for a counteroffensive and their intimate knowledge of the buildup in Japan, observed that "a military stalemate" might soon develop on the peninsula and might last for several months. Memorandum for the Secretary of Defense from the Service Secretaries, 24 August 1950, 091 Korea (TS), RG 319, NA.

139. See Taubman, *Stalin's American Policy*, 208–11, 215–16.

140. For figures on defense expenditures in western Europe, the United States, and Canada on the eve of the Korean War and a general discussion of the immediate economic impact of the conflict in the West, see J. I. Nimmo (of the Australian Department of the Treasury), "Economic Effects of Korea," 21 July 1950, A1838/T184, 3123/5/3, AA; on German and French opinion, see Adenauer, *Memoirs*, 277; Richardson, *Germany and the Atlantic Alliance*, 22; U.S. State Department, Office of Intelligence Research, "World Reactions to Korean Developments," 4 and 7 August 1950, Box 4, SRRKW; *NYT*, 24 July 1950, 10; 26 July 1950, 12; 13 August 1950, 13; 20 August 1950, 28. On political and economic problems of rearmament in England, see Boxes 105–8, Attlee Papers; regarding Soviet propaganda aimed at economic problems in western Europe, see Moscow to Secretary of State, 15 August 1950, Box 6004, RG59, NA.

141. As the U.S. embassy in Moscow reported during the previous spring, the Kremlin had an "exaggerated belief in the power of its propaganda." See *FR, 1950*, 4:1174.

142. *NYT*, 10 August 1950, 3.

143. CIA, Foreign Broadcast Information Division, "Foreign Radio Comments Related to the Situation in Korea," 10 July 1950, Box 251, PSF; U.S. Department of State, Office of Intelligence Research, "World Reaction to Korean Developments," 30 July 1950, Box 4, SRRKW, HST; A. W. Dulles to John Foster Dulles, 8 September 1950, Box 48, JFD; Adenauer, *Memoirs*, 275–77.

144. Werth, *France*, 472–73.

145. U.S. Department of State, Office of Intelligence Research, "Sino-Soviet Radio Comment on 'American Aggression' in China and the Korean War," 27–31 August 1950, Box 251, PSF.

146. *NYT*, 6 August 1950, 4:3; 13 August 1950, 4:5; 20 August 1950, 4:5; 28 August 1950, 1, 5.

147. John Melby to William S. B. Lacy, 29 September 1950, Box 10, Melby Papers.

148. On the Communist Party in India, see Overstreet and Windmiller, *Communism in India*, chap. 13; Kautsky, *Moscow and the Communist Party of India*, pts. 3–4. On Soviet-Indian relations, see Stein, *India and the Soviet Union*, chap. 1; Naik, *Soviet*

*Policy towards India*, chap. 2. On strains in Indian-U.S. relations, see U.S. Department of State, Division of Historical Policy Research, "American Policy and Diplomacy in the Korean Conflict," pt. 5 (August 1950), 37–40, Box 7, KP.

149. *NYT*, 15 August 1950, 1, 7; 20 August 1950, 4:5. A report of the Australian High Commissioner's office concluded that "it is very doubtful if the Government would have escaped considerable and damaging criticism from political parties and the press, and in Parliament, had it decided to move as enthusiastically to the side of the United States, as . . . have Australian and New Zealand." See Francis Stuart (acting Australian High Commissioner in India) to A. S. Watt, 27 July 1950, A1838/T184, 3123/5/3, AA.

150. For a useful survey of Indian foreign policy, see Kundra, *Indian Foreign Policy*.

151. Pandit, *Scope of Happiness*, 252–53; Henderson to Acheson, 21 October 1950, Box 4158, RG59, NA.

152. Nehru to Chief Ministers, 15 July 1950, as quoted in Gopal, *Nehru*, 2:102.

153. McMahon, *Colonialism and the Cold War*. Nehru's suspicions of the United States on the issue of Western imperialism extended back to the 1920s. See Gopal, *Nehru*, 1:103–4.

154. Gopal, *Nehru*, 2: chap. 6; Indian Council of World Affairs, *India and the United Nations*; Luard, *History of the United Nations*, 1: chap. 14. The Security Council's recommendations for resolution of the Kashmir dispute, which Nehru often found unacceptable, illustrated to him the danger to India of a United Nations of greatly expanded authority.

155. The secretaries of the armed services in the United States even expressed concern that Indian and other efforts to terminate the fighting in Korea at an early date might help to produce "an uncontrollable demand for a settlement that would nullify the heroic resistance of American and South Korean troops and injure US interests." Memorandum for the Secretary of Defense from the Service Secretaries, 24 August 1950, 091 Korea (TS), RG319, NA.

156. Acheson, *Present*, 334–36; McGhee, *Envoy to the Middle World*; Merrill, "Indo-American Relations," 203–26.

157. Henderson to Acheson, 10 August 1950, Box 4158, RG59, NA. For an excellent survey of Indian-U.S. relations, see Brands, *India and the United States*.

158. Brecher, *Israel's Foreign Policy*, 121–22. In 1950 Israeli imports were seven times as great as its exports. On Israel's economy and concerns about U.S. support, see *NYT*, 23 March 1950, 20; Richard Ford (Counselor at U.S. Embassy, Tel Aviv) to Acheson, 31 July 1950, Box 7, Israel 350, RG84, WNRC; Bialer, *Between East and West*, chap. 1.

159. UNSC, *OR*, vol. 17, 30 June 1950, 2, 9, 13–14; Louis, *British Empire in the Middle East*, 60–63. Issues of the *Middle East Journal* (vols. 4 and 5) contain useful summaries and chronologies of events in the region during 1950. For a convenient outline of the response of Middle Eastern nations to UN action in Korea, see Shann, "Korea: Middle Eastern Reactions," 21 July 1950, A1838/T184, 3123/5/3, AA.

160. *FR, 1950*, 5:293–302.

161. Louis, *British Empire in the Middle East*, 640–45.

162. Waggoner to State Department, 29 September 1950, Box 4106, RG59, NA.

163. Swedish Institute of International Affairs, *Sweden and the United Nations*, 69–73; *NYT*, 5 August 1950, 2; 10 August 1950, 8; 12 August 1950, 5; 21 August 1950, 3; 26 August 1950, 5.

Chapter 3
Diplomacy Fails: The UN Counteroffensive and Chinese Intervention

1. Heinl, *Victory at High Tide*, 25, 40, 42.
2. *USAKW*, 3:150–54.
3. Heinl, *Victory at High Tide*, 87–120.
4. *NYT*, 21 September 1950, 6–7; 22 September 1950, 1, 8; 24 September 1950, 4:1; 26 September 1950, 15; Jessup memorandum of conversation with Malik, 19 September 1950, Box 2824, RG59, NA.
5. *NYT*, 15 September 1950, 1; 14 September 1950, 1, 8; 19 September 1950, 1.
6. UNGA, *OR*, sess. 5, plenary meetings, 1:23 ff. For early discussions on this matter within the State Department, see *FR, 1950*, 2:303–37.
7. For comments to this effect regarding Korea, see *FR, 1950*, 7:761, 771.
8. *NYT*, 16 September 1950, 14.
9. For a summary of the talks, see Acheson, *Present*, 442–45; for detailed minutes, see file 449, FO800, PRO.
10. 383.21 Korea, RG218, NA.
11. 091 Korea (TS), RG319, NA.
12. Paul Nitze interview with the author, 9 January 1975; *FR, 1950*, 7:781–82.
13. *FR, 1950*, 7:785, 793 n; Bolté to Collins and Memorandum for the Record, 27 September 1950, Box 33A, RG319, MMB, NA.
14. *FR, 1950*, 7:698, 724–25.
15. Ibid., 65 n.
16. Ibid., 742–43.
17. Ibid., 765, 768.
18. Ibid., 793–94, 797–98.
19. *PPPUS: Harry S. Truman, 1950*, 644.
20. *FR, 1950*, 7:727.
21. Ibid., 736–41, 743–47, 751–52.
22. Ibid., 763–64, 768–74. In his dispatch to Attlee on 25 September, Bevin noted that agreement on a draft "has only been arrived at after many hours of discussions with the Americans." See folder 511, FO800, PRO.
23. *NYT*, 20 September 1950, 1.
24. See "Minutes of Meeting between Bevin, Acheson, and Schuman, 14 September 1950," in folder 449, FO800, PRO, for a relatively amicable exchange on the matter; for a Bevin report after the meetings, see Bevin, "New York Meetings: Developments in Far Eastern Policy," 6 October 1950, PREM8/1171, PRO.
25. See the minutes of meetings between 22 and 26 September in ibid.
26. File 511, ibid.
27. Jebb to Foreign Office, 25 September 1950, FO371/84097, PRO.
28. Chiefs of Staff Committee, "Minutes of the 152d Meeting on 20 September 1950, and Slim, "Policy Following on Enemy Defeat in South Korea," in vol. 36, DEFE4, PRO; "Cabinet Minutes," 26 September 1950, CAB 128/18, PRO.
29. *FR, 1950*, 7:826–28.
30. *FR, 1950*, 7:809–10; Bevin to Nehru, 27 September 1950, FO 371/84097, PRO.
31. *FR, 1950*, 7:811–12.
32. Ibid., 810–11.
33. Ibid., 6:522.
34. Nye to Foreign Office, 30 September 1950, FO371/84097, PRO.

35. *FR, 1950*, 7:821–22.
36. Ibid., 858.
37. Ibid., 848–49, 851.
38. Foreign Office to Franks, 4 October 1950, FO371/84110, PRO; Sulzberger, *Long Row of Candles*, 578.
39. *FR, 1950*, 7:826.
40. UNGA, *OR*, sess. 5, comm. 1–2, 1950, 24–25, 55; Lie, *In the Cause of Peace*, 344–45.
41. UNGA, *OR*, sess. 5, comm. 1–2, 1950, 51, 54, 56, and supplement no. 20, 1950, 9–10. See also Pearson to Reid, 5 October 1950, vol. 11, WIKF, DEA, which characterized both the Arab and Latin American blocs as divided on the Indian resolution.
42. Gascoigne to the British Foreign Office, 3 October 1950, FO 371/84099, PRO.
43. Ministry of Defence, London, to Lord Tedder, 5 October 1950, FO 371/84100, PRO.
44. Chiefs of Staff Committee, Minutes of 162d Meeting, 5 October 1950, DEFE4, PRO.
45. Bevin, "New York Meetings: Developments in Far Eastern Policy," 6 October 1950, PREM8/1171, PRO.
46. *FR, 1950*, 7:893; Lord Tedder to Bradley, 5 October 1950, 383.21 Korea, RG218, NA.
47. A.D.P. Heeney to Pearson, 4 October 1950, vol. 11, WIKF.
48. Pearson to Heeney, 5 October 1950, ibid; Pearson "Memorandum—Canada and Korea—September to December 1950," Vol. 15, Pearson Papers, PAC.
49. Pearson to Heeney, 9 October 1950, and Wrong to Pearson, 5 October 1950, vol. 11, WIKF; *FR, 1950*, 7:883–85.
50. Pearson to Heeney, 9 October 1950, ibid.
51. Pearson, *Mike*, 2:160.
52. On Acheson's apology, see ibid., 161–62; Pearson to Heeney, 10 October 1950, and Wrong to Pearson, 9 October 1950, vol. 11, WIKF. Pearson was more inclined to place the blame on the Pentagon.
53. Burke oral history, 192–93, 212.
54. *FR, 1950*, 7:848–49, 864–66.
55. Ibid., 868–69.
56. See the translations of Soviet documents in Weathersby, "Soviet Role," 19–27.
57. Hao and Zhai, "China's Decision to Enter the Korean War," 104–5; Weiss, "Storm Around the Cradle," 79–82.
58. As quoted in Hao and Zhai, "China's Decision to Enter the Korean War," 106.
59. Ibid.
60. *MZM*, 1:539–41.
61. Chen, "Sino-Soviet Alliance," 27.
62. See *FR, 1950*, 7:698, 724–25, 742, 765, 768; see also *IS*, 26 August 1950.
63. Chen, "China's Road to the Korean War," 255–57.
64. See Hunt, "Beijing and the Korean Crisis," 473.
65. See Zhang, "Military Romanticism," chap. 1.
66. Mao, *Selected Works*, 4:21–22, 97–101. For a broader discussion of these views, see Ryan, *Chinese Attitudes toward Nuclear Weapons*, 14–17.
67. Ryan, *Chinese Attitudes toward Nuclear Weapons*, 28–29; Panikkar, *In Two Chinas*, 108.
68. Chen, "China's Road to the Korean War," 257–62.

69. For a text of the treaty, see Garthoff, ed., *Sino-Soviet Military Relations*, 214–16.

70. A translation of this document is in Weathersby, "Soviet Role," 9.

71. This account is based on Chen, "China's Road to the Korean War," 278–82, and Goncharov, Lewis, and Xue, *Uncertain Partners*, 188–91. Where the accounts differ, I follow the former, which strikes me as the best researched and most plausible reconstruction.

72. *MZM*, 1:552.

73. *MZM*, 1:556.

74. *MZM*, 1:558–61.

75. On press reports from Taiwan and perceptions in Beijing, see Warwick Chipman (Canada's High Commissioner to India) to Pearson, 5 October 1950, vol. 11, WIKF; see also Hao and Zhai, "China's Decision to Enter the Korean War," 103.

76. *SCMP*, 6 November 1950.

77. Zhou, *Selected Works of Zhou Enlai*, 2:59–64.

78. Chow, *Ten Years of Storm*, 116–17. Hao and Zhai have confirmed this story through interviews with unidentified Chinese officials (see "China's Decision to Enter the Korean War," 111).

79. *FR, 1950*, 7:876–80.

80. Ibid., 897–99, 906–11.

81. Khrushchev, *Khrushchev Remembers: The Glasnost Tapes*, 146–47.

82. Stalin's dispatch to Mao quoted on p. 101 above was, as Kathryn Weathersby remarks, at least in part "bravado . . . largely for Chinese consumption," but we should not rule out the possibility that it reflected an important element in the Soviet leader's perspective. See Weathersby, "Soviet Role," 9.

83. *FR, 1950*, 6:368, 371–72, 374–75, FO371/84087, PRO, and vol. 3, WIKF.

84. Escott Reid to Pearson, 26 September 1950, vol. 10, WIKF.

85. Had General Nie's and Foreign Minister Zhou's first discussion with Panikkar after 15 September been with an American, not only would its substance have been relayed soon to Washington, before the momentum for crossing the 38th parallel had reached virtually insurmountable proportions; it also would have been evaluated with less inherent skepticism.

86. *FR, 1950*, 7:913–14, 931; Mao, *Selected Works*, 5:43.

87. *FR, 1950*, 7:915, 933–34.

88. Charles Murphy Oral History, HSTL. The best secondary account of the conference is in James, *Years of MacArthur*, 3:500–17.

89. *FR, 1950*, 7:948–60; Acheson, *Present*, 457. This portrayal of MacArthur's self-confidence is consistent with his statements to foreign diplomats in Tokyo during October and early November. See, for example, "Confidential Conversation Between General MacArthur and A. G. Katzin, Sunday, 8 October 1950," vol. 11, WIKF, DEA; see also Sir A. Gascoigne to the Foreign Office, 3 November 1950, FO371/84102, PRO.

90. John Muccio Oral History, HSTL.

91. Collins, *War in Peacetime*, 179–80.

92. UNGA, *OR*, 3d sess., pt. 1, 25–27.

93. *FR, 1950*, 7:939.

94. Australian Mission to the United Nations to the Department of External Affairs, 12 October 1950, AA.

95. *FR, 1950*, 7:959–60.

96. Ibid., 953, 959–60.

97. Ibid., 696–97; see also the reports from the U.S. embassy in Korea to Washington in Korea Post Files, RG84, WNRC.

98. Sir Esler Dening, "Tripartite Meeting, Document 12—Courses of Action in Korea," 14 September 1950, FO371/84101, PRO.

99. *FR, 1950*, 7:994–95; for ROK pressure on UNCURK, see "Summary of Informal Meetings of Interim Committee on Korea," 26 October 1950, DAG-1/2.1.2–6, UNA.

100. *The Times of London*, 25 October 1950, 5; for an unflattering general report on the behavior of ROK troops in North Korea, see H. W. Bullock (Alternate Australian representative to UNCURK), "Conditions in Pyongyang," 16 November 1950, A1838/T184, 3123/9, AA.

101. Ringwalt (London) to Department of State, 7 November 1950, London Post Files, RG84, WNRC.

102. *FR, 1950*, 7:1004–6; R. H. Scott memo, 19 October 1950, FO371/84108, PRO.

103. Holmes to Pearson, 21 October 1950, vol. 11, WIKF; "Problems Facing UNCURK," 27 November 1950, A1838/T184, 3123/5/6, AA.

104. Tomlinson to Shattock, 7 November 1950, and Foreign Office Minutes by Milward, 16 November 1950, FO371/84102, PRO.

105. Plimsoll, "Views of General MacArthur on Korea and the Far East," 21 November 1950, A1838/T184, 3123/5/6; Plimsoll, "The Work of UNCURK in Seoul," 5 January 1951, A1838/T184, 3123/3/2, AA.

106. Ibid.

107. *IS*, 4 November 1950. For a more detailed account of guerrilla activities during the fall, see *USAKW*, 1:721–28.

108. *FR, 1950*, 7:1055–58.

109. *USAKW*, 3:233–34.

110. Blair, *Forgotten War*, 378–79.

111. Ibid., 377.

112. Cumings, *Origins of the Korean War*, 2:105.

113. On MacArthur surrounding himself with sycophants, see James, *Years of MacArthur*.

114. *SCMP*, 1 November 1950. Mao's classic statement on war is "On Protracted War," which was published originally in 1938 and is reprinted in English in Mao, *Selected Works*, 2:113–94.

115. *FR, 1950*, 7:1023–25, 1030, 1034–35.

116. Ibid., 1075–77.

117. Ibid., 1097–98, 1107–10.

118. For Acheson's message to Bevin of 6 November, see ibid., 1050–53.

119. On the election of 1950, see Caridi, *Korean War and American Politics*, chap. 4. Official documents on top-level discussions rarely mention the political implications of various policy options. Foreign observers and the U.S. press, however, were virtually unanimous in viewing domestic politics as crucial in the Truman administration's response to the fall crisis. See, for example, the correspondence between Washington and Ottawa in vols. 2143 and 2152, RG25, especially the PAC and KYD entries of 5 and 19 November 1950. Acheson's account in *Present* (468) implies that fear of an open debate with MacArthur was an important, if unstated factor in deliberations within the administration. On talk among Democrats of Acheson's responsibility for

defeats in the congressional election, see Edward Barrett to F. H. Russell, 13 November 1950, Box 92, GE.

120. *FR, 1950*, 7:1101–6.
121. Memorandum for the President, 10 November 1950, Box 72, GE.
122. *FR, 1950*, 7:1097, 1124 n, 1133–34, 1141–42, 1167–68, 1210, 1213–15, 1224–25.
123. Ibid., 7:1198–1201; *Manchester Guardian*, 19 November 1950, 5; Farrar, "Britain's Proposal," 327–51.
124. *FR, 1950*, 6:528, 534–36, 573 n.
125. Ibid., 7:1127; *DSB*, 23 (27 November, 4 December 1950): 853, 889; *PPPUS: Harry S. Truman, 1950*, 711.
126. *SCMP*, 17–18 November 1950.
127. *IS*, 4, 15, 19, 25 November 1950; *FR, 1950*, 7:1147.
128. *FR, 1950*, 7:1151–52.
129. Ibid., 7:1184, 1188–90.
130. *IS*, 15 November 1950; *USAKW*, 3:263–64.
131. Acheson infotel to various U.S. missions abroad, 20 November 1950, Box 1336, RG84, WNRC; Pearson, "Memorandum—Canada and Korea—September to December 1950," vol. 15, Pearson Papers, PAC.
132. *FR, 1950*, 7:1138–40, 1151, 1159–62, 1172. For pressures on Attlee and Bevin, see the minutes of British cabinet meetings of 13 and 20 November 1950, CAB128/18, PRO.
133. Ibid., 7:1181–83.
134. Bolté to Collins, 20 November 1950, RG 218, NA.
135. Ibid.
136. *FR, 1950*, 7:1204–8, 1222–24.
137. Ibid., 7:1231–33.
138. See the memorandum of the conversation between MacArthur and William Sebald (State Department representative to the occupation of Japan), 14 November 1950, Box 16, KP.
139. *FR, 1950*, 7:1237–38.
140. Ibid., 5:1474.
141. There is uncertainty over when Stalin reversed himself. Soviet-made MIG-15 jets appeared over North Korea on 1 November, but it is possible that Soviet pilots were not actually flying them until later in the month. For recent evidence on the matter, see Goncharov, Lewis, and Xue, *Uncertain Partners*, 199–200, and Jon Halliday, "Air Operations in Korea: The Soviet Side of the Story," in Williams, *Revolutionary War*, 149–51.
142. Mao to Zhou, 14 October 1950, *MZM*, 1:559.
143. Thomas J. Christensen uses Mao's telegrams to Stalin on 2 October and to Zhou on 13 and 14 October (*MZM*, 1:539–41, 558–59) to argue that, from the beginning, Mao had an offensive attitude regarding the Korean intervention and that this made a major Sino-U.S. military engagement inevitable, at the latest in the spring of 1951. My reading of the telegrams, and of other evidence, indicates that Mao's thinking in October was very much in a state of flux. It must be remembered that Mao's telegrams to Stalin and to Zhou while Mao was in the Soviet Union were designed to enhance Chinese prospects for obtaining Soviet aid. See Christensen, "Threats, Assurances, and the Last Chance for Peace," 135–40.

144. *MZM*, 1:558–61.
145. Ibid., 576.
146. Ibid., 588–89.
147. Peng, *Memoirs of a Chinese Marshall*, 476; Hao and Zhai, "China's Decision to Enter the Korean War," 113.
148. For the charge regarding British espionage, see Whitney, *MacArthur*, 393–94, 455–57; MacArthur, *Reminiscences*.
149. Hao and Zhai, "China's Decision to Enter the Korean War," 112.
150. On preparations for U.S. action against Manchuria, see *FR, 1950*, 7:1034–35; see also *SCMP*, 5–6 November 1950.
151. Foot, *Wrong War*, 82–84; *FR, 1950*, 7:714–18.
152. *SCMP*, 10–12 November 1950.
153. *FR, 1950*, 7:1133–34.
154. Ibid., 7:1124 n, 1141–42, 1359–60. Rusk's speech included mention of the buffer zone idea and implied U.S. flexibility on the matter.
155. *SCMP*, 15 November 1950.
156. This analysis draws extensively from Whiting, *China Crosses the Yalu*, 116–50, but integrates the leak through the Polish delegation at Lake Success into the equation. Wu Xiuquan, the head of the Chinese delegation, claims in his memoirs that he worried that the delay in his arrival "might lose our delegation this opportunity to wage a struggle against the U.S. imperialists." Bad weather slowed their progress through the Soviet Union, but in Prague, Wu asserts, "It took us three days to go through entry visa formalities." Surely the Chinese government could have gotten its delegation to New York more rapidly had it so desired. See Wu, *Eight Years*, 51–52.
157. *CDSP*, 4 November 1950, 21, 55; *FR, 1950*, 7:1025; *IS*, 19 October 1950.
158. Hao and Zhai, "China's Decision to Enter the Korean War," 111. For a sensible analysis of the Soviet position in the fall, see Zimmerman, "The Korean and Vietnam Wars," 328–36.
159. *FR, 1950*, 3:415–31; *NYT*, 21 October 1950, 1, 5; 22 October 1950, 1, 25; 24 October 1950, 6; 31 October 1950, 1, 9; 4 November 1950, 1, 5.
160. *FR, 1950*, 6:1296, 1332–36.
161. Stebbins et al., *The United States in World Affairs, 1950*, 369–72.
162. *CDSP*, 22 November 1949 and 9 December 1950.
163. *CDSP*, 9 December 1950.
164. *NYT*, 3 November 1950, 1.
165. U.S. Embassy, Moscow, "Report on Internal Developments in the Soviet Union for November 1950," RG 84, WNRC; Shulman, *Stalin's Foreign Policy*, 154–56.
166. Shulman, *Stalin's Foreign Policy*, 154–56; U.S. Embassy, Moscow, Report on Internal Developments in the Soviet Union for November 1950," RG84, WNRC.

CHAPTER 4
LIMITING THE WAR

1. For a succinct description of the Chinese Communist army, see U.S. Marine Corps, *U.S. Marine Operations in Korea*, vol. 3, 83–94. For more detailed accounts, see Griffith, *Chinese People's Liberation Army*, and George, *Chinese Communist Army in Action*. For an account that draws on new Chinese sources, see Zhang, "Military Romanticism."

2. Marshall, *River and the Gauntlet*, 5, 18.

3. For a detailed account of the demise of the offensive on the Western front, see ibid., and Appleman, *Disaster in Korea*. The Briton, identified only as "Spey," wrote his report in Tokyo on 27 December 1950. It is attached to John Raynor (of the Office of the Commissioner General for the United Kingdom in Southeast Asia) to F.R.H. Murray (of the Foreign Office in London), 26 January 1951, FO371/92729, PRO.

4. Detailed accounts of the Chosin campaign include U.S. Marine Corps, *U.S. Marine Operations in Korea*, vol. 3; Hammel, *Chosin*; Hopkins, *One Bugle No Drums*; Appleman, *East of Chosin*.

5. Military events during the winter and spring of 1950–51 are covered most authoritatively in Appleman, *Ridgway Duels for Korea*. Rees's *Korea* and Goulden's *Korea* cover both military and diplomatic aspects of the period. The problems encountered by Communist forces come through clearly in UNC/FEC, *Staff Section Reports*, in Box 385, RG 407, WNRC. The best account of UN air activity is in Futrell, *United States Air Force in Korea*, chaps. 8 and 9. For a poignant statement of the command and morale problems Ridgway found among U.S. forces in Korea and his plans for improvement, see Ridgway to Collins, 8 January 1951, Box 20, Ridgway Papers. For British reports of the turnaround of morale in January, see FO371/92724 and 92726. The Chinese side is covered in Zhang, "Military Romanticism," chap. 5.

6. UNSC, *OR*, 1950, 5:1–26.

7. *U.S. News and World Report*, 29 (8 December 1950): 16–17; see also *NYT*, 2 December 1950, 1, 4. For a more detailed secondary account, see James, *Years of MacArthur*, 3:540–42.

8. Acheson and Truman's calls for unity are reported in *NYT*, 30 November 1950, 1, 14; and 1 December 1950, 1. For Cain's speech, see *CR*, 96 (28 November 1950): 15939–42; for complaints of the treatment of MacArthur, see *NYT*, 30 November 1950, 14; for McCarthy's tirade, see *NYT*, 3 December 1950, 49.

9. *NYT*, 29 November 1950, 1, 8; *Hansard*, 5th series, vol. 481, 1426, 1434.

10. *NYT*, 30 November 1950, 6.

11. For the minutes of these meetings, see FO800/456, PRO.

12. *NYT*, 1 December 1950, 1, 3, 4, 8; 3 December 1950, 1, 19; *FR, 1950*, 7:1306–7; Acheson, *Present*, 478–79.

13. *The Nation*, 171 (9 December 1950): 520–21. For the radio reaction in Europe, see CIA, FBID, "Foreign Radio Reaction to President Truman's 30 November Press Statement on the Atom Bomb (30 November–1 December 1950)," and "Foreign Radio Reactions to the President's Meeting with Prime Minister Attlee and to the 30 November Statement on the Atomic Bomb (1–4 December 1950)," PSF. For an analysis of British opinion by the U.S. embassy in London, see Julius C. Holmes to Acheson, 3 December 1950, RG84, WNRC.

14. *NYT*, 3 December 1950, 23.

15. *FR, 1950*, 7:1317, 1334; Nehru to Attlee, 3 December 1950, FO800/470, PRO.

16. *NYT*, 3 December 1950, 23–24.

17. O'Neill, *Australia in the Korean War*, 1:146–47.

18. Jebb to Foreign Office, 29 November 1950, FO371/84104, PRO.

19. *FR, 1950*, 7:1300–1301.

20. *The Nation*, 171 (9 December 1950), 520.

21. *FR, 1950*, 7:1247–48. The most detailed minutes of this meeting are in Box 72, GE.

22. *FR, 1950*, 7:1293–94, 1311, 1324, 1335–36, 1345–46.

23. Ibid., 1279; Acheson, *Present*, 472.
24. *FR, 1950*, 7:1279.
25. Ibid., 1335–36.
26. Ibid., 1244–45.
27. Ibid., 1253–54. See also Dingman, "Atomic Diplomacy," 65–69.
28. Ibid., 1242, 1263–65, 1279, 1300, 1312–13, 1327–28.
29. See Trachtenberg, "'Wasting Asset,'" 20–36.
30. Ibid., 6:581–83; Bolté to Collins, 1 December 1950, 091 Korea TS, RG319, NA.
31. See enclosure A to JCS2173/3, 4 December 1950, 091 Korea TS, RG319, NA.
32. *FR, 1950*, 7:1330, 1335; Memorandum for the Secretary of Defense, 4 December 1950, 092 Korea, RG330, NA.
33. *FR, 1950*, 7:1321.
34. Kennan, *Memoirs (1950–1963)*, 30–31; Acheson, *Present*, 476; *FR, 1950*, 7:1345–46.
35. Acheson, *Present*, 476–77.
36. *FR, 1950*, 7:1250–51.
37. Ibid., 676, 1310–11.
38. Lie, *In the Cause of Peace*, 351–52; *FR, 1950*, 7:1303–5, 1310–11, 1315–16.
39. *FR, 1950*, 7:1325, 1354–57.
40. Acheson, *Present*, 478. Compare this description to Acheson's affection for Bevin as conveyed in ibid., 270–72, 337–38.
41. Harris, *Attlee*, 247–48, 276–86, 390–400, 463–65.
42. Ibid., 463–65; Acheson, *Present*, 478–80.
43. British minutes of the meetings are in FO800/1200, PRO; U.S. minutes are in *FR, 1950*, 7:1361–1481. On 18 November the British Foreign Office received a message from Karachi that the Soviet ambassador to China recently had informed Burma's ambassador there that, if UN forces bombed Manchuria, the Soviet Union immediately would enter the war. This came a week after the British representative in Beijing reported a similar threat by the counselor in the Soviet embassy to the Indian ambassador. See FO371/83310, PRO.
44. In her "Anglo-American Relations," Rosemary Foot suggests the impact of the meetings on Acheson and Marshall. The analysis of Truman is my own.
45. *FR, 1950*, 7:1468–75.
46. Ibid., 1476–79.
47. Acheson, *Present*, 484.
48. *FR, 1950*, 7:1462–65, 1476–79.
49. Minutes of the meeting devoted to NATO are in *FR, 1950*, 3:1746–58. For the favorable reception of the communiqué in France, see *NYT*, 9 December 1950, 4.
50. *USAKW*, 3:225.
51. On the climate of "pessimism, indecision and divided counsels at Lake Success," see *NYT*, 3 December 1950, 5.
52. On Bebler's effort, see Lie, *In the Cause of Peace*, 351–52); *FR, 1950*, 7:1230–31; and *NYT*, 27 November 1950, 1.
53. *FR, 1950*, 7:1254–56, 1272.
54. *NYT*, 5 December 1950, 1; see also *SCMP*, 28 November, 1–2 and 5 December 1950.
55. Lie, *In the Cause of Peace*, 352.
56. *FR, 1950*, 7:1415–17. For descriptions of Rau's conversations with Wu on 1 and 3 December, see ibid., 1299, 1354–57.

57. Jebb to the British Foreign Office, 5 December 1950, FO371/84105, PRO.
58. *NYT*, 6 December 1950, 1.
59. Pearson to Nehru, 30 November 1950, vol. 13, WIKF.
60. Nehru to Attlee, 3 December 1950, FO371/84105, PRO.
61. British High Commissioner to India to the Commonwealth Relations Office, 8 December 1950, FO371/84106, PRO. This message to London included the text of Nehru's message to Panikkar.
62. Attlee to Nehru, 5 December 1950, FO371/84105, PRO.
63. *FR, 1950*, 7:1432–34, 1443; Pearson to the Department of External Affairs, 7 December 1950, and Reid to Pearson, 6 December 1950, vol. 14, WIKF, DEA.
64. *FR, 1950*, 7:1421–22; UNGA, *OR*, sess. 5, comm. 102, 1950, 395–401.
65. *FR, 1950*, 7:1482. On the perception of Qiao as the "bad guy" of the Chinese delegation, see Pearson to the Department of External Affairs, 7 December 1950, vol. 14, WIKF.
66. *FR, 1950*, 7:1490–91, 1495.
67. UNGA, *OR*, sess. 5, comm. 102, 1950, 433–34.
68. Ibid., 435.
69. *FR, 1950*, 7:1525–26; Romulo to Quirino, 11 December 1950, and Romulo to Bernabe Africa (Filipino representative on UNCURK), 14 December 1950, Box 15, PR; Romulo to Quirino, 15 December 1950, Box: Special Correspondence, EQ-CPR, EQ.
70. Ibid., 1538–40.
71. UNGA, *OR*, sess. 5, comm. 1–2, 1950, 440–42.
72. *FR, 1950*, 7:1525, 1550–53.
73. Ibid., 1534–35, 1543; Warwick Chipman (Canadian High Commissioner to India) to Department of External Affairs, 12 December 1950, vol. 15, WIKF.
74. *FR, 1950*, 7:1556–58, 1567; Lie, *In the Cause of Peace*, 355–57.
75. *FR, 1950*, 7:1594–98.
76. Ibid., 1541, 1600.
77. Ibid., 1549–50.
78. Ibid., 1440, 1541, 1600; Pearson to Chipman, vol. 16, WIKF. 80. *FR, 1950*, 7:1576–77, 1590, 1605.
79. *FR, 1950*, 7:1576–77, 1590, 1605.
80. On Mao's aims in Korea, see his telegram to Stalin of 2 October (*MZM* 1:539–41). In this document, Mao talked of wiping out "American and aggressive forces in Korea."
81. Quoted in Zhang, "Military Romanticism," 113–14.
82. Quoted in ibid., 114–15.
83. *MZM*, 1:719–22; Zhang, "Military Romanticism," 115–16.
84. Nie, *Memoir*, 744–45.
85. *MZM*, 1:722–24, 731.
86. See, for example, *SCMP*, 26–27 November 1950, and *FBIS*, 1 December 1950.
87. *NYT*, 9 December 1950, 3.
88. *SCMP*, 10–11 December 1950.
89. *SCMP*, 13 December 1950.
90. *SCMP*, 17–18 December 1950.
91. *FR, 1950*, 7:1595.
92. "Report on Internal Developments in the Soviet Union for December 1950," Moscow Embassy Files, RG84, WNRC.

93. See, for example, *FBIS*, 8 December 1950.
94. See the analysis by Harry Schwartz in *NYT*, 14 December 1950, 4.
95. Walworth Barbour to Acheson, 26 December 1950, Box 6004, RG59, NA.
96. Barbour to Acheson, 20 December 1950, Moscow Embassy Files, RG84, WNRC.
97. *NYT*, 14 December 1950, 1.
98. Ryan, *Chinese Attitudes*, 45–46; Barbour to Acheson, 7 December 1950, Moscow Embassy Files, RG84, WNRC.
99. UNC/FEC, General Headquarters, *Staff Section Reports*, 5, 6, 27 December 1950, RG 407, WNRC; *NYT*, 14 December 1950, 1.
100. *NYT*, 13 December 1950, 8.
101. *NYT*, 21 December 1950, 1, 22.
102. *NYT*, 24 December 1950, 20.
103. *NYT*, 21 December 1950, 28.
104. *NYT*, 18 December 1950, 15; *CDSP*, 20 January 1951.
105. *SCMP*, 28 December 1950.
106. Ibid.; *FBIS*, 26 December 1950.
107. See a report on a meeting of Vyshinsky and certain diplomatic representatives from eastern Europe in *FR, 1951*, 4:1522–23.
108. On the Prague meeting and Soviet call for a four-power conference of foreign ministers, see p. 123 above. On public opinion in western Europe and the domestic pressures on Adenauer, see Schwartz, *America's Germany*, 148–52; for an account of the French domestic scene cast in the broad sweep of European politics in late 1950, see Werth, *France*, 485–500.
109. *FR, 1950* 4:1507–8.
110. Ibid., 5:423–35.
111. Ibid., 4:438–39; 5:1337–38; Albert W. Sherer, Jr. (U.S. chargé in Budapest), "Summary of Political and Economic Developments in Hungary in 1950," 2 February 1951, Box 4, classified general records (Belgrade, Yugoslavia); John Peurifoy (U.S. ambassador to Greece) to Acheson, 12 December 1950, and Walworth Barbour (counselor of U.S. embassy, Moscow) to Acheson, 16 December 1950, Box 1, Top Secret General Records (Belgrade, Yugoslavia), RG84, WNRC.
112. Bela Kiraly, "The Aborted Soviet Military Plans Against Tito's Yugoslavia," in Vucinich, *At the Brink of War and Peace*, 273–88. Planners in the U.S. State Department did worry that the overcommitment of U.S. forces in Asia would encourage the Soviet Union to move in the Balkans, especially against Yugoslavia. See *FR, 1951*, 7:1534.
113. See, for example, the analysis of *New York Times* correspondent C. L. Sulzberger in *NYT*, 7 December 1950, 1, 20; see also *FR, 1950*, 5:273–76.
114. *FR, 1950*, 5:615–16.
115. Ibid., 1337–38. The word *détente* was used to characterize Soviet policy by Turkey's foreign minister Koprulu.
116. Strachey to Bevin, 2 January 1950, FO800/517, PRO.
117. See the exchanges between 5 and 8 January among William Strang, Pierson Dixon, and Roger Makins, all high-level Foreign Office officials, in ibid. Strong wrote on 8 January, "I understand that this paper has been sent to the chancellor of the exchequer, the minister of defense, and the minister of state; and maybe to others."
118. KYD, 7 January 1951.
119. Attlee to Bevin, 4 January 1951, and Bevin to Attlee, 9 January 1951, FO800/445, PRO.

120. James, *Years of MacArthur*, 3:547–59.
121. *FR, 1950*, 7:1630–33. For the JCS message to MacArthur of 29 December 1950, see ibid., 1625–26.
122. Sherman to JCS, 3 January 1951, 452 China, RG218, NA.
123. *FR, 1951*, 7:70–72.
124. NSC minutes, 18 January 1951, PSF; for an abbreviated version, see *FR, 1951*, 7:79 n, 92–94. For a detailed secondary account, see Foot, *Wrong War*, 120–21.
125. Frank to Bevin, 1 January 1951, FO371/92756, PRO.
126. Gascoigne to Bevin, 31 December 1950, FO371/92724, PRO. The London *Spectator* was more sarcastic, characterizing MacArthur's communiqués "as a form of psychological warfare apparently directed against his own troops." See James Plimsoll (Australian Representative to UNCURK) in "Korea: The Military Situation," 12 March 1951, A1838/T184/5/9, AA.
127. See the reports of Air Marshall C. A. Bouchier to the Ministry of Defense in FO371/92724, PRO.
128. *FR, 1951*, 7:37.
129. Bradley and Blair, *A General's Life*, 614–18.
130. CCS (51) 10, 12 January 1951, DEFE5/39, PRO.
131. Acheson, *Present*, 516.
132. Collins, *War in Peacetime*, 251–52; *FR, 1951*, 7:58.
133. Collins quotes extensively from his and Vandenberg's report of the 19th in his *War in Peacetime*, 253–55.
134. *FR, 1951*, 7:27–28.
135. Wrong to Pearson, 28 December 1950 and 29 December 1950, vol. 16, WIKF. For an unsuccessful effort by Pearson to get Nehru to convey to China a sense of U.S. reasonableness regarding the scope of possible negotiations, see Pearson to Chipman, 23 December 1950; Chipman to Pearson, 24 December 1950; Escott Reid to Hume Wrong, 27 December 1950, ibid.
136. *FR, 1951*, 7:9–13.
137. Pearson, *Mike*, 2:288. Pearson kept a diary of UN proceedings during December 1950 and January 1951, most of which is reprinted as appendix 1 in the volume cited. A complete typescript is in Pearson's papers at PAC.
138. British Foreign Office to British delegation at the United Nations, 5 January 1950, FO371/92763, PRO.
139. Strang to Sir Keith Officer, 10 January 1951, Officer Papers; Pearson, *Mike*, 2:290.
140. *FR, 1951*, 7:19.
141. Ibid., 45.
142. Pearson, *Mike*, 2:292; Bajpai to William Strang and enclosure, 8 January 1950, FO371/92768, PRO.
143. Ibid., 292–95; Stairs, *Diplomacy of Constraint*, 162 n; O'Neill, *Australia in the Korean War*, 1:175–76.
144. *FR, 1951*, 7:64.
145. UNGA, *OR*, First Committee, sess. 5, 422d meeting, 11 January 1951, 475–76.
146. Jebb to R. H. Scott, 15 January 1951, FO371/92768, PRO; Pearson, *Mike*, 2:293–96; UNGA, *OR*, First Committee, sess. 5, 422d–424th meetings, 11–13 January 1951, 475–93.
147. Jebb to R. H. Scott, 15 January 1951, FO371/92768, PRO; Pearson, *Mike*, 2:296–98; UNGA, *OR*, First Committee, sess. 5, 425th meeting, 13 January 1951, 495–500.

148. Acheson, *Present*, 513.
149. *NYT*, 14 January 1950, 1 and 9.
150. *NYT*, 17 January 1950, 1.
151. *FR, 1951*, 7:91–92.
152. The text is reprinted in ibid., 115–16. On British reservations, see ibid., 85–87, 98–100.
153. *FR, 1951*, 7:1885–87.
154. *NYT*, 20 January 1951, 1. *CR*, 1951, 97 (1): 457–64.
155. Pearson, *Mike*, 2:300–301; Bevin to J. Hutchison (British chargé in Beijing), 20 January 1951, and two dispatches from Hutchison to Bevin, 22 January 1951, FO371/92768, PRO.
156. *FR, 1951*, 7:117.
157. Ibid., 125.
158. Pearson, *Mike*, 2:301–2. Austin's outburst is *not* apparent in UNGA, *OR*, First Committee, 429th meeting, 22 January 1951, 531–32, but it is in the verbatim account in *NYT*, 23 January 1951, 5. See also Jebb's characterization in his wire to the Foreign Office of 22 January 1951 in FO371/92769, PRO.
159. *FR, 1951*, 7:130–31.
160. CM8(51), 25 January 1951, CAB 128/19, PRO.
161. Jebb to Foreign Office, 24 January 1950, FO371/92769, PRO.
162. The Soviet delegate did express general approval, although he offered two minor amendments. See UNGA, *OR*, First Committee, 431st meeting, 25 January 1951, 549; *NYT*, 25 January 1951, 1.
163. Williams, ed., *Hugh Gaitskill*, 229–31; Roger Makins to Younger, 25 January 1951, FO371/92771, PRO.
164. Williams, *Hugh Gaitskill*, 242–55.
165. On this point, see Attlee's speech in the House of Commons on 23 January, which is reprinted in full in *NYT*, 24 January 1951, 4.
166. *NYT*, 21 January 1951, IV, 3; 24 January 1951, 1, 3.
167. *FR, 1951*, 7:135.
168. UNGA, *OR*, First Committee, 433d meeting, 27 January 1951, 570; *FR, 1951*, 7:144–45.
169. CM 9(51), 26 January 1951, and CM 10(51), 28 January 1951, CAB128/19, PRO.
170. J. Hutchison (British chargé in Beijing) to Foreign Office, 28 January 1951, FO371/92771, and William Strang (permanent under secretary of state in the Foreign Office) minute on conversation with Attlee, 30 January 1950, FO371/92773, PRO.
171. UNGA, *OR*, First Committee, 438th meeting, 30 January 1951, 602, and UNGA, *OR*, 327th plenary meeting, 1 February 1951, 695–96.
172. *SCMP*, 2–4 February 1951.
173. Hutchison to Foreign Office, 4 February 1951, FO371/92775, PRO.
174. Hutchison to Foreign Office, 5 January 1951, FO371/92761, and Hutchison to Foreign Office, FO371/92766; *FR, 1951*, 7:116.
175. *SCMP*, 1–3 January 1951.
176. *SCMP*, 5–6 January 1951.
177. *FR, 1951*, 7:1476–88. On the identification of Taylor as the second party, see Dingman, "Atomic Diplomacy," 76 n.
178. Ibid., 1491–1503.
179. Hutchison to Foreign Office, 18 January 1951, FO371/92768 (FK1071/113 and 114), PRO.

180. *SCMP*, 26–27 January 1951. 180. *FR, 1951*, 7:1530–33.
181. *FR, 1951*, 7:1530–33.
182. Yao, "Peng Dehuai's Leadership," 714; see also Chen, "China's Changing Aims," 30–31.
183. On the stepped-up campaign against counterrevolutionaries, see Weiss, "Storm Around the Cradle," 91.
184. U.S. intelligence reports plus the memoirs of Chinese commander Peng Dehuai indicate that the Communist offensive bogged down because of logistical and weather problems. See UNC/FEC, *Staff Section Reports*, Box 385, RG407, WNRC, and Peng Dehuai, *Memoirs*, 478–79. Historian Chen Jian agrees on the basis of Chinese archival sources (see Chen, "China's Changing Aims," 29–30; also Zhang, "Military Romanticism," 121–25).
185. Zhang, "Military Romanticism," 127–28.
186. See the lengthy excerpt from Mao's telegram to Peng of 28 January in Chen, "China's Changing Aims," 32–33.
187. For general reports on guerrilla activities and the morale of South Koreans, see the various CIA memos entitled "Daily Korean Summary" in Box 248, PSF. For a more detailed analysis, see UNC/FEC, *Command Report of Intelligence Activities for January 1951*, Box 385, RG407, WNRC. For suggestive secondary accounts of the Chinese Communists' use of and faith in guerrilla warfare at that time, see Whitson, *Chinese High Command*, 94–97, and George, *Chinese Communist Army in Action*, 175.
188. Malik did meet privately with John Foster Dulles on the Japanese peace treaty, but he was "more reserved" than he had been in discussions during the previous fall. He did not bring up Korea (*FR, 1951*, 4:797–99).
189. *CDSP*, 17 February 1951; see also Shulman, *Stalin's Foreign Policy*, 164–65.
190. *NYT*, 22 January 1951, 1.
191. See, for example, Department of State, Office of Intelligence Research, "Trends in Soviet-Communist Tactics," 24 January 1951, Box 3801, 611.61, RG59, NA.
192. *NYT*, 17 February, 1951, 3.
193. Shulman, *Stalin's Foreign Policy*, 163–71.
194. Kaplan, *Dans les Archives du Comite Central*, 155–79.
195. For contemporary reports, see *NYT*, 11 February 1951, IV, 2; 26 February 1951, 10; 3 March 1951, 4; 4 March 1951, IV, 5; 10 March 1951, 5; 23 March 1951, 7; 27 March 1951, 16.
196. For the U.S. embassy's analysis of Stalin's interview, see Kirk to Acheson, 19 February 1951, 320 USSR, RG84, WNRC; see also *FR, 1951*, 4:1533–36. For additional evidence of Stalin's belief in the increased likelihood of global war, see Pietro Secchia's letter to the Italian Communist Party weekly *Rinascita* (3 April 1970). A member of the central committee of the Italian Communist Party, Secchia was called to Moscow in early 1951 along with compatriot, Luigi Longo. Party Secretary Palmiro Togliatti had been in the Soviet capital for about a month. During his stay, Soviet leaders asked him to become head of the Cominform in Prague. One reason given for the proposed move was that an international conflict might occur at any time and, under such circumstances, he must not be allowed to fall into enemy hands. Togliatti rejected the proposal and was permitted, grudgingly, to return to Italy. The Soviets may have been motivated partly by a desire to weaken Togliatti's influence in the Italian Communist Party, but it is quite possible that the incident represents one more piece of evidence of Stalin's fears of a direct confrontation with the United States. I wish to thank

Geoffrey Warner for bringing the incident to my attention and referring me to the pertinent source.

197. Kopper to Reinhardt, 7 March 1951, and attached memo (author unidentified) dated 21 February 1951, Box 28, Records of the Office of Chinese Affairs, RG59, NA.

198. The consensus among U.S. military leaders was that the Soviets could overrun western Europe, with the exception of Spain, in a matter of weeks. For reflections of this view, see Moscow to the Department of State, "Embassy Estimate of Soviet Intentions," 25 April 1951, Box 23, Records of the Policy Planning Staff 1947–1953, RG59, NA, and JIC 435/52, "Estimate of the Likelihood and Nature of a Soviet Attack on the United Kingdom between Now and Mid-1952," 7 February 1951, 381 U.S., 092 USSR, RG218, NA. However, Rear Admiral L. C. Stevens, who served as a U.S. naval attaché in Moscow from 1947 to 1950, held a different view. He argued that, although Soviet armed forces had considerable defensive capability, the nation's backward economy and its primitive logistical system restricted their offensive potential. Stevens contended that "the national strategy of the Soviet Union not only would not contemplate the scope of operations commonly credited to it [in the West], but does not contemplate any global war of her own choosing under the conditions that now obtain in the world, and which should continue to obtain." See his address to the National War College of 25 January 1951 in Box 23, Records of the Policy Planning Staff, 1947–1953, RG59, NA. Much can be said for Stevens's view, although his failure to take into account the Kremlin's assessment of the political weakness of the anti-Communist alliance in western Europe may compromise his estimate of Soviet plans.

199. *SCMP*, 15 February 1951.

200. *CDSP*, 31 March 1951. If less explicit than Zhou, however, Soviet comments in *Pravda* did imply a broad interpretation of the treaty (see the British chancery in Moscow to the Northern Department of the Foreign Office in London, 16 February 1951, FO 371/92245, PRO; see also *FR, 1950*, 4:1524).

201. Nehru to Krishna Menon, 31 January 1951, as quoted in Gopal, *Nehru*, 2:136.

202. Chipman to Pearson, 7 February 1951, vol. 22, WIKF. For other Asian reactions, see H. Merle Cochran (U.S. ambassador to Indonesia) to Acheson, 9 February 1951; Avra M. Warren (U.S. Ambassador to Pakistan) to Acheson, 10 February 1951; Henry B. Day (U.S. chargé in Burma) to Acheson, 20 February 1951, Box 4272, RG59, NA.

203. Reid to Pearson, 19 February 1951, vol. 6, Escott Reid Papers, PAC.

204. *NYT*, 4 February 1951, IV, 1.

205. Box D6, Eric Sevareid Papers, LC.

206. Eisenhower recommended moving slowly on German rearmament. For reports on his trip and his reception by Congress on his return, see *NYT*, 21 January 1951, IV, 5; 28 January, 1951, IV, 3; 2 February 1951, 1, 4, 5; *FR, 1951*, 3:392–459. For an assessment of the importance of rearmament in the West and an expression of appreciation for U.S. leadership in this area, see Pearson to Wrong, 9 February 1951, vol. 22, WIKF.

207. *NYT*, 1 February 1951, 6; *FR, 1951*, 4:291–348. In his treatment of the Plevan visit to Washington, Irwin Wall emphasizes the U.S. refusal to accommodate France on a variety of issues, especially economic and military aid. He concedes, however, that the public relations aspect of the trip was positive (see Wall, *Making of Postwar France*, 204–7).

208. Finn, *Winners in Peace*, 272–83.

209. Franks to Foreign Office, 24 January 1951, FO371/92770, PRO.

210. For use of this argument by U.S. diplomats, see *NYT*, 28 January 1950, IV, 3; *FR, 1951*, 7:99–100.

211. Franks to Foreign Office, 27 January 1951, FO371/92771, PRO.

212. On Spender, Menzies, and the aggressor resolution, see O'Neill, *Australia in the Korean War*, 1:170–82; for an account of the Spender-Menzies relationship, see Barclay, *Friends in High Places*, chap. 2; for an overview of Australian strategic thinking, see Reese, *Survey of International Relations*, chaps. 4–6.

213. Shann to the Department of External Affairs, 26 January 1951, A1838/T184, 3123/8/1, AA.

214. Jebb to Foreign Office, 27 January 1951, FO371/92771, PRO.

CHAPTER 5
THE DIMENSIONS OF COLLECTIVE ACTION

1. This account of the battle of Chipyong-ni is based on the following: Appleman, *Ridgway Duels for Korea*, chap. 11; Gugeler, *Combat Actions in Korea*, chaps. 9 and 10; Hoyt, *The Bloody Road to Panmunjom*, chaps. 13 and 14; *Newsweek*, 37 (19 and 26 February 1951): 27–28 and 26, respectively; *Time*, 57 (19 and 26 February): 34 and 28, respectively.

2. *Newsweek* 37 (26 February 1951): 26. For an analysis of the positive impact on the morale of U.S. troops of the "amazingly good show" of French, Dutch, and British units, see Major W.R.L. Turp (British military attaché, Korea) to Major I. R. Ferguson (War Office, London), 19 February 1951, FO371/92732, PRO.

3. Zhang, "Military Romanticism," 134.

4. *Newsweek*, 19 February 1951, 27. Far Eastern Command intelligence estimated that the Communists suffered more than 130,000 casualties between 26 January and 24 February. See UNC/FEC, *Staff Section Report*, February 1951, Box 399, RG407, WNRC.

5. Peng, *Memoirs of a Chinese Marshal*, 479–80.

6. Zhang, "Military Romanticism," 186–87.

7. Ibid., 194; *FR, 1951*, 7:326.

8. Unless otherwise noted, this account of the spring offensive is based on Appleman, *Ridgway Duels for Korea*, chaps. 18–20; Rees, *Korea*, 243–63; *USAKW*, 3:379–90, 387–90; Ridgway, *The Korean War*, 171–81; Zhang, "Military Romanticism," 190–99.

9. Quoted in Rees, *Korea*, 250.

10. On material conditions, see Ridgway to the Joint Chiefs, 30 May 1951, Box 16, SRRKW; on U.S. psychological warfare, see Colonel R. S. Bratton to Department of the Army, 13 June 1951, FEC, AG Administrative File, RG338, WNRC; on the use of former Nationalist troops, see Acheson Info Circular, 24 April 1951, 320 China, RG84, WNRC.

11. *USAKW*, 3:397–99; Collins, *War in Peacetime*, 1969, 306–9; Ridgway to the Joint Chiefs, 14 June 1951, Box 16, SRRKW.

12. For a good summary of the process of constituting the GOC, see C. Glover (Canadian Department of External Affairs), "Notes for Heads of Division Meetings," 12 February 1951, vol. 22, WIKF.

13. *FR, 1951*, 7:160.

14. *FR, 1951*, 7:161. The government's stand on the aggressor resolution provoked considerable debate in the Swedish parliament and press. See Swedish Institute of International Affairs, *Sweden and the United Nations*, 82–93.

15. *FR, 1951*, 7:161, 170; *NYT*, 9 February 1951, 3, and 13 February 1951, 4.
16. *FR, 1951*, 7:213–19; Austin to Acheson, 14 February 1951, Box 9, SRRKW.
17. *FR, 1951*, 7:214.
18. Lamb to the British Foreign Office, 18 March 1951, FO371/92778, PRO.
19. *FR, 1951*, 7:328.
20. Australian delegation to the United Nations to Department of External Affairs, 30 March 1951, A1838/T184, 3123/5/10, AA.
21. Ibid.; British Foreign Office to Franks, 30 March 1951, FO371/92778, PRO.
22. CIRC 462 from SECSTATE, 7 February 1951, 320 China, RG84, WNRC; see also *FR, 1951*, 7:1893–94.
23. *NYT*, 15 February 1951, 3.
24. Wrong to Pearson, 14 February 1951, Pearson Papers, PAC.
25. *FR, 1951*, 7:1899–1902, 1914–15, 1936–41, 1943, 1949–50.
26. See a paper by the British chiefs of staff: "Strategic Implications of the Application of Economic Sanctions Against China," 9 February 1951, DEFE5/27, PRO.
27. *FR, 1951*, 7:1932.
28. On the evolution of allied trade policy toward Communist nations, see Yasuhara, "Export Controls in Asia"; for a brief but useful summary, see Secretary of State for External Affairs to Canadian Permanent Delegation to the UN, 3 May 1951, vol. 23, WIKF.
29. *FR, 1951*, 7:1885–87.
30. Ibid., 1907–11. A subcommittee of the AMC actually did a study of League sanctions against Italy to point out the problems with making collective economic measures effective. See "Procedures for the Application and Co-ordinator of Collective Measures (The League of Nations Experiment in 1935–36)," A1838/T184, 3123/5/9, AA.
31. Australian delegation to the United Nations to Department of External Affairs, 30 March 1951, A1838/T184, 3123/5/10, AA; British Foreign Office to Franks, 30 March 1951, FO371/92778, PRO.
32. On the early maneuvering, see *FR, 1951*, 7:1895–97; Australian mission to the UN to the Department of External Affairs, 5 February 1951, A1838/T184, 3123/1, AA; *NYT*, 17 February 1951, 1–2. For a good summary, see Memorandum for Mr. Norman, 19 April 1951, vol. 23, WIKF.
33. *NYT*, 9 March 1951, 11; J. O. Lloyd minute on latest developments in Korea for the Minister of State, 23 February 1951, FO371/92731, PRO; see also documents in A1838/T184, 3123/5/9, AA.
34. Secretary of State for External Affairs to Permanent UN Representative of Canada, 2 March 1951, vol. 21, WIKF; memorandum for Mr. Norman (of the Canadian Department of External Affairs), 19 April 1951, vol. 23, WIKF; *FR, 1951*, 7:1932.
35. *FR, 1951*, 7:1931–36, 1941–46.
36. *CR*, 97 (12 March 1951): 2257–58.
37. On British efforts, see Prime Minister Attlee's statement to Parliament on 12 February in *NYT*, 13 February 1951, 1; for Truman's statement, see *NYT*, 16 February 1951, 1, 3.
38. *FR, 1951*, 7:178–81.
39. *NYT*, 20 February 1951, 1.
40. *FR, 1951*, 7:220.
41. *NYT*, 16 March 1951, 1.
42. *FR, 1951*, 7:235–38.

43. Ibid., 263–64.
44. Ibid., 265–66.
45. Ibid., 267, 269–70, 272.
46. *NYT*, 28 March 1951, 1. See also Truman's statement of 29 March in *PPPUS: Harry S. Truman, 1951*, 203–7.
47. *FR, 1951*, 7:212, 249–50, 272; Rusk's briefing of ambassadors, 20 March 1951, Box 3, SRRKW.
48. See A. R. Menzies (chief of the U.S. and Far Eastern Division of the Canadian Department of External Affairs) to Escott Reid, 10 March 1951, vol. 22, WIKF. For a representative assessment of the impact on U.S. opinion of battlefield events in Korea, see Australian embassy in the United States to Department of External Affairs, 17 March 1951, A1838/T184, 3123/5/9, AA.
49. U.K. High Commissioner to India to British Foreign Office, 28 February 1951, FO371/92778, PRO; *FR, 1951*, 7:187–88.
50. Lamb to the British Foreign Office, 18 March 1951, FO371/92778, PRO; Canadian high commissioner to India to Canadian Department of External Affairs, 26 March 1951, vol. 22, WIKF.
51. *FR, 1951*, 7:223–26; Jebb to British Foreign Office, 9 and 16 March 1951, FO371/92778, PRO.
52. *FR, 1951*. 7:247–48, 290 n; Jebb to British Foreign Office, 16 March 1951, FO371/92778, PRO. In April UNCURK did consider an approach to North Korea but was dissuaded by Lie and others. See *FR, 1951*, 7:292–93, 333–35, 348.
53. *FR, 1951*, 7:290, 293.
54. Ibid., 304–5.
55. Ibid., 376, 379–80.
56. Zhang, "Military Romanticism," 189–92.
57. *SCMP*, 28–31 March 1951.
58. This conclusion derives from my survey of materials in *CDSP*, *SCMP*, and *FBIS*, and from reports of the U.S. embassy in Moscow in 320 USSR, RG84, WNRC.
59. Peng, *Memoirs of a Chinese Marshall*, 479–80. For an editorial in *Renmin ribao* illustrating PRC efforts to mobilize the country for a protracted effort in Korea, see *SCMP*, 18–19 March 1951.
60. *MZM*, 2:151–53.
61. Pearson to Wrong, 22 March 1951, vol. 20, WIKF. On the five principles, see above, pp. 153–54. Australia, France, and South Africa suggested some of the same changes as Pearson (see *FR, 1951*, 7:258 n).
62. British Foreign Office to Franks, 24 March 1951, FO371/92813, PRO.
63. *FR, 1951*, 7:280–82.
64. Ibid., 278–80.
65. Ibid., 328–30. For British exchanges with the Americans and others, particularly the Indians, plus Foreign Office deliberations, see FO371/92779, PRO. For evidence that for some time the State Department had been trying to distance the United States from the five principles, see Clubb to Rusk, 23 February 1951, Box 22, Office of Chinese Affairs, RG59, NA.
66. *FR, 1951*, 7:301–4, 311–15, 322–24.
67. James, *Years of MacArthur*, 3:586–89; *USAKW*, 3:374.
68. Truman, *Memoirs*, 2:441–42.
69. Truman to George Elsey, 16 April 1951, Box 72, GE.
70. *MSFE*, 3536, 3542.

71. *FR, 1951*, 7:227–28, 236–37, 278.
72. Ibid., 298–99.
73. Acheson, *Present*, 520.
74. Bradley and Blair, *A General's Life*, 632.
75. Memo for the Record, by Bradley, 24 April 1951, RG218, NA.
76. Ibid.; see also Bradley and Blair, *A General's Life*, 631–35.
77. On administration concern in late March over the impact of the MacArthur issue on congressional opinion regarding troops to Europe, see Christopher E. Steel (minister in the British embassy in Washington) to Foreign Office, 24 March 1951, FO371/92813, PRO. This dispatch described a meeting with Rusk in the aftermath of MacArthur's statement undermining the planned U.S. peace initiative. Steel paraphrased Rusk as saying that "the political situation at home was such that, were they [the administration] explicitly to disown him [MacArthur], the whole of their foreign policy might be jeopardized including troops for Europe."
78. *NYT*, 8 April 1951, IV, 3.
79. See, for example, documents of late March and early April in the JCS1776/202 series in CCS383.21, RG218, MMB, NA.
80. *HJCS*, 3:444–68.
81. *FR, 1951*, 7:232–34.
82. Bradley and Blair, *A General's Life*, 634; Record of Acheson telephone conversation with Robert Lovett, 24 March 1951, DA.
83. See, for example, Anders, *Forging the Atomic Shield*, 127, and Dingman, "Atomic Diplomacy," 69.
84. Bradley and Blair, *A General's Life*, 630–31; *FR, 1951*, 7:309.
85. *FR, 1951*, 7:291–92.
86. See "Diary" for 7 April 1951, Box B103, LeMay Papers. (LeMay was head of the Strategic Air Command), and Anders, "The Atomic Bomb," 1–6.
87. Bradley and Blair, *A General's Life*, 630–31; *MSFE*, 1187, 1253–54, 1391, 1419, 1441, 1443; Memo for the Record, by Bradley, 24 April 1951, RG218, NA.
88. Morrison to Franks, 6 April 1951, and Franks to Morrison, 6 April 1951, FO371/92757, PRO.
89. *FR, 1951*, 7:306–7.
90. Ibid., 296–98, 1616–19.
91. Koo diary entry for 11 April 1951, Box 218, Koo papers; *NYT*, 8 April 1951, 1, and 10 April 1951, 1.
92. *NYT*, 12 April 1951, 1, 3.
93. 20 April 1951, Box 2, SRRKW. This source offers a useful day-to-day summary of events at home and abroad relating to Korea, based primarily on *NYT*.
94. "Schedule for Welcoming of General MacArthur," date and author unknown, Box 73, GE.
95. *NYT*, 12 April 1951, 8.
96. 22 April 1951, Box 2, SRRKW.
97. *NYT*, 15 April 1951, 12.
98. 16 April 1951, Box D6, Sevareid Papers. For extensive materials on White House efforts to counteract pro-MacArthur sentiment, see Box 73, GE; Box 5, Tannenwald papers, and Boxes 304–5, Harriman Papers.
99. *PPPUS: Harry S. Truman, 1951*, 223–37.
100. *MSFE*, 3553, or *NYT*, 20 April 1951, 4.
101. For details on MacArthur's activities after the speech, see James, *Years of MacArthur*, 3:617–21. On public opinion, see *DSOD*s for April and May 1951.

102. On Spain, see "Foreign Radio Reactions to the Replacement of General MacArthur (11–12 April 1951)," PSF; *NYT*, 12 April 1951, 17.

103. *New Yorker*, 27 (28 April 1951): 70.

104. *NYT*, 15 April 1951, IV, 2.

105. *NYT*, 12 April 1951, 1, and 15 April 1951, IV, 5; "Foreign Radio Reactions to the Replacement of General MacArthur (11–12 April 1951)," PSF; *FBIS*, 13 and 16 April 1951.

106. *NYT*, 12 April 1951, 17.

107. *Newsweek*, 37 (30 April 1951): 29; *NYT*, 22 April 1951, 3; 12 April 1951, 6; 16 April 1951, 1; *FBIS*, 13 April 1951.

108. *FBIS*, 12 April 1951.

109. *SCMP*, 13–16 April and 17–18 April 1951.

110. A.R. Menzies (Head, Canadian Liaison Mission, Japan) to Pearson, 13 April 1951, vol. 12, WIKF.

111. *NYT*, 15 April 1951, IV, 4.

112. Canadian Consulate General, the Philippines, to Under Secretary of State for External Affairs, 13 April 1951, vol. 23, WIKF.

113. *NYT*, 12 April 1951, 6, 7; *Time*, 57 (23 April and 20 April 1951): 34 and 29, respectively; Sae Sun Kim (ROK chargé in Washington) to Acheson, 16 April 1951, Box 9, SRRKW.

114. *NYT*, 13 April 1951, 6. Filipino ambassador to the United States, J. Elizalde, wrote to President Quirino on the 14th urging "strict neutrality and non-intervention" in the dispute in the United States lest he "jeopardize our non-partisan situation in Congress." See Box: Special Correspondence EQ-J. Elizalde May 1950–1953, EQ. Filipino diplomats in the United States took heart with MacArthur's brief yet favorable mention of their country in his speech to Congress. See *NYT*, 20 April 1951, 4, and A. L. Valencia (Philippine embassy in Washington) to Romulo, 5 May 1951, Box 1:5, CR.

115. *NYT*, 22 April 1951, 12; 25 April 1951, 1.

116. *NYT*, 15 April 1951, 1.

117. *NYT*, 14 April 1951, 1.

118. *PPPUS: Harry S. Truman, 1951*, 223–27; Dingman, "Atomic Diplomacy," 75.

119. For details, see the next section of this chapter.

120. *FR, 1951*, 7:352.

121. UN document S/2092/Corr. 1; *NYT*, 17 April 1951, 1, 4; Holmes to Pearson, 19 April 1951, vol. 24, WIKF.

122. *FR, 1951*, 7:370–72.

123. Ibid., 369–70, 375; Lamb to the British Foreign Office, 19 April 1951, FO371/92780, PRO; Austin to Acheson, 19 April 1951, Box 10, SRRKW. It appears that no such attacks occurred (*FR, 1951*, 7:370).

124. *FR, 1951*, 7:373–74.

125. Ibid., 376–77, 384.

126. Ibid., 376–77.

127. U.S.-Soviet specialist Charles Bohlen, then in Paris, believed the Kremlin would interpret MacArthur's firing as a tactical response to allied pressure. See Fisher Howe memo of conversation with Bohlen, 13 April 1951, Box 3801, 761.00, RG59, NA.

128. *SCMP*, 19–20 April 1951. For the debate in Congress, see McMahon, "Food as a Diplomatic Weapon," 349–50, 360–71.

129. On UNCURK activities, see *FR, 1951*, 7:333–36, 348.

130. *USAKW*, 3:380–82.

131. *NYT*, 8 April 1951, 1 and IV, 1; *FR, 1951*, 7:316–17.

132. *NYT*, 26 April 1951, 1; "Memo on Meeting at John Barriere's," 1 May 1951, Harriman Papers.

133. Franks to British Foreign Office, 15 April 1951, FO371/92757, PRO; Wrong to Canadian Department of External Affairs, 13 April 1951, vol. 24, WIKF.

134. 13 April 1951, Box 4198, RG59, NA.

135. *FR, 1951*, 7:338–42.

136. Ibid., 338–44; Franks to British Foreign Office, 13 April 1951, FO371/92757, PRO.

137. Ridgway to JCS, 26 April 1951, Ridgway Papers; *FR, 1951*, 7:385.

138. *FR, 1951*, 7:386–87.

139. Franks to British Foreign Office, 30 April 1951, FO371/92757, PRO.

140. *FR, 1951*, 7:387, 400.

141. On the resignation from the British cabinet of Aneurin Bevan, Harold Wilson, and John Freeman on 22–24 April, see Harris, *Attlee*, 473–80.

142. Ibid., 427–31. For ongoing fears in the British Foreign Office that public opinion was dictating U.S. policy, see R. Scott to Captain M. E. Butler Bowden, 2 May 1951, FO371/92758, PRO.

143. Acheson to Bradley, 12 May 1951, Box 11, SRRKW. A curious gap exists in the available documentation on the question of Ridgway's authority. Although the Joint Chiefs' directive of 28 April (see note 138 above) gave the UN commander some leeway, a subsequent one of 1 May, which nullified "all previous directives or portions of directives in conflict herewith," did not (*FR, 1951*, 7:395). Ridgway questioned the new directive on this and other points, but much of the available evidence suggests that he did not receive satisfaction regarding the retaliation issue (see *HJCS*, 3:488–95; *USAKW*, 3:385–87). However, Acheson's note to Bradley on 12 May strongly implies that the secretary of state assumed that Ridgway could act on his own under certain circumstances. I have discussed this matter with James F. Schnabel, the author of the official histories cited above (telephone conversation, 19 May 1986), and, although he has seen no specific documentation indicating that Ridgway had such authority after the directive of 1 May, he believes that it existed. I agree. It is my hope that definitive documentation on the subject eventually will appear.

144. *FR, 1951*, 7:1963–64.

145. Ibid., 1968–70; Holmes to Pearson, 17 April 1951, vol. 24, WIKF; Memorandum of Conversation: Additional Measures Committee Participants, 13 April 1951, Box 49, WA. For a useful summary of the earlier deliberations of the AMC, see Salvatore Lopez to Romulo, 26 April 1951, Box 1:5, *CR*.

146. *FR, 1951*, 7:1964–67. Shann's fears of U.S. action are outlined in his message to the Department of External Affairs on 14 April 1951 in A1838/T184, 3123/5/10, AA.

147. *NYT*, 19 April 1951, 4.

148. *FR, 1951*, 7:1974–75; Memo of conversation between James N. Hyde of the U.S. Mission to the UN and Francis LaCoste and Jacques Tine of the French delegation and J. E. Coulsen and D. S. Laskey of the U.K. delegation, 23 April 1951, and Austin to Acheson, 27 April 1951, Box 10, SRRKW.

149. Austin to Acheson, 1 and 4 May 1951, Box 10, SRRKW.

150. *NYT*, 3 May 1951, 1.

151. *MSFE*, 42, 51–52, 104, 110, 121–22.

152. *NYT*, 7 May 1951, 24.

153. *CR*, 97 (9 May 1951): 5101–2.

154. Austin to Acheson, 8 May 1951, Box 10, SRRKW.

155. *FR, 1951*, 7:430.

156. *NYT*, 15 May 1951, 1, 4.

157. For the parliamentary debate, see *Hansard*, 5th series, vol. 487, 1190–2186.

158. I have found no explicit evidence that the British were swayed on sanctions in part because of their need for U.S. support on Iran, but given the importance of the Iranian crisis to London and the comparatively marginal significance of sanctions against China, it would be surprising if policymakers failed to link the two matters in their own minds. For a useful discussion of the Iranian crisis, see Louis, *British Empire in the Middle East*, 651–66.

159. UNGA, *OR*, sess. 5, 330th plenary meeting, 18 May 1951, 738–42; *NYT*, 18 May 1951, 1, 3. For the text of the resolution, see *FR, 1951*, 7:1988–89.

160. See UN documents A/1841 and A/1841, A1 through A5; see also Harrison Lewis, "Action under UN Strategic Embargo Resolution of 18 May 1951," 15 September 1951, 320.2, RG59, NA, and U.S. Department of State, Division of Historical Policy Research, "American Policy and Diplomacy in the Korean Conflict," part 12, Box 34, KP.

161. Weiss, "Storm Around the Cradle," 220–23; *FR, 1951*, 7:242–46.

162. *MSFE*, 351, 470–71, 531.

163. *NYT*, 22 April 1951, 12; 6 May 1951, 4:5.

164. *DSB*, 24 (28 May 1951): 846–48; for the report on Jiang's call for a second front on the mainland, see *NYT*, 17 May 1951, 1.

165. *MSFE*, 712; *DSB*, 24 (28 May 1951): 848.

166. For MacArthur's approval of the apparent shift in U.S. policy, see *NYT*, 12 May 1951, 8; for Jiang's aggressive statements, see *NYT*, 17 May 1951, 5.

167. On military assistance, see *FR, 1951*, 7:1584–86, 1591.

168. On consideration of U.S. support for a possible Nationalist attack on the mainland, see ibid., 1574–81, 1598–1605, 1637–39, 1673–82; *HJCS*, 3:447–48. The United States had been tolerant of Nationalist raids on the mainland for some time (see 793.00/6-451, RG59, NA).

169. For a revealing discussion of domestic politics in relation to East Asian policy and the evolution of NSC 48/5, which constituted an updated statement of that policy, see "Under Secretary's Advisory Committee: Notes of Meeting of Tuesday, 1 May 1951," Box 28, KP. NSC 48/5 is printed in *FR, 1951*, 6:33–63.

170. *MSFE*, 731–33, 756, 898, 937–38.

171. *USAKW*, 3:356.

172. *MSFE*, 100, 152, 180.

173. *MSFE*, 306, 423–24, 950–51, 1102, 1772, 2135–36.

174. *MSFE*, 423–24. By early July this was no longer true, as contributions had risen to about 40,000. If naval and air force personnel is added, the figure was higher by more than 12,600 (see *NYT*, 9 July 1951, 4).

175. By the end of April thirty-two UN members (out of sixty) and three nonmembers had offered something to the organization's emergency relief program in Korea. Seven other members and one nonmember had offered aid of another sort (see *Yearbook of the United Nations*, 1951, 249–57).

176. See above, 110–14.

177. *USAKW*, 3:225–27; U.S. Department of State, Division of Historical Policy Research, "American Policy and Diplomacy in the Korean Conflict," pt. 8 (November 1950), 81–83, Box 16, KP.

178. In fact, it was the Pentagon that, at the end of January 1951, took the initiative within the U.S. government in suggesting that new units be solicited abroad (see *FR, 1951*, 7:147). For the State Department response, see ibid., 194–95.

179. The British estimated that, whereas the Soviets had an initial force of twenty-four divisions in East Germany and Poland and could build that to from seventy-five to ninety divisions in seven to thirty days, NATO had only fourteen to fifteen divisions available immediately and only seventeen to twenty-two after a thirty-day buildup. The Soviets also had a considerable advantage in tactical air strength. See Joint Planning Staff, "Defense of Europe in the Short Term," 17 May 1951, DEFE 5/42, PRO.

180. Larson, *United States Policy Toward Yugoslavia*, 215–49.

181. Allen to Acheson, 28 June 1950, Box 1, Top Secret Records (Belgrade, Yugoslavia), RG84, WNRC.

182. Swedish Institute of International Affairs, *Sweden and the United Nations*, 72–73, 80–95.

183. The noncontributors were Afghanistan, Egypt, Indonesia, Iran, Iraq, Saudi Arabia, Syria, and Yemen (see *Yearbook of the United Nations*, 1951, 251–52).

184. On the Egyptian and Iranian crises, see Louis, *British Empire in the Middle East*, 604–747.

185. See David Wainhouse (State Department Office of United Nations Political and Security Affairs) to John Hickerson, 22 May 1951, Box 4273, 795.00, RG59, NA; Venkataramini, *American Role in Pakistan*, 154–69.

186. Stairs, *Diplomacy of Constraint*, 1974, 191–97; O'Neill, *Australia in the Korean War*, 1:208–19; McGibbon, *New Zealand and the Korean War*, 216–20.

187. The most detailed discussion of the U.S. effort is Bohlen, "United States-Latin American Relations," 193–200. Documents covering U.S. negotiations with Latin America are in box 4309, 795B.5, RG59, NA.

188. Marshall to the JCS, 14 December 1950, Box 37, RG319, MMB, NA.

189. *MSFE*, 3530–32.

190. Memorandum of Conversation by Arthur Emmons, 11 April 1951, Box 4273, 795.00, RG59, NA; *FR, 1951*, 7:362–64; daily summary of events for 25 April 1951, Box 2, SRRKW.

191. *USAKW*, 3:394–95.

192. See, for example, *MSFE*, 538–40.

193. *FR, 1951*, 7:418–19; Draft Memorandum for General Bradley, 19 April 1951, Box 38, RG319, MMB, NA; Ridgway to Collins, 1 May 1951, Box 16, SRRKW.

194. See NSC 48/5, approved by the president on 17 May, in *FR, 1951*, 6:37; see also Bradley to Marshall, 23 May 1951, Box 16, SRRKW.

195. Stebbins et al., *United States in World Affairs, 1951*, 222–25; *NYT*, 9 May 1951, 9; 13 May 1951, 3:1; 9 June 1951, 23; 17 June 1951, 3:1; 9 July 1951, 1, 34.

196. For numerous reports of late 1950 and early 1951 of Turkish pride in the performance of its troops in Korea and the expectations deriving therefrom, see 795.00, Box 4062, RG59, NA; see also *FBIS*, 4 and 20 December 1950; 20 January and 7 February 1951.

197. *NYT*, 16 May 1951, 20.

198. See, for example, the discussion of the JCS with State Department officials on 6 February 1951 in *FR, 1951*, 5:27–42.

199. Ibid., 52.

200. Kirk to the Department of State, 27 February 1951, 795.00, Box 4062, RG59,

NA. For evidence of a Soviet backdoor approach through Israel to renew a nonaggression pact with Turkey, see George Wadsworth (U.S. ambassador to Turkey) to Acheson, 24 January 1951, ibid.

201. *FR, 1951*, 3:501–2, 508–17; see also Leffler, "Strategy, Diplomacy, and the Cold War," 822–25.

202. *NYT*, 16 May 1951, 1, 20; 17 May 1951, 9; 20 May 1951, 4:5; see also papers presented to the British cabinet dated 17 May 1951 by the Foreign Office and the Defense Committee, CAB129/45, PRO.

203. For a discussion of the command issue and its relationship to Turkey and Greece, see Stebbins et al., *United States in World Affairs, 1951*, 334–37; see also Leffler, *Preponderance of Power*, 419–25. British support for Turkish and Greek entry into NATO was announced on 18 July.

204. Larson, *United States Policy Toward Yugoslavia*, 237–39; Heuser, *Western "Containment" Policies*, 160–61, 189–90.

205. *NYT*, 17 May 1951, 9.

206. Yoshitsu, *Japan and the San Francisco Peace Settlement*, 50–66.

207. On ANZUS, see O'Neill, *Australia in the Korean War*, 1:185–200; *FR, 1951*, 6:132–265, and McGibbon, *New Zealand and the Korean War*, 208–15. On the security treaty that was eventually offered to the Philippines, see Meyer, *Diplomatic History*, 104–7; *FR, 1951*, 6:223–26, 229–50; Dingman, "Diplomacy of Dependence."

208. *NYT*, 12 May 1951, 1, 3; 19 May 1951, 4.

209. *DSB*, XXIV (25 June 1951): 1019. For documentation on the negotiations, see *FR, 1951*, 6:777–1120.

210. See, for example, W. A. Harriman's memo "Talk with President Auriol (Ambassador Barnet present most of the time), Saturday, 31 March 1951; 4:00 P.M. at the Embassy," Box 307, Harriman Papers.

211. On the shift in German opinion, see *NYT*, 15 April 1951, 16.

212. For a balanced contemporary account, see Stebbins et al., *United States in World Affairs, 1951*, 43–68; for an excellent later analysis, see Schwartz, *America's Germany*, chap. 7.

213. Stebbins et al., *United States in World Affairs, 1951*, 68–79; Acheson, *Present*, 554–56; *FR, 1951*, 3:1086–1162; Wall, *Making of Postwar France*, 211–12.

214. Stebbins et al., *United States in World Affairs, 1951*, 230–31.

215. See the minutes of W. A. Harriman's conversation with French Minister of Finance Maurice Petsche of 26 June 1951, Box 307, Harriman Papers.

216. *FR, 1951*, 7:470–72.

217. *NYT*, 3 June 1951, 1, 2; *MSFE*, 1756, 1761, 1782, 2085.

218. Steel to Foreign Office, 8 June 1951, and Strang minute, 20 June 1951, FO371/92783; Morrison to Franks, 9 June 1951, FO371/92782, PRO.

CHAPTER 6
ARMISTICE TALKS: ORIGINS AND INITIAL STAGES

1. *NYT*, 2 May 1951, 1; 3 May 1951, 1, 6, 7, 10, 57.

2. *FR, 1951*, 7:401–10, 421–22.

3. Ibid., 421–22. For the Alsop article, see the *New York Herald-Tribune*, 6 May 1951, 11, 7; see also Kennan, *Memoirs, 1950–1963*, 35–36.

4. On the Moscow talks over Berlin in 1948, see Shlaim, *The United States and the Berlin Blockade*, 305–54.

5. Acheson, *Present*, 532; *FR, 1951*, 7:460–62; see also Kennan's recounting of his mission in a memorandum of 20 February 1968, 795.00/5–2551, RG59, NA.
6. *CR*, 97 (17 May 1951): 5424.
7. *CDSP*, 23 June 1951; Acheson to Certain Diplomatic and Consular Officers, 25 May 1951, 350.21, RG84, WNRC. See also David Bruce (U.S. ambassador to France) to Acheson, 24 May 1951, 795.00, RG59, NA, on an editorial appearing in the French Communist newspaper *Humanité*.
8. *NYT*, 24 May 1951, 1, 3; 25 May 1951, 3. Apparently the indirect Soviet approach to the Swedish Foreign Ministry was through Ilya Ehrenburg, a prominent Soviet writer and leader of the World Peace Council (see W. Walton Butterworth, U.S. ambassador to Sweden, to Acheson, 14 June 1951, Box 9, SRRKW).
9. *NYT*, 23 May 1951, 1, 30; 24 May 1951, 3.
10. See note 5 above.
11. *FR, 1951*, 7:483–86.
12. Ibid., 507–11.
13. See above, pp. 157–58.
14. Acheson, *Present*, 532.
15. The most complete record of this trip is in a folder entitled "China 1951 (CMB Hong Kong Report)," S/P Files, Lot 64D563, RG59, NA.
16. *FR, 1951*, 7:1667–71.
17. Marshall to Nitze, 8 June 1951, Box 28, PPS.
18. *SCMP*, 1–5 June 1951.
19. *FR, 1951*, 7:1711 n.
20. *FR, 1951*, 7:1711–12, 545.
21. Ibid., 522, 563.
22. *NYT*, 24 June 1951, 1, 4, 5.
23. Ibid., 4.
24. *FR, 1951*, 7:547; *Time*, 58 (2 July 1951): 21.
25. *FR, 1951*, 7:553–54, 555–56, 560–63.
26. *FR, 1951*, 7:569.
27. Ibid., 566–71, 577–78, 583–87.
28. Joy, "My Battle," 36.
29. Dean Rusk confirmed in an interview with the author (18 April 1988) that the site was okayed rather quickly in Washington without intense evaluation, simply to expedite the beginning of talks.
30. For the pertinent documents, see *DSB*, 25 (9 July 1951): 43–45; for more details, see *USAKW*, 3:16–21.
31. Acheson telephone conversation with Senator Kerr, 29 June 1951, DA.
32. See the maps in *NYT*, 1 July 1951, 4:4, and 8 July 1951, 4:5; see also "Public Draft of Off-the-Record Remarks by the Secretary of State before Editors and Publishers," 29 June 1951, Box 69, DA.
33. Weyland to Ridgway, 3 July 1951, Ridgway Papers.
34. *DSOD*, 2 July 1951, Box 5; *MSAO*, June and July 1951, Box 12.
35. Ridgway to the Joint Chiefs, 4 July 1951, Box 15, SRRKW.
36. Memo for the Executive Secretariat, by Lucius Battle, 6 July 1951, DA; Notes on Cabinet Meeting, 6 July 1951, Box 1, Connelly Papers; for an illustration of the campaign that ensued, see President Truman's 4 July speech in *PPPUS: Harry S. Truman, 1951*, 370–74.
37. *FR, 1950*, 7:1549–50.

38. *FR, 1951*, 7:285, 469, 497–98, 500–503, 598–600.
39. Ibid., 598.
40. Ibid., 640.
41. Ibid., 599–600.
42. Ibid.; for Acheson's statement following the Malik speech, see *NYT*, 27 June 1950, 1, 3.
43. *FR, 1951*, 7:618.
44. See, for example, ibid., 629–33.
45. Ibid., 598.
46. On the first case, which involved the mass execution of convicted prisoners north of Seoul, see *FR, 1950*, 7:1579–81, 1586–87; UN document A/1881, 20–22; and James Plimsoll's report of 17 February 1951 to the Australian government, a copy of which is in FO371/99548, PRO.
47. *NYT*, 11 April 1951, 4; 25 April 1951, 3; 26 April 1951, 3; 27 April 1951, 3.
48. Weatherly (second secretary to U.S. embassy in Korea) to Arthur Emmons, 8 May 1951; E. Allan Lightner (Counselor to U.S. embassy in Korea) to Department of State, 26 May 1951, Box 4304, 795.00, RG59, NA.
49. *NYT*, 11 May 1951, 5.
50. *NYT*, 13 June 1951, 3; 14 June 1951, 2; 16 June 1951, 2. For extensive reporting on Korean politics during the spring and summer of 1951, see Box 4300, 795B.5, RG59, NA.
51. Plimsoll to Australian Department of External Affairs, 10 December 1950, A1838/T184, 3127/2/1/5, AA.
52. Alec Adams to John Lloyd, 6 April 1951, FO371/92736, PRO.
53. *The Times of London*, 6 May 1951, 1.
54. A. Humphreys to Morrison, 13 May 1951, FO371/92764, PRO.
55. R. S. Milward minute, 8 May 1951, FO371/92736, PRO.
56. Muccio to Acheson, 12 February 1951, Box 4272, 795.00, RG59, NA.
57. *FR, 1951*, 7:230–31, 526–27.
58. Pusan 213 to Department of State, 16 June 1951, Box 4273, 795.00, RG59, NA; Pusan 8 to the Department of State, 6 July 1951, ibid.; Muccio to Acheson, 6 June 1951, Box 9, SRRKW; *NYT*, 2 July 1951, 3.
59. *NYT*, 1 July 1951, 3; *FR, 1951*, 7:601–4.
60. *FR, 1951*, 7:645.
61. *SCMP*, 26–27 June and 1–3 July 1951.
62. *NYT*, 1 July 1951, 4:1; Simmons, *Strained Alliance*, 206.
63. *DSB*, 25 (9 July 1951): 43–44.
64. Simmons, *Strained Alliance*, 200–201, 206.
65. Zhang, "Military Romanticism," 205–7.
66. *MZM*, 2:350, 355; Chen, "China's Changing Aims in the Korean War," 38–39; Zhang, "Military Romanticism," 208–9.
67. Chen, "China's Strategies," 21.
68. For one example of such a Soviet threat, see *FR, 1951*, 7:236–37; *Washington Post*, 11 March 1951, 5B.
69. For discussions of Soviet aid to China, all of which suggest Beijing's discontent, see Simmons, *Strained Alliance*, 180–82; George, *Chinese Communist Army in Action*, 183–89; Weiss, "Storm Around the Cradle," 94–96, 100; and Eckstein, *Economic Growth and Foreign Trade*, 141–42, 324. For a more recent discussion based on Chinese sources, see Zhang, "Military Romanticism," 238–39, 302–3.

70. "Background Report on the Korean War," 9 August 1966, reprinted in translation in Weathersby, "Soviet Role," 15–16.

71. Simmons, *Strained Alliance*, 182–85; Monat, "Russians in Korea," 76–102 passim; U.S. Far Eastern Command, G-2, "Staff Section Report," October 1951, Box 568, and U.S. Far Eastern Command, G-2, "Far Eastern Command Intelligence Digest," 1–15 December 1951, Box 585, RG407, WNRC.

72. See, for example, Monat, "Russians in Korea," 76–102 passim; see also "Summary of Certain Statements by Hugo Valvanne (minister of Finland to India and the People's Republic of China), attached to Henderson to the Department of State, 12 May 1951, Box 1340, RG84, WNRC. The statements by Valvanne were based on a recent visit to Beijing in which he observed a "cultural 'Russianization' " in progress.

73. Lamb, "Record of Conversation with Indian Ambassador, Sardor Panikkar, on 14 July 1951," FO371/92201, PRO.

74. On the June agreements, see W. P. Montgomery (U.K. Trade Commissioner, Hong Kong), to Under Secretary, Commercial Relations and Exports Department, Board of Trade, 18 July 1951, FO371/92199, PRO; on the air buildup in the fall, see Futrell, *United States Air Force in Korea*, 374–87; on overall Soviet aid, see Griffith, *Chinese People's Liberation Army*, 177–78.

75. See, for example, the analysis in the Australian embassy in Washington's analysis for the Australian Department of External Affairs of 14 June 1951, in A1838/T84, 3123/5/5.

76. On the U.S. buildup, see *NYT*, 1 May 1951, 1; 6 May 1951, 4:7; 7 May 1951, 1; 8 May 1951, 13; 8 June 1951, 4; 10 June 1951, 6:12–41 passim; 24 June 1951, 4:2; 28 June 1951, 11.

77. *NYT*, 1 May 1951, 10.

78. See the analysis of British chargé Leo Lamb in his dispatches to the Foreign Office of 22 June 1951 (FO371/92191, PRO) and 14 July 1951 (FO371/92201, PRO); see also U.S. State Department, Office of Intelligence Research, "Current Public Opinion in Communist China," OIR Rpt. No. 5532, 14 May 1951, Box 303, Harriman Papers.

79. Chen, "China's Strategies," 25. By mid-July, the Communist buildup on the battlefield was on a sufficient scale to create fears among U.S. observers of another Communist offensive. See, *FR, 1951*, 7:614–15, 674–75; Ridgway to JCS, 6 July 1951, 383.21 Korea, RG218, MMB, NA.

80. Stebbins et al., *United States in World Affairs, 1951*, 136–37.

81. Peng, *Memoirs of a Chinese Marshall*, 481. According to Zhang ("Military Romanticism," 148), this telegram was dated 13 June.

82. McLane, *Soviet Strategies*, 468–69.

83. Quoted in Zhang, "Military Romanticism," 202.

84. In a conversation of early July with Israeli ambassador to the United States Abba Eban, Malik expressed a desire to end the war but showed more interest in the impact of his speech of 23 June on U.S. public opinion. See Memo of Conversation, John Hickerson with Abba Eban, 11 July 1951, Box 4274, 759.00, RG59, NA.

85. Zhang, "Military Romanticism," 300.

86. Joy, "My Battle," 40.

87. Ibid.; see also Joy, *Negotiating while Fighting*, 13–14.

88. Joy, *How Communists Negotiate*, 4–5.

89. *FR, 1951*, 7:651.

90. *USAKW*, 2:19.

91. *FR, 1951*, 7:658–59.
92. Ibid., 660.
93. Ibid., 664–65.
94. Ibid., 671–73.
95. Ibid., 682–85.
96. *MZM*, 2:381.
97. See the description of Mao's instructions to his negotiators in Korea in Chen, "China's Strategies," 22.
98. Ibid., 17.
99. *FR, 1951*, 673–74. This view of the Chinese as being more accommodating than the North Koreans jibes with a report to Moscow from Soviet Ambassador to North Korea, Razuvaev, of 10 September 1951. I wish to thank Kathryn Weathersby for providing me with a translation of this document from the archives of the Soviet Foreign Ministry.
100. Joy, *Negotiating while Fighting*, 19; *FR, 1951*, 7:685.
101. *FR, 1951*, 7:689.
102. The two UNC agendas are presented in *USAKW*, 2:23–24.
103. *FR, 1951*, 7:727–28.
104. Ibid., 735.
105. *FR, 1951*, 7:740.
106. *NYT*, 27 June 1951, 1 and 3.
107. *FR, 1951*, 7:599.
108. *MZM*, 2:426 and 428.
109. *FR, 1951*, 7:740–45.
110. Ibid., 748–52.
111. *FR, 1951*, 7:751–52.
112. Joy, *Negotiating while Fighting*, 23–24.
113. *FR, 1951*, 7:762.
114. For a perceptive analysis on this point, see Lindesay Parrott's article in *NYT*, 12 August 1951, 4:5.
115. *FR, 1951*, 781.
116. Ibid., 787–89.
117. Ibid., 789–90.
118. For Communist accusations and the UN rebuttals, see ibid., 794–98.
119. Ibid., 801–10; Joy, *Negotiating while Fighting*, 26.
120. *FR, 1951*, 7:810–12.
121. *FR, 1951*, 7:814–15, 819–21, 828–29; Joy, *Negotiating while Fighting*, 26–28.
122. *FR, 1951*, 7:829–30, 842–48; Joy, *Negotiating while Fighting*, 28–33.
123. Joy, *Negotiating while Fighting*, 33–34; *FR, 1951*, 7:848–49. For a discussion of Communist charges and the evidence, see *USAKW*, 2:42–44.
124. *FR, 1951*, 7:852–53, 855–56. On the growing Communist air strength, see *USAKW*, 2:80, and Futrell, *United States Air Forces in Korea*, 372–73. For some public speculation on Communist motives that overlapped with Ridgway's, see *NYT*, 4:1.
125. Joy, *Negotiating while Fighting*, 35.
126. Acheson, *Present*, 535–36.
127. Chen, "China's Strategies," 27–28.
128. See Zhang, "Military Romanticism," 151.
129. *USAKW*, 2:40–42; *NYT*, 26 August 1951, 4:1.
130. *NYT*, 4 August 1951, 4:3.

131. *Time*, 58 (23 July 1951): 14.
132. *Time*, 58 (20 August 1951): 25.
133. *USAKW*, 2:80–86.
134. Zhang, "Military Romanticism," 300–302.
135. *FR, 1951*, 7:855–56.
136. Zhang, "Military Romanticism," 231–32; Chen, "China's Strategies," 26–28.
137. *MZM*, 2:433.
138. Zhang, "Military Romanticism," 150, 205–6.
139. *NYT*, 24 August 1951, 1; 26 August 1951, 1, 4:1; 27 August 1951, 1; 28 August 1951, 1, 2; 29 August 1951, 1, 2.
140. Stalin's wire, undated but clearly shortly after 27 August, is in the Soviet Foreign Ministry archives. I wish to thank Kathryn Weathersby for providing me with a translation of this document.
141. *NYT*, 30 August 1951, 1; 2 September 1951, 4:1.
142. *NYT*, 12 August 1951, 4:5; 19 August 1951, 4:1, 3; 26 August 1951, 4:3, 5. On Nehru's view, see Nehru, *Letters to Chief Ministers*, 465–67, 483–84; on Indonesia, see Sastroamidjojo, *Milestones on My Journey*, 233–39; on the Philippines, see Dingman, "Diplomacy of Dependence," 307–21, and CR boxes 1:5 and 1:6; on Japan's economic recovery, see Borden, *Pacific Alliance*, 144–49.
143. *NYT*, 19 August 1951, 4:1, 3; Acheson to certain diplomatic and consular officers, 24 August 1951, Moscow Embassy Files, RG84, WNRC.
144. See the analysis in a U.S. State Department study, "Estimate No. 27," attached to W. Park Armstrong, Jr., to Acheson, 22 August 1951, Box 4275, 795.00, RG59, NA.
145. *NYT*, 3 September 1951, 1:4; September 1951, 2:5; September 1951, 1, 4; 7 September 1951, 1, 8; September 1951, 1, 2, 57; Futrell, *United States Air Force in Korea*, 373–74. In mid-September the UNC estimated that there were 25,900 Caucasian troops in North Korea, 15,400 of which were Soviet. They were in service and support rolls rather than on the front lines (*FR, 1951*, 7:922). On the increasing use of Chinese pilots, see Zhang, "Military Romanticism," 241–42.
146. *NYT*, 9 September 1951, 24; 13 September 1951, 14.
147. *NYT*, 9 September 1951, 4:2.
148. *NYT*, 5 August 1951, 4:5; 12 August 1951, 4:4.
149. *NYT*, 9 September 1951, 4:3.
150. Stebbins et al., *United States in World Affairs, 1951*, 129–41.
151. Scott minute, 30 August 1951, FO371/92201, PRO.
152. Moscow to Acheson, 30 July 1951, 611.61, RG59, NA.
153. *NYT*, 9 September 1951, 1:1, 26–27; 4:3.
154. *USAKW*, 2:80–89.
155. *FR, 1951*, 7:991–92.

Chapter 7
Progress

1. *FR, 1951*, 7:875–77.
2. Ibid., 882.
3. Ibid., 884–86.
4. Ibid., 909.
5. Ibid., 901–3.
6. Ibid., 925–27, 929–30.

7. Ibid., 925–30.
8. Ibid., 952–55.
9. Ibid., 957. For an account of Ridgway's continued bitterness toward the Communists over their negotiating tactics, see George Clutton (of the British mission in Tokyo) to Morrison, 6 October 1951, FO371/92747, PRO.
10. *FR, 1951*, 7:904, 916; Merchant to Rusk et al., 13 September 1951, Box 26, Records of the Office of Chinese Affairs, RG59, NA.
11. *FR, 1951*, 7:955–62.
12. Ibid., 990–94.
13. *USAKW*, 2:92–103; *NYT*, 30 September 1951, 1, 3; 7 October 1951, 4:1.
14. *MZM*, 2:465; *FR, 1951*, 7:1005.
15. Ibid., 1008–15, 1031–36, 1038–41, 1050–51, 1050–59, 1061; Joy, *Negotiating while Fighting*, 55–64.
16. Joy, *Negotiating while Fighting*, 63–64.
17. Ibid., 71–74; *FR, 1951*, 7:1097–1100.
18. Joy, *Negotiating while Fighting*, 72–73; *FR, 1951*, 7:1092–93.
19. *FR, 1951*, 7:1100–1102.
20. See, for example, Bo to Ridgway, 13 October 1951, Ridgway Papers.
21. *FR, 1951*, 7:1120; *Newsweek* 38 (19 November 1951): 32; *NYT*, 11 November 1951, 4:11, and 12 November 1951, 3.
22. Shattock minute, 31 July 1951, FO371/92791, PRO.
23. *NYT*, 30 September 1951, 1; 14 October 1951, 4:1; Stebbins et al., *United States in World Affairs, 1951*, 278–79.
24. Scott to Tomlinson, 29 September 1951, FO371/92795; Victor Balfour to Scott, 26 October 1951, FO371/92811, PRO.
25. *The Times of London*, 27 and 28 September 1951, 4 and 4, respectively.
26. *NYT*, 14 October 1951, 4:3; 28 October 1951, 4:5.
27. *Hansard*, 5th series, vol. 493, 70–80. In fact, President Truman opposed a "Big Three" meeting (see Ambassador Alan Kirk's memorandum of conversation with the president, 26 October 1951, Box 2825, 611.61, RG59, NA).
28. Ibid., 67–79, 191–210.
29. *NYT*, 11 November 1951, 4:1, 1:1; see also *The Nation*, 175 (17 November 1951): 413–19; *FR, 1951*, 4:428–41. Since the early stages of the war in Korea, the U.S. Congress had consistently made substantial cuts of Truman administration requests for foreign economic aid.
30. *PPPUS: Harry S. Truman, 1951*, 520–23.
31. *NYT*, 6 October 1951, 3; 7 October 1951, 1:1, 3; 12 October 1951, 17; Eric Sevareid commentary of 11 October 1951, D5, Sevareid Papers, LC.
32. *PPPUS: Harry S. Truman, 1951*, 566; *NYT*, 11 October 1951, 18.
33. *NYT*, 4 October 1951, 1; 6 October 1951, 1, 3; 7 October 1951, 3.
34. *Collier's* (27 October 1951). On the impact of this issue in Europe, see *The Nation*, 173 (10 November 1951): 385, and Eric Sevareid's news analysis of 12 November 1951 in D5, Sevareid Papers, LC.
35. *NYT*, 4 November 1951, 4:1; *The Times of London*, 3 November 1951, 10.
36. On the Vienna meeting, see *NYT*, 4 November 1951, 14; 6 November 1951, 3; 7 November 1951, 10; 8 November 1951, 2; Stebbins et al., *United States in World Affairs, 1951*, 379; Shulman, *Stalin's Foreign Policy Reappraised*, 202–3.
37. *PPPUS: Harry S. Truman, 1951*, 623–27.
38. UNGA, *OR*, sess. 6, 335th meeting, 13–17; *NYT*, 9 November 1951, 1.

39. CIA, Foreign Broadcast Information Division, "Foreign Radio Reactions to President Truman's Program for a Reduction of World Armaments (7–9 November 1951)," Box 251, PSF; *The Nation*, 173 (17 November 1951): 416–17; *NYT*, 11 November 1951, 4:1, 3; 12 November 1951, 9; 18 November 1951, 4:1, 3.

40. Acheson stated in his speech to the General Assembly that "no general progress can be put into effect while UN forces are resisting aggression in Korea" (UNGA, *OR*, sess. 6, 17).

41. For Vishinsky's proposal, see ibid., 26; for the Chinese response, see *NYT*, 12 November 1951, 1.

42. *FR, 1951*, 7:1124.

43. See *FR, 1950*, 7:1107–10.

44. *FR, 1951*, 7:1128–30.

45. *FR, 1951*, 7:1122–24, 1128–32, 1147–48.

46. *USAKW*, 2:118.

47. *FR, 1951*, 7:1147–48, 1159–63, 1172, 1176–77, 1186–88; *USAKW*, 2:118–21.

48. KAN, 2:84.

49. *FR, 1951*, 7:1174–75.

50. The quotes are from Burke's description of his meeting with the president in Burke to Joy, 17 December 1951, Burke Papers.

51. On the Communist insistence on a cease-fire simultaneously with the settlement of item 2, see *FR, 1951*, 7:1127, 1132.

52. Quoted in *USAKW*, 2:177.

53. For a general discussion of the incident, see *USAKW*, 2:177–78; for Truman's response to press reports, see *FR, 1951*, 7:1199–1200; for Van Fleet's justification of his order, see Van Fleet to Ridgway, 30 November 1951, Box 20, Ridgway Papers.

54. See Bo to Ridgway, 13 October 1951, Box 20, Ridgway Papers, and Ridgway, *Korean War*, 190.

55. Blair, *Forgotten War*, 802.

56. See above, pp. 224–25.

57. For press discussions indicating that item 5 would pose no problems to an early settlement, see *NYT*, 24 November 1951, 3; 25 November 1951, 4:1.

58. See above, p. 212.

59. *FR, 1951*, 7:1149, 1175.

60. Ibid., 1141–42.

61. Ibid., 1154–56; Franks to British Foreign Office, 21 November 1951, FO371/92759, PRO.

62. *NYT*, 24 November 1951, 3.

63. Quoted in *USAKW*, 2:135.

64. Alapatt, "Legal Implication of Repatriation," 84–85.

65. *FR, 1951*, 7:666–67; General Headquarters, FEC, Joint Strategic Plans and Operations Group, "Location of and Authority 1 to Visit Prisoner of War Camps," 8 July 1951, Box 8, RG338, WNRC.

66. *FR, 1951*, 7:626–27.

67. Ibid., 622.

68. Headquarters, Eighth Army (Korea), Staff Study, "Arrangements Pertaining to Prisoners of War," n.d. but clearly summer 1951, Box 8, RG338, WNRC.

69. *USAKW*, 2:136–37.

70. *FR, 1951*, 7:792–93. This argument was made in the Pentagon during the sum-

mer, but was later countered by Ridgway's claim that the UNC had scrupulously avoided any promise of asylum.

71. Collins to Lovett, 15 November 1951, Box 1, RG218, MMB, NA.

72. The State Department had been dubious about nonforcible repatriation from the start. See, for example, Acheson draft of a letter to Marshall, 16 August 1951, Box 1, Records of the Director of the Office of Northeast Asian Affairs (U. Alexis Johnson), 1945–1953, RG59, NA. On the trend toward an all-for-all exchange in November, see *FR, 1951*, 7:1167–70.

73. *FR, 1951*, 7:1073.

74. For a hint of the Communists' position passed on through their correspondents at Panmunjom, see *NYT*, 24 November 1951, 3.

75. *FR, 1951*, 7:1137.

76. See "Daily Opinion Summary," 15 November 1951 and 19 November 1951, Box 5, Records of the Office of Public Opinion Studies, 1943–1965, RG59, Diplomatic Branch, NA.

77. Ridgway to Collins, 16 November and 19 November 1951, Ridgway Papers.

78. On congressional concerns about atrocities in the aftermath at the Hanley incident, see H. A. Houser, "Memorandum for the Record: Congressional investigation of atrocities in Korea," 8 December 1951, Korea (Atrocities), RG330, MMB, NA; see also Eric Sevareid's commentaries of 14 and 15 November 1951, D5, Sevareid Papers.

79. UNGA, *OR*, sess. 6, plenary meetings, 8 November 1951, 15, 17; and comm. 1–2, 19 November 1951, 9.

80. On the congressional appropriation, which passed on 10 October, see Stebbins et al., *United States in World Affairs, 1951*, 397; on the Kirk-Vishinsky exchange, see *FR, 1951*, 7:1003.

81. For an English translation of the speech, see *CDSP*, 3 (1 December 1951): 1–8, 32; for Bohlen's analysis, see Bohlen to Kennan, 9 November 1951, Box 36, Bohlen Papers.

82. This point is made in Willging, "Soviet Foreign Policy," 120. Willging translates the key word in Beria's speech as "nonaligned" while the translator for the CDSP uses "independent." See *CDSP*, 3 (1 December 1951): 32.

83. Army Chief of Staff J. Lawton Collins visited Yugoslavia in October and, on 14 November, the United States and Yugoslavia signed a military assistance agreement. See *FR, 1951*, 4:1837, 1840, 1854–1856, 1858–59, 1862–63; *NYT*, 15 October 1951, 1; 17 October 1951, 18; 18 October 1951, 17; 19 October 1951, 8; 15 November 1951, 11.

84. Willging, "Soviet Foreign Policy," 115–20.

85. McGeehan, *German Rearmament Question*, 149–68.

86. On the French economic crisis, see Wall, *Making of Postwar France*, 220–24.

87. *NYT*, 18 November 1951, 4:4.

88. James Reston's front-page article in the *New York Times* on 3 December was entitled "More Arms to Go to Europe If War in Far East Ends."

89. I wish to thank Kathryn Weathersby for providing me with a translation of this document from the Soviet Foreign Ministry archives.

90. *FR, 1951*, 7:1205.

91. On the simulated atomic missions over North Korea, see *HJCS*, 3 (pt. 2): 614, and Ryan, *Chinese Attitudes toward Nuclear Weapons*, 52–53; on U.S. public opinion and the use of nuclear weapons, see ibid., 53–54.

92. *SCMP*, 4–5 November 1951.
93. *SCMP*, 9–10 November 1951. For greater detail, see Weiss, "Storm Around the Cradle," 94–99.
94. Zhang, "Military Romanticism," 303–4; Weiss, "Storm Around the Cradle," 123–28, 180–90. The Three Anti campaign centered on waste, corruption, and bureaucracy, the Five Anti campaign on bourgeois bribery, tax evasion, theft of state property, cheating on government contracts, and stealing economic information.
95. Zhang, "Military Romanticism," 218–21.
96. For evidence of Kim's difficulties in North Korea, see his *Works*, 6:417–27; Lee and Scalapino, *Communism in Korea*, 416–29.
97. Mao, *Selected Works*, 4:61–62.
98. *MZM*, 2:497.
99. Weiss, "Storm Around the Cradle," 100.
100. Futrell, *United States Air Force in Korea*, 378–80.
101. *NYT*, 24 November 1951, 3.
102. *FR, 1951*, 7:1229–30, 1234.
103. Ibid., 1278–79, 1307; *USAKW*, 2:125–27.
104. *FR, 1951*, 7:1189–93, 1200–1201, 1221–23; Shattock (British Foreign Office) to Eden, 30 November 1951, and Minutes of Chiefs of Staff Meeting, 30 November 1951, FO371/92758, PRO.
105. Wrong to Pearson, 17 December 1951, copy in FO371/99564, PRO; *FR, 1951*, 7:1429–31.
106. *FR, 1951*, 7:1408–9.
107. Ibid., 1415–17; Watt (Australian Department of External Affairs) to Officer (Australian Embassy, Paris), 31 December 1951, A1838/T184, 3123/4/12, AA.
108. *NYT*, 16 December 1951, 10; 29 December 1951, 2; "Summary of Daily Meeting with the Secretary," 27 December 1951, Box 5, General Records of the Office of the Executive Secretariat, RG59, NA; *FR, 1951*, 7:1458–60.
109. Ibid., 1447–48.
110. Ibid., 1382.
111. Ibid., 1373–74; *USAKW*, 2:141.
112. *USAKW*, 2:141–42.
113. Ibid., 142–43.
114. *FR, 1951*, 7:1244 n.
115. Ibid., 1290–96.
116. Ibid.; see also Franks to British Foreign Office, 11 December 1951, FO371/92800, PRO.
117. *FR, 1951*, 7:1197.
118. Ibid., 1226.
119. Ibid., 1232–33.
120. Ibid., 1296.
121. Ibid., 1370–71; Joy, *Negotiating while Fighting*, 136–37.
122. Joy, *Negotiating while Fighting*, 176–77.
123. On the failure of Chinese leaders to anticipate the complexities in resolving the POW issue, see Chen, "China's Strategies," 26–27.
124. Ibid., 184.
125. *NYT*, 3 January 1952, 1.
126. Lamb to British Foreign Office, 19 December 1951 and 10 January 1952, FO371/99230/1013/1, PRO.

127. Joy, *Negotiating while Fighting*, 85.

128. On speculation in the U.S. press and UNC fears of its impact on the Communists, see Joy, *Negotiating while Fighting*, 189.

129. Ibid., 199.

130. The most comprehensive study of the POW issue in Soviet-U.S. relations during World War II is Elliott, *Pawns of Yalta*.

131. Here I am speaking of the $100 million appropriated by Congress during October 1951 for use by exiles from the Soviet bloc or dissidents within it as part of a U.S. plan to take the offensive in the cold war (see Yurechko, "From Containment to Counteroffensive," chap. 2). The Soviets played up this evidence of America's aggressive intentions in their propaganda during late 1951 and early 1952.

132. Joy, *Negotiating while Fighting*, 190.

133. *FR, 1952-1954*, 13-14.

134. *USAKW*, 2:146, 154-55.

135. "Memorandum of Conversation at Dinner at British Embassy, Sunday, 6 January 1952," 7 January 1952, DA.

136. *USAKW*, 2:180; Rees, *Korea*, 301; *NYT*, 6 January 1952, 4:4.

137. *MZM*, 2:642.

138. On passage of the "Uniting for Peace" resolution, see above, p. 123. The CMC report is published as UN document A/1891.

139. By 30 September 1951, only thirty-eight of sixty UN members had responded to Secretary-General Lie's call for the earmarking of fully trained and equipped military units within national forces for action against aggression under the UN banner. Of the eighteen that were essentially favorable, the vast majority were vague in their commitments. See UN document A/1891, annex 2.

140. UNGA, *OR*, sess. 6, First Committee meetings, 1951-1952, 125-28. On U.S. aid to Nationalist forces under General Li Mi, about four thousand strong by the end of 1950 and three times that a year later, see Prados, *Presidents' Secret Wars*, 73-76, and Leary, *Perilous Missions*, 129-32. These forces invaded Yunnan Province in southwest China from Burma in April and July 1951 and were quickly repulsed. The next invasion occurred in August 1952 with the same result. The U.S. government consistently denied charges that it was aiding General Li, and it is not certain that President Truman or Secretary of State Acheson knew of the activity, which was conducted by the Central Intelligence Agency.

141. *NYT*, 5 January 1952, 1, 3.

142. *NYT*, 3 January 1952, 47, 58.

143. On cuts in economic aid, see ibid.; on the trade issue, see Funigiello, *American-Soviet Trade in the Cold War*, 69-71.

144. *NYT*, 3 January 1952, 1.

145. *NYT*, 15 January 1952, 26.

146. Stebbins et al., *United States in World Affairs, 1951*, 204-6; Borden, *Pacific Alliance*, 155-65; *NYT*, 3 January 1952, 47.

147. *FBIS*, 2 January 1952, AA16; *NYT*, 31 December 1951, 4; 1 January 1952, 3; 2 January 1952, 1; 6 January 1952, 5.

148. *NYT*, 1 January 1952, 3; 6 January 1952, 4:3, 3. On Soviet efforts to split the British and the Americans, see *NYT*, 20 December 1951, 20.

149. On British concerns during early 1952, see FO371/99231, PRO.

150. *FR, 1951*, 7:1360.

151. Scott to Jebb, 2 January 1952, FO371/99564, PRO.

152. For an account of the sixth session of the General Assembly, see Stebbins et al., *United States in World Affairs, 1951*, chaps. 10 and 11; for the debate on the Moroccan issue, see UNGA, *OR*, sess. 6, 354th meeting, 243–69.

153. *NYT*, 28 November 1951, 11; 29 November 1951, 6.

154. C. C. Parrott (U.K. delegation to the UN) to J.S.H. Shattock (China and Korea Department, British Foreign Office), 1 December 1951, and "Record of a Meeting of Heads of Commonwealth Delegations Held at the United Kingdom Delegation Offices in Paris on Friday, 30 November 1951," FO371/92799, PRO; U.K. High Commissioner in India to British Foreign Office, 31 December 1951, FO371/99564, PRO.

155. UNGA, *OR*, sess. 6, First Committee, 486th meeting, 173.

156. Ibid., 174.

157. See above, p. 240.

158. *NYT*, 10 January 1952, 1.

159. *NYT*, 18 January 1952, 1; UNGA, *OR*, sess. 6, First Committee, 493d meeting, 209–13.

160. *NYT*, 3 February 1952, 1; UNGA, *OR*, sess. 6, 507th meeting, First Committee, 300.

161. *NYT*, 18 January 1952, 1; 3 February 1952, 4:5.

162. *NYT*, 3 February 1952, 18, 4:1, 5; Acheson, *Present*, 608–10.

163. In mid-January Taft stated that all-out war should be waged against China if armistice talks failed (*NYT*, 20 January 1952, 41). He expressed confidence that the Soviet Union would not intervene in such a conflict.

164. *CDSP*, 8 March 1952, 3–6, 46; *NYT*, 3 February 1952, 10.

165. *NYT*, 13 January 1952, 4:3; 17 January 1952, 1; 20 January 1952, 4:1.

166. *NYT*, 20 January 1952, 4:5. For detailed accounts of the Churchill visit, see Acheson, *Present*, 594–605, and Gilbert, *Churchill*, vol. 8, chap. 37.

167. A Gallup poll conducted in mid-November 1951 showed 23 percent approving Truman's performance, 58 percent disapproving, and 19 percent holding no opinion. A similar poll conducted from 20 to 25 January 1952 returned figures of 25 percent, 62 percent, and 13 percent, respectively (see Gallup, *Gallup Poll*, 2:1032, 1040).

168. *NYT*, 20 January 1952, 4:3.

169. Truman's journal is in Box 333, PSF. For a published text of this passage with some analysis, see Bernstein, "Truman's Secret Thoughts," 31–33, 44.

170. *FR, 1952–1954*, 15:32–33; "Minutes of Meeting with the Secretary," 22 January 1952, Box 5, Records of the Office of the Executive Secretariat, RG59, NA.

171. Stelle to Nitze, 24 January 1952, Box 20, PPS.

172. Marshall to Nitze, 28 January 1952, ibid.

173. On Bohlen, see Johnson, *Right Hand of Power*, 133; see also Johnson's oral history, 71 and 74.

174. *FR, 1952–1954*, 15:32–38. An article by columnist Walter Lippmann may have had an impact here. See the *New York Herald-Tribune*, 24 January 1952, 11. Lippmann's article was discussed at the secretary's meeting on 24 January (see Box 5, Records of the Executive Secretariat, RG59, NA).

175. *FR, 1952–1954*, 15:40–43, 639; Bernstein, "Struggle over the Korean Armistice," in Cumings, ed., *Child of Conflict*, 280.

176. H.O.H. Frelinghuysen to Johnson, 5 February 1952, Box 2, Records of the Bureau of Far Eastern Affairs, Lot 55D128, RG59, NA. On Soviet treatment of POWs held by that nation at the end of World War II, see C. H. Peake to Johnson, 27 June 1952, Box 7, ibid.

177. Barrett to Matthews, 5 February 1952, Box 2, Records of the Bureau of Far Eastern Affairs, Lot 55D128, RG59, NA.

178. Ibid., 44–45. For retrospective accounts by participants, see Acheson, *Present*, 652–54; Johnson, *Right Hand of Power*, 133–41; Bohlen, *Witness to History*, 300; Truman, *Memoirs*, 2.

179. *FR, 1952–1954*, 15:77–78; Joy, *Negotiating while Fighting*, 258–59, 272.

180. For a press report of trouble in the camps, see *Time* 59 (28 January 1952): 21.

181. Johnson, *Right Hand of Power*, 131.

182. *FR, 1952–1954*, 15:98–99; Johnson, *Right Hand of Power*, 136.

183. In addition to the sources already cited, the paragraphs on the POW camps are based on *USAKW*, 2:232–40; Callum A. MacDonald, "'Heroes Behind Barbed Wire': The U.S., Britain and the POW Issue in the Korean War," in Cotton and Neary, *Korean War in History*, 135–50; Myers and Bradbury, "Political Behavior"; UNC/FEC, MIS, "The Communist War in POW Camps," 28 January 1953, 383.6 TS, RG319, WNRC; and Brigadier General Haydon L. Boatner to Senator John Tower, 4 February 1970; Boatner to the Hoover Institution on War, Revolution and Peace, 5 December 1975; and Boatner to "Folks," 1 July 1952, Box 1, Boatner Papers. Boatner became commander of UNC POW camps in May 1952.

184. For defenses, on legal grounds, of the principle of no forced repatriation, see Gutteridge, "Repatriation of Prisoners of War," 207–16; Mayda, "Korean Repatriation Problem," 414–38. 184. *FR, 1952–1954*, 15:58–59.

185. *FR, 1952–1954*, 15:58–59.

186. Ibid., 66–67.

187. "Memorandum of Conversation, Korea: Prisoners of War," 13 February 1952, Box 2, Records of the Bureau of Far Eastern Affairs, Lot 55D128, RG59, NA.

188. *FR, 1952–1954*, 15:70–71.

189. See above, p. 245.

190. In his memoirs, Johnson says, "When I returned to Washington I stressed to the Joint Chiefs privately that I thought the camps were out of control and required overhaul" (*Right Hand of Power*, 137). It is unlikely that Acheson had been briefed on conditions in the camps before the meeting of the 27th, as he had arrived in Washington from a NATO meeting in Lisbon only hours before.

191. Major General Bryan L. Milburn, G-1 FEC, for Van Fleet, 29 February 1952, as quoted in *USAKW*, 2:240.

192. See Boatner correspondence cited in note 182 above.

193. On Van Fleet's estimate, see Memo for Diary, 11 March 1952, Box 22, Ridgway Papers.

194. *FR, 1952–1954*, 15:44; Bernstein, "Struggle over the Korean Armistice," in Cumings, ed., *Child of Conflict*, 280.

195. See above, p. 251.

196. See, for example, *NYT*, 20 November 1951, 3; *Newsweek* 38 (26 November 1951; 31 December 1951): 31 and 21, respectively; *U.S. News and World Report* 31 (30 November 1951): 11.

197. On editorial opinion, see *MSAO* for January and February 1952.

198. *FR, 1952–1954*, 15:44.

199. Bernstein reaches the same conclusion in "Struggle over the Korean Armistice," in Cumings, ed., *Child of Conflict*, 282, based largely on Princeton Seminars, 14 March 1952, DA. In his oral history (76–79, HSTL), Johnson argues to the contrary on

calculations in Washington. However, he places the meeting of 27 February in the summer of 1952, much closer to the November election than in fact it occurred.

200. For a detailed narrative, see *USAKW*, 2:159–63.

201. *NYT*, 27 February 1952, 1, 5.

202. "Briefing of Ambassadors on Korea, by Johnson," 29 February 1952, Box 3, SRRKW.

203. For the most balanced treatment of the bacteriological warfare campaign, see Ryan, *Chinese Attitudes toward Nuclear Weapons*, chap. 4. The available evidence does not permit a definitive conclusion on the accuracy of the basic charge or the real beliefs of Chinese leaders. A private Mao note of 4 March published in *MZM*, 3:303, has the Chinese leader instructing subordinates to prepare to provide vaccinations for civilian and military personnel in two northeastern provinces and to prepare sufficient vaccine for the populations of Beijing and Nanjing. The implication is that Mao believed the Americans were waging bacteriological warfare against China.

204. *NYT*, 16 March 1952, 1; LMB to Scott, 17 March 1952, FO371/99234, PRO; Dening (Tokyo) to Scott, 17 March 1952, FO371/99569, PRO.

205. On hints by the Communist press, see *FR, 1952–1954*, 15:108.

206. Joy, *Negotiating while Fighting*, 307–52.

207. Ibid., 292, 306, 318–20.

208. Ibid., 328–44; *FR, 1952–1954*, 15:136–39, 142–43.

209. Joy, *Negotiating while Fighting*, 341, 346.

210. *FR, 1952–1954*, 15:136–39, 142–43.

CHAPTER 8
DEADLOCK

1. *FR, 1952–1954*, 15:142–43, 160–64; *USAKW*, 2:169–70.
2. *FR, 1952–1954*, 15:143–44.
3. Dodd's prediction is recorded in Joy, *Negotiating while Fighting*, 350.
4. The quoted material is from Joy, *Negotiating while Fighting*, 355.
5. *FR, 1952–1954*, 15:153 n.
6. Joy, *Negotiating while Fighting*, 355–56.
7. *FR, 1952–1954*, 15:154.
8. Ibid., 156, 158–59.
9. Ibid., 159.
10. Joy, *Negotiating while Fighting*, 367–68; *USAKW*, 2:171.
11. Joy, *Negotiating while Fighting*, 369–405; *USAKW*, 2:264.
12. On covert actions in China, see Leary, *Perilous Missions*, 132–42.
13. *USAKW*, 2:199–200.
14. Joy, *Negotiating while Fighting*, 266.
15. Ibid., 343.
16. *USAKW*, 2:169.
17. Joy, *Negotiating while Fighting*, 350.
18. Ibid., 355–56; *FR, 1952–1954*, 159.
19. On Ridgway's response to the incident of August 1951, see Goldhammer, "Korean Armistice Conference," 142–46.
20. See above, p. 228; *FR, 1952–1954*, 15:30, 80–81.
21. The charges may be followed in *SCMP* and *FBIS*. In mid-March the State Department estimated that 25 percent of Chinese radio broadcasts directed toward a do-

mestic audience and 20 percent of broadcasts aimed at a foreign audience centered on these charges. See "Briefing of Ambassadors on Korea, by Hickerson," 18 March 1952, Box 3, SRRKW.

22. Joy, *Negotiating while Fighting*, 401.

23. For the estimate of the Chinese interpreters who led Joy to propose rescreening, see ibid., 355. For a more conservative estimate, see *FR, 1952–1954*, 15:192. The figure after that screening was 5,236 (see *FR, 1952–1954*, 15:204); the actual number of Chinese repatriates after the armistice and after neutral screening in the demilitarized zone was 6,670 (see *USAKW*, 2:514). The total number of Communist repatriates was 82,493. Whether those figures would have been substantially higher had rescreening occurred in April–May 1952 is impossible to determine, but UNC rescreening in the spring of 1952 would have been motivated by a desire to increase the number of repatriates whereas, after the armistice occurred, the UNC had a stake in demonstrating the accuracy of the initial screening. Although the UNC did not conduct the post-armistice screening, it did have control over the POWs until they reached the demilitarized zone.

24. *FR, 1952–1954*, 15:207.

25. Soon after Pandit's meeting with Zhou, New Delhi received word from Panikkar that the Chinese drew a sharp distinction between Chinese and North Korean POWs, that all of the former must be returned (ibid., 248–49).

26. Ibid., 189–90, 208.

27. *PPPUS: Harry S. Truman, 1952–1953*, 321–22; Hansard, Parliamentary Debates, House of Commons, 5th series, vol. 500, 383–86.

28. Even the British, ever alert for signs of dissension between the Communist giants, regarded Sino-Soviet relations as extremely close and Soviet influence paramount. Eden to Arthur Bottomly, 1 May 1952, FO371/99235, PRO.

29. *NYT*, 2 March 1952, 4:3; 9 March 1952, 4:6.

30. *NYT*, 11 March 1952, 1, 6; Schwartz, "The German Question," 10–11. For an alternative to the view presented here of Stalin's initiative, see Steininger, *German Question*.

31. *NYT*, 12 March 1952, 11; Schwartz, "The German Question," 11–14.

32. Schwartz, "The German Question," 14–16; Acheson, *Present*, 630–31; Eden, *Full Circle*, 50–51.

33. *NYT*, 11 April 1952, 4.

34. *NYT*, 6 April 1952, 1:1, 4; 4:2.

35. *NYT*, 13 April 1952, 4:2, 3, 4.

36. See above, pp. 32–33.

37. Tucker, *The Soviet Political Mind*, chap. 4.

38. Knight, *Beria*, 160–65.

39. Stalin, *Economic Problems of Socialism*, 37–39.

40. On the Soviet press and the general climate for Western diplomats in Moscow, see the various reports of the U.S. embassy in Moscow in 611.61, Box 6005, RG59, NA, and from the British embassy in Moscow in FO371/100813, 100837, 100847, PRO.

41. For estimates, see Weiss, "Storm Around the Cradle," 64–67.

42. On the collections campaign in China, see ibid., 94–101; on CPV casualties during the fall 1951 campaigns, see *USAKW*, 2:96, 102, 103; for estimates of the Chinese buildup in Korea between the summer of 1951 and the spring of 1952, see *FR, 1952–1954*, 15:181.

43. See Weiss, "Storm Around the Cradle," 123–28, 173–90; for reports on the

turmoil in China created by the Three Anti-Five Anti campaign, see Lamb to Eden, 19 February 1952, FO371/99234, PRO, and Lamb to Scott, 17 March and 17 April 1952, FO371/99235, PRO.

44. See Lamb to Scott, 17 April 1952, FO371/99235, PRO, and Lamb to Scott, 28 May 1952, FO371/99236, PRO; Edwin W. Martin to George W. Perkins, 28 March 1952, Box 3024, RG59, NA.

45. Zhang, "Military Romanticism," 249.

46. On the limited impact of the UNC air war in North Korea, see Futrell, *United States Air Force in Korea*, 435–38.

47. For U.S. expressions of concern on the impact of the bacteriological warfare campaign, see *FR, 1952–1954*, 15:73–74, 79, 101–2; "Summary of Daily Meeting with the Secretary," 17 March 1952, Box 5, Records of the Office of the Executive Secretariat, RG59. For PRC expressions of confidence on the impact of this campaign, see Zhang, "Military Romanticism," 249–50.

48. *NYT*, 6 April 1952, 4:1; 9 April 1952, 1; 1 May 1952, 1; 11 May 1952, 4:1.

49. UNC/FEC, MIS, "The Communist War in POW Camps," 28 January 1953, RG407, WNRC.

50. *USAKW*, 2:242–43.

51. For events on Koje-do, see ibid., 243–55; Headquarters, Second Logistical Command, "Command Report," May 1952, RG407, WNRC.

52. As late as 14 May, State Department official Charles Bohlen pointed out in a meeting with the Joint Chiefs that reports from abroad indicated "strong support for our position." See *FR, 1952–1954*, 15:197. For doubts in the British Foreign Office on no forced repatriation, see C. H. Johnston, "The Korean Armistice Talks," 29 January 1952, FO371/99565; R. H. Scott, "Korea: Armistice," 1 March 1952, FO371/99568; Scott to Tomlinson, 7 May 1952, FO371/570, PRO.

53. *NYT*, 16 May 1952, 3.

54. For debates in the House of Commons, which included frequent references to the British press, see *Hansard*, Parliamentary Debates, House of Commons, vol. 501, 6–9, 625–36, 917–30, 1815–35. For an example of the impact of the Koje-do incident on the British press, compare editorials in the *Times of London* of 8 and 23 May 1952, 7. For U.S. analyses of the impact abroad of the Koje-do incident, see *FR, 1952–1954*, 15:222–24, 243, 309–10.

55. *NYT*, 14 June 1952, 1; 15 June 1952, 4:2; *USAKW*, 2:257–62; Boatner to the Hoover Institution on War, Revolution and Peace, 5 December 1975; Boatner to "Folks," 1 July 1952; Boatner to Senator John Tower, 4 February 1970, Box 8, Boatner Papers.

56. By early June the POW issue had replaced the charges regarding bacteriological warfare as the number one item on the Communist propaganda agenda. See *FR, 1952–1954*, 15:309–10.

57. For a detailed analysis of U.S. policy in the crisis, see Keefer, "Democracy's Failure?" For a narrative of the crisis and its background, see UNC/FEC, MIS, "FEC Intelligence Digest," 16–31 July 1952, 15–62, Box 707, RG407, WNRC; also UN document A2187, 2–20, the report of the UN commission on the crisis.

58. The quote is from Muccio to Acheson, 12 June 1952, *FR, 1952–1954*, 15:337.

59. For concern about the morale of the ROKA, see Muccio to Acheson, 12 June 1950, 795.00, Box 4281, RG59, NA.

60. For an evaluation of the broad and negative impact of the crisis on U.S. and UN

standing abroad, see Hickerson to Matthews, 13 June 1952, *FR, 1952–1954*, 15: 326–28.

61. On the Zhou-Pandit meeting, see above, p. 272.

62. Bowles's cultivation of Nehru and its impact on Indian-U.S. relations are documented in the correspondence in the ambassador's papers. For public expressions of improvement in Indian-U.S. relations, see *NYT*, 29 February 1952, 3; 9 March 1952, 4:4.

63. *NYT*, 7 April 1952, 1, 3.

64. Gopal, *Nehru*, 2:138–39.

65. Lamb to Scott, 15 May 1952, FO371/99260, PRO. The quote is from Lamb's report of Panikkar's description of Mao's conversation with Pandit.

66. *FR, 1952–1954*, 15:206–7. In a conversation with the British high commissioner to India (acting), Sir Girja S. Bajpai, secretary-general of the Indian Ministry for External Affairs, stated that Pandit had reported that the Chinese regarded the British as "less rigid and hostile than the Americans" and wondered if the influence of the former might be "brought to bear" on the latter. See U.K. High Commissioner to India (acting) to Commonwealth Relations Office, 14 May 1952, FO371/99573, PRO.

67. *FR, 1952–1954*, 15:202–3 n, 206–7.

68. Ibid., 224, 243–44, 250.

69. U.K. High Commissioner in India (acting) to Commonwealth Relations Office, 17 June 1952, FO371/99576, PRO.

70. Gross's report to the State Department of this conversation, sent on 30 June, is in *FR, 1952–1954*, 15:364–67. The account that follows is taken from this report.

71. *FR, 1952–1954*, 15:384.

72. Ibid., 407–8; U.K. High Commissioner in India (acting) to Commonwealth Relations Office, 14 July 1952, FO371/99580, PRO.

73. *FR, 1952–1954*, 15:374–76, 386–87, 396.

74. For expressions of outrage in England and India over the UNC bombing, see *NYT*, 25 June 1952, 3; 26 June 1952, 1; 27 June 1952, 3; 6 July 1952, 3; and Selwyn Lloyd to Eden, 2 July 1952, FO371/99578; U.K. High Commissioner in India (acting) to Commonwealth Relations Office, 16 July 1952, FO371/99581, PRO. For evidence that some U.S. pilots were flying north of the Manchurian border in "hot pursuit" of Communist planes, see Mahurin, *Honest John*, 68–73. For Canadian and British suspicions on this matter, see Wrong to Pearson, 5 June 1952, vol. 31, WIKF.

75. On the planning and implementation of the air attacks, see Futrell, *United States Air Force in Korea*, 448–53.

76. U.K. High Commissioner to India (acting) to Commonwealth Relations Office, 11 August 1952, FO371/99583, PRO.

77. J. O. Lloyd, "Korean Armistice Negotiations," 14 July 1952, FO371/99581, PRO. When Nehru confronted Panikkar on the 12th he reportedly speculated that Mao must have vetoed Chou's Plan B (see *FR, 1952–1954*, 15:406).

78. *FR, 1952–1954*, 15:366.

79. *NYT*, 16 December 1952, 13; 19 June 1955, 27; 22 May 1957, 3.

80. Earlier in June Jebb noted in a report to London that "Zinchenko has not proved reliable as interpreter of Soviet thought in the past." See Jebb to Foreign Office, 11 June 1952, FO371/99575, PRO.

81. Chen, "China's Strategies," 34–35.

82. For the *very* limited Communist offensive of November 1951, see Zhang, "Mil-

itary Romanticism," 219–20. We will see in chapter 9 that the offensives of 1953 were on a far larger scale.

83. Futrell, *United States Air Force in Korea*, 452, 482; Simmons, *Strained Alliance*, 216.

84. *USAKW*, 285–93; Zhang, "Military Romanticism," 157.

85. *FR, 1952–1954*, 15:376–79, 402–4; *NYT*, 4 July 1952, 3; 5 July 1952, 1; 6 July 1952, 4:8.

86. Acheson, *Present*, 640–47.

87. *NYT*, 22 June 1952, 4:2.

88. Ibid., 4:3; 29 June 1952, 4:5.

89. On Great Britain, see *NYT*, 3 July 1952, 5; 13 July 1952, 13, 4:2; on France, see *NYT*, 25 July 1952, 4.

90. McCoy, *Presidency of Harry S. Truman*, 292–94; *NYT*, 30 June 1952, 1; 2 July 1952, 1; 6 July 1952, 4:6. The strike was settled on 24 July.

91. I want to thank Chen Jian for sharing his insight with me on this point.

92. Schwartz, "The German Question," 22–23.

93. *NYT*, 13 July 1952, 2.

94. For various accounts of Nenni's conversation with Stalin of early July, see FO371/97850, 100826, PRO.

95. On the Soviet hate-America campaign, see *NYT*, 21 June 1952, 2; 22 June 1952, 4:1; 29 June 1952, 4:5; 6 July 1952, 4:7. For expressions of concern about the campaign by U.S. diplomats, see Kennan to Acheson, 22 May 1952; Kennan to Matthews, 6 June 1952; Acheson to Kennan, 9 June 1952; Kennan to Acheson, 19 June 1952, 611.61, Box 2825, RG59, NA.

96. *NYT*, 22 June 1952, 4:1.

97. *NYT*, 22 June 1952, 4:6.

98. *NYT*, 3 July 1952, 2.

99. *NYT*, 22 June 1952, 4:1.

100. *NYT*, 5 July 1952, 3.

101. Zhang, "Military Romanticism," 302–3, 305.

102. Ibid., 304–5; Weiss, "Storm Around the Cradle," 128–32, 213–16.

103. "Stalin's Conversations with Chinese Leaders," 10–19.

104. Ibid; Chen, "China's Strategies," 37.

105. Stairs, *Diplomacy of Constraint*, 249–56; Pearson to Wrong, 6 June 1952, vol. 31, WIKF.

106. *USAKW*, 2:320–24; Kaufman, *Korean War*, 276–78; Foot, *Wrong War*, 178–79.

107. *DSOD*, 10 July 1952, Box 6.

108. *MSAO*, July 1952, Box 12.

109. *Life* 32 (19 May 1952):146–48, 151–52, 154, 157, 160.

110. Divine, *Foreign Policy*, 34.

111. *FR, 1952–1954*, 15:193–94, 270 n.

112. Clark, *From the Danube to the Yalu*, 3.

113. Ibid., 26–27. For the Ridgway quote, see above, p. 240. For a report outlining the attitudes of Clark and his top subordinates in Tokyo and Korea on negotiations with the Communists, see "Memorandum for Mr. Karl R. Bendetsen, by Dr. Ralph L. Watkins," 28 August 1952, PSF.

114. *FR, 1952–1954*, 15:272–73.

115. For the Chinese warning, see Lamb to British Foreign Office, 27 June 1952,

FO371 99635, PRO. The idea of asking military observers from these nations to investigate conditions on Koje-do originated with U.S. Senator Richard B. Russell. See Russell to Truman, 10 June 1952, Box 2, 000.5, RG218, NA. Acheson's correspondence with the five countries is available in Box 11, SRRKW. Although the initial tasks of the group, had it been formed, did not include rescreening prisoners, it was understood that its formation might represent a first step in that direction. See Percy Spender (Australian ambassador in Washington) to R. G. Casey (Australian foreign minister), 20 June 1952, A1838/T184, AA.

116. *HJCS*, 4:109–16.

117. Ibid., 119–21; Marc Trachtenberg, "'Wasting Asset,'" 29–30.

118. Foot, *Wrong War*, 176–77.

119. *USAKW*, 2:320–21; Bradley to Lovett, 19 June 1952, and Joint Chiefs to Clark, 19 June 1952, Box 17, SRRKW.

120. Futrell, *United States Air Force in Korea*, 488–90.

121. *USAKW*, 2:320–21; Foot, *Wrong War*, 177. For Pentagon consideration of the issues of use of Nationalist troops in Korea as opposed to augmentation of the ROK army, see Memo for the Record, by Lovett, 7 August 1952; Lovett to the Joint Chiefs, 23 August 1952,; Joint Chiefs to Lovett, 25 August 1952, Box 318, RG330, NA; see also Clark's conversation with Karl Lott Rankin, the U.S. minister to China, as recorded in the latter's diary of 26 September 1952, Box 1, Rankin Papers.

122. "Next Stop in Korean Armistice Negotiations," 21 August 1952, Box 8, Records of the Bureau of Far Eastern Affairs, Lot 55D128, RG59, NA.

123. *FR, 1952–1954*, 15:422–26, 427 n.

124. For Clark's response, see *FR, 1952–1954*, 15:427–29; for Kennan's response, see ibid., 426–27, 435.

125. Ibid., 451–52.

126. Kennan to Acheson, 18 and 19 August 1952, Box 8, Records of the Bureau of Far Eastern Affairs, Lot 55D128, RG59, NA.

127. For State Department references to the Hallinan proposal and its coverage in the Communist press, see *FR, 1952–1954*, 15:462–66; Kennan to Acheson, 23 and 24 August 1952, 795.00, Box 4238, RG59, NA. The U.S. Communist Party endorsed Hallinan's candidacy on 6 September (*NYT*, 7 September 1952, 4).

128. *FR, 1952–1954*, 15:463–65; R. H. Scott, "Korean Armistice Negotiations," 30 August 1952, FO371/99583, PRO.

129. *FR, 1952–1954*, 15:465–67.

130. Ibid., 485–86. Apparently Mexican President Miguel Alémán submitted this proposal to advance his chances for a Nobel Peace Prize, for which he had been nominated (*NYT*, 10 September 1952, 3).

131. *FR, 1952–1954*, 15:487.

132. Ibid., 466–70.

133. Ibid., 475, 479.

134. Ibid., 453–56, 505; British Foreign Office to Washington, 6 September 1952, FO371/99582, PRO; Chester Ronning to Jules Leger (both of the Canadian Department of External Affairs), 3 September 1952, vol. 40, WIKF; Australian Department of External Affairs to Washington, 26 August 1952, A1838/T184, 3123/5/14, AA.

135. *FR, 1952–1954*, 15:522–25.

136. For Truman's December 1951 statement of concern regarding the rearmament program in the event of an armistice in Korea, see *FR, 1951*, 7:1295.

137. *FR, 1952–1954*, 15:532–38. According to Henry Lieberman, the *New York*

*Times* correspondent in Hong Kong, Nationalist raids on the Chinese coast from the islands numbered more than fifty between 1 June and 14 October. Although most of these raids involved small groups of between ten and two hundred Nationalist troops, about four thousand participated in a raid on the Communist-held Nanchi Island off the Fujie coast on 11 October. The role of the United States in the planning and execution of such raids remains uncertain. See *NYT*, 7 December 1952, 1; 8 December 1952, 3.

138. *FR, 1952–1954*, 15:545–48.

139. Ibid., 554–57.

140. *DSB* (20 October 1952): 600.

141. Admiral Fechteler's minutes of the meeting on 17 September in Box 17, SRRKW, indicate that Acheson envisaged an eventual unilateral release of nonrepatriates if the situation arose.

142. See unsigned memo of "about Sept 16, 1952," in DA.

143. Clark, *From the Danube to the Yalu*, 80–82; Foot, *Wrong War*, 184.

144. Collins, *War in Peacetime*, 324; *USAKW*, 2:330.

145. See Lovett's and Fechteler's comments in Fechteler's minutes of the meeting with Acheson on 17 September in Box 17, SRRKW.

146. On General Bradley's concern about the U.S. negotiating position in the heat of the election campaign, see *FR, 1952–1954*, 15:481.

147. *USAKW*, 2; 140.

148. Ibid., 513–14, 522–25, 536–37.

149. On Truman's sense of guilt regarding U.S. disarmament after World War II, see ibid., 534.

150. *FR, 1952–1954*, 15:454–55.

151. Ibid., 552.

152. Ibid., 506.

153. For the British reaction to Lie's plea, see U.K. Foreign Office to Washington, 12 September 1952, FO371/99583, PRO.

154. C. H. Johnston, "Korea," 29 September 1952, FO371/99585, PRO. Australian Department of External Affairs to Australian High Commissioner's Office (London), 18 September 1952, CRS/A816, item 19/323/86, AA. For a Quaker proposal bearing similarities to the Mexican plan and presented to Churchill in September, see Bailey, *Korean Armistice*, 113–14.

155. Washington to U.K. Foreign Office, 3 October 1952, FO371/99586, PRO.

156. Jebb to U.K. Foreign Office, 26 September 1952, FO371/99585, PRO.

157. *FR, 1952–1954*, 15:599–606.

158. Ibid., 541–44. The Soviets approached the Mexican ambassador in Washington to find out whether it had been cooked up by the United States. See "Memorandum of Conversation, by Philip Raine," 24 September 1952, 611.12, Box 2727, RG59, NA. I wish to thank Lester Langley for pointing out this document to me. For a report on a conversation between Malik and an Israeli diplomat indicating that the Soviets might be more sympathetic to an armistice on UNC terms than the Chinese, see USUN to Acheson, 10 October 1952, Box 8, Records of the Bureau of Far Eastern Affairs, Lot 55D128, RG59, NA.

159. *SCMP*, 24 September 1952; CDSP, 1 November 1952; *NYT*, 16 September 1952, 4. Mao's published telegrams of mid-September show him to be anxious to consult with "Soviet comrades" on upcoming events in the UN General Assembly and on possible PRC nonaggression treaties with Burma and India (*MZM*, 3:544–47).

160. For a translation of Malenkov's address, see *CDSP*, 1 and 8 November 1952.

161. The first invitations to the Beijing conference had been sent out in March (see *SCMP*, 2–4 October 1952; *NYT*, 12 October 1952, 4:7). Plans for the Nineteenth Party Congress in Moscow were not announced until 20 August. According to Khrushchev, the decision for the congress was very much Stalin's. See Khrushchev, *Khrushchev Remembers*, 276–77.

162. *NYT*, 12 October 1952, 4:1; *USAKW*, 2:303–18.

163. Thomas Hamilton reported in the *NYT* on 13 October (9) that the Soviet delegation included "an unusually large number of experts on UN affairs" and that the Soviet press agency TASS was planning more in-depth coverage than ever before. On the other hand, in late September, Andrei Gromyko, now Soviet ambassador in the United Kingdom and soon to be a Soviet delegate to the General Assembly, told a Swedish diplomat that he saw no reason for discussing Korea in the General Assembly, that it was better suited to resolution by the great powers alone. See Foreign Office minute by P. Mason, 30 September 1952, FO371/99586, PRO.

164. For expressions of U.S. concern, see *FR, 1952–1954*, 3:32–34.

165. *NYT*, 14 October 1952, 1.

166. See *FR, 1952–1954*, 8:1048–59; Kennan, *Memoirs 1950–1963*, chap. 7. According to two accounts of Italian Socialist Pietro Nenni's private conversation with Stalin in July, the latter hinted that he did not want Kennan in Moscow. The Soviet Union's hesitation in accepting Kennan's appointment late the previous year suggests that Stalin was never happy with the return to Moscow of the author of containment. For accounts of the Nenni interview, see J. W. Russell (at the British embassy in Rome) to P. Mason (British Foreign Office, London), 2 October 1952, and H. T. Morgan (British Foreign Office, London), "Nenni-Stalin Interview of July, 1952," 24 November 1952, FO371/100826, PRO.

167. Divine, *Foreign Policy*," 2:69–70.

168. UNGA, *OR*, sess. 7, plenary meetings, 1952, 5–7.

169. On past flirtations among Latin American delegations with mediation attempts on Korea, see Houston, *Latin America and the United Nations*, 120–27. For an assessment of the state of U.S.-Latin American relations in late 1952, see Stebbins et al., *United States and World Affairs, 1952*, 261–73.

170. Stebbins et al., *United States in World Affairs, 1952*, 76. On the impact of the Korean War on U.S.-Latin American relations, see Bohlin, "United States-Latin American Relations," chaps. 4–6.

171. For Acheson's maiden address to the sixth session of the General Assembly, see UNGA, *OR*, sess. 6, 335th meeting, 13–17.

172. *NYT*, 16 October 1952, 1.

173. UNGA, *OR*, sess. 7, 382d meeting, 71–86; UN document A/2229.

174. UNGA, *OR*, sess. 7, 383d meeting, 90–100. In fact, the Communist proposal of 8 October offered no significant concession on the POW issue. See *FR, 1952–1954*, 15:554–57.

175. Acheson, *Present*, 765–66.

176. Ibid., 766. Only Colombia, Honduras, Uruguay, and Nicaragua among the Latin Americans and Thailand and the Philippines among the Asians emerged as cosponsors (see UNGA, *OR*, First Committee, 512th meeting, 27).

177. For a text of the resolution, see UN document A/C.1/725. For reservations about it in the British Foreign Office, see Lloyd to Jebb, 23 October 1952, FO371/99587, PRO.

178. On Commonwealth desires going into the assembly, see T. Clifton Webb

(Minister for External Affairs, New Zealand) to Alfred Rive (Canadian High Commissioner to Australia), 29 September 1952, vol. 41, WIKF.

179. The description of Menon's background and personality provided below is based on George, *Krishna Menon*, and Lengyel, *Krishna Menon*. Technically, Menon's surname was Krishna Menon, but he was nearly always referred to in the press as if it were Menon alone.

180. Gopal, *Nehru*, 2:141–44.

181. George, *Krishna Menon*, 166.

182. For a critical view of Menon's dealings with Asian diplomats, which contrasts him sharply with Sir Benegal Rau, see Jansen, *Nonalignment and the Afro-American States*, 108–13.

183. Chairman, Canadian Delegation to the General Assembly, New York, to Secretary of State for External Affairs, Ottawa, 24 October 1952, vol. 42, WIKF. See also "Record of Meeting of Heads of Commonwealth Delegations Held at United Nations Headquarters on 24th October, 1952," 24 October 1952, FO371/99587, PRO.

184. *FR, 1952–1954*, 15:555–56.

185. *NYT*, 30 October 1952, 9, and 1 November 1952, 2.

186. *NYT*, 29 October 1952, 1; see also the comment by Paul Martin of the Canadian delegation in "Minutes of the Third Meeting of Heads of Commonwealth Delegations held on Tuesday, the 28th October, 1952, at United Nations Headquarters," FO371/99587, PRO.

187. For the Vishinsky speech, see UNGA, *OR*, First Committee, 514th meeting, 31–38. For the Soviet draft resolution, see A/C.1/729.

188. Austin to State Department, 5 November 1952, Box 1284, 320, RG59, NA.

189. British High Commissioner to China to the Foreign Office, 28 October 1952, FO371/99587, PRO.

190. *FR, 1952–1954*, 15:590–91.

191. Ibid., 581–82. On Indonesia's perspective, see Memorandum of Conversation, Dean Acheson with Indonesia Foreign Minister Murkarto and ambassadors Palar and Sastroamidjojo, 31 October 1952, 320, Box 1283, RG59, NA.

192. *NYT*, 5 November 1952, 3. For Palar's report to the U.S. delegation in Arab-Asian group activities, see Austin to the State Department, 5 November 1952, 320, Box 1284, RG59, NA; for an earlier estimate by Iran's Nasrollah Entezam to the effect that the twenty-one-power resolution lacked wide support among Arab-Asian delegations, see Memorandum of Conversation, Dean Acheson with Entezam, 29 October 1952, ibid.

193. *FR, 1952–1954*, 15:570, 581.

194. *NYT*, 20 October 1952, 22. The above paragraph is based on reports in *NYT*, especially 17 October 1952, 1; 21 October 1952, 1; 23 October 1952, 1; 26 October 1952, 1, 4:6; on Alexander Werth's report in the *Nation*, 175 (1 November 1952): 408–9, and in his *France 1940–1955*, 590–96; on Stebbins et al., *United States in World Affairs, 1952*, 390–401; on numerous reports in 320, Box 1284, RG59, NA; and on Wall, *Making of Postwar France*, 229–32.

195. *NYT*, 21 October 1952, 1, 4; 23 October 1952, 5; 30 October 1952, 9; Stebbins et al., *United States in World Affairs, 1952*, 399–401.

196. *NYT*, 30 October 1952, 1.

197. *NYT*, 29 October 1952, 1; Stebbins et al., *United States in World Affairs, 1952*, 79–92. For a discussion of this matter in the Soviet press, see *FBIS*, 5 November 1952, AA1-AA2.

198. On the limited results and follow-up to the Moscow international economic conference, see U.S. Department of State, Office of Intelligence Research, "The USSR in 1952," 20 March 1953, RG59, NA, 27. On Soviet hopes, see *NYT*, 27 October 1952, 3; see also *FBIS*, 27 October 1952, AA3-AA8, BB6-BB9; 4 November 1952, AA3-AA12.

199. Divine, *Foreign Policy*," 2:50–55.

200. For the mixed reaction abroad to Eisenhower's victory, see *NYT*, 6 November 1952, 1, 8, 10. For Nehru's attitude, see Nehru, *Letters to Chief Ministers*, 3:166–67.

201. Divine, *Foreign Policy*," 2:69–70.

202. Colville, *Fringes of Power*, 654.

203. *NYT*, 9 November 1952, 4:3.

204. *FR, 1952–1954*, 15:611, 634–35.

205. *FR, 1952–1954*, 15:585–89, 595–97.

206. For Vishinsky's speech, see UNGA, *OR*, First Committee, 521st meeting, 10 November 1952, 85–91.

207. *FR, 1952–1954*, 15:612.

208. Ibid., 629.

209. See Bullen, "Great Britain, the United States and the Indian Armistice Resolution on the Korean War," 34–37.

210. *FR, 1952–1954*, 15:637–45; Pearson to Department of External Affairs, Ottawa, November 15 and 17, Box 41, WIKF.

211. Record of telephone conversation between the secretary of state and General Eisenhower, 18 November 1952, FO371/99591, PRO.

212. Bullen, "Great Britain, the United States and the Indian Armistice Resolution," 37. The *New York Herald-Tribune* complained on 19 November (22) of the "want of tact" of the U.S. delegation at the United Nations in attacking the resolution before it was even "formally presented or explained." The editors recognized "defects" in the Indian plan, but thought that it "might be an effective vehicle for reaching a settlement." For indications of the impact of press opinion on British and Canadian actions, see Shuckburgh, *Descent*," 54, and Pearson, *Mike*, 2:326.

213. Pearson, *Mike*, 2:325; *NYT*, 18 November 1952, 3; UN document A/C.1/734.

214. Pearson, *Mike*, 2:326, 328.

215. Shuckburgh, *Descent*, 53–54. Simon was British foreign minister from 1931 to 1935. For Eden's description of the incident, see "Memorandum by the Secretary of State for Foreign Affairs: Korea: Proceedings at the seventh session of the General Assembly of the United Nations," 15 December 1952, C. (52) 441, CAB 129157, PRO.

216. UNGA, *OR*, 526th meeting, First Committee, 117–18. See also the report on Eden's speech and clarifications by a British spokesman in *NYT*, 21 November 1952, 1.

217. Pearson, *Mike*, 2:324.

218. Acheson, *Present*, 703–5.

219. Pearson, *Mike*, 2:184, 329.

220. The Chairman, Canadian delegation to the General Assembly, New York, to the Secretary of State for External Affairs, Canada, 20 November 1952 and 22 November 1952, vols. 42 and 43, respectively, WIKF; *NYT*, 23 November 1952, 1.

221. See UN document A/C.1/734, rev. 1.

222. *FR, 1952–1954*, 15:681–83.

223. For Acheson's statement, see ibid., 683; for the speech, see UNGA, *OR*, First Committee, 529th meeting, 135–38.

224. O'Shaughnessy (U.S. embassy, Moscow) to the secretary of state, 21 November 1952, Box 1285, 320, RG59, NA.
225. UNGA, *OR*, First Committee, 529th meeting, 135–38.
226. *FR, 1952–1954*, 15:684.
227. For Acheson's speech, see UNGA, *OR*, First Committee, 529th meeting, 139–41.
228. UN document A/C.1/734, rev. 1.
229. Ibid.
230. *FR, 1952–1954*, 15:679.
231. On the final negotiations, see Pearson, *Mike*, 2:330–31; the chairman, Canadian delegation to the General Assembly, New York, to the Secretary of State for External Affairs, Canada, 27 November 1952, vol. 43, WIKF. For the second revision of article 17, see UN document, A/C.1/734, rev. 2.
232. Nehru, *Letters to Chief Ministers*, 3:185.
233. *FR, 1952–1954*, 15:700–705.
234. For Menon's acknowledgement in his speech of 19 November, see UNGA, *OR*, First Committee, 525th meeting, 111–15.
235. *NYT*, 25 December, 1; 26 December 1952, 14; Selwyn Lloyd to Jebb, 13 January 1953, FO371/105480, PRO.
236. *NYT*, 4 December 1952, 3.
237. *NYT*, 7 December 1952, 50.
238. Nehru, *Letters to Chief Ministers*, 3:184, 187–91.
239. *NYT*, 5 December 1952, 1; 7 December 1952, 1, 4:4; 9 December 1952, 1; 10 December 1952, 1. A report from the Australian High Commissioner's Office in New Delhi of 12 December (CRS A1838, item 852/20/4/2 Pt. D, AA) concluded that "a dent had been made in India's policy of neutrality," but "public opinion remains more concerned with colonialism and race relations than with Korea or Communism and the press as a whole continues to give incomparably more space to affairs in South Africa, Kenya, and North Africa."
240. See UNGA, *OR*, First Committee meetings, 537–53, 187–321.
241. See, for example, Scott minute, 25 November 1952, FO371/99592, PRO. In a note to Zhou Enlai on 3 December, Mao referred to the Indian resolution as "ridiculous" (see *MZM*, 3:624).
242. UNGA, *OR*, First Committee, 531st meeting, 149. In February 1953 the Indians confirmed to the British that the Chinese had informed Raghavan a few hours before Vishinsky's speech that they opposed the Indian resolution (see U.K. High Commissioner, India to Commonwealth Relations Office, London, 4 February 1953, FO371/105481, PRO).
243. *SCMP*, 29–30 November 1952.
244. See, for example, Nehru's comments at Columbia University in the United States of 17 October 1949 in Nehru, *Visit to America*, 31–32, and to the Constituent Assembly in New Delhi of 8 March 1948 in his *Independence and After*, 215.
245. On the Indian press, see Escott Reid to Pearson, 4 December 1952, vol. 44, WIKF.
246. "Stalin's Conversations with Chinese Leaders," 10–19. See also Reid to Pearson, 12 December 1952, ibid. For a poignant account of the usefulness of anti-Americanism in fostering national unity in China by an Indian journalist and member of the Indian cultural delegation that toured China during the spring of 1952, see Moraes, *Report on Mao's China*.

247. On the Sino-Soviet economic relationship, see Weiss, "Storm Around the Cradle," 129–32; on the "unprecedented" volume of propaganda in celebrating Sino-Soviet friendship, see Lamb to the British Foreign Office, 20 November 1952, FO371/99256, PRO.

248. *NYT*, 25 November 1952, 1.

249. *USAKW*, 2: chap. 13; Zhang, "Military Romanticism," 308–17.

250. Chen, "China's Strategies," 37.

251. Zhang, "Military Romanticism," 317–18; *MZM*, 3:632, 638, 656–58, 667–68.

252. On Eisenhower's activities of late November and early December, see Ambrose, *Eisenhower*, 2:30–35.

253. Clark, *From the Danube to the Yalu*, 97–99, 237; *NYT*, 7 December 1952, 1, 72, and 8 December 1952, 3; *FR, 1952–1954*, 14:79; Field, *United States Naval Operations, Korea*, 442.

254. *NYT*, 8 December 1952, 4.

255. The quote is from Mao's instructions to his commanders of 16 December, quoted in Zhang, "Military Romanticism," 321; see also *MZM*, 3:632, 638, 656–58.

256. *NYT*, 3 February 1953, 1, 14.

257. *NYT*, 4 February 1953, 3.

258. *NYT*, 8 February 1953, 4.

259. *NYT*, 1 March 1953, 1.

260. "Records of Action, 29 January 1953," Box 1, WSC Series White House Office, Office of the Special Assistant for National Security Affairs, DDEL; *USAKW*, 2:357–61.

261. *NYT*, 15 March 1953, 1.

262. *NYT*, 8 February 1953, 2, 4:4; Commissioner General Singapore, to Head of China and Korea Department (Foreign Office, London), "China News Commentary, 29th January–12th February 1953," 23 February 1953, FO371/105215, PRO.

263. Quoted in Zhang, "Military Romanticism," 299.

264. Chen, "China's Strategies," 42.

265. *FR, 1952–1954*, 15:716–17, 785–86, 788–90.

266. Volkogonov, *Stalin*, 570.

CHAPTER 9

CONCLUDING AN ARMISTICE

1. *NYT*, 8 March 1953, 4:3.

2. Bowles to Dulles, 9 March 1953, 761.00 Box 3799, RG59, NA.

3. For a poignant description of Molotov, see Bohlen, *Witness to History*, 380–81. For a report on "responsible foreign opinion in Moscow" on Stalin's death and Molotov's takeover of the Foreign Ministry, see Jacob Bean (U.S. embassy, Moscow) to the State Department, 13 March 1953, Box 3799, 761.00, RG59, NA.

4. The funeral orations are printed in *NYT*, 10 March 1953. See also Harrison Salisbury's analysis from Moscow in ibid., 1, 10.

5. *NYT*, 15 March 1953, 4:1; Stebbins et al., *United States in World Affairs, 1953*, 115.

6. *NYT*, 22 March 1953, 1, 4:1; 29 March 1953, 3. For comprehensive listings of conciliatory Soviet gestures toward the West in the aftermath of Stalin's death, see U.S. Department of State, Office of Intelligence Research, "Intelligence Report No. 6278," 21 April 1953, and "Intelligence Report No. 6389," 14 August 1953, RG59, NA.

7. *NYT*, 5 April 1953, 4:1.
8. *DSB*, 38 (6 April 1953): 494. For background on the UNC proposal of 22 February, see Clark, *From the Danube to the Yalu*, 240–41.
9. Ibid., 13 April 1953, 526–27.
10. *MZM*, 4:148–49; Zhang, "Military Romanticism," 326.
11. *NYT*, 5 April 1953, 1; UNGA, *OR*, 424th plenary meeting, 681–82.
12. *NYT*, 5 April 1953, 4:1.
13. Ibid.; *PPPUS, Dwight D. Eisenhower, 1953*, 147.
14. *FR, 1952–1954*, 15:834–37.
15. Ibid., 835.
16. Ibid., 894; Dulles telephone conversation with Robert Cutter, 7 April 1953, Reel 1, Dulles Telephone Conversations (microfilm edition), JFD. Dulles had shown interest in this idea as far back as August 1952. See Dulles to Eisenhower, 21 August 1952, Box 1, Dulles-Herter series, DDE.
17. Hughes, *Ordeal of Power*, 105; see also *FR, 1952–1954*, 13:419–20, 436–37, 455–56, 505–6.
18. *FR, 1952–1954*, 15:815, 817–18, 842–43, 865–69; *HJCS*, 3:953–54.
19. *USAKW*, 3:414–15.
20. *DSB*, 28 (20 April 1953): 75–76.
21. *FR, 1952–1954*, 15:894.
22. *NYT*, 15 April 1953, 1.
23. For the draft resolutions, see UN documents A/C.1/L.39 and A/C.1/L.40, respectively. For maneuvers in New York on the two resolutions, see Lodge's reports to the State Department of 14 and 15 April 1953 in 320, RG59, NA.
24. *NYT*, 17 April 1953, 1; UNGA, *OR*, First Committee, 603d meeting, 648–53.
25. UNGA, *OR*, 427th plenary meeting, 707–11.
26. Hughes, *Ordeal of Power*, 102–7; Ambrose, *Eisenhower*, 2:94; Rostow, *Europe after Stalin*.
27. *PPPUS: Dwight D. Eisenhower, 1953*, 179–88.
28. On the overwhelmingly favorable domestic response, see U.S. Department of State, Office of Public Opinion Studies, "Monthly Survey of American Opinion in International Affairs," April 1953, Box 12, Records of the Office of Public Opinion Studies, 1943–1965, RG59, NA.
29. *NYT*, 17 April 1953, 1, 4, 5; 18 April 1953, 2, 2; 19 April 1953, 1, 4:1, 3, 8.
30. U.K. Embassy in Moscow, "Weekly Summary—23rd to 29th April," 29 April 1953, FO371/106505, PRO.
31. *DSB*, 28 (27 April 1953): 603–8.
32. *CDSP* 5 (16 May 1953): 3–6.
33. *FR, 1952–1954*, 15:950–51; *USAKW*, 2:423.
34. *USAKW*, 2:423–24; "Transcript of Proceedings, 123rd Session of Mil Armistice Conf, 28 April 1953," Box 704, KAN.
35. Transcript of Proceedings, 124th Session of Mil Armistice Conf, 29 April 1953," Box 704, KAN.
36. Ibid., 2 May 1953.
37. HKAN, pt. 3, vol. 1, 299–302.
38. Ibid., 314–17; *FR, 1952–1954*, 15:962–64.
39. "Transcript of Proceedings, 129th Session of Mil Armistice Conf, 2 May 1953," Box 704, KAN.
40. *NYT*, 1 and 5 May 1953, 1.

41. *NYT*, 3 May 1953, 3.

42. *FR, 1952–1954*, 15:956. For a report on the Soviet approach to Indonesia, see Charles Bohlen (U.S. ambassador to the Soviet Union) to Dulles, 5 May 1953, Box 1392, Moscow Lot 56F20, RG84, WNRC.

43. On Indonesian politics, see Feith, *Wilopo Cabinet*; Hinley, *Communist Party in Indonesia*, 240–43.

44. For Dulles's fears on precisely this point, see *FR, 1952–1954*, 15:970.

45. The Indian resolution actually had named the first four countries and had provided for a fifth, unnamed, as an umpire in cases where the others were deadlocked. It was widely assumed that India would be a prime candidate. Since in most cases the first four nations were sure to find themselves deadlocked, the umpire would be the crucial member of the commission. For the text of the Indian resolution, see *FR, 1952–1954*, 15:702–5. For the text of the Communist proposals of 7 May 1953, see ibid., 980–81.

46. Ibid., 956–60.

47. G. C. Graham (British embassy in South Korea) to Churchill, 1 May 1953, FO371/105490; LLoyd to Sir Roger Makins (British ambassador to the United States), 1 May 1953, FO371/105488; Sir Esler Dening (British ambassador to Japan) to Rob Scott, 7 May 1953, FO371/105492, PRO.

48. On Eden's illness, see James, *Eden*, 361–64.

49. Colville, *Fringes of Power*, 661–62, 664–65.

50. Gilbert, *Churchill*, 8:793.

51. Shuckburgh, *Descent to Suez*, 74.

52. Gilbert, *Churchill*, 8:827–28; *Hansard*, 11 May 1953, 883–98.

53. Ibid.

54. Secretary of State for Commonwealth Relations, London, to High Commissioner for the United Kingdom, Ottawa, 8 May 1953, vol. 48, WIKF; Churchill minute, 10 May 1953, FO371/105490, PRO.

55. "The Visit of the Prime Minister of Canada to Washington, May 7 to May 9: Record of the Talks between the Honorable L. B. Pearson and the Department of State—Thursday, May 7," vol. 48, WIKF; Pearson to New Delhi, 12 May 1953, ibid.

56. On the reaction to the 7 May proposal at the United Nations, see *NYT*, 8 May 1953, 2.

57. *FR, 1952–1954*, 15:692–93.

58. Eisenhower, *White House Years*, 1:95–96; Ambrose, *Eisenhower*, 2:30–31; Oliver, *Syngman Rhee*, 406–7; Paik, *From Pusan to Panmunjom*, 215–17.

59. On the issue of advances of Korean currency, see *FR, 1952–1954*, 15:747–52, 771–72, 792, 797, 813. The two sides reached agreement on 25 February after months of talks. On the issue of the ROK government's return to Seoul, see ibid., 729–31, 745–46, 802, 812. In early March Rhee agreed to limit the movement of government officials from Pusan to Seoul.

60. Ibid., 897–900.

61. Ibid., 902–3; Eisenhower, *White House Years*, 1:181–82.

62. *FR, 1952–1954*, 15:933–35.

63. Graham to the British Foreign Office, 4 April 1953, FO371/105484, PRO.

64. HKAN, pt. 4, vol. 1, 67–71.

65. Ibid., 70–74, 88–89; *FR, 1952–1954*, 15:906.

66. Critchfield to The Secretary, Department of External Affairs, Canberra, 1 May 1953, A1838, Item 852/20/4/2pt., AA.

67. HKAN, pt. 4, vol. 1, 109.

68. *FR, 1952–1954*, 15:907.
69. Ibid., 910–14, 917–19, 938–40, 947–50.
70. For background on Republican divisions in Congress, see Kepley, *Collapse of the Middle Way*, and Reichard, *Reaffirmation of Republicanism*.
71. Guhin, *John Foster Dulles*, 184–85. The transcripts of Dulles's telephone conversations in JFD are full of calls to and from members of Congress.
72. The standard work on the Bricker amendment is Tannenbaum, "The Bricker Amendment Controversy," 73–93. See also Guhin, *Dulles*, 202–9; Reichard, *Reaffirmation of Republicanism*, 59–66; Stebbins et al., *United States in World Affairs, 1953*, 52–58.
73. Stebbins et al., *United States in World Affairs, 1953*, 80–87; Kolodziej, *Uncommon Defense and Congress*, chap. 4; Ferrell, ed., *Eisenhower Diaries*, 235–37.
74. Stebbins et al., *United States in World Affairs, 1953*, 92–99; *NYT*, 4 May 1953, 1; 10 May 1953, 4:3.
75. *NYT*, 5 May 1953, 1.
76. Nationalist Chinese ambassador Wellington Koo remarked to Madame Chiang in March regarding the withdrawal of restrictions on Nationalist operations against the mainland that it represented "only a gesture without any intention to follow it up with any definite plan of a positive character." See Koo diary entry, 8 March 1953, Box 219, Koo Papers.
77. *NYT*, 9 April 1953, 1, 4; 10 April 1953, 1. Senator Knowland immediately called Dulles, complaining that the story indicated that "we are planning a Far Eastern Munich." If it was not repudiated immediately, Knowland threatened to call a conference of Republican senators. Senator H. Alexander Smith also called to express concern. See Dulles's telephone conversations of 9 April in Reel 1, Dulles Telephone Conversations (microfilm edition), JFD.
78. See Hickenlooper's conversation with Dulles of 9 May in Dulles Telephone Conversations, Reel 1 (Microfilm edition), JFD. See also Smith's diary entry of 11 May in Box 282, HAS.
79. *DSB* 28 (25 May 1953): 755–57.
80. *FR, 1952–1954*, 15:1008–10.
81. Compare sections XIII and XVII in the Indian resolution (ibid., 704–5) to sections IV(11) and XI(24) of the UNC proposal of 13 May (*DSB* 28 [25 May 1953]: 756–57).
82. "Transcript of Proceedings, 137th Session of Mil Armistice Conf, 14 May 1953," Box 704, KAN.
83. *NYT*, 8 May 1953, 1, 3; 9 May 1953, 2.
84. Memo of conversation, U. A. Johnson with R. H. Belcher (First Secretary of the British Embassy), 16 May 1953, Box 3024, RG59, NA.
85. *FR, 1952–1954*, 15:1016.
86. *NYT*, 10 May 1953, 4:3.
87. *Hansard*, 12 May 1953, 1061–71.
88. *CR*, 83d Congress, 1st sess., 13 and 14 May 1953, 4837, 4860–62, 4909–14.
89. Ibid., 4914–15, 4964–66.
90. *The Times of London*, 16 May 1953, 6.
91. For key documents in the preliminary assessment, see *FR, 1952–1954*, 15:815, 817–18, 825–27, 838–57, 892–95, 908–10, 945–46, 975–77, 1012–17. The most detailed secondary account of the planning documents is *HJCS*, 3:948–62. Also useful is Keefer, "President Dwight D. Eisenhower," 271–78.

92. On public opinion, see U.S. Department of State, Office of Public Opinion Studies, "Recent Opinion Polls on Korea," 23 March 1953, and "American Attitudes toward Big Power Meetings," 1 June 1953, Box 1, RG59, NA. Polls were ambiguous on whether the public believed the United States should pursue total victory in Korea even if a settlement proved possible along the current battle line and with no forced repatriation of prisoners of war. The latter report cited above suggested the shallowness of support for a total solution if a lesser one seemed possible.

93. *FR, 1952–1954*, 15:1014.

94. Futrell, *U.S. Air Force in Korea*, 625–28.

95. *FR, 1952–1954*, 15:1053. Smith was acting secretary of state while Dulles was on a trip to the Middle East and South Asia.

96. *FR, 1952–1954*, 15:1059–63, 1064–68.

97. Despite a substantial effort, the Communists failed to establish air superiority over North Korea. Still, reinforced by sophisticated Soviet antiaircraft artillery from the ground, Communist planes could have destroyed a substantial number of enemy bombers operating over Manchuria. For discussions of Communist air power, see Futrell, *U.S. Air Force in Korea*, 374–80; Ryan, *Chinese Attitudes*, 167; Bueschel, *Communist Chinese Air Power*, 20–29.

98. Ibid., 2:328–35.

99. Ibid., 15:1053.

100. Ibid., 1082–86.

101. For coverage of the ongoing unrest in the POW camps and UNC efforts to control it, see *USAKW*, 2:405–7, 410; *FR, 1952–1954*, 15:716–18, 722–26, 732–33, 768–69, 790–95, 797–98, 801.

102. Ibid., 1075–79.

103. *PPPUS: Dwight D. Eisenhower, 1953*, 296.

104. *CR*, 84th Congress, 1st sess., 19 May 1953, 5115–17.

105. *FR, 1952–1954*, 15:1075–79; see also Senator Smith's diary entries of 22 and 23 May in HAS.

106. For a well-informed press report on the continuing tension, see James Reston's article in *NYT*, 24 May 1953, 1.

107. *FR, 1952–1954*, 15:1086–90.

108. Ibid., 1097–1102.

109. *NYT*, 26 May 1953, 4.

110. *FR, 1952–1954*, 15:1098–1100.

111. *NYT*, 20 May 1953, 3; 21 May 1953, 1; Lamb to British Foreign Office, 28 May 1953, FO371/105189, PRO.

112. *FR, 1952–1954*, 15:742, 1022–24, 1082–86.

113. This conclusion is based on my reading of Eisenhower's comments in the National Security Council meeting of 20 May. See ibid., 1067–68. For a well-researched account that emphasizes Eisenhower's caution and uncertainty, see Dingman, "Atomic Diplomacy," 78–89.

114. *Hansard*, 18 May 1953, 1692–95; 20 May 1953, 2071, 2074–77; 21 May 1953, 2253–56, 2262.

115. Dening to British Foreign Office, 19 May 1953, FO371/105493, PRO; *NYT*, 22 May 1953, 1; *The Times of London*, 22 May 1953, 3, 8.

116. *FR, 1952–1954*, 15:1080–81.

117. Ibid., 1084.

118. Ibid., 1103–4.

119. "Transcript of Proceedings, 142nd Session of Mil Armistice Conf," 4 June 1953, Box 704, KAN.
120. *USAKW*, 2:429–30.
121. *SCMP*, 30 May–1 June 1953; *NYT*, 1 June 1953, 1, 3.
122. *USAKW*, 2:462–65.
123. Mao Zedong, *Jianguo Yilai Mao Zedong Wengao*, vol. 4 (Beijing: Zhongyang Wenxian Press, 1990), 201, as quoted in Zhang, *Deterrence*, 138.
124. Zhang, "Military Romanticism," 222–24.
125. "Transcript of Proceedings, 143rd Session of Mil Armistice Conf," 4 June 1953, Box 704, KAN.
126. Zhang, "Military Romanticism," 224–25.
127. Progress on these matters is covered in detail in *USAKW*, 2:431–35, and HKAN, pt. 3, vol. 2, 418–68.
128. Zhou's message to Pearson at the UN General Assembly came only four days after his return from Moscow. Jacob Malik, now a Soviet deputy foreign minister, insisted in a July meeting with the Italian ambassador that the initiative to end the Korean War had originated with his government, not the PRC (see Frank Roberts to William Strang, 28 July 1953, FO371/106524, PRO). He did not claim, however, that the Chinese needed much persuading. Another indication that the Soviets were leading the Chinese on Korea came in an overture of 30 March by Kasaniev, now the senior Soviet national in the UN Secretariat, to Hans Engen of the Norwegian delegation, who had been used by the Soviets in the past as a conduit to the Americans. Kasaniev nudged Engen out of a plenary session of the General Assembly and informed the Norwegian that Zhou's message, which had been announced at the United Nations only two hours earlier, was "the real thing," that only the "technicalities" now remained to be resolved. He also raised the possibility of an Eisenhower-Malenkov meeting, emphasizing the importance of bilateral talks and of subjects other than Korea. Engen informed the American Tom Cory that he was certain Kasaniev "was speaking under instructions and that he appeared to be reciting a lesson." Engen also believed that Kassaniev's instructions had been prepared before Zhou's message (see Lodge to the Secretary of State, 30 March 1953, 695A.0024, RG59, NA). It is doubtful that the Soviets would have made such an approach, obviously "intended for American ears," unless they were promoters rather than merely followers of the Zhou message.
129. I wish to thank Kathryn Weathersby for providing me with a description of this document from the Presidential Archive in Moscow.
130. Chen, "China's Strategies," 39.
131. Mao Zedong, *Jianquo Yilai Mao Zedong Wengao*, 4:148–49, quoted in Zhang, *Deterrence*, 136.
132. For the debate on the eve of the Korean War and Malenkov's and Beria's position in it, see Letteney, "Foreign Policy Factionalism under Stalin."
133. See Stalin, *Economic Problems of Socialism*, 37–39. For a discussion of this document in the context of Soviet diplomacy during 1952, see above, pp. 275, 290.
134. Baring, *Uprising in East Germany*, xx–xxii, 7–9, 17–19.
135. On trade and economic aid matters, see Weiss, "Storm Around the Cradle," 128–33.
136. *NYT*, 7 March 1953, 3; 10 March 1953, 12; 11 March 1953, 10.
137. Paul Grey (U.K. embassy in Moscow) to R. H. Scott (U.K. Foreign Office, London), 11 April 1953; Leo Lamb (U.K. consulate in Peking) to U.K. Foreign Office,

27 April 1953; Wilkins (U.K. Foreign Office, London) minute, 4 December 1953, FO371/105344, PRO.

138. Western analysts in Hong Kong thought economic pressures were central to China's decision to end the war. See Henry Lieberman's article in *NYT*, 27 July 1953, 5.

139. Knight, *Beria*, 186–94.

140. On Lodge, see Jebb to Eden, 28 March 1953, FO371/106534, PRO; on Bohlen, see Gascoigne to U.K. Foreign Office, 19 April 1953, FO371/106532, PRO.

141. For Clark's note, see *USAKW*, 2:430; on Bohlen's meeting with Molotov, see *FR, 1952–1954*, 15:1109–11.

142. *FR, 1952–1954*, 15:1068–69.

143. Memorandum of conversation between Eisenhower and President Lyndon B. Johnson, 17 February 1965, Post-Presidential Papers, 1961–1969, DDEL; memorandum for the record of memorandum of conversation between Andrew Goodpaster and Eisenhower, 13 May 1965, National Security File, Name File, President Eisenhower, Lyndon B. Johnson Library, Austin, Texas.

144. Reid, *Envoy to Nehru*, 45; Lamb to U.K. Foreign Office, 28 May 1953, FO371/105496, PRO; *FR, 1952–1954*, 15:1104–6.

145. For a discussion of the literature on the atomic threat and the end of the Korean War, see Ryan, *Chinese Attitudes toward Nuclear Weapons*, 152–62, 264–69. The most persuasive accounts to me are Keefer, "President Dwight D. Eisenhower," and Foot, "Nuclear Coercion," 92–112.

146. Futrell, *United States Air Force in Korea*, 627–28.

147. On difficulties with the spring harvest in China, see articles in the *People's Daily* published and translated in *SCMP*, 23–25 May 1953, 28 May 1953, 5 June 1953, and 11 June 1953; Lamb to U.K. Foreign Office, 28 May 1953, FO371/105189, PRO. On the broader context of these problems, see Weiss, "Storm Around the Cradle," 164–69.

148. Clark, *From the Danube to the Yalu*, 279–80; *USAKW*, 2:451; *FR, 1952–1954*, 15:1196–1200.

149. Clark, *From the Danube to the Yalu*, 268–69.

150. Briggs to Secretary of State, 26 May 1953, 795.00/5–2553, RG59, NA.

151. Briggs to Secretary of State, 28 May 1953, 795.00/5–2853, RG59, NA.

152. *FR, 1952–1954*, 15:1122–23.

153. *PPPUS: Dwight D. Eisenhower, 1953*, 377–80.

154. *FR, 1952–1954*, 15:1165–66, 1168–69.

155. *FR, 1952–1954*, 1368–69.

156. Ibid., 1159–60; *USAKW*, 2:449; Briggs to Secretary of State, 6 and 11 June 1953, 795.00/6–653 and 795.00/6–1153, RG59, NA.

157. *USAKW*, 2:448–49. For Paik's recollections of Rhee's plans for and release of POWs, see his *From Pusan to Panmunjom*, 229–32.

158. See Kotch, "The Origins of the American Security Commitment to Korea," in Cumings, *Child of Conflict*, 246–47.

159. *FR, 1952–1954*, 15:1124.

160. Ibid., 1153.

161. On U.S. perceptions of the viability of this option after Rhee's action of 18 June, see ibid., 1318.

162. Ibid., 1099.

163. *DSB*, 28 (29 June 1953): 907.

164. Eisenhower, *White House Years*, 1:185–86.
165. *USAKW*, 2:452.
166. *FR, 1952–1954*, 15:1199.
167. See Clark's account of his 12 May discussion with Rhee in *From the Danube to the Yalu*, 264. See also Briggs's account of a 1 March meeting with Rhee in *FR, 1952–1954*, 15:803–4.
168. *FR, 1952–1954*, 15:1197–98.
169. *FR, 1952–1954*, 15:1209.
170. On the Tasca report, see ibid., 1244–63.
171. Ibid., 1236–37.
172. Ibid., 1180–88.
173. Ibid., 1232.
174. Ibid., 1241–42.
175. Ibid., 1248; *NYT*, 25 and 28 July 1953, 1, 4:3, respectively.
176. *NYT*, 21 July 1953, 5.
177. *NYT*, 28 July 1953, 4:3.
178. For background on Robertson, see Candee, *Current Biography, 1953* (New York: Wilson, 1954), 533–35.
179. *FR, 1952–1954*, 15:1278. For a comprehensive summary of Robertson's talks with Rhee, see an undated memorandum entitled "Robertson-Clark-Rhee," located in Box 5, Mark Clark Papers,
180. *FR, 1952–1954*, 15:1271.
181. Ibid., 1285–86.
182. Ibid., 1282–83.
183. Robertson Oral History, DDEL.
184. Clark to Howard, 7 July 1953, Box 8, Clark Papers.
185. *FR, 1952–1954*, 15:1291–92. Clark had received prior approval for these measures from Washington. See Memorandum for the President, from John Foster Dulles, 28 June 1953 (and additional note at bottom dated 6/29/53), in Dulles-Herter series, Box 1, DDE.
186. *FR, 1952–1954*, 15:1332–33.
187. Ibid., 1355.
188. Ibid., 1362–63.
189. In a letter to Eisenhower on the 11th, Rhee omitted the qualifying phrase: "I have decided not to obstruct, in any manner, the implementation of the terms [of an armistice], in deference to your requests" (ibid., 1368–69).
190. Ibid., 1357–60.
191. For a summary on the Asian reaction, see W. K. Scott to Dulles and Smith, 9 July 1953, 795.00/7–953, RG59, NA. For reactions at the United Nations, see *NYT*, 18 June 1953, 3; 19 June 1953, 1. For various other reactions outside the United States and Korea, see *NYT*, 19 June, 4; 21 June 1953, 4, 4:1.
192. Clark, *From the Danube to the Yalu*, 272.
193. See above, p. 324.
194. *NYT*, 21 June 1953, 1. On Rhee's apparent restraint, see W. K. Scott to Dulles and Smith, 29 June 1953, 795.00/6–2953, RG59, NA.
195. See Clark, *From the Danube to the Yalu*, 287; *FR, 1952–1954*, 15:1328, 1447–48.
196. *USAKW*, 2:465–73. For a day-to-day summary of battlefield events from a UNC perspective, see UNC, Public Information Office, "A Chronology of the Korean Campaign, 1 January–27 July 1953," Box 8, Clark Papers.

197. *FR, 1952–1954*, 15:1444.
198. *DSB* 28 (29 June 1953): 906–7.
199. *USAKW*, 2:451; *FR, 1952–1954*, 15:1210–11, 1223–24.
200. *SCMP*, 24 June 1953.
201. Clark, *From the Danube to the Yalu*, 284.
202. Memorandum of Conversation, Soviet Communication Concerning Truce Negotiations (plus attachment), 29 June 1953, 795.00/6-2953, RG59, NA.
203. *DSB* 29 (13 July 1953): 46–47.
204. Du, *Zai Zhiyuanju Zongbu*, 594.
205. *DSB* 29 (20 July 1953): 73–74.
206. "Transcript of Proceedings, sessions 151–56 of the Mil Armistice Conf, 10–15 July 1953," Box 704, KAN.
207. *USAKW*, 2:474–76; Paik, *From Pusan to Panmunjom*, 236–42.
208. "Transcript of Proceedings, 158th Session, Mil Armistice Conf, 19 July 1953," Box 704, KAN.
209. The most detailed accounts of the final preparations for the armistice are in *USAKW*, 2:484–90, and HKAN, pt. 3, vol. 2, 564–674.
210. Hastings, *Korean War*, 329.
211. On 14 July the Canadian minister in Sweden wired home with the following description of Chinese calculations, as reported by the Swedish embassy in Beijing: "Swedes believe the Chinese will go so far as to carry out the terms of the armistice even though subsequent political conferences might break down and Syngman Rhee might attack the North. Chinese evidently realize that Rhee could not go far without American ammunition and, therefore, there will be little trouble in beating him back and any such action will not be considered as a reason for breaking off the armistice agreements" (WIKF, vol. 52). For Chinese and North Korean press coverage of U.S. assurances and of Communist exploits on the battlefield, see *SCMP*, 21, 22, 23, 24 July 1953; *FBIS*, 27 July 1953.
212. Stebbins et al., *United States in World Affairs, 1953*, 140; *NYT*, 31 May 1953, 1; 1 June 1953, 12; 6 June 1953, 4.
213. On connections made in the Soviet press between events in East Berlin and the POW incident in Korea, see Bohlen to the Secretary of State, 23 June 1953, Box 6007, 961.61, RG59, NA.
214. Baring, *Uprising in East Germany*, 24–55, 97–108. For the impact on Hungary of the unrest elsewhere in eastern Europe, see Nagy, *On Communism*, xii, 38–39, 66–74.
215. *NYT*, 11 July 1953, 1, 3. For an insider's account of Beria's fall, see Khrushchev, *Khrushchev Remembers*, 322–38. For the most recently available information on the incident, see Knight, *Beria*, 194–200.
216. Canadian Minister, Stockholm, to Pearson, 14 July 1953, vol. 52, WIKF.
217. *NYT*, 27 July 1953, 3.
218. *The Times of London*, 28 July 1953, 6.
219. *USAKW*, 2:489–91.
220. *NYT*, 27 July 1953, 5; *SCMP*, 28 July 1953.
221. Clark, *From the Danube to the Yalu*, 296.
222. *The New York Herald-Tribune*, 27 July 1953, 1.
223. *FR, 1952–1954*, 15:1442–43.
224. *NYT*, 29 July 1953, 2.
225. *NYT*, 30 July 1953, 1, 2.
226. *DSB*, 29 (27 July 1953): 104–6.

227. *NYT*, 29 July 1953, 1, 2.
228. *NYT*, 2 August 1953, 4:3.
229. *The Nation*, 177 (8 August 1953): 105–6.
230. *NYT*, 31 July 1953, 1, 3; 2 August 1953, 4:3.
231. *NYT*, 30 July 1953, 3.

232. Nehru wasted no time after the armistice was signed in expressing his view that the PRC should be admitted to the United Nations. On the political conference, he did say that, "to begin with," Korea should be the only issue discussed. See *NYT*, 31 July 1953, 3.

233. *The Times of London*, 31 July 1953, 9.
234. *CDSP*, 5 September 1953, 20–21.
235. *SCMP*, 28 July 1953.
236. *NYT*, 30 July 1953, 1; *FBIS*, 28 July 1953.
237. *NYT*, 2 August 1953, 4:5.
238. Ibid.

239. For Soviet conciliatory gestures during June and July, see U.S. Department of State, Office of Intelligence Research, "Intelligence Report No. 6389: A List of 'Conciliatory' Soviet Bloc Gestures in Foreign Affairs," 14 August 1953, 15–17, RG59, NA.

240. *FR, 1952–1954*, 8:1193.
241. *DSB* 29 (10 August 1953): 175–76.
242. *Hansard*, 27 July 1953, 893–94.

243. *FBIS*, 28 July 1953; "World Press Reactions to the Korean Truce," 29 July 1953, Box 821, Central Files, DDE.

244. U.S. embassy (Ankara) to the State Department, 30 July 1953, Box 154, RG84, WNRC.

245. "World Reactions to the Korean Truce," 29 July 1953, Box 821, Central Files, DDE.

246. U.S. embassy (Belgrade) to State Department, 14 August 1953, Box 154, RG84, WNRC. For a summary of reactions in Arab nations, see "World Reactions to the Korean Truce," 29 July 1953, Box 821, Central Files, DDE.

247. See, for example, *FR, 1952–1954*, 15:1456.

248. On Knowland's suggestion and Rhee's reaction, see *NYT*, 6 July 1953, 1; *FR, 1952–1954*, 15:1455–56. On Rhee's ongoing opposition and the State Department's futile exploration after the signing of an armistice, see Hwang, "U.S. Initiative for Korean Neutralization."

249. U.S. planners were already intent on containing Rhee, in part by maintaining tight control over the dispensation of U.S. aid to the ROK (see *FR, 1952–1954*, 15:1453–54).

## Chapter 10
### The Korean War as International History

1. Frank Pace Oral History, HSTL.

2. On both Soviet and U.S. air activities, see Halliday, "Air Operations in Korea," in Williams, *Revolutionary War*, 149–70.

3. Stebbins et al., *United States in World Affairs, 1953*, 164–65; Stebbins et al., *United States in World Affairs, 1950*, 121. *The Statistical History of the United States*, 1141.

4. See Timothy Ireland's analysis in his *Creating the Entangling Alliance*, chaps. 4 and 5.

5. *NATO Facts and Figures*, 256.

6. Kaplan, *United States and NATO*, 154–56.

7. Lord Ismay, "NATO: The Right Road to Peace," *DSB* 28 (March 23, 1953): 429; *The Statistical History of the United States*, 1141.

8. Heuser, *Western "Containment" Policies*, chaps. 5, 6.

9. McGeehan, *German Rearmament Question*, chaps. 2–5.

10. *NATO Facts and Figures*, 256; Kaplan, *United States and NATO*, 172.

11. Ismay, *NATO*, 34–46.

12. For the full text of Ridgway's report, see *DSB* 28 (29 June 1953): 899–904.

13. *HJCS*, 4:328.

14. For an interesting study of the Soviet tactics in Europe during 1945 and 1946 based on recently declassified intelligence sources in the United States, see Mark, "American Policy Makers."

15. See, for example, *FR, 1950*, 1:145–46, 293.

16. This analysis is based on Rosenberg, "The Origins of Overkill," 14–18; Rosenberg, "American Atomic Bomb Strategy," 62–87; and Trachtenberg, "'Wasting Asset,'" 5–49. The view, commonly held in the United States and western Europe at the time, that Soviet bloc forces held the capacity to launch a *blitzkrieg* attack that would quickly position them on the English channel, has been challenged by Evangelista in "Stalin's Postwar Army Reappraised," 110–38. There seems little doubt, however, that Soviet bloc forces held local advantages in central Europe and the Balkans.

17. Kiraly, "The Aborted Soviet Military Plans Against Tito's Yugoslavia," in Vucinich, *At the Brink of War and Peace*, 273–88. For a secondary analysis, see Heuser, *Western "Containment" Policies*, chaps. 4, 5.

18. "Interview with DPRK Lt. Gen. (Ret.) Kang Sang Ho, DPRK Lt. Gen. (Ret.) Yoo Song Chol, DPRK Brig. Gen. (Ret.) Chung Sangchine. Also Present ROK Maj. Gen. (Ret.) Kim Ha-In and Mr. Ju Young-Bok. Stanford, Calif., April 13, 1992," 3–5.

19. Ibid., 16.

20. Kennan, *Memoirs (1925–1950)*, 511.

21. On Marshall's sense of history, see May and Neustadt, *Thinking in Time*, 247–56.

22. Chae-Jin Lee, "The Effects of the War on South Korea," in Lee, ed., *Korean War*, 113.

23. Cumings, *Origins of the Korean War*, 1:xix.

24. Koh, "The War's Impact on the Korean Peninsula," in Williams, ed., *Revolutionary War*, 246.

25. See ibid., 10–16, and Brands, "Eisenhower, Rhee, and the 'Other' Geneva Conference of 1954."

26. The United States also was a good deal more generous in its economic assistance to the ROK than it had been before June 1950 (see Chae-Jin, Lee, "The Effects of the War on South Korea," in Lee, *Korean War*, 125–26).

27. Koh, "The War's Impact on the Korean Peninsula," 20.

28. Foot, *Substitute for Victory*, 196.

29. In a speech of 12 September 1953, Mao pointed out that, "fighting together with the Korean people, we fought our way back to the 38th parallel and held firmly at the parallel. . . . If we had not fought our way back to the 38th parallel and the front lines had remained at the Yalu River and the Tumen River, then the people at places such as

Shenyang, Anshan, and Fushun would not have been able to feel secure in carrying out production" (see Kau, *The Writings of Mao Zedong*, 1:388).

30. Quoted in Zhang, "Military Romanticism," 231.
31. Khong, *Analogies at War*, 140–46.
32. Quoted in ibid., 231.
33. Clubb, *China and Russia*, 401–2.
34. Zhai, "Geneva Conference of 1954."
35. Clubb, *China and Russia*, 409; Jansen, *Nonalignment and the Afro-Asian States*, chap. 9.
36. See, for instance, Zhang, "Military Romanticism," 231, and Jia, "Unmaterialized Rapprochement," 190.
37. Clubb, *China and Russia*, 402–5.
38. See Weiss, "Storm Around the Cradle."
39. Clubb, *China and Russia*, 406–7. In his *Politics at Mao's Court*, Frederick C. Teiwes emphasizes factional politics rather than Gao's pro-Soviet orientation as the key factor in the purge. He does not deny Gao's pro-Soviet sympathies as a secondary force, however.
40. See Ulam, *The Communists*, 77–80, 104–7.
41. He Di, "The Evolution of the People's Republic of China's Policy toward the Offshore Islands," in Iriye and Cohen, eds., *The Great Powers in East Asia*, 222–45.
42. Jia, "Unmaterialized Rapprochement," chap. 1.
43. Hahn, *The United States, Great Britain, and Egypt*, chap. 9.
44. On Israel's growing orientation toward the West, see Bialer, *Between East and West*, 38, 218–20.
45. See Qing, "The Eisenhower Administration and Changes in Western Embargo Policy Against China, 1954–1958," and Foot, "The Search for a 'Modus Vivendi': Anglo-American Relations and China Policy in the Eisenhower Era," in Iriye and Cohen, *The Great Powers in East Asia*, 121–63.
46. See Gaddis, "The American 'Wedge' Strategy, 1949–1955," in Harding and Yuan, *Sino-American Relations 1945–1955*, 157–83.
47. On the importance of the Korea analogy in the U.S. decisions on Vietnam of 1964 and 1965, see Khong, *Analogies at War*.
48. Dingman, "The Dagger and the Gift," 20.
49. Ibid., 17–18, 13–15; Finn, *Winners in Peace*, 263–65, 275–82, 306–307.
50. Borden, *The Pacific Alliance*, 168.
51. Ibid., 210–19; Watanabe, "Southeast Asia in U. S.-Japanese Relations," and Cohen, "China in Japanese-American Relations," in Cohen, ed., *The United States and Japan*, 80–95 and 36–60, respectively.
52. Luard, *History of the United Nations*, 1:98–105.
53. For similar conclusions growing out of a broader study of the history of the United Nations, see ibid., 1:271–74.

# • BIBLIOGRAPHY •

### MANUSCRIPT SOURCES

*Abilene, Kansas, USA*

    Dwight D. Eisenhower Library
        Dwight D. Eisenhower Papers

*Annapolis, Maryland, USA*

    U.S. Naval Academy Archives
        Arleigh Burke Papers
        William Sebald Papers

*Athens, Georgia, USA*

    Richard B. Russell Library, University of Georgia
        Richard B. Russell Papers

*Burlington, Vermont, USA*

    Bentley-Howe Library, University of Vermont
        Warren Austin Papers

*Canberra, ACT, Australia*

    Australian National Library
        Keith Officer Papers
        Percy Spender Papers

*Carlisle, Pennsylvania, USA*

    U.S. Army War College Archives
        Omar Bradley Papers
        Matthew B. Ridgway Papers

*Charleston, South Carolina, USA*

    The Citadel Archives
        Mark Clark Papers

*Charlottesville, Virginia, USA*

    University of Virginia Library
        Louis Johnson Papers

*Hull, Canada*

    Historical Office, Department of External Affairs
        War in Korea File

*Independence, Missouri, USA*

    Harry S. Truman Library
        Dean G. Acheson Papers
        George Elsey Papers

John Melby Papers
Theodore M. Tannenwald Papers
Harry S. Truman Papers

*Kew, England, U.K.*

Public Records Office
CAB 128 (Cabinet Minutes), 1950–1953
CAB 129 (Cabinet Papers), 1950–1953
DEFE 4 (Defense Records), 1950–1953
FO 371 (Foreign Office Records), 1947–1953
FO 800 (Ernest Bevin Papers)
PREM 8 (Records of the Prime Minister), 1950–1953

*London, England, U.K.*

London School of Economics
Hugh Dalton Papers

*Manila, The Philippines*

Ayala Museum and Library
Elpidio Quirino Papers
José P. Laurel Memorial Library-Museum
José P. Laurel Papers
University of the Philippines Library
Carlos P. Romulo Papers

*Milton Keynes, England, U.K.*

The Open University
Kenneth Younger Diary

*Mitchell, ACT, Australia*

Australian Archives (Mitchell Branch)
Records of the Department of External Affairs, 1950–1953

*New Haven, Connecticut, USA*

Sterling Library, Yale University
Dean G. Acheson Papers
Hanson Baldwin Papers
Chester Bowles Papers
Walter Lippman Papers

*New York, New York, USA*

Butler Library, Columbia University
Wellington Koo Papers
United Nations Archives
DAG-1

*Ottawa, Canada*

Public Archives of Canada
Escott Reid Papers

Lester B. Pearson Papers
W. L. Mackenzie King Papers

*Oxford, England, U.K.*

Bodleian Library, Oxford University
Clement Attlee Papers

*Philadelphia, Pennsylvania, USA*

University of Pennsylvania Library
William R. Matthews Papers

*Princeton, New Jersey, USA*

Seeley Mudd Library, Princeton University
George F. Kennan Papers
H. Alexander Smith Papers
John Foster Dulles Papers
Karl Lott Rankin Papers

*Stanford, California, USA*

Hoover Library
Haydon Boatner Papers
Claire L. Chennault Papers
C. Turner Joy Papers

*Suitland, Maryland, USA*

Washington National Records Center
Record Group 84, "Post Files of the Department of State"
Record Group 260, "Records of the Occupation of Japan"
Record Group 332, "Records of the U.S. Theaters of War, World War II"
Record Group 407, "Records of the Far Eastern Command"

*Washington, D.C., USA*

Library of Congress
Joseph and Stewart Alsop Papers
Charles E. Bohlen Papers
W. Averell Harriman Papers
Curtis Lemay Papers
Robert P. Patterson Papers
Eric Sevareid Papers
Robert A. Taft Papers
Hoyt Vandenberg Papers
National Archives
Record Group 46, "Records of the Foreign Relations Committee of the United States Senate"
Record Group 59, "Records of the Department of State"
Record Group 218, "Records of the Plans and Operations Division, United States Army"
Record Group 319, "Records of the Joint Chiefs of Staff"
Record Group 330, "Records of the Office of the Secretary of Defense"
Record Group 338, "Records of the Far Eastern Command"

## Dissertations and Other Unpublished Secondary Works

Afroz, Sultana. "U.S.-Pakistan Relations, 1947–1960." Ph.D. diss., University of Kansas, 1985.

Agyeman-Duah, Baffour. "United States Military Assistance Relationship with Ethiopia, 1953–77. Historical and Theoretical Analysis." Ph.D. diss., University of Denver, 1984.

Alapatt, G. K. "The Legal Implications of the Repatriation of War Prisoners in Relation to the Korean Armistice and in View of the Division of Korea." Ph.D. diss., St. Louis University, 1958.

Bohlen, Thomas Gerard. "United States-Latin American Relations and the Cold War: 1949–1953." Ph.D. diss., University of Notre Dame, 1985.

Chen, Jian. "The Sino-Soviet Alliance and China's Entry into the Korean War." Paper presented at a Workshop on Chinese Foreign Policy, Michigan State University, October 1991.

———. "China's Road to the Korean War: The Making of Sino-American Confrontation, 1948–1950." Copy in author's possession. Forthcoming, Columbia University Press.

———. "China's Strategies to End the Korean War." Paper presented at the annual meeting of the Association of Asian Studies, Boston, March 1994.

Dingman, Roger. "The Dagger and the Gift: The Impact of the Korean War on Japan." Paper delivered at the Fifteenth Military History Symposium, U.S. Air Force Academy, October 14–16, 1992.

Egan, Joseph Bernard. "The Struggle for the Soul of Faust," Ph.D. diss., University of Connecticut, 1985.

Goldhammer, Herbert. "The Korean Armistice Conference." Santa Monica, Calif.: The Rand Corporation, 1951. Copy in author's possession.

Huebner, Jon Walter. "The Genesis of China's Taiwan Problem, 1949–1953: Chinese Perspectives and Policy." Ph.D. diss., New York University, 1979.

Jia, Qing-Guo. "Unmaterialized Rapprochement: Sino-American Relations in the Mid-1950s." Ph.D. diss., Cornell University, 1988.

Kim, Dong-Soo. "U.S.-South Korea Relations in 1953–1954: A Study of Patron-Client State Relationship." Ph.D. diss., University of Connecticut, 1985.

Koh, Kwang Il. "In Quest of National Unity and Power: Political Ideas and Practices of Syngman Rhee." Ph.D. diss., Rutgers University, 1963.

Letteney, Ronald Lee. "Foreign Policy Factionalism Under Stalin, 1949–1950." Ph.D. diss., The Johns Hopkins University, 1971.

Mark, Eduard. "The Intelligence Horizon of American Policy Makers, 1944–1946." Paper delivered at the annual meeting of the Society for Historians of American Foreign Relations, University of Virginia, June 1993.

Michalak, Stanley Jacob, Jr. "The Senate and the United Nations: A Study of Changing Perceptions about the Utilities and Limitations of the United Nations as an Instrument of Peace and Security and Its Role in American National Security Policy." Ph.D. diss., Princeton University, 1967.

Morris, William George. "The Korean Trusteeship, 1941–1947: The United States, Russia, and the Cold War." Ph.D. diss., University of Texas at Austin, 1975.

Myers, Samuel M., and William C. Bradbury. "The Political Behavior of Korean and Chinese Prisoners of War in the Korean Conflict: A Historical Analysis." Technical Rpt. No. 50, Human Resources Research Office, George Washington University, August 1958.

Paddock, Alfred H., Jr. "Psychological and Unconventional Warfare, 1941–1952: Origins of a 'Special Warfare' Capability for the United States Army." Ph.D. diss., Duke University, 1979.

Pendill, C. Grant, Jr. "Foreign Policy and Political Factions in the USSR, 1952–1956: The Post-Stalin Power Struggle and the Developing Nations." Ph.D. diss., University of Pennsylvania, 1969.

Rabel, Roberto Giorgio. "Between East and West: Trieste, the United States and the Cold War, 1943–1954." Ph.D. diss., Duke University, 1984.

Raith, Charles Adolphe. "The Anti-UN Coalition before the Senate Foreign Relations and the House Foreign Affairs Committees during the Years 1945–1955." Ph.D. diss., University of Pennsylvania, 1962.

Schwartz, Thomas A. "The German Question in the American-Soviet Relations: Fears, Opportunities, and the Search for Stability." Paper presented to the Conference on U.S.-USSR Relations, 1950–1955, Ohio University, 7–9 October, 1988.

Soh, Jin Chull. "Some Causes of the Korean War of 1950: A Case Study of Soviet Foreign Policy in Korea (1945–1950), with Emphasis on Sino-Soviet Collaboration." Ph.D. diss., University of Oklahoma, 1963.

Soonthornrojana, Adulyasak. "The Rise of United States-Thai Relations, 1945–1975." Ph.D. diss., University of Akron, 1986.

U.S. Army Forces in Korea. "History of the United States Army Forces in Korea," vols. 1–3. 1948. Available in the Office of the Chief of Military History, Washington, D.C.

Weathersby, Kathryn. "Soviet Policy Toward Korea, 1944–1946." Ph.D. diss., Indiana University, 1990.

Weiss, Lawrence Stephen. "Storm Around the Cradle: The Korean War and the Early Years of the People's Republic of China, 1949–1953." Ph.D. diss., Columbia University, 1981.

Willging, Paul Raymond. "Soviet Foreign Policy in the German Question: 1950–1955." Ph.D. diss., Columbia University, 1973.

Yurechko, John Joseph. "From Containment to Counteroffensive: Soviet Vulnerabilities and American Policy Planning, 1946–1953." Ph.D. diss., University of California, Berkeley, 1980.

Zhang Shuguang. "Military Romanticism: China and the Korean War, 1950–1953." Draft manuscript, March 1992, in possession of the author.

## GOVERNMENT AND UNITED NATIONS PUBLICATIONS

*North Korea*

Kim Il-sung. *Works*. Vols. 1–7. Pyongyang: Foreign Languages Publishing House, 1981.

*People's Republic of China*

Mao Zedong. *Jianguo Yilai Mao Zedong Wengao* (Mao Zedong's manuscripts since the founding of the PRC). Vols. 1–3. Beijing: Central Government Publishing House, 1987.

*United Kingdom*

U.K. Parliament. *Hansard*, 1950–1953.

*United Nations*

UN General Assembly. *Official Record*, 1947–1953.
UN *Yearbook*, 1947–1954.

*United States*

U.S. Central Intelligence Agency. *Foreign Broadcast Information Service*, 1950–1953.

U.S. Congress. *Congressional Record*, 1945–1953.

———. Senate. Armed Services and Foreign Relations Committee. *Military Situation in the Far East*. 82d Congress, 1st session, 1951.

U.S. Consulate General, Hong Kong. *Survey of the China Mainland Press*, 1950–1953.

U.S. Department of the Army. *Military Advisers in Korea: KMAG in Peace and War*, by Robert K. Sawyer, 1962.

———. *United States Army in the Korean War*. Vol. 1: *South to the Naktong, North to the Yalu*, by Roy Appleman. Vol. 2: *Truce Tent and Fighting Front*, by Walter Hermes. Vol. 3: *Policy and Direction, the First Year*, by James F. Schnabel. 1961–1972.

———. Supreme Commander Allied Powers, Japan. *South Korean Interim Government Activities*. Vols. 23–35. 1947–1948.

———. *Summation of Non-Military Activities in Japan and Korea, 1945–1946*. Vols. 1–5. 1945–1946.

———. *Summation of U.S. Army Military Government Activities In Korea*. Vols. 6–22. 1946–1947.

U.S. Department of State. *American Policy, 1950–1955: Basic Documents*. 1957.

———. *Department of State Bulletin*. Vols. 12–31. 1945–1954.

———. *Foreign Relations of the United States, 1942*. Vol. 1: *The British Commonwealth, The Far East*. 1969.

———. *Foreign Relations of the United States: Conferences at Cairo and Tehran, 1943*. 1961.

———. *Foreign Relations of the United States, 1944*. Vol. 5: *The Near East, South Asia, Africa, The Far East*. 1969.

———. *Foreign Relations of the United States, 1945*. Vol. 6: *The British Commonwealth, The Far East*. 1969.

———. *Foreign Relations of the United States, 1945: The Conference of Berlin (The Potsdam Conference)*. 2 vols. 1957.

———. *Foreign Relations of the United States: Conferences at Malta and Yalta, 1945*. 1955.

———. *Foreign Relations of the United States, 1946*. Vol. 8: *The Far East*.

———. *Foreign Relations of the United States, 1947*. Vol. 6: *The Far East*.

———. *Foreign Relations of the United States, 1948*. Vol. 6: *The Far East and Australia*. 1974.

———. *Foreign Relations of the United States, 1949*. Vol. 2: *The United Nations, The Western Hemisphere*. Vol. 7: *The Far East and Australasia*. 1974.

———. *Foreign Relations of the United States, 1950*. Vol. 1: *National Security*. Vol. 2: *The United Nations, The Western Hemisphere*. Vol. 3: *Western Europe*. Vol. 4: *Central and Eastern Europe and the Soviet Union*. Vol. 6: *East Asia and the Pacific*. Vol. 7: *Korea*. 1976–1980.

———. *Foreign Relations of the United States, 1951*. Vol. 1: *National Security Affairs; Foreign Economic Policy*. Vol. 2: *The United Nations; The Western Hemisphere*.

Vol. 3: *European Security and the German Question.* Vol. 4: *Europe: Political and Economic Developments.* Vol. 6: *Asia and the Pacific.* Vol. 7: *Korea and China.* 1977–1985.

———. *Foreign Relations of the United States, 1952–1954.* Vol. 2: *National Security Affairs.* Vol. 3: *United Nations Affairs.* Vol. 5: *Western European Security.* Vol. 6: *Western Europe and Canada.* Vol. 7: *Germany and Austria.* Vol. 8: *Eastern Europe; Soviet Union; Eastern Mediterranean.* Vol. 11: *Africa and South Asia.* Vol. 12: *East Asia and the Pacific.* Vol. 13: *Indochina.* Vol. 14: *China and Japan.* Vol. 15: *Korea.* 1979–1988.

———. *Korea, 1945–1948.* 1948.

———. *Korea's Independence.* 1947.

———. *Moscow Meeting of Foreign Ministers, December 16–26 1945.* 1946.

———. *North Korea: A Case Study in the Techniques of Takeover.* 1961.

———. *United States Policy in the Korean Conflict.* 1951.

———. *United States Policy in the Korean Crisis.* 1950.

———. *United States Relations with China with Special Reference to the Period 1944–1949.* 1949.

U.S. General Services Administration. *Public Papers of the Presidents of the United States: Harry S. Truman, 1950–1953.* 1965.

———. *Public Papers of the Presidents of the United States: Dwight D. Eisenhower, 1953–1954.* 1960.

U.S. Joint Chiefs of Staff. *The History of the Joint Chiefs of Staff.* Vol. 1: *The Joint Chiefs of Staff and National Policy, 1945–1947*, by James F. Schnabel. Vol. 2: *The Joint Chiefs of Staff and National Policy, 1947–1949*, by Kenneth W. Condit. Vol. 3: *The Joint Chiefs of Staff and National Policy, The Korean War*, by James F. Schnabel and Robert J. Watson. Wilmington, Del.: Michael Glazier, 1979.

U.S. Marine Corps. *U.S. Marine Operations in Korea 1950–53.* 4 vols. By Lynn Montross and Nicholas A. Canzona. 1957.

U.S. Office of the Secretary of Defense. *History of the Office of the Secretary of Defense.* Vol. 2: *The Test of War 1950–1953.* 1988.

INTERVIEWS

Charles L. Bolté, 6 August 1974.
Niles Bond, 30 July 1977.
W. Walton Butterworth, 16 November 1971.
O. Edmund Clubb, 16 March 1977.
J. Lawton Collins, 21 July 1974.
John B. Coulter, 26 December 1973.
George M. Elsey, 23 July 1974.
Philip C. Jessup, 6 June 1972.
John J. Muccio, 27 December 1973.
Paul Nitze, 9 January 1975.
John H. Ohly, 4 August 1975.
Matthew B. Ridgway, 26 November 1971.
Dean Rusk, 24 July 1972.
Raymond Thurston, 4 May 1978.
Thomas B. Timberman, 30 December 1973 and 13 August 1974.
James E. Webb, 7 August 1974.

ORAL HISTORIES

*Independence, Missouri*

Harry S. Truman Library
  Robert W. Barnett
  Edward W. Barrett
  Robert K. E. Bruce
  Laurence E. Bunker
  John Cabot
  O. Edmund Clubb
  William H. Draper
  George M. Elsey
  Gordon Gray
  Loy W. Henderson
  U. Alexis Johnson
  Edwin W. Martin
  H. Freeman Matthews
  John Muccio
  Charles Murphy
  Frank Pace
  Arthur R. Ringwalt
  Francis J. Russell
  Philip C. Sprouse

*New York, New York*

Butler Library, Columbia University
  Columbia University Oral History Project (microfiche edition)
  "Reminiscences of Ernest R. Gross"

NEWSPAPERS AND POPULAR MAGAZINES

*The Nation*, 1950–1953.
*Newsweek*, 1950–1953.
*The New York Times*, 1945–1953.
*Time*, 1950–1953.
*U.S. News and World Report*, 1950–1953.

BOOKS AND ARTICLES

Acheson, Dean. *Present at the Creation: My Years in the State Department*. New York: Norton, 1969.
Adenauer, Konrad. *Memoirs 1945–1953*. Translated by Beate Ruhmvon Oppen. London: Weidenfeld and Nicolson, 1966.
Alliluyeva, Svetlana. *Twenty Letters to a Friend*. Translated by Priscilla Johnson MacMillan. New York: Harper and Row, 1967.
Ambrose, Stephen E. *Eisenhower*. Vol. 2: *The President*. New York: Simon and Schuster, 1984.
Anders, Roger M. "The Atomic Bomb and the Korean War: Gordon Dean and the Issue of Civilian Military Control." *Military Affairs* 52 (January 1988): 1–6.

Andrew, Christopher, and Oleg Gordievsky. *KGB: The Inside Story*. New York: Harper Collins, 1990.

Appleman, Roy E. *East of Chosin: Entrapment and Breakout in Korea, 1950*. College Station: Texas A & M University Press, 1987.

———. *Disaster in Korea: The Chinese Confront MacArthur*. College Station: Texas A & M University Press, 1989.

———. *Ridgway Duels for Korea*. College Station: Texas A & M University Press, 1990.

Bailey, Sydney D. *The Korean Armistice*. New York: St. Martin's, 1992.

Barclay, Glen St. J. *Friends in High Places: Australian-American Diplomatic Relations Since 1945*. Melbourne: Oxford University Press, 1985.

Baring, Arnulf. *Uprising in East Germany: June 17, 1953*. Ithaca, N.Y.: Cornell University Press, 1972.

Bernstein, Barton J. "Truman's Secret Thoughts on Ending the Korean War." *Foreign Service Journal* 57 (November 1980): 31–33, 44.

Bialer, Uri. *Between East and West: Israel's Foreign Policy Orientation, 1948–1956*. New York: Cambridge University Press, 1990.

Blair, Clay. *The Forgotten War: America in Korea, 1950–1953*. New York: Times Books, 1987.

Bo Yibo. "The Making of the 'Lean-to-One-Side' Decision." Translated by Zhai Qiang. *Chinese Historians* 5 (Spring 1992): 57–62.

Boardman, Robert. *Britain and the People's Republic of China, 1949–1974*. London: Macmillan, 1976.

Bohlen, Charles E. *Witness to History 1929–1969*. New York: Norton, 1973.

Bonwetsch, Bernd, and Peter M. Kuhfus. "Die Sowjetunion, China und Der Koreakrieg." *Vierteljahrshefte für Zeitgeschichte* 33 (January 1985): 28–87.

Borden, William S. *The Pacific Alliance*. Madison: University of Wisconsin Press, 1984.

Boyle, Andrew. *The Fourth Man: The Definitive Account of Kim Philby, Guy Burgess, and Donald Maclean and Who Recruited Them to Spy for Russia*. New York: Dial, 1979.

Bradley, Omar N., and Clay Blair. *A General's Life*. New York: Simon and Schuster, 1983.

Brands, H. W. "The Dwight D. Eisenhower Administration, Syngman Rhee, and the 'Other' Geneva Conference of 1954." *Pacific Historical Review* 56 (February 1987): 59–85.

———. *Cold Warriors: Eisenhower's Generation and American Foreign Policy*. New York: Columbia University Press, 1988.

———. *The Specter of Neutralism: The United States and the Emergence of the Third World, 1947–1960*. New York: Columbia University Press, 1989.

———. *India and the United States: Cold Peace*. Boston: Twayne, 1990.

———. *Inside the Cold War: Loy Henderson and the Rise of the American Empire*. New York: Oxford University Press, 1991.

Brecher, Michael. *Decisions in Israel's Foreign Policy*. London: Oxford University Press, 1974.

Browder, Robert Paul, and Thomas C. Smith. *Independent: A Biography of Lewis W. Douglas*. New York: Knopf, 1986.

Brzezinski, Zbigniew. *The Soviet Bloc, Unity and Conflict*. Rev. and enlarged ed. Cambridge, Mass.: Harvard University Press, 1967.

Bueschel, Richard M. *Communist Chinese Air Power*. New York: Praeger, 1968.

Bullen, Roger. "Great Britain, the United States and the Indian Resolution on the Korean War: November 1952." In *Aspects of Anglo-Korean Relations, International Studies* (International Center for Economics and Related Disciplines, London School of Economics and Political Science, 1984), 29–43.

Bullock, Alan. *Ernest Bevin, Foreign Secretary.* New York: Norton, 1983.

Candee, Marjorie Dent, ed. *Current Biography, 1953.* New York: H. W. Wilson, 1953.

Caridi, Ronald J. *The Korean War and American Politics: The Republican Party as a Case Study.* Philadelphia: University of Pennsylvania Press, 1968.

Chang, Carson. *Third Force in China.* New York: Bookman, 1952.

Chang, Gordon H. *Friends and Enemies: The United States, China, and the Soviet Union, 1948–1972.* Stanford, Calif.: Stanford University Press, 1990.

Chay, Jongsuk. *Diplomacy of Asymmetry: Korean-American Relations to 1910.* Honolulu: University of Hawaii Press, 1990.

Chen, Jian. "China's Changing Aims during the Korean War, 1950–1951." *The Journal of American East Asian Relations* 1 (Spring 1992): 8–41.

Chien, Frederick Foo. *The Opening of Korea: A Study of Chinese Diplomacy 1876–1885.* Hamden, Conn.: Shoe String Press, 1967.

Chow, Ching-wen. *Ten Years of Storm: The True Story of the Communist Regime in China.* Translated by Lai Mind. New York: Holt, Rinehart and Winston, 1960.

Christensen, Thomas. "Threats, Assurances, and the Last Chance for Peace: The Lessons of Mao's Korean War Telegrams." *International Security* 17 (Summer 1992): 122–54.

Clark, Mark W. *From the Danube to the Yalu.* New York: Harper and Brothers, 1954.

Clubb, O. Edmund. *China and Russia: The Great Game.* New York: Columbia University Press, 1971.

Cohen, Warren I. "Conversations with Chinese Friends: Zhou Enlai's Associates Reflect on Chinese-American Relations in the 1940s and the Korean War." *Diplomatic History* 11 (Summer 1987): 286–92.

Collins, J. Lawton. *War in Peacetime: The History and Lessons of Korea.* Boston: Houghton Mifflin, 1969.

Colville, John. *The Fringes of Power, 10 Downing Street: Diaries 1939–1955.* New York: Norton, 1985.

Condit, Doris M. *History of the Office of the Secretary of Defense.* Vol. 2: *The Test of War, 1950–1953.* Washington, D.C.: U.S. Government Printing Office, 1988.

Cumings, Bruce. *The Origins of the Korean War.* Vol. 1: *Liberation and the Emergence of Separate Regimes.* Princeton, N.J.: Princeton University Press, 1981.

———. *The Origins of the Korean War.* Vol. 2: *The Roaring of the Cataract*, Princeton, N.J.: Princeton University Press, 1990.

———, ed. *Child of Conflict: The Korean-American Relationship, 1943–1953.* Seattle: University of Washington Press, 1983.

Cumings, Bruce, and Jon Halliday. *Korea: The Unknown War.* London: Viking, 1988.

Darling, Frank C. *Thailand and the United States.* Washington, D.C.: Public Affairs Press, 1965.

Dayal, Shiv. *India's Role in the Korean Question.* Delhi: S. Chaud, 1959.

Devillers, Philippe. "De Conflit Vu D'Europe." *Revue Francaise de Science Politique* 20 (December 1970).

Dingman, Roger. "The Diplomacy of Dependence: The Philippines and Peacemaking with Japan, 1945–1952." *Journal of Southeast Asian Studies* 27 (September 1986): 307–21.

———. "Atomic Diplomacy during the Korean War." *International Security* 13 (Winter 1988/89): 61–89.

Dittmer, Lowell. *China's Continuous Revolution: The Post-Liberation Epoch, 1949–1981*. Berkeley: University of California Press, 1987.

Divine, Robert A. *Foreign Policy and U.S. Presidential Elections*. Vol. 2. New York: New Viewpoints, 1974.

Domes, Jurgen. *Peng Te-huai: The Man and the Image*. Stanford, Calif.: Stanford University Press, 1985.

Donovan, Robert J. *Tumultuous Years: The Presidency of Harry S. Truman, 1949–1953*. New York: Norton, 1982.

Du Ping. *Zai Zhiyuanju Zongbu* (At the headquarters of the volunteer army). Beijing: Jiefangjun chubanshe (Liberation Army Press), 1989.

Eckstein, Alexander. *Communist China's Economic Growth and Foreign Trade*. New York: McGraw-Hill, 1966.

Eden, Anthony. *Memoirs: The Reckoning*. Boston: Houghton Mifflin, 1963.

———. *Memoirs: Full Circle*. Boston: Houghton Mifflin, 1960.

*Egypt and the United Nations Report of a Study Group Set Up by the Egyptian Society of International Law*. New York: Manhattan Publishing, 1957.

Eisenhower, Dwight D. *The White House Years*. Vol. 1: *Mandate for Change, 1953–1956*. Garden City, N.Y.: Doubleday, 1963.

Elliott, Mark R. *Pawns of Yalta: Soviet Refugees and America's Role in Their Repatriation*. Urbana: University of Illinois Press, 1982.

Evangelista, Matthew A. "Stalin's Postwar Army Reappraised." *International Security* 7 (Winter 1982): 110–38.

Farrar, Peter. "Britain's Proposal for a Buffer Zone South of the Yalu in November 1950." *Journal of Contemporary History* 18 (1983): 327–51.

Farrar-Hockley, Anthony. *The British Part in the Korean War*. Vol. 1: *A Distant Obligation*. London: Her Majesty's Stationary Office, 1990.

Fedorenko, N. "The Stalin-Mao Summit in Moscow." *Far Eastern Affairs* (January 1989): 134–48.

Fehrenbach, T. R. *This Kind of War*. New York: Macmillan, 1963.

Feith, Herbert. *The Wilopo Cabinet, 1952–1953*. Ithaca, N.Y.: Cornell University Press, 1958.

Ferrell, Robert H., ed. *The Eisenhower Diaries*. New York: Norton, 1981.

Fifield, Russell H. *The Diplomacy of Southeast Asia: 1945–1958*. New York: Harper and Brothers, 1958.

Foot, Rosemary. *The Wrong War: American Policy and the Dimensions of the Korean Conflict, 1950–1953*. Ithaca, N.Y.: Cornell University Press, 1985.

———. "Anglo-American Relations in the Korean Crisis: The British Effort to Avert an Expanded War, December 1950–January 1951." *Diplomatic History* 10 (Winter 1986): 43–57.

———. "Nuclear Coercion and the Ending of the Korean Conflict." *International Security* 13 (Winter 1988/89): 99–112.

———. *A Substitute for Victory: The Politics of Peacemaking at the Korean Armistice Talks*. Ithaca, N.Y.: Cornell University Press, 1990.

Funigiello, Philip J. *American-Soviet Trade in the Cold War*. Chapel Hill: University of North Carolina Press, 1988.

Futrell, Robert Frank. *The United States Air Force in Korea*. New York: Duell, Sloan, and Pearce, 1961.

Gaddis, John Lewis. *Strategies of Containment: A Critical Appraisal of Postwar American National Security Policy.* New York: Oxford University Press, 1982.

Gallup, George M. *The Gallup Poll: Public Opinion 1935–1971.* 2 vols. New York: Random House, 1972.

Garthoff, Raymond, ed. *Sino-Soviet Military Relations.* New York: Praeger, 1966.

Garver, John. *Chinese-Soviet Relations, 1937–1945: The Diplomacy of Nationalism.* New York: Oxford University Press, 1988.

George, Alexander L. "American Policy-Making and the North Korean Aggression." *World Politics* 7 (January 1955): 209–32.

———. *The Chinese Communist Army in Action: The Korean War and Its Aftermath.* New York: Columbia University Press, 1967.

George, T.J.S. *Krishna Menon.* New York: Taplinger, 1965.

Gilbert, Martin. *Winston S. Churchill.* Vol. 8: *Never Despair, 1945–1965.* Boston: Houghton Mifflin, 1988.

Gillingham, John. *Coal, Steel, and the Rebirth of Europe, 1945–1955.* New York: Cambridge University Press, 1991.

Gopal, Sarvepalli. *Jawaharlal Nehru.* 2 vols. Cambridge, Mass.: Harvard University Press, 1976–1984.

Goncharov, Sergei, John W. Lewis, and Xue Litai, *Uncertain Partners: Stalin, Mao, and the Korean War.* Stanford, Calif.: Stanford University Press, 1993.

Gordenker, Leon. *The United Nations and the Peaceful Unification of Korea: The Politics of Field Operations.* The Hague: Marinus Nijhoff, 1959.

Goulden, Joseph. *Korea: The Untold Story of the War.* New York: Times Books, 1982.

Griffith, Samuel B., II. *The Chinese People's Liberation Army.* New York: McGraw-Hill, 1967.

Gromyko, Andrei. *Memories.* Translated by Harold Shukman. London: Hutchinson, 1989.

Gugeler, Russell A. *Combat Actions in Korea.* Washington, D.C.: Combat Forces Press, 1954.

Guhin, Michael A. *John Foster Dulles: A Statesman and His Times.* New York: Columbia University Press, 1972.

Gutteridge, J.A.C. "The Repatriation of Prisoners of War." *International and Comparative Law Quarterly* 2 (1953): 207–16.

Hahn, Peter L. *The United States, Great Britain, and Egypt, 1945–1956.* Chapel Hill: University of North Carolina Press, 1991.

Hahn, Werner G. *Postwar Soviet Politics: The Fall of Zhdanov and the Defeat of Moderation, 1946–1953.* Ithaca, N.Y.: Cornell University Press, 1982.

Hamby, Alonzo. *Beyond the New Deal: Harry S. Truman and American Liberalism.* New York: Columbia University Press, 1973.

Hammel, Eric M. *Chosin.* New York: Vanguard, 1981.

Hao Yufan and Zhai Zhihai. "China's Decision to Enter the Korean War: History Revisited." *China Quarterly* 121 (March 1990): 94–115.

Harding, Harry, and Yuan Ming, eds. *Sino-American Relations, 1945–1955: A Joint Reassessment of a Critical Decade.* Wilmington, Del.: Scholarly Resources, 1989.

Harris, Kenneth. *Attlee.* London: Weidenfeld and Nicolson, 1982.

Hastings, Max. *The Korean War.* New York: Simon and Schuster, 1987.

He Di. "The Last Campaign to Unify China: The CCP's Unmaterialized Plan to Liberate Taiwan." *Chinese Historians* 5 (Spring 1992): 1–16.

———. "The Most Respected Enemy: Mao Zedong's Perception of the United States." *China Quarterly* 137 (March 1994): 144–58.

Heinl, Robert Debe, Jr. *Victory at High Tide: The Inchon-Seoul Campaigns.* Philadelphia: Lippincott, 1968.

Heller, Francis H., ed. *The Korean War: A 25-Year Perspective.* Lawrence: Regents of Kansas Press, 1977.

Henderson, Gregory. *Korea: The Politics of the Vortex.* Cambridge, Mass.: Harvard University Press, 1968.

Hess, Gary. *The United States' Emergence as a Southeast Asian Power, 1940–1950.* New York: Columbia University Press, 1987.

Heuser, Beatrice. *Western "Containment" Policies in the Cold War: The Yugoslav Case, 1948–53.* London: Routledge, 1989.

Heuser, Beatrice, and Robert O'Neill, eds. *Securing Peace in Europe, 1945–62.* New York: St. Martin's, 1992.

Hinley, Donald. *The Communist Party in Indonesia, 1951–1963.* Berkeley: University of California Press, 1964.

Hogan, Michael. *The Marshall Plan: America, Britain, and the Reconstruction of Western Europe, 1947–1952.* New York: Cambridge University Press, 1987.

Holloway, David. *Stalin and the Bomb.* New Haven: Yale University Press, 1994.

Hopkins, William B. *One Bugle No Drums: The Marines at Chosin Reservoir.* Chapel Hill, N.C.: Algonquin Books, 1986.

Houston, John A. *Latin America and the United Nations.* New York: Carnegie Endowment for International Peace, 1956.

Hovet, Thomas, Jr. *Bloc Politics in the United Nations.* Cambridge, Mass.: Harvard University Press, 1960.

Hoyt, Edwin P. *The Bloody Road to Panmunjom.* New York: Stein and Day, 1985.

Huang, Chen-Hsia. *The Chinese High Command: A History of Communist Military Politics, 1927–71.* New York: Praeger, 1973.

Hughes, Emmet John. *The Ordeal of Power: A Political Memoir of the Eisenhower Years.* New York: Atheneum, 1963.

Hull, Cordell. *Memoirs.* 2 vols. New York: Macmillan, 1948.

Hunt, Michael H. "The Long Crisis in U.S. Diplomatic History: Coming to Closure." *Diplomatic History* 16 (Winter 1992): 115–40.

———. "Beijing and the Korean Crisis, June 1950–June 1951." *Political Science Quarterly* 107 (Fall 1992): 453–78.

Hwang, In Kwang. "The 1953 U.S. Initiative for Korean Neutralization." *Korea and World Affairs* 9, 10 (Winter 1986): 798–826.

Indian Council of World Affairs. *India and the United Nations.* New York: Manhattan Publishing, 1957.

Ireland, Timothy P. *Creating the Entangling Alliance.* Westport, Conn.: Greenwood, 1981.

Iriye, Akira, and Warren I. Cohen, eds. *The United States and Japan in the Postwar World.* Lexington: University of Kentucky Press, 1989.

———. *The Great Powers in East Asia, 1953–1960.* New York: Columbia University Press, 1990.

Ismay, Lord. *NATO: The First Five Years, 1949–1954.* The Netherlands: Bosch-Utrecht, 1956.

James, D. Clayton. *The Years of MacArthur.* 3 vols. Boston: Houghton Mifflin, 1967–1985.

James, Robert Rhodes. *Anthony Eden.* New York: McGraw Hill, 1987.

Jansen, G. H. *Nonalignment and the Afro-American States.* New York: Praeger 1966.

Jervis, Robert. "The Impact of the Korean War on the Cold War." *Journal of Conflict Resolution* 24 (December 1980): 563–92.

Johnson, U. Alexis, with Jef Olivarius McAllister. *The Right Hand of Power*. Englewood Cliffs, N.J.: Prentice-Hall, 1984.

Joy, Charles Turner. "My Battle Inside the Korea Truce Tent." *Collier's* 130 (16, 23, and 30 August 1952): 36–43 passim, 26–31 passim, and 70–73, respectively.

———. *How Communists Negotiate*. New York: Macmillan, 1955.

———. *Negotiating while Fighting: The Diary of Admiral Turner C. Joy at the Korean Armistice Conference*. Edited and with an introduction by Allan E. Goodman. Stanford, Calif.: Hoover Institution Press, 1978.

Kaplan, Karel. *Dans les Archives du Comite Central: Trent ans de secrets du bloc sovietique*. Paris: Albin Michel, 1978.

Kaplan, Lawrence S. *The United States and NATO: The Formative Years*. Lexington: University of Kentucky Press, 1984.

Katzenbach, Edward L., Jr., and Gene Z. Hanrahan. "The Revolutionary Strategy of Mao Tse-tung." In *Modern Guerrilla Warfare*, ed. Franklin Mark Osanka (New York: Free Press, 1962), 131–46.

Kau, Michael Y. M., ed. *The Writings of Mao Zedong, 1949–1976*. Vol. 1. Armonk, N.Y.: M. E. Sharpe, 1986.

Kaufman, Burton I. *The Korean War: Challenges in Crisis, Credibility, and Command*. New York: Temple University Press, 1986.

Kautsky, John H. *Moscow and the Communist Party of India*. Cambridge, Mass.: MIT Press, 1956.

Keefer, Edward C. "President Dwight D. Eisenhower and the End of the Korean War." *Diplomatic History* 10 (Summer 1986): 267–89.

———. "The Truman Administration and the South Korean Political Crisis of 1952: Democracy's Failure?" *Pacific Historical Review* 60 (May 1991): 145–68.

Kennan, George F. *Memoirs (1925–1950)*. Boston: Little, Brown, 1967.

———. *Memoirs (1950–1963)*. Boston: Little, Brown, 1972.

Kepley, David R. *The Collapse of the Middle Way*. Westport, Conn.: Greenwood, 1987.

Kerksvlict, Benedict J. *The Huk Rebellion: A Study of Peasant Revolt in the Philippines*. Berkeley: University of California Press, 1977.

Khong, Yen Foon. *Analogies at War: Korea, Munich, Dien Bien Phu, and the Vietnam Decisions of 1965*. Princeton, N.J.: Princeton University Press, 1992.

Khrushchev, Nikita. *Khrushchev Remembers*. Introduction, commentary, and notes by Edward Crankshaw. Translated and edited by Strobe Talbott. Boston: Little, Brown, 1970.

———. *Khrushchev Remembers: The Last Testament*. Translated and edited by Strobe Talbott. Boston: Little, Brown, 1974.

———. *Khrushchev Remembers: The Glasnost Tapes*. Foreword by Strobe Talbott. Translated and edited by Jerrold L. Schecter, with Vyacheslav V. Luchkov. Boston: Little, Brown, 1990.

Kim, C. I. Eugene, and Han-Kyo Kim. *Korea and the Politics of Imperialism, 1876–1910*. Los Angeles: University of California Press, 1967.

Kim, Chullbaum. *The Truth about the Korean War: Testimony 40 Years Later*. Seoul: Eulyoo, 1991.

Kim, Chullbaum, and James I. Matray, eds. *Korea and the Cold War: Division, Destruction, and Disarmament*. Claremont, Calif.: Regina Books, 1993.

Kim, Joungwon Alexander. *Divided Korea: The Politics of Development, 1945–1972.* Cambridge, Mass.: Harvard University Press, 1975.

Kim, Key-Hiuk. *The Last Phase of the East Asian World Order: Korea, Japan, and the Chinese Empire, 1860–1882.* Los Angeles: University of California Press, 1980.

Knight, Amy. *Beria: Stalin's First Lieutenant.* Princeton, N.J.: Princeton University Press, 1993.

Kolodziej, Edward A. *The Uncommon Defense and Congress, 1945–1963.* Columbia: Ohio State University Press, 1966.

Kovalev, Ivan. "Stalin-Mao Dialogue." *Far Eastern Affairs* 82, nos. 1 and 2 (1992): 100–16 and 94–111, respectively.

Kramer, Mark. "The USSR Foreign Ministry's Appraisal of Sino-Soviet Relations on the Eve of the Split, September 1959." *Bulletin of the Cold War International History Project* 6–7 (Winter 1995–1996): 170–85.

Krammer, Arnold. *The Forgotten Friendship: Israel and the Soviet Bloc, 1947–53.* Urbana: University of Illinois Press, 1974.

Kundra, J. C. *Indian Foreign Policy, 1947–1954.* Groningen, Netherlands: J. B. Wolters, 1955.

Kwak, Tae Hwan, ed. *U.S.-Korean Relations, 1882–1982.* Seoul: Kyungnam University Press, 1982.

Lacey, Michael J., ed. *The Truman Presidency.* New York: Cambridge University Press, 1989.

Larson, David L. *United States Policy Toward Yugoslavia, 1943–1963.* Washington, D.C.: University Press of America, 1979.

Lauterback, Richard E. *Danger from the East.* New York: Harper and Brothers, 1947.

Leary, William M. *Perilous Missions: Civil Air Transport and CIA Covert Operations in Asia.* Tuscaloosa: University of Alabama Press, 1984.

Lee, Chae-Jin, ed. *The Korean War: 40-Year Perspectives.* Claremont, Calif.: The Keck Center for International and Strategic Studies, 1991.

Lee, Chong-sik. *The Politics of Korean Nationalism.* Los Angeles: University of California Press, 1963.

Lee, Chong-sik, and Robert Scalapino. *Communism in Korea.* 2 vols. Los Angeles: University of California Press, 1972.

Lee, Yur-Bok. *Diplomatic Relations Between the United States and Korea, 1866–1887.* New York: Humanities Press, 1970.

Leffler, Melvyn P. "Strategy, Diplomacy, and the Cold War: The United States, Turkey, and NATO, 1945–1952." *Journal of American History* 71 (March 1984): 807–25.

———. *A Preponderance of Power: National Security, the Truman Administration, and the Cold War.* Stanford, Calif.: Stanford University Press, 1992.

Lengyel, Emil. *Krishna Menon.* New York: Walker, 1961.

Lensen, George Alexander. *Balance of Intrigue: International Rivalry in Korea and Manchuria, 1884–1899.* 2 vols. Tallahassee: University Presses of Florida, 1982.

Li Xiaobing, Wang Xi, and Chen Jian, annotators and translators. "Mao's Dispatch of Chinese Troops to Korea: Forty-Six Telegrams, July–October 1950." *Chinese Historians* 5 (Spring 1992): 63–86.

Lie, Trygve. *In the Cause of Peace: Seven Years with the United Nations.* New York: Macmillan, 1954.

Lim Un, *The Founding of a Dynasty in North Korea—An Authentic Biography of Kim Il-sung.* Tokyo: Jiyusha, 1982.

Liu Shao-ch'i. *Collected Works of Liu Shao-ch'i, 1945–1967.* Hong Kong: Union Research Institute, 1969.
Liu Xiaoyuan. "Sino-American Diplomacy over Korea during World War II." *Journal of American-East Asian Relations* 1 (Summer 1992): 223–64.
Lodge, Henry Cabot. *The Storm Has Many Eyes: A Personal Narrative.* New York: Norton, 1973.
Louis, William Roger. *The British Empire in the Middle East, 1945–1951.* New York: Oxford University Press, 1984.
Lowe, Peter. *The Origins of the Korean War.* London: Longman, 1986.
Luard, Evan. *A History of the United Nations.* Vol. 1: *The Years of Western Domination, 1945–1955.* New York: St. Martin's, 1982.
Mabon, David. "Elusive Agreements: The Pacific Pact Proposals of 1949–1951." *Pacific Historical Review* 57 (May 1988): 147–77.
MacArthur, Douglas. *Reminiscences.* New York: McGraw-Hill, 1964.
McCagg, William O., Jr. *Stalin Embattled, 1943–1948.* Detroit: Wayne State University Press, 1978.
McCormack, Gavan. *Cold War/Hot War.* Sydney, Australia: Hale and Iremonger, 1983.
McCoy, Donald R. *The Presidency of Harry S. Truman.* Lawrence: University Press of Kansas, 1984.
McCullough, David. *Truman.* New York: Simon and Schuster, 1992.
McGeehan, Robert. *The German Rearmament Question.* Urbana: University of Illinois Press, 1971.
McGhee, George. *Envoy to the Middle World: Adventures in Diplomacy.* New York: Harper and Row, 1983.
McGibbon, I. A. *New Zealand and the Korean War.* New York: Oxford University Press, 1992.
McGlothlen, Ronald. *Controlling the Waves: Dean Acheson and U.S. Foreign Policy in Asia.* New York: Norton, 1993.
McLane, Charles B. *Soviet Strategies in Southeast Asia.* Princeton, N.J.: Princeton University Press, 1966.
McMahon, Robert J. *Colonialism and the Cold War: The United States and the Struggle for Indonesian Independence, 1945–1949.* Ithaca, N.Y.: Cornell University Press, 1981.
―――. "Food as a Diplomatic Weapon: The India Wheat Loan of 1951." *Pacific Historical Review* 56 (August 1987): 349–77.
―――. "The United States and South Asia: Making a Military Commitment to Pakistan, 1947–1954." *Journal of American History* 75 (December 1988): 812–56.
McNeal, Robert H. *Stalin: Man and Ruler.* New York: New York University Press, 1988.
Mahurin, Walker M. *Honest John: The Autobiography of Walker M. Mahurin.* New York: Putnam's, 1962.
Mancall, Mark. *China at the Center: 300 Years of Foreign Policy.* New York: Free Press, 1984.
Mao Tse-tung. *Selected Works of Mao Tse-tung.* Vols. 1–5. Peking: Foreign Languages Press, 1961–1977.
―――. *On the People's Democratic Dictatorship.* Edited and annotated by Tien-yi Li. New Haven, Conn.: Yale University Press, 1968.
Marshall, S.L.A. *The River and the Gauntlet.* New York: William Morrow, 1953.

Martin, Edwin W. *Divided Counsel: The Anglo-American Response to Communist Victory in China*. Lexington: University of Kentucky Press, 1986.
Matray, James Irving. "Truman's Plan for Victory: National Self-Determination and the Thirty-Eighth Parallel Decision in Korea." *Journal of American History* 66 (September 1979): 314–33.
———. *The Reluctant Crusade: American Foreign Policy in Korea, 1941–1950*. Honolulu: University of Hawaii Press, 1985.
May, Ernest R. *"Lessons of the Past": The Use and Misuse of History in American Foreign Policy*. New York: Oxford University Press, 1973.
———. "The American Commitment to Germany, 1949–55." *Diplomatic History* 13 (Fall 1989): 431–60.
———. "The U.S. Government, a Legacy of the Cold War." *Diplomatic History* 16 (Spring 1992): 269–77.
May, Ernest R., and Richard E. Neustadt. *Thinking in Time: The Uses of History for Decision Makers*. New York: Free Press, 1986.
Mayda, Jare. "The Korean Repatriation Problem and International Law." *American Journal of International Law* 47 (1953): 414–38.
Mazuzan, George T. *Warren R. Austin at the UN, 1946–1953*. Kent, Ohio: Kent State University Press, 1977.
Merrill, Dennis. "Indo-American Relations: A Missed Opportunity in Asia." *Diplomatic History* 11 (Summer 1987): 203–26.
Merrill, John. *Korea: The Peninsular Origins of the War*. Newark: University of Delaware Press, 1989.
Meyer, Milton Walter. *A Diplomatic History of the Philippine Republic*. Honolulu: University of Hawaii Press, 1965.
Monat, Pawel. "Russians in Korea: The Hidden Bosses." *Life* (27 June 1960): 76–102 passim.
Monnet, Jean. *Memoirs*. Garden City, N.Y.: Doubleday, 1978.
Moraes, Frank. *Report on Mao's China*. New York: Macmillan, 1954.
Morgan, Kenneth O. *Labour in Power, 1945–1951*. Oxford, England: Oxford University Press, 1984.
Mozingo, David. *Chinese Policy toward Indonesia, 1949–1967*. Ithaca, N.Y.: Cornell University Press, 1969.
Mullik, B. N. *My Years with Nehru, 1948–1964*. Bombay: Allied Publishers, 1972.
Munro-Leighton, Judith. "A Postrevisionist Scrutiny of America's Role in the Cold War in Asia, 1945–1950." *The Journal of American-East Asian Relations* 1 (Spring 1992): 73–98.
Nagy, Imre. *On Communism*. New York: Praeger, 1957.
Naik, J. A. *Soviet Policy towards India from Stalin to Brezhnev*. Delhi: Vikas Publications, 1970.
Nash, Philip. "The Use of Counterfactuals in History: A Look at the Literature." *Newsletter of the Society for Historians of American Foreign Relations* 22 (March 1991): 2–12.
Nehru, Jawaharlal. *Independence and After: A Collection of Speeches, 1946–1949*. New York: John Day, 1950.
———. *Visit to America*. New York: John Day, 1950.
———. *Letters to Chief Ministers, 1947–1964*. Vols. 2–3, 1950–1952. London: Oxford University Press, 1986.

Nie Rongzhen. *Huiyilu* (Memoirs). Beijing: Jiefangjun chubanshe (Liberation Army Press), 1986.

Nimmo, William S., ed. *The Occupation of Japan*. Norfolk, Va.: MacArthur Memorial Foundation, 1990.

"N. K. Preemptive Strike Plan in '50 Made Public in Russia." *The Korean Herald*, 30 August 1992, 1.

Noble, Harold Joyce. *Embassy at War*. Edited, annotated, and with an introduction by Frank Baldwin. Seattle: University of Washington Press, 1975.

Noer, Thomas J. *Cold War and Black Liberation: The United States and White Rule in Africa, 1948–1968*. Columbia: University of Missouri Press, 1985.

Oliver, Robert T. *Syngman Rhee and American Involvement in Korea, 1942–1960*. Seoul: Panmun Books, 1978.

O'Neill, Robert. *Australia in the Korean War, 1950–1953*. Vol. 1: *Strategy and Diplomacy*. Canberra: Australian Government Publishing Service, 1981.

Ovendale, Ritchie. "Britain, the United States, and the Recognition of Communist China." *The Historical Journal* 26, 1 (1983): 139–58.

———. *The English-Speaking Alliance: Britain, the United States, the Dominions and the Cold War, 1945–1951*. London: Allen and Unwin, 1985.

Overstreet, Gene D., and Marshall Windmiller. *Communism in India*. Los Angeles: University of California Press, 1959.

Paige, Glenn D. *The Korean Decision*. New York: Free Press, 1968.

Paik, Sun-yup. *From Pusan to Panmunjom*. Washington, D.C.: Brassey's, 1992.

Pandit, Vijaya Lakshmi. *The Scope of Happiness: A Personal Memoir*. New York: Crown, 1979.

Panikkar, K. M. *In Two Chinas*. London: Allen and Unwin, 1950.

Pearson, Lester B. *Mike: The Memoirs of the Right Honorable Lester B. Pearson*. 3 vols. Toronto: University of Toronto Press, 1973.

Peng Dehuai. *Memoirs of a Chinese Marshall—The Autobiographical Notes of Peng Dehuai*. Translated by Sheng Longpu. Edited by Sara Grimes. Beijing: Foreign Languages Press, 1984.

Pickersgill, J. W., and D. F. Foster, eds. *The Mackenzie King Record*. Vol. 4. Toronto: University of Toronto Press, 1970.

Porter, Brian. *Britain and the Rise of Communist China: A Study of British Attitudes, 1945–1954*. London: Oxford University Press, 1967.

Prados, John. *Presidents' Secret Wars: CIA and Pentagon Covert Operations from World War II Through Iranscam*. New York: William Morrow, 1986.

Ra'anan, Gavriel D. *International Policy Formation in the USSR: Factional "Debates" during the Zhdanovshchina*. Hamden, Conn.: Archon Books, 1983.

Rahman, M. M. *The Politics of Non-alignment*. New Delhi: Associated Publishing House, 1969.

Randall, Stephen J. *Colombia and the United States: Hegemony and Independence*. Athens: University of Georgia Press, 1992.

Rees, David. *Korea: The Limited War*. New York: St. Martin's, 1964.

Reese, Trevor R. *Australia, New Zealand, and the United States: A Survey of International Relations, 1941–1968*. London: Oxford University Press, 1969.

Reichard, Gary W. *The Reaffirmation of Republicanism*. Knoxville: University of Tennessee Press, 1975.

Reid, Escott. *Envoy to Nehru*. Delhi: Oxford University Press, 1981.

Resis, Albert, ed. *Molotov Remembers: Inside Kremlin Politics.* Chicago: Ivan R. Dee, 1993.

Richardson, James L. *Germany and the Atlantic Alliance.* Cambridge, Mass.: Harvard University Press, 1966.

Ridgway, Matthew B. *The Korean War.* Garden City, N.Y.: Doubleday, 1967.

Rioux, Jean-Pierre. *The Fourth Republic, 1944–1958.* Translated by Godfrey Rogers. New York: Cambridge University Press, 1987.

Riskin, Carl. *China's Political Economy: The Quest for Development since 1945.* New York: Oxford University Press, 1987.

Romulo, Carlos P., with Beth Day Romulo. *Forty Years: A Third World Soldier at the UN* Westport, Conn.: Greenwood, 1986.

Rosenberg, David Alan. "American Atomic Bomb Strategy and the Hydrogen Bomb Decision." *Journal of American History* 66 (June 1979): 62–87.

———. "The Origins of Overkill: Nuclear Weapons and American Strategy, 1945–1960." *International Security* 7 (Spring 1983): 3–71.

Rostow, W. W. *Europe after Stalin: Eisenhower's Three Decisions of March 11, 1953.* Austin: University of Texas Press, 1982.

Ruhl, Lothar. "Offensive Defense in the Warsaw Pact." *Survival* 33 (September 1991): 442–50.

Rusk, Dean. *As I Saw It.* New York: Norton, 1990.

Ryan, Mark A. *Chinese Attitudes toward Nuclear Weapons: China and the United States during the Korean War.* Armonk, N.Y.: M. E. Sharpe, 1989.

Sandusky, Michael C. *America's Parallel.* Alexandria, Va.: Old Dominion Press, 1983.

Sastroamidjojo, Ali. *Milestones on My Journey: The Memoirs of Sastroamidjojo, Indonesian Patriot and Political Leader.* St. Lucia, Queensland: University of Queensland Press, 1979.

Schaller, Michael. *The American Occupation of Japan.* New York: Oxford University Press, 1985.

———. *MacArthur: Far Eastern General.* New York: Oxford University Press, 1989.

Schnabel, James E., and Robert J. Watson. *The History of the Joint Chiefs of Staff.* 4 vols. Wilmington, Del.: Michael Glazier, 1979.

Schonberger, Howard B. "The General and the Presidency: Douglas MacArthur and the Election of 1948." *Wisconsin Magazine of History* 57 (Spring 1974): 201–19.

Schram, Stuart. *Mao Tse-tung.* New York: Simon and Schuster, 1966.

Schwartz, Thomas Alan. *America's Germany: John J. McCloy and the Federal Republic of Germany.* Cambridge, Mass.: Harvard University Press, 1991.

Segal, Gerald. *Defending China.* New York: Oxford University Press, 1985.

Shao Kuokanf. "Chou En-lai's Diplomatic Approach to Non-aligned States in Asia: 1953–1960." *China Quarterly* 78 (June 1979): 324–38.

Shi Zhe. "With Mao and Stalin: The Reminiscences of a Chinese Interpreter." Translated by Chen Jian. *Chinese Historians* 5 (Spring 1992): 35–46.

———. "I Accompanied Chairman Mao." *Far Eastern Affairs* (Moscow), no. 2 (1989): 125–33.

Shlaim, Avi. *The United States and the Berlin Blockade, 1948–1949.* Los Angeles: University of California Press, 1983.

Short, Anthony. *The Communist Insurrection in Malaya, 1948–1960.* London: Frederick Muller, 1975.

Shuckburgh, Evelyn. *Descent to Suez: Diaries 1951–56*. New York: Norton, 1986.

Shulman, Marshall. *Stalin's Foreign Policy Reappraised*. Cambridge, Mass.: Harvard University Press, 1963.

Siegfried, Andre, Edouard Bonnefous, and J. B. Duroselle. *L'Annee Politique 1951*. Paris: Presses Universitaires de France, 1952.

Simmons, Robert R. *The Strained Alliance: Peking, P'yongyang, Moscow, and the Politics of the Korean Civil War*. New York: Free Press, 1975.

Smith, Robert Aura. *Philippine Freedom, 1946–1958*. New York: Columbia University Press, 1958.

Snyder, Jack. "The Gorbachov Revolution: A Waning of Soviet Expansionism?" *International Security* 12 (Winter 1987/88): 93–131.

Spender, Percy. *Exercises in Diplomacy*. Sydney: Sydney University Press, 1969.

———. *Politics and a Man*. Sydney: Collins, 1972.

Stairs, Denis. *The Diplomacy of Constraint: Canada, the Korean War, and the United States*. Toronto: University of Toronto Press, 1974.

Stalin, J. *Economic Problems of Socialism in the USSR*. Moscow: Foreign Languages Publishing House, 1952.

"Stalin's Conversations with Chinese Leaders." *Bulletin of the Cold War International History Project* 6–7 (Winter 1995–1996): 4–29.

Stebbins, Richard P., et al. *The United States in World Affairs, 1950*. New York: Harper and Brothers, 1951.

———. *The United States in World Affairs, 1951*. New York: Harper and Brothers, 1952.

———. *The United States in World Affairs, 1952*. New York: Harper and Brothers, 1953.

Stebbins, Richard P., et al., with the assistance of Grant S. McClellan. *The United States in World Affairs, 1953*. New York: Harper and Brothers, 1955.

Stein, Arthur. *India and the Soviet Union: The Nehru Era*. Chicago: University of Chicago Press, 1969.

Steininger, Rolf. *The German Question: The Stalin Note of 1952 and the Problem of Reunification*. Translated by Jane T. Hedges. Edited by Mark Cioc. New York: Columbia University Press, 1990.

Stueck, William. *The Road to Confrontation: United States Policy toward China and Korea, 1947–1950*. Chapel Hill: University of North Carolina Press, 1981.

———. "The Limits of Influence: British Policy and American Expansion of the War in Korea." *Pacific Historical Review* 55 (February 1986): 65–95.

Suh, Dae-sook. *The Korean Communist Movement, 1918–1948*. Princeton, N.J.: Princeton University Press, 1967.

Sulzberger, C. L. *A Long Row of Candles: Memoirs and Dairies, 1934–1954*. New York: Macmillan, 1969.

Swearingen, Robert, and Paul Langer. *Red Flag in Japan: International Communism in Action, 1919–1951*. Cambridge, Mass.: Harvard University Press, 1952.

Swedish Institute of International Affairs. *Sweden and the United Nations*. New York: Manhattan Publishing, 1956.

Tannenbaum, Duane A. "The Bricker Amendment Controversy: Its Origins and Eisenhower's Role." *Diplomatic History* 9 (Winter 1985): 73–93.

Taubman, William. *Stalin's American Policy: From Entente to Détente to Cold War*. New York: Norton, 1982.

Teiwes, Frederick C. *Politics at Mao's Court: Gao Gang and Party Factionalism in the Early 1950s*. Armonk, N.Y.: M. E. Sharpe, 1990.

Trachtenberg, Marc. "A 'Wasting Asset'? American Strategy and the Shifting Nuclear

Balance, 1949–1954." *International Security* 13 (Winter 1988/89): 5–49.
Truman, Harry S. *Memoirs*. 2 vols. Garden City, N.Y.: Doubleday, 1956.
Tsui, Chak-Wing David. "Strategic Objectives of Chinese Military Intervention in Korea." *Korea and World Affairs* 16 (Summer 1992): 338–64.
Tuchman, Barbara. *Stilwell and the American Experience in China, 1911–1945*. New York: Macmillan, 1970.
Tucker, Robert C. *The Soviet Political Mind*. New York: Norton, 1971.
———. *Stalin in Power: The Revolution from Above, 1928–1941*. New York: Norton, 1990.
Ulam, Adam. *Expansion and Coexistence: The History of Soviet Foreign Policy, 1917–1967*. New York: Frederick A. Praeger, 1968.
———. *Stalin*. New York: Viking, 1973.
———. *The Communists: The Story of Power and Lost Illusions, 1948–1991*. New York: Scribner's, 1992.
Van Ree, Erik. *Socialism in One Zone: Stalin's Policy in Korea, 1945–1947*. Oxford, England: Berg, 1989.
Venkataramini, M. S. *The American Role in Pakistan, 1947–1958*. New Delhi: Radiant Publishers, 1982.
Volkogonov, Dmitri. *Stalin: Triumph and Tragedy*. Edited and translated from the Russian by Harold Shukman. New York: Grove Weidenfeld, 1988.
Vucinich, Wayne S., ed. *At the Brink of War and Peace: The Tito-Stalin Split in Historic Perspective*. New York: Brooklyn College Press, 1982.
Wall, Irwin M. *The United States and the Making of Postwar France, 1945–1954*. New York: Cambridge University Press, 1991.
Weathersby, Kathryn. "New Findings on the Korean War." *Bulletin of the Cold War International History Project* 3 (Fall 1993): 1, 14–18.
———. "The Soviet Role in the Early Phase of the Korean War: New Documentary Evidence." *Journal of American-East Asian Relations* 3 (Winter 1994): 1–33.
———. "To Attack, or Not to Attack? Stalin, Kim Il-sung, and the Prelude to War." *Bulletin of the Cold War International History Project* 5 (Spring 1995): 1–9.
———. "New Russian Documents on the Korean War." *Bulletin of the Cold War International History Project* 6–7 (Winter 1995–1996): 30–84.
———. "Soviet Aims in Korea and the Origins of the Korean War, 1945–1950: New Evidence from Russian Archives." Working Paper no. 8, Cold War International History Project, Washington, D.C.
Weis, W. Michael. *Cold Warriors and Coups d'Etat: Brazilian-American Relations, 1945–1964*. Albuquerque: University of New Mexico Press, 1993.
Werth, Alexander. *France, 1940–1955*. New York: Henry Holt, 1956.
Westad, Odd Arne. *Cold War and Revolution: Soviet-American Rivalry and the Origins of the Chinese Civil War*. New York: Columbia University Press, 1993.
Whiting, Allen S. *China Crosses the Yalu: The Decision to Enter the Korean War*. New York: Macmillan, 1960.
Whitney, Courtney. *MacArthur: His Rendezvous with History*. New York: Knopf, 1956.
Whitson, William. *The Chinese High Command*. New York: Praeger, 1973.
Williams, Philip M. *Hugh Gaitskill: A Political Biography*. London: Jonathan Cape, 1979.
———. *The Senate and U.S. Troops in Europe*. New York: St. Martin's, 1985.
———. ed. *The Diary of Hugh Gaitskill, 1945–1956*. London: Jonathan Cape, 1983.

Williams, William J., ed. *A Revolutionary War: Korea and the Transformation of the Postwar World*. Chicago: Imprint Publications, 1993.

Wiltz, John Edward. "Did the United States Betray Korea in 1905?" *Pacific Historical Review* 44 (August 1985): 243–70.

Wolfe, Thomas W. *Soviet Power and Europe, 1945–1970*. Baltimore, Md.: Johns Hopkins Press, 1970.

Wu Xiuquan. *Eight Years in the Ministry of Foreign Affairs (January 1950–October 1958)—Memoirs of a Diplomat*. Beijing: New World Press, 1985.

Xu Yan. *The First Contest*. Beijing: Chinese Radio and Television Press, 1990.

Yao Xu. "Peng Dehuai's Leadership Contribution to the War to Resist America and Aid Korea." *Kangshi Yanjiu ziliao* 1 (1983): 2–12.

Yasuhara, Yoko. "Japan, Communist China, and Export Controls in Asia, 1948–1952." *Diplomatic History* 10 (Winter 1986): 75–89.

*Yearbook of the United Nations, 1947–1953*. New York: Columbia University Press, 1952.

Yoshitsu, Michael M. *Japan and the San Francisco Peace Settlement*. New York: Columbia University Press, 1963.

Yu Song-chol. "My Testimony." Translated from Korean. *Foreign Broadcast Information Service* 90 (15 November–27 December 1990).

Zhai Qiang. "China and the Geneva Convention of 1954." *China Quarterly* 129 (March 1992): 103–22.

———. *The Dragon, the Lion, and the Eagle: Chinese-British-American Relations, 1949–1958*. Kent, Ohio: Kent State University Press, 1994.

Zhang Shuguang. " 'Preparedness Eliminates Mishaps': The CCP's Security Concerns in 1949–1950 and the Origins of Sino-American Confrontation." *The Journal of American-East Asian Relations* 1 (Spring 1992): 42–72.

———. *Deterrence and Strategic Culture: Chinese-American Confrontations, 1949–1958*. Ithaca, N.Y.: Cornell University Press, 1992.

Zhang Tong. "Recollection of the Self-Defense War against India." In *Xin Zhongguo waijiao feng yun* (Main events of new China's diplomacy), comp. Waijiobu Waijiaski bianjibu, 66–78 (Beijing: Shijie Zhishi chubanshe [World Knowledge Press], 1990).

Zhou Enlai. *Selected Works of Zhou Enlai*. Vol. 2. Beijing: Foreign Languages Press, 1989.

Zimmerman, William. "The Korean and Vietnam Wars." In *Diplomacy of Power: Soviet Armed Forces as a Political Instrument*, ed. Stephen S. Kaplan, 314–56 (Washington D.C.: Brookings Institution, 1981).

# • INDEX •

Acheson, Dean, 88; and armistice line, 212, 225, 230; and arms reductions, 240, 418n. 40; and Asia, 366; and bombing of Manchuria, 189, 408n. 143; and bombing of Yalu power stations, 283; and British peace probe, 50–51, 52–54; and buildup of Western military strength, 54–56, 74; and cease-fire in Korea, 142, 153, 210, 212; and covert activity in Southeast Asia, 421n. 140; and embargo on PRC, 173, 189–90, 191; and greater sanctions statement, 249; impact of personality of, 8, 76; and Japan, 55–56, 71; and Kennan-Malik talks, 205–6; and MacArthur firing, 179, 180–81, 182, 186, 190; and Middle East, 365; negotiations of regarding NATO, 89, 234; and POW issue, 260, 261, 263, 264, 287, 288, 298–300, 423n. 190; and Taiwan, 36, 76, 153; and UN campaign in North Korea, 90, 91, 93, 96, 97, 107, 115, 116, 118; and UN General Assembly (fall 1952), 288, 291, 293–94, 295, 298–301; under attack at home, 115, 131, 135; and "Uniting for Peace" proposal, 89; and U.S. policy toward Korea, 30, 35, 36, 37, 56, 58, 62, 74, 76, 78, 101, 116, 133, 134–38, 150, 151–52, 202, 246; and U.S. position in armistice talks, 251, 253
Adenauer, Konrad, 147, 201, 257, 273, 281, 282, 296–97, 344
Afghanistan, 57, 132, 196, 197, 353
Albania, 73, 196, 233, 352
Alden, Robert, 343
Alemán, Miguel, 429
Allen, George, 196
Allison, John, 61–62, 63, 90, 97
Anderson, Orvil, 62, 385n. 102
Arab-Asian group, 81, 94, 119, 126, 132, 139, 140–42, 152–57 passim, 164–65, 169–70, 173, 175, 178, 186, 192, 196, 256–57, 282, 291, 292–94, 295–302 passim, 311
Arab League, 82
Argentine, 197
armistice talks: adoption of agenda in, 224–25; and agreement on armistice line, 240–41, 251, 252, 266; airfields issue in, 243, 249, 250, 253, 256, 265–67; on armistice line, 225–42 passim; beginning of, 221–25; breakoff of, 229–35; and crisis of summer 1953, 336, 337, 339–41; disruptive incidents involving, 227–28, 229, 230–31, 232, 236, 237; inspection issue in, 243–44, 248, 249, 253, 265–67, 271; and item 5, 5, 264–65; package proposals in, 269, 271, 284, 287; and POW issue, 244, 250, 266–67, 270–72, 311, 313–15, 319–20, 322–23, 326; resumption of, 236–38, 310–11; rotation and replenishment issues in, 249, 250, 252–53; successful conclusion of, 340–41; U.S. recesses, 288, 291, 292
Armstrong, Orland A., 314
Asian neutrals, 4
atomic weapons, 311; as deterrent to expanded war in Korea, 48, 67, 240; Mao's view of, 99–100, 113, 121, 145–46, 306; and NATO, 350; and offshore islands crisis, 364; and Soviet peace movement, 60; Soviet view of, 161–62, 312, 351; tests of, 41, 240; and U.S. Korea policy in 1945, 18; U.S. stockpile of, 285, 351, 352; use of in Korean War, 62, 98, 121, 131–32, 133–34, 137, 145–46, 181, 183, 186, 239–40, 246, 247, 285, 306, 310, 321, 322, 324, 326
Attlee, Clement, 52, 67, 92–93, 95, 131–33, 136–38, 139–40, 148–49, 151, 156, 160, 184, 239, 320–21, 389n. 22
Austin, Warren, 57, 59–61, 63–64, 96, 139, 152, 156, 166
Australia, 335; and aid to UN in Korea, 12, 72, 73; and greater sanctions statement, 249; and Japanese peace treaty, 164, 200–201, 233; and process of unifying Korea, 108–11 passim; as restraint on U.S., 118, 165–66, 173; in UN, 57, 63, 290; and UN elections in South Korea, 26, 27; on UNCOK, 35; U.S. defense treaty with, 5, 200–201, 233, 234
Austria, 57, 275, 284, 312

bacteriological warfare, 265, 272, 275–76, 278, 424n. 203, 424–25n. 21, 426n. 56
Bajpai, Girja S., 93, 132, 162, 427n. 66
Baldwin, Hanson, 258
Balkans, 147, 196, 233, 345–46, 352, 398n. 112, 445n. 16
Bandung conference, 362–63
Barrett, Edward, 113, 260–61
Bebler, Ales, 138
Belgium, 173

Bell, Daniel, 386n. 116
Beria, Lavrentii, 32, 246, 274–75, 308, 327, 328, 341–42, 359
Berlin, 59, 88, 92, 205, 206, 221, 232, 282, 292, 341, 351, 360
Bevin, Ernest: and condemning of PRC, 153; end of era of, 136, 171; and peace probe on Korea, 50–51; and UN campaign above 38th parallel, 89, 91, 92, 95, 109, 389n. 22; under attack at home, 131; and U.S., 76–78, 89, 92, 135, 148–49
bipolarity, 83–84, 370
Boatner, Hayden, 277, 284
Bohlen, Charles, 176, 205, 237, 246, 260, 325, 329, 330, 345, 407n. 127
Bolivia, 197, 293
Bolté, Charles, 118
Bowles, Chester, 278, 308
Bradley, Omar, 88, 107; and armistice talks, 236–37; and expansion of war in Korea, 150, 194; and MacArthur firing, 179–81 passim; and MacArthur hearings, 205; and trip to Korea, 237, 240; at UN (fall 1952), 299; and UN operations above 38th parallel, 90, 95, 112, 115, 118, 202
Brazil, 173, 191, 197, 293, 311
Bricker, John, 318
Bridges, Styles, 318
Briggs, Ellis, 317, 319, 323, 331, 335, 338, 342
British Broadcast Company, 147
Bruce, David L. K., 54
buffer zone, in Korea, 116, 117–18
Bulganin, Nikolai, 123–24
Bulgaria, 23, 73, 147, 148, 196, 200, 352
Burgess, Guy, 52
Burgin, Julian, 91
Burke, Arleigh, 97, 241, 250
Burma, 41, 157, 172, 173, 192, 210, 211, 233, 254, 255, 270, 313, 421n. 140, 430
Butler, R. A., 131, 239

Cain, Harry, 131
Cairo conference: and Korea, 17; and Taiwan, 116, 123, 140, 153
Canada: aid to UN in Korea by, 12, 197; and greater sanctions statement, 249; influence on U.S., 4, 118, 130, 165–66, 171–72, 173, 177–78, 188, 298–302, 324-25; and Koje-do, 283; and MacArthur firing, 185; as source of weapons for PRC, 127; in UN, 63, 95–96, 118, 152–53, 156, 164–65, 170, 173, 294, 298–303 passim; and UN elections in South Korea, 26, 27; on UNCOK, 35
Capehart, Homer, 182, 191
Capps, Arlie, 85
Cepicka, Alexej, 161
Ceylon, 192
Chase, William C., 305, 306
Cheju Island, 28, 336
Chen Jian, 64
Chen Yun, 247
Chile, 110, 197, 293
China, 335; changing position of, 355; civil war in, 3, 11, 28, 33–34, 35, 37, 38, 75–76, 98, 139, 218, 244, 245, 261, 270; economic backwardness of, 45; emergence as major power, 127; historic involvement in Korea, 13, 16, 39, 45; importance of Korea to, 25; and Korea between world wars, 15; and Korea during World War II, 16–17; and Korean trusteeship, 17, 22; Manchu dynasty of, 13; Nationalist government of, and Korea, 16–17; Soviet jets in, 41; Stalin and, 4; treaty with Soviet Union (1945), 34; treaties with Soviet Union (1950), 34, 38–39, 41–44; UN condemnation of, 149; U.S. intentions toward, 125; U.S. naval blockade of, 134, 137, 149–50
China, Nationalist, 169, 366; activities in Southeast Asia, 254; compared to ROK, 28, 356; and Japanese peace treaty, 201, 258; and MacArthur firing, 185; mainland collapse of, 29; offers troops to Korea, 72, 194–95; operations against mainland by, 102, 104, 150, 305, 306; as participant in Four-Power conference, 154; and POW issue, 244, 252, 259, 261–62, 268, 270; saved by Korean War, 363–64; U.S. aid to, 6, 30, 37–38, 52, 53, 66–70, 150, 193
China, People's Republic of: admitted to UN, 50–51, 52–53, 58, 59–61, 64, 92, 102, 104–5, 135, 139, 143, 158, 193; aid to India by, 187; and armistice, 344; and armistice line, 225, 227; attitude of (fall 1952), 291–92, 303–6; and beginning of armistice talks, 216–21, 223–24; and break-off of armistice talks, 230–35 passim; concern about atomic weapons, 98, 99–100; condemnation by UN, 135, 140, 142, 151–66 passim, 177; conditions in, 219–20, 247–48; decision to cross 38th parallel, 143–45, 357–58; delegation travels to USSR (1952), 285–86; and entry into Korean War, 8, 62–65, 83, 90, 91, 93–106, 347, 351, 354, 357; and

final concessions on Korea, 328–30, 362, 443n. 211; and Four-Power conference, 140; and GOC, 170–71, 176; growing air power of, 231–32, 237, 248; "hate America" campaign in, 52, 65, 434n. 246; impact of Korean War on, 362–64; and India, 197, 278–80; and interest in negotiations on Korea, 207–8; invasion of Tibet by, 119; and item 3 in armistice talks, 252–53; and Japanese peace treaty, 201, 219, 232–33; and MacArthur, 175–77 passim, 183, 185; miscalculations of, 354, 359; negotiations in UN by, 138–42 passim; as permanent factor in Korean War, 7, 361; position in armistice talks at end of 1951, 249–50; and POW issue, 251–52, 262, 269–73, 278–81, 284, 291–92, 303–7, 320, 324, 362; recognized by U.K. and India, 39; relations with Soviet Union, 6–7, 33–34, 37, 44, 100, 101, 120, 121, 136, 145, 162, 171, 206, 207, 211, 217, 218–19, 273, 327–28, 346, 355, 358, 362–65, 366, 425n. 28; relations with U.S., 6, 42–43, 69, 93, 97–103 passim, 117, 121–22, 162, 171, 175–76, 186, 206, 207, 258–59, 346–47; sanctions against, 152, 169–74 passim, 183, 189–93, 237, 285, 287, 289–90, 296, 343; and seven-power conference, 171, 177; and Southeast Asia, 254; spring 1951 offensive of, 185, 187, 188–89, 190, 193, 195, 198, 204, 205; surprised at Western response to North Korean attack, 52; and Taiwan, 39, 41, 45, 50, 52, 65, 69, 93, 97–102, 116, 130–31, 135, 139, 143, 153, 158, 162, 177, 186, 201, 220, 312, 319, 346–47, 358; as target of greater sanctions statement, 244; Three Anti–Five Anti campaign in, 275, 420n. 94; and trade with Japan, 255; troops of in Korean War, 4; UN prisoners held in, 245

Chinese People's Volunteers: change in tactics of, 216–17, 220, 221; condition of, 144, 159; confusion in U.S. regarding size and aims of, 111–13; counteroffensive of (Nov. 1950), 127–29, 145; DPRK troops under authority of, 143; and epidemics, 276; fall 1952 offensive of, 291, 305; February 1951 offensive of, 167; first campaign of, 111, 113–15 passim; interaction with North Koreans, 217–18; Korean War as training ground for, 282; and limited offensives of 1951 and 1953, 280; make contact with enemy, 111; Mao's original plans for, 120–21; New Year's offensive of, 129–30, 145, 149, 151, 157; ordered into Korea, 106; ordered to stay on defensive, 247; and POW issue, 252, 295; prepares for sixth phase offensive, 232; second campaign of, 119; and spring 1951 offensives, 168–69, 175–76, 177, 179, 181, 354; and spring 1953 offensive, 325–26; and summer 1953 offensive, 340

Chipman, Warwick, 162
Chipyong-ni, battle of, 167–68
Chistiakov, Ivan, 20
Cho Man-sik, 21, 40
Cho, Pyung Ok, 108, 213
Church, John, 47
Churchill, Winston: and British politics, 76–77, 277; dislike of trusteeship of, 18; and Eisenhower, 312, 315; recaptures power, 239; and spring 1953 crisis in Anglo-American relations, 320–21, 324–25; trips to U.S., 254, 257–58, 315
Clark, Mark: aggressive inclinations of, 284, 285, 286, 288–89, 330; and armistice, 342; and British, 324; and POW issue, 286, 288–89, 306–7, 329; and Rhee, 317, 319, 323, 324, 330–38 passim, 442n. 185; succeeds Ridgway, 284; and summer 1953 negotiations with Communists, 339–40, 341
Clubb, O. Edmund, 69, 97, 113
Cold War, 3, 274, 275, 302–3, 304, 348, 357, 360, 368–69
Collins, J. Lawton, 62, 86, 118, 133, 137, 143, 151, 179, 180, 322, 337
Colombia, 195, 431n. 176
Colson, Charles, 276
Colville, Jock, 315
Cominform, 125, 147, 282, 401n. 196
Connally, Tom, 36, 154
Conservative Party (U.K.), 131, 191–92, 239, 321
Cooper, John Sherman, 321
Corrigan, Frank, 204
Cory, Thomas, 204, 440n. 128
counterfactual analysis, 7, 70, 351–52
Critchley, T. K., 317
Cuba, 353
Cumings, Bruce, 361, 373n. 1, 376n. 74
Czechoslovakia, 26, 160, 281, 298, 314, 331, 341

Davies, John Paton, 118, 205
Dean, Gordon, 239
Democratic Front for the Unification of the Fatherland, 31, 40

Democratic Party (U.S.), 77, 106, 114–15, 182, 264, 284, 318–19
Deng Chao, 112
Deng Hua, 167, 224, 230, 232, 305
Dening, Esler, 319, 324
Dingman, Roger, 367
Dirksen, Everett, 321
Dodd, Francis, 263, 269, 271, 276, 277
Douglas, Lewis, 77
Doyle, James, 85
Duce, Terry, 161–62
Dulles, John Foster: and armistice in Korea, 343, 345; attacked by Vishinsky, 124; characterized by Churchill, 315; in election campaign of 1952, 283, 297; and Japan, 54, 56, 123, 164, 185, 200–201, 401n. 188; and Nehru, 329; and post-armistice U.S. policy, 367; and Republican Right, 318–19, 438n. 77; and resumption of armistice talks, 310; and Rhee, 316–17, 331, 337; Soviet attack on, 312; and Taiwan, 116
Durbrow, Elbridge, 205

East Germany, 54, 281–82, 327, 328, 341–42
Eban, Abba, 154, 414n. 84
Eden, Anthony, 249, 272, 278, 290, 298, 299, 300, 315, 344
Egypt, 279; and Arab nationalism, 196, 255, 365–66; and Korean issue, 57, 81–82, 173, 365–66; and six-power conference, 178; and Suez Canal zone, 239, 256, 315, 366
Ehrenburg, Ilya, 412n. 8
Eisenhower, Dwight: applies pressure on Communists in Korea, 328–29, 330; and armistice in Korea, 342; compared to Truman, 137; early actions as president, 306, 309; election of, 297–98; and expansion of war, 321–22, 324, 348; first crisis of as president, 315–25 passim; as NATO commander, 146, 156, 164, 350; as perceived by PRC, 305; post-armistice policies of, 366–67; as president-elect, 299, 305, 316; as presidential candidate, 284, 297; and resumption of armistice talks, 310–11; and Rhee, 316–17, 319–20, 331, 333, 334, 338–39, 442n. 189; 16 April 1953 speech of, 311–12
Elizalde, Mike, 72, 407n. 114
Engen, Hans, 103, 440n. 128
Entezam, Nasrollah, 96, 124, 141, 170–71, 432n. 192
Eritrea, 74
Ethiopia, 74, 173, 195
Europe, as factor in great power calculations

regarding Korea, 4, 28, 33, 36, 42, 46, 63, 66, 73–74, 75, 78, 79, 96, 102, 104, 114, 146, 147, 148, 149, 150, 161, 163, 180, 183, 194, 196, 198, 217, 233, 239–40, 245, 273, 281–82, 349, 356
European Coal and Steel Community, 201, 254, 281, 350
European Defense Community, 246, 257, 273, 274, 281, 296, 344

Faure, Edgar, 257
Fawzi Bey, Mahmoud, 81
Fechteler, William, 287
France: and admission of Greece and Turkey to NATO, 200; in Africa, 57; and call for PRC withdrawal from Korea, 117; and condemnation of PRC, 156; contribution to UN effort in Korea, 72, 73–74, 167, 194–95; and fall 1952 UN General Assembly, 291, 296–97; fears in, 54, 79–80, 131–32, 202; and German rearmament, 55, 71, 79, 88, 89, 92, 123, 147, 201, 234, 246, 273, 281, 297; and greater sanctions statement, 249; and Indochina, 5, 17, 41–42, 362, 366; and MacArthur firing, 184; military buildup in, 70, 79; and Morocco, 256; peace movement in, 79; political crisis in, 257; proposed meeting with U.S. and U.K., 324; and raw materials issue, 199, 239; reaction in to Korean armistice, 345; as restraint on U.S., 46, 118, 135, 173, 190, 239–40; and Saar, 257, 296–97; and Soviet overtures of 1953, 309, 312; Stalin's characterization of, 275, 296; and Stalin's proposal on Germany, 273; support for Yugoslavia, 5, 200; on UNCOK, 35; vulnerability of to air attack, 113; vulnerability to air attack, 113
Franks, Oliver, 109, 149, 150, 155–56, 165, 181–82, 188
Freeman, Paul, 167

Gaitskill, Hugh, 156
Gao Gang, 143, 217, 223, 304, 364, 446n. 39
Gascoigne, Alvary, 95, 150–51
Geneva conference of 1954, 361, 362
Geneva convention of 1949, 244, 252, 260
Germany: and attack on Soviet Union, 33–34; connection to Korea, 205, 221, 256, 265; effect of air attacks on, 112; fate of POWs of, 244; foreign ministers' meeting on, 176, 177; May 1952 Soviet note on, 281–82; and neutralization, 246, 273–75; and 1930s, 4, 16; peace treaty with, 312; possible elections in, 273–74; and Soviet overtures of

1953, 309, 328; and Soviet-U.S. conflict, 24, 123, 312
Grafstrom, Sven, 171, 178, 205
Graves, Hubert, 90–91
Great Britain (*see* United Kingdom)
Greece: conditions in, 147; contribution to UN effort in Korea, 72, 73, 194, 195, 196; great power tensions over, 24; and MacArthur firing, 184; and NATO, 5, 73, 88, 147, 199–200, 219, 234, 246, 349; and Soviet Union, 345; support of U.S. by, 132; U.S. aid to, 24
Gromyko, Andrei, 50, 176, 209, 210, 234, 282, 431n. 163
Gross, Ernest, 187, 278, 279–80, 290, 299, 300
Guam, 67

Hainan, 39
Hallinan, Vincent, 286, 429n. 127
Hammarskjold, Dag, 309
Hanley, James, 245
Harriman, W. Averell, 68, 179
Harrison, William: and POW issue, 313, 314, 329; recesses armistice talks, 288, 322, 325; and summer 1953 negotiations, 340, 342
Henderson, Loy, 132
Herriot, Edward, 296
Hickenlooper, Bourke, 319
Hickerson, John, 171, 181, 299
Hitler, Adolph, 112, 114, 292, 352
Ho Chi Minh, 35, 39
Hodge, John, 20–21, 23
Holland, Sydney, 73
Honduras, 431n. 176
Hong Kong, 66, 72, 90, 122, 172, 191, 206–7, 211, 366
Hoover, Herbert, 146, 257
Howard, Roy, 336
Hughes, Emmett John, 310
Hull, John, 261, 262, 263
Humphrey, Hubert, 182
Hungary, 147, 196, 352
Hunt, Michael, 9

Iceland, 219
ideology, 8, 354–55
Inchon landing, 78–79, 85–86, 88, 91–92, 98, 100, 104, 106, 114–15, 143, 160, 354, 356–57
India, 171; and admission of PRC to UN, 51, 59, 80, 319; and aid from PRC, 187; conflict with Pakistan, 196–97; contribution to UN effort in Korea, 58, 72, 196; and Eisenhower, 312; and embargo on PRC, 192; and fall 1952 UN General Assembly, 290, 294, 298–305 passim, 388n. 154, 434n. 239; impact of Korean armistice on, 211; and Japanese peace treaty, 233; and Mexican peace proposal, 290; and nonaggression pact with PRC, 430n. 159; peace probes of, 51–54, 63–64, 78, 86–87, 118, 119, 139–40, 196, 278–80, 284, 291; and post-armistice political conference, 344; recognizes PRC, 35; refuses to serve on GOC, 170; on repatriation commission, 313, 314, 315, 319, 331, 338, 437n. 45; and resolution condemning PRC, 152–66 passim; and resolution on POWs, 298–305 passim, 319–20, 322; as restraint on U.S., 4, 130, 132, 165, 298–303; and six-power conference, 178; and South Koreans, 317, 331; supports UN response to North Korean attack, 51, 52, 80; and Taiwan, 67, 80; and UN campaign above 38th parallel, 93–94, 97, 118, 119; and UN elections in South Korea, 26; on UNCOK, 35; and U.S. action against Manchuria, 188
Indochina: conditions in, 80, 164, 210, 211, 249, 310; French forces in, 57; PRC interest in, 39, 41, 98, 172, 249, 346, 364–65; U.S. policy toward, 6, 30, 36, 41–42, 43, 53, 80, 81, 312, 346, 366; and World War II, 17, 18
Indonesia, 80, 152, 233, 234, 254, 284, 311, 313, 314
Interim Committee on Korea, 107–10 passim
International Materials Conference, 199
Iran: and Arab nationalism, 196, 255; crises over, 24, 192, 239; impact of armistice on, 210, 211; and Soviet Union, 57–58, 82, 147; support of U.S. by, 132
Iraq, 57–58, 81, 239, 296
Israel, 343; orientation of toward West, 366; reaction in to Korean armistice, 345; and UN action on Korea, 52, 81, 94, 154, 156, 196
Italy: and African colonies, 17; fall of government in, 344; fears of, 147; and MacArthur firing, 184; and 1930s, 4, 16, 151–52, 173; and Trieste, 344–45

Jacobs, Joseph, 24
Japan, 11, 118, 137, 221; annexes Korea, 13, 331; Communist Party of, 35; economic conditions in, 5, 24, 55, 71, 233, 344, 367–68; fate of POWs of, 244, 260; fears in, 54; historic involvement in Korea, 13, 102; impact of Korean War on, 5, 43, 63, 71, 78, 233, 367–68; importance of Korea to, 24–25; and Indochina, 17; involvement in Ko-

rean War, 3–4, 5, 195, 233; and Korea between world wars, 15; and MacArthur firing, 185; and 1930s, 16, 102, 151–52, 246; and origins of Korean War, 31–32, 36; peace treaty with, 5, 55–56, 71, 123, 143, 161, 162, 164, 180, 185, 199, 200–201, 219, 230, 232–34, 254–55, 283; rearmament of, 56, 71, 122, 124, 219, 232, 344, 368; response in, to armistice, 344; and Rhee, 32, 277; as source of weapons for PRC, 127, 219; and Soviet Union, 312, 322; Stalin's characterization of, 275; and trade with Communists, 254–55, 367, 368; UN military action in Korea from, 12, 48, 70, 71, 72, 195, 344, 356, 368; and U.S. defense perimeter, 30, 53; U.S. defense treaty with, 5, 71, 123, 164, 232–33, 246, 255; vulnerability of, 134, 135, 146, 151, 322; and World War II, 18, 73, 346

Jebb, Gladwyn, 59, 132, 139, 153, 155–56, 166, 190, 191, 427n. 80

Jessup, Philip, 88, 205, 291

Jiang Jieshi, 28, 29, 30, 37–38, 53, 67, 69, 116, 122, 139, 149, 179, 193, 194, 261, 270, 295, 306, 319, 343, 346, 367, 374n. 34

Jinmen, 50, 364

Johnson, Edwin, 205

Johnson, Louis, 62, 66, 68, 71, 88

Johnson, U. Alexis, 97, 259, 261, 262, 263, 264, 423n. 190, 423–24n. 199

Jordan, 81

Joy, Turner, 222, 224, 225, 227–29, 230, 238, 241, 250, 261, 266, 268, 271, 284

Judd, Walter, 323

Kaesong, 227, 228, 230, 232, 235; chosen as site for negotiations, 209–10, 215; contest for in talks, 238, 242; end of neutralization of, 324, 329; movement of negotiations out of, 236–38; neutralization of, 228; opening of armistice talks at, 221–22; seized by Communists, 10, 221

Kaplan, Karel, 161

Kasaniev, Vasily, 103, 440n. 128

Kashmir, 73, 81, 197, 343, 347, 388n. 154

Katsuo, Okayaki, 344

Kelly, David, 50

Kem, James, 174, 191

Kennan, George, 61, 133, 134–35, 205–6, 216, 217, 221, 285–86, 292, 431n. 166

Kennedy, Joseph, 146

Khan, Liaquat Ali, 73, 197

Khrushchev, Nikita, 5, 36, 37, 104–5, 327, 353, 431n. 161

Ki Fu-chun, 364

Kim Il-sung, 353; background of, 21, 37, 143, 362; and beginning of armistice talks, 216, 223; Clark's letters to, 306–7, 329; and Communist China, 3, 29, 31, 37, 39, 45, 98, 106, 120, 143–44, 203, 357; concern about Japan, 31–32; and crisis of summer 1953, 339; dependence on Soviets and Chinese, 247–48, 270, 273, 361; dissimulation campaign of June 1950, 40–41, 379–80n. 137; impact of his personality on Korean War, 8, 31, 359; impatience with Chinese, 218; miscalculations of, 355–56; rise of, in North Korea, 21; and second march into South Korea, 143–44, 145; and Soviet Union, 3, 4, 21, 31, 36, 98, 106, 203, 357; and Stalin's advice, 307

Kim Ku, 21, 23, 26–27

Kim Kyu-sik, 23, 26–27

Kim Tu-bong, 22

King, W. L. Mackenzie, 26

Kiraly, Bela, 352

Kirk, Alan, 200, 209

Knowland, William, 306, 318, 319, 321, 323, 336, 347, 438n. 77

Koh, B. C., 361

Koje-do, 261–62, 263–64, 266, 268, 271, 276–78, 281, 283, 284, 429n. 115

Kojong (king of Korea), 22–23

Koo, Wellington, 182, 438n. 76

Korea: arrival of U.S. troops in 1945, 19; balance of military forces in, 28, 29, 202–3, 210, 221, 234–35, 241–42, 253, 262, 275–76, 280–81, 291, 305, 354; Communist movement in, 14–15, 22; in Confucian system, 13, 16; division of, 3, 19, 270; factional politics in, 14; as "hermit kingdom," 13; impact of World War II on, 16–19; Independence Club in, 14; invasions of, 13; as loser in Korean War, 360–61; as peripheral to calculations of other nations, 4; possible negotiations on, 204–10, 347; pre-1940 U.S. relations with, 16; ruled by Japan, 13–14; Soviet-U.S. Joint Commission on, 22, 23, 24; strategic significance of, 4, 16, 24–25; traditional Chinese role in, 13, 39; and treaty with U.S. (1882), 16, 22–23; trusteeship for, 17, 22; U.S. considers unification of, 61–64, 76–78, 87, 89–90, 92–93, 107–11; withdrawal of foreign troops from, 122, 145, 177, 206, 210, 224, 243, 256; Yi dynasty in, 14, 15, 21

Korea, Democratic People's Republic of (*see also* North Korea): and armistice line, 225,

227, 230; and beginning of armistice talks, 216–21 passim, 223–24; and breakoff of armistice talks, 230–35 passim; conditions in, 20, 21–22, 27, 247–48; creation of, 27; deceit in preparing attack on South, 40–41; and final Communist concessions (1953) 327, 329–30; interest in continued fighting, 50, 70, 120, 142–43; labeled aggressor, 177; message to UN, 186–87; military superiority over South Korea, 11, 29, 47, 48, 50, 52, 77–78; miscalculations of, 354, 356; position in armistice talks at end of 1951, 249–50; and POWs, 245, 250, 261–62, 270, 273; promotes subversive activities in South, 28, 31; relations with China, 6–7, 105–6, 120, 142–43, 270, 331, 362; relations with Soviet Union, 6–7, 43, 78–79, 105, 142–43, 176, 206, 270, 331, 362; role in buffer zone, 116, 120; second move into South Korea, 128–29, 142–43; status at UN, 60–61, 369; U.S. view of intentions of, 30, 356

Korea, People's Republic of, 19–20

Korea, Republic of (*see also* South Korea): army of, overrun by North Koreans, 11, 47, 48; army of, pummeled by Chinese, 128, 168, 169, 338, 340, 341; army of, in spring 1953 CPV offensive, 325; and beginning of armistice talks, 213–15; builds up army, 179, 285, 323, 329; and campaign in North Korea, 111, 118, 120; creation of, 27; elections in, 37; fails to appear at armistice signing, 342; interest in continued fighting, 50, 70, 142–43, 213–15; and item 5 in armistice talks, 243; and MacArthur firing, 185; military contribution in war, 194, 198; 1952 crisis in, 277, 281; and POWs, 244, 250, 251, 261–62, 319, 330; relations with Japan, 31–32; status at UN, 60–61, 90, 107, 294–95, 369; surprise of officials at North Korean attack, 10–11; troops cross 38th parallel, 94, 97, 99, 204; UN aid to, 3–4, 11–12, 56–58, 75; and unification of Korea, 90, 92, 107–11, 114, 214–15, 316–17; U.S. aid to, 29, 445n. 26; U.S. attitude toward, 35–36, 75–76, 356; U.S. defense pact with, 5, 316, 323, 331, 336, 337, 338, 342; withdraws troops after armistice, 343

Korean Democratic Party, 21, 27–28

Korean independence movement, 14–15

Korean National Democratic Front, 22

Korean War: and analogy with 1930s, 4–5, 12, 43; as civil war, 59–60, 130–31; as confrontation of alien cultures and ideologies, 228, 267, 354–55, 357–59; as context for POW issue, 244–45, 269–72; global impact of, 3, 4–7, 46, 347, 360, 361, 370; impact of ideology in, 8, 355; impact on Middle East, 365–66; impact on Soviet empire, 327; impact on UN, 368–70; and Japan, 5, 43, 63, 71, 78, 233, 367–68; multilateral nature of, 3–4, 12–13; paradoxes of, 370; and prestige of China, 6, 65, 362–63; risk of global war as result of, 4, 46, 101, 138, 148, 160–62, 240, 256, 259, 320, 322, 348, 370; and Sino-American relations, 6, 363–65, 366; and Sino-Soviet relations, 6–7, 327–28, 362–63, 367, 370; as substitute for World War III, 3, 46, 348–53; as tragedy, 353–60; and U.S.-Latin American relations, 293

Kurile Islands, 18

Kuznetsov, Vassillii, 328, 339–40

Labor party (U.K.), 76, 79, 131, 191–92, 199, 239, 246, 279

Lacoste, Francis, 190

Lamb, Lionel, 218, 247

Laos, 310, 319

Latin America, 71–72, 74, 197–98, 292–93

League of Nations, 151, 170, 173

Lebanon, 81

Lee, Chae-Jin, 361

Lee Joo Yun, 144

Lehman, Herbert, 182

Li Kenong, 224

Li Mi, 255, 421n. 140

Li Sang Zho, 250, 251

Libby, Ruthven, 250, 251, 266, 287, 289

Liberia, 74, 132

Lie, Trygve, 37, 56, 68, 96, 139, 141, 176, 286, 290, 309, 378–79n. 109, 421n. 139

Lin Biao, 98, 100, 145

Liu Zhaoqi, 34, 37

Lloyd, Selwyn, 296, 298–99, 300, 345

Lodge, Henry Cabot, 309–10, 329

Longo, Luigi, 401n. 196

Lovett, Robert, 43, 251, 260, 261, 263, 287, 299

Lu Zuofu, 105

Luxembourg, 58

Macao, 192

MacArthur, Douglas, 103; address to Congress of, 183, 185, 190; aggressive inclination of, 57, 62, 75, 95, 107, 113–14, 125, 174–76, 211, 357, 359; appointed UN commander in Korea, 56; authority of, 156; background of, 65–66; and campaign in

North Korea, 90, 91, 94, 95, 96, 106–19 passim, 121, 127–28, 347, 362; criticized by U.S. allies, 131, 132, 150–51, 181–82, 184; desire to expand war beyond Korea, 129–30, 131, 149–50, 175, 284; and early days of war, 44; and Eisenhower, 305; at end of World War II, 18; and expansion of ROK army, 198; firing of, 159–60, 170, 178, 214, 219, 406n. 77; firing of, foreign reaction to, 184–87, 219; firing of, reasons for, 178–82, 194; impact of his personality on Korean War, 8, 11, 76, 106–7, 359; and Inchon landing, 85–86, 355–56; and Japan, 55, 56, 66; orders aid to South Korea, 11; pessimism of, 134, 135, 144, 149, 150–51, 399n. 126; and plans for counteroffensive, 63; and Taiwan, 66–70; and testimony before Congress, 194–95; ultimatum to North Korea, 99, 106; and UN contributions to Korea, 58; and U.S. defense perimeter, 30; visits South Korea, 27; at Wake Island, 106–7, 348

McCarthy, Joseph, 53, 131, 182, 318–19, 321

McClure, Robert, 244–45

Maclean, Donald, 52

Malan, Daniel, 74

Malaya, 41, 66, 72, 172, 191, 211, 311, 312

Malenkov, Georgii, 32, 123, 274, 290, 308, 327, 359

Malik, Jacob: in General Assembly, 88, 94, 141, 145, 256–57, 290, 430n. 158; and Japan, 123, 401n. 188; and 1953 Zhou initiative to end war, 440n. 128; and possible negotiations on Korea, 204–9 passim, 212, 216, 217, 220, 225, 414n. 84; and Taiwan, 67; in UN Security Council, 59–61, 63–64, 282

Manchuria, 43, 279; bacteriological warfare in, 265, 272; Korean Communist movement in, 14, 15, 21, 105; PRC forces in, 65, 79, 90, 98, 101, 115, 117, 231–32, 279, 280, 283; as source of CPV supplies in Korea, 130; Soviet and Chinese preparations in, 146, 180–81, 364; Soviet presence in, 4, 24, 34, 104, 172, 180–81, 217, 218, 351, 363; strategic location of, 16, 111, 143; UN action prohibited in, 89–90, 95; UN bombing of, 69, 93, 111, 113, 115, 119, 133–34, 146, 150, 183, 186, 187–89, 193, 232, 279, 280, 283, 310, 322, 324, 329, 348–49, 396n. 43, 439n. 97; and Yalta agreements, 18

Mao Zedong: aims in Korea, 125–26, 143, 159, 220; approves North Korean attack, 31, 37; and armistice line, 225, 227, 230; and bacteriological warfare, 424n. 203; and beginning of armistice talks, 216–17, 223; calls off fall 1951 offensive, 232, 235, 247; compared to Nixon, 355; and CPV action in winter 1951, 158–59; cultivates Indians, 52; and decision to enter Korean War, 8, 98–106, 363; desire for armistice, 275–76; and final Communist concessions in Korea, 327; impact of his personality on Korean War, 8, 99–100, 144, 168, 220, 280, 359; Korea policy in summer 1950, 50, 51, 52, 64–65; motives in decisions on Korean War, 8, 37–40, 45–46, 64–65, 119–21, 125, 143–46 passim, 157–60, 235, 247–48, 280–81, 282–83, 305–6, 309, 325–26, 354, 357–58, 445–46n. 29; and nonaggression pact with India, 430n. 159; as perceived by U.S., 42; perceives U.S. weakness in armistice talks, 231, 253, 281; and POW issue, 273, 280, 309, 359; reaction to early Eisenhower actions, 306–7; relationship with Korean Communists, 15, 29, 45; relationship with Soviet Union, 33–34, 37–38, 157–58, 363–64; and resumption of armistice talks, 237, 309; and spring 1951 offensives, 168–69, 177, 202–3; and spring 1953 CPV offensive, 325–26; strategy in war, 112–13, 216, 358; and summer 1953 CPV offensive, 340; and United Kingdom, 278; visits Soviet Union, 34, 38; warns of UN landing at Inchon, 78

Marshall, Charles Burton, 157–58, 206–7, 208, 259–60

Marshall, George, 335; and aid to Europe, 24; and armistice talks, 211; becomes secretary of defense, 89; and crisis of late 1950, 133, 135, 137; and expansion of war beyond Korea, 150; fears of, 348, 359–60; and firing of MacArthur, 179–80; impact of his personality on Korean War, 8, 114–15; and MacArthur hearings, 193; and Taiwan, 193; and UN operations above 38th parallel, 90, 94, 107, 114–15, 175, 348

Marshall Plan, 173, 202

Martin, Joseph, 179

Martin, Kingsley, 343, 347

Matsu, 364

Matthews, Francis, 62, 69, 88

Matthews, H. Freeman, 263

Menderes, Adnan, 345

Menon, M. Gopala, 140

Menon, V. K. Krishna, 51, 294–96, 298–305 passim, 309–10, 432n. 179

Menzies, A. R., 105–6

Menzies, Robert, 73, 165
Merchant, Livingston, 90–91, 97
Merrill, John, 40
Mexico, 94, 173, 197, 286, 287, 289, 290, 293, 295–96, 302, 429n. 130, 430n. 158
Milward, R. S. 214
Molotov, V. M., 24, 32, 308, 315, 325, 329
Moody, Blair, 182
Morocco, 256, 291, 303
Morrison, Herbert, 178, 181, 186, 189, 191, 208–9, 214, 312
Moscow Agreements (1945), 22, 24
Moscow International Economic Conference, 273, 274
Mossadeq, Mohammed, 192, 239
Muccio, John, 28, 107–8, 215, 373n. 3
Murphy, Robert, 286, 319, 322
Munsan-ni, 222, 223, 229, 237, 271
Murrow, Edward R., 321

Nam Il, 222–25 passim, 227–29, 238, 248, 313, 314, 325, 340, 341, 342
Nazi-Soviet pact, 309
Nehru, Jawaharlal: domestic concerns of, 80–81, 381n. 8, 388n. 149, 388n. 153; and Dulles threat, 329; and fear of Soviet Union and China, 80–81; policy on Korea, 51, 79–80, 91, 93, 119, 139–40, 153–57 passim, 162–63, 165, 196, 278–79, 301–2; response to armistice, 444n. 232; and Stalin's death, 329; and suspicions of West, 80, 302–3, 388n. 153
Nenni, Pietro, 282, 431n. 166
Nesterov, Michael, 274
Netherlands, 12, 95, 96, 117, 118, 131, 209
New Zealand, 5, 12, 73, 153, 197, 200–201, 233, 234, 249
Nicaragua, 431n. 176
Nie Rongzhen, 91, 99–100, 144
Nitze, Paul, 42, 181, 260
Nixon, Richard, 182, 355
Noble, Harold Joyce, 10–11
Nomura, Kichisaburo, 97, 112
North Atlantic Treaty Organization, 35; buildup during Korean War, 5–6, 43, 71, 73–74, 78, 79, 88, 96, 123, 137–38, 164, 199–200, 219, 234, 246, 264–65, 273, 297, 349–50, 360; and crisis over POWs (1953), 331; disunity in, 52, 79, 96, 105, 123, 148, 181, 212–13, 215, 246, 257, 299, 322, 324; and MacArthur firing, 184; ministers applaud Eisenhower, 312; and possible entry of Sweden into, 196; and Ridgway, 272; significance of POW issue to, 245; support for resistance to North Korea, 5; weakness in relation to Soviet bloc forces, 4–5, 46, 54–55, 82, 137, 148, 410n. 179, 445n. 16
North Korea (see also Korea, Democratic People's Republic of): bacteriological warfare in, 265, 272; conditions in, 20–22, 27, 234, 309, 329–30; CPV behavior in, 217–18; CPV enters, 101; first CPV campaign in, 111, 113–14; losses incurred in war, 361; possible elections in, 77, 108–11; possible PRC operations in, 100, 101, 117; Soviets in, 20–22, 218; sponsors North-South conference, 26–27; UN march into, 76, 89–90, 94–111 passim; U.S. bombing of, 80, 247, 248, 270, 276, 279, 280, 285, 286–87, 322, 324, 329, 345, 439n. 97; U.S. demands inspection of, 212, 253
North Korean Communist Party, 21
Norway, 57, 103
NSC-68, 42–43, 349
NSC-81, 63, 76, 89–90, 121
Nye, Archibald, 93

O'Dwyer, William, 204
Ongjin, 10, 168
Organization of American States, 71
Osan, 47, 86
Outer Mongolia, 39

Pace, Frank, 348, 359
Pacific Pact, 35
Padilla Nervo, Luis, 171, 178, 186, 292–93
Paek Tu Chin, 334
Paik Yun Sup, 332
Pak Hon-yong, 22, 23, 186
Pak Il-u, 218
Pakistan, 58, 72–73, 81, 93, 110, 153, 196–97, 211, 284, 313, 314, 315
Palar, Lambertus, 187, 295
Palestine, 81–82, 136, 347
Pandit, Vijaya Lakshmi, 272, 278, 294, 425n. 25, 427n. 66
Panikkar, V. M.: leaves PRC, 279; peace probe of, 51, 140; and PRC entry into Korean War, 90–91, 93, 94, 97, 99, 100, 105, 357; and PRC interest in negotiations (1951), 171, 176, 186; and PRC probe of 1952, 278–80, 284, 425n. 25; and PRC terms for ending Korean War, 153, 278–79; and resolution condemning PRC, 157, 158; singled out by PRC, 52, 158; and Sino-Soviet relations, 218
Panmunjom, 222–23, 224, 237, 238, 243, 244, 247, 250, 252, 255, 258, 262–66 passim,

269–73 passim, 276, 278, 280, 284, 285, 287–94, 296, 302, 309, 310, 311, 313, 315, 316, 318–32 passim, 337–40 passim
Panyushkin, Alexander, 328
Pearson, Lester: and Acheson, 56; and condemnation of PRC, 152–53, 165–66; and crisis of late 1950, 139–40, 141, 142; and Malik's speech, 208; and March 1951 U.S. overtures to PRC, 177; response to armistice, 343–44; and spring 1953 negotiations in Korea, 315, and UN campaign in North Korea, 95–96; in UN General Assembly (fall 1952), 298–300, 309
Peers, Roy, 105
Peng Dehuai: and armistice, 342; and armistice line, 225, 230; and beginning of armistice talks, 216–17, 223; and change in CPV tactics, 220, 221; Clark's letters to, 306–7, 329; and CPV crossing of 38th parallel, 144; and crisis of summer 1953, 339; and fall 1951 offensive, 232, 234–35; and North Koreans, 218; ordered to stay on defensive, 247; and PRC intervention in Korea, 99, 100; and PRC victory in Korea, 362; reassured by Mao, 248, 253; and rotation of CPV troops, 282; and spring 1951 offensives, 168–69, 177; and spring 1953 CPV offensive, 325–26; and winter 1951 offensives, 158, 168
Permanent Committee of the Peace Movement, 60
Perón, Juan, 197
Peru, 197, 296, 298, 302
Phibun Songhram, Luang, 74
Philippines: on AMC, 173; contribution to UN effort in Korea, 58, 72, 73, 194, 431n. 176; and Japanese peace treaty, 200, 233, 254; and MacArthur firing, 173; and process of unification in Korea, 110; revolt in, 41, 72, 80; and sanctions against PRC, 191; U.S. defense treaty with, 5, 200, 233, 234; U.S. position in and toward, 13, 15, 30, 35, 36, 41–42, 43, 53, 136, 141, 164
Pinay, Antoine, 296
Pleven, René, 89, 131, 164, 257
Plimsoll, James, 108, 109–10, 214
Poland, 16, 22, 23, 116, 122, 123, 293, 295, 298, 305, 311, 314
Port Arthur, 39
Pospelov, Peter, 160
Potsdam conference, 18, 136, 312
Prague, 123, 147
preventive war, 41, 62
prisoners of war: atrocities against, 244, 245; and desperate conditions among CPV soldiers, 169; screening of, 268, 425n. 23, 429n. 115
prisoners-of-war issue, 7, 224, 258; and civilian internees, 245, 250, 266, 268, 284; Communist flexibility on, 266, 309–10; Hallinan's proposal on, 286; initial U.S. position on, 212; and no forced repatriation principle, 244–45, 250–51, 256, 258–65, 266, 270–72, 279, 287, 294, 298–306 passim, 323, 326; in spring 1953, 313–33 passim; in summer 1953, 330–39 passim
Pusan, 47, 48, 157, 215, 261, 277, 310, 316, 317, 322, 335, 361, 437n. 59
Pusan perimeter, 48, 86, 151, 356
Pushtunistan, 197
Pyongyang, 118, 120, 121, 128, 143, 144, 361
Pyun Yung Tai, 324, 331, 338

Qiao Guanhua, 139, 224
Quemoy, 38
Quirino, Elpidio, 43, 72, 73, 185, 200, 407n. 114

Radhakrishnan, Sarvepalli, 51, 278
Radio Moscow, 80
Raghavan, Nedgan, 295, 304–5, 434n. 242
Rankin, Karl Lott, 67
Rau, Benegal, 63, 94, 95, 132, 139, 140–42 passim, 152–55 passim, 185–86, 192, 196, 256
Razmara, Ali, 82
Reciprocal Trade Agreements Act (U.S.), 318
Red Cross, 224, 244, 251, 288, 307
Reid, Escott, 163, 304
Republican Party (U.S.): attacks Truman on East Asia policy, 53–54, 75–77, 114–15, 116, 174, 254, 283–84; Eisenhower's troubles with, 316, 317–19, 320, 321, 322, 366; and Japan, 255; and MacArthur, 65–66, 114–15, 182, 183–84; and 1952 presidential campaign, 257, 264, 283–84, 289, 297–98; and UN contribution in Korea, 194
Reston, James, 342
Rhee, Syngman, 186, 218; antiguerrilla campaigns of, 30, 213; and beginning of armistice talks, 214–15; demands unification of Korea, 62, 77, 316, 332, 334–35, 337, 342; and DFUF proposals of June 1950, 40–41; and difficulties in governing, 27–28, 36, 37, 213, 277–78, 281, 332; elected president of ROK, 27; foreign criticism of, after armistice, 346; and Japan, 32, 277; and Korean Provisional Government, 15; and neutrali-

zation of Korea, 347; and People's Republic, 19-20; and process of unifying Korea, 108–11; pushes for independent South Korea, 24; relations with U.S., 22–23, 24, 29–30, 198, 213–15, 243, 277–78, 316–20, 323–24, 330–39, 341, 367; and release of POWs, 324, 330–33; response to armistice, 342–43, 443n. 211; returns to Korea (1945), 21; and ROK army, 198, 213, 215; stature of, in Korea, 19–20; and talks with Robertson, 334–38, 442n. 189

Ridgway, Matthew: anger at Communists, 228, 236, 271–72, 284; appointed NATO commander, 272; and armistice line, 225, 227–29, 238, 240; assessment of talks, 241–43; and beginning of armistice talks, 209–10, 211, 212, 213, 216, 222–23, 224; and civilian internees, 245; and Communist breakoff of talks, 230; impact in early 1951, 167–68; and item 3, 249, 250, 253, 271; as NATO commander, 350; and POW issue, 245, 251, 262–64, 266, 268–69, 271–72, 276, 288; and reopening of talks, 236–38; replaces MacArthur, 159–60, 169, 185; reports on military conditions, 151; and ROK army, 198; and spring 1951 Chinese offensives, 169, 188, 189, 408n. 143; takes command of Eighth Army, 130; and Van Fleet, 242–43, 276

Robertson, Walter, 331, 334–37
Romulo, Carlos, 72
Roosevelt, Franklin D., 17, 18, 137
Roschin, N. V., 218
Rumania, 23, 147, 196, 233, 352
Rusk, Dean, 53–54, 61, 90–91, 97, 116, 135, 151, 171–72, 174, 175, 181–82, 193, 406n. 77
Russell, Richard, 62, 429n. 115
Russia, 13, 14–15, 16
Russo-Japanese War, 13, 16
Ryukyus, 30, 53

St. Laurent, Louis, 96, 153, 165, 300
Sakhalin Island, 18
Salisbury, Harrison, 160
Salisbury, Lord, 344
Saudi Arabia, 132
Schuman, Robert, 131, 184, 208, 254, 296, 298, 373n. 8
Sebald, William, 212
Secchia, Pietro, 401n. 196
Second World Peace Congress, 124
Semenov, Vladimir, 176
Seoul, 10, 12, 92, 108, 163; CPV capture of, 157; damage to, 361; demonstrations in, 317, 335; falls to Communists, 11, 47, 129, 143, 353; and Inchon landing, 85–86; Korean Provisional Government established in, 14; North Korean rule of, 109; return of ROK government to, 316, 437n. 59; second UN recapture of, 130, 168, 215; and spring 1951 Chinese offensives, 168; turmoil in 1945, 20; UNCURK in, 110; U.S. arrival in in 1945, 19

Sevareid, Eric, 163, 183
Shanghai, 14–15, 38
Shann, K. C. O., 12, 153, 166, 190
Shenyang, 101
Sherman, Forrest, 86, 150, 180
Shim Um Mium, 213
Shinwell, Emanuel, 95
Shuckburgh, Evelyn, 299
Sihn Sung Mo, 47, 108, 213
Simon, John, 300, 433n. 215
Singapore, 191, 254
Sinjiang, 34, 38
Sino-Japanese War, 13, 17
Slim, William, 93
Smith, H. Alexander, 319, 321, 323, 438n. 77
Smith, Howard K., 131–32
Smith, O. P., 128
Smith, Walter Bedell, 115, 133, 322, 323
Somaliland, 74
Songhyon-ni, 236–37
Soong Jingling, 207
South Africa, 74
South Korea (*see also* Korea, Republic of): Communist inspections in, 243, 253; conditions in, 20–22, 23, 24–25, 27–29, 30, 31, 110-11, 213, 277, 317, 355, 367; Interim Legislative Assembly in, 23, 28; losses incurred in war, 361; partisans in, 230–31; possible U.S. economic assistance for, 24–25; POWs originating in, 266
South West Africa, 74
Southeast Asia Treaty Organization, 5
Soviet Union: and armistice, 344; and beginning of armistice talks, 216–21; and breakoff of armistice talks, 230–35 passim; and division of Korea, 3, 18–19, 20; capacity to attack U.S., 322; and Collective Measures Committee, 253–54; and creation of DPRK, 27; and crisis at end of 1950, 141–43, 145–48; détente with U.S., 6; divisions in, 32–33, 309; explodes atomic weapon, 41, 240; and fall 1952 UN General Assembly session, 290–92, 293–95, 298, 301, 303–6, 430n. 158, 431n. 163; and final con-

cessions on Korea, 327, 329–30; foreign policy after of Stalin's death, 308–9, 311, 312; and Four-Power talks on Korea, 140, 147; at Geneva conference, 362; and German rearmament, 88, 123, 124, 145, 147, 148–49, 161–62, 201–2, 273–75; and Greece, 345; "hate-America" campaign in, 275, 280, 282, 309; and Indian subcontinent, 197; and inspection issue in armistice talks, 269, 271; intentions of, 350–53; interest in negotiations on Korea, 88–89, 94, 103–4, 122–24, 145, 204–9 passim, 246–47, 356–57; interests in Korea, 16; and Iran, 57–58, 82, 147, 351; and Japanese peace treaty, 232–33, 234; and Korea between world wars, 15; and Korea during World War II, 17–19; Korea policy in early 1951, 160–62; and Korean Communists, 22; and Korean People's Republic, 21–22; as loser in Korean War, 6–7, 62, 78; and MacArthur firing, 184–85, 407n. 127; membership in UN, 369–70; military action prohibition in, 89–90, 95; military buildup of, 5–6; Nineteenth Party Congress in, 290–91, 431n. 161; 1945 treaty with China, 34; 1950 treaties with China, 34, 38–39, 41, 44, 100, 120, 162, 355; and peace movement, 124–25, 220, 230, 240, 255, 344; perceived intentions of, 42, 43–44, 62–63, 90, 91, 92–93, 98, 119, 148, 160, 213, 258–59, 260, 264–65; and POW issue, 244–45, 256, 260, 272–73, 290–92, 293–95, 298, 301, 303–6; presence in North Korea, 218; problems in economic relations with PRC, 327–28; as prominent factor in Korean War, 7; seeks to exploit Western disunity, 52, 78–83, 102, 105, 121–22, 146–48, 160–62, 165, 187, 199, 201–2, 220, 230, 232–33, 234, 246–47, 253–58, 283, 297, 344, 345, 358; supports China in Korean War, 4, 6, 100–101, 105, 119–20, 122–23, 127, 145, 148, 160–62, 168, 176, 177, 211, 217, 218–19, 220, 232, 233, 235, 243, 247, 248, 282, 346, 348, 362, 363, 425n. 28; supports and aids North Korea, 3, 4, 6, 11, 31, 83, 106, 235, 243, 247, 329–30, 348, 362; surprised at Western reaction to North Korean attack, 52; and Sweden, 82; and Turkey, 147–48, 345; and UN on Korea, 26, 59–61, 82–83, 94–96, 135, 246–47; and view of Korean War origins, 204; view of U.S. hardens (1946), 24; visited by Chinese delegation (1952), 285–86; war with U.S., 44, 105, 119, 121–24, 134, 137, 145, 160–62, 172, 200, 351; and Yugoslavia, 5, 6, 33, 147, 210, 345

Spain, 88, 183

Spender, Percy, 73, 132, 165–66

Stalin, Joseph, 132; accepts 38th parallel in Korea, 18–19; ambivalence toward Communists in China, 34, 37, 38–39, 220–21, 356, 357, 359; approves North Korean attack, 4, 31; and atomic bomb, 240; and Balkans, 147; and beginning of armistice talks, 217, 220–21; and CPV halt in January 1951, 158; death of, 307, 308, 315, 326, 327, 341, 344; and designs on Korea, 18; and divisions within Soviet Union, 32–33, 233, 274–75, 327, 358, 377n. 81; and *Economic Problems of Socialism in the USSR*, 275, 290; encourages Mao's firmness in Korea, 232; and France, 275, 296; and Germany, 246, 273–75; and global context of armistice talks, 273–75, 281–83; hostility toward West, 234; impact of his personality on Korean War, 8, 359, 360; and India, 278; and Iran, 82, 147; and Kennan recall, 431n. 166; Korea policy in summer 1950, 50, 51, 52, 58–59, 65, 69–70, 78–84; and Korean trusteeship, 17; miscalculations of, 355, 358; motives in decisions on Korean War, 8, 32–33, 35–37, 104–5, 120, 122, 123, 124, 143, 203, 220–21, 246–47, 351, 353, 358; and Nineteenth Party Congress, 431n. 161; options during Korean War, 7; possible initiative to end Korean War, 307, 326; possible U.S. overture to (1952), 285–86; and PRC entry into Korea, 36, 65, 69, 79, 101, 103, 104–5, 119, 121, 125–26, 351; and Scandinavia, 82, 143; and Soviet entry into war against Japan, 18; and war with U.S., 44, 65, 101, 104–5, 122–23, 124, 160–62, 233, 246, 349, 352, 396n. 43, 401n. 196, 402n. 198

Stelle, Charles, 259

Stevens, L. C., 402n. 198

Stilwell, Joseph, 374n. 34

Stockholm Peace Petition, 59, 79

Strachey, John, 148

Strong, Robert, 67, 150

Sulzberger, C. L., 297, 308

Sun Yat-sen, 207

Sunde, Arne, 57, 186

Suslov, Mikhail, 32

Suwon, 47

Sweden: and declaration on Korea, 178; on neutral repatriation commission, 298, 314, 315; and PRC, 158, 171, 176, 192, 208, 284,

339–40, 341–42; and Soviet Union, 205, 339–40; and UN action in Korea, 52, 82, 93, 115, 196
Switzerland, 284, 298, 311, 313, 314, 315
Syria, 27, 35, 81

Taegu, 28, 48
Taejon, 47
Taft, Robert, 154, 257, 283–84, 297, 318, 422n. 163
Taiwan: hopes of Nationalists on, 48, 102, 254, 270; impact of Korean War on, 364–65, 366, 367; and Japan, 344; and Japanese peace treaty, 201; and Malik speech, 208; and POW issue, 252, 262, 266, 268, 288, 295; PRC designs on, 39, 41, 45, 50, 52, 65, 69, 97, 102, 105, 139, 153, 158, 177, 186, 187, 210, 220, 223, 232, 346–47, 358; raids on mainland from, 305; UN considers status of, 93, 115–16, 130–31, 153–54; and UN effort in Korea, 56–57, 139; U.S. defense pact with, 5; U.S. policy toward, 6, 30, 35, 38, 43, 50–51, 53, 58, 63, 66–70, 75–76, 102, 104, 139, 140, 182, 185, 186, 193, 219, 255, 257, 306, 319, 329, 346–47, 367, 385n. 97
Tasca, Henry, 334
Taylor, George, 157, 158
Taylor, Maxwell, 317, 333–34, 342
Tedder, Arthur, 95, 151, 188
Teheran conference, 17, 18
Thailand, 41, 58, 72, 110, 192, 211, 254, 431n. 176
Thayer, Charles, 205
38th parallel, 223, 249; and beginning of Korean War, 10, 43; chosen as dividing line in 1945, 18–19; halt of UN or Chinese troops at, 7; military skirmishes along, 30; PRC move beyond, 121, 128–29, 143–45, 148, 217; and proximity to armistice talks, 209–10; restoration of, 50, 52, 58, 60–61, 62, 70, 75, 78, 102, 135, 136–37, 140, 142, 144, 158, 159, 163–64, 168, 169, 172, 174, 175, 178, 180, 202, 206, 207, 208, 211, 212, 215, 217, 224–25, 227–35 passim, 238, 240, 242, 256–57, 357–58; in Russo-Japanese relations at turn of century, 19; UN move beyond, 89–111 passim, 134, 138, 169, 172, 174, 175, 178, 180, 187, 348, 357, 391n. 85
Tibet, 119
Tito, Joseph Broz, 6, 33, 37, 42, 147, 196, 346, 352, 356
Togliatti, Palmiro, 401n. 196
Trieste, 344–45

Truman, Harry S., 88; and allied pressures of fall 1951, 239–40; anger at Communists, 258–59; approves concession on armistice line, 240; and atomic weapons, 67, 131–32, 181, 186, 324; attacks on his administration, 42, 53–54, 75, 131, 146, 154, 170, 174, 180, 184, 188, 194, 198, 254, 258, 264, 289, 335, 357, 366; and bombing in North Korea, 285; compared to FDR and Eisenhower, 137; compared to Stalin, 104; and congressional protectionism, 297; contrasted with Mao, 99, 144; and covert action in Southeast Asia, 421n. 140; declares national emergency, 145, 146; desire to avoid war with China, 125; desire to sustain U.S. rearmament, 250–51, 287, 289, 359; and election of 1952, 276, 281, 283–84, 289, 359; fiscal conservatism of, 43, 356; and German rearmament, 55; impact of his personality on Korean War, 8; and inviolability of Korean border, 116, 121–22; and Japan, 164; and Korea policy before June 1950, 18, 29, 35; Korea policy in summer 1950, 50–51, 56, 58, 62, 71, 75–76; and limiting war in Korea, 130, 135, 136–38, 146, 149, 150, 151, 180–81, 183, 202, 218, 284, 349; and MacArthur, 56, 65, 75, 106–7, 113, 170, 178–83 passim, 184, 185, 186, 190, 193, 348; and Middle East, 365–66; and move north of 38th parallel, 63, 89, 95, 121, 174; orders aid to South Korea, 11; and POW issue, 245, 250–51, 259–65 passim, 272, 287, 288, 289, 359; seizes steel mills, 276; and Taiwan, 30, 66–70, 75, 366; and U.S. troops to Europe, 154, 180; unpopularity of, 422n. 167; use of history by, 43
Truman-Attlee meetings, 132, 136–38
Truman Doctrine, 184
trusteeship, 17
Tsarapkin, Semen, 204
Tunisia, 291, 296, 303
Turkey: on AMC, 173, 191; contribution to UN effort in Korea, 72, 73, 130, 168–69, 194–95, 196, 199–200, 345; and Korean armistice, 345; and MacArthur firing, 184; and NATO, 5, 73, 88, 147, 199–200, 234, 246, 349, 385n. 111; and process of unification in Korea, 110; and Soviet Union, 147–48, 351; support of U.S. by, 132, 365; U.S. aid to, 24

Ulbricht, Walter, 328
Unden, Osten, 82
United Kingdom: and admission of Greece

and Turkey to NATO, 200; aid to UN in Korea, 12, 58, 72–74, 76, 194–95; alliance with Japan, 13; and armistice terms, 211, 239; and Communist peace probe of 1952, 279; criticism of U.S. in, 131, 239; differences on China with U.S., 52, 66–67, 92, 136–38, 172, 173, 177–78, 185, 188–94 passim, 201, 237, 254–55, 290, 294–303 passim, 318, 319, 321, 344, 366, 367, 427n. 66; and Four-Power talks, 140; and German rearmament, 88, 92, 123, 147, 201, 234, 281; and greater sanctions statement, 244, 249; influence of Arab-Asian bloc on, 164; influence on U.S., 4, 46, 51, 76–78, 79, 92–96, 118, 119, 130, 135, 136-38, 148–57 passim, 165–66, 171, 174, 177–78, 181–82, 188–94 passim, 239–40, 246, 283, 294, 298–303 passim, 315–26 passim, 365–66, 427n. 66; and Iran, 82, 192, 239; and Japanese peace treaty, 201, 254–55; and Korean trusteeship, 17, 22; and MacArthur firing, 181–82, 184; military buildup in, 71, 79, 201; and negotiations with PRC, 170, 176, 177–78; peace probe by, 51–54; position in Middle East, 81–82, 239, 315, 365–66; and process of unifying Korea, 108–10 passim, 117–18; and raw materials issue, 199, 239, 254, 257–58; recognizes PRC, 35; response to Korean armistice in, 343, 345; soldiers of, in Korea, 128, 130, 168–69; as source of weapons for PRC, 127; and South Koreans, 214, 317; and Soviet overtures of 1953, 309; Stalin's characterization of, 275; support for Yugoslavia, 5, 200; in UN, 59, 63, 92–96, 117, 255–56, 319; and UN elections in South Korea, 26; U.S. air bases in, 219; vulnerability to air attack, 113, 352; withdraws aid to Greece, 24

United Korean Committee, 15

United Nations: and air power in Korea, 130, 181; and China after Korean War, 366; and Egypt, 82; and embargo on PRC, 155, 159, 169–70, 172–73, 189–93, 343; as forum for Soviet propaganda, 60; impact of Korean War on, 43, 56, 138, 151, 163, 253–54, 345, 368–70; as instrument of Soviet policy, 83; as instrument of U.S. policy, 4, 25–26, 46, 123, 164–65, 253–54; Korea holds center stage in, 48, 56, 59–61, 138–42, 151–66 passim, 163; military contributions for Korea, 56–58, 71–75, 138, 191, 194–99, 290; and move above 38th parallel, 89–97 passim; and Palestine, 81–82; as restraint on U.S., 4, 46, 130, 132, 142, 164–66, 169–70, 240, 243, 290, 349, 369, 370; sentiment in at beginning of armistice talks, 212–13; support for South Korea, 3–4, 11–12; and unification of Korea, 77, 138; World Peace Council as competitor of, 160–61

United Nations Commission on Korea, 12, 35, 40, 77

United Nations Commission on the Unification and Rehabilitation of Korea, 108, 110, 187, 277

United Nations General Assembly: Additional Measures Committee, 154, 170, 171, 173–74, 186, 189–92, 204, 287, 290; calls for elections in Korea, 26; calls for withdrawal of foreign troops from Korea, 28; cease-fire group of, 141–42, 149, 152, 170, 211; and Chinese intervention in Korea, 140–42; Chinese representation in, 92, 102; Collective Measures Committee, 253–54, 368, 421n. 139; creates UNCOK, 12; creates UNTCOK, 26; and disarmament, 309; early 1953 session, 307, 311, 440n. 128; and embargo on PRC, 191–92; fall 1951 session of, 238, 240, 243, 246, 291; fall 1952 session of, 287, 289–306 passim; and final disposition of POWs, 322, 326; Good Offices Committee, 156, 157, 166, 170–71, 173, 176, 178, 186–87, 205, 208; and Indian resolution on POWs, 298–306 passim; North Korean message to, 186–87; possible strengthening of, 89; reconvenes in early 1952, 253; reconvenes after armistice, 343–44; and resolution condemning PRC, 151–66 passim, 170, 192; and resolution on unification of Korea, 91–96, 98, 102, 175; as restraint on U.S., 46, 148, 255–56, 349; as setting for diplomatic maneuvers, 86–87; Soviets overplay hand in, 256–57; supports ROK, 35, 107; takes on Korean issue, 24; and "Uniting for Peace" resolution, 123, 170, 253

United Nations Security Council: and call for PRC to withdraw from Korea, 117, 135, 139, 152; creates UN command in Korea, 57; early resolutions in Korean War broadly supported, 12; and Egypt, 365; impact of Soviet return to, 368; and inviolability of Korean frontier, 116; and Iran, 239; and Kashmir, 81; North Korean message to, 186–87; and Palestine, 204; possible circumventing of, 89; PRC attack on U.S. in, 130–31; response to North Korean attack, 12, 91; Soviet boycott of, 35, 44, 46, 51, 56, 59, 83, 369, 378–79n. 109, 381n. 161; sum-

mer 1950 debate in, 59–61, 63–64; summer 1952 debate in, 282; and Taiwan, 68, 93, 115–16
United Nations Temporary Commission on Korea, 26, 35, 66
United States: abandonment of Korea, 22–23, 331, 374n. 16; aid to Korea by, 29; attitudes harden in early 1950, 41, 53, 366; and breakoff of talks, 230–35 passim; changing position of, 355; and Chinese civil war, 38, 45; and commencement of armistice talks, 204–15 passim; concern about credibility of, 4, 25, 28, 43, 61–62, 97–98, 133, 136, 183, 356, 357; on condemning China as aggressor, 135, 140, 149, 164–65; considers effort to unify Korea, 61–64, 76, 89–119 passim; and creation of ROK, 27; defense treaties of, 5; and differences with allies, 50–51, 52, 66–67, 79–80, 83, 94–97, 116, 136–38, 148–57, 162–66, 199, 200–203, 239–40, 242, 246–47, 249–50, 254–58, 276–77, 283–84, 287, 289–303 passim, 315–16, 320–22, 324–26; and division of Korea, 3, 18–19, 20; divisions on Korea policy within, 29, 58, 61–64, 146, 356; and embargo on PRC, 171–73, 183, 187, 189–93, 237, 285, 287, 289–90, 296, 343, 366–67, 368; as emergent power in Asia, 13; failure of deterrence by in Korea, 353; and fear of PRC, 97, 346; fears regarding negotiations with Soviets, 89, 104; and Five-Power conference, 187; and Four-Power conference, 140; and German rearmament, 55, 71, 79, 164, 200–202; and GOC, 170–71; hardens view of Soviet Union in 1946, 24; initial position in armistice talks, 212; and Iran, 192; and Korea between world wars, 15; Korea's importance to, 16–19, 24–25, 133; and Korean Provisional Government, 16–17; and Korean trusteeship, 17, 22; limited patience in Korea, 194, 246; and Malik speech, 208–9; marginal interest in Korea, 16, 34–35, 207, 356; military buildup of, 55, 71, 79, 89, 163–64, 183, 194, 219, 234, 246, 281, 289, 349–50, 353, 367; military buildup, in Korea, 48; military weakness of, 54–55, 63–64, 133–34, 137, 350; military-industrial potential of, 351; miscalculations of, 354, 359; naval action off China coast, 188, 285; and neutralization of Korea, 334; officials surprised by North Korean attack, 10–11, 30; overcommitment in Asia, 367; and package proposal in armistice talks, 253, 269; and Pakistan, 196–97; and POW issue, 212, 244–45, 250–51, 253, 258–65, 276–77, 284, 285–90, 292, 293–94, 296, 298–303 passim, 310, 313–15, 319–20, 321–24, 330–39 passim, 362; and PRC admission to UN, 53, 58, 59–61, 102, 119, 135, 136, 140, 187, 343, 346–47, 381n. 161; pressured by Arab-Asian nationalists, 256; as prominent force in Korean War, 7, 194–95, 369; proposes greater sanctions, 243–44, 249–50, 251, 253, 287; reaction to North Korean attack, 12, 43–44, 48; recesses armistice talks, 288, 292; and recognition of PRC, 42–43; response to PRC intervention in Korea, 111–19; and Sino-Soviet split, 367; as source of weapons for PRC, 127, 219; and Soviet overtures of 1953, 309; and summer 1953 crisis with ROK, 330–39; supports and aids South Korea, 3, 4, 34–35, 194–95, 198, 361, 445n. 26; and Taiwan, 6, 30, 52, 53, 66–70, 116, 119, 130–31, 136, 140, 187, 193, 255, 285, 306, 319, 385n. 97; takes Korean issue to UN, 24; and Third-World nationalism, 365–67; as threat to PRC, 44–45, 52, 98, 100, 102, 364; treaty with Korea (1882), 16, 22–23; troops arrive in Korea (July 1950), 47; and UN role and course in Korea, 46, 48, 56–58, 59–61, 71–75, 91–97, 102, 107–11, 117–18, 137, 148–57 passim, 164–66, 170–78 passim, 186–99 passim, 286–303 passim; vulnerability to Soviet attack, 322; weakness in Southeast Asia, 80; withdraws troops from Korea, 28–29; and Yugoslavia, 246, 352
United States Congress: and aid to India, 187; and aid to South Korea, 24–25, 29; and appropriation for exiles from Soviet bloc, 246, 254, 421n. 131; and armistice in Korea, 366; China bloc in, 30, 53; Churchill's speech to, 257; and condemnation of PRC, 154, 156; and Eisenhower's speech of 16 April 1953, 312; and fall 1950 elections, 115; and foreign economic aid, 239, 254, 293, 417n. 29; Great Debate in, 154, 156, 180, 201; lack of sense of urgency in, 43; and MacArthur firing, 182, 183, 185, 190, 194; nationalism of, 202, 254, 297; and POW issue, 264; and PRC admission to UN, 323; Truman's statement on Taiwan to, 67; and U.S. military buildup, 71, 234, 284, 349
United States House of Representatives: defeats aid bill for ROK, 36; and fall 1950 elections, 115; and MacArthur firing, 182; MacArthur's letter read in, 179; political balance in, 318

United States Senate: and defense buildup, 88; and fall 1950 elections, 115; and Japan, 255; and MacArthur firing, 182, 184; and MacArthur hearings, 191, 195, 202, 219; peace resolution in, 205; political balance in, 318; and POW issue, 260; and PRC admission to UN, 323; and troops to Europe, 180

Uruguay, 197, 293, 431n. 176

Van Fleet, James, 169, 198, 202, 242–43, 263–64, 268–69, 276, 306, 336
Vandenberg, Hoyt, 62, 151, 180
Venezuela, 173, 191
Vietminh, 41, 80, 249, 310, 319, 362
Vietnam, 162, 367
Vietnam, Democratic Republic of, 35, 38
Vishinsky, Andrei: and armistice in Korea (1953), 340; replaced by Molotov, 308; at UN (fall 1950), 88, 103, 124; at UN (fall 1951), 240; at UN (winter 1951–52), 253–54, 256–57; at UN (fall 1952), 293, 295, 296, 298, 301, 303, 304, 305, 434n. 242; U.S. overture to, 285
Voice of America, 80, 147, 312

Waggoner, Joseph, 82
Wake Island: conference at, 106–7, 348
Walker, Walton, 130
Wang Ming, 33
West Germany: fate of POWs of, 260; French forces in, 57; and MacArthur firing, 184; military vulnerability of, 54, 148; and rearmament, 5, 55, 71, 79, 88, 89, 123, 124, 145, 147, 148–49, 161–62, 164, 199, 201–2; and Saar, 257, 296–97; Stalin's characterization of, 275
Weyland, O. P., 210–11
Whiting, Allen, 69
Wiley, Alexander, 321
Wilkinson, James, 90, 93–94, 113
Willoughby, Charles, 97, 111–12, 117
Wilson, Charles E., 199, 306, 310
Wilson, Woodrow, 14
Wolmi Do, 85, 86
Won Yong Duk, 332, 333
Wonsan, 118, 120, 121
World Peace Council, 124, 160–61, 186, 187, 240, 282, 412n. 8
World War II, 108, 109, 115, 128, 257, 335; impact of bombing in, 112–13; impact on Korea, 15–16, 43; and Japan, 18, 73, 346; Korea at end of, 18; and Latin America, 197; lessons of, 346, 348, 359; and peace treaties regarding, 200; and Philippines, 185; and POW issue, 244–45, 259, 260, 359; and Soviet Union, 44, 234, 309; U.S. demobilization after, 211, 348, 360
Wrong, Hume, 171–72, 188, 263
Wu Xiuquan, 130, 138–39, 141, 394n. 156

Xie Fang, 241
Xu Xiangqian, 217

YAK fighter planes, 10
Yalta conference, 17, 18
Yang You Chang, 316–17, 334
Yo Un-hyong, 23
Yoon Chi Yung, 317
Yoshida, Shigeru, 54, 55, 258
Yosu, 28
Younger, Kenneth, 148–49
Yu Chan Yang, 215
Yugoslavia: and aid from West to, 5, 147, 196, 200, 246, 345; and AMC, 173; border incidents involving, 233; conditions in, 147, 196; détente with Soviet Union, 6; and Greece and Turkey, 349; impact of Korean War on, 7, 43; and NATO, 349; neutrality of, 196, 356; and reaction to Korean armistice, 345–46; Soviet attack on, 5, 33, 147, 210, 352, 359, 363, 398n. 112; and Trieste, 345; UN Security Council rejects resolution of, 12

Zhang Shuguang, 216
Zhou Enlai: at Bandung and Geneva, 362–63; and crisis at end of 1950, 140, 141–42, 143, 145; and overtures to India, 278–80, 295; and POW issue, 272, 304–5, 309–10, 313, 425n. 25, 440n. 128; and PRC entry into Korean War, 64, 90, 91, 94, 97, 98–99, 102, 105, 106, 115–16, 122; on PRC need for armistice, 247; reaction to early Eisenhower actions, 306; and resolution condemning PRC, 157, 158, 162; and Sino-Soviet alliance, 162; and Taiwan, 68; visits to Soviet Union, 38, 100–101, 283, 290, 327
Zinchenko, Constantin, 186–87, 279–80, 427n. 80
Zorin, Valerin, 265